# Chinese Politics in the Era of Xi Jinping

Renowned for his coverage of China's elite politics and leadership transitions, veteran Sinologist Willy Lam has produced the first book-length study in English of the rise of Xi Jinping—State President and General Secretary of the Chinese Communist Party (CCP). With rare insight, Lam describes Xi's personal history and his fascination with quasi-Maoist values, the factional politics through which he ascended, the configuration of power of the Fifth-Generation leadership, and the future directions of domestic and foreign policy under the charismatic "princeling."

Despite an undistinguished career as a provincial administrator, Xi has rapidly amassed more power than his predecessors. He has overawed his rivals and shaken up the party-state hierarchy with a thorough anti-corruption campaign. With a strong power base in the People's Liberation Army and a vision of China as an "awakening lion," Xi has been flexing China's military muscle in sovereignty rows with countries including Japan, Vietnam, and the Philippines while trying to undermine the influence of the United States in the Asia-Pacific region. While Xi is still fine-tuning his art of governance, his zero tolerance for dissent and his preoccupation with upholding the privileges of the "red aristocracy" and the CCP's status as "perennial ruling party" do not bode well for economic, political, or cultural reforms. Lam takes a close look at Xi's ideological and political profile and considers how his conservative outlook might shape what the new strongman calls "the Great Renaissance of the Chinese people."

**Willy Wo-Lap Lam** is Adjunct Professor in the Centre for China Studies and the Department of History of the Chinese University of Hong Kong.

# Chinese Politics in the Era of Xi Jinping

## Renaissance, Reform, or Retrogression?

**Willy Wo-Lap Lam**

NEW YORK AND LONDON

First published 2015
by Routledge
711 Third Avenue, New York, NY 10017

and by Routledge
2 Park Square, Milton Park, Abingdon, Oxon, OX14 4RN

*Routledge is an imprint of the Taylor & Francis Group, an informa business*

**Library of Congress Cataloging-in-Publication Data**

Lam, Willy Wo-Lap.
  Chinese politics in the era of Xi Jinping : renaissance, reform, or retrogression?
by Willy Wo-Lap Lam.
    pages cm
  Includes index.
1. China—Politics and government—2002– 2. Xi, Jinping. I. Title.

DS779.46.L349 2015
951.06′12—dc23                                                    2014028353

ISBN: 978-0-7656-4208-0 (hbk)
ISBN: 978-0-7656-4209-7 (pbk)
ISBN: 978-1-315-71936-8 (ebk)

Printed and bound in the United States of America by Publishers Graphics,
LLC on sustainably sourced paper.

For Chan Kin-Man, Rev. Chu Yiu-Ming, Martin Lee, Benny Yiu-Ting Tai, and Cardinal Joseph Zen

# Contents

# ———— Acknowledgments ————

Watching, analyzing, and writing about China require patience, forbearance, clairvoyance, and, occasionally, inspiration from the heavens. The first two years of the administration of Xi Jinping proved much more eventful—and at times more exciting—than expected. Xi has pulled off a series of Machiavellian maneuvers to bolster his power in the Chinese Communist Party, the government, and the army. He has waged perhaps the largest anti-corruption crackdown since the end of the Cultural Revolution. And in foreign and military policy, Xi has not shied away from head-on confrontations with countries in the Asia-Pacific including the United States. China-watching since the Eighteenth Party Congress, however, could also be depressing. Xi has continued to mothball political and institutional reforms. He has repeatedly said no to universal values and global norms. As a big fan of Chairman Mao Zedong, he has also redoubled ideological control in areas ranging from the media to the classroom. While scholars and analysts of China should remain highly objective, it is comforting to know that I can share my upbeat as well as pessimistic views with so many China specialists and enthusiasts.

In the course of researching and writing this book, I have benefited from expert advice and timely tips, tea and sympathy, and much more from the following friends, colleagues, teachers, students, fellow China watchers, and folks concerned with the fate of China and Hong Kong (I have omitted the honorifics except for religious teachers; after all, we are mostly proletarians): Paul André, Fulton Armstrong, Bao Pu, Robbie Barnett, Bo Zhiyue, Jean-Philippe Béja, Nicholas Bequelin, John Berthelsen, Philip Bowring, Keith Bradsher, Kerry Brown, Jean-Pierre Cabestan, Anson Chan, Corina Chan, Chan Kin-Man, Lucy Chan, Priscilla Chan, Vivien Chan, Gordon Chang, Benjamin Charlton, Nicholas V. Chen, Helen Ngai-lun Cheng, Joseph Yu-Shek Cheng, Ching Cheong, Pearl Chih, Ivan Choy, Linda Choy, Venerable K.L. Dhammajoti, Audrey Eu, Jonathan Fenby, Isaac Stone Fish, Fong Chongyi, Edward Friedman, Brad Glosserman, Stephen Green, David Hale, Ryoichi Hamamoto, Harry Harding, Venerable Hin Hung, Michael Hsiao, Russell Hsiao, Cyd Ho, W. John Hoffman, Victoria Hui, Hung Ching-Tin, Y. Karunadasa, Sharon Kei, Maria Kruczkowska, Timmy Kwai, Daniel Kwan, Carol Lai, David Lampton, Diana Lary, Kevin C.T. Lau, Emily Lau, Lee Cheuk-Yan, Franky F.L. Leung, Theresa Leung, Angela Li, Li Chun Wai, Linda Li, Joe Lian Yi-Zheng, Allen P.F. Lee, Albert Lim, Louisa Lim, Kevin Lin, Perry Link, Sonny Lo, Paul

Loong, Bruce Lui, Bernard Luk, Alexander Lukin, Christie LuStout, Mak Yin-Ting, Yasuhiro Matsuda, Claudia Mo, Jeanne Moore, Robert Morton, Mou Chi-Wang, Kit-Fai Naess, Ng Ka-po, Eiichi Oshima, Kenneth Quinones, Pan Siu-to, Minxin Pei, Hugo Restall, Joshua Rosenzweig, Louisa Sakai, Shinnosuke Sakai, John Seaman, David Shambaugh, Victor Shih, Masaru Soma, Song Yao, Akio Takahara, Tetsuya Toyoda, Steve Tsang, King Tsao, Tsoi Yiu-cheong, Sebastian Veg, Arthur Waldron, Father Harry Wong, Kan-Tai Wong, Linda Wong, Symon Wong, Wong Yiu-Chung, Wing Thye Woo, Alfred Wu, Guoguang Wu, Wu Lik-Hon, Yan Pengfei, Yeung Sum, Wei Hongyun, Ray Yep, Maochun Yu, Verna Yu, Ricky Yue, Zhang Baohui, Zheng Yongnian, Zhiwei Zhang, and Zhu Zhiqun.

I am fortunate to have been associated with the Chinese University of Hong Kong since January 2007. I would like to thank the following professors and colleagues: Leung Yuen Sang, Yip Hon Ming, and Ma Muk Chi in the History Department; David Faure, Jan Kiely, and Kristof van den Troost at the Centre for China Studies; and Simon Shen, Shirley Lin, Miron Muskat, and James Seymour at the Master's in Global Political Economy Program. I am grateful for the support of the Jamestown Foundation, a leading foreign policy think-tank in Washington DC, where I have been a senior fellow for almost a decade. Encouragement over the years from Glen Howard is especially appreciated.

I am very much obliged to the management and staff of two renowned publishers, M.E. Sharpe and Routledge, for their tremendous help. Heartfelt thanks are due to Vice-President Patricia Kolb, Managing Editor Angela Piliouras, Copyeditor Debra E. Soled, Editorial Coordinator Brianna Ascher, as well as other experts at M.E. Sharpe for generous assistance. I am also indebted to Stephanie Rogers, Publisher, Asian Studies, and Senior Production Editor, Alf Symons, at Routledge and their editorial and production team for much-appreciated support.

I also salute my siblings for several decades of warm support and  close camaraderie: my sisters Pansy, Kin-Hung, Miranda, and Leslie and brothers Wo Hei and Justin. Above all, I must express my gratitude for the spiritual and other support that my dear, sweet wife, Grace, has given me for so many years. We are very thankful to have two loving, smart, and kind-hearted children, Ching-Wen and Wen-Chung. I am cautiously optimistic that my grandson James will see a China that is more in tune with universal values, such as the rule of law, freedom of expression, and democratic elections.

# ——— Introduction ———
## Why Is Xi Jinping So Fearful of Change?

### The Party's Legitimacy Remains Fragile Twenty-Five Years After Tiananmen

A feeling of *plus ça change plus c'est la même chose* permeated Beijing in June 2014 as the world—minus Chinese officialdom—marked the twenty-fifth anniversary of the Tiananmen Square crackdown. There is little doubt that within less than three decades, China has emerged as a quasi-superpower that is spearheading global power projection the likes of which have seldom been seen in history. Yet observers knowledgeable about contradictions in the China polity would hardly agree with the late patriarch Deng Xiaoping's conclusion about the events in Tiananmen Square: "the gunshots will buy us twenty or more years of stability."[1] From early May to mid-June 2014, the Chinese capital became a virtual combat zone, with anti-riot squads in armored vehicles criss-crossing the city's thoroughfares and alleyways at frequent intervals.

As many as a hundred dissidents, human rights lawyers, nongovernmental organization (NGO) activists, and free-thinking journalists were picked up by security forces on dubious charges such as "picking quarrels and provoking troubles." Taking a leaf from Chairman Mao Zedong's people's warfare playbook, the administration of President Xi Jinping recruited 85 million Beijing residents as part-time vigilantes and spies. On average, two informants were assigned to cover a 100-meter-size neighborhood. This was to complement the estimated 500,000 surveillance cameras that the police had installed in public venues in the capital over the past few years. Following the long-standing Chinese Communist Party (CCP) practice of imposing collective amnesia with respect to the Tiananmen killings, Xi's propaganda machinery went into overdrive, scrubbing clean any reference to the massacre in schools, the media, and cyberspace. Operators of China's Internet search engines were told to ban more than sixty politically sensitive terms.[2] This paranoia illustrated the fact that even though Deng had committed the grave error of ordering troops under order of martial law to shoot to kill fellow Chinese, the CCP's goal of attaining "long reign and perennial stability" remains illusory.

The twenty-fifth anniversary of the June 4 massacre is a good prism through which to examine the ideology and orientations of Xi, a member of the Fifth Generation of post-1949 Chinese leaders who seems to be a disciple of Mao more than of Deng. A month after being named the CCP general secretary and chairman of the Central Military Commission (CMC; thus commander in chief) at the Eighteenth

Congress of the CCP in late 2012, Xi went to Guangdong Province to demonstrate his credentials as heir to Deng's reforms. "The decision made by Deng Xiaoping on the reform and open door policy is correct, and we will continue to walk down this correct road," he told local cadres.[3] Yet it is clear that Xi is interested in only one facet of the Deng legacy: promoting "state capitalism" while clamping down on dissent. Equally significantly, Xi is anxious to maintain a blackout on the more progressive aspects of Deng's legacy. Although Deng as a Second-Generation leader masterminded the 1989 massacre and rendered CCP-style authoritarianism more repressive than ever, in the early to mid-1980s Deng had sponsored political reforms aimed at remedying ills exposed by the Cultural Revolution (1966–76). What Xi is consigning to oblivion is the fact that the liberal wing of the CCP—led by former CCP general secretaries Hu Yaobang and Zhao Ziyang—was implementing Deng's forward-looking agenda, to the applause of most Chinese.[4] Thus, while Tiananmen Square is a symbol for some of the worst excesses of the CCP, it is also a potent emblem of universal political ideals, such as freedom of expression, that were gallantly championed by Hu and Zhao as well as the student protestors.

Beijing's handling of the Tiananmen anniversary testified to the fact that the CCP leadership is fine-tuning, and, in some cases, reversing, policies that Deng laid down during the early stages of reform. After the tanks and armored personnel carriers crushed the "counterrevolutionary turmoil" in Tiananmen Square, the Party's liberal faction was obliterated—and political liberalization has been frozen to this day. The extent to which at least parts of Deng's political-reform agenda might be resuscitated could be gauged if we were to pinpoint the deviations that post-Tiananmen leaders— particularly President Xi and his allies—have made to Deng's edicts.

## How Xi Jinping Has Adulterated Deng Xiaoping's Legacy

While Deng is best known for economic liberalization, he also initiated impressive institutional changes to prevent the return of Chairman Mao's so-called "one-voice chamber." The rationale behind institutional reform was laid out in a 1980 *People's Daily* article by Deng titled "On the Reform of the Leadership System of the Party and State." Deng argued that to avoid a rerun of the Cultural Revolution, China had to replace "rule of personality" with rule of law and rule of institutions. "If systems [of governance] are sound," he wrote, "they can place restraints on the actions of bad people; if they are unsound, they may hamper the efforts of good people or indeed, in certain cases, may push them in the wrong direction."[5]

Until almost the eve of the June 4, 1989, crisis, Deng—aided by his first two chosen successors, Hu and Zhao—was pushing the following changes in the political structure:

- Collective leadership instead of "rule of personality." The Party and state should be run collectively by the Politburo Standing Committee (PBSC). The general secretary of the Party is at most a "first among equals." Each PBSC member has a clear-cut portfolio. When votes are cast to settle controversial issues, the vote of each PBSC member carries equal weight.[6]

- Separation of Party and government (*dangzhengfenkai*). This ethos was laid out in Zhao Ziyang's Political Report to the Thirteenth Party Congress in 1987. The CCP should focus on long-range goals and planning. Day-to-day governance should be left to professional administrators on the State Council (or cabinet) and regional governments. After Tiananmen, Deng said: "not one word of the Thirteenth Congress report should be changed."[7]
- The organizational principle of the "five lakes and four seas" and the delegation of authority to localities. There should be a balance of factions within the top echelons of the Party-state apparatus. More administrative powers should be delegated to local governments under the principle of "to each [locality] in accordance with its characteristics."[8]
- One of Deng's greatest contributions to Chinese modernization is that he said good-bye to Mao's penchant for periodically launching *qunzhong yundong* (mass movements) and other political campaigns to rectify and purify the thinking of cadres and intellectuals. Deng, as the great architect of reform, simply declared that "economic construction is the core task of the Party." At least until 1989, Deng opposed several waves of "anti-bourgeois liberalization campaigns" launched by leftist Party elders because they were seen as disrupting China's economic growth.[9]
- Not too long after taking power in late 1978, Deng began the demobilization of a million soldiers. Annual budget increases for the military were kept to single digits. Most significantly, the "New Helmsman" indicated that the defense establishment should be subservient to China's pursuit of economic goals. While Deng was a beneficiary of actions taken by a group of senior generals in the People's Liberation Army (PLA) to remove the Gang of Four radicals upon the death of Chairman Mao in 1976, he did not favor the top brass's involvement in either politics or foreign affairs.[10]

Xi's track record since gaining power at the Eighteenth Party Congress has amounted to a renunciation of many of Deng's axioms about governance. Almost from day one, the new supreme leader started a power grab that is as stunning as it is inimical to Deng's ideals about putting institutions ahead of individuals. For example, the two superagencies that Xi created at the apex of the Party—the Central National Security Commission (CNSC) and the Central Leading Group on Comprehensively Deepening Reforms—have given the leader the authority to ride roughshod over the entire Party-state-military establishment. The theory and practice of the collective leadership have been dealt a body blow. The Leninist—and Maoist—concentration of powers at the Party's topmost echelon also runs counter to Deng's *dangzhengfenkai* precept (see Chapter 3).[11]

In terms of internal Party affairs, Xi has run afoul of two of Deng's aphorisms: avoid factionalism and give more clout to regional administrations. While it is true that Xi's two predecessors—Jiang Zemin and Hu Jintao—put together large personal factions, there are indications that the Fifth-Generation potentate is about to outshine his two predecessors in terms of assembling a formidable coterie of trusted confidants (see Chapter 2). Xi's grooming of cadres with a revolutionary bloodline for top jobs has also violated Deng's internal instruction in the early 1980s that the offspring of Party elders (called "princelings") should focus on business, not politics. Compared to Jiang and Hu, Xi has sent more officials with central government experience to take up regional positions so as to cement the grip of the *zhongyang* (Party central authorities) over the localities. Xi's preoccupation with "top-level design" in policy-making means that the wiggle room of local officials has been reduced.[12]

Xi is the first top leader since the Cultural Revolution to give equal importance to economic construction and ideological pursuits. The conservative son of the liberal Party elder Xi Zhongxun has resurrected the ideological imperative, implying that the pursuit of politically correct *yishixingtai* (ideology and thought) and related goals is as important as building up the economy. He has also reiterated that economic developments that are "subversive"—meaning detrimental to the CCP's perennial ruling party status—should be jettisoned. This is contrary to what is perhaps Deng's most famous aphorism: "whether black or white, a cat is a good one if it catches mice." The late patriarch had used this pragmatic logic to justify unorthodox policies, including privatization of much of the economy. General Secretary Xi has revived Maoist political campaigns with gusto. He has launched political movements—such as the Mass-Line Education and Practice Campaign— that are reminiscent of the *qunzhong yundong* of Great Helmsman Mao.[13]

Ex-presidents Jiang and Hu began undercutting Deng's PLA-related policies by giving the army double-digit budget increases. Particularly during the second half of the Hu administration (2007–12), the generals began to have a bigger say in national security issues. Yet the political clout of the generals has reached an apogee under Xi, who started his career as secretary to then-defense minister Geng Biao from 1979 to 1982. Since the Eighteenth Party Congress, a record number of officials who had served in the PLA or military enterprises have been given senior Party and government jobs. Xi underscored his connections with the PLA estab-lishment at a 2014 conference on providing employment for demobilized soldiers. "I, too, am a military man who has become a cadre [in civilian departments]," said the commander-in-chief.[14]

### Decline in Social Justice and Equality—and the Temptation of Nationalism

While China is on course to overtake the United States as the world's largest economy soon, Chinese who do not belong to the "red aristocracy"—a reference to the unholy alliance between top cadres and their offspring, on the one hand, and big business groups, on the other—see no cause for optimism. The

CCP's "legitimacy via economic performance" is being imperiled as the growth rate of the gross domestic product (GDP) is expected to dip to 6 percent or lower by the end of this decade. Owing to sky-high real-estate prices, even members of the middle and professional classes find it difficult to own an apartment in big cities and commercial centers. According to independent social scientists, the Gini coefficient of economic inequality has risen above 0.6 (where 0 is completely equal and 1 is completely unequal), exceeding the level in the United States. Despite the fact that Xi has taken more forceful measures to crack down on corruption and rent-seeking, Chinese society lacks the basics of rule of law and distributive justice to prevent members of disadvantaged sectors such as peasants and migrant workers from being exploited by the moneyed and politically empowered classes. Peking University political scientist Pan Wei, who is usually deemed an establishment intellectual, has complained that "the lack of the feeling of justice in everyday life is the core contradiction of this country's governance."[15]

For Tsinghua University sociologist and reform theorist Sun Liping, meaningful changes in the economic, political, or social system have been trumped by what he calls the *quanguitizhi* (system of special privilege). "The reality of so many years has told us that the *quanguitizhi* is a wall that blocks up everything," he said in the spring of 2014. "Up against this wall, China can't go anywhere." This is despite the fact that most members of the country's educated class are fully aware of the deleterious effects of the "red aristocracy," which Sun summed up as "depressing social vigor; polarization of rich and poor; retrogression in rule of law; social debilitation and paralysis; and environmental degradation."[16] The economist Wu Jinglian argued that the Xi administration could not afford to lose time in reinstating reform. "Reform is in a race with revolution," said Wu. "The administration needs more political courage and wisdom . . . to build up a competitive market system." Wu, who once advised Zhu Rongji while he was premier, warned that further procrastination on reform could spawn a popular uprising of devastating magnitude.[17]

As we discuss in the ensuing chapters, Xi seems to have little interest in political liberalization—or any institutional change that could jeopardize the monopoly of power enjoyed by the CCP and its elite clans. Even in the relatively less controversial area of economic reform, Xi has erred on the side of caution by stipulating that reform strategies must be meticulously mapped out by top Party organs. The general secretary has also insisted that reform measures not be permitted to endanger sociopolitical stability (see Chapter 4).

In the absence of real reform, it is not surprising that Xi and his conservative colleagues are turning more and more to nationalism to divert public attention from domestic woes and to bolster the Party's legitimacy. As veteran sinologist Jean-Philippe Béja pointed out: "Xi Jinping has raised the Chinese Dream slogan and bolstered China's position on the world stage. . . . The CCP is relying on nationalism to uphold its legitimacy."[18]

Xi has thrown Deng's famous "keep a low profile" diplomatic dictum out of the window. While protesting that "expansionism is not in the genes of Chinese," the commander-in-chief has flexed China's muscle in asserting sovereignty rights in the East China Sea and the South China Sea. Although the president has earned the support in particular of the xenophobic *fenqing* (angry young people) through what official commentators call "brandishing the sword," China may have painted itself into a corner. A number of Asian countries, including Japan, India, Vietnam, the Philippines, and Australia, are seeking enhanced defense ties with the area's status-quo power—the United States—in order to protect themselves against an aggressive China (see Chapter 5). For the first time in recent memory, leaders of the Group of Seven (G7) countries indicated at their summit in Brussels in June 2013 that they were "deeply concerned by tensions in the East and South China Sea." Without mentioning China, the G7 statement said: "We oppose any unilateral attempt by any party to assert its territorial or maritime claims through the use of intimidation, coercion or force."[19]

## The Conundrum of Neo-Authoritarianism: The World Awaits an Answer from Xi Jinping

While talking to a group of American journalists in early 2014, the chairperson of the National People's Congress (NPC's) Foreign Affairs Committee, Fu Ying, said: "The West will never believe that China is advancing until we produce a Gorbachev."[20] A former deputy foreign minister and ambassador to Australia and the United Kingdom, the English-speaking Fu is one of the most articulate defenders of authoritarianism with Chinese characteristics. Although it is an ingrained belief among senior cadres that the West—principally the United States—is bent on changing the colors and emblems of the Party via "peaceful evolution" or "color revolutions" (a reference to the changes in Eastern Europe), Fu may have missed the point about foreign countries' misgivings about the People's Republic of China (PRC).

Despite Beijing's insistence on the early twentieth-century principle of "non-interference in the internal affairs of other countries," China's neighbors as well as the West have a legitimate interest in the domestic developments of a country that is home to one-fifth of humanity. And this goes beyond issues such as pollutants that originate in China spreading as far as California—and the possibility that food shortages in China could have a ripple effect on agricultural prices worldwide. Given the increasing assertiveness of the PLA, China specialists have qualms about the fact that the Chinese military remains a "Party army" that answers only to the Politburo Standing Committee. Even foreign politicians, academics, and opinion leaders who are deemed China-friendly worry about a mass outbreak of disorder in the eventuality of the sudden loss of the Party's "mandate of heaven" (i.e., the erstwhile emperors' basis of legitimacy).

Owing in part to the fact that Xi has so successfully positioned himself as a Maoist—or Vladimir Putin-like—strongman, much of the world's anxiety about China can be summed up in a simple question about whether—and when—Xi will make a commitment to real reform. The implicit social contract behind Xi's one-upmanship has been a variation on the theory of neo-authoritarianism that was first proposed by Zhao Ziyang: Because China is such a complicated country—and resistance to reform is so entrenched—the top leader needs extraordinary powers to ring in the new.[21] Ironically, despite his genuine commitment to political as well as economic liberalization, Zhao, like Hu Yaobang before him, was never able to break free of the interference of Deng and other conservative elders. Xi, by contrast, seems to have already amassed enough power to push through unpopular reform measures. Unfortunately, the Fifth-Generation titan's message for the twenty-first century is: the CCP will cleave to time-tested formulas and make advancement through "self-perfection." The leader has repeatedly warned that "Western" precepts of governance are unsuitable for China and that disasters would occur "if the CCP were to blindly copy foreign development models." While Xi's words of wisdom saturate the print and electronic media on a daily basis, the main thrust of his governing philosophy is that Chinese must have "self-confidence in the road, theories, and institutions" of "socialism with Chinese characteristics." He has also urged young men and women to become modern versions of Lei Feng and Jiao Yulu—near-mythic paragons of unquestioned devotion to the party (see Chapter 6).[22]

But will more of the same be enough to usher in the "Chinese Dream," which Xi has defined as the "great renaissance of the Chinese people"? If New Helmsman Xi is aware of the urgent appeals of top intellectuals such as Wu Jinglian and Sun Liping, the famously self-confident leader does not seem to have been moved one bit. The well-known blogger Han Han is speaking for millions of disgruntled Chinese when he encapsulates the plight that is gripping China: "[the Party] taught us cruelty and [power] struggle in the first few decades—and greed and selfishness in the ensuing few decades. Our culture and traditional morality have been shattered. The same goes for trust among us. Gone too is any semblance of faith and consensus."[23] Some 1.35 billion Chinese are pining desperately for an end to the sophistry and suppression that have characterized CCP rule for more than sixty-five years. Yet Xi's answer to friend and foe alike echoes Mao's autarkist idiosyncrasy: "The Party will purify itself. It will perfect itself, reform itself, and seek self-elevation."[24] In other words, do not expect outside-the-box thinking or Deng-style "thought liberation" to take place during Xi's tenure, which is set to last until the Twentieth Party Congress in 2022.

## Notes

1. Cited in Liang Jing, "The historic price to pay for mass killings to order to preserve stability," Radio Free Asia, June 26, 2011, www.waicannews.com/news/html/78/t-578.html.

2. For a discussion of extraordinary measures the leadership took to prevent outbreak of disorder on the twenty-fifth anniversary of the Tiananmen crackdown, see, for example, Christina Larson, "Beijing, 25 years on, seems more nervous than ever about Tiananmen

voices, *Businessweek,* June 5, 2014, www.businessweek.com/articles/2014-06-05/25-years-on-beijing-seems-more-nervous-than-ever-about-tianamen-voices; Megan Carber, "There are 64 Tiananmen terms censored on China's Internet today," *Atlantic,* June 4, 2014, www.theatlantic.com/technology/archive/2014/06/china-has-found-64-tiananman-related-terms-to-block-on-its-internet-today/372137/; Xin Lin, "Beijing mobilizes 850,000 residents to prevent and control mass incidents," Radio Free Asia, May 30, 2014, www.rfa.org/mandarin/yataibaodao/shehui/xl-05302014101715.html.

3. Cited in "Xi Jinping pays inspection trip to Guangdong," Xinhua News Agency, December 11, 2012, http://politics.people.com.cn/n/2012/1211/c133637–19865390.html.

4. For a discussion of political reform initiated by Deng Xiaoping and implemented by Hu Yaobang and Zhao Ziyang, see, for example, Merle Goldman, *Sowing the Seeds of Democracy in China: Political Reform in the Deng Xiaoping Era* (Cambridge: Harvard University Press, 1994), pp. 25–61, 133–165.

5. Cited in "Deng Xiaoping proposes reform of the leadership system of the party and state," *People's Daily,* August 25, 2009, http://news.163.com/09/0825/20/5HJBL0OI00013LJ5.html; for a discussion of Deng's ideas about political institutions, see, for example, Kjeld Erik Brødsgaard, "Governing capacity and institutional change in China in the era of reform," *Copenhagen Journal of Asian Studies* 28, no. 1 (2010), http://rauli.cbs.dk/index.php/cjas/article/viewFile/2834/3063/.

6. For a discussion of Deng's idea about a collective leadership, see, for example, Chen Xianku, "Deng Xiaoping's theory about a central collective leadership," *CCP Central Party School Journal* (January 2005), www.cntheory.com/news/Llzzfz/2008/87/0886100468II8D4JD40K4HC797B24.html.

7. Cited in "Zhao Ziyang's Report to the 13th Party Congress," *People's Daily,* November 4, 2012, http://news.ifeng.com/mainland/special/zhonggong18da/content-4/detail_2012_11/04/18822143_0.shtml. For a discussion of the significance of the separation of party and government, see, for example Tao Zheng, "An interpretation of the principle of 'separation of party and government' raised at the 13th Party Congress," 21ccom.Net (Beijing), January 15, 2013, www.21ccom.net/articles/lsjd/lsjj/article_2013012575854.html.

8. For a discussion of Deng's views on human resources, see, for example, He Gengwen, "Deng Xiaoping's comprehensive thoughts on personnel issues," *Journal of Liaoning Normal University* 32, no. 6 (November 2009), www.cnki.com.cn/Article/CJFDTotal-LNSS200906002.htm. See also Huang Benyu, "The personnel-related views of Mao Zedong, Deng Xiaoping, Jiang Zemin and Hu Jintao," *People's Daily,* September 3, 2010, http://dangshi.people.com.cn/GB/138903/138911/12624846.html.

9. For a discussion of Deng's rationale for giving up mass movements, see, for example, Tan Yuxi, "The historic change from organizing lots of political campaigns to stopping the holding of political campaigns: Learn from Deng Xiaoping's idea of no more political movements," *Harbin Academy Journal* (June 2001), www.cnki.com.cn/Article/CJFDTotal-HEBS200106011.htm; Kan Heqing and Chen Changshen, "Rethinking on the history of political movements after 1949: Deng Xiaoping's thoughts on 'Stop organizing movements,'" *Journal of Yunnan Administration Academy* (June 2004), www.doc88.com/p-1748774204372.html.

10. For a discussion of Deng's stance on the PLA's role in the polity, see, for example, Yitzhak Shichor, "Demobilization: The dialectics of PLA troop reduction," *China Quarterly* 146 (June 1996): 336–359.

11. For a discussion of the significance of the two newly created super-agencies, see for example, Willy Lam, "New high-level groups threaten line between party and government," *China Brief,* Jamestown Foundation, April 9, 2014, www.jamestown.org/programs/chinabrief/single/?tx_ttnews%5Btt_news%5D=42208&tx_ttnews%5BbackPid%5D=25&cHash=9c04fb8086372aa9cd6deb00e61e01e7/.

12. For a discussion of how Xi has revised many of Deng's political-reform ideals, see, for example, Willy Lam, "Forgetting Tiananmen, and what came before it," *China Brief,* Jamestown Foundation, June 4, 2014, www.jamestown.org/single/?tx_ttnews%5Btt_news%5D=42467&tx_ttnews%5BbackPid%5D=7&cHash=98f4dcc55ef666c8a4920d4c7b0891ce/.

13. For a discussion of Xi's views on *qunzhong yundong,* see, for example, "Xi chairs Politburo meeting, which decides to launch a mass-line education and practice [campaign]," China News Service, April 19, 2013, www.chinanews.com/gn/2013/04–19/4747527.shtml.

14. Cited in "Xi Jinping: I am also a cadre transferred from the army," *Liberation Daily* (Shanghai), May 28, 2014, http://news.ifeng.com/a/20140528/40488634_0.shtml.

15. See Pan Wei, "The major contradiction of governance is people's lack of a feeling of justice in everyday life," *People's Daily,* May 7, 2014, http://news.takungpao.com/mainland/focus/2014–05/2461949.html.

16. See "Sun Liping: the challenge posed by vested interests to reform has not yet begun," Aisixiang.com (Beijing), April 22, 2014, www.aisixiang.com/data/74187.html.

17. Cited in Wu Jinglian, "China's reform is in a race with revolution," Phoenix TV Net (Beijing), April 11, 2013, http://news.ifeng.com/mainland/detail_2013_04/11/24113061_0.shtml.

18. Author's interview with Jean-Philippe Béja in Beijing, May 31, 2014.

19. Cited in "G7 'deeply concerned' at tensions in East, South China Seas," Reuters, June 4, 2014, www.reuters.com/article/2014/06/04/uk-g7-japan-china-idUSKBN0EF2D620140604/

20. Cited in "How the world's most powerful leader thinks," *Huffington Post,* January 21, 2014, www.huffingtonpost.com/2014/01/21/xi-jinping-davos_n_4639929.html/.

21. For a discussion of different versions of neo-authoritarianism as proposed by Zhao Ziyang and others, see, for example, Yu Keping, "The logic of political development in the PRC's 60 years of history," *People's Daily,* March 5, 2010; see also Barry Sautman, "Sirens of the strongman: Neo-Authoritarianism in recent Chinese political theory," *China Quarterly,* no. 129 (March 1992): 72–102.

22. For a discussion of Xi's theory of self-confidence on the socialist path, theory and institutions, see, for example, Research Center on the Theory of Chinese-Style Socialism, Chinese Academy of Social Sciences, "Firm up the 'three kinds of self-confidence' and unswervingly go down the Chinese path," *People's Daily,* May 31, 2013, http://theory.people.com.cn/n/2013/0531/c49150–21684041.html; "Xi Jinping: China will not blindly copy foreign models," China News Service, March 9, 2013, www.chinanews.com/gn/2013/03–19/4657500.shtml. See also "Xi Jinping: Everybody can learn from the Lei Feng spirit," *Qingdao Morning Post* (Qingdao), March 5, 2014, www.anhuinews.com/zhuyeguanli/system/2014/03/05/006336911.shtml.

23. Cited in "Quotations from Han Han: I'm also a bloody public intellectual," Topnews9.com (Beijing), May 24, 2012, www.topnews9.com/html/2012/0524/2755.html.

24. For a discussion of Xi's theory of "self-perfectionism," see for example, Tang Wenyu, "Why does the Chinese Communist Party put its emphasis on 'self-advancement,'" *Study Times* (Beijing), July 1, 2013, http://theory.people.com.cn/n/2013/0701/c49150–22036240.html.

# List of Acronyms

| | |
|---|---|
| air defense identification zone | ADIZ |
| All-China Sports Association | ACSA |
| Asia-Pacific Economic Cooperation | APEC |
| Association of Southeast Asian Nations | ASEAN |
| BRICS Development Bank | BDB |
| Central Commission for Disciplinary Inspection | CCDI |
| Central Coordinating Group on Talent-related Work | CCGTW |
| Central Leading Group on Comprehensively Deepening Reforms | CLGCDR |
| Central Leading Group on Finance and Economics | CLGFE |
| Central Leading Group on Foreign Affairs | CLGFA |
| Central Leading Group on Internet Security and Informatization | CLGISI |
| Central Military Commission | CMC |
| Central National Security Commission | CNSC |
| Central Party School | CPS |
| Central Policy Research Office | CPRO |
| Central Political-Legal Commission | CPLC |
| China Aerospace Science and Technology Corporation | CASC |
| China Aerospace Science and Industry Corporation | CASIC |
| China Institutes of Contemporary International Relations | CICIR |
| China National Overseas Oil Corporation | CNOOC |
| China National Petroleum Corp | CNPC |
| China North Industries Group Corporation | Norinco |
| China Securities Regulatory Commission | CSRC |
| China's Writers' Association | CWA |
| China-ASEAN Free Trade Area | CAFTA |
| Chinese Academy of Sciences | CAS |
| Chinese Academy of Social Sciences | CASS |
| Chinese Communist Party | CCP |
| Chinese People's Political Consultative Conference | CPPCC |
| Code of Conduct | CoC |
| Commercial Aircraft Corporation of China | COMAC |
| Communist Party of the Soviet Union | CPSU |
| Communist Youth League | CYL |

| | |
|---|---|
| Conference on Interaction and Confidence Building Measures in Asia | CICA |
| Democratic Party of Japan | DPJ |
| European Union | EU |
| exclusive economic zones | EEZs |
| five-year plan | FYP |
| free trade areas | FTA |
| free trade zone | FTZ |
| gross domestic product | GDP |
| Group of Seven | G7 |
| initial public offerings | IPOs |
| intellectual property rights | IPRs |
| International Consortium of Investigative Journalists | ICIJ |
| International Liaison Department | ILD |
| Liberal Democratic Party | LDP |
| Ministry of Foreign Affairs | MOFA |
| Ministry of Foreign Trade and Economic Cooperation | MOFTEC |
| Ministry of Public Security | MPS |
| Ministry of State Security | MSS |
| most-favored nation | MFN |
| National Defense University | NDU |
| National Development and Reform Commission | NDRC |
| National People's Congress | NPC |
| New Silk Road Economic Belt | NSREB |
| nongovernmental organization | NGO |
| Offices to Maintain Social Stability and to Rectify Law and Order | OMSS |
| Organization for Economic Cooperation and Development | OECD |
| outbound foreign direct investment | OFDI |
| overseas development aid | ODA |
| People's Armed Police | PAP |
| People's Bank of China | PBOC |
| People's Liberation Army | PLA |
| People's Republic of China | PRC |
| Pi Ka Wang International Group | PKWIG |
| Politburo Standing Committee | PBSC |
| privately owned enterprises | POEs |
| Program for International Student Assessment | PISA |
| Regional Comprehensive Economic Partnership | RCEP |
| Rural Education Action Program | REAP |
| special administrative regions | SARs |
| Shanghai Cooperation Organization | SCO |
| small and medium-size enterprises | SMEs |
| special administrative regions | SARs |

| | |
|---|---|
| special economic zone | SEZ |
| State Assets Supervision and Administration Commission | SASAC |
| State Oceanic Administration | SOA |
| State Security Leading Groups | SSLG |
| state-owned enterprise | SOE |
| Supreme People's Court | SPC |
| Tibet Autonomous Region | TAR |
| Trans-Pacific Partnership | TPP |
| U.S.-China Strategic and Economic Dialogue | S&ED |
| village administrative committees | VAC |
| Western Returned Scholars Association | WRSA |
| World and China Institute | WCI |
| World Intellectual Property Organization | WIPO |
| World Trade Organization | WTO |
| Xiamen International Airport | XIA |
| Xinjiang Uighur Administration Region | XUAR |

# Chinese Politics in the Era of Xi Jinping

# 1

# Factors Behind Xi Jinping's Rise

## Factional Intrigue and
## Controversies Over the Future of Reform

### Introduction: Is Xi Jinping Up to the Challenge?

Xi Jinping signaled his intention to shake up the trajectory of twenty-first century history when he announced, during an official visit to Paris in March 2014, "The lion has woken up." While he went on to reassure his audience that China would remain a "peaceful, pleasant and civilized lion," the undisputed leader of 1.3 billion people had served notice that the fast-rising quasi-superpower was going to prove true the prediction attributed to Napoleon Bonaparte: "China is a sleeping lion, and when she awakes, the world will shake." Had he not been in Paris, Xi might have delivered the same message with a quotation from his idol, Mao Zedong, who pronounced sixty-five years ago at the rostrum of Tiananmen Square, "the Chinese people have stood up!"[1]

Xi came to power at the Eighteenth Congress of the Chinese Communist Party (CCP) in late 2012, which was a critical—and paradoxical—juncture in Chinese history. Dozens of books have predicted that China will "rule the world." Both Chinese and Western experts have touted the "Chinese model" (a.k.a. the "Beijing Consensus" or "Chinese Socialism 3.0") as a viable alternative to laissez-faire capitalism.[2] The Renmin University international relations expert Jin Canrong is confident that the forthcoming "hegemonic transition," shorthand for China replacing the United States as the ultimate arbiter of global standards, will definitely occur. "The United States knows full well that it is unable to contain China's rise," said Jin, adding, "The premise of a successful containment policy is that the object of containment is relatively stupid and that it likes to antagonize [other countries]. . . . The transition of power lies in the hands of China. . . . If China does not make mistakes, the power transition will surely take place. To a big extent, the fate of China and the fate of the world lies in our hands."[3]

Jin and other optimistic observers can certainly refer to a number of relatively positive developments on which to base their bullish predictions. Despite the near-consensus view that double-digit growth is a thing of the past, many economists reckon that the GDP growth rate can be maintained at the still-healthy level of 6 percent or 7 percent through the 2010s.[4] Moreover, starting with the second half of the Hu Jintao administration (2007–12), Beijing has skillfully used its hard-power projection, including massive outbound foreign direct investment (OFDI), to win friends and deflect criticism on different continents (see Chapter 5). The massive military modernization programs under Hu and particularly under Xi have vastly boosted China's say in geopolitical issues.

Things, however, are hardly looking good on different fronts. Compared to most Western and Asian countries, China seemed to have gone through the global financial crisis of 2008 relatively unscathed. Yet the decision by ex-premier Wen Jiabao to inject RMB 4 trillion to resuscitate the economy has dealt a blow to economic liberalization. The bulk of the funds went into relatively inefficient infrastructure projects that were run by state-owned enterprise (SOE) conglomerates. As the Peking University economist Zhang Weiying pointed out when he summed up the ten years of the Hu-Wen administration: "The economy retrogressed from being market-oriented to being government-oriented; the trend of 'private enterprises advancing at the expense of the public sector' changed to 'the public sector advancing at the expense of private firms.'" The gap between rich and poor yawned wider even as the unholy alliance between top party clans and business groupings became more pronounced. Professor Zhang added that the ten years of the Hu-Wen administration was "the decade of stagnation in structural reform, the lost decade in terms of [promoting] social harmony." The slogan of 'building up a country with rule of law' has deteriorated into 'preserving stability is the overriding task,'" he argued.[5]

Most crucially, despite having vowed to promote "intra-Party democracy" and a "scientific outlook on development," ex-president Hu put political and institutional reforms largely on the back burner. According to the legal expert Jiang Ping, "not only is there lack of progress in political reform, there has been a turning back of the clock in certain areas."[6]

Wuhan University law professor Qin Qianhong called the past ten years "the decade of severe retrogression in the rule of law."[7] Independent historian Zhang Lifan was equally blunt. "It can almost be said that nothing was accomplished on the political front under Hu Jintao," he contended. "The ten-year-long procrastination on reform has resulted in the exponential growth of vested interests, meaning that his successors will face even tougher challenges." Zhang said Hu's only significant contribution was his surprise decision to vacate all his party positions, including the chairmanship of the policy-setting Central Military Commission (CMC)—which is China's equivalent of commander-in-chief—in late 2012.[8]

Indeed, Xi was lucky that Hu (born in 1942) decided to retire from his CMC post at the Eighteenth Party Congress. At the Sixteenth Party Congress a decade earlier, then vice-president Hu succeeded Jiang Zemin as general secretary; but the head of the Fourth-Generation leadership (a reference to cadres born in the 1940s) had to wait two more years before Jiang relinquished the all-powerful CMC seat.[9] Big question marks, however, hang over whether Xi can successfully pick up the threads of economic, and particularly political, reform that were laid down by the late patriarch Deng Xiaoping and his first two designated successors, former general secretaries Hu Yaobang and Zhao Ziyang.

This chapter looks at political changes introduced at the Eighteenth Party Congress, which, at least in theory, paved the way for the transition of power from the Fourth-Generation leadership to the Fifth-Generation leadership (i.e., senior officials born in the 1950s). The traits and orientations of the Gang of Princelings (a reference to the offspring of party elders and senior cadres), of which Xi is the *de facto* leader, are examined. Also analyzed are the proclivities—and political fortunes—of the Communist Youth League (CYL) Faction, which is the only party clique that can pose some kind of challenge to Xi and his powerful allies. The phenomenon of state entrepreneurs and returnees (Chinese with degrees from foreign universities) being inducted into the upper echelons of the Party-state apparatus is appraised. The issue of whether Xi and his new team are in a position to battle the entrenched vested interests and resuscitate the reform agenda is discussed in detail.

## The Eighteenth Party Congress and the Advent of the Xi Jinping Era

### Xi's Problematic Emergence as Supreme Leader

Xi was officially selected as general secretary and CMC chairman at the first session of the Eighteenth Central Committee, which took place on November 15, 2012, a day after the conclusion of the Eighteenth Party Congress. During the week-long conclave, the 2,270 delegates representing the CCP's 85 million members met for their quinquennial convention to pick the 205 full members of the ruling Central Committee, as well as 171 alternate, or nonvoting Central Committee members.[10]

At least in theory, Xi (b. 1953) should have been very happy with the results because of the political identities and traits of the six other members of the supreme Politburo Standing Committee (PBSC): Premier Li Keqiang (b. 1955), NPC chairman Zhang Dejiang (b. 1946); chairman of the top consultative organ, the Chinese People's Political Consultative Conference (CPPCC), Yu Zhengsheng (b. 1945); executive secretary of the Central Committee Secretariat Liu Yunshan (b. 1947); secretary of the Central Commission for Disciplinary Inspection (CCDI) Wang Qishan (b. 1948); and Executive Vice-Premier Zhang Dejiang (b. 1946). Except for Premier Li, who is a senior representative of the CYL Faction led by ex-president Hu, all six PBSC members have ties to either ex-president Jiang Zemin's Shanghai Faction or Xi's Gang of Princelings.[11]

While the Eighteenth Party Congress was billed as one of the CCP's most momentous events in the twenty-first century, it was also swathed in the patriarchal—and undemocratic—traditions of the ninety-one-year-old party. As with past practice, the composition of the new ruling organ—the seven PBSC members—was determined by the outgoing PBSC members as well as party elders, especially ex-president Jiang (b. 1926), who effectively ran China from 1989 to 2004.[12] Three of the seven members of the new PBSC are deemed Jiang protégés. Apart from Xi, NPC chairman Zhang Dejiang and ideology and propaganda tsar Liu Yunshan owed their elevation to Jiang's recommendation. Jiang and former Premier Li Peng (born in 1928) were instrumental in preventing two of Hu's loyalists—Li Yuanchao (b. 1950) and Wang Yang (b. 1955)—from making it to the PBSC. Both Li and Wang, who have reformist reputations, have managed to hang on to their Politburo seats. Wang, who established a reformist reputation when he was Guangdong Party secretary from 2007 to 2012, became vice-premier in charge of foreign trade after the congress. Li, a former head of the CCP Organization Department, was given the consolation prize of vice-president—a post that does not have substantial powers.[13]

Xi's apparent ability to get his way at the congress, however, was a function of several developments that illustrated the efficacy of the rule of man—not the rule of law or of institutions. First, there was a resurgence of geriatric politics. Jiang, who was instrumental in Xi's promotion to the PBSC at the Seventeenth Party Congress in 2007 (see Chapter 2), again played the role of kingmaker in 2012. Jiang's pre-eminent position was illustrated by protocol arrangements at the opening session of the Eighteenth Party Congress on November 8. The first to greet the delegates at the Great Hall of the People was outgoing general secretary Hu, who was closely followed by Jiang. A distance of several meters separated the two potentates from the other eight soon-to-retire PBSC members and Party elders including former PBSC member Song Ping (b. 1917).[14]

Moreover, the choice of the seven-member PBSC and the twenty-five-member full Politburo was also influenced by three political incidents, none of which were handled according to the spirit of "intra-Party democracy." The first was the fall of the ambitious Chongqing Party secretary Bo Xilai (b. 1949). This became inevitable owing to revelations about the murder of British businessman Neil Heywood by his wife, Gu Kailai, in late 2011 and efforts by Wang Lijun, Bo's police chief and right-hand man, to seek political asylum at the U.S. consulate in Chengdu in February 2012. Before his downfall, Bo, the charismatic son of Party elder Bo Yibo, had catapulted himself to center stage through his campaign of *changhong dahe* (singing [Maoist] red songs and combating criminal gangs). Bo also told intimates that he was a more qualified person to lead the country than fellow princeling Xi.[15] In the wake of the Heywood and Wang scandals, Hu, Wen, and Xi pooled their resources to ensure the end of Bo's career. Bo was relieved of all his Party positions in March 2012 and given a life sentence for corruption and abuse of power in September 2013. Gu received a suspended death sentence the same year. The entire handling of the Bo scandal, however, reeked of old-style skullduggery and back-stabbing. There was little "democratic" discussion of the Bo affair within the Party. And the punishment meted out to Bo and Gu was based on political, not judicial, considerations (see Chapter 3).[16]

For a brief period, the downfall of Bo the bad-apple princeling gave the CYL Faction some momentum. Given the widespread public perception that princeling-cadres had abused their special privileges—particularly in accumulating massive wealth and laundering their ill-gotten gains—Bo and Gu's shenanigans brought disrepute to cadres with "revolutionary bloodlines." Several princeling cadres and military officers suffered collateral damage due to their chummy ties with Bo. They included Generals Liu Yuan and Zhang Haiyang, who are the sons, respectively, of State President Liu Shaoqi and former general and Politburo member Zhang Zhen. Immediately after the announcement on March 15 that Bo's Politburo membership had been suspended, there were wild stories of an aborted coup in Beijing. While these rumors turned out to be untrue, the Bo affair adversely affected the careers of Generals Liu and Zhang.[17]

Yet the so-called Ling Gu affair of March 2012 turned out to be even more of a disaster for the CYL Faction, particularly ex-president Hu. Ling Gu, the only son of Ling Jihua, who was then director of the CCP General Office and a close adviser to Hu, was killed in a traffic accident in Beijing. The twenty-three-year-old Ling was driving a Ferrari sports car that was worth more than RMB 1 million. Two of Ling's girlfriends, who were students at Central University for Nationalities (or Minzu University), were severely injured in the incident.[18] There was no evidence that other CYL Faction members such as then-director of the Organization Department Li Yuanchao, had tried to cover up the embarrassing incident. However, the Ling Gu episode exposed the huge personal assets of both Ling Gu and his mother, Gu Liping. For example, she ran a big charity organization that was believed to be a front for a lucrative business consultancy, and Ling Gu was the proud owner of several high-priced imported cars. Hu's enemies, led by ex-president Jiang, launched a ferocious attack not only on Ling Jihua but also other members of the CYL Faction. In August the same year Ling Jihua was transferred to the less important position of director of the United Front Department, and he failed to win a spot in the Politburo at the Eighteenth Party Congress. Even more significant was the fact that Jiang severely criticized Hu for failing to keep an eye on his underlings. In response, Hu reportedly noted that Ling worked twelve-hour days and that he did not have time to keep an eye on his family members. However, the damage had been done. Hu's moral authority had been dealt a big blow—and his influence over personnel arrangements at the Eighteenth Party Congress was severely affected.[19]

The third incident that raised questions about institutions and processes in the Party revolved around the mysterious "disappearance" of Xi from September 1 to September 15. At a time when world media were pulling out all the stops to find out more about the top leader-in-waiting, Xi was nowhere to be found. All sorts of unofficial explanations were given. CPPCC vice-chairman Tung Chee-hwa told CNN that Xi had injured his back while swimming. The real reason, however, could be that Xi did something unprecedented: He was using his silence as a protest against what he perceived to be irregularities in the preparations for the Eighteenth Party Congress, particularly personnel arrangements that were not to his liking. One of Xi's gripes was President Hu's apparent intention of hanging on to the CMC chairmanship after his retirement from the posts of general secretary and PBSC member.[20]

Given Xi's advocacy of unity at all costs and his reputation as a team player, the "silent protest" conducted by the princeling was singularly out of character. However, his strategy worked to some extent. Hu finally agreed to perform a "naked"—that is, total—retirement. The price Hu asked for was that he would be in charge of the upcoming round of personnel changes at the CMC's upper echelons. Thus, two Hu protégés in the PLA, General Fang Fenghui, then commander of the Beijing Military Region, and General Zhang Yang, political commissar of the Guangzhou Military Region, were promoted respectively to chief of the General Staff Department and director of the General Political Department at the seventh and last plenum of the Seventeenth Central Committee, which ended just four days before the opening of the Eighteenth Party Congress. If the top leadership had followed long-standing convention, the composition of the new CMC should have been unveiled at the first plenum of the Eighteenth Central Committee held on November 15, the same day that the PBSC lineup was announced.[21]

### Setback for "Intra-Party Democracy"

The Eighteenth Party Congress demonstrated stunning setbacks for political reform, even the much less ambitious goal of "intra-Party democracy"—or boosting the democratic rights of the 85 million CCP members. In his Political Report to the Eighteenth Party Congress (hereafter Report), Hu repeated many points made in his Political Report to the Seventeenth Party Congress five years earlier. Emphasis was laid on reforming the Party's personnel system, particularly fairer and more transparent ways for picking leaders by the rank and file. For example, Hu said that the authorities must substantiate Party members' "right to know, right to take part [in Party deliberations], electoral rights, and supervisory rights." Regarding the selection of senior cadres, Hu indicated that the Party must "comprehensively and correctly implement democratic, open, competitive and meritorious" goals.[22] However, while discussing leadership issues in 2007, Hu had put emphasis on systems of "democratic centralism and collective leadership" and indicated that the Party must "oppose and prevent dictatorial [practices] by individuals or a minority [of leaders.]" There were no more references to preventing the dictatorial practices of strongman-like figures in the 2012 Report.[23]

The failure to push forward with political reform was highlighted by remarks made by ex-premier Wen Jiabao, the only member of the old Politburo who had consistently rooted for liberalization. While discussing Hu's Report with congress delegates from his native Tianjin, Wen again highlighted the imperative of institutional changes. "We must strengthen and improve the leadership of the party," Wen said. "In particular, we must push forward the reform of the leadership system of the Party and state."[24] Wen's comment on the "reform of the leadership system of the Party and state" seemed as timely as it was hard-hitting. While Wen had made dozens of appeals to speeding up political reform, including upholding Deng Xiaoping's edicts on the subject, this was the first time that he made an indirect—but obvious—reference to one of the most celebrated articles of the chief architect of reform. In a 1980 piece titled "On the Reform of the System of Party and State Leadership," Deng cited the following daunting obstacles to political and institutional liberalization: "bureaucracy, overconcentration of power, patriarchal methods, life tenure for leading positions and [special] privileges of various kinds." Deng had this to say about the Party's "patriarchal" traditions: "Besides leading to overconcentration of power in the hands of individuals, patriarchal ways within the revolutionary ranks place individuals above the organization, which then becomes a tool [for dictatorial leaders]."[25]

The Chinese media made much of the fact that there were *cha'e* elections (polls in which candidates outnumber the positions up for grabs) at this congress. Thus when the conclave opened, the delegates were given a name list of 224 candidates from which to pick the 205 members of the Central Committee. Among those eliminated was then-commerce minister Chen Deming. His unexpected failure to make it to the Central Committee meant that the original script in which Chen would become a Politburo member and vice-premier in charge of foreign trade had to be scrapped.[26] The margin of elimination for the Central Committee elections, however, was a mere 9.3 percent, barely one percentage point higher than that at the Seventeenth Party Congress in 2007. Moreover, the speculation that the CCP would for the first time hold *cha'e* elections to pick members of the Politburo turned out to be false.[27] In terms of democratic procedures for picking top leaders, the CCP has lagged further behind the Vietnamese Communist Party, which introduced competitive elections to choose its Party general secretary in 2006.[28]

The new leadership did not even pass muster in terms of the most basic criterion of rejuvenation. The average age of the seven PBSC members was 63.4. Only two of them—General Secretary Xi and Premier Li, who first made it to the PBSC in 2007—were born in the 1950s. The age of the five new inductees ranged from sixty-four to sixty-seven. Given the convention that cadres aged sixty-eight are barred from consideration for the PBSC, all five can only serve one term.[29] Equally problematic of the new leadership corps was its lack of representativeness. Despite pledges made by both Hu and Xi about doing more for the disadvantaged sectors, there were no bona fide workers and peasants on the 205-member Central Committee. Forty-one Central Committee members hailed from the PLA and the paramilitary People's Armed Police (PAP). This was in keeping with the long-held tradition that 20 percent of Central Committee seats be reserved for the armed forces, who were seen as the pillar of the "dictatorship of the proletariat."[30]

Another power bloc that made impressive gains at the Eighteenth Party Congress consisted of representatives of China's *yangqi* (centrally held SOE conglomerates; see Chapter 4). Six newly minted full Central Committee members were *yangqi* bosses, compared to just one five years ago. They were the general manager of the China Aerospace Science and Technology Corporation, Ma Xingrui; general manager of China Aerospace Science and Industry Corporation, Xu Dazhe; president of the China Aviation Industry Corporation, Lin Zuoming; president of the China North Industries Group Corporation (Norinco), Zhang Guoqing; general manager of Petro China and China National Petroleum Corporation (CNPC), Jiang Jiemin; and president of the Bank of China, Xiao Gang. In addition, the president of China's sovereign fund China Investment Corporation, Lou Jiwei, was promoted from alternate to full Central Committee member. Most of these SOE bosses were transferred to government posts in 2013 and 2014 (see Chapter 3). *Yangqi,* particularly those with links to the military, are traditionally close to the Gang of Princelings. For example, the eldest son of ex-president Jiang Zemin, Zhang Mianheng, has had a long association with the defense and aerospace industries.[31]

By contrast, there is only one private entrepreneur in the Central Committee: alternate member Zhang Ruimin, who is the leader of the Hai'er Corporation, which makes household appliances. This was the third time since 2002 that Zhang had been named a Central Committee alternate member. Liang Wen'gen, chairman of the Sany Group and one of China's richest men, failed to be elected alternate Central Committee member, despite widespread reports in the official Chinese media that he would be inducted into this inner sanctum of power. The increasing political clout of the *yangqi* CEOs seems to testify to the fact that the trend, characterized by Chinese economists as "SOEs making advances even as private enterprises retreat," will continue in the foreseeable future.[32]

Fighting graft was another area in which Hu Jintao's efforts seem to have fallen short. Hu echoed warnings sounded by ex-president Jiang in the late 1990s that the Party's failure to eradicate endemic corruption could "deal a body blow to the Party and even lead to the collapse of the Party and country." "We must never slacken in fighting graft and in building clean governance," he warned. "The alarm bells must be rung unceasingly." Yet the retiring Party chief failed to introduce measures such as Party regulations requiring all senior cadres to publicize the assets of their close kin—and to disclose whether the latter have foreign residency status. It was also significant that while reading his speech, Hu omitted this clause, which was in the printed version: "Senior cadres must not only discipline themselves stringently but also strengthen the education of and constraints over their relatives and close associates."[33]

In the run-up to the congress, Bloomberg and the *New York Times* published detailed reports about the business activities of the relatives of then-vice president Xi and ex-premier Wen. Despite immediate action taken by state censors to block online access to these articles in China, millions of netizens are believed to have read them. While Hu's warnings about the exacerbation of graft could be the Party's answer to growing criticisms about greed in high places, no investigations were believed to have been launched on the well-publicized business activities of the close relations of top officials despite the fact that while participating in discussions among provincial and municipal deputies to the Congress, top cadres such as CPPCC chairman-designate Yu Zhengsheng claimed that effective steps had been taken to prevent their relatives from making money improperly.[34]

In his Report, Hu urged Party cadres and members to work harder at "innovation of the implementation [of policies], theoretical innovations, and the innovation of institutions." Yet he also repeated this same point that he made five years earlier: "While [the Party] will not go down the old road of ossification, it will also avoid devious paths that will change the flag and standard [of socialist orthodoxy]." On other occasions, Hu and Xi declared that cadres must do whatever it takes to preserve the status of the CCP as China's "perennial ruling party." Both the Fourth- and the Fifth-Generation leader pointed out that "the CCP's ruling status may not necessarily last forever: what we had in the past does not mean we have them now; what we possess now does not mean we'll have them forever."[35] Given the predominance of conservatism in the Report—and the Byzantine fashion in which the new corps of leaders was chosen—the chances are not high that the new leadership under Xi Jinping will push reformist goals and policies in the foreseeable future.

## The Rise of the Gang of Princelings

It is an interesting coincidence that the leaders of the three most important Asian countries are all princelings. Apart from Xi, the prime minister of Japan, Shinzo Abe, and the president of South Korea, Park Geun-hye, are the offspring of notable politicians. The Chinese situation, however, is significantly different from that in the two other Asian countries that have been heavily influenced by Confucian culture: there are no checks and balances in Chinese politics to prevent abuse of power by members of the "red aristocracy," who believe that their pedigree entitles them to ride roughshod over the people. An appreciation of the composition and the preoccupations of the *taizidang* (Gang of Princelings) is a prerequisite for understanding Xi and his policies.

At a time when the CCP's top echelon is orchestrating a return to conservative norms, cadres with a "revolutionary bloodline" are considered trustworthy custodians of the values first propagated by Mao Zedong and his Long March veterans. It is therefore not surprising that high-profile *gaoganzidi* (children of Party leaders) such as Xi Jinping and the disgraced former Chongqing Party secretary Bo Xilai were at the forefront of the resuscitation of Maoist norms (see Chapter 3).[36] However, the return of the princelings—who are seen as representatives of the "red aristocracy"—to the limelight does not seem to augur well for political liberalization.

The political fortune of the Gang of Princelings suffered a blow during the first decade of the era of reform. Deng Xiaoping was against allowing too many princelings to monopolize Party and government posts. In the early 1980s, Deng reportedly indicated in an internal Party meeting that the proportion of *taizidang* Central Committee members should be limited. This was to prevent nepotism and factionalism from wreaking havoc on the Party. The patriarch also stipulated the now-famous "five lakes and four seas" principle for grooming future leaders, who, he instructed, must come from diverse factional and geographical backgrounds.[37] Instead of seeking a political career, princelings were instead encouraged to go into business. It was no accident that the patriarch's sons, Deng Pufang and Deng Zhifang, were successful but also controversial, businessmen. The same goes for the children of Third- and Fourth-Generation leaders including Li Peng, Jiang Zemin, Zhu Rongji, Hu Jintao, and Wen Jiabao. Li Peng's son and daughter, for example, were active in the energy field while Jiang's two sons were entrepreneurs in information technology in Shanghai.[38]

The careers of many princelings were adversely affected by Deng's stricture. Bo Xilai, for example, did not get into the Central Committee until 2002, when he was fifty-three years old despite the fact that he had years earlier established himself as a formidable "warlord" in industrialized Liaoning Province. A number of high-profile princelings, including Xi Jinping, Wang Qishan (son-in-law of the late vice-premier Yao Yilin) and Deng Pufang made it onto the Central Committee at a relatively late point in their careers. The trio were first inducted into the Central Committee in 1997 as alternate, or second-tier and nonvoting, members. Moreover, Xi got the lowest—and Deng and Wang respectively the second and seventh lowest—number of votes among the 151 alternate members.[39]

This is not to say, of course, that princelings have ever ceased to play a sizable role in Chinese politics. So-called second-tier princelings—officials whose fathers were senior cadres but not at the level of Politburo members—have continued to become important government ministers or heads of CCP departments. Examples have included several leaders of the Shanghai Faction such as ex-president Jiang and ex-vice president Zeng Qinghong. Jiang's foster father was the "revolutionary martyr" Jiang Shangqing, while Zeng's father was former interior minister Zeng Shan.[40] And by the early 2000s, the princelings had made a big comeback. The Seventeenth Party Congress in 2007 witnessed the joining of the forces of the Gang of Princelings and the Shanghai Faction, which was responsible for the selection of Xi Jinping—and not Li Keqiang—as "crown prince." As we saw earlier, apart from Xi and then vice-premier Wang Qishan, Yu Zhengsheng, who is the son of the former head of the now-defunct First Ministry of Machine-Building, Yu Qiwei, joined the PBSC at the Eighteenth Party Congress. A crony of Deng Pufang's, Yu is considered the "big brother" among princelings as well as a prominent representative of the Deng clan.[41]

However, princelings have obvious drawbacks as a political bloc. Despite the freeze on political reform since 1989, a large portion of the population harbors prejudice against symbols of special privileges. The princelings faction also suffers from institutional shortcomings. Foremost is a lack of connections based on common values beyond perpetuating the special privileges that they enjoy. All *gaoganzidi* share this lowest common denominator: They want to preserve the prerogatives that have traditionally been arrogated by descendants of the CCP's empire-builders, which has been encapsulated by this popular saying: "Since the fathers built heaven and earth, the sons have a right to inherit them."[42]

Yet the camaraderie and commonality of purpose among princelings are significantly less pronounced than those among members of organizationally or geographically based groupings such as the CYL Faction and the Shanghai Faction. Even though Xi is the highest-ranked princeling, the fact that he lacks obvious national achievements means that he may not necessarily command the allegiance of the majority of the pedigreed cadres. The sons and daughters of Party elders who were rivals may harbor grudges against one another. For example, the relationship between Xi and Bo has been affected by the fact that their fathers—Xi Zhongxun and Bo Yibo—hailed from rival CCP factions. Xi Zhongxun was a liberal and ally of late Party chief Hu Yaobang while Bo Yibo was close to conservative Second-Generation titans such as Chen Yun and Li Xiannian. Similarly, princelings may clash over their assessment of Party history, including the stature of Mao Zedong. While quite a few *gaoganzidi* are fervent followers of Mao, others, like General Liu Yuan, whose father suffered grievously during the Cultural Revolution, have openly pilloried the Great Helmsman.[43]

The one branch of the polity in which princelings may be most united is the PLA, where the sons—and occasionally daughters—of Long March veterans still enjoy a substantial advantage in promotions. It is estimated that several dozen PLA major-generals, lieutenant-generals, and full generals boast distinguished pedigrees.[44] And, given Xi's ties to the PLA, it is likely that some of these generals could become the supreme leader's close advisers. The CYL Faction, by contrast, is thinly represented, if at all, in the defense establishment. "Princeling generals" who made it to the Eighteenth Central Committee include the newly promoted director of the General Armaments Department and CMC member, General Zhang Youxia (b. 1950), who is the son of General Zhang Zongxun; Air Force commander and CMC member Ma Xiaotian (b. 1949), who is the son of Ma Zaiyao, a political commissar at the now-defunct PLA Military Academy; political commissar of the General Logistics Department General Liu Yuan (b. 1951); Navy Political Commissar Admiral Liu Xiaojiang (b. 1949), who is the son-in-law of Hu Yaobang; political commissar of the Second Artillery Corps General Zhang Haiyang (b. 1949); and political commissar of the National Defense University General Liu Yazhou (b. 1951), a strategist who is the son-in-law of the late president Li Xiannian.[45]

Given the cozy relationship between Xi and these princeling generals, the military forces are set to become his major power base. Among pedigreed members of the top brass, Xi is believed to rely most on the advice of Generals Zhang Youxia, Ma Xiaotian, and Liu Yuan. Among members of the top brass from a plebeian background, Xi is said to be particularly close to the commander of the Second Artillery Corps or missile forces, General Wei Fenghe (b. 1954). In any event, compared to his predecessors Jiang and Hu, Xi has spent considerably more time inspecting different divisions of China's labyrinthine defense establishment.[46]

However, the strength of the princeling generals—which continues into the Sixth- and Seventh-Generation officers, or those born in the 1960s and 1970s—has thrown into sharp relief the dearth of Sixth- and Seventh-Generation princeling cadres in the Party and government apparatus. Unlike the case of the CYL Faction (see the following section), not many Sixth-Generation princelings on the political stage are being groomed for big things. The great majority of princelings born from the 1960s to 1980s have gone into the world of business. There are, however, exceptions. In 2013, the grandson of Deng Xiaoping, Deng Zhuodi (b. 1975), who has a law degree from Duke University, became deputy chief of Pingguo County, Guangxi Province. Deng's father is the patriarch's second son, Deng Zhifang, who is believed to have permanent residency in the United States.[47] At about the same time, Hu Haifeng (b. 1972), the businessman son of ex-president Hu, was named deputy Party secretary of Jiaxing, Zhejiang Province. The younger Hu's name came up in 2009 in a corruption case involving the operations of his old high-tech company, Nuctech Corporation, in Namibia.[48] Yet the likelihood is slim that another princeling will be inducted into the Politburo, let along the PBSC, in the coming decade or so.

### The Political Fortunes of the Communist Youth League Faction

#### The CYL Faction's Setback at Eighteenth Party Congress

The *tuanpai* (CYL Faction), headed by ex-president Hu Jintao, suffered a stunning setback regarding the distribution of the spoils at the Eighteenth Party Congress. Premier Li Keqiang is the only CYL Faction affiliate among the seven members of the Politburo Standing Committee. However, the *tuanpai*, which has been meticulously nurtured by Hu from the mid-1990s onward, has remained the CCP's single-largest faction. This close-knit network is particularly strong among Fifth- and Sixth-Generation cadres. And the *tuanpai* could make a partial comeback at the Nineteenth Party Congress, set for 2017.

The CYL Faction's strength is apparent with the full Politburo of twenty-five members, twelve of whom were born in the 1950s. At least eight Politburo members are considered to have ties of various degrees of intimacy to the *tuanpai*. Apart from Li Keqiang, they include two second-term Politburo members who narrowly missed PBSC membership: State Vice-President Li Yuanchao and Vice-Premier Wang Yang. The other five *tuanpai*-affiliated Politburo members are Vice-Premier Liu Yandong (b. 1945); director of the Propaganda Department, Liu Qibao (b. 1953); Beijing Party secretary Guo Jinlong (b. 1947); Shanghai Party secretary Han Zheng (b. 1954), who also has links with the Shanghai Faction; and Guangdong Party secretary Hu Chunhua (b. 1963). The CYL Faction is also the largest bloc within the 205 full Central Committee members, 80 percent of whom are Fifth-Generation stalwarts.[49]

Owing to their seniority as well as generally accepted track record, Li Yuanchao and Wang Yang are deemed to have reasonably good chances of making the PBSC at the Nineteenth Party Congress. Equally significant is the quickly rising political fortune of one of the brightest stars among the Sixth-Generation cadres: Hu Chunhua, who is called a potential "core" of the Sixth-Generation leadership. Hu Chunhua, a former CYL Party secretary who was posted to Guangdong, China's most prosperous province, soon after the Eighteenth Party Congress, has been mentioned as a successor to Xi. Hu and newly appointed Chongqing Party secretary Sun Zhengcai (b. 1963) are the only two Sixth-Generation officials in the Politburo. As such, they are tipped for induction to the PBSC in 2017. Sun, who is a protégé of ex-premier Wen Jiabao, does not have obvious factional inclinations.[50]

Indeed, the advantage of the *tuanpai* is even more obvious among the rising Six-Generation cadres. Of the nine Central Committee members who were born in the 1960s, four are associated with the CYL Faction. Apart from Hu Chunhua, they are president of the Supreme People's Court and former Party secretary of Hunan Zhou Qiang (b. 1960); chairman of the Xinjiang Autonomous Region Nur Bekri (b. 1960); and Heilongjiang governor and former CYL First Party secretary Lu Hao (b. 1967).[51] Sixth-Generation Alternate Central Committee members who have worked in the CYL include the following up-and-coming cadres: the current CYL Party secretary Qin Yizhe (b. 1965); deputy Party secretary of Hebei Province, Zhao Yong (b. 1963); deputy Party secretary of Hunan Province, Sun Jinlong (b. 1962); Party secretary of Fuzhou, the capital of Fujian Province, Yang Yue (b. 1968); chairman of the Beijing municipal CPPCC Ji Lin (b. 1962); and Party secretary of Hami district, Xinjiang, Liu Jian (b. 1970).[52]

The career trajectory of Hu Chunhua (who is not related to Hu Jintao) merits close examination as he is a reasonably strong candidate for the PBSC at the next Party congress. At least in the run-up to the Eighteenth Party Congress, ex-president Hu's intention was to position him to succeed Xi at the Twentieth Party Congress in 2022. This would be in the tradition of the "cross-generation designation of successors," which was initiated by Deng Xiaoping at the Fourteenth Party Congress in 1992. On that occasion, Deng surprised Jiang Zemin by elevating then-Party secretary of Tibet Hu Jintao to the PBSC, thus in effect naming the forty-nine-year-old "core" of the Fourth-Generation leadership as Jiang's successor. And at the Seventeenth Party Congress, Jiang maneuvered to have then-Party secretary of Shanghai Xi inducted to the PBSC as Hu's successor.[53]

Hu Chunhua's career is typical of that of most CYL-affiliated rising stars. He first rose to ministerial-level status as Party boss of the CYL and then was transferred to the provinces to gain extra experience. Hu gained national prominence when he was named first Party secretary of the CYL in 2006. He later became governor of Hebei Province (2008–9) and Party secretary of Inner Mongolia (2009–12).

The swiftness of his rise up the hierarchy was possible only with the personal endorsement of ex-president Hu.[54]

It is noteworthy, however, that it was in the Tibet Autonomous Region (TAR) that Hu Chunhua first distinguished himself. And while Deng was said to have favored Hu Jintao due to his resolute suppression of "splittists" in Tibet, ex-president Hu may also have been impressed by Hu Chunhua's experience in taming the restive region. Even though the older Hu was never able to adapt to the harsh climate in the TAR, the younger Hu stayed there for nineteen years. Upon his graduation from Peking University in 1983, Hu volunteered to go to work as a young cadre in the Organization Department of the Tibet Communist Party Committee. Subsequently, he became editor of *Tibet Daily* and manager of the Lhasa Hotel. It is a mark of ex-president Hu's trust in his protégé that the younger Hu rose to become first deputy Party secretary of Tibet in 2005, when the latter was merely forty-two. A fluent speaker of Tibetan, Hu was credited with reviving the Tibet economy, thwarting separatist tendencies among Tibetans, and moving more Han Chinese into the region.[55] It was perhaps due to his special relationship with the president that the younger Hu did not need to take responsibility for the tainted milk scandal that first erupted in Hebei in 2008. Among the first goals that Hu established for himself as Party boss of the Inner Mongolia Autonomous Region was "upholding political stability." Hu mandated that the No. 1 Party and government official in each locality in the autonomous region "personally take charge of maintaining sociopolitical stability." And it was apparently due to his administrative ability that Hu successfully handled the series of disturbances that rocked Inner Mongolia in early 2011. As we shall see in Chapter 2, however, President Xi, who does not seem to have a high estimation of the CYL Faction's ability, is building up a close coterie of followers. And the head of the princelings' faction seems determined to marginalize a number of *tuanpai* rising stars including Hu.[56]

The only other Sixth-Generation cadre on the Politburo is Sun Zhengcai, a technocrat who does not have close links to either the *tuanpai,* the princelings, or the Shanghai Faction. A respected expert in agriculture, Sun worked in the Party-and-government apparatus of Beijing municipality before being named agriculture minister in 2006 by ex-premier Wen. In 2009, Sun was promoted to become Party secretary of Jilin, a position that he held until he was inducted into the Politburo and transferred to Chongqing to run the directly administered municipality. Given that Sun has top-level experience in both the central government and the provinces, he has a good chance of further advancement, particularly on the State Council. Indeed, there is talk that he could be a potential successor to Li Keqiang as prime minister in 2023.[57]

By contrast, there were relatively few big stars among Shanghai Faction or *taizidang* members among either Fifth- or Six-Generation officials. Since the early 1990s princelings have been perceived by ordinary Party members as symbols of special privilege. Since early 2012, the *taizidang*'s public image has been damaged by the political scandal of former Chongqing Party boss Bo Xilai. The *taizidang*'s reputation has taken a further drubbing thanks to numerous reports by both the Chinese and foreign press about the questionable business dealings of the spouses and children of top officials. It is therefore not surprising that a mere handful of Fifth-Generation princelings made it to the Central Committee—but only as alternate members—at the Eighteenth Party Congress. A good example is Li Xiaopeng (b. 1959), then vice-governor of Shanxi Province and a former president of the state-owned energy giant, the Huaneng Group. The fact that Li, the eldest son of former premier Li Peng, garnered the fewest votes among the 171 alternate Central Committee members testified to the unpopularity of princeling politicians.[58]

A sure-fire way for the CYL Clique to maintain its profile and momentum in the higher echelons of the Party-state apparatus is to seize the moral high ground of reform. In a State Council conference held just a week after the congress, premier-in-waiting Li Keqiang hoisted high the banner of institutional and economic reform. In language that is reminiscent of that used by both ex-premier Wen and Deng Xiaoping, Li pointed out that "our only [choice] is to go forward since there is no way back." "We must be brave in experimentations, because this is where our responsibility lies," he added. "We may be able to avoid mistakes if we do nothing; yet we have to shoulder the responsibility that history has given us." Li put particular emphasis on the propagation of "equality of rights, equality of opportunity, and equality of regulations—so that every citizen can be able to derive benefits through hard work."[59]

### The Challenges of Premier Li Keqiang

As the highest-ranking Fifth-Generation leader of the CYL Faction, Li Keqiang sometimes has to engage in fierce competition with the Gang of Princelings to ensure maximum benefits for his clique. Like ex-president Hu and another CYL stalwart, Wang Yang, Li is a native of eastern Anhui Province. After spending four years in the countryside "learning from the masses," Li was able to get into Peking University (Beida) in 1978. He was among the first batch of university students after college education resumed in the wake of the Cultural Revolution. Li was a top student at Beida's Law School.[60] While he thought seriously of furthering legal studies in the United States, Li gave up the idea after being told by top Beida officials that he was being groomed for a high-level government post. Li also caught the eye of mentor Hu Jintao, who inducted him into the CYL Central Committee in 1983. Li became first Party secretary of the CYL in 1993, when he was barely thirty-eight years old. His long years in the CYL enabled him to build up a formidable nationwide network of followers.[61]

In 1998 Li was transferred to Henan Province, where he stayed until 2004. In these six years, he served as acting governor, governor, and, finally in 2003, as Party secretary. While Li deserved some credit for reviving the economy of this landlocked, predominantly agricultural province, it was overshadowed by the scandal of the "AIDS villages." Tens of thousands of poor Henan peasants contracted

AIDS through selling blood at illegal—and unhygienic—blood-collection centers. This evil practice started before Li went to Henan; however, Li was criticized by international human rights organizations for failing to put a quick end to the practice. Moreover, he was said to have harassed if not also persecuted a host of human rights activists, including the well-known "AIDS heroine," Gao Yaojie. These "people's heroes" were prevented from talking to the foreign media.[62] As preparation for his eventual elevation to the PBSC, mentor and ex-president Hu transferred Li in 2004 to the industrialized northeastern province of Liaoning. His track record in Liaoning was somewhat better. For example, he did a great deal to persuade multinational corporations to set up high-tech plants in the old industrial base of Liaoning. On the social front, he was able to resettle tens of thousands of "squatters" in the provincial capital of Shenyang to newly built low-cost government housing.[63]

Li's tenure as executive vice-premier from 2008 to early 2103 was considered lackluster. This was due in part to the fact that, because the global financial crisis erupted in September 2008, he had to devote the bulk of his energies to helping ex-premier Wen shield the Chinese economy from the fallout of recession then affecting much of the Western world. Li, however, barely achieved a passing grade in several specific portfolios that he had assumed: reforming the medical system, tackling the housing bubble, and ensuring food safety. While Li deserved some credit for extending health insurance to the villages, the No. 2 member of the State Council was unable to stop creeping corruption particularly at hospitals. Urban housing has become unaffordable even for members of the middle and professional classes despite Li's determination to boost the number of low-cost apartments for urban workers. The then-vice-premier was unable to prevent developers, including many state-owned enterprises, from the unethical if not illegal practice of hoarding valuable plots of land, waiting for them to gain value instead of building on them. As director of the National Food Safety Commission, Li had to take responsibility for the never-ending scandals involving fake liquor, plaster soybean curd (tofu), milk enriched with hydrolyzed leather, and oil that has been "recycled" from used lard scooped up from the gutters.[64]

As far as preparation for their top jobs is concerned, Premier Li enjoys certain distinct advantages over President Xi. First, while their age difference is small, Li is a lot more knowledgeable about international issues, including global economics and international law. His training in law and economics at Peking University was impressive. Moreover, Li is at least more aware of the importance of political and institutional reform. While studying law at Beida, Li impressed his professors and classmates by having a good grasp of Western political ideals. A couple of the British textbooks that he translated into Chinese are still being used at Chinese law schools. His enthusiasm for political reform was demonstrated in speeches that he gave as a Beida student leader.[65]

After he was inducted into the top echelon of the CYL—and groomed as a future Party and state leader—Li stopped talking about political reform. The reason is obvious. Except for Wen Jiabao, almost none of the Fourth- or Fifth-Generation leaders have any interest in genuine political liberalization. However, immediately after he became executive vice-premier in March 2008, Li helped Wen design structural changes in the central government, such as giving more powers to the Ministry of Environmental Protection and the formation of superagencies to handle the energy and food-safety portfolios. In 2008 Li also wanted to establish a "superministry" to oversee transportation, including aviation, railways, and highways. The plan failed in part because of the opposition of then-minister of railways Liu Zhijun, who enjoyed a close relationship with both Jiang Zemin and Hu Jintao. However, Liu was convicted of corruption in 2011. And a reorganization of State Council agencies took place in March 2013 as Li became premier. For example, the enlarged Ministry of Transport has incorporated offices including the State Postal Bureau, the Civil Aviation Administration of China, and the National Railway Administration.[66]

One big question regarding the Xi-Li administration is: Will there be clashes between these two leaders? If a power struggle were to erupt between the Gang of Princelings and the CYL Faction, it could take the form of intensifying rivalry between Xi and Li. For example, while Li, as premier, is supposed to have overall responsibility for the economy, it is possible for Xi to interfere with Li's work because in China, the Party leads the government in almost all arenas. It is well-known that Party general secretaries and premiers since the early 1980s—including Hu Yaobang and Zhao Ziyang; Zhao Ziyang and Li Peng; Jiang Zemin and Zhu Rongji; and Hu Jintao and Wen Jiabao—had occasional quarrels regarding specific financial and economic policies.[67] As we shall see in Chapters 3 and 4, Xi has come up with new institutions such as the Central Leading Group on Comprehensively Deepening Reforms so as to arrogate to himself ultimate control over economic policy-making.

### Communist Youth League Alumnae Among the Six-Generation Leadership

Sixth-Generation cadres are poised to take power at the Twentieth Party Congress in 2022. While this may seem a long way off, it is in the Chinese tradition to groom future leaders well in advance. Having spent twenty years in the PBSC, ex-president Hu was in a position to elevate a host of Sixth-Generation cadres from his CYL Clique to prominent posts. At the time of the Eighteenth Party Congress, a disproportionately large number of officials born in the 1960s who had risen to ministerial-level slots were Hu protégés. According to Renmin University professor of public administration Mao Shaolong, it is not an accident that so many CYL-affiliated cadres have been catapulted to positions of prominence. "The CYL is the Party's unit for training talent," he said. "Young officials who have gone through the League system mature quickly [in the hierarchy]." Mao also noted that they had had many opportunities to prove their worth in central- and regional-level positions.[68]

Given that most members of the CYL Faction are veteran *danggong* (party functionaries), *tuanpai* cadres are generally considered politically correct and knowledgeable about the requirements of the central authorities. Much more significant for the future of the country, however, is the question of whether CYL affiliates will be capable of tackling the increasingly complex challenges facing twenty-first-century China. *Tuanpai* cadres have traditionally been experts in three areas: ideology (including "modernizing Marxism for the new era"), propaganda, and personnel and disciplinary matters. In its long history, there were brilliant—and liberal—minds within the CYL such as Hu Yaobang and former director of the Department of Propaganda, Zhu Houze, who distinguished themselves in ideological and political liberalization. Taking the cue from President Hu, however, most Fifth-Generation *tuanpai* officials, let alone Sixth-Generation ones, have steered clear of the controversial issue of political reform. In order to satisfy the "morality" criterion, *danggong* veterans seem more adept at demonstrating political trustworthiness and avoiding mistakes than at testing new ideas that may be deemed controversial and ideologically suspect.[69]

With the possible exception of Li Keqiang and Wang Yang, senior CYL-affiliated cadres lack expertise in global business and high technology, the two areas in which China must excel in order to maintain its competitiveness. So far as substantive matters of governance are concerned, the *tuanpai* seems less well-equipped and competent than technocrats or "returnees," a reference to officials with advanced degrees from Western universities. In terms of their upbringing, education and work experience, Hu Chunhua and Zhou Qiang, the two most outstanding Sixth-Generation *tuanpai* cadres, do not seem to have sufficient exposure to and knowledge of Western culture and institutions.[70]

It should also be noted that ex-president Hu seems to have violated the oft-cited principle of "intra-Party democracy"—which would at least in theory allow cadres a bigger say in choosing their leaders—by letting two favorite Sixth-Generation underlings take the proverbial "helicopter ride" to the top. This is particularly glaring given that many Fifth-Generation CYL heavyweights have proven to be lackluster cadres who owe their rise to patronage rather than performance. Examples include the former Party secretaries of Tibet and Xinjiang, respectively Zhang Qingli (b. 1951) and Wang Lequn (b. 1944), as well as former Sichuan Party boss Liu Qibao (b. 1953) and Anhui Party secretary Zhang Baoshun (b. 1950). Zhang Qingli and Wang have been criticized for suppressing the religious and cultural heritage of ethnic minorities within their jurisdiction. Liu, together with his predecessor Du Qinglin, yet another CYL alumnus, has been faulted for the large number of shoddily constructed buildings that collapsed during the Sichuan earthquake in 2008. And Zhang Baoshun, who served in Shanxi Province from 2001 to 2010, was widely blamed for failing to curtail the number of deadly accidents in the coalmines of his resource-rich province.[71]

## The Rise of the Technocrats and Returnees

In the tradition of Jiang Zemin's "Theory of the Three Represents," one of whose major thrusts is to absorb well-educated and entrepreneurial-minded talents into the mid- to upper echelons of the Party, the Hu Jintao administration began appointing more cadres with business experience to government positions.[72] Moreover, academics and professionals with no Party affiliation but who have impressive professional expertise were inducted to ex-premier Wen's second cabinet. For example, the German-educated automobile specialist Wan Gang (b. 1952) was appointed minister of science and technology from 2008 to 2013, and the French-educated medical researcher Chen Zhu (b. 1953) became minister of health during the same period.[73]

Until around about the turn of the twenty-first century, cadres with business and professional experience who excelled in senior slots in the Party-state apparatus usually came from two sectors: petroleum and electricity as well as automobiles. Two former PBSC members—ex-vice president Zeng Qinghong (b. 1939) and former head of the political-legal apparatus Zhou Yongkang (b. 1942)—as well as PBSC member and Executive Vice-Premier Zhang Gaoli, earned their spurs in the oil business. The son of ex-premier Li Peng, Li Xiaopeng (b. 1959), a former CEO of the energy giant Huaneng, was appointed vice-governor of Shanxi Province in 2008. There have been more recent appointments from the energy sector. Thus Sinopec President Su Shulin (b. 1962) was named governor of Fujian in 2011. And CNPC chairman Jiang Jiemin (b. 1954) became the ministerial-level head of the State Assets Supervision and Administration Commission (SASAC) a few months after the Eighteenth Party Congress. (Jiang was arrested in September 2013 in association with the Zhou Yongkang corruption case; see Chapter 3.)[74] Former PBSC members with auto experience include ex-president Jiang and former executive vice-premier Li Lanqing. Wang Zhaoguo (b. 1941), a former Politburo member and head of the official trade union, was a deputy head of the Second Auto Works in 1982, when he was picked by Deng Xiaoping for a senior post in Beijing. Sixth-Generation cadres from the auto-manufacturing sector include the deputy Party secretary of Jilin, Zhu Yanfeng (b. 1961), who was posted to the northeastern province in 2007 after a brilliant career at the First Auto Works.[75]

Reflecting Xi's concern for promoting synergy between the military and the civilian sectors (see Chapter 5), an unprecedented number of cadres with experience in the military-industrial complex and the aerospace sector have entered the government. Zhang Qingwei (b. 1961), a famed rocket scientist who had held top managerial posts at the China Aerospace Science and Technology Corporation (CASC) and the Commercial Aircraft Corporation of China, was named governor of Hebei in 2011. Ma Xingrui (b. 1959), another CASC veteran, became deputy Party secretary of Guangdong in 2013, while the president of Norinco, Zhang Guoqing (b. 1964), was appointed deputy Party secretary of Chongqing the same year. Qinghai governor Liu Peng (b. 1960) is an aeronautic engineer who cut his teeth at a Lanzhou-based factory under the Aviation Industry Corporation of China, where he worked from 1982 to 1999. Wang Yong (b. 1955), a former senior executive at the China Aerospace Science and Industry Corporation, which is a sister company of CASC, was made a state councilor in charge of industry and SOE groups in early 2013. Wang was head of SASAC from 2010 to 2013.[76]

While tapping state entrepreneurs—particularly those in sectors with national-security significance, such as energy and aerospace—for government jobs could bring valued expertise to central and regional administrations, it is doubtful that these managers-turned-administrators are capable of new thinking. The sorry state of the so-called Petroleum Faction has been exposed to the full by investigations into the Zhou Yongkang corruption empire. Apart from Jiang Jiemin, at least four senior executives at CNPC were arrested for corruption and abuse of power. Moreover, given the fact that *yangqi* executives have long been accustomed to enjoying privileges including monopoly and preferential access to state resources, they might not favor the introduction of more competition into the marketplace (see Chapter 4).

While the Hu-Wen administration broke with tradition and appointed a few Western-trained non-CCP members as ministerial-level cadres, the number of returnees being promoted to senior slots after the Eighteenth Party Congress seems to have leveled off. A 2014 survey by the respected liberal Guangdong paper *Southern Weekend* showed that only 31—or 18 percent—of the 169 officials with ministerial rank or above had studied or worked abroad. Moreover, only 15, or 9 percent, of these cadres—who include 29 ministers, 31 regional party secretaries, 31 regional governors or mayors, state councilors as well as Politburo members and senior leaders of the NPC and CPPCC—obtained degrees from foreign universities. Of these fifteen degree holders, however, eleven are either cadres with no party affiliation or those who are members of the eight *minzudangpai* (democratic parties). (The eight democratic parties are considered subsidiaries of the CCP; their leaders are usually CPPCC or NPC vice-chairpersons.)[77] They include the state councilor in charge of diplomacy Yang Jiechi (b. 1950); State Council Deputy Secretary-General Xiao Jie (b. 1957); President of the Chinese Academy of Sciences Bai Chunli (b. 1953); and two *minzudangpai* leaders, NPC vice-chairman Zhang Baowen (b. 1946) and CPPCC vice-chairman Han Qide (b. 1945). Six regional cadres including Chongqing Party chief Sun Zhengcai, Hubei Party secretary Li Hongzhong, Jiangxi governor Lu Xinshe and Shanxi governor Li Xiaopeng have studied overseas. However, their academic training abroad lasted less than a year.[78]

It is significant that, among the seven members of the CCP's first post-1949 PBSC, all except Chairman Mao had either studied or worked abroad. For example, Zhou Enlai studied and worked in Japan and France, while Deng Xiaoping studied in France and the Soviet Union. Among the seven members of the current PBSC, only NPC chairman Zhang Dejiang has studied abroad; he graduated with a degree in economics from Kim Il Sung University in North Korea in 1980.[79] Premier Li is the only member of the twenty-five full Politburo members who is fluent in English. The paucity of returnees at the top echelons of the Party or government reflects the fact that public service is not the first choice of young men and women who have made a huge investment in their education in Western countries. Most returnees have joined either the business world or academia. Moreover, at a time when the Xi leadership is putting priority on recruiting officials who have faith in the socialist path, overseas-educated Chinese may fear that their having been exposed to the proverbial sugar-coated bullets of capitalism may be held against them. This development, however, could mean that some of the most talented and best-trained Chinese will not be in a position to influence policy-making at the highest levels.[80]

## Conclusion: The World Awaits Xi's Reforms

### Why Most Members of All CCP Factions Want to Preserve the Status Quo

Like all large political parties in the world, the CCP has been riven with factions or what Mao used to call "mountain strongholds" since the days when the guerrilla leaders schemed and plotted in the caves of Yan'an, Shaanxi Province. Factionalism almost led to the ruin of the Party—and China—during the violent clashes of the Cultural Revolution (1966–76). Until Deng's death in 1997, rivalry among the CCP's disparate camarillas was in large measure predicated upon ideological differences. There was the "struggle between two lines" between Chairman Mao, on the one hand, and "capitalist roaders" such as State President Liu Shaoqi and Deng, on the other. For much of the 1980s and 1990s, Deng fought numerous battles with the conservative patriarch Chen Yun—a keen advocate of "reform within a birdcage"—over the pace and orientation of economic liberalization.[81]

After the Tiananmen Square crisis in 1989 and the collapse of the Soviet and East European Communist parties in the early 1990s, however, a solid consensus has emerged among all CCP factions that they must preserve a high degree of unity on a range of "core interests" in the ideological and policy arenas, including maintaining the Party's monopoly on power; cracking down on dissent and foreign "conspiracies" to turn China into a capitalist country; taking tough measures against secessionist or "anti-Beijing" activities in Tibet, Xinjiang, Hong Kong, and Taiwan; maintaining economic growth of at least 7 percent a year, which is seen as essential for preventing social instability; and, equally importantly, preserving the vested interests of existing power blocs and stakeholders, which include the major clans of the Party.[82]

Thus, until about the time of the Tiananmen Square incident in 1989, the question of whether or not to reform belonged in the realm of ideology and worldviews. But after the June 4, 1989, massacre, and especially after the collapse of the Soviet Union, holders of vested interests—including the heads of major Party factions—came to an agreement that preserving the status quo was of the utmost priority. An unprecedented number of spouses and children of top cadres of different political stripes have gone into business. Some have become senior managers of SOE conglomerates. Even more have used their sterling political connections to start private firms in lucrative areas such as finance and real estate. Critics of the government do not seem to be exaggerating when they say that 100 or so of the biggest clans within the country's "red aristocracy" control the largest chunk of economic pie. According to the *China Daily*, the top 1 percent of Chinese families control 41.4 percent of the country's wealth. Other official media reported in the late 2000s that 91 percent of Chinese citizens who owned more than RMB 100 million came from "high-cadre families."[83]

Whether or not to reform thus revolves around the question of money: whether members of the privileged classes are willing to give up fortunes worth billions upon billions of renminbi. Reform has become well-nigh impossible because any change of the political or economic status quo will threaten the finances of the big clans. This state of impasse was expertly analyzed by then-Guangdong Party secretary Wang Yang in 2012. "Thirty years ago, reform consisted of shaking off ideological shackles," Wang said. "Now, the major task of reform is breaking up the constraints of vested interests."[84] Because of the rigidity of China's one-party authoritarian rule—as well as the political elite's determination to uphold the status quo—expectations of significant changes to the system have fallen to new lows among the intelligentsia as well as ordinary citizens.

### Great Expectations of Xi's Leadership

Despite President Xi's lack of reformist credentials, expectations were high in the run-up to the Eighteenth Party Congress that the son of revered Party elder Xi Zhongxun (1913–2002) might be willing and able to go further than Hu Jintao or Wen Jiabao in economic and political reform. For Wu Jinglian, the grand old man of market-style liberalization, the message of the Eighteenth Party Congress was that "we must have greater political courage and wisdom." "We face major economic and political difficulties," he said not long after the watershed conclave. "We have to rely on market-oriented economic reform and political reform based on the rule of law and democracy to solve these problems."[85]

Calls for ringing in the new have come from different quarters of the polity. Consider, for example, General Liu Yazhou, who is political commissar of China's most important military academy, the National Defense University. In a book published in Hong Kong in late 2012 called *Liu Yazhou's Thoughts on China*, the renowned strategist surprised Chinese audiences by giving top priority to changes in the political system. "Whether China can really rise up depends on the battle called the reform of the political structure," he wrote. "Political reform is the battle front with overriding significance. The core of the reform of the political structure is democratization, particularly democratization within the party." On another occasion, General Liu made this prediction: "Within ten years, the shift from authoritarian politics to democratic politics will inevitably take place. China will undergo major changes."[86]

Coinciding with the fifth plenum of the Seventeenth Central Committee in October 2010—one of whose decisions was to confirm Xi's status as heir apparent to Hu by making him first vice-chairman of the CMC—several hundred senior Party members wrote an open letter to the leadership. The veterans, led by Mao Zedong's secretary, Li Rui, called upon the central authorities to "implement Article 35 of the constitution and . . . put into place freedom of speech and publication for citizens." The missive revealed that in early 2003, then-president Hu had made this promise at an internal meeting: "Abolishing news censorship and opening up avenues of public opinion is the mainstream view and demand of society." "If the Communist Party does not reform and transform itself, it will lose vigor and go toward perdition," Hu said.[87] Obviously, Li and the other signatories hoped that Xi could deliver what Hu had pledged but failed to bring to pass.

Yet the most moving plea for reform came from former PLA senior colonel and famed writer Xin Ziling, who has followed the exploits of Xi Zhongxun for years. In an article titled "Learn from Xi Zhongxun: And Hoping That What Xi Jinping Will Do Will Bring Solace to His Father's Glorious Spirit," Xin outlined three magnanimous deeds of the older Xi. Soon after 1949, Mao gave instructions to regional officials on wiping out "anti-revolutionary elements." The chairman said that the "extermination quota" was 0.1 percent of the population under their jurisdictions. Xi, who was in charge of Northwest China, ended up executing only 0.04 percent of the populace under his control. The second memorable event took place after Xi had become Party secretary of Guangdong in 1978. Upon his arrival, he was told that the PLA was authorized to shoot to kill residents who sought to flee to Hong Kong. Xi immediately stopped the practice, saying "Thirty years after liberation, Hong Kong has become prosperous whereas we are dirt poor." The third incident was Xi's famous defense of Hu Yaobang when Deng and other conservative Party elders decided to sack the liberal leader in January 1987. Xi, who was then in charge of the Central Committee Secretariat, argued that the Party elders had violated the CCP charter by kicking out a general secretary at an "enlarged Politburo meeting."[88]

Other intellectuals also urged Xi to pick up the threads of reform begun by Deng Xiaoping and Xi Zhongxun. For the liberal writer Wu Zuolai, the fact that Xi managed to grab hold of military power so early meant that he could initiate reform from a position of strength. "Xi Jinping should become the worthy son of Xi Zhongxun," Wu said. "Xi should not become the grandson of Mao Zedong." But Wu warned that there was no way that Xi could both uphold the vested interests of the red aristocracy and serve the people. "Xi has to make a choice between the two goals," Wu said.[89] Which way Xi goes will have a major impact on not only 1.3 billion Chinese but also the trajectory of much of the twenty-first century.

## Notes

1. See "Xi Jinping's speech in Paris: China the lion has woken up," Xinhua News Agency, March 28, 2014, http://finance.21cn.com/stock/ssbd/a/2014/0328/07/26822741.shtml.

2. Cited in "Jin Canrong: The future of China and the world are in the hands of our generation," *Global Times,* December 7, 2013, http://world.huanqiu.com/roll/2013-12/4640329.html. For a discussion of the "hegemonic transition" theory, see, for example, Ian Clark, "China and the United States: A succession of hegemonies?" *International Affairs* 87, no. 1 (January 2011): 13–28; William A. Callahan, "Chinese visions of world order: Post-hegemonic or a new hegemony?" *International Studies Review* 10, no. 4 (December 2008): 749–761; Randall L. Schweller, "After unipolarity: China's visions of international order in an era of U.S. decline," *International Security* 36, no. 1 (Summer 2011): 41–72.

3. For some examples of upbeat assessment of the China model, see, for example, Martin Jacques, *When China Rules the World: The End of the Western World and the Birth of a New Global Order* (London: Penguin Press, 2009); Joshua Cooper Ramo, *The Beijing Consensus* (London: Foreign Policy Centre, 2004). See also Wang Shaoguang, "Chinese socialism 3.0," in *China 3.0,* ed. Mark Leonard (London: European Council on Foreign Relations, 2012), pp. 68–75.

4. A World Bank report titled *China 2030,* written in partnership with the Development Research Center of the State Council, projected that the country's GDP would grow at an average of 8.6 percent from 2011 to 2015 and 7 percent for the 2011–15 period. See also Daniel H. Rosen, "China's economic outlook in 2020 and beyond," Peterson Institute for International Economics, March 14, 2012, www.economonitor.com/piie/2012/03/14/chinas-economic-outlook-in-2020-and-beyond/. Other forecasts say the growth rate will taper off at 5 percent to 6 percent by 2020. See Russell Flannery, "China faces years of slowing GDP growth, top strategist says," *Forbes,* August 11, 2013, www.forbes.com/sites/russellflannery/2013/08/11/china-faces-years-of-slowing-gdp-growth-top-strategist-says/.

5. See Zhang Weiying, "China's social ethos has experienced a big retrogression in the past ten years," Caijing.com (Beijing), July 1, 2013, http://politics.caijing.com.cn/2013-07-01/112979923.html.

6. For a discussion of democracy within the Party promoted by ex-president Hu, see, for example, Willy Lam, "Intra-party democracy with Chinese characteristics," in *Whither China's Democracy: Democratization in China Since the Tiananmen Incident,* ed. Joseph Y.S. Cheng (Hong Kong: City University of Hong Kong Press, 2011), pp. 33–64. See also Gu Bin, "Wu Jinlian and Jiang Ping on reform at the Eighteenth Party Congress," *China Insight* (Beijing) no. 2 (February 2013), www.zcom.com/article/97146/.

7. Cited in Qin Qianhong, "My interpretation of judicial reform stated at the Eighteenth Party Congress," Aisixiang.com (Beijing), December 8, 2013, www.aisixiang.com/data/70256.html.

8. Cited in Staff Reporter, "Scientific development has yet to be accomplished; political reform has stagnated," *Ming Pao* (Hong Kong), March 15, 2013, http://specials.mingpao.com/cfm/News.cfm?SpecialsID=272&News=854a70300d802ebf9dc470388c0843af17c5f0ba896e4d3386e24338b92c27/.

9. For a discussion of the significance of Jiang's retirement from the CMC in 2004, see, for example, James Mulvenon, "The king is dead! Long live the king! The CMC leadership transition from Jiang to Hu," *China Leadership Monitor,* Hoover Institution, no. 13, 2004, http://media.hoover.org/sites/default/files/documents/clm13_jm.pdf.

10. For a discussion of preparations for the Eighteenth Party Congress, see, for example, Cheng Li, "Preparing for the Eighteenth Party Congress: Procedures and mechanisms," *China Leadership Monitor,* Hoover Institution, no. 36, 2012, http://media.hoover.org/sites/default/files/documents/CLM36CL.pdf.

11. For a discussion of the traits and affiliation of the new Politburo leadership, see, for example, Alice Miller, "The new Party Politburo leadership," *China Leadership Monitor,*

Hoover Institution, no. 40, 2012, http://media.hoover.org/sites/default/files/documents/ CLM40AM.pdf. See also Cheng Li, "A biographical and factional analysis of the post-2012 Politburo," *China Leadership Monitor,* Hoover Institution, no. 41, Spring 2013, http://media. hoover.org/sites/default/files/documents/CLM41CL.pdf.

12. For a discussion of the influence of party elders at the Eighteenth Party Congress, see, for example, Xu Shugan, "While Hu Jintao has retired, geriatric politics has not come to an end," *Ming Pao,* November 15, 2012, http://news.sina.com.hk/news/20121115/-1761-2823849/1.html.

13. For a discussion of reasons for the failure of Li Yuanchao and Wang Yang to be inducted to the Politburo Standing Committee, see, for example, Benjamin Kang Lim, "Exclusive: China's backroom powerbrokers block reform candidates—sources," Reuters, November 20, 2012, www.reuters.com/article/2012/11/21/us-china-congress-poll-idUSBRE8AK01F20121121/.

14. For a discussion of Jiang Zemin's influence on the Eighteenth Party Congress, see, for example, Edgar Yuen, "New developments of party elders intervening in Chinese politics," *Ming Pao,* November 10, 2012, www.e123.hk/ElderlyPro/details/200217/74/sc/.

15. For a discussion of power struggle surrounding the downfall of Bo Xilai, see, for example, Anton Wishik, "The Bo Xilai crisis: A curse or a blessing for China?" National Bureau of Asian Research, Washington, April 18, 2012, www.nbr.org/research/activity. aspx?id=236/.

16. For a discussion about the ramifications of the Bo trial, see, for example, Willy Lam, "Compromising the case against Bo Xilai," *Wall Street Journal,* August 20, 2013, http:// online.wsj.com/news/articles/SB10001424127887323608504579024320304674550/.

17. For a discussion of collateral damage suffered by Bo's princeling friends, see, for example, Kathrin Hille, "China's 'princeling' generals hit by Bo purge," *Financial Times,* May 7, 2012, www.ft.com/intl/cms/s/0/4a932e72-9298-11e1-9e0a-00144feab49a. html#axzz2zueBKe00/.

18. For a discussion of the effect of the car accident of Ling Jihua's son, see, for example, John Garnaut, "Death of Chinese playboy leaves fresh scratches in party paintwork," *Sydney Morning Herald,* September 4, 2012, www.smh.com.au/world/death-of-chinese-playboy-leaves-fresh-scratches-in-party-paintwork-20120903-25a8v.html#ixzz2zQoOKNVY/.

19. For a discussion of the interaction between Hu Jintao and Ling Jihua, see, for example, Jonathan Ansfield, "How crash cover-up altered China's succession," *New York Times,* December 4, 2012, www.nytimes.com/2012/12/05/world/asia/how-crash-cover-up-altered-chinas-succession.html?pagewanted=all&_r=0/; see also "Top China official Ling Jihua in surprise demotion," BBC News, September 3, 2012, www.bbc.com/news/world-asia-china-19467312.

20. For a discussion of Xi Jinping's "mysterious" absence before the congress, see, for example, Staff Reporter, "Party may have asked former HK chief executive to talk to CNN: Report," *China Times* (Taipei), September 20, 2012, www.wantchinatimes.com/ news-subclass-cnt.aspx?id=20120920000086&cid=1101/; see also "Where in the world is China's Xi Jinping?" ABC News, September 11, 2012, http://abcnews.go.com/blogs/ headlines/2012/09/where-in-the-world-is-chinas-xi-jinping/.

21. For a discussion of Hu Jintao's role in the formation of the new CMC, see, for example, B. Raman, "Will Hu Jintao emulate Jiang and retain control of PLA after party transition?" South Asia Analysis Group (New Delhi), October 31, 2013, www.southasiaanalysis.org/ node/1037/. For a discussion of the appointment of the new CMC before the Eighteenth Party Congress, see, for example, "The organizational structure of the Central Military Commission has been formed," *Hong Kong Commercial Daily,* November 5, 2012, www. hkcd.com.hk/content/2012-11/05/content_3077551.htm.

22. Cited in "Hu Jintao's report to the Eighteenth Party Congress," China.com, September 20, 2012, http://news.china.com.cn/politics/2012-11/20/content_27165856.htm. See also

"Hu Jintao's Report to the 17th Party Congress," Xinhua News Agency, October 24, 2007, http://news.xinhuanet.com/newscenter/2007-10/24/content_6938568.htm.

23. Ibid.

24. See "Wen Jiabao: The task of pushing forward the reform of the party and state leadership systems is heavy and urgent," *New Beijing Post* (Beijing), November 10, 2012, http://news.qq.com/a/20121110/000042.htm.

25. See Deng Xiaoping, "On the reform of the party and state leadership systems," *People's Daily,* August 18, 1980, www.people.com.cn/GB/historic/0818/2706.html.

26. For a discussion of *cha'e* (competitive elections) at the Eighteenth Party Congress, see, for example, He Liangliang, "The degree of competitiveness in elections at the Eighteenth Party Congress will increase," Phoenix TV News, November 13, 2012, http://news.ifeng.com/mainland/special/zhonggong18da/content-2/detail_2012_11/13/19101367_0.shtml.

27. For a discussion of the possibility of the competitive elections of Politburo members, see, for example, Benjamin Kang Lim and Michael Martina, "Exclusive: China leaders consider internal democratic reform," Reuters, November 6, 2012, http://uk.reuters.com/article/2012/11/06/us-china-congress-idUSBRE8A50J420121106/.

28. For a discussion of intraparty democracy within the Vietnamese Communist Party, see, for example, Willy Lam, "China's debate over Vietnam's Reforms," *China Brief,* Jamestown Foundation, August 4, 2006, https://uyghuramerican.org/article/chinas-debate-over-vietnams-reforms.html.

29. For a discussion of the age of the Politburo Standing Committee members, see, for example, Shen Zewei, "Are the Politburo Standing Committee members transitory figures?" *Lianhe Zaobao* (Singapore), November 18, 2012, www.zaobao.com/special/report/politic/cnpol/story20121118-117742/.

30. For a discussion of the PLA members of the new Central Committee, see, for example, "Bright stars among the new military Central Committee members," *Wen Wei Po* (Hong Kong), November 21, 2012, www.afinance.cn/new/xwpl/201211/512283.html.

31. For a discussion of *yangqi* CEOs who were inducted to the Central Committee, see, for example, Lu Mengjun, "Seven Central Committee members with *yangqi* background have got into the government after the Eighteenth Party Congress," *Dongfang Daily* (Shanghai), March 30, 2014, www.dfdaily.com/html/33/2014/3/30/1135817.shtml.

32. For a discussion of the role of private entrepreneurs at the Eighteenth Party Congress, see, for example, Willy Lam, "Private sector show at Communist Party congress," Asianews. it.com, October 25, 2012, www.asianews.it/news-en/Private-sector-show-at-Communist-Party-Congress-26190.html.

33. See "Hu Jintao's report to the Eighteenth Party Congress," China.com.

34. Cited in "Yu Zhengsheng: establishing an adequate system is an effective way to take control of leaders' relatives and aides," *People's Daily,* November 10, 2012, http://cpc.people.com.cn/18/n/2012/1110/c350828-19538701.html. For a discussion of the private lives of the seven Politburo Standing Committee members, see "The new leadership collective: Ordinary lifestyle, great aspirations," Guancha.cn (Beijing), December 24, 2013, www.guancha.cn/politics/2013_12_24_194822_s.shtml.

35. Cited in "Hu Jintao: The advanced nature of the party and its ruling status may not necessarily last forever," China News Service, December 18, 2008, www.chinanews.com/gn/news/2008/12-18/1492805.shtml; "Xi Jinping: The party's ruling status may not be everlasting," *Southern Metropolitan News* (Guangzhou), September 9, 2008, www.nfdaily.cn/china/shizheng/content/2008-09/09/content_4589087.htm.

36. For a discussion of princelings' revival of Maoism, see, for example, Willy Lam, "The Maoist revival and the conservative turn in Chinese politics," *China Perspectives,* no. 2 (2012), http://chinaperspectives.revues.org/5851/.

37. For a discussion of Deng's personnel principles, see, for example, Willy Lam, "Interpreting the significance of CCP personnel changes," *China Brief,* Jamestown Foundation, June 19, 2006, www.asianresearch.org/articles/2898.html.

38. For a discussion of princelings who excel in the business world, see, for example, James Ball, "China's princelings storing riches in Caribbean offshore haven," *Guardian,* January 21, 2014, www.theguardian.com/world/ng-interactive/2014/jan/21/china-british-virgin-islands-wealth-offshore-havens. See also Michelle FlorCruz, "China's private equity princelings use elite connections to help raise billions," IBTimes.com, April 10, 2014, www.ibtimes.com/chinas-private-equity-princelings-use-elite-connections-help-raise-billions-1570092/.

39. See "List of alternate members of the Fifteenth Party Congress," Xinhua News Agency, October 29, 2002, http://news.xinhuanet.com/ziliao/2002-10/29/content_612072.htm.

40. For a discussion of Jiang Zemin's family and upbringing, see, for example, "Jiang Zemin: How a member of a learned family becomes general secretary," *Southern Weekend,* September 23, 2004, www.china.com.cn/chinese/2004/Sep/666859.htm. For a discussion of Zeng Qinghong's relationship with his father, see, for example, "Zeng Qinghong's mother remembers: Zeng Shan and his seven children," *Shenzhen News,* July 17, 2009, www.sznews.com/culture/content/2009-07/17/content_3920249_5.htm.

41. For a discussion of the political network of Yu Zhengsheng, see, for example, "The illustrious family of Yu Zhengsheng," Now TV (Hong Kong), November 15, 2012, http://news.now.com/home/international/player?newsId=50993/. See also Benjamin Kang Lim, "China princeling emerges from defection scandal," Reuters, June 19, 2007, www.reuters.com/article/2007/06/19/us-china-party-yu-idUSPEK15174020070619/.

42. For a discussion of the traits and mentality of the princelings under Xi, see, for example, Cheng Li, "Rule of the princelings," Brookings Institution, February 10, 2013, www.brookings.edu/research/articles/2013/02/china-xi-jinping-li/. See also Ananth Krishnan, "From Mao to Xi: For China's princelings, red legacy is strength and weakness," *The Hindu,* December 31, 2013, www.thehindu.com/news/international/world/for-chinas-princelings-red-legacy-is-strength-and-weakness/article5519744.ece/.

43. For a discussion of divisions within the princelings, see, for example, "Some princelings are divided owing to the rivalries of their fathers during the Cultural Revolution," USChinapress.com (Los Angeles), November 21, 2013, http://news.uschinapress.com/2013/1121/527655.shtml.

44. For a discussion of princelings among the generals, see, for example, "How many princeling generals in the PLA do you recognize?" News.21cn.com (Beijing), October 12, 2012, http://news.21cn.com/social/daqian/2012/10/12/13235850.shtml. For a discussion of Xi's relations with princeling generals, see, for example, David Lague and Charlie Zhu, "Special Report: Rising China's pride and challenge—Its mighty army," Reuters, December 24, 2013, http://uk.reuters.com/article/2013/12/24/us-breakout-generals-special-report-idUKBRE9BN0DN20131224/.

45. For a discussion of the traits and orientations of members of the new military commission, see, for example, James Mulvenon, "The new Central Military Commission," *China Leadership Monitor,* Hoover Institution, no. 40, 2012, http://media.hoover.org/sites/default/files/documents/CLM40JM.pdf.

46. For a discussion of the frequency with which Xi inspects different PLA divisions, see, for example, Ji Shuoming, "The intensity with which Xi Jinping looks after the PLA exceeds that of Jiang Zemin and Hu Jintao," *Ta Kung Pao* (Hong Kong), April 13, 2014, http://news.takungpao.com/mainland/focus/2014-04/2418529.html.

47. See Patrick Boehler, "Deng Xiaoping's grandson a county-level official, state media reveals," *South China Morning Post,* May 3, 2013, www.scmp.com/news/china/article/1229044/deng-xiaopings-grandson-county-level-official-state-media-reveals/.

48. For a discussion of the careers of the offspring of Hu Jintao and Deng Xiaoping, see, for example, Kor Kian Beng, "China's princelings in high posts: Hu Jintao's son and Deng Xiaoping's grandson carving political careers," *Straits Times,* May 29, 2013, www.stasiareport.com/the-big-story/asia-report/china/story/chinas-princelings-high-posts-20130529/. See also Simon Montlake, "China censors Namibia corruption case that may touch president's son," *Christian Science Monitor,* August 3, 2009, www.csmonitor.com/World/Asia-Pacific/2009/0803/p06s01-woap.html.

49. For a discussion of the strength of the CYL Faction, see, for example, Willy Lam, "China Youth clique maintains clout," *Asia Times,* December 4, 2012, www.atimes.com/atimes/China/NL04Ad01.html.

50. For a discussion of the promotion potentials of Hu Chunhua and Sun Zhengcai, see, for example, Leslie Hook, "China looks to fill next generation gap," *Financial Times,* November 12, 2012, www.ft.com/intl/cms/s/0/51f468c8-167f-11e2-b6f1-00144feabdc0.html#axzz2zoQ3aqRj/. For an earlier assessment of their career trajectories, see "Hu Chunhua and Sun Zhengcai have demonstrated their potentials," *Caijing* (Beijing), December 11, 2006, http://magazine.caijing.com.cn/2006-12-11/110061102.html.

51. Cited in Willy Lam, "China Youth clique maintains clout." See also "An expansion of the corps of post-1960s generation of ministerial-level officials," *Ta Kung Pao,* March 20, 2013, http://news.takungpao.com.hk/mainland/zgzq/2013-03/1501581.html.

52. For a discussion of the political orientation of Sixth-Generation cadres among alternate Central Committee members, see, for example, "60 among alternate Central Committee members were born after 1960," China Economy Net (Beijing), December 1, 2012, http://news.ifeng.com/gundong/detail_2012_12/10/20006910_0.shtml.

53. For a discussion of the "cross-generation designation of successors," see, for example, "The Eighteenth Party Congress: Xi Jinping has benefited from the cross-generation designation of leaders," Now TV (Hong Kong), October 12, 2012, http://news.now.com/home/international/player?newsId=48064/; see also Willy Lam, "China picks core new leaders," *Asia Times,* May 23, 2009, www.atimes.com/atimes/China/KE23Ad02.html.

54. For a discussion of the development of Hu Chunhua's career, see, for example, "First Party Secretary of the Communist Youth League Hu Chunhua discusses three experiences of his career," Caijing.com (Beijing), November 21, 2007, www.caijing.com.cn/2007-10-21/100034398.html. See also "Hu Chunhua becomes governor at the age of 45," *Party Life* (Beijing), December 19, 2012, http://news.sohu.com/20121219/n360841958.shtml.

55. For a discussion of Hu Chunhua's career in Tibet, see, for example, "Hu Chunhua spent 19 years working in Tibet," Caixin.com (Beijing), November 15, 2012, http://video.caixin.com/2012-11-15/100460783.html.

56. For a discussion of Hu's work in Inner Mongolia, see, for example, "Little Hu and the mining of the grasslands," *Economist,* July 14, 2012, www.economist.com/node/21558605/. For a discussion of President Xi's low estimation of—and efforts to marginalize—the CYL Faction, see, for example, Willy Lam, "With Zhou's circle down, Xi's purge may turn to Hu," *China Brief,* July 3, 2014, www.jamestown.org/programs/chinabrief/single/?tx_ttnews%5Btt_news%5D=42581&cHash=636a58b80110a5ea45f3662dfcf26f0a.

57. For a discussion of the political career of Sun Zhengcai, see, for example, "The development path of three Sixth-Generation regional leaders," *People's Daily,* November 28, 2011, www.dangjian.cn/syjj/tp/201111/t20111128_403065_17.shtml. See also Zachary Keck, "Sun Zhengcai, a rising star," *Diplomat,* November 28, 2012,http://thediplomat.com/2012/11/sun-zhengcai-a-rising-star/.

58. For a discussion of Li Xiaopeng's career, see, for example, "Li Xiaopeng says being the governor of Shanxi is like sitting on a volcano," China.com, March 8, 2013, http://news.china.com/zh_cn/focus/2013lh/news/11136226/20130308/17718096.html.

59. See "Li Keqiang stresses that reform will bring the biggest bonus to China," Xinhua News Agency, November 22, 2012, http://finance.people.com.cn/n/2012/1122/c1004-19667962.html.

60. For a discussion of Li's career in the Peking University law school, see, for example, Jaime Florcruz, "High expectations for China's presumptive premier," CNN, April 6, 2012, http://edition.cnn.com/2012/04/06/world/asia/china-li-keqiang-profile/.

61. For a discussion of the development of Li's political career, see, for example, "Li Keqiang and his seven teachers and patrons," *Northeast Net* (Shenyang), November 19, 2012, http://story.dbw.cn/system/2012/11/19/054380102.shtml. See also Simon Rabinovitch, "Li prepares to become Chinese premier," *Financial Times,* November 13, 2012, www.ft.com/intl/cms/s/0/8135b318-2d35-11e2-9211-00144feabdc0.html#axzz30HrBOOgZ/.

62. For a discussion of the AIDS-related scandals when Li served in Henan Province, see, for example, Jill Reilly, "China's new leader led cover-up into hospital scandal that saw up to 300,000 people infected with HIV," *Daily Mail* (London), November 30, 2012, www.dailymail.co.uk/news/article-2240830/Chinas-new-leader-Henan-Li-led-hospital-cover-saw-300k-people-infected-HIV.html.

63. For a discussion of Li Keqiang's achievements in Liaoning Province, see, for example, Li Yang, "Memorable events when Li Keqiang ran Henan and Liaoning," Ifeng.com (Beijing), November 15, 2012, http://news.ifeng.com/mainland/special/zhonggong18da/dujia/detail_2012_11/15/19188705_0.shtml.

64. For a discussion of Li's performance as executive vice-premier from 2008 to 2013, see, for example, Huo Kan and Yang Zheyu, "How China's new premier climbed the rungs of power," CNBC news, March 19, 2013, www.cnbc.com/id/100570822/. See also "Li Keqiang: the results of medical reform have gradually become evident," Securities Times Net (Beijing), January 20, 2011, http://finance.ifeng.com/stock/roll/20110120/3239524.shtml.

65. For a discussion of the Li Keqiang as a student radical in Peking University, see, for example, Keith Richburg, "Li Keqiang, China's next premier, carries reformers' hopes," *Washington Post,* November 9, 2012, www.washingtonpost.com/world/asia_pacific/li-keqiang-chinas-next-premier-carries-reformers-hopes/2012/11/09/126800fc-29a3-11e2-aaa5-ac786110c486_story.html.

66. For a discussion of State Council structural reforms contemplated by Li Keqiang in 2008, see, for example, "A scheme for reforming the structure of the State Council," Zhong Cai Net (Beijing), March 11, 2008, www.cfi.net.cn/newspage.aspx?id=20080311001575/; see also Bai Tiantian,"Transport ministry reform finishes," *Global Times,* March 13, 2014, www.globaltimes.cn/content/848085.shtml.

67. For a discussion of the rivalry between Xi Jinping and Li Keqiang, see, for example, Kenji Kawase, "Are we seeing the emergence of 'dictator' Xi?" *Nikkei Asian Review* (Tokyo), November 28, 2013, http://asia.nikkei.com/print/article/7005/. See also Zachary Keck, "Is Li Keqiang being marginalized?" *Diplomat,* January 7, 2014, http://thediplomat.com/2014/01/is-li-keqiang-being-marginalized/.

68. Cited in "Sixth-generation senior cadres in Chinese politics," *People's Daily,* March 30, 2010, www.360doc.com/content/10/0330/13/1081498_20859483.shtml.

69. For a discussion of the political traits of associates of the CYL Clique, see, for example, Willy Lam, "The life of the Party," Project Syndicate, October 9, 2007, www.project-syndicate.org/commentary/the-life-of-the-party/. See also Victor Funnel, "The Chinese Communist youth movement, 1949–1966," *China Quarterly,* no. 42 (June 1970): 105–130.

70. For a discussion of the traits and careers of Hu Chunhua and Zhou Qiang, see, for example, *"People's Daily Overseas Edition* portrays Zhou Qiang and six other Sixth-Generation ministerial-level officials," *People's Daily,* September 20, 2012, http://news.xinhuanet.com/local/2012-09/20/c_113146165.htm.

71. For a discussion of the prospects of CYL Faction members nurtured by ex-president Hu, see, for example, Irene Liu and Chris Ip, "Analysis: China's next inner circle," Reuters, March 3, 2013, www.reuters.com/article/2013/03/03/us-china-factions-idUSBRE9220GJ2013033/.

72. For a discussion of the effect of the "Theory of the Three Represents" on political participation, including managers and professionals joining the Party, see, for example, Gilles Guiheux, "The political 'participation' of entrepreneurs: Challenge or opportunity for the Chinese Communist Party?" Social Research: An International Quarterly 73, no. 1 (Spring 2006): 219–244.

73. For a discussion of non-Party members becoming senior officials, see, for example, Lin Meilian, "Non-Communist parties try to remain relevant," Global Times, March 14, 2013, www.globaltimes.cn/content/768204.shtml; see also "Non-Communists take part in state administration," CCTV, March 7, 2008, www.cctv.com/english/20080307/101002.shtml.

74. For a discussion of the petroleum faction, see, for example, Willy Lam, "China's energy bosses taking political wheel," Asia Times, May 6, 2011, http://atimes.com/atimes/China_Business/ME06Cb02.html.

75. For a discussion of Zhu Yanfeng's career, see, for example, "Jilin Deputy Party Secretary Zhu Yanfeng was named 'young marshal of the auto industry' at age 38," Editors and Publishers' Net (Beijing), March 31, 2013, www.bianjichuban.com/info/viewnews-11801.html.

76. For a discussion of the career of Wang Yong, see, for example, Wang Jun, "State Councilor Wang Yong is in charge of state-assets and industrial safety," Ta Kung Pao, May 3, 2013, http://news.takungpao.com/mainland/zgzq/2013-05/1586796.html. For a discussion of the careers of Ma Xingrui and Zhang Guoqing, see, for example, "Several Beijing-based officials are transferred to the regions: Three Central Committee members are within the leaderships of Guangdong and Chongqing," China News Service, November 22, 2013, http://news.hexun.com/2013-11-22/159930292.html. See also Willy Lam, "The rise of the military-space faction," China Brief, September 25, 2014, www.jamestown.org/programs/chinabrief/single/?tx_ttnews%5Btt_news%5D=42875&tx_ttnews%5BbackPid%5D=25&cHash=ab4e465ba64b133acae02b703de72551.

77. Cited in "A report on returnees getting into politics," Southern Weekend (Guangzhou), April 18, 2014, http://news.takungpao.com/mainland/focus/2014-04/2430868.html.

78. Ibid.

79. For a portrait of Zhang Dejiang, see, for example, "China face to watch: Zhang Dejiang," BBC News, March 2, 2012, www.bbc.com/news/world-asia-china-17219632.

80. For a discussion of the impact of returnees on the future of Chinese politics, see, for example, Huiyao Wang, "Chinese returnees, a globalization force in changing modern China," Center for China and Globalization (Beijing), April 1, 2011, http://en.ccg.org.cn/_d276009973.htm.

81. For a discussion of factional struggles in CCP politics, see, for example, Jing Huang, Factionalism in Chinese Communist Politics (Cambridge: Cambridge University Press, 2006), pp. 350–386; Lucian W. Pye, The Spirit of Chinese Politics (Cambridge: Harvard University Press, 1992), pp. 197–232.

82. For a discussion of the changing nature of China's disparate factions, see, for example, Willy Lam, "Ideology, vested interests: Why China's reforms have hit a brick wall," CNN, November 16, 2012, http://edition.cnn.com/2012/11/12/opinion/china-reforms-lam/.

83. See Chen Weihua, "Income gap, a woe for China and U.S.," China Daily, October 12, 2010, http://usa.chinadaily.com.cn/2010-10/12/content_11399998.htm.

84. Cited in Hu Jian and Xie Sijia, "Wang Yang: The crux of the matter is the fundamental interests of the broad masses," Nanfang Daily (Guangzhou), March 6, 2012, http://epaper.nfdaily.cn/html/2012-03/06/content_7063612.htm.

85. See Wu Jinlian, "How can China pick up on the threads of reform?" Phoenix TV Net, March 22, 2013, http://news.ifeng.com/exclusive/lecture/special/wujinglian/.

86. Cited in He Liangliang, "Liu Yazhou: Whether China can rise depends on the battle of political reform," 21ccom.net (Beijing), January 8, 2013, www.21ccom.net/articles/read/article_2013010874534.html.

87. Cited in Jiang Xun, "Veterans from the Communist Party publish open petition," *Yazhou zhoukang* (Hong Kong), October 15, 2010, www.cntvboxnow.com/thread-1145769-1-1.html.

88. Cited in Ching Cheong, "Can Xi Jinping expand upon his father's spirit?" *Hong Kong Economic Journal,* October 22, 2010, http://forum.hkej.com/node/57806/. See also Xin Ziling, "The path opened up by Xi Zhongxun," *Open Magazine* (Hong Kong), November 2013, pp. 33–36.

89. See Wu Zuolai, "Is Xi Jinping the 2.0 edition of Mao Zedong?" BBC Chinese Service, October 7, 2013, www.bbc.co.uk/zhongwen/trad/focus_on_china/2013/10/131007_cr_xijinping_maozedong.shtml.

## ——— 2 ———

# The Making of a New Helmsman

**Introduction: What Kind of Leader Is Xi Jinping?**

It is easy to underestimate Xi Jinping. Before examining the remarkable career of the New Helmsman, it is instructive to look at two assessments of the Fifth-Generation leader. Wikileaks documents have provided snippets of the conversations held in 2009 between a group of senior scholars in Shanghai and the U.S. consul-general in Shanghai, Beatrice Camp. Their subject matter was the political orientation of Xi, who served briefly as Shanghai's Party secretary in 2007 before being inducted to the Politburo Standing Committee (PBSC) at the Seventeenth Party Congress in 2007. Prior to this major promotion, Xi was Party secretary of Zhejiang Province in 2002 to 2007 after serving in Fujian Province for seventeen years.

Ding Xinghao, who was president of the Shanghai Institute of American Studies, argued that Xi's accomplishments in Zhejiang and Shanghai could be summed up by the expression *wuweierzhi,* which can be translated as "doing nothing [special] by letting things take their course."[1] Ding added that Xi was cautious by nature—and that he simply tried "not to mess things up." Zhu Xueqin, a top social scientist at Shanghai University, indicated that there was "no chance" that Xi would be willing or able to promote needed political reforms. According to Xu Mingqi, deputy director of the World Economy Institute at the Shanghai Institute of Social Sciences, the "situation is serious" because the stakes for the successor of ex-president Hu Jintao would be enormous in the next decade due to the mushrooming sociopolitical contradictions in Chinese society.[2]

A number of observers share Professor Ding's *wuweierzhi* assessment of Xi's statecraft and political philosophy. This is not necessarily a pejorative description of a cadre or ruler's approach to governance. *Wuweierzhi* is one of the central tenets of Lao Zi's (the founder of Daoism) approach to good governance. It means letting nature take its course and allowing the people to follow their natural inclinations so as to better develop their innate talents and to create wealth in society. The ruler should adopt a nonobtrusive stance and not intervene with the activities of the people unless he is convinced that his charges are heading in the wrong direction.[3] Over the years, however, *wuweierzhi* has also developed a derogatory connotation: It is used to describe officials, including top leaders, who merely follow conventional wisdom—and who lack both new ideas and the authority and audacity to push them through.

Then there is this official appraisal by He Guoqiang, then Politburo member and director of the CCP Organization Department, when Xi was named Shanghai Party secretary. "Comrade Xi Jinping passes muster politically, and he has a relatively good grasp of ideology and policy," said the Party's personnel chief. "Comrade Xi is also conversant with Party affairs and economic work. He has relatively strong ability in macro-level decision-making as well as rich leadership experience. He has strong capabilities in organization and in being on top of the whole situation." Other attributes that He ascribed to Xi included: he has a pragmatic work style, and he handles policies with an eye toward stability; he attaches importance to the art of leadership and work methodologies; he has good ties with colleagues and the masses as well as high moral standards.[4]

These two assessments are not necessarily contradictory. First, it is a common trait of up-and-coming officials to stick to the middle of the road, to steer clear of radical ideas—and to avoid being seen as upstaging their superiors. Among Xi's contemporaries, only the disgraced former Party chief of Chongqing Bo Xilai and Vice-Premier Wang Yang were known to be charismatic—and not afraid of pronouncing unconventional and even unorthodox views. As we shall see in the ensuing chapters, after Xi became CCP general secretary and commander-in-chief in late 2012, he lost no time in amassing power and impressing the body politic with his personal stamp. Yet even after establishing his authority, Xi has remained conscientious about cleaving to the goals of "socialism with Chinese characteristics." This fits in with Organization chief He's description of Xi as a trustworthy cadre who would not stray from Party dogma. The traits that He attributed to Xi do not include qualities that were associated with earlier leaders including Mao Zedong, Deng Xiaoping, Hu Yaobang, Zhao Ziyang, and, to a lesser extent, even Third-Generation representatives such as Jiang Zemin or Zhu Rongji. To varying extents, these former leaders could be described as visionaries or at least risk-takers who dared to go the extra mile in order to attain their objectives, even those that appeared to be unpopular.[5]

Xi, however, has his strong points. His peculiar personality, upbringing, and work experience are such that he is good at holding down the fort and maintaining the status quo, particularly the CCP's status as "perennial ruling Party." More significantly, as He pointed out, Xi is good at upholding stability and "uniting people." He may be the best Fifth-Generation leader to hold together the disparate factions and power blocs in the Party, government, and the PLA. Moreover, his experience in running two relatively important coastal provinces—Fujian and Zhejiang—and his long years of dealing with foreign dignitaries and businessmen both before and after his emergence as "crown prince" in 2007 mean that he has the knowledge and skills to keep the ship of state on an even keel.[6] He will continue the CCP's time-tested policy of pursuing "market-oriented state capitalism" while putting a moratorium on political liberalization and using tough tactics to muzzle dissent. Best of all, Xi passes the "loyalty test" with flying colors. Despite his exposure to the "bourgeois-liberal" values and norms that have penetrated China's affluent eastern coast, the princeling supreme leader remains a firm believer in Marxism, Mao Zedong Thought, and socialism with Chinese characteristics (see Chapter 3).

This chapter looks at Xi's family, especially his revered father, the late vice-premier Xi Zhongxun, and his glamorous wife, the renowned folk singer Peng Liyuan. Xi's career in the Central Military Commission (CMC) and the provinces of Hebei, Fujian, and Zhejiang as well as Shanghai are examined. Also analyzed are Xi's intimate circle of advisers and confidants in the Party, the government, and the military. As we shall see in the ensuing sections, what Xi lacks may be the training and experience that might predispose him to bringing about thoroughgoing economic and political reform.

## Xi's Family and Intimate Circles

Even after Xi's emergence as vice-premier and heir-apparent to the CCP throne at the Seventeenth Party Congress in 2007, Xi remained relatively unknown. He was dwarfed by two figures: his much-admired father, Xi Zhongxun, and his wife, Peng Liyuan, a singer in the PLA and a national heart-throb. Xi Zhongxun (1913–2002) is best remembered outside China as the governor and Party secretary of Guangdong from 1978 to 1980. In those early days in the era of reform, the elder Xi played a seminal role in implementing Deng Xiaoping's vision of turning Guangdong into a national pacesetter for reform.[7] Thanks to his father's influence, Xi picked up some conversational Cantonese (the dialect spoken in Guangdong), which served him well during his tenure in Fujian. Xi could speak in Cantonese with influential Hong Kong tycoons who were investing in Fuzhou and other cities.

### *"A Tiger Won't Beget a Dog": Disparate Political Orientations of Xi Zhongxun and Xi Jinping*

Xi owes a lot to his father, who is remembered as a leading liberal cadre much in the mold of former general secretary Hu Yaobang (1915–1989), with whom Xi served in the Party's Northwestern Bureau (which supervised provinces including Xinjiang, Sichuan, Ningxia, Gansu, and Shaanxi before "Liberation" in 1949). In the run-up to and after 1949, Xi clashed with hawks such as General Wang Zhen on ways and means to "tame" ethnic minorities such as the Tibetans, Uighurs, and Muslims. General Wang advocated naked suppression of the "barbarians," whereas Xi wanted peaceful reconciliation with the minorities.[8] It was said that until his death, the older Xi carried with him a memento that the Dalai Lama had given him. The two had engaged in long conversations before the spiritual leader's flight to India in 1959.[9] In December 1986 and January 1987, Xi was almost the only Party elder who openly defended General Secretary Hu when the latter was vilified by the Party's conservative wing for failing to contain the "wave of bourgeois liberalization" that was allegedly sweeping the country. While Xi's act of courage failed to prevent Hu from being sacked, Party liberals still feel a sense of gratitude toward the liberal and righteous titan.[10]

Xi's courage in defending his fellow liberal comrades could have sprung in part from his own sad experience. Thanks to his brilliant administrative abilities after 1949, he was rewarded with the post of vice-premier and secretary-general of the State Council in 1959. However, in 1962 the Shaanxi native fell victim to factional politics and was purged as an "enemy of the Party" four years before the Cultural Revolution (1966–76) started. Xi was a political "nonperson" from 1962 to 1978, when he was rehabilitated by Deng Xiaoping.[11] During this period, his wife, Qi Xin, and four children—Qiaoqiao, An'an, Jinping, and Yuanping—also suffered from discrimination and material deprivation. In a memoir written in 2008, Qi Xin revealed that, thanks to the intercession of Zhou Enlai, she and her children were able to have a brief meeting with the imprisoned Xi in 1972. "He could not distinguish between Qiaoqiao and An'an," Qi wrote. "And he was totally surprised that his sons had grown so tall."[12]

The most important contribution made by the older Xi may have been his stewardship over the development of Guangdong as the province that had implemented Deng Xiaoping's open-door policy. Upon his arrival in the southern province in 1978, he tried hard to attract Hong Kong and overseas-Chinese investments. The elder Xi also gave a green light to quasi-capitalist pursuits such as the large-scale revival of private enterprise. Xi was one of Deng's key aides who persuaded the chief architect of reform to set up China's special economic zones (SEZs), which included the Guangdong cities of Shenzhen, Zhuhai, and Shantou.[13] Even more surprising, however, was the fact that Xi adopted a tolerant attitude toward dissidents in Guangdong. The best example was his "rehabilitation of the reputation" of three young radicals, Li Zhengtian, Chen Yiyang, and Wang Xizhe. The trio gained national fame by writing big-character posters, a form of popular political communication, under the pen-name of Li Yizhe that criticized the mistakes of the Cultural Revolution. Within eight months of his arrival in Guangzhou, Xi declared that the three were not counterrevolutionaries, and they were released in December 1978.[14]

After leaving Guangdong, Xi served on the Central Committee's Secretariat from 1981 to 1988, and he continued to support Deng's new economic policy—as well as Hu Yaobang's political reform. The elder Xi moved to the NPC as one of its vice-chairmen in March 1988—a pre-retirement job. His reactions to the June 4, 1989, massacre remain unknown. Yet it is reasonable to think that he was one of the few Party elders who condemned Deng's use of the PLA to crush innocent student demonstrations. After his retirement from the NPC in 1993, Xi moved to Shenzhen, where he remained until his death in 2002. As a filial son, Xi visited his father regularly until his death.[15]

*Xi's Siblings: Sister Qi Qiaoqiao Acts as Xi's "Bridge"*
*to the Other Princeling Clans*

Xi has three elder siblings, the children of Xi Zhongxun and his first wife, but one son and one daughter from the elder Xi's first marriage died young. Xi Qianping, the daughter who is still alive, is a former journalist who is active in gatherings of fellow princelings. Xi Zhongxun and his second wife, Qi Xin, had four children: the daughters Qiaoqiao, An'an; and the sons Jinping and Yuanping. Qiaoqiao (b. 1949) and Yuanping (b. 1955) have gone into business. It is a credit to the strict training of the elder Xi—and the discipline of Xi Jinping—that while Qiaoqiao An'an, and Yuanping seemed to have benefited economically from their princeling connections, there is no innuendo about Jinping providing explicit help to their businesses, unlike most princeling businessmen, who have profited from assistance provided by their high-powered relatives. During an anti-graft campaign in 2004, then-Zhejiang Party boss Xi noted that officials must "rein in their spouses, children, relatives and close colleagues so as to prevent them from seeking private gains."[16] Qiaoqiao has set up a large real-estate business in Beijing and Shenzhen. According to a mid-2012 report by the Bloomberg news agency, Xi's siblings and other close relatives owned "investments in companies with total assets of $376 million; an 18 percent indirect stake in a rare-earth company with $1.73 billion in assets; and a $20.2 million holding in a publicly traded technology company." The three richest Xi relatives are Qiaoqiao, her husband, Deng Jiagui, and their daughter, Zhang Yannan. An'an (b. 1951), who is a manager in a cultural enterprise owned by Qiaoqiao, adopts a low profile. Her husband, Wu Long, is a wealthy telecommunications executive.[17]

Yet the most important "function" of Qiaoqiao, particularly after Xi's induction to the PBSC in 2007, is to act as liaison with the other princeling families. It has been a custom among the clans that since their most important members are usually actively involved in politics, second-tier figures take up the role of unofficial public-relations officers. Moreover, Qiaoqiao is as suave and outgoing as Jinping is reserved and introverted. And the fact that she has a nationwide property business means that she has established good networks at least in the cities.[18] Qiaoqiao's role is important in view of the fact that, owing to Xi Zhongxun's open break with conservative Party elders—including Deng Xiaoping, Chen Yun, Bo Yibo, Li Xiannian, and Wang Zhen—over the dismissal of Hu Yaobang, the Xi family had become isolated from the mainstream princeling clans.[19] Thus, throughout his long stay in Fujian from 1985 to 2002, Xi did not have a lot of contact with other princelings. It is interesting that when Xi "returned" to Beijing in the run-up to his induction into the PBSC in 2007, he invited Deng Pufang, Deng's eldest son, for dinner, but the wheelchair-bound Deng did not show up. He only sent his sister, Deng Rong, and her husband, He Ping, to act as his representatives. That Xi and Deng Pufang are on good terms, however, was demonstrated by the effusive letter that the president sent Deng Pufang in March 2014 marking the thirtieth anniversary of the establishment of the China Welfare Fund for the Handicapped.[20]

Xi Yuanping has never hit the big time. He is believed to have immigrated to Hong Kong before the British territory's handover to Chinese sovereignty in 1997. However, his long-time association with a Zhejiang Province tycoon, Jia Yun, might have caused some embarrassment to his elder brother. Jia was the head of the Pi Ka Wang International Group (PKWIG), which had interests in leather goods, real estate, logistics, and film. At its height, PKWIG had assets of RMB 1.7 billion. And Yuanping helped Jia look after his film and TV businesses. In 2003, however, Jia was arrested for economic crimes including tax evasion. Fortunately for Xi Jinping, who was then the No. 1 cadre in Zhejiang, his brother's involvement with PKWIG did not seem to affect his political standing. Now that he is comfortably retired, Yuanping's only title is president of the International Energy Conservation Environmental Protection Association, a semiofficial think tank that is involved in global dialogue with green organizations in Western countries.[21]

### Peng Liyuan, Xi's "Secret Weapon"

Another major influence in Xi's life is his wife, Peng Liyuan. Official biographies usually say very little about the spouses of top figures, so it is interesting to note that Peng is Xi's second wife. Xi was briefly married to the talented, multilingual Ke Xiaoming, daughter of the senior diplomat Ke Ping, whose posts included a period as Chinese ambassador to the UK. Xi and Ke Xiaoming (aka Ke Lingling) tied the knot in 1980, when Xi was serving as General Geng Biao's secretary.[22] At that time, Xi and Ke lived in a big house owned by Ke's parents. Most reports in the Hong Kong media said that Xi and Ke did not get along well—and that Xi's mother had to intervene to keep the marriage together. By the time Xi made his decision in 1982 to "rusticate" to Hebei as deputy Party secretary of the remote Zhengding County, Ke had already gone to England to pursue further studies. Soon after Xi settled in Zhengding, he received an ultimatum from Ke: Xi either had to join Ke in London or they would separate. After securing the approval of his mother, Xi decided to get a divorce.[23] Given the short and unhappy marriage experience, Xi did not keep up ties with his father-in-law. Although this marriage lasted only two years, it provides some important hints about Xi's character: he had no sympathy for his wife's "Western" proclivities, and he was intent on building a career in rural China.

In 1986, Xi met glamorous singer Peng Liyuan in Beijing on an "arranged date." Peng, who was born in 1962, came from a rural family in Shandong Province and entered the Shandong Provincial Arts School at the age of fourteen.[24] She won a major national folksong contest two years later and joined the Song and Dance Troupe of the PLA Jinan Military Region. Peng's big break came in 1984, when she was recruited by the Song and Dance Troupe of the PLA General Political Department, which has produced some of China's best-known singers. Even before this, she had been invited to join singing tours in Europe and Asia. In 1991, Peng was admitted to the elite Chinese Music Academy, where she eventually earned a master's degree in musicology. Given her unusual talent—and formal training—Peng's fame spread far and wide in China.[25]

In an interview regarding her marriage with Xi, Peng claimed that it was "love at first sight" even though her parents had qualms about her marrying the son of a prominent Party elder. It is true that even after Xi was promoted to become Party secretary of Zhejiang in 2002, Peng remained more famous—and popular—than her husband. After a simple wedding ceremony in September 1986, they lived apart—Peng at the PLA headquarters in Beijing and Xi in Fujian.[26] Xi liked to tell people that he did not want Peng to become a housewife. "She has too many devoted fans, and it would be wrong for me to deprive them of the chance to appreciate her art," Xi said. "Moreover, she had benefited from many years of support from and training by the PLA—and it is only right that she should continue to render services to the troops."[27]

After Xi's promotion to the PBSC in 2007, the Chinese media carried many stories whose apparent purpose was to deny rumors that, because the two had lived apart at least during Xi's seventeen years in Fujian, Xi had had a number of romantic entanglements. In Hong Kong and overseas-Chinese media, reports surfaced about his close friendship with a glamorous TV anchorwoman, Meng Xue, when he was based in Fuzhou.[28] After Xi's ascendancy to the top, the official media ran a plethora of articles testifying to the close relationship between Xi and Peng. For example, Peng told the Chinese press that, following the age-old custom of rural couples, she made a thick winter cotton quilt for Xi soon after their marriage—and brought the heavy blanket all the way from Beijing to Fuzhou. The quilt was made from a particularly fine cotton that Peng asked her mother to procure in their native Shandong. Peng also revealed that while their daughter, Mingze, lived with her in Beijing, she remained very close to her father.[29]

Peng has great political savvy. As we shall see in later sections, the entertainer was instrumental in introducing Xi to the powerful Shanghai Faction. And after Xi's elevation to the PBSC, Peng reportedly discouraged officials from treating her as a "future first lady." Nonetheless, she became much more active in social welfare and charity pursuits. Her work in boosting the welfare of AIDS patients was well known. For example, she visited AIDS orphans in remote villages in southwestern Yunnan Province in late 2009. "AIDs is actually not so fearsome," she told the victims. "What is terrible is the cold-hearted looks and unsympathetic expressions of people. It's prejudice and discrimination that are horrible."[30]

Considering that none of China's current or former first ladies—for example, the wives of Jiang Zemin or Hu Jintao—have been active in social and charitable work, the example set by Peng will have long-lasting significance. Since becoming first lady, she has been instrumental in popularizing Chinese fashion and even Chinese-made mobile phones. Peng's high-profile meeting with the American first lady, Michelle Obama, in 2014 has spawned much discussion about China's newfound "first lady diplomacy."[31]

### Humble Beginnings in a Shaanxi Village

"One step, one footprint at a time . . . I don't go after perfection."[32] This now-famous motto of the "princeling" general secretary says a lot about both Xi Jinping's career and statecraft before his ascendancy to the proverbial "peacock throne" at the Eighteenth Party Congress. Xi was not one to rock the boat, to spin out visionary ideas—or to take risky steps in reform. Unlike his liberal and outspoken father, Xi was always anxious to project the image of a humble student of his elders—and a team player. Throughout his provincial career, Xi steered clear of controversial policies or sayings so as not to spoil his chances of moving up the hierarchy.

Xi's innate conservatism could be due to the persecution that his father suffered at the hands of Chairman Mao and other conservative Party elders. From 1962 to 1979 (when his son was age nine to twenty-six), the elder Xi was in jail, exiled to the countryside, or under constant state-security surveillance. The main lesson that the younger Xi drew from his father's exploits was not to push forward a reformist agenda but to stick to a safe, middle-of-the-road, and even conservative political course.[33]

The young Xi was sent down to the countryside (or "rusticated") in his native Shaanxi Province from 1968 to 1975 in the village of Liangjiahe, Yanchuan County, some 70 miles from Yan'an, where his father had played a sizable role in helping to build up one of the CCP's major rural bases. In interviews with the media after Xi became famous, Liangjiahe natives who had helped the teenager adjust to a spartan life on the Loess Plateau said he had a tough time adjusting. The cave where he lived was infested with bugs, and shortly after his arrival, his body was covered with rashes. After several months, however, he was able to walk for 10 miles while carrying a large sack of wheat. Lu Nengzhong, in whose cave-house Xi lived for three years, said Xi struggled to balance two buckets of water on a bamboo pole across his shoulders. "He slid down hills on his butt instead of walking down them," he added. "He was very careful, very cautious." Lu also remembered that Xi liked to read thick books that he had brought with him from Beijing.[34]

Nonetheless, Xi claimed that he gained his wisdom about life—and his commitment to public service—through learning from illiterate peasants. "I felt very lonely," Xi wrote later about his first brush with the rough countryside. "But after I got used to the local life, especially after I lost myself in the local people, I began to feel a happy fulfillment." "We mustn't stand high above the masses or consider the masses as our fish and meat," he argued. "The hard life of the grassroots can cultivate one's will. With that kind of experience, regardless of the difficulties that I encounter in the future, I am fully charged with courage to take on any challenge, to believe in the impossible, and to conquer obstacles without panic."[35]

During his stay at Liangjiahe, Xi became a member of the CYL. Yet due to his father's dubious political status, his applications to join the CCP were turned down ten times. It was not until January 1974 that he was able to join the Party, a status that enabled him to become the Party secretary of his village. Xi learned from his parents first-hand about the treachery of CCP politics: you can be betrayed by your closest comrades, and the best way forward is to lie low and hide your feelings as well as political orientation. In any event, Xi was successful in cultivating ties with the peasants—to the point that they unanimously supported his application to enroll at Tsinghua University.[36] In 1975, the young man was able to get into the Department of Chemical Engineering as a *gongnongbing xueyuan* (a student with the background of worker, peasant, or soldier). It must be noted, however, that China's universities did not formally reopen until 1979, when qualified professors resumed teaching. And although the diploma that Xi got was recognized by the government, the quality of the education he received from 1975 to 1979 was inferior to that available to post-1979 Tsinghua students.[37] And like the majority of the large number of Fourth- and Fifth-Generation cadres who majored in engineering, Xi never practiced his profession after graduation.

### Early Years at the Central Military Commission and Hebei Province

The year 1979 was a turning point in Xi's life: he graduated from Tsinghua University with a degree in chemical engineering. Equally important, his father, who had been rehabilitated in 1977, was able to get him the plum job of secretary concurrently at the State Council General Office and the CCP CMC General Office. The CMC, which reports directly to the Politburo Standing Committee, is China's highest decision-making body on defense issues. Xi's specific job at the CMC was personal assistant to Defense Minister Geng Biao (1909–2000). Given the sensitive nature of both posts, only young men with the best political connections could secure them.[38]

Although he spent only three years at the CMC, it was an invaluable item on his curriculum vitae, enabling Xi in his later career to maintain cozy relations with the large number of princelings who became senior PLA officers in the 1990s and 2000s. The period when Xi served in the CMC coincided with a quasi-honeymoon between China and the United States, immediately after their formal establishment of diplomatic relations in January 1979. General Geng Biao visited the United States in 1980, and Xi helped Geng in preparation of his visit. This means that very early in his career Xi was exposed to the tricky nature of U.S.-China relations.[39]

More significantly, few among China's Fifth- or Sixth-Generation leaders have military credentials. It is noteworthy that his official Xinhua biography in late 2012 emphasized that he had taken on different military roles throughout his career. For example, he was political commissar of the PLA Brigade in Zhengding County, Hebei; first secretary of the Party Committee of the Fuzhou Military District; first political commissar of the Fujian Province Artillery Reserves Corp; first Party secretary of the Zhejiang Province Military District; and the head of the National Defense Mobilization Committee of the Nanjing Military Region.[40] This experience ensured that even before Xi's return to the CMC as vice-chairman in 2010, he maintained close ties with members of the top brass.

Career-wise, Xi made a decision in 1982 that would change his political for-tunes—and enable him to ascend to the top echelons of the Party-state apparatus later. He decided to leave the CMC and "go down to the countryside." He was ap-pointed deputy Party secretary of Zhengding County, Hebei Province, which was not far from Beijing. Xi was promoted to become county Party secretary after just a year, a position in which he served until his transfer to Fujian in 1985.[41] Although, given the passage of time, it has become difficult to assess the performance of the neophyte cadre, this stint would enable followers and publicists of Xi to portray him as a "man of the masses," who, in the words of Mao Zedong, "hails from the people and goes among the people [to render service]."[42]

In one of the rare interviews that he gave the Chinese media about his early life, Xi told *China Profiles* magazine that his decision to leave the CMC—and to establish his grassroots credentials—took a lot of people by surprise. His boss, Geng Biao, advised him to stay in the PLA—and to work in the field army in the provinces if he wanted grassroots experience. Xi noted that most of his contemporaries who had already rusticated during the Cultural Revolution had no more appetite for rural life. "Some who had suffered during the Cultural Revolution wanted to 'compensate' themselves by enjoying the pleasures associated with the big cities," he said. Xi noted that in his circle of friends, only Liu Yuan, the son of the disgraced president Liu Shaoqi, made the same decision by assuming the post of a village administra-tor in Henan Province. Xi pointed out that the grassroots were the best place for him to develop his career. "We were rusticated during the Cultural Revolution by force of circumstances," he said. "Yet we were able to learn a lot of things in the countryside. Now that leftist ideology has been jettisoned, it is a good opportunity for us to do our best and build up our careers [in rural China]."[43]

Indeed, if Xi had stayed in the PLA, he would at most have become an army general and a member of the CMC. This is exactly what happened to Liu Yuan, who joined the PAP—and subsequently the PLA—in 1992 after having attained the position of vice-governor of Henan Province four years earlier. Liu became a full general in 2009 and in 2012 narrowly missed promotion to become director of the General Political Department.[44] By contrast, the fact that Xi's CV includes the governorship and Party leadership of two important provinces stood him in good stead when it came to time to compete for the very top echelon of the Party-state apparatus.

## Seventeen Lackadaisical Years in Fujian Province

Upon leaving Fujian to take up the appointment as Party secretary of Zhejiang in 2002, Xi was asked by reporters about his achievements during his seventeen-year stint in Fujian. Xi's reply was characteristically low-key and noncontroversial: "It's up to the people to pass judgment on my performance. If there were merits, they were the merits of our collective leadership."[45] Like a large number of Fifth-Generation leaders, including Premier Li Keqiang, Xi built up his career in the provinces. He was in Fujian from 1985 to 2002 and rose from being the deputy mayor of Xiamen (1985–88) to being governor of Fujian in 2000. Although the princeling was promoted every two or three years, his performance in the "frontline province"—so-called because it is opposite Taiwan—could not be called meteoric; nor did he leave behind any major achievements.

### Learning the Ropes in Xiamen and Ningde

#### Xiamen and the Lessons of Xiang Nan and Hu Yaobang

Xi was ecstatic about his transfer to Xiamen in 1985. At that time, Xiamen was just a minor city—and the position of deputy mayor of Xiamen was just one notch above that of Party secretary of a county. But two things mattered. Xiamen had been designated an SEZ (on par with the Shenzhen SEZ) in 1980. And in May 1985—just a month before Xi's arrival—the size of the SEZ had been extended from a paltry 1 square mile to 50.5 square miles (2.5 square kilometers to 131 square kilometers). The first investments from the United States and Japan had started to arrive.[46] Second, Xiang Nan, a reformer and a good friend of Xi's father, was Party secretary of Fujian. That was why the younger Xi spent a couple of days with Xiang in the provincial capital of Fuzhou before making his way to Xiamen in the south. There was also another trait of Xiang's that would later help Xi's career. Because Xiang was a prominent leader of the CYL Faction, Xi had developed good ties with a major figure of a Party faction with which he would have to do business after entering the top echelons of the Party in 2007.[47]

Unfortunately, the development of Xiamen coincided with the most vicious power struggle at CCP headquarters since the end of the Cultural Revolution. Conservatives led by the orthodox patriarch Chen Yun—whose most famous dictum was "let's pursue reform within the bird-cage [of socialism]"—were trying to restrict Deng Xiaoping's market-oriented initiatives. And one of their early targets was none other than Xiang Nan. The conservatives, who had control of the national media, made use of a series of fake medicine and fake liquor scandals in Fujian to cast aspersions on "the uncontrolled development of private enterprise." Xiang had to bear overall responsibility—and he resigned in bitter frustration in 1986.[48] Xiang's fall also coincided with the conservatives' putting pressure on Deng to abolish the entire SEZ experiment. This forced the great architect of reform to be on the defensive: Deng said then that if the SEZs proved to be defective, they could be dismantled at any time.[49]

In January 1987, Hu Yaobang was illegally relieved of his post as CCP general secretary at an extended Politburo meeting. The immediate cause was Hu's apparent failure to curb a tidal wave of student demonstrations that hit about ten cities in December 1986. Deng allowed a bunch of conservative elders such as General Wang Zhen to savage Hu, who was accused of being "weak and soft" in the face of the wave of "bourgeois liberalization" sweeping the country. Given the intimate relations between Xi Zhongxun and Hu Yaobang, the younger Xi was devastated.[50] The ignoble fate that befell Hu, whose death in April 15, 1989, ignited the enormous pro-democracy movement that year, left a great impression on Xi. The Xiamen deputy mayor was again given a lesson in realpolitik: that it is wisest to lie low and not to stick one's neck out in the corridors of CCP politics.

It was therefore not surprising that Xi did not have much to show for his three years as the No. 2 man in Xiamen. He did, however, contribute to the drafting of the long-term development plan for Xiamen, "Xiamen's Strategy for Economic and Social Development." Even more important was that he had the chance to develop personal friendships with a host of Hong Kong and Taiwan businessmen who were prospecting for investment opportunities in Xiamen. This would serve to broaden his outlook. While his faith in orthodox socialism apparently remained solid, the neophyte cadre became aware of the importance of learning management and technology from multinational firms.[51]

Xi's unpretentious ways—and his natural friendliness with ordinary cadres and common people—also earned him immense popularity in Xiamen. In late 1987, a few dozen deputies to the Xiamen People's Congress nominated Xi as an "alternative candidate" to Mayor Zou Erjun, whose "re-election" had to be confirmed by a majority of deputies in the Xiamen legislature. Real competition was unheard of in the CCP politics of that era. And the authorities from the provincial capital of Fuzhou did everything to convince the deputies not to abandon Zou. Xi was also anxious not to appear to challenge the authority of his superiors. Nonetheless, Xi lost to Zou by a narrow margin. But it seemed evident that in terms of "promoting unity among cadres" as well as "building up relations between cadres and the masses," Xi was doing a better job than the incumbent mayor.[52]

*Xi Pulled in his Horns at Ningde*

In early 1988, Xi was given a promotion: he was named Party secretary of Ningde District, one of nine administrative units of Fujian. It was, however, a mixed blessing. Ningde, which is in eastern Fujian, is a hilly region with a dire lack of both natural resources and human talent. Fully one-third of the officially designated "poor population" of Fujian lived within the nine counties in Ningde. Local cadres were ecstatic at the prospect that the arrival of a "princeling," who had good connections in Beijing and Hong Kong, might bring favorable policies as well as domestic and foreign investments. But Xi was realistic enough to see that the area lacked the potential for industrialization. Even more important was that the national zeitgeist was out of kilter. In 1988 inflation around the country was high, so the mood was to rein in investment. Then came the student demonstrations of 1989, the Tiananmen Square massacre, and the massive outflow of foreign investment. It was hardly the time to contemplate ambitious development projects.[53]

Xi recalled later that Ningde cadres expected that upon assuming office he would introduce "three rounds of fire"—a popular Chinese proverb meaning multiple initiatives of great magnitude. But Xi was cautious. He said, "I only used a small amount of fire to keep the water warm." "The most important thing is not to let the fire be extinguished," he added. "Sometimes it may be necessary to add a bit of cold water" to cool the unrealistic expectations of Ningde cadres.[54] As a result, Xi focused on improving the lot of the Ningde masses. One good thing that he did was to move fisherfolk along the Ningde coast—who for generations had lived in tiny and hygienically substandard junks—to new housing on land.

An even more politically savvy thing that the thirty-six-year-old did in 1989 was to launch an investigation into large-scale corruption among Ningde officials. More than 7,300 local cadres were found to have appropriated farmland to build their own small villas—and often with either official funds or ill-gotten gains acquired through corruption. Due to the large number of officials involved, the Ningde case became big news even nationally. Xi was determined to root out what he called "corruption on either side of the road." "I would rather hurt the vested interests of hundreds of cadres than allow a few million people to suffer [the consequences of corruption]," he said.[55] In May 1990, Xi the "Conqueror of Corrupt Officials" became nationally known as a result of a *People's Daily* article, "Winning the Hearts of Ten Thousand People Through Doing a Good Deed." Zhang Mingqing, who reported the story, wrote that "the masses are clapping their hands because their top leaders are willing to get to the bottom of corruption."[56] As we shall see, however, Xi was not always so efficient or determined in combating graft in other parts of the province.

### *Great Expectations for Fuzhou's Development*

Xi finally had a good opportunity to make his mark on Fujian in 1990, when he was appointed Party secretary, the No. 1 job—in Fuzhou, the provincial capital. He would stay in this post for six years. The June 4, 1989, massacre dealt a body blow to national efforts at reform. The United States and many other countries imposed a partial ban on doing business with China. Yet by the early 1990s, China was on the move again. In 1992, Deng Xiaoping tried to resuscitate economic reform, which was threatened by the return of conservative, anti-market opinion in Beijing. Deng left the capital and went to the prosperous provinces in the south. In forward-looking cities such as Shenzhen and Zhuhai, Deng preached no-holds-barred, quasi-capitalist ideas about running the economy. This spelled great opportunities for Fujian, which had traditionally lagged behind Guangdong in luring investment from Hong Kong, Taiwan, and overseas Chinese investors.[57]

In 1993 Xi took full advantage of Deng's *nanxun*—(imperial tour to southern China)—when he embarked on trips to Hong Kong, Singapore, Malaysia, and the United States. It was also the first time that Xi gained global exposure. Ethnic Chinese and foreign businessmen were impressed by his earnestness and zeal in attracting overseas capital. Xi did not have his father's natural suaveness and brilliance, but he tried to make up for them by painting rosy pictures of Fuzhou. Despite being the capital of a major province, Fuzhou was merely a medium-size city that did not have many skyscrapers. It also fell behind Xiamen not just in foreign direct investment but, more importantly, the ability of local cadres to do business according to international standards. While visiting Hong Kong in 1993, Xi boasted that his city would "catch up with advanced metropolises within China" by the turn of the century and that it would attain the levels of the Four Asian Dragons by 2010.[58] Xi even put up a big poster at the entrance of the Fuzhou Party Headquarters Building: "Everything will be done as soon as possible." "This slogan does not mean only raising efficiency," Xi explained. "Now that we are competing in the international marketplace, we must make our reactions [to market requirements] both cautiously and quickly."[59]

One of Xi's biggest coups was to invite Taiwanese, Hong Kong, and overseas Chinese in Southeast Asia to invest in the provincial capital. The young cadre could take some credit for setting up China's first overseas Chinese investment zone, the Rongqiao Economic and Technological Development Zone on the outskirts of Fuzhou. Investors included the legendary Chinese-Indonesian magnates Sudono Salim (Liem Swie Liong) and Sutanto Djuhar—and Xi was personally involved in protracted negotiations to persuade them to pour money into the relative backwater of Fuzhou. The Xi team also impressed investors with the speed with which they cleared up old residential districts to make space for industrial and commercial developments.[60]

However, a much more ambitious project to redevelop the Three Lanes and Seven Allies—a neighborhood in Fuzhou that dated back to the Ming and Qing dynasties—turned out to be nothing short of disastrous. This rabbit warren of ancient mansions, artisans' quarters, and factories housed many of China's first inventers and artisans in industries such as paper, silk, and garments. In the early 1990s, the Fujian leadership successfully invited Hong Kong tycoon Li Ka-shing—the richest man in Asia—to invest nearly RMB 5 billion in building modern apartment blocks. Li acquired 661 *mu* (1 *mu* = 0.0667 hectare) of land at the relatively low cost of RMB 98.95 million. According to Fujian newspapers, the first stage of the development, which went on stream in 2003, afforded the government profits of RMB 70 million. However, local authorities had doled out almost RMB 100 million in compensation to the original residents. Much more important, so many treasured historic buildings were destroyed that this became a *cause célèbre* for intellectuals and environmentalists all over the country. Strong protests were lodged by municipal and provincial legislators and members of the CPPCC. The project came to a halt a year later; and the contract with foreign investors was suspended in 2005. In 2006, the Fuzhou government took upon itself the task of rebuilding the entire area at a cost of RMB 4.5 billion.[61] By that time, of course, Xi had already left Fuzhou—but this ill-starred project cast a shadow on his entire career in the province.

### Changle International Airport: A "Prestige Project" that Went Terribly Wrong

The genesis of Changle International Airport was typical of the "work style" of cadres posted to the outlying areas: They aim to construct at least one multimillion-renminbi project during their tenure. Ultramodern prestige projects are important for their promotion. Moreover, they will be remembered in local history for the gargantuan skyscrapers, container terminals, high-tech development zones, or—in the case of Xi Jinping in Fuzhou—an ultramodern airport.

Changle International Airport was the biggest capital project during Xi's six years as leader of Fuzhou. As with the grandiose airport in the Zhuhai SEZ next to Macau, there were not enough flights to keep Changle viable. Even today, northern Fujian—which the airport serves—remains a relatively underdeveloped region compared to booming, vibrant southern Fujian. The Fujian leadership chose a good time for the opening of the airport: on June 23, 1997, almost the same time that Hong Kong's sovereignty reverted to China. Unlike Hong Kong, however, Changle Airport was an unmitigated disaster from day one. Total investment, which would be shouldered by the provincial administration, was RMB 2.7 billion. In its first four years of operation, however, the airport accumulated debts of more than RMB 3 billion. The white elephant project was even classified by the official media as a "negative example" of unscientific and nondemocratic decision-making.[62]

First, the airport was predicated upon a pie in the sky notion: the prospect of almost immediate direct flights between the mainland and Taiwan. This "dream" was not accomplished until 2009. The location, Changle, is a remote suburb some 30 miles (45 kilometers) from downtown Fuzhou. Yet the worst part of the decision-making involved the messy finances. When the go-ahead was given in 1992, the provincial and municipal government had accumulated only RMB 400 million, less than 15 percent of the total estimated cost. This contravened existing regulations that in order to commence megaprojects, government units or corporations needed to have at least 30 percent of the required cash in hand. Some RMB 2.35 billion was made available through bank loans and bonds. In 2002, the airport's major creditors—the China Development Bank and China Construction Bank—stepped in to restructure the airports' debt and to look for new buyers. A year later, a white knight appeared in the guise of the cash-rich Xiamen International Airport (XIA). A joint venture—Fuzhou International Airport—was formed by the XIA and the Fuzhou government to take over the wreckage.[63]

### Xi and the Yuan Hua Smuggling Scandal

Despite his apparently mediocre performance, Xi was able to rise steadily up the hierarchy in Fujian. In late 1996, he was transferred out of Fuzhou and given an opportunity to serve the entire province in his capacity as deputy-Party secretary of Fujian. At the Fifteenth Party Congress in 1997, Xi became a member of the Central Committee of the CCP—an indispensable step for future advancement. However, he was only chosen as an alternate—or second-tier and nonvoting—member; and among the 151 alternate members, he got the fewest votes.[64] Given that a number of fellow princelings—including the second son of Deng Xiaoping, Deng Zhifang—were also among the least popular alternate members, this phenomenon seemed to reflect the general bias against high-born cadres among delegates to Party congresses. Nonetheless, the path had been cleared for his further promotion to acting governor in 1999 and then governor one year later. At forty-seven, he was one of China's youngest governors. However, his once-and-future competitor, Li Keqiang, had become governor of Henan—then the most populous province in China—in 1999, when the CYL Faction stalwart was barely forty-four. Xi served as the No. 1 cadre in the Fujian provincial government until his transfer to Zhejiang in 2002.[65]

While he was governor, his primary objective was to boost the economy, in particular to narrow the gap between Fujian and the neighboring rich provinces of Guangdong and Zhejiang. However, as when Xi served in Xiaman and Ningde, he was unable to focus on economic development due to the intervention of factional politics. By 1998, a storm was gathering force surrounding the smuggling and corruption deals of Lai Changxing, a rags-to-riches businessman and fixer in Xiamen, who founded the Yuanhua Group in 1994. Some RMB 50 billion in ill-gotten gains were involved in the Yuanhua scandal. Lai reportedly enjoyed the patronage of senior officials in the Fujian Party-and-government apparatus, the navy (naval vessels were used for smuggling purposes), and the Ministry of Public Security. Perhaps because some of his cronies were supporters of Lai, ex-president Jiang Zemin was unenthusiastic about pursuing what some called the largest criminal case in CCP history. Then-premier Zhu Rongji, however, personally took charge of the investigations, which were handled by agents of the Central Commission for Disciplinary Inspection (CCDI), China's highest-level anti-graft agency. Lai was tipped off and fled to Canada via Hong Kong in 1999. CCDI cadres, who set up special investigation units in Fuzhou and Xiamen, interviewed mid- to senior-ranking officials on a daily basis.[66]

Among top-level officials indirectly implicated in the Lai scandal was former Politburo Standing Committee member Jia Qinglin, who was based in Fujian from 1985 to 1996, during which time Jia rose from deputy Party secretary to governor in 1991 and finally Party secretary in 1993. His wife, Lin Youfang, was said to be a friend and business associate of Lai's. In 1999, Jia's wife put out a statement denying her complicity with the Lai gang. Xi also told interviewers at the time that Lin Youfang had nothing to do with the Yuanhua case. Given Jia's close ties with ex-president Jiang, he and his wife did not suffer any political damage. But senior cadres in Beijing—for example, vice-minister of public security Li Jizhou and the PLA head of military intelligence, Ji Shengde—were arrested. Then Fujian Party secretary Chen Mingyi had to resign from his job in early 2000 to take political responsibility. And Xi was given the task of restoring morale among shaken Fujian officials.[67] It was a job that Xi—who excelled at the arcane art called *tuanjiexue* (promoting unity among colleagues)—did very well.

Observers of Xi's career have often asked whether the princeling was tainted. It is true that when he was deputy mayor of Xiamen from 1985 to 1988, Lai had not yet set up his mafia-like operation. However, a large number of Xiamen cadres were arrested for facilitating Lai's wrongdoing, including two former Xiamen deputy Party secretaries, Liu Feng and Zhang Zongxu, as well as three former Xiamen deputy mayors, Lan Pu, Zhao Keming and Su Shuili. Zhang Zongxu served together with Xi as deputy mayor of Xiamen, though by 1990 Xi had left Xiamen for Fuzhou.[68] But it seems inconceivable that he would have been unaware of the monkey business of his former colleagues in Xiamen. And it was possible that, for his own political purposes, he chose not to share his knowledge of Lai's evil deeds with his superiors in Beijing as well as with cadres of the CCDI.[69]

### Xi's Fujian Report Card

Almost by any measure, it cannot be said that Xi acquitted himself well in Fujian, whose economy—and most development indicators—lagged behind those of other coastal provinces, despite the province's proximity to Taiwan and the exponential increase in Taiwan investment on the mainland. One problem was that the majority of the highest-quality Taiwan-related projects have gone to Shanghai and Guangdong—and Fujian officials and businessmen were not able to convince Taiwan compatriots to put money into their "home villages." Xi and his colleagues could, of course, point to external circumstances over which they had no control: the Taiwan crisis of 1996 and 2000, during which the PLA engaged in war games in the Taiwan Strait to discourage the allegedly secessionist activities of then-president Lee Teng-hui.[70] These crises disrupted not only Taiwan investment in Fujian but also the development of the entire provincial economy. Extenuating circumstances notwithstanding, it cannot be denied that Fujian's unsatisfactory progress was due above all to the lack of new ideas—and local cadres' failure to do things according to the requirements of the international marketplace.

It is because of Fujian's abject poverty that the "frontline province" has produced the largest number of illegal refugees who end up—if they are lucky—in the Chinatowns of the United States and Europe. This was dramatically illustrated by a tragic incident in June 2000, when fifty-eight Fujian residents were found suffocating to death inside a container truck near the British port of Dover. When commenting on the incident to the press, all that Xi could say was that his government would crack down on the "snakeheads" (people smugglers) and boost education among the peasants. "Fujian farmers have quite a good life," the governor said. "Yet they have been duped by snakeheads to try to 'make a big fortune abroad.'" Xi even blamed unnamed foreign governments for granting Chinese refugees political asylum simply on the grounds that they were the members of the Falun Gong sect or were victims of forced abortions.[71]

There is also the issue of the massive outbreak of corruption throughout Fujian. Xi is believed to be a Mr. Clean; one of his adages is "Either you get into business or you become a [clean] official. If you have chosen to be a cadre, you should not think about making money."[72] And if Xi had, like so many other princelings, chosen commercial activity, it would not have been very difficult for him to become a billionaire. Unlike other ostentatious princelings such as Bo Xilai, Xi has painstakingly cultivated a thrifty image his entire career. However, as a senior Fujian official, he has to bear political responsibility for the series of corruption scandals there.

What Xi has done best is to demonstrate fully—particularly to his superiors in Beijing—that he plays by the rules of the Party and that he is a man of the people. While he may not have inherited the "bourgeois-liberal" tendencies of his father, Xi certainly has Xi Zhongxun's knack for winning over the confidence of the masses.[73] Xi's associates were impressed by the many trips he made to different corners of Fujian and the fact that he seemed to exude genuine empathy and good will for the lowly peasants or fisherfolk with whom he talked. This was how *People's Daily* described a typical inspection trip that Xi took to the outskirts of the city of Sanming. Upon reaching the village of Long Mei, Xi told the peasants, "This time, I've come in all sincerity to have a chat with you," Xi was quoted as saying. "I hope my visit has not created any burden for you." "This simple introduction has dissolved the uneasiness of the villagers," the article in *People's Daily* said. The article ended with this memorable Xi quotation: "Since we do things for the people, the key is whether the people are satisfied. We don't do things in order to please our superiors."[74]

## Five Crucial Years in Zhejiang Province

The years 2002 to 2007 will be remembered as a critical juncture during which the princeling managed to show the Party—and his countrymen—that he was up to the task of running a rich coastal province. In the Chinese hierarchy, the Party secretary rather than the governor makes policies. Xi's stint in Zhejiang may also go down in history as the only period when he demonstrated a relatively high degree of innovative and progressive thinking.

### Xi's "Two Birds" Theory

As in much of his career, Xi was lucky in Zhejiang. His predecessor as its Party boss Zhang Dejiang—who was promoted to the Politburo in 2007—was a notable conservative. So it was relatively easy for Xi to portray himself as an enthusiastic and competent standard-bearer of Deng Xiaoping's reform and open-door policy. In early 2001, Zhang, a graduate of Kim Il-sung University in Pyongyang, wrote an article in the conservative journal *Huaxia Forum* called "We Must Make It Clear That Private Businessmen Cannot Join the Party."[75] This appeared despite the fact that then-general secretary Jiang Zemin was at that time finalizing plans to allow non–state sector entrepreneurs and professionals to join the CCP, a radical policy made official in a controversial speech that Jiang delivered on July 1, 2001, the eightieth anniversary of the founding of the CCP, in which the Party chief said it was in the Party's interest to throw open its door to private businessmen.[76] Compared to Zhang, Xi, who had no objections to the development of private enterprises, looked much more progressive even though he had a conservative bent with respect to ideological issues.

And while Deng was renowned for his "two cats" theory ("whether black or white, a cat is a good cat if it catches mice"), Xi espoused his "two birds" theory in 2005 so as to push forward his grand plan of moving Zhejiang industries up-market because at a time of energy shortages and rising labor costs, smokestack industries would have no place in the go-go coastal province. The first bird referred to the slogan *tenglong huanniao* (lit., to find a bigger cage for a bigger bird). This meant that Zhejiang, especially industrialized cities such as Hangzhou, Dongshan, and Wenzhou, needed to develop hardware and software for capital-intensive and high-tech production activities. Moreover, it needed to make more efforts toward synergy with Shanghai and Pudong, which are national leaders in pace-setting industries. The second bird referred to the companion phrase: "a phoenix seeking Nirvana," meaning that Zhejiang was ready to kickstart a more ambitious phase of modernization.[77]

In 2005, the Xi team informed manufacturers in 430 "backward" product lines that they had to either upgrade their technology or move out of the province. The relatively low-tech sectors included iron and steel, nonferrous metals, light industry, textiles and garments, petrochemicals, machine-building, pharmaceuticals, and printing. The production scale of plants engaged in 145 of these product lines would be decreased, while factories turning out the other 285 types of merchandises would be shut down or moved elsewhere. "We have to shake off our dependence on the *cuguang* [rough and wild] style of growth, and put more effort into boosting our capacity for innovation," Xi said.[78]

It is significant that Wang Yang, a CYL Faction stalwart who was Party secretary of Guangdong from 2007 to 2012, borrowed the spirit—and almost the exact wording—of Xi's campaign to modernize Zhejiang's industrial base. However, unlike Xi, who adopted a low profile and stuck to the time-honored CCP tradition of "doing instead of talking," the charismatic Wang played up his "go high-tech" movement in the Guangdong as well as national media. Wang's efforts, however, were marred by bad timing, specifically, the global financial crisis that hit China hard from mid-2008 to mid-2009. There were reports of clashes between Wang and local Guangdong officials whose priority was preserving jobs—and ensuring sociopolitical stability—rather than moving their factories up the technological chain.[79]

Xi was one of the provincial bosses who seemed genuinely committed to environmental issues. This might have been due to the long years he had spent in the villages—and his personal experience that the air and water quality in the countryside had deteriorated due to excessive and irresponsible industrialization. His motto for striking a better balance between man and nature was: "Green water and blue skies equal golden and silver mountains," meaning that a clean environment is tantamount to unlimited riches. While Zhejiang is a relatively rich coastal province, villages in backward regions still used firewood and bamboo for fuel. In 2003, the Zhejiang government began asking remote villages to use marsh gases, a relatively clean source of energy, for heating and other household purposes. Xi told reporters that when he was a village cadre in Yanchuan County, Shaanxi, in the 1970s, he had pioneered the use of marsh gases. "All of rural Zhejiang should go down the path of ecologically friendly economic construction," he said.[80]

### Democratic Experiments in Zhejiang

Having absorbed the lessons of ousted Party chiefs Hu Yaobang and Zhao Ziyang, Xi has never gone on the record as an advocate of political liberalization. Yet during his Zhejiang stint, he did make contributions to developing grass-roots democracy. His message was that "the more comprehensive grassroots democracy is, the more harmonious society will be." The Party secretary explained: "Given that the democratic consciousness and [education] qualities of some grassroots people may not be high enough, problems of one sort or another may emerge," he said. But, referring to the famous Chinese proverb that "one must not stop eating in order to avoid choking," Xi said he would continue practicing grassroots democracy in incremental steps.[81]

In early 2005, Xi introduced a relatively liberal model for the popular election of members of the village administrative committees (VACs) in Zhejiang. Village elections—picking the heads and deputy heads of VACs—were first introduced by Deng Xiaoping in 1979. However, the VAC candidates were usually Party members nominated by relevant CCP authorities, for example, the Party committees running the villages or the Party committees of higher administrative units such as townships or counties. In March 2005, residents of Tangjiadi Village were allowed to run for elections as *zijian* (self-recommended) candidates, that is, they did not need to be nominated by Party or government units.[82] It is significant that the CCP Organization Department has never indicated explicitly that "independent candidates" can run in grassroots elections. In 2011, for example, some 100 "independent candidates" running to become deputies to regional people's congresses were disqualified. In many instances, such candidates—and their supporters—were subject to heavy-handed intimidation by police and other security units, and they had no choice but to withdraw.[83]

Equally significant was the pioneering work of residents in Bailian, a village under the jurisdiction of the township of Rui'an near Wenzhou, in impeaching the head of its VAC. The mid-2007 impeachment, which was later ratified by the Zhejiang administration, was the first such case in the country: 221 villagers moved to impeach He Guangtou, who was suspected of corruption and failure to consult villagers over major financial matters. For example, He sold off 100 *mu* of collective land without proper consultation with and authorization from the peasants. He was impeached in a vote of 413 to 248.[84] After the Bailian experiment, cases of the impeachment of VAC heads became more frequent at least in coastal China. This exercise of grassroots democracy was referred to by experts on political reform as the "Rui'an experience." As Xi put it at the time, "We must boost the level of organization among peasants so as to construct the 'new socialist village.' . . . This will really resolve issues of raising the efficiency of agriculture as well as the income of peasants."[85]

In 2006, the Xi administration initiated a new evaluation system for municipal- and county-level cadres who were being groomed for promotion. Apart from appraisals from their superiors, these cadres' performance—measured on the basis of twenty-one criteria—was also assessed by as many as 150 "people's representatives"—for example, deputies to local people's congresses and consultative conferences. And apart from the GDP level, cadres had to demonstrate a track record in improving the environment.[86] It must be noted, however, that Xi never departed from his play-it-safe philosophy regarding the enhancement of grassroots democracy. For example, Xi shied away from bolder experiments such as conducting one-person-one-vote elections of the heads of *xiang* (townships) or *zhen* (towns)—which are one rung higher than villages in the administrative hierarchy. Direct polls at the *xiang* and *zhen* levels were first held on an experimental basis in Sichuan and Guangdong in 2000.[87]

### Xi's Track Record in Zhejiang

During his frank exchange with then-U.S. ambassador Clark Randt in 2006, Xi gave a long summary of his province's achievements. For example, he said, according to the ambassador's record, which was subsequently revealed by Wikileaks, "provincial GDP increased 13.6 percent in 2006, with per capita GDP now at $4,000—well, $3,975 to be exact." Only Guangdong, Jiangsu, and Shandong had bigger GDP than Zhejiang. And on a per capita GDP basis, Zhejiang ranked first among all provinces—and lagged behind only the centrally administered cities of Shanghai, Beijing, and Tianjin. Per capita GDP was about $6,000 in the provincial capital of Hangzhou in 2006 and about $6,500 in Ningbo. Zhejiang also ranked first in the country in tax revenue and in per capita disposable income.[88]

Xi went on to tell Randt that nearly all other provinces had sent delegations to Zhejiang to study the province's successful economic track record. "Recently, delegations from Xinjiang, Sichuan, and Jiangxi have scheduled appointments to visit and study Zhejiang, bringing large delegations that will include county-level Communist Party secretaries," Xi reportedly said. He also quoted then-Jiangxi provincial Party secretary Meng Jianzhu as saying that he and others had much to learn from Zhejiang's development path.[89]

Was Xi's enthusiasm for economic expansion a sign of the kind of "GDP worship" that has received widespread criticism even in the official Chinese media? Both in his talk with Randt and on other occasions, Xi made much of the development of privately owned enterprises (POEs) in Zhejiang. As in Guangdong, by the 1990s the non-state sector had accounted for half the province's GDP. Two caveats must, however, be stated. First, POEs, such as those in the world-famous manufacturing center of Wenzhou, developed in the mid-1980s, well before Xi's time. Second, while it was undeniable that Xi gave POEs a great deal of support —particularly those in more promising sectors, such as information technology and the automobile industry (see Chapter 4)—he failed to raise the quality of the great majority of private firms. This explains in part the big crash that the Zhejiang private sector suffered in 2011, when some 25,000 POEs folded.[90] In 2010, a POE worker in the Zhejiang manufacturing sector typically produced RMB 76,000 worth of added value a year, RMB 25,000 less than the national average. The head of the Zhejiang Federation of Industry and Commerce told *Caijing National Weekly* in 2011 that many of the private small and medium-size enterprises (SMEs) in Zhejiang suffered from low productivity. "These SMEs have difficulty moving up the value chain," he said. "They lack motivation, funds, and room for maneuver."[91]

Irrespective of criticisms, it cannot be denied that Xi's five years in Zhejiang provided him with a platform—and some semblance of a national track record—with which to knock on the door of the Politburo. Even ex-president Hu pronounced himself satisfied with the performance of the Zhejiang economy when he talked with Zhejiang parliamentarians at the NPC session in 2005. Hu lauded Zhejiang for having broken the RMB 1 trillion GDP mark the year before, meaning that "the province is able to attain the main goals and tasks of the tenth five-year plan one year in advance." He also praised the coastal province's achievements with respect to sociopolitical stability and "the construction of spiritual civilization."[92] Hu was probably aware at this stage that Xi would be a contender to become the next general secretary, thereby posing a threat to his own candidate, then-Party secretary of Liaoning Li Keqiang. That he appeared to be unstinting in his assessment of Zhejiang seemed to testify to the fact that Xi had acquitted himself reasonably well in five short years of running the province.

### Seven Months as Honcho of Shanghai

Xi served in Shanghai for a mere seven months: from March 2007 to mid-October the same year, when he was elevated to the PBSC and the post of executive secretary or head of the Central Committee Secretariat at the Seventeenth Party Congress. However, the Shanghai interlude was an indispensable step that enabled him to elbow aside CYL Faction rising star Li Keqiang—and become "crown prince" at the Seventeenth Party Congress.

First, his appointment in Shanghai to replace the corrupt Chen Liangyu confirmed to the entire Party-state apparatus his intimate ties to the Shanghai Faction and especially the kingmaker extraordinaire, ex-president Jiang Zemin. This led to the effective merger of the two potent forces in the Party: the Gang of Princelings and the Shanghai Faction.[93] Second, even before 1949 Shanghai politicians played a disproportionately large role in both Party and national politics. One has only to recall the tremendous influence wielded by the Gang of Four radicals, whose power base was Shanghai. After the Cultural Revolution, several Shanghai Party secretaries, including Jiang Zemin, Zhu

Rongji, Huang Ju, Wu Bangguo, and Yu Zhengsheng—Xi's successor—have become PBSC members. And even after the retirement of Jiang Zemin in 2002, the Shanghai Faction retained formidable clout in internal Party affairs. As discussed in Chapter 1, Xi lacks a national network of cronies and protégés in the Party and government. Support rendered to Xi by Jiang Zemin, ex-vice president Zeng Qinghong, and other Shanghai Faction stalwarts proved essential for Xi to consolidate his position after his ascendancy to the top in late 2012. A number of affiliates in the Shanghai Faction were also persuaded to cross over to the Xi camp both before and after the Eighteenth Party Congress (see the following section).

Xi mainly pursued two goals during his brief time in Shanghai. The first was reassuring officials there that after dumping Chen Liangyu the central authorities would not launch a large-scale purge. "My first job is to promote unity among our cadres," he told officials in Shanghai upon arriving, thus implying that there would be no massive blood-letting.[94] Again, Xi's talent at uniting people was being used to good effect even though it was well known that Chen-related investigations had exposed corruption and other instances of economic malfeasance by hundreds of mid- to high-ranking Shanghai officials. Chen, an erstwhile protégé of ex-president Jiang, was arrested in September 2006 on charges of corruption.[95] Among other alleged crimes, he helped his business associates secure land illegally for real-estate development; he also gave the green light for his cronies to secure large loans from the city's social-security funds. Xi was apparently successful in raising the morale of Shanghai cadres.

The new Party boss's second and equally important goal was to prepare for his move to Beijing after the Seventeenth Party Congress.[96] He was conscientious in asking Shanghai Faction heavyweights, including then-vice-president Zeng Qinghong, to introduce him to capable officials who could be inducted into his inner circle of close advisers (see below).

Despite his short tenure in Shanghai, Xi was eager to go down in history as having contributed to the glories of China's most important business center. In a speech delivered not long after taking up his new position, Xi vowed to raise Shanghai's profile as the undisputed economic, financial, trade, and shipping center of the country. "In the next five years, it is imperative that we materialize the magnificent blueprint of realizing Shanghai's [role of being] the 'four centers' as well as a modernized international metropolis," he said. Xi added that Shanghai would abide by Beijing's instructions and work with other regions in China to take advantage of the opportunities of globalization. "Shanghai will once again return to the center stage of China's economy," he said. "However, this time Shanghai's role is not 'dancing alone' but 'leading the entire country to dance' [together]."[97] It was not possible for Xi to achieve much in half a year. But his having participated in high-level decision-making regarding the fate of China's foremost business city bolstered his national stature considerably.

**How Xi Became "Crown Prince" at the Seventeenth Party Congress—and His Testy Relations with Boss Hu**

*Xi Curried Favor with the Shanghai Faction*

During Xi's formative years in Chinese officialdom—his seventeen years in Fujian Province—he had very little contact with members of the Shanghai Faction. If anything, he was closer to the CYL Faction due to the relatively large number of Fujian cadres who had benefited from the patronage of former Party secretary and CYL Faction stalwart Xiang Nan. It must also be noted that being "close-to-the-earth" Shaanxi people, both Xi Zhongxun and Xi Jinping are temperamentally different from the typically suave, worldly, and big-spending Shanghainese politicians (*hai-pai*).

It was Xi's wife, Peng, who first got her husband connected with the Shanghai Faction. Peng continued her career with the PLA Song and Dance Troupe in Beijing even after her marriage to Xi. After Party elders picked Jiang Zemin in 1989 to succeed Zhao Ziyang, he brought only one official with him from Shanghai, his aide and political adviser Zeng Qinghong, who would later become PBSC member and vice-president. Zeng's younger brother, Zeng Qinghuai, who had always had an interest in the performing arts, became a senior official in the Ministry of Culture. Shortly thereafter, Zeng Qinghuai extended his tentacles over the entire cultural scene in the capital.[98] The "master impresario" also became a key patron of the two most glamorous stars in the PLA Song and Dance Troupe: Peng and Song Zuying. Much has been written about the allegedly intimate relationship between ex-president Jiang and the comely Song. What is less well-known is that Peng made use of her friendship with Zeng Qinghuai to introduce her husband to Shanghai Faction chieftains, including Jiang and Zeng Qinghong. It is not an exaggeration to say that this "spousal diplomacy" played a substantial role in Xi's landing the job of Zhejiang Party secretary in 2002.[99]

*Jiang's Brief "Retirement" in Zhejiang and His "Discovery" of Xi*

The turning point in Xi's battle for the privilege of succeeding Hu Jintao came in September 2004, when Jiang Zemin was forced by Hu—and several senior generals who had crossed over to the Hu camp—to vacate his position as CMC chairman. After all, Jiang had already ceased to be a member of the Politburo and Central Committee at the Sixteenth Party Congress in 2002. And his refusal to yield the CMC chairmanship to Hu was seen as a shameful retrogression from the principle of "intra-Party democracy."[100]

Jiang, who wanted to remain commander-in-chief until the Seventeenth Party Congress in 2007, was obviously unhappy about his ouster. His Shanghai Faction associates tried to improve his mood by building a grand mansion for him in a choice Shanghai suburb. While work on the "Shanghai Palace" was progressing,

Jiang decided to take refuge in a guesthouse in Hangzhou. After all, Hangzhou is the favorite retreat of a number of illustrious Party elders, including Chen Yun. One other objective that Jiang wanted to accomplish in Hangzhou was testing the loyalty of Xi Jinping, who had been newly installed as Party secretary of Zhejiang Province. It was significant that Jiang's aides had communicated the wish of the "core of the Third-Generation leadership" to stay temporarily in Hangzhou directly to Peng Liyuan. Throughout Jiang's year-long stay in Hangzhou, Xi did everything possible to curry favor with the old man. Apart from accompanying Jiang to famous tourist spots around Hangzhou, Xi also discussed Chinese literature and arts with the ex-president, who liked to show off his knowledge of ancient culture. Jiang was so satisfied with Xi that he decided to designate the young man as Hu Jintao's successor at the Seventeenth Party Congress.[101]

Xi also profited from his widespread image as a proverbial *laohaoren* (man with no enemies) who has no excessively strong political orientation or affiliation. In an effort to promote intra-Party democracy, in early 2007 Hu and his associates conducted a series of opinion polls among as many as 400 senior cadres—full and alternate members of the Central Committee, Party elders, as well as leaders of the NPC and CPPCC—on the issue of "the most appropriate candidates to be promoted to the Politburo and the PBSC." The names of both Li Keqiang and Xi Jinping were on the list. The result of the "beauty contest" showed that Xi did significantly better than Li. Apart from members of the Gang of Princelings and the Shanghai Faction, other respondents who were not close to the CYL Faction had good reason to pick Xi rather than Li, who was universally known as Hu's favorite.[102]

Due in part to the results of the poll, it was difficult for Hu to say no to Jiang's recommendations. Despite Hu's success in forcing Jiang to give up the CMC chairmanship, Jiang still commanded the loyalty of a number of key generals, demonstrated by the fact that after his nominal departure from the CMC in September 2004, Jiang held on to his original—and the biggest—office at CMC headquarters, the August 1 Building in northwestern Beijing, until the eve of the Eighteenth Party Congress.[103]

Jiang was reportedly ecstatic about his ability to follow the tradition laid down by Deng Xiaoping regarding the "cross-generation designation of successors."[104] In the run-up to the Fourteenth Party Congress in 1992, Deng named Hu Jintao as Jiang's successor without so much as consulting the latter. Apart from ensuring that the CYL Faction would not be so powerful as to marginalize his own protégés, Jiang also had selfish motives for propping up Xi. It is well-known among intellectuals and pundits in Beijing that Jiang's two sons had engaged in hugely lucrative commercial deals when they were active on the Shanghai business scene. At one point, Jiang's eldest son, Jiang Mianheng, was even known as the "IT king of Shanghai." It was within the realm of possibility that, in return for Jiang's support, Xi had pledged to support the activities of the ex-president's two sons in the decade after the Eighteenth Party Congress.[105]

## Xi's Uneasy Coexistence with Boss Hu

It goes without saying that Xi's relationship with Hu Jintao was uneasy at best. It also did not help that both are introverts—and both have similar err-on-the-side-of-caution mentalities. Their friction was obvious to the world. Given that his own position on the CMC was insecure, Hu delayed as long as possible the ritual of inducting Xi into the commission partly due to the fact that Xi was on good terms with the dozens of princeling generals in the PLA. According to tradition, the fourth plenum of the Seventeenth Central Committee—which took place in October 2009—would have been the logical time for Xi to have become CMC vice-chairman. The rationale was that, given the likelihood that Xi would become general secretary and CMC chairman at the Eighteenth Party Congress, he would need at least three years to familiarize himself with military work. But reporters were told that personnel issues would not be discussed at the fourth plenum. Immediately after the pivotal meeting, news leaked out that Xi had written a letter to the PBSC, announcing that he did not want to be considered for the position of CMC vice-chair. The vice-president indicated that "I want to focus on improving the performance of my existing jobs, and I do not yet feel fit to take up extra portfolios."[106]

Then came something that was most uncharacteristic of Xi: apparently open defiance of his boss. In October 2009, soon after the conclusion of the fourth plenum, Xi set out on a five-country European tour. According to long-standing protocol, Xi would extend greetings from Hu to his hosts. Xi did just that with a number of senior European officials. However, according to Xinhua News Agency, the words "Hu Jintao" never appeared during Xi's tête-à-tête with German chancellor Angela Merkel, the leader of the most important European country. Before official discussions began, Xi handed Merkel the English editions of two books—one on energy and the other on IT—written by ex-president Jiang Zemin. According to Xinhua, Xi then "passed along Comrade Jiang Zemin's greetings and good wishes" to the German leader. Merkel reciprocated by asking Xi to send her greetings to Jiang. There was no reference to Hu. This was doubly strange, given that Jiang had already retired when Merkel came to power and the two did not have any previous dealings with each other.[107]

The Merkel incident must have been doubly irritating for Hu. Less than two weeks earlier, Hu had been publicly humiliated by Jiang during celebrations to mark the sixtieth anniversary of founding of the People's Republic of China on October 1. During the three-hour-long festivities, the official Chinese media gave Jiang about the same prominence as Hu. For example, the eighty-three-year-old former president appeared twenty times on CCTV's coverage of the all-important military parade. And Hu was caught a couple of times on TV assuming a humble posture next to the talkative and high-spirited Jiang. The next day, *People's Daily* put similarly sized photos of Hu and Jiang side by side on its front page.[108]

Hu, of course, lacked the guts to confront either Jiang or Xi openly. Apart from delaying Xi's entry to the CMC, the only thing that Hu did was to bruise Xi's ego by having Li Keqiang perform duties—such as meeting foreign dignitaries—that should have been handled by Xi, since, as vice-president, he was supposed to share some of the diplomatic functions of the president. And then there was the visit to the Sichuan earthquake zone in May 2009 to mark the first anniversary of the temblor. Then-executive vice-premier Li was the only senior cadre whom Hu brought along to this symbolically important occasion.[109] Yet both Hu and Xi knew that there was very little that Hu could do to disrupt the arrangements made at the Seventeenth Party Congress. So finally, at the fifth plenum of the Central Committee in October 2010, Xi got what he wanted: the first vice-chairmanship of the CMC and confirmation that he would emerge as general secretary at the Eighteenth Party Congress. The only thing left hanging in the air at the time was whether Hu would follow Jiang's footsteps by remaining on the CMC for a few years beyond the Eighteenth Party Congress. Hu's eventual decision in favor of a "naked" or total retirement at the congress enabled Xi to quickly gather virtually all the reins of power in his hands.[110]

### Xi Jinping's Governing Team

One of Xi Jinping's major power bases is the Gang of Princelings, particularly cadres with a "revolutionary bloodline" who are serving in the PLA (see Chapters 1 and 5). Compared to previous general secretaries, including Jiang Zemin and Hu Jintao, however, Xi's networking skills do not appear to have been superior. Having spent most of his career in Fujian and Zhejiang Provinces, the princeling does not seem to have built up a large coterie of associates and followers in the Party-state hierarchy. This could have been due to the fact that Xi had learned the lesson from his father about not forming inner circles that could be construed as conspiratorial in nature. Indeed, one of his favorite axioms about being a responsible cadre is "do not do things using my name and my banner."[111]

While Jiang had his Shanghai Faction and Hu his CYL Faction, there is no obvious clique in the Party-state apparatus associated with Xi. Instead, he has put together a corps of loyalists based mainly on the following three groups of cadres: those who have served in Shaanxi, his home province; Xi's former associates and underlings in Fujian, Zhejiang, and Shanghai, in addition to high-school and college friends; and mostly Shanghai-affiliated cadres recommended to him by his mentors, Jiang Zemin and Zeng Qinghong.[112]

Among senior cadres who enjoy the title "state leader," thirteen have intimate ties with Shaanxi in one way or another. Apart from Xi, Politburo member and Organization Department director Zhao Leji (b. 1957), chief of the PLA General Staff Department General Fang Fenghui (b. 1951), director of the General Armaments Department General Zhang Youxia (b. 1950), and Vice-Chairman of the NPC Zhang Baowen (b. 1946) claim Shaanxi as their "home province." PBSC member and CPPCC chairman Yu Zhengsheng (b. 1945) was born in Shaanxi even though his home province was Zhejiang. Senior cadres with substantial work experience in Shaanxi include Zhao, Politburo member and NPC vice-chairman Li Jian'guo (b. 1946) as well as Politburo member and director of the Central Committee General Office Li Zhanshu (b. 1950). Both Zhao and Li Jian'guo are former Party secretaries of Shaanxi while Li Zhanshu is a former Party secretary of Xian, the capital of the province. In addition, Defense Minister Chang Wanquan (b. 1949) served in Shaanxi-based PLA divisions from 1974 to 2002. A few top cadres also spent time in the province either as "rusticated youths" or as students in colleges in the province, including PBSC member and top graft-buster Wang Qishan (b. 1948), who first got to know Xi when they worked in rural communes in Shaanxi during the Cultural Revolution.[113]

Wang Qishan, Li Zhanshu, and Zhao Leji are three Shaanxi Faction affiliates who are deemed closest to Xi. As Party secretary of the CCDI, Wang, who is also a princeling, has spearheaded the anti-corruption campaign, which has taken the Party by storm (see Chapter 3). Given his age, however, Wang is expected to retire at the Nineteenth Party Congress, scheduled for 2017. Xi first became acquainted with Li during the former's stint as deputy Party secretary and then Party secretary of Zhengding County, Hebei Province, from 1982 to 1985. During much of this period, Li, who is a Hebei native, was Party boss of neighboring Wuji County. Later on in their careers, Xi and Li were able to renew their friendship when the latter served in Shaanxi from 1998 to 2003. Although Xi left his home province in 1975, he paid regular visits to Xian and other Shaanxi cities to maintain ties with his relatives. Li is said to have won the trust of Xi by moving the grave of Xi Zhongxun from Beijing to his native county of Fuping.[114] Much of Xi's relationship with Zhao is based on their being fellow natives of Shaanxi. Zhao, who spent the bulk of his career in the remote western Qinghai Province, was Party boss of Shaanxi from 2007 to 2012. During these five years, Zhao apparently won Xi's gratitude by providing help to less well-off members of the labyrinthine Xi Zhongxun clan.[115] Both Li and Zhao have high chances of being inducted to the PBSC at the Nineteenth Party Congress.

Perhaps because Xi's seventeen years in Fujian were not exactly a happy experience, he has brought almost none of his former associates from the coastal province to Beijing. By contrast, about a dozen of his Zhejiang underlings have won big promotions. Reuters news agency even reported in early 2014 that Xi had plans to promote 200 "progressive officials" from Zhejiang to "senior positions across the spectrum in the years ahead." Take, for example, Zhong Shaojun (b. 1968), who was appointed deputy director of the CMC General Office in early 2013. While Zhong had had no prior military experience, Xi made him a senior colonel so as to bolster his credentials as his PLA troubleshooter for the rest of the decade. Zhong was deputy director of the Zhejiang organization department and Xi's personal secretary when the latter was Party secretary of the province.[116] Then there is Huang Kunming (b. 1956), who was mayor of the Zhejiang city of Huzhou and Party secretary of Jiaxing when Xi was Party boss of Zhejiang. Huang, who subsequently became Party secretary of Hangzhou, was appointed deputy director of the CCP Propaganda Department in late 2013.[117] Another veteran Zhejiang cadre, Cai Qi (b. 1955), who was mayor of Hangzhou when Xi left for Shanghai in 2007, in early 2014 was named a deputy secretary-general of the Central National Security Commission (CNSC), which is the country's highest office on internal security (see Chapter 3). Also set to have a bright future is Chen Min'er (b. 1960), who was one of the nine Sixth-Generation cadres to have been elected a full member of the Eighteenth Central Committee. A former head of the Zhejiang propaganda department, Chen was made governor of Guizhou Province in 2013.[118]

While Xi served in Shanghai for a mere seven months, several of his subordinates in the city have been transferred to the Zhongnanhai Party headquarters. Foremost among them is Ding Xuexiang (b. 1962), who was secretary-general of the Shanghai Party committee when Xi was Party secretary. After the Eighteenth Party Congress, Ding was promoted to deputy director of the CCP General Office and director of the General Secretary's Office.[119] Senior judge Shen Deyong (b. 1954), who was head of the Shanghai Commission for Disciplinary Inspection from 2006 to 2008, is one of the few Xi cronies with expertise on legal-judicial issues. A veteran jurist who first became vice-president of the Supreme People's Court (SPC) in 1998, Shen has been deputy Party secretary and executive vice-president of the SPC since 2008.[120]

Several of Xi's policy advisers were introduced to him by trusted Party elders such as Zeng Qinghong. The most senior within this group included two veterans of the Central Policy Research Office (CPRO), Shi Zhihong and He Yiting. Shi (b. 1950), whose specialty is drafting Party documents, was Zeng's personal secretary when the latter was director of the Central Committee General Office from 1993 to 1999. Shi worked in senior positions in the CPRO from 2007 until 2013, when he was named to a pre-retirement post on the CPPCC. However, the Shanghai native still advises Xi on issues such as the modernization of socialist dogma.[121] He (b. 1952), who served on the CPRO for twenty-four years, was promoted to executive vice-president of the Central Party School (CPS) in late 2013. Like Shi, He is Xi's point man on doctrinal matters.[122] Another close adviser and speechwriter is Li Shulei (b. 1964), who served as Xi's key aide when the latter was president of the CPS from 2007 to 2012. In early 2014, Li left the school after twenty-five years of service to become head of the Propaganda Department of Fujian Province.[123] Yet compared to his predecessors Jiang and Hu, Xi seems to lack close aides whose personal loyalty to the Party boss has been anchored in decades of service.

Then there are two prominent Xi classmates. Liu He (b. 1952), who studied with Xi at the elite Beijing 101 Middle School, is a trusted adviser on economic and financial issues. A graduate of the Kennedy School of Government at Harvard, Liu served at the People's Bank of China and in other economic departments before assuming his current post as secretary general of the CCP's Central Leading Group on Finance and Economics.[124] The relatively small size of Xi's network—especially in the higher reaches of the Party—was reflected by the fact that he tapped his former college classmate, Chen Xi—an academic who spent almost his entire career in higher education—for the key slot of deputy director of the Organization Department. Chen (b. 1953), a former Party secretary at Tsinghua University and the China Association for Science and Technology, functioned as Xi's "gatekeeper": making sure that Party, government, and enterprise posts went to politically correct candidates.[125]

Another remarkable point about the nature of Xi's inner circle is that he lacks a circle of academics, public intellectuals, and other professionals who might help him think outside the box. Former vice-president Zeng Qinghong often sought the advice of scholars at the Chinese Academy of Social Sciences (CASS) or editors at Beijing-based official newspapers. Former premier Zhu Rongji is known to have sought the views of nationally known liberal economists such as Wu Jinglian. Premier Li Keqiang has reportedly assembled a large personal think tank that consists of professors and former classmates from Peking University, his alma mater.[126] By contrast, Xi likes to consult thinkers with military backgrounds, who offer him blueprints about realizing the Chinese Dream of a strong China that can close the gap with the world's sole superpower, the United States. Xi's princeling associate, General Liu Yuan, who is himself a noted military thinker, has reportedly drawn Xi's attention to the writings of professors teaching at military academies.[127]

The preponderance of military figures in his kitchen cabinet, coupled with the country's increasingly tense confrontation with Japan and the United States, could predispose the commander-in-chief to pursuing more muscular foreign and military policies. The relative dearth of liberal aides among his inner circle could also affect the extent to which Xi might be inclined to entertain political liberalization. During his tour of Guangdong Province in December 2012, Xi pointed out that he was looking for "high-caliber cadres [who] have confidence in the [socialist] road, and in [the Party's] theories and institutions."[128] Xi has yet to show Chinese as well as foreign observers that he and his aides are capable of not only holding down the fort of CCP supremacy but also blazing new paths for reform.

### Conclusion: Xi's Qualifications Compared to Those of His Predecessors

After examining Xi's rise to power, one cannot help pointing out that compared to previous top leaders after the Cultural Revolution—Deng Xiaoping, Hu Yaobang, Zhao Ziyang, Jiang Zemin, and Hu Jintao—Xi's training and experience appeared to be neither sufficient nor impressive. Given the indisputable fact that Deng, Hu Yaobang, and Zhao made massive contributions to both economic and political reform, it does not seem as though Xi will be able to match their records. Before Hu Yaobang or Zhao became general secretary, they had already established a formidable national reputation among CCP members as well as ordinary citizens. And the reform visions spun out by the two bold leaders won them the admiration of the great majority of the intelligentsia.[129]

What about Xi compared to Hu Jintao, his immediate predecessor? It is true that both have a cautious temperament and middle-of-the-road political orientations; both are inclined to uphold the CCP's status as "perennial ruling Party." And both were picked by their superiors for the top job due to their experience in the provinces as Party secretaries. However, Hu had had substantially more experience in Beijing: he had run the CYL, which has a labyrinthine national network; moreover, he had served as a PBSC member for ten years before ascending the "throne" in 2002.[130] Prior to his elevation to the PBSC in 2007, however, Xi had had no national-administration experience. He spent seventeen of his formative years in Fujian, during which he had no chance to develop either skills or visions that marked him out as a potential heavyweight reformer. Much the same could be said of Xi compared to Jiang Zemin. Jiang had the distinct advantage of having worked at central government ministries as well as localities. Moreover, he had the added merit of speaking English—and being personally involved in the execution of Deng Xiaoping's open-door policy. For example, Jiang worked closely with then-vice premier Gu Mu, a liberal official, in setting up China's SEZs.[131]

Xi also scores very poorly in terms of exposure to the West—and overall knowledge about international norms even though he was barely twenty-five when Deng kick-started the era of reform and the open door. During his trip to Iowa in 1985, when he was head of Yongding County, Xi declared that he was impressed with American technology. However, this direct contact with the West did not seem to have affected his views on politics and governance.[132] As we shall discuss in Chapter 3, Xi resembles Mao inasmuch as both attach the highest esteem to Confucian classics: His homilies to young cadres are replete with references to virtues extolled in the classics of imperial China. By contrast, ex-president Jiang, who exemplifies the worldview of a Shanghainese, is much more conversant about the ways of the Western world.

The putative "core" of the Fifth-Generation leadership also suffers from a general lack of first-rate education. As stated above, he attended Tsinghua University before the college system was revived in 1979. Much has been written about the fact that his Ph.D. dissertation on Marxist economics—which earned him a law degree from Tsinghua in 2002—was hardly an exemplar of scholarly erudition.[133] By contrast, Li Keqiang, who was Xi's major competitor for the no. 1 slot, has considerably more rigorous academic training. For example, Li was a top student at Peking University Law School from 1979 to 1983. His doctoral studies in economics under Professor Li Yining are considered a solid academic endeavor.[134]

Even more of a liability is perhaps Xi's princeling background, a political handicap particularly given the fact that there were two other princelings on the PBSC. Irrespective of the elevated status that cadres with "revolutionary bloodline" can command among certain sectors of the polity, princelings represent the notion of a Chinese-style aristocracy. One of the most deep-seated contradictions in Chinese society, however, is precisely the masses' revolt against cadres and clans with special privilege. It also does not help that princelings sit on many boards of companies that are seen as amassing indecently high levels of wealth. The likes of Bo Xilai and Xi Jinping also raised eyebrows by sending their kids to expensive private colleges abroad. From this perspective, Xi's *gaoganzidi* background may be held against him despite the care that he has taken all his life to cultivate his image as "a man of the masses."

Yet Xi also has advantages to which his predecessors could not have aspired. As we shall see in Chapter 3, he has a Machiavellian streak that he had successfully kept to himself until the Eighteenth Party Congress. Despite his largely lackluster career before 2012, Xi has proven to be a lot more comfortable with power than ex-president Hu. The quick moves that he made soon after the Eighteenth Party Congress to consolidate his hold over the PLA top brass indicate that he has a solid power base from which to further expand his authority. Equally significant is that, compared with his predecessors, Xi seems to be relatively free of constraints imposed by his patrons. Former Party chiefs Hu Yaobang and Zhao Ziyang were effectively sacked by Deng, who kept an eye on Jiang Zemin until the patriarch's death in 1997. Hu lacked the strength of character to prevent ex-president Jiang's frequent interventions. Time, however, is on Xi's side. While he still has to humor kingmaker Jiang, it is unlikely that the eighty-eight-year-old Shanghai Faction potentate can last for long. While Xi does not seem to have ambitions about retooling the CCP according to international norms, he seems well-placed at least to attain the goal of tightening the Party's—and his own—grip on power.

## Notes

1. Cited in Kevin G. Hall, "Sizing up China's next leader no easy task, WikiLeaks cables show," McClatchy Newspapers, February 16, 2012, www.mcclatchydc.com/2012/02/16/139137/sizing-up-chinas-next-leader-no.html.

2. Ibid.

3. For a discussion of the approaches of Daoism to governance, see, for example, Craig Johnson, "Taoist leadership ethics," *Journal of Leadership and Organizational Studies* 7, no. 1 (Winter 2000): 82–91; Nada Korac-Kakabadse, Alexander Kouzmin, and Andrew Kakabadse, "Spirituality and leadership praxis," *Journal of Managerial Psychology* 17, no. 3 (2002): 165–182.

4. See He Guoqiang, "The Party central authorities think it is appropriate for Xi Jinping to become Shanghai Party secretary," China News Service, March 24, 2007, www.chinanews.com/gn/news/2007/03-24/899401.shtml.

5. It can be argued that Xi was picked in 2007 as Hu's successor because he was seen as a fairly mediocre cadre with no strong political inclinations one way or another. For a discussion on the circumstances of Xi's emergence as heir apparent to Hu, see, for example, Cheng Li, "China's team of rivals," *Foreign Policy*, no. 171 (March/April 2009): 88–93, www.jstor.org/discover/10.2307/20684856?uid=3738176&uid=2&uid=4&sid=21103934864997/.

6. For contemporary assessments of Xi Jinping's ability and ambitions, see, for example, Andreas Lorenz, "'Redder than red': An American portrait of China's next leader," *Der Spiegel*, www.spiegel.de/international/world/redder-than-red-an-american-portrait-of-chinas-next-leader-a-732972.html; William A. Callahan, "Who is Xi Jinping, and where will he lead China?" Le Centre Tricontinental, Brussels, November 8, 2012, www.cetri.be/spip.php?article2815&lang=fr/; "Singapore founding father Lee Kuan Yew says Xi Jinping is

in Mandela's class," *South China Morning Post,* August 7, 2013, www.scmp.com/news/asia/article/1294831/lee-kuan-yew-says-xi-jinping-mandelas-class?page=all/; Ankit Panda, "Xi Jinping's one year performance review," *Diplomat,* March 5, 2014, http://thediplomat.com/2014/03/xi-jinpings-one-year-performance-review/.

7. For a discussion of Xi Zhongxun's career, see, for example, "Xi Zhongxun, a life full of heroism but marred by misfortunes," *People's Daily,* May 29, 2006, http://cpc.people.com.cn/GB/85037/85038/7880593.html; see also Xi Yuanping, "My father, Xi Zhongxun," *Xinmin Evening Post* (Shanghai), December 30, 2009, http://sh.xinmin.cn/minsheng/2009/12/30/3209232.html.

8. For a discussion of Xi Zhongxun's views on ethnic minorities, see, for example, Fan Ming, "Remembering Xi Zhongxun's revolutionary achievements," CRT.com.cn (Beijing), January 8, 2009, www.crt.com.cn/news2007/News/sqmh/2009/18/091811301376EK13F4J003CC9BJ664_3.html.

9. Ibid.; see also Benjamin Lim and Frank Daniel, "Does China's next leader have a soft spot for Tibet?" Reuters, September 1, 2012, http://in.reuters.com/article/2012/09/01/china-tibet-xi-jinping-idINDEE88002I20120901/.

10. Cited in Lin Mu, "Xi Zhongxun before and after Hu Yaobang's fall from grace," Chinareform.org (Beijing), February 17, 2013, www.chinareform.org.cn/Explore/history/201302/t20130218_160927.htm.

11. For a discussion of how Xi Zhongxun was persecuted beginning in 1962, see, for example, "How Kang Sheng persecuted Xi Zhongxun in 1962," *People's Daily,* January 30, 2013, www.gd.xinhuanet.com/newscenter/2013-01/30/c_114549141.htm.

12. Cited in "Qi Xin remembers: My life with Xi Zhongxun for 55 years," China.com, March 27, 2008, http://news.xinhuanet.com/book/2008-03/27/content_7866038_3.htm.

13. Cited in "Xi Zhongxun and the establishment of Shenzhen and other special economic zones," Xinmin Net (Shanghai), December 14, 2012, http://news.xinmin.cn/rollnews/2012/12/14/17638794.html.

14. For discussion of Xi's rehabilitation of Li Yizhe, see Lu Diwen, "The story of how Xi Zhongxun rectified the 'Li Yizhe case,'" *Yangcheng Evening Post* (Guangzhou), January 20, 2008, www.chinawriter.com.cn/bk/2008-03-07/12956.html.

15. Cited in Xu Qingquan, "Why did Xi Zhongxun spend his last years in Shenzhen?" *China News Weekly* (Beijing), October 21, 2013, www.zj.xinhuanet.com/newscenter/rb/2013-10/21/c_117797651.htm.

16. For a discussion of the siblings of Xi Jinping see Chen Yuan, "The family life of Xi Zhongxun: he asks his children to keep a low profile," *People's Daily,* March 15, 2013, http://news.xinhuanet.com/politics/2013-10/15/c_125534820.htm. See also "The Zhejiang Communist Party Committee has made six anti-graft pledges to people in the province," Xinhua News Agency, July 15, 2004, http://news.xinhuanet.com/newscenter/2004-07/15/content_1604262.htm.

17. For a discussion of Xi's rich relatives, see, for example, "Xi Jinping millionaire relatives reveal fortunes of elite," Bloomberg News, June 29, 2012, www.bloomberg.com/news/2012-06-29/xi-jinping-millionaire-relations-reveal-fortunes-of-elite.html; John Garnaut, "Chinese leader's family worth a billion," *Sydney Morning Herald,* June 30, 2012, www.smh.com.au/world/chinese-leaders-family-worth-a-billion-20120629-218qi.html. See also Staff Reporter, "Xi relatives own assets of more than HK$400 million," *Apple Daily,* November 16, 2012, http://hk.apple.nextmedia.com/news/art/20121116/18068392.

18. For a discussion of Xi Qiaoqiao, see, for example, Kentaro Koyama, "Xi's sister developed 'iron will' during banishment in Cultural Revolution," *Asahi Shimbun* (Tokyo), October 18, 2012, http://ajw.asahi.com/article/special/red_aristocrats/AJ201210150001o; see also "A brief introduction of Xi Qiaoqiao and Xi An'an," Qiandaohu Net (Hangzhou), October 20, 2013, www.qiandaoh.com/news/201310/20/2629.html.

19. For a discussion of the relations between Xi Jinping and other major clans in the "red aristocracy," see, for example, Cheng Li, "Rule of the princelings," *Cairo Review of Global Affairs* (Cairo), February 10, 2013, www.brookings.edu/research/articles/2013/02/china-xi-jinping-li/.

20. See "Xi Jinping sends letter of congratulations on the 30th anniversary of the China Welfare Fund for the Handicapped," Xinhua News Agency, March 21, 2014, http://news.xinhuanet.com/politics/2014-03/21/c_119889772.htm.

21. For a discussion of Xi Yuanping's career, see, for example, "Revelations about Xi Yuanping, the low-profile brother of Xi Jinping," *Ta Kung Pao* (Hong Kong), October 14, 2013, http://photo.takungpao.com/politics/2013-10/1349115.html. See also Wu Ming, *A Biography of Xi Jinping* (Hong Kong: Hong Kong Culture and Arts Press, 2008), pp. 386–91. For a discussion of the career of Jia Yun, see, for example, Peng Zhiqiang, "Jia Yun discloses his plans for 'escape' and his relations with Fan Bingbing," *Chengdu Commercial Post* (Chengdu), April 13, 2007, http://news.eastday.com/s/20070413/u1a2762501.html.

22. Cited in "The real reason behind the divorce of Xi Jinping and his first wife," DWNews.com (New York), November 2, 2012, http://forum.dwnews.com/threadshow.php?tid=1004250/; see also "A short marriage that is not well-known: Xi Jinping and first wife, Ke Lingling," Boxun news (New York), December 29, 2011, www.peacehall.com/news/gb/china/2011/12/201112290546.shtml.

23. Ibid.

24. For a discussion of Peng Liyuan's Shandong roots, see, for example, "Peng Liyuan: The daughter of Shandong," *Dazhong Daily* (Jinan), April 3, 2013, www.zgnt.net/content/2013-04/03/content_2180689.htm.

25. For a discussion of Peng's music career, see, example, "The first master's degree holder in indigenous music," Chinese Jiangsu Net, March 21, 2013, http://news.163.com/13/0321/14/8QGFO3C600014AED.html.

26. Cited in "Xi Jinping and Peng Liyuan got married in 1986," *Shenzhen Special Zone Daily,* December 24, 2012, http://news.cntv.cn/china/20121224/101855.shtml; see also "Peng Liyuan: The family is the support for women," *Global Personalities* (Beijing), March 28, 2013, http://eladies.sina.com.cn/qg/2013/0328/18191217742_5.shtml.

27. Cited in Wang Yonghua, "Xi Jinping said it was a case of love at first sight—and they talked on the phone every day," *Huashang News* (Xian), December 25, 2012, http://ent.sina.com.cn/s/m/2012-12-25/09393819759.shtml.

28. Cited in "Love affair between Xi Jinping and TV anchorwoman in Fuzhou," *Apple Daily* (Hong Kong), November 17, 2012, www.eulam.com/html/201211/17/391022.html.

29. Cited in "Peng Liyuan: The family is the support base for women"; see also "Peng Liyuan reveals her married life with Xi Jinping," *Shenzhen News* Net, July 12, 2007, www.sznews.com/home/content/2007-07_b/12/content_1333740_3.htm.

30. For a discussion of Peng Liyuan's role as AIDS goodwill ambassador, see, for example, Mo Bei and Hu Tingting, "Peng Liyuan: From singer to good will ambassador for lung and AIDS diseases," *Global Times People* (Beijing), November 24, 2012, http://news.ifeng.com/history/zhongguoxiandaishi/detail_2012_11/24/19501713_8.shtml.

31. For a discussion of Peng's new mission as first lady, see, for example, "Peng Liyuan's new mission," *Qianjiang Evening Post* (Hangzhou), July 4, 2012, http://news.xinhuanet.com/mil/2011-07/04/c_121621627_8.htm. See also Malcolm Moore, "China claims victory in battle of first ladies," *Telegraph* (London), March 21, 2014, www.telegraph.co.uk/news/worldnews/asia/china/10714688/China-claims-victory-in-battle-of-first-ladies.html.

32. Cited in Lu Minghe, Zhao Lei, and Cai Huiqun, "Xi Jinping's road to politics," *Southern Weekend* (Guangzhou), March 29, 2007, http://news.sina.com.cn/c/2007-03-29/102212644233.shtml.

33. For a discussion about Xi Jinping's views about his father, see, for example, Andrew Higgins, "For Xi Jinping, set to become China's next leader, father's past is sensitive," *Washington Post,* February 13, 2012, www.washingtonpost.com/world/asia_pacific/for-chinas-next-leader-the-past-is-sensitive/2012/02/10/gIQAdJZ09Q_story.html.

34. Cited in "Xinhua News Agency puts out special article on the private life of Xi Jinping," *People's Daily,* December 24, 2012, http://news.xinhuanet.com/video/2013-06/09/c_124840730.htm; see also Edward Wong, "Tracing the myth of a Chinese leader to its roots," *New York Times,* February 16, 2011, www.nytimes.com/2011/02/17/world/asia/17village.html?_r=2&pagewanted=1/.

35. For Xi's recollection of his life in the countryside as part of Mao's rectification campaign, see "Xi Jinping wrote an article about his early life, saying that his stay in the villages has had a big impact on him," I-Feng.com, October 21, 2010, http://history.people.com.cn/GB/198307/13015010.html.

36. Cited in "Xinhua news agency puts out special article on the private life of Xi Jiping."

37. For a look at the life of the *gongnongbing* students, see, for example, "The life of *gongnongbing* students at Tsinghua University during the Cultural Revolution," Tsinghua University Net, July 15, 2009, http://news.ifeng.com/history/gongye/jiyi/geren/200907/0715_6834_1251094.shtml.

38. For a discussion of Xi's three years as Geng Biao's secretary, see, for example, Geng Ying and Geng Yan, "How Xi Jinping assesses his three-year service as secretary to Geng Biao," *People's Daily,* December 23, 2013, http://news.ifeng.com/history/zhongguoxiandaishi/detail_2013_12/23/32380395_0.shtml.

39. Cited in "Defense Minister Geng Biao visited the United States in 1980 and looked at advanced equipment of the American forces," Ifeng.com (Beijing), January 11, 2011, http://news.ifeng.com/history/gaoqing/detail_2011_01/11/4222095_0.shtml.

40. See "Biography of Xi Jinping," Xinhua News Agency, February 1, 2013, http://news.xinhuanet.com/rwk/2013-02/01/c_114586554.htm.

41. For a discussion of Xi's life and work at Zhengding, see, for example, "Zhengding, Hebei: The starting point of Xi Jinping's political career," *Ta Kung Pao,* July 11, 2013, http://news.takungpao.com/mainland/focus/2013-07/1753931.html; see also "Hebei Daily publishes front-page article on comrade Xi Jinping's work in Zhengding," Xinhua News Agency, January 2, 2014, http://news.xinhuanet.com/local/2014-01/02/c_125944449.htm.

42. Cited in "Xi Jinping insists on the mass line when he was working in Zhengding," Northeast News Net (Shenyang), September 2, 2013, http://news.nen.com.cn/system/2013/09/02/010767455.shtml.

43. Cited in Feng Xi, "Xi Jinping: The masses are the sources of our strength," *China Profiles* (Beijing), January 6, 2013, http://elite.youth.cn/introd/201301/t20130106_2780404.htm.

44. For a discussion of the relationship between Xi Jinping and Liu Yuan, see, for example, James Mulvenon and Leigh Ann Ragland, "Liu Yuan: Archetype of a 'Xi Jinping man' in the PLA?" *China Leadership Monitor,* Hoover Institution, May 8, 2009, http://media.hoover.org/sites/default/files/documents/CLM36JM.pdf.

45. Cited in Shao Fangqing, "Xi Jinping in Fujian: Step by step for 17 years," *China Business News* (Beijing), April 5, 2007, http://finance.sina.com.cn/leadership/crz/20070405/01593473971.shtml.

46. For a discussion of the expansion of the Xiamen SEZ, see, for example, Zhao Lin, "On June 29, 1985, the Xiamen special zone was extended to the entire island," Xiamen Net, December 26, 2011, www.xmnn.cn/zt11/jjtq30/z11_19/201112/t20111226_2119861.htm.

47. For a discussion of the influence that Xiang Nan had on Xi Jinping, see, for example, "Xiang Nan: The Hakka man who is a pioneer," China Longyan Net (Longyan, Fujian), February 17, 2012, http://news.sohu.com/20130804/n383342411.shtml.

48. Cited in "Xiang Nan fell from grace because of the fake medicine scandal in Jinjiang," Sina.com.cn (Beijing), September 12, 2008, http://finance.sina.com.cn/money/roll/20080912/14515301486.shtml.

49. For a discussion of controversies surrounding the special economic zones, see, for example, Yue-man Yeung, Joanna Lee, and Gordon Kee, "China's special economic zones at 30," *Eurasian Geography and Economics* 50, no. 2 (2009): 222–240.

50. For a discussion of the relations between Xi Zhongxun and Hu Yaobang, see, for example, Zhang Jie, "Xi Zhongxun resolutely stands by Hu Yaobang," *Financial Digest* (Hong Kong), December 2012, http://kan.weibo.com/con/3617295256040432?_from=title/.

51. For a discussion of Xi's career in Xiamen, see, for example, "Xi Jinping: Xiamen has given me many tough tests in life," *Xiamen Daily* (Xiamen), November 23, 2012, http://fj.sina.com.cn/news/m/2012-11-23/141616087_2.html.

52. Cited in Wu, *A Biography of Xi Jinping*, pp. 142–143.

53. For an official assessment of Xi's performance in Ningde, see, for example, Wu Xiaoyu, Wang Minxia and Wang Guoping, "Ningde cadres push forward Xi Jinping's teachings about 'going down to the grassroots,'" *Fujian Daily*, April 17, 2014, http://fj.ce.cn/n02/201404/17/t20140417_1463995.shtml.

54. Cited in Yu Wei, "Xi Jinping: Taking the 'Red Boat' and going to the forefront," *Da Di* (Beijing), December 1, 2006, http://paper.people.com.cn/dd/html/2006-12/01/content_12102960.htm.

55. For a discussion of Xi's fight against graft, see, for example, Han Yuting and Lu Liyi, "Xi Jinping served in Fujian for 17 years; he is well-known for fighting corruption," *Fujian Daily* (Fuzhou), November 20, 2012, http://news.qq.com/a/20121120/000794.htm.

56. Cited in "When Xi Jinping ran Ningde, he was adamant in fighting graft," *Zhengzhou Evening Post* (Zhengzhou), December 8, 2012, http://zzwb.zynews.com/html/2012-12/08/content_426411.htm.

57. For a discussion of the impact of Deng's southern tour on development of China's regions, see, for example, Tian Xiaowen, "Deng Xiaoping's Nanxun: Impact on China's regional development," in *The Nanxun Legacy and China's Development in the Post-Deng Era*, ed. John Wong and Zheng Yongnian (Singapore: Singapore University Press), pp. 75–94.

58. For a discussion of Xi's efforts to attract Hong Kong and foreign investors to Fuzhou, see, for example, Wu Ming, *China's Future: Life Story of Xi Jinping* (Hong Kong: CNHK, 2012), pp. 196–206.

59. Cited in "Xi Jinping's 17 years in Fujian: he received kudos for fighting corruption and maintaining high government efficiency," *Economic Observer* (Beijing), November 20, 2012, http://fj.sina.com.cn/news/m/2012-11-20/073115606_3.html.

60. For a discussion of Xi's work in attracting overseas-Chinese capital to Fuzhou, see for example, Wu Ming, *A Biography of Xi Jinping*, pp. 165–169.

61. Cited in Chen Guoming, "CPPCC members in Fujian appeal for the preservation of the 'Three Lanes and Seven Allies'," China News Service, January 9, 2004, www.chinanews.com/n/2004-01-09/26/389909.html. See also Wang Yong, "Analysis of government behavior in the case of the Three Lanes and Seven Allies of Fuzhou," *Reform and Opening Up* (Beijing), no. 22, 2010, www.xzbu.com/1/view-290078.htmwww.xzbu.com/1/view-290078.htm.

62. For a discussion of the scandal surrounding the Changle Airport near Fuzhou, see, for example, Zhong Minyuan, "A study on mistaken decision-making regarding the Fuzhou Changle Airport," *South Reviews* (Guangzhou), April 5, 2004, www.ce.cn/ztpd/hqmt/gnmt/nfc/more/t20040105_275604.shtml.

63. Ibid.

64. Cited in "Xi Jinping came in last in the votes garnered by alternate members of the new Central Committee," VOA Chinese Service, November 19, 2012, www.wenxuecity.com/news/2012/11/19/2086966.html.

65. For a discussion of his career before Fuzhou, see, for example, "The people are the fountainhead of our strength: on General Secretary Xi Jinping," Xinhua News Agency, December 25, 2012, http://news.xinhuanet.com/politics/2012-12/25/c_114148683_7.htm.

66. For a discussion of the Yuan Hua smuggling case, see, for example, Shawn Hsieh, "The rise of collective corruption in China: The Xiamen smuggling case," *Journal of Contemporary China* 14, no. 42 (2005): 67–91.

67. Cited in "Governor Xi Jinping says Fujian will do whatever it can to help central authorities investigate the Yuan Hua Case," China News Service, January 20, 2000, www.chinanews.com/2000-1-29/26/17163.html. See also Anthony Kuhn, "14 Chinese receive death sentence in smuggling case," *Los Angeles Times,* November 9, 2000, http://articles.latimes.com/2000/nov/09/news/mn-49474/.

68. For a discussion of Xiamen officials who have been arrested due to their connections with the Yuan Hua case, see, for example, "People whose careers have been ruined by Lai Changxing," *Economic Observer* (Beijing), July 22, 2011, http://money.163.com/11/0723/00/79JURA5S00253B0H.html. See also Wang Jia, "An introduction to officials who fell from grace because of the Yuan Hua case," *China Business Journal* (Beijing), July 30, 2011, http://finance.sina.com.cn/roll/20110730/020010232952.shtml.

69. It is probable that Xi chose to keep mum on the Lai Changxing case because of the powerful protectors of the smuggling kingpin. For a discussion, see Sheng Xue, "The end of road for Lai Changxing," *Open* (Hong Kong), June 9, 2012, www.open.com.hk/content.php?id=830/. See also Edward Wong, "Former insider indicted in Chinese corruption scandal," *New York Times,* December 30, 2011, www.nytimes.com/2011/12/31/world/asia/lai-changxing-indicted-in-china.html?_r=0/.

70. For a discussion of the confrontation between China and Taiwan during the 1995–96 crisis, see, for example, Robert S. Ross, "The 1995–96 Taiwan strait confrontation: Coercion, credibility, and the use of force," *International Security* 25, No. 2 (Fall 2000): 87–123.

71. Cited in "Xi Jinping says Fujian will redouble efforts to combat smuggling and human trafficking," China News Service, March 10, 2002, www.chinanews.com/2002-03-10/26/168352.html.

72. Cited in "Xi Jinping's view on fighting corruption: If you want to become a cadre do not think of making money," *People's Daily,* December 28, 2012, http://fanfu.people.com.cn/BIG5/n/2012/1228/c64371-20048078.html.

73. For Xi's description of his approach to the masses, see, for example, "Former Fujian governor Xi Jinping: Introduce capital and talents to Fujian," CCTV, December 20, 2012, http://fj.qq.com/a/20121120/000233.htm.

74. Cited in "Xi Jinping worked in Fujian for 17 years: He is praised for fighting corruption and making attempts in implementing reforms," Fjsen.com (Fuzhou), November 20, 2012, http://fj.qq.com/a/20121120/000184.htm.

75. Cited in Lam, "Intraparty democracy with Chinese characteristics," in *Whither China's Democracy,* p. 59.

76. For a discussion of private entrepreneurs in Zhejiang joining the Party, see, for example, Yuxin Wu, "Methods and characteristics of political participation by private entrepreneurs—A case study of Zhejiang Province," *Asian Culture & History* 3, no. 1 (2011): 138–143.

77. Cited in "Xi Jinping: Raise well the 'two birds' so that Zhejiang can create a new round of prosperity," *People's Daily,* March 3, 2006, http://cpc.people.com.cn/GB/64242/64253/4448987.html.

78. Cited in "Zhejiang: 430 'backward manufacturing product lines' put on the black list," Xinhua News Agency, November 21, 2005, www.sh.xinhuanet.com/zhuanti/csj/2005-11/21/content_5636860.htm.

79. For a discussion of Wang Yang's approach to economic restructuring in Guangdong, see, for example, "Guangdong's GDP has lost momentum due to the policy of 'enlarging the bird cage and changing the bird' strategy; Wang Yang is resolute about continuing with reform," *Huaxia Times*, May 26, 2013, http://business.sohu.com/20120526/n344130349.shtml.

80. For a discussion of Xi's view on the environment, see Bao Hongjun, "Zhejiang Party secretary Xi Jinping: Blue water and green hills are the equivalent of silver and gold," *People's Daily*, April 4, 2006, http://politics.people.com.cn/GB/14562/4322248.html.

81. "Xi Jinping talks about harmonious society: The more well-established grassroots democracy is, the more harmonious society will be," Xinhua News Agency, September 25, 2006, http://news.xinhuanet.com/local/2006-09/25/content_5381864.htm.

82. For a discussion of village-level elections in Zhejiang when Xi was Party secretary of the province, see, for example, Dong Huaping, "Zhejiang leads the country in allowing 'self-recommended' candidates to run for village-level officials," China News Service, March 28, 2005, www.chinanews.com/news/2005/2005-03-28/26/555799.shtml.

83. For a discussion of restrictions on local-level elections, see, for example, Michael Wines, "China appears to be moving to halt grassroots candidates," *New York Times*, June 10, 2011, www.nytimes.com/2011/06/10/world/asia/10china.html?_r=0/; see also "China rejects 'independent candidate' amid local legislature elections," Xinhua News Agency, June 8, 2011, http://news.xinhuanet.com/english2010/china/2011-06/08/c_13918045.htm.

84. For a discussion of the dismissal of the Rui'an village chief, see, for example, Chen Dongsheng, "The Rui'an phenomenon in Zhejiang: The first time in China that a village administrator has been impeached," *Legal Daily*, June 28, 2007, http://society.people.com.cn/GB/37454/37459/5921704.html.

85. Cited in "Xi Jinping emphasizes the comprehensive implementation of the construction of the new socialist village in Zhejiang," Zhejiang Online, March 24, 2006, http://zjnews.zjol.com.cn/05zjnews/system/2006/03/24/006531917.shtml.

86. Cited in "Zhejing Party secretary demands an appraisal system for assessing cadres' responsibility for achieving environmental goals," *China Environment News*, June 9, 2006, http://news.sina.com.cn/c/2006-06-09/10439161973s.shtml.

87. For a discussion of experiments of elections at the town or township level, see Willy Lam, *Chinese Politics in the Hu Jintao Era* (Armonk, NY: M. E. Sharpe, 2006), pp. 113–116. See also, Lianjiang Li, "The politics of introducing direct township elections in China," *China Quarterly*, no. 171 (September 2002): 704–723.

88. Cited in "Zhejiang Party Secretary touts economic successes and work toward rule of law at ambassador's dinner, March 19, 2007," Wikileaks. https://www.wikileaks.org/plusd/cables/07BEIJING1840_a.html; see also "Special report: Cables show United States sizing up China's next leader," Reuters, February 17, 2011, www.reuters.com/article/2011/02/17/us-wiki-china-xi-idUSTRE71G5WH20110217/.

89. Ibid.

90. For a discussion of the failure of many Wenzhou enterprises, see, for example, Peng Liang, "Why Wenzhou bosses have fled," *Economic Observer* (Beijing), October 8, 2011, www.eeo.com.cn/2011/1008/213001.shtml.

91. See "The collapse of small and medium-size enterprises in Zhejiang reflects their failure to transform themselves," *Economy and Nation Weekly* (Beijing), July 25, 2011, http://finance.sina.com.cn/china/dfjj/20110725/165810203379.shtml.

92. See "General Secretary Hu Jintao visits Zhejiang parliamentarians," *Zhejiang Daily*, March 5, 2005, http://biz.zjol.com.cn/05biz/system/2005/04/11/006089788.shtml.

93. For a discussion of the interaction among the factions in the CCP, see, for example, Alexis Lai, "'One Party, two coalitions'—China's factional politics," Alexis Lai, CNN.com, November 9, 2012, http://edition.cnn.com/2012/10/23/world/asia/china-political-factions-primer/; see also Cheng Li, "A biographical and factional analysis of the post-2012 Politburo,"

*China Leadership Monitor,* Hoover Institution, no. 41, 2013, http://media.hoover.org/sites/default/files/documents/CLM41CL.pdf.

94. Cited in "Shanghai authorities convene a meeting of cadres: He Guoqiang and Xi Jinping make speeches," *Liberation Daily* (Shanghai), March 26, 2007, www.china.com.cn/policy/zhuanti/zgrsrm/2007-03/26/content_8085795.htm.

95. For a discussion of the Chen Liangyu case, see, for example, Jonathan Watts, "Shanghai's Communist Party chief sacked in corruption purge," *Guardian,* September, 25, 2006, www.theguardian.com/world/2006/sep/25/china.jonathanwatts/; Joseph Kahn, "Shanghai Party boss held for corruption," *New York Times,* September 25, 2006, www.nytimes.com/2006/09/25/world/asia/25china.html?_r=0/.

96. Cited in "Xi Jinping looks back on his work in Shanghai in the past seven months," China News Service, October 28, 2007, http://news.sina.com.cn/o/2007-10-28/102812799660s.shtml.

97. Cited in "Xi Jinping: Shanghai will lead the nation in a new dance," *People's Daily,* June 1, 2007, http://cpc.people.com.cn/GB/64093/67507/5808679.html.

98. For a discussion of the role and clout of Zeng Qinghuai, see, for example, "Zeng Qinghuai has sterling connections in Beijing," *Apple Daily* (Hong Kong), August 27, 2004, http://hk.apple.nextmedia.com/news/art/20040827/4268616#Scene_1/.

99. For a discussion of how Xi Jinping endeared himself to Jiang Zemin, see, for example, Shi Weijian, "The story of Jiang Zemin's 'discovery' of Xi Jinping," *Frontline* (Hong Kong), February 1, 2010, pp. 6–10.

100. For a discussion of how Jiang was forced out of the Central Military Commission, see, for example, Joseph Kahn, "Resignation of China's senior leader seems imminent," *New York Times,* September 19, 2004, www.nytimes.com/2004/09/19/international/asia/19china.html?_r=0/.

101. Cited in Shi Weijian, "The story of Jiang Zemin's 'discovery' of Xi Jinping."

102. Cited in "The CCP selects its highest-level leaders through internal ballots," BBC Chinese Service, June 8, 2012, www.bbc.co.uk/zhongwen/trad/chinese_news/2012/06/120608_china_ccp_polls_top_leaders.shtml; see also Gu Lu, "Why Communist Youth League Faction members always lose in internal ballots," *The Sun* (Hong Kong), May 27, 2012, http://city.mirrorbooks.com/news/html/71/n-51671.html.

103. Cited in Tong Qian, "China's Central Military Commission has abolished Jiang Zemin's office," BBC Chinese Service, November 1, 2012, www.bbc.co.uk/zhongwen/trad/chinese_news/2012/11/121101_jiang_office.shtml.

104. For a discussion of the phenomenon of the "cross-generation designation of leaders," see, for example, Willy Lam, "China picks core new leaders," *Asia Times* Online (Hong Kong), May 23, 2009, www.atimes.com/atimes/China/KE23Ad02.html.

105. For a discussion of the business activities of Jiang Mianheng, see, for example, Matt Forney, "Chinese leader's son builds telecommunications empire," *Wall Street Journal,* November 1, 1999, http://online.wsj.com/article/SB941414623101926633.html. For a discussion of princelings including the two Jiang sons who are involved in military enterprises, see, for example, Tai Ming Cheung, *China's Entrepreneurial Army* (Oxford: Oxford University Press, 2001), pp. 88–91.

106. Cited in "Xi Jinping writes letter to central authorities saying he has no wish to become the next general secretary," *Open,* September, 2009, www.cenews.eu/?p=17561/.

107. Cited in Willy Lam, "Cracks in the Great Politburo Wall," Asiasentinel.com (Hong Kong), October 13, 2009, https://www.google.com/#q=Willly+lam+asia+sentinel+xi+jinping+merkel+2009+jiang+zemin/.

108. For a discussion of Jiang's reappearance on National Day, October 1, 2009, see, for example, Mak Yin-ting, "Jiang Zemin's high-profile appearance at National Day celebrations have fed rumors about a 'power struggle,'" Radio Free Asia, October 2, 2010, www.rfi.fr/actucn/articles/118/article_16518.asp.

109. For a discussion of the close relationship between Hu Jintao and Li Keqiang, see, for example, Li Feng and Ren Yuyang, "Power transition in China: Li Keqiang as the doppelganger of Hu Jintao," VOA News, October 11, 2012, www.voachinese.com/content/china-power-transition-20121011/1524709.html.

110. For a discussion of Xi's rapid consolidation of power when compared with predecessors Hu Jintao and Jiang Zemin, see, for example, "Xi assumes China's presidency to cement transition of power," Bloomberg, March 14, 2013, www.bloomberg.com/news/2013-03-14/xi-assumes-china-presidency-to-cement-rapid-transition-of-power.html.

111. Cited in "Xi Jinping: Do not do things by using my flags and standards," *Zhengzhou Evening Post* (Zhengzhou), March 15, 2013, http://news.china.com/focus/2013lh/news/11136226/20130315/17731157.html.

112. For a discussion of the officers and cronies Xi Jinping has transferred to Beijing, see, for example, Sun Jiaye, "Is Xi Jinping transferring his confidantes to Beijing," *Ming Pao* (Hong Kong), October 9, 2013, http://premium.mingpao.com/cfm/Content_News.cfm?Channel=ca&Path=134475140124/caq_er.cfm.

113. For a discussion of the "Shaanxi Faction" in Chinese politics, see, for example, "13 among the new leadership corps have 'Shaanxi experience,'" *Hua Shang Daily* (Xian), March 17, 2013, www.sxdaily.com.cn/n/2013/0317/c226-5093757.html. See also Liu Junning, "Can the Shaanxi Faction restart political reform," 199.com (Beijing), October 7, 2012, www.l99.com/EditText_view.action?textId=564693/.

114. For a discussion of Li Zhanshu's traits, see, for example, Willy Lam, "Xi Jinping's imperfect inner circle," *Asia Times,* February 19, 2013, www.atimes.com/atimes/China/CHIN-01-190213.html.

115. For a discussion of Zhao Leji's career, see, for example, Sun Hongwei, "Zhao Leji leaves Shaanxi to take up position at Organization Department," China Net (Beijing), November 20, 2012, http://news.qq.com/a/20121120/000148.htm.

116. For a discussion of Xi's plans to promote Zhejiang cadres to Beijing, see, for example, Benjamin Kang Lim and Megha Rajagopalan, "China's Xi purging corrupt officials to put own men in place: Sources," Reuters, April 16, 2014, www.reuters.com/article/2014/04/16/us-china-corruption-xi-insight-idUSBREA3F1UT20140416/. For a discussion of Zhong Shaojun's relationship with Xi, see, for example, "Xi Jinping's secretary has become head of the General Office of the Central Military Commission," *Want Daily* (Taipei), June 20, 2013, www.hotmap.ca/article.php?act=detail&id=17787/.

117. For a discussion of Huang Kunming's career, see, for example, "Former Party secretary of Hangzhou appointed Deputy Director of the CCP Propaganda Department," China Economy Net, October 23, 2013, http://news.sina.com.cn/c/p/2013-10-23/184028513192.shtml.

118. See "Chen Min'er has been nominated as governor of Guizhou Province," CCTV News, December 18, 2012, http://news.ifeng.com/mainland/special/renshitiaozheng/content-3/detail_2012_12/17/20255302_0.shtml. For a discussion of Cai Qi's career, see, for example, "Cai Qi tipped to become deputy secretary-general of the Central National Security Commission," *Ta Kung Pao,* March 28, 2014, http://news.takungpao.com.hk/mainland/focus/2014-03/2385386.html.

119. For a discussion of the career of Ding Xuexiang, see, for example, "Member of the Shanghai Party Standing Committee Ding Xuexiang has been appointed deputy director of the CCP General Office," China News Service, May 16, 2013, www.chinanews.com/gn/2013/05-16/4823400.shtml; see also "Ding Xuexiang appointed director of the Office of the General Secretary," *Hubei Daily,* July 24, 2013, http://news.takungpao.com/mainland/focus/2013-07/1783446.html.

120. For a discussion of the career of Judge Shen, see "The C.V. of Shen Deyong," Xinhua News Agency, February 28, 2002, http://news.xinhuanet.com/ziliao/2002-02/28/content_295029.htm. See also Patrick Boehler, "Supreme People's Court judge urges end

to wrongful convictions," *South China Morning Post*, May 7, 2013, www.scmp.com/news/china/article/1232279/supreme-peoples-court-judge-urges-end-wrongful-convictions/.

121. Cited in Ma Haoliang, "Shi Zhihong, member of Zhongnanhai think tank," *Ta Kung Pao*, November 11, 2012, www.takungpao.com/paper/content/2012-11/11/content_1370530. htm.

122. For a discussion of the career of He Yiting, see, for example, "He Yiting has been transferred to the Central Party School and become a deputy to Liu Yunshan," *Ta Kung Pao*, September 29, 2013, http://news.takungpao.com/mainland/focus/2013-09/1936303.html

123. For a discussion of the rise of Li Shulei, see, for example, "Peking University academic has become an assistant to Xi Jinping," *People's Daily*, January 8, 2009, www. hinews.cn/news/system/2009/01/08/010393016.shtml. See also "Li Shuli appointed Director of Propaganda Department of Fujian Province," China News Service, February 7, 2014, www.chinanews.com/gn/2014/02-07/5808541.shtml.

124. For a discussion of Liu He's role and importance, see, for example, "Liu He as China's Larry Summers makes Politburo appreciate the United States," Bloomberg News, September 24, 2009, www.bloomberg.com/apps/news?pid=newsarchive&sid=aKp9wybwC4HM/; see also "CCP brain trust member Liu He said to be a reformer," *Nanfang Daily* (Guangzhou), October 11, 2011, www.nfdaily.cn/pic2/content/2013-10/11/content_81183407.htm.

125. Cited in "Chen Xi appointed as executive vice-director of the Organization Department," Xinhua News Agency, April 26, 2013, http://news.xinhuanet.com/renshi/2013-04/26/c_124632546.htm.

126. For a discussion of Li Keqiang's links with his classmates, see, for example, "Li Keqiang, Yuan Chunqing, Hu Chunhua, and the emergence of Peking University graduates," *Southern Weekend*, October 25, 2007, www.china.com.cn/book/txt/2007-10/25/content_9121505.htm.

127. For a discussion of Xi's think tank members, see, for example, Bo Zhiyue, "Xi Jinping's Advisors," East Asia Institute, National University of Singapore, EAI Background Brief no. 847, September 4, 2013, www.eai.nus.edu.sg/BB847.pdf.

128. See "Xi Jinping stresses in Guangdong that the pace of reform and open door must not decelerate," Xinhua News Agency, December 11, 2012, http://news.xinhuanet.com/politics/2012-12/11/c_113991112.htm.

129. For a study of the contributions of Hu Yaobang, see, for example, Shu-shin Wang, "Hu Yaobang: New chairman of the Chinese Communist Party," *Asian Survey* 22, no. 9 (September 1982), pp. 801–822; Merle Goldman, "Hu Yaobang's intellectual network and the theory conference of 1979," *China Quarterly*, no. 126 (June 1991): 219–242.

130. For a discussion of the stature of Hu Jintao, see, for example, Richard D. Ewing, "Hu Jintao: The making of a Chinese general secretary," *China Quarterly*, no. 173 (March 2003): 17–34.

131. For a discussion of Jiang Zemin's contribution to the establishment of the special economic zones, see, for example, Zhang Mingjie, "Jiang Zemin and our country's experiment with special economic zones," *Party Archives* (Beijing), May 2010), www. wxyjs.org.cn/dhgjzyldryj_558/201210/t20121031_135515.htm.

132. For a discussion of Xi's several trips to the United States, see, for example, Zhao Lingmin, "Xi's footprints in the United States," *Nanfang People* (Guangzhou), June 7, 2013, www.nfpeople.com/story_view.php?id=4530/.

133. For a discussion of the plagiarism allegations against Xi's Ph.D. dissertation, see, for example, "Doubts' about Xi Jinping's LL.D. thesis exposed," BBC Chinese Service, August 11, 2013, www.bbc.co.uk/zhongwen/trad/press_review/2013/08/130811_press_xi_degree. shtml.

134. For a portrait of Li Keqiang when he was at the Peking University law school, see, for example, "Li Keqiang was conscientious and thirsty for knowledge when he was at Beida," *People's Daily*, April 20, 2013, www.chinanews.com/gn/2013/04-20/4747751.shtml.

# 3

# Xi Jinping's Ideology and Politics

## Introduction: Xi's Stunning Power Grab— and His Conservative Agenda

Particularly in comparison to ex-president Hu Jintao, who is known for his diffidence and indecisiveness, "New Helmsman" Xi Jinping likes to strike the pose of a gung-ho strongman who does not mince words.[1] Immediately upon becoming general secretary of the CCP as well as chairman of its Central Military Commission (CMC) at the Eighteenth Party Congress in November 2012, the Fifth-Generation leader told different divisions of the People's Liberation Army (PLA) "to be ready when called upon, to fight effectively and to win wars." On improving Party discipline, Xi indicated that "to forge iron, you need a strong hammer." Regarding his favorite concept of "self-confidence in the [socialist] road," the CCP leader laid down this down-to-earth aphorism: "Where is the road? It's just under our feet." While the late patriarch Deng Xiaoping advised his colleagues "to cross the river while feeling for stones," Xi's recommendation is as bold as it is straightforward: "Open up a road if you are blocked by mountains; build a bridge if you are crossing a river." He gave this response when asked whether socialism with Chinese characteristics is good for his country: "Whether a pair of shoes fits only the feet can tell; whether a country's developmental path [is suitable] only people in that country will know." As for whether China can meet its myriad challenges, Xi had this to say: "There is no mountain that is too tall for mankind, and no road that is too long for our feet."[2]

Part of his apparent confidence springs from the fact that, compared to both ex-presidents Jiang Zemin and Hu, the leader of one-fifth of mankind is a relatively simple person committed to defending what he regards as self-evident truths. The guiding philosophy of his rule can be summed up in several paragraphs. As he noted upon becoming Party chief, "the CCP must do well in the series of tests it is undertaking." "The nature of the Party will never change," he said, alluding to conspiracy theories that the CCP might undergo "peaceful evolution" and morph into an entity that is no longer under the guidance of Marxism, Leninism, and Mao Zedong Thought. "Our red *jiangshan* [heaven and earth] will never change color," he pledged.[3] And if 1.3 billion Chinese are of one heart and one mind—and unreservedly following the edicts of the Party and its supreme leader—they can soon attain the "Chinese Dream," which is destined to be a prime slogan of the Xi Jinping era. To realize these herculean tasks, however, Xi has arrogated to himself powers that are significantly more sweeping than those held by his two predecessors.

Making his messages simple and straightforward, Xi does not get involved in relatively complicated explanations about how "Chinese-style socialism" can meet the challenges of the twenty-first century. It is unlikely that he will enunciate complicated doctrines like ex-president Jiang's "Theory of the Three Represents" or ex-president Hu's "Scientific Outlook on Development." Xi simply tells Party members and ordinary Chinese to have faith in the system as demonstrated by the "three self-confidences." "Chinese of different races must boost their self-confidence in socialism with Chinese characteristics," Xi said throughout 2013. "They must have self-confidence in the [Chinese] path and in the theories and institutions [of Chinese-style socialism]."[4]

On the one hand, Xi (b. 1953) has expressed confidence that the Fifth-Generation leadership can build on achievements in the economy to realize bigger triumphs, which will in turn confer extra legitimacy on the CCP as the country's "perennial ruling Party." On the other, Xi has betrayed nervousness that China—and the Party—may go the same way as the Soviet Union and the Communist Party of the Soviet Union (CPSU). This was revealed in an internal speech that Xi gave while touring southern Guangdong Province immediately after the Eighteenth Party Congress. Like many other members of the CCP's conservative wing, Xi blamed the demise of the CPSU, which was considered the CCP's "big brother" in the 1950s, on efforts by "traitors" such as Mikhail Gorbachev and Boris Yeltsin to repudiate Soviet-style communism. "How come the Soviet Party collapsed overnight?" Xi asked. "An important reason is that [Soviet Party members'] beliefs and ideals were not firm enough." Equally important was the fact that the Soviet defense forces failed to defend the Party against the challenges of the West. "The Soviet army was depoliticized, divorced from the Party, and turned into a national army," said Xi, adding that the CCP must never give up its monopoly of "the tools of the dictatorship of the proletariat." He indicated that Party members and intellectuals who lacked strong beliefs in the Party were suffering from "calcium deficiency of the spirit." "Party members should aim to achieve communism," he pointed out, adding that it was wrong to assume that "communism is something ethereal and cannot be attained."[5]

Since becoming commander-in-chief in late 2012, Xi has repeatedly stressed that the PLA is a "Party army" and that "the Party must have absolute control over the gun." At the third plenum of the Eighteenth Central Committee, held in November 2013, Xi set up the Central National Security Commission (CNSC), which is geared toward boosting domestic security (see following section). He wants to ensure that not only Party members but ordinary Chinese will serve the CCP with undivided devotion and loyalty. "*Dangxing* [nature of the Party] and *renminxing* [nature of the people] have always tallied with each other and are unified," he said in a 2013 conference on ideology and propaganda. While Xi agrees with Deng Xiaoping that "economic construction is the center of the Party's work," he has also upheld the "extremely important" role of ideological pursuits.[6] As we shall see, much of Xi's statecraft consists of enhancing the fealty of CCP members and Chinese citizens through efforts including improvement of their "moral and ideological qualities," buttressing people's "confidence in the road of socialism with Chinese characteristics" and extolling the virtues of the Chinese Dream as interpreted by the CCP. All these exercises represent a dramatic shift to the leftist radicalism associated with remnant Maoism, one of whose most disturbing manifestations is heavy-handed control over people's lives and intolerance of the kind of cultural and social diversity that has come in the wake of thirty-five years of Deng's reform and open-door policy.

This chapter looks at Xi's ideology, goals, and policies. The ramifications of the Chinese Dream are explored in detail. His efforts to promote "democratic centralism" through means including the creation of two superagencies at the apex of the Party are discussed. The CCP's Mao-style "mass-line campaign" and other attempts to impose tight control over the ideological and propaganda arenas are appraised. Xi's concept of "total national security" and his draconian crackdown on dissent are examined. Also analyzed is Xi's turning back the clock regarding almost all aspects of political reform. The large-scale anti-corruption movement—perhaps Xi's most notable achievement to date—is assessed. The conclusion compares Xi's approach to governance with that of his immediate predecessors.

## Xi's Key Mission: Concentration of Power at the Top and the Selling of the Chinese Dream

### Xi's No-Holds-Barred One-Upmanship—and the Emergence of a Strongman

When he was a senior official in Fujian and Zhejiang, Xi was famous for his "theory of unity": maintaining harmony among cadres of different traits and backgrounds and respecting the CCP's established institutions. Immediately after becoming Party chief in November 2012, however, the Fifth-Generation stalwart began an eighteen-month-long power grab that was as spectacular as it was disruptive of the Party's traditions.

By virtue of being Party general secretary, chairman of the CMC and head of the CCP Central Leading Group on Foreign Affairs, Xi directly oversees the Party apparatus (including areas relating to ideology and personnel) as well as military and foreign affairs. These were more or less the portfolios held by his predecessors, ex-presidents Jiang and Hu. The power calculus changed dramatically upon the establishment of two mammoth Party organs at the third plenum of the Eighteenth Central Committee in November 2013—the CNSC and the Central Leading Group on Comprehensively Deepening Reforms (CLGCDR)—both of which are chaired by Xi.[7] The CNSC has to some extent superseded the Central Political-Legal Commission, which controls the country's quasi-police state apparatus (see below). The CNSC has enabled Xi to gain direct control over the police, the People's Armed Police (PAP), the secret police as well as other law-enforcement units, such as the courts and the prosecutors' offices. Using a saying popular in Beijing's political circles, Xi has taken charge of "both the gun and the knife." Xi's stewardship of the CLGCDR—which is in charge of reform of the economy as well as areas ranging from "social governance" to culture and the environment—essentially means that the Party boss has become the final arbiter on economic decision-making. This also clearly implies that Premier Li Keqiang, who is no. 2 in the Politburo Standing Committee (PBSC) pecking order, has to defer to Xi regarding economic matters (see Chapter 4). In February 2014, Xi added one more feather to his cap when he made himself head of the Central Leading Group on Internet Security and Informatization (CLGISI), which essentially dictates what China's 600 million-odd netizens can and cannot see online.[8]

Both the CLGCDR and the CNSC are superagencies that tower over—and in some cases also duplicate—the existing Party and state apparatuses. While all the leading groups and commissions set up by Deng in the early 1980s are led by only one PBSC member, the CLGCDR's has four: Chairman Xi and three Vice-Chairmen, namely, Premier Li, ideology and propaganda tsar Liu Yunshan and Executive Vice-Premier Zhang Gaoli. Under these four PBSC stalwarts are ten ordinary Politburo members, including the three other vice-premiers of the State Council and the heads of CCP units such as the Central Committee General Office and the Organization and Propaganda Departments. The heads of major ministerial-level departments, such as the People's Bank of China, the National Development and Reform Commission (NRDC), the Finance Ministry, and the Education Ministry also sit on the mammoth unit. Subgroups of the CLGCDR have been established in all thirty-one major administrative regions. While the CNSC has a slightly less grandiose set-up, it has jurisdiction over the army, the police, and all foreign-policy and national-security agencies in the Party and government.[9]

It seems clear that Xi has created these two monstrous organizations to circumvent existing government institutions in order to better exercise his authority. The secretary-generals and general office chiefs of the CNSC and the CLGCDR are respectively director of the Central Committee General Office Li Zhanshu (b. 1950) and director of the Central Policy Research Office (CPRO) Wang Huning (b. 1955), both of whom are Politburo members and Xi confidants. Moreover, the Central Committee General Office and the CPRO have become the nexus and clearinghouse of the CNSC and the CLGCDR, respectively. Xi has thus ensured that a coterie of loyalists at the apex of the Party are in control of these two gargantuan policy establishments.[10]

Xi's no-holds-barred one-upmanship has run counter to some of the most ingrained institutional reforms undertaken by Deng, including the collective leadership system and the separation of the Party and the government. Upon coming to power in late 1978, Deng worked hard to introduce a collective leadership and to prevent the re-emergence of a Mao-like personality cult. Deng never became Party general secretary or prime minister. According to Deng's design, the general secretary is only a first-among-equals within the PBSC. Each PBSC member has full control over his portfolio, even though top-level decisions have to be discussed and cleared by the entire PBSC. Votes are cast to settle contentious issues, and the general secretary's vote is no weightier than those of his PBSC colleagues. Thanks in part to his control over the two superagencies, Xi rides roughshod over existing institutions and their leaders.[11] And to the extent that both the CLGCDR and the CNSC are Party and not state organs, all power has been centered at the upper echelons of the CCP. This goes against the principle of the separation of the Party and the government, which is enshrined in the Political Report to the Thirteenth Party Congress in 1987.[12]

Even before the watershed third plenum of the Eighteenth Central Committee, however, Xi's overarching ambitions had become clear. With the possible exception of Premier Li, Xi seems to be doing almost all the talking—and hogging most of the media limelight. The other five PBSC members have kept the lowest of profiles. Until mid-2013, Li maintained a reasonably high level of visibility in the official press, which gave a great deal of exposure to Li Keqiang Economics or "Likonomics." Li's power began to wane in the run-up to the third plenum, and "Likonomics" all but disappeared from the public discourse (see Chapter 4).[13]

A key reason for Xi's quick consolidation of power is that, unlike his predecessors, he does not have to spend much energy fending off interference from Party elders. The latter include former general secretaries and other retired PBSC members. Ex-president Jiang Zemin did not really come into his own until Deng Xiaoping became incapacitated two years before his death in 1997. Ex-president Hu lived very much under Jiang's shadow during his ten-year tenure (see Chapter 2).[14]

Due in part to the fact that Jiang was one of his principal patrons, Xi has to listen to the ex-president's views on a wide range of issues, including an anti-graft campaign that is ensnaring an unprecedented number of the offspring of Party elders (see below). However, it is unlikely that Jiang (b. 1926), who lives mostly in Shanghai, is in a position to breathe down the neck of his protégé frequently. Ex-president Hu (b. 1942) agreed to retire from all his positions, including the CMC chairmanship, at the Eighteenth Party Congress. That Hu has little influence over Xi is reflected by the latter's success in sidelining several key members of the Communist Youth League (CYL) Faction headed by the former Party chief. Apart from Premier Li, CYL Faction heavyweights who have been marginalized include the following Politburo members: Vice-President Li Yuanchao, the director of the Propaganda Department Liu Qibao, and Guangdong Party secretary Hu Chunhua. Apart from taking part in official functions involving foreign dignitaries—for example, attending the funeral of Nelson Mandela in early 2014—Li's main job is looking after "mass organizations" such as trade unions and women's organizations. Liu Qibao has been totally overshadowed by Liu Yunshan, the PBSC member in charge of ideology and propaganda. Being only one of two Politburo members who were born after 1960, Hu Chunhua, a former CYL Party secretary, was often cited as a possible successor to President Xi. It is understood, however, that Xi wants to anoint his own protégé as the next general secretary.[15]

Xi's publicists have gone into overdrive in meticulously constructing a virtual personality cult around the putative "man of the people." In late 2013, Xi lined up for thirty minutes at the Qingfeng Steamed Stuffed Bun Shop in Beijing. He paid RMB 21 out of his own pocket for a nondescript meal of pork and onion buns and vegetables. Qingfeng immediately became a new tourist attraction for visitors to the capital. A few months later, Xi braved the heavy smog enveloping the capital when he visited Nanluoguxiang, a popular shopping district, without wearing a mask. The next day, one local paper ran this headline: "Breathing the same air, sharing the same fate." One of the most memorable pictures of Xi was taken when he visited Wuhan in mid-2013. It was raining heavily and the general secretary, with his trouser legs rolled up, was holding his own umbrella. Moments later, he came across some young factory workers, whereupon he was heard to say: "Hello, good-looking ladies." Another captivating snapshot was Xi kicking a soccer ball with gusto in Dublin's Croke Park while on a state visit to Ireland in 2012. During tours to the provinces in China, he likes to talk soccer, China's most popular sport, with ordinary people. Known in cyberspace as Xi Dada (Big Xi), the president has his own Weibo microblog site, called the "Learning from Xi Fan Club," which regularly feeds his fans with exclusive pictures of Xi particularly during foreign or domestic trips.[16]

Xi's excuse for his self-aggrandizing gamesmanship is that he needs the extra clout to untie the Gordian knot of reform. However, the princeling's preoccupation is clearly preservationist—not reformist—in nature—that is, upholding socialism with Chinese characteristics and safeguarding the CCP's status as the "perennial ruling Party." It is therefore difficult not to reach the conclusion that Xi is grabbing power for power's sake, to ensure his unquestioned supremacy and to protect his legacy. The self-serving nature of Xi's statecraft becomes clearer in light of the fact that the creation of superagencies such as the CLGCDR and the CNSC could delay—not speed up—reform of the economy and other sectors. As we shall see below and in Chapter 4, the president's obsession with "top-level design" and a hierarchical top-down chain of command could exacerbate the already serious degree of bureaucratism in the polity. As Jiang Zhiyong, an expert at the State Information Center, pointed out, "the momentum for reform this time is coming from the very top [of the Party]." "Initiatives from the top are being implemented layer by layer by central and regional [administrations]," he added. Jiang expressed fears that since midlevel and local cadres were already very familiar with this top-down approach, new reforms could be adulterated by the delaying tactics of various officials. He cited "going through the motions and putting on shows" as typical strategies adopted by regional cadres to water down orders from on high.[17]

### Different Meanings of "The Renaissance of the Chinese People"

Since becoming the boss of the world's largest and most powerful political Party, Xi Jinping has repeatedly talked about the Chinese Dream (*Zhongguo meng*). On most of these occasions, Xi has equated the Chinese Dream with "fulfilling the great renaissance of the Chinese race," adding that "this is the greatest dream of the Chinese people in recent history."[18] Given that Xi lacks a reputation as a sophisticated theorist, the Chinese Dream has already been considered a major slogan of the Xi epoch, which is set to run until the Twentieth Party Congress in 2022. Questions, however, have arisen as to whether the "fulfillment of the Chinese Dream" can be raised to the same level as seminal dictums laid down by Xi's predecessors, such as ex-presidents Hu Jintao and Jiang Zemin. Hu coined catchphrases such as "constructing a harmonious society" and implementing a "scientific outlook on development," while Jiang is best remembered for his "Theory of the Three Represents."[19] Of more significance is the fact that, owing to the vague yet all-embracing connotations of the Chinese Dream, cadres and intellectuals of different persuasions are locked in a fierce debate over the rallying cry's relevance to the future of reform, particularly political liberalization.

At the simplest level, the Chinese Dream or the renaissance of the Chinese people simply means *fuguo qiangbing* (an economically prosperous and militarily strong China). *Fuguo qiangbing* was a slogan of the ill-fated Qing dynasty (1644–1911) modernizers during the short-lived Hundred Days' Reform in 1898.[20] When Xi first put forward his pet theory while inspecting an exhibition on recent history at the National Museum of China in November 2012, he expressed two specific objectives about economic progress. By 2021, the centenary of the founding of the CCP, China should meet the target of "constructing a *xiaokang* [moderately well-off] society." Furthermore, by 2049—the centenary of the founding of the PRC—the country should have developed into a "modernized socialist country that is rich, strong, democratic, civilized and harmonious." According to Wang Yiming, a senior economist at the National Development and Reform Commission (NDRC), China's GDP is expected to reach RMB 90 trillion by 2020, at which point per capita GDP will likely breach the psychologically important benchmark of $10,000. Wang further projected that by 2050, the country's GDP could reach RMB 350 trillion, and per capita GDP could be as much as RMB 260,000.[21] In other words, in terms of comprehensive strength, China the quasi-superpower will have bridged the gap with the long-standing superpower, the United States, by the middle of the twenty-first century.

What about sociopolitical development, particularly the flowering of democratic ideals? Upon being elected state president at the NPC in March 2013, Xi dropped hints about some form of commitment to egalitarianism when he revisited the

Chinese Dream leitmotif. He indicated that "the Chinese Dream is the dream of the [Chinese] people as well as the dream of every Chinese [person]." He further pledged that all Chinese should have "the chance to distinguish themselves in their lives." "They should enjoy the opportunity to have their dream come true," he added, "They should have the opportunity to grow up and make progress in tandem with the motherland and the times."[22]

It is apparent, however, that Xi was not referring to Western or universal precepts of equality and democratic rights. After all, Xi has repeatedly vowed that while the CCP administration "will avoid old roads that are closed and fossilized, it will also not go down the slippery path that involves changing the flags and emblems" of socialism with Chinese characteristics.[23] In his talk to NPC delegates in early 2013, Xi stipulated three prerequisites for attaining the Chinese Dream: "The Chinese Dream can be fulfilled only by going down the Chinese road; realizing the Chinese Dream necessarily means propagating the China spirit; and realizing the Chinese Dream requires concentrating and crystallizing China's strength."[24] This essentially ruled out universal norms about democratic governance. Moreover, the Xi administration has, through administrative restructuring, concentrated more power in a few high-level, nontransparent Party organs, such as the CCP Central Committee Secretariat and the two superagencies discussed above.

Conservative opinion makers have warned that Xi's slogan must not be interpreted as an endorsement of "bourgeois-liberal" values. Wang Yiwei, a political scientist at Renmin University, has laid into liberal intellectuals "who want to equate 'the Chinese Dream' with all-out Westernization." It was wrong to equate the Chinese Dream with ideals such as "the dream of constitutional governance or the dream of human rights and democracy," he noted. Wang added that the Chinese Dream actually meant "the Sinicization of Marxism through taking into consideration China's own conditions, so as to open up the path of socialism with Chinese characteristics."[25] In a commentary on the same subject, the usually hardline *Beijing Daily* noted that Xi's axiom was aimed at promoting patriotism as well as obedience to CCP edicts. The paper said: "We must meld together the country's dream and the dream of the [Chinese] people with each individual's dream." The commentary added: "The Chinese Dream is about goals that Communist Party members struggle hard to achieve . . . It also represents the [collective] aspirations of all Chinese men and women."[26]

Despite the fact that Xi has the past decade avoided touching upon the sensitive issue of political reform or ideological liberalization, a number of free-thinking intellectuals have given the "Chinese Dream" a liberal twist. Leading dissident Bao Tong, who was the personal secretary to disgraced CCP general secretary Zhao Ziyang, called upon Xi to "return the dream to the people." Bao, who is under twenty-four-hour police surveillance, indicated that Xi at least recognized that the "subject" (*zhuti*) of the Chinese Dream was individual Chinese and not the state. "Xi has made clear that the Chinese Dream should be realized according to the private ownership system," Bao noted in early 2013. "The country should allow us common people to each dream his own dream," he said. Bao added that his own dream was that all Chinese "can have freedom of expression . . . and freedom from fear of being harassed and censored."[27] Similarly, He Weifang, a Peking University law professor and internationally known public intellectual, offered this personal reading: "The most important goal of a modernized nation is to allow the people to have dignity, freedom and [civil] rights so that each person can work hard to fulfill his own dream."[28]

It is significant that even scholars who are working within the Party establishment have apparently given the Chinese Dream a relatively unorthodox spin. For theorist Zhou Tianyong, who teaches politics at the CCP Central Party School (CPS), the Chinese Dream meant that "every Chinese can work and live in democracy, equality, fairness, justice, [and] righteousness—and in a well-ordered, harmonious society." Zhou argued that "the state should come up with policies so that each person who tries hard should have the chance [to realize his dream]."[29] Xin Ming, another well-known CPS scholar, put forward a similar characterization of the Chinese Dream. Xin pointed out that the Chinese Dream should have the following connotations: "a sufficient level of democracy, well-developed rule of law, [the enshrinement of citizens'] sacrosanct human rights . . . and the free and full development of every citizen."[30]

### Playing the Nationalist Card to Shore Up the Party's Legitimacy

A heavy dosage of patriotism—and nationalism—is integral to the Chinese Dream mantra. While every leader since Mao Zedong has played up nationalism, Xi has done so in a way that is more overt and aggressive than that of his two predecessors.[31] "Realizing the Chinese Dream means propagating the Chinese spirit," he said. "This means the spirit of the Chinese people, whose core is patriotism. This is also the spirit of making the country prosperous and strong." Xi indicated that "patriotism is a spiritual force that can resolutely unify all Chinese." Xi added that a prime responsibility of the CCP was to "take up the baton of history and continue to assiduously fight for the great renaissance of the Chinese people, so that they can stand up in the community of nations with more strength and resoluteness."[32] As a proud nationalist, Xi is adamant that the CCP administration never tailor China's governance and its value systems to suit foreign models. In speaking with visiting Serbian president Tomislav Nikolic in mid-2013, Xi reiterated that "we will neither change the shape of our feet to suit a [foreign] pair of shoes nor will we copy wholesale [foreign experiences]." He reiterated that socialism with Chinese characteristics was "firmly implanted in China's deep culture and tradition and that it is solidly anchored in Chinese conditions."[33]

Xi is smart enough to realize that dwelling too much on nationalism could stoke fears of a "Chinese threat." So he is also at pains to underscore the internationalist dimensions of the Chinese Dream. In March 2013 while on his first trip overseas since becoming state president, "Chinese put a lot of store by patriotism," Xi said in Russia and Africa. "Yet we also have a global outlook and global perspective."[34] Xi made it clear that the ideal of the Chinese Dream was not confined to the PRC and its citizens. In an interview with journalists from the BRICS (Brazil, Russia, India, China, and South Africa) countries, Xi pointed out that "because China is the world's second-largest economy, the Chinese Dream will also bring opportunities to the world" and that "the Chinese Dream will be realized by means of a road of peace."[35] While speaking at the Moscow State Institute of International Relations, he reiterated that "the Chinese Dream will bring blessings and benefits not only to the Chinese people but also to peoples in other countries." While touring Tanzania the new Chinese head of state gave the clearest indication of the global significance of the Chinese Dream. While waxing eloquent on the "African dream" and the "world dream," Xi said: "Together with the international community, the Chinese and African peoples will work toward realizing the global dream of sustained peace and joint prosperity." Xi even touched on the similarities between the Chinese Dream and the American Dream when he met for an informal summit with President Barack Obama in California in June 2013. These statements, which were tailor-made for a global audience, seemed indicative of Xi's desire to highlight Beijing's commitment to "peaceful development."[36]

However, there is clearly a military—and globally assertive—aspect to the Chinese Dream and pursuit of "the renaissance of the Chinese people." While inspecting PLA divisions in late 2012, Xi reiterated that the Chinese Dream comprised "the dream of a strong China" and "the dream of a strong military." "To attain the great renaissance of the Chinese people, we must uphold [the principle of] the synthesis of a prosperous country and a strong army, and we must assiduously build up and consolidate national defense and a strong military," Xi noted. On numerous occasions, Xi also called upon PLA officers and soldiers to "get ready to fight and to win wars" (see Chapter 5).[37] Moreover, the PLA top brass seems keen on interpreting the Chinese Dream so as to justify its lobbying for more economic resources and a greater say in national affairs. In a 2013 editorial called "The Whole Army Must Provide Resolute and Strong Support to Guarantee the Realization of the Chinese Dream," *Liberation Army Daily* indicated that the defense forces would "struggle hard for the fulfillment of the dream of a strong China and a strong army." "Only when national defense construction is up to scratch will there be a strong guarantee for economic construction," the PLA mouthpiece added, "Boosting national defense construction also will give a significant push to economic and social development."[38]

Compared to the "Theory of the Three Represents" and the "Scientific Outlook on Development," the Chinese Dream is much more easily understood by ordinary Chinese. This slogan can also be interpreted in a self-serving fashion by different sociopolitical groups. It cannot, however, be denied that while Xi's mantra can be regarded as representative of the lowest common denominator of Chinese politics, it is basically an affirmation of the status quo, rather than a clarion call for ringing in the new. The Chinese Dream says very little about the administration's commitment to either political or economic reform.[39] The putative head of the Gang of Prince-lings has yet to prove to both Chinese and foreign audiences that he is at least as capable as his father of thinking outside the box and offering unconventional yet effective solutions to China's myriad problems.

**Preservation of the CCP's "Perennial Ruling Party" Status**

*Boosting Confidence in the Party's Path—But No Reexamination of Past Errors*

Shortly after taking power, Xi indicated that Party authorities would do whatever it takes to firm up Chinese citizens' "self-confidence in the road" (*daolu zixin*) of socialism with Chinese characteristics. There was no bigger threat to the CCP's status as China's "perennial ruling Party" than a "calcium deficiency of the spirit" among certain Party members, which, Xi warned in his lively language, could result in a kind of "soft bone disease."[40] It is therefore not surprising that ideologues and commissars in CCP offices such as the Propaganda Department and the Ministry of Education are pushing through draconian measures to prevent Chinese intel-lectuals, especially college students, from going down what Xi calls "the deviant path" of Westernization. In the unpublished Central Party Document no. 9, titled "Concerning the Situation in the Ideological Sphere," the CCP Central Commit-tee General Office called upon Party and government agencies handling educa-tion, ideology, and the media to tackle "seven serious problems in the ideological sphere that merit attention." The circular added that these problems reflected "the sharpness and complexity of the struggle in the ideological sphere." The nature of these challenges was revealed by the fact that the document asked teaching staff at universities nationwide to steer clear of "seven unmentionable topics" (*qige buyaojiang*): universal values, press freedom, civil society, citizens' rights, the Party's historical aberrations, the *quangui zichanjieji* (privileged capitalist class), and independence of the judiciary.[41]

Xi is not the first leader to establish "forbidden zones" for Chinese intellectuals. In his speech in December 2008 commemorating the thirtieth anniversary of the era of reform, then-general secretary Hu Jintao warned that the CCP would never "go down paths that involve altering the [Party's] flags and standards." Former PBSC member and chairman of the NPC Wu Bangguo raised eyebrows in 2011 when he issued the "Five No's": "no to multiparty politics; no to diversification of [the Party's] guiding thought; no to the separation of powers; no to a federal model; and no to privatization."[42]

Xi, however, has gone further. First, specific instructions have been given to college teachers all over China not to discuss the "seven unmentionables" in class. As the newly appointed deputy Party secretary of Chongqing, Zhang Guoqing, pointed out, "enemy forces inside and outside China are joining hands [to infil-trate] universities, and the struggle in ideology has intensified." Zhang, who used to head Norinco, China's largest arms trader, urged Party cells at colleges to boost students' education in the "three self-confidences."[43] Similar strictures regarding "seizing control of the lectern" were laid down and enforced only during the first year or so after the Tiananmen Square Incident in 1989. A number of leading liberal intellectuals have criticized the new edict as a stunning retrogression. The Beijing Institute of Technology economist Wu Xingdou argued that "this move to bring the *weiwen* [upholding stability] campaign to the colleges indicates that the Party is going down a blind alley." For the respected Party historian Zhang Lifan, the "seven unmentionables" represented "a return to the days of [Mao's chosen successor] Hua Guofeng, who said that whatever Mao said and did was correct."[44]

Much more so than previous leaders such as Deng Xiaoping, Hu Yaobang, Zhao Ziyang, Jiang Zemin and Hu Jintao, Xi has refused to let Party members or ordinary intellectuals talk publicly about mistakes by the CCP, especially those committed by Chairman Mao and his close allies. That Xi is as deferential to Mao as the disgraced Politburo member Bo Xilai became evident just days after he rose to become Party chief. In a late November 2012 speech on the "spirit of the Eighteenth Party Congress," Xi proclaimed that "we must never give up Marxism-Leninism and Mao Zedong Thought." Otherwise, he warned, "we will lose the foundation [of Party rule]."[45]

It is significant that Xi attributed the collapse of the CPSU to the deStalinization campaign. "The wholesale negation of the history of the Soviet Union and the CPSU, the negation of Lenin and Stalin . . . spawned historical nihilism and confusion of thoughts," Xi said in an internal speech in late 2012. "Various levels of Party organizations [in the Soviet Union] almost lost all their functions."[46] In January 2013, Xi put forward his now-famous theory that the Party should "not differentiate [post-1949 CCP] history into the pre-reform period and the post-reform period." "While socialism with Chinese characteristics was initiated during the period of the reform and open door, this [creed] was established on the basis of more than twenty years of [socialist] construction [after 1949]," he said, "These two periods should not be [arbitrarily] cut off from each other—and one period should not be used to negate the other."[47]

Xi's instructions—which have come to be known as "the theory of the two cannot negates" (*liangge bunengfouding*)—amounted to an unreserved defense of the stature and contributions of Chairman Mao despite the horrific catastrophes of the Anti-Rightist movement (1957–59), the Great Leap Forward (1958–61), the Three Years of Famine (1958–61), and the Cultural Revolution (1966–76). In a mid-2013 commentary in the official *Guangming Daily*, Party theorist Qi Biao lauded Xi for "correctly upholding and defending Party history and consolidating the foundation of Party rule." Qi, who is a senior staffer in the Party History Research Office of the CCP, contended that the Great Leap Forward and the Cultural Revolution were "minor tributaries in the river of time" that did not detract from "the CCP's great attainments" during that epoch. Other articles by conservative ideologues have accused intellectuals who have vilified Mao of indulging in "historical nihilism."[48]

The problem with this politically motivated interpretation of history is that, while the CCP propaganda machinery for the past two decades or so has prevented academics from holding conferences and other commemorative events to learn from the mistakes of the Mao period, well-documented books about the disastrous blunders of Mao and his ultraleftist colleagues have appeared regularly in Hong Kong and elsewhere. For example, the retired Xinhua editor Yang Jisheng published in Hong Kong the much-acclaimed *Tombstone,* which has been translated into English and other languages. This book records the horrendous famine of 1959–61, which killed an estimated 36 million people (see Chapter 6).[49] It is perhaps for this reason that the Xi administration has begun a large-scale campaign to whitewash history. In an article in the Party's theoretical journal *Seeking Truth,* the vice-president of the Chinese Academy of Social Sciences (CASS), Li Shenming, heaped praise on Mao's myriad "political and economic accomplishments." Li blamed "unbalanced media reports" on supposed misperceptions of historical events, such as the Anti-Rightist movement. Professor Li wrote: "During the Anti-Rightist movement, 550,000 [intellectuals] were labeled rightists, but not a single person was sentenced to death. However, the [campaign] was described as a bloody one by [biased] media." Li also claimed that estimates that more than 30 million Chinese starved to death during that period were "gross exaggerations."[50]

### Resuscitation of Maoist Orthodoxy

Particularly in his first term (2012–17) as Party chief, it is likely that Xi will seek to build his power base—and consolidate his legitimacy—by emphasizing Maoist orthodoxy. This was evidenced by the talk that Xi gave in the first Politburo study session conducted soon after the Eighteenth Party Congress. "The First-Generation collective leadership headed by comrade Mao Zedong has provided valuable experience, theoretical preparation and material basis for pioneering socialism with Chinese characteristics," Xi said.[51] The veneration of Mao was already obvious during Xi's apprenticeship years while he was serving as president of the CPS. And the rehoisting of the banner of the Great Helmsman provides perhaps the most convincing proof of the conservative orientations of the would-be "core" of the Fifth-Generation leadership.

### The Campaign to Restore Maoist Norms

Xi was a major figure behind the revival of Maoism in many provinces in China from around 2008 to 2010 despite the widespread perception that the prime originator of the campaign to *changhong* (sing red songs) and restore Maoist norms was Bo Xilai. Bo made a name for himself not only in China but also overseas by organizing *changhong* concerts, popularizing quotations from Mao's *Little Red Book,* and even asking college students to emulate Red Guards by "learning from the masses" by living and working in the villages. However, Bo started his "red" crusade with a distinct political motive—joining the Politburo Standing Committee at the Eighteenth Party Congress.[52] For Xi, it is more a reflection of his long-held belief in Mao's larger-than-life exploits.

In his talks at the CPS, Xi liked to sprinkle his homilies to students of the elite cadre-training institution with words of wisdom from the Marxist and Maoist canon. Supreme leader-in-waiting Xi also made a big push for the *yiyuanhua* (monolithic approach) to ideology. Since 2007 he has been stepping up old-style Marxist—and Maoist—indoctrination. For example, at the beginning of the semester at CPS in April 2011, Xi urged students to "pay attention to the Marxist canon," especially Mao's classic writings. "Cadres must seriously study Marxist theory to ensure that they can maintain political resoluteness," he said. Xi added that since Marxist classics were voluminous, "we should focus on the salient points, and concentrate on studying the quintessence—particularly the important works of Mao Zedong."[53]

Xi's repeated stress on grooming neophytes who are "both politically upright and professionally competent" echoed Mao's dictum on picking officials who were "both red and expert." While talking about "Party construction," or ways to ensure the ideological purity of CCP cells, Xi noted that the leadership must learn from the "great Party-construction engineering project that was successfully pioneered by the First-Generation leadership with comrade Mao Zedong as its core."[54] When he was touring the provinces, Xi liked to celebrate "proletariat paragons" first lionized by Mao. While inspecting the Daqing Oilfield in Heilongjiang Province in late 2009, the then-vice-president lauded the "spirit of the Iron Man of Daqing," a reference to the supposedly superhuman exploits of Wang Jinxi, the legendary oilfield worker. Xi has also heaped praise on "heroes of the masses" such as the self-sacrificing fireman Lei Feng and the altruistic county Party secretary Jiao Yulu.[55]

It was Xi's ally Zhang Quanjing, a former director of the CCP Organization Department, who gave perhaps the most eloquent explanation of the relevance of Maoism to twenty-first century China. In a 2011 article, Zhang said Mao's ideas consisted of the "paradigm of synthesizing Marxism-Leninism with revolution and construction in China." "Mao Zedong Thought has incorporated the wisdom of China and the world during different historical periods," Zhang asserted. In areas including ideology, military affairs, politics, economics, culture, technology, and sports, he indicated, Maoism was "the crystallization of the intelligence of the whole Party and all Chinese."[56]

It is not surprising that Xi took advantage of the celebration of Mao's 120th birthday in December 2013 to tell the nation that "the Party will hold high the banner of Mao Zedong Thought forever." While acknowledging that the Great Helmsman had made mistakes, Xi noted that Mao was a "great patriot and national hero," somebody who "changed the face of the country and led the Chinese people to a new destiny." "The banner of Mao Zedong Thought cannot be lost, and losing it means a negation to the Party's glorious history," he said at a lavish ceremony in the Great Hall of the People. "The principle of holding high the banner of Mao Zedong Thought should not waver at any time."[57] According to the independent historian

Xu Youyu, intellectuals had "more negative things to say about Mao because there is more information out there about certain parts of history." He argued, however, that celebrating Mao remained a way for ambitious cadres to burnish their careers. "They are more willing to talk about Mao's contributions because the suffering seems increasingly distant, but the opportunities for advancement are increasingly numerous," Xu said.[58]

*How the Maoist Revival Helps Strengthen the Gang of*
*Princelings and the Legitimacy of the "Red Aristocrats"*

Like most political trends in China, the resuscitation of Maoist norms is intricately related to factional intrigue within the Party. Jockeying for position between the two major CCP cliques—the Gang of Princelings and the CYL Faction—had in‑tensified in the run-up to the Eighteenth Party Congress. And it was not an accident that then-vice-president Xi Jinping and then-Politburo member Bo Xilai, two prominent princelings, were among the most ardent architects of the quasi-Maoist renaissance. Implicit in the princelings' rehoisting of the Maoist flag was a veiled critique of the policies undertaken by ex-president Hu and his CYL Faction, which seemed to have exacerbated the polarization of rich and poor and spawned a kind of crass commercialism that ran counter to Maoist spiritual values.[59]

Much more significantly, the princelings are using the Maoist crusade to lobby for more clout in the polity. The pedigreed cadres are cunningly using the Maoist restitution to further exploit their advantage of having an illustrious lineage. As the famous Chinese proverb goes: "After the father has won heaven and earth, the son has the right to rule over them." This was the basis of the "revolutionary legitimacy" of the First- and Second-Generation leadership under Mao and Deng, respectively. As the sons and daughters of Long March veterans, princelings re-gard their "revolutionary bloodline" as a prime political resource.[60] Thus, while visiting the "revolutionary mecca" of Jinggangshan in Jiangxi Province in 2008, Xi paid homage to the "countless martyrs of the revolution who gave their blood and lives to win over this country." "They laid a strong foundation for the good livelihood [that we now enjoy]," he said. "Under no circumstances can we forsake this tradition."[61] Similarly, while marking National Day on October 1, 2008, Bo urged Chongqing's cadres "to forever bear in mind the ideals and hot-blooded [devotion] of our elders." "Forsaking [their revolutionary tradition] is tantamount to betrayal," Bo stated.[62]

It is also not surprising that the military offspring of Party elders and Red Army generals since 2010 have been a vocal force behind the *changhong* movement. Take, for instance, this high-powered group called the "Singing Troupe of 100 Offspring of Generals." Senior members of the group include the sons and daugh-ters of Marshals Chen Yi, Nie Rongzhen, Luo Rongzhen, He Long: Chen Haosu, Nie Li, Luo Dongjin, and He Xiaoming.[63] Because of the aura of respectability attached to their fathers, these military princelings felt a sense of pride in singing "revolutionary songs," many of which were associated with the Great Helmsman. Like their civilian counterparts, such as Xi Jinping, military princelings want to play up the symbolic value of their pedigree—and their fitness to play a big role in military and political affairs.[64]

There are, however, limits to how much President Xi can exploit his relationship with the "red princelings" for political advantage. Quite a few high-born cadres, including those in the PLA, appear to have reservations about Xi's relentless amassing of power—and they may not share Xi's enthusiasm for Maoism. Take, for example, the political commissar of the General Logistics Department, General Liu Yuan, whose father, Liu Shaoqi, was tormented to death early in the Cultural Revolution. In a mid-2010 interview with the Party journal *Study Times,* Liu (b. 1951) could hardly suppress his disdain for the Great Helmsman. "Great as Chairman Mao was, he committed serious errors because he went against democracy, refused to listen to criticism, and was not subject to supervision," Liu said. Although Liu is considered a crony of President Xi's, he was also close to the disgraced Bo Xilai. This might explain the fact that the charismatic Liu failed to earn a promotion at the Eighteenth Party Congress.[65]

### The Supremacy of the "Theoretical System of Marxism and Socialism with Chinese Characteristics"

Xi Jinping established his reputation as an orthodox Marxist when the helmsman-in-waiting was vice-president and then president of the CPS from 2007 to 2012. He is a keen proponent of the principle—seconded by ex-president Hu Jintao as well as most senior members of the Party establishment—of "Sinicizing" and "modernizing" Marxism and socialism by ensuring that these beliefs will be suitably adapted to twenty-first-century China. These arguments were spelled out in detail in Xi's speeches and articles in theoretical journals such as *Seeking Truth* and *Study Times.* In a 2010 article in *Seeking Truth,* Xi quoted Friedrich Engels to the effect that "Marxism is a worldview and methodology but not [a set of] orthodox precepts." Paraphrasing Mao, Xi noted that "Marxist methodology amounts to a telescope and a microscope that we use in politics as well as the art of war: it is a fundamental method for guiding us in knowing our world and changing the world." Xi was convinced that "the theoretical system of socialism with Chinese characteristics"—which the CCP is implementing—was the newest and best possible way to "Sinicize Marxism." This had been achieved through "using Marxist principles, viewpoints, and methods to study and solve practical questions that have emerged in the course of China's evolution, construction, and reform," Xi argued with typical verbosity. Only through Marxist and socialist methodology, he added, could Party members "boost the systematic nature, perspicacity, and creativity in their work and avoid irresoluteness, superficiality, and myopia."[66]

In various speeches, Xi has adduced plenty of evidence to show how Mao Zedong and his successors have adopted the right strategies for waging a successful revolution. Not surprisingly, Xi referred to the "economic miracle" that the country had attained in the past two to three decades. "In the past thirty years, our country has developed in a sustained and speedy fashion with a clip that is rarely seen in the world," Xi wrote in a long article in the April 1, 2008, issue of *Seeking Truth*. "Socialism and Marxism have manifested robust liveliness on Chinese soil."[67] Xi also heaped praise on the *kexue fazhanguan* (scientific outlook on development), which was the main mantra of the Hu Jintao era. The then-vice-president asserted that *kexue fazhanguan,* which was characterized by "a rich ideological content and a formidable innate logic," was able to fulfill the goals of "putting people first" and attaining "comprehensive, well-coordinated, and sustainable development." No wonder he called this the "newest"—and most successful—instance of the Sinicization of Marxism.[68]

Yet an intriguing paradox has emerged. If, as Xi and his orthodox colleagues have maintained, the superiority of socialism with Chinese characteristics is so self-evident, how come the CCP leadership has to pull out all the stops to defend the canon—and to crush the voices of dissent? Xi has reiterated the importance of "popularizing" Marxism and socialism, that is, making them relevant and palatable to twenty-first-century Chinese. This has betrayed the fear of Xi and his colleagues that many Chinese have found the fossilized creed woefully obsolete. Moreover, there is a nagging suspicion that what Xi is upholding is not so much Chinese-style socialism as the CCP's monopoly on power. It is perhaps in this context that the leadership's frequent warnings about cadres having to *ju'an siwei* (have a sense of danger in the midst of comfort and plenty) is best understood. Xi counseled in a speech to the CPS in 2008 that the Party's ability to retain absolute power should not be taken for granted. "The Party's ruling status did not come about as a matter of course, and this status is not [automatically] guaranteed," Xi argued. "Whatever [power] we possessed in the past we might not have now; and whatever we have now we may not possess forever."[69]

The sense of crisis in the midst of plenty was also revealed when PBSC member and fellow princeling Wang Qishan asked his underlings to read Alexis de Tocqueville's *The Old Regime and the Revolution.*[70] The famous treatise is a morality tale about how Louis XVI, the last king of France, lost his legitimacy because the apparent prosperity of the "old regime" had bred inequality and other social malaise. Xi himself picked up on the well-known theme of "dynastic cycles": that in the past, dynasties rose and fell in accordance with whether the emperors could satisfy the people's demands. "The more advanced and developed our [socialist] enterprise, the more new situations and problems will arise—and we face more risks and challenges," he said. "We will have to contend with even more circumstances that we cannot predict."[71]

Despite the fact that Marxism and socialism—or at least the authoritarian versions developed in China and the Soviet Union—were discarded by the entire Soviet bloc in the early 1990s, Xi is adamant that "Chinese-style socialism" is right for China. "[The creed] is deeply implanted all over China and is suitable to

China's conditions," he indicated not long after the Eighteenth Party Congress. "It has tremendous strength and vitality. In contemporary China, only Chinese-style socialism can develop China, create happiness for the people, and bring forth the renaissance of the Chinese people." Moreover, he argued that Chinese-style socialism was geared toward the future. "We must uphold Marxism and socialism from the point of view of [further] developing it," Xi pledged. "It is a great canvas that Communists of our generation must continue to enrich and expand."[72] The idea that Beijing might consider options and solutions other than orthodox socialism has been totally ruled out by the Fifth-Generation titan.

### The Importance of Learning and Innovation

While Xi's articles and speeches are replete with references to the glorious accomplishments of the CCP and Chinese-style socialism, he has at the same time called upon cadres and Party members to be humble in learning new things and to be bold in theoretical innovations. The Party chief is keen to turn the CCP into a "Marxist political party that is geared toward learning." As he put it in a talk to the CPS: "Faced with profound changes in world affairs as well as conditions in China and within the Party—and faced with the difficulty, complicity, and seriousness of the task of reform and modernization—the CCP must put even more emphasis on learning."[73] The then-vice-president's stress on "Marxist learning" harks back to the famous slogan put forward by Jiang Zemin during his first full five-year term as president (1993–8), when the "core" of the Third-Generation leadership laid down the "Three Emphases" dictum, that is, "putting emphasis on studying the Marxist canon, political correctness, and righteousness." Jiang insisted on raising the theoretical aptitude of cadres through diligent studies of the Marxist-Maoist canon.[74]

Despite his apparent lack of reformist credentials, Xi likes to evoke the mantra of *sixiang jiefang* (thought liberation), which has been identified with trailblazers such as Deng Xiaoping and former general secretary Hu Yaobang. In his typically bombastic fashion, Xi stated in 2009 that "liberation of thinking is the fundamental ideological weapon to enable us to adapt ourselves to new circumstances, to tackle new challenges, to get to know new things, and to accomplish new goals." Thought liberation is linked to the magic word "innovation," which is invoked by CCP propagandists on an almost daily basis to prove that the Party is capable of breaking new ground despite its conservative mentality. And whenever Xi cites the word *chuangxin* (innovation), he means multifaceted innovation: "innovation in concepts of development, innovation in approaches to development, innovation in development policies, and innovation in leadership methodology." Xi specifically laid down a theory of fourfold *chuangxin* for Party and government institutions. They are "innovation in organizational design," "innovation in the construction of leadership teams," innovation in work systems, and "innovation in the management and education of Party members."[75]

Yet Xi never fails to qualify his enthusiasm for *sixiang jiefang* and innovation with caveats aplenty: for example, innovators must abide by the overall tenets of "the theoretical system of socialism with Chinese characteristics." The Party boss is not afraid to touch upon the sensitive issue of learning from the West. Like ex-presidents Jiang and Hu, Xi is at pains to point out that in this age of globalization, the CCP will never close its door to new currents in the world. In a memorable talk at the CPS in late 2009, the leader-in-waiting indicated that the CCP must keep up with the times. "The Party is constantly learning [new things] to establish morality, to boost wisdom, and to create new enterprises," he said. Xi called on cadres and Party members to "boldly absorb and take as examples all the fruits of civilization of humankind, including those from developed, capitalist countries in the West." "The CCP will be a political Party that is at the forefront of the times," he contended. "We are bold in [making] changes and brave in innovation. We will never become fossilized; we will never stagnate."[76]

As for what Chinese can learn from the West, Xi cited two examples: modes of production and management methods.[77] Certainly, Western values and institutions, including anything that smacks of taboo subjects such as democracy or checks and balances, are out of bounds. Here, we are reminded of late Qing dynasty minister Zhang Zhidong's famous theory on limited Westernization and modernization: "Chinese learning for the essence and Western learning for the application." This meant that Chinese modernizers of the 1880s and 1890s should delve into Western sciences and technologies only to strengthen China's infrastructure and defense capabilities. As for "software"—including values and methods of governance—China should still stick to time-tested Confucian orthodoxy. It was this refusal to tinker with traditional beliefs, norms, and institutions that doomed the Qing dynasty's "Self-Strengthening Movement."[78]

A bone of contention among officials and scholars in the past decade or so is the extent to which China should adopt *pushijiazhi* (universal values) such as human and labor rights that are enshrined in the United Nations Charter. Among top-level cadres, only ex-premier Wen Jiabao has gone on the record as advocating the no-holds-barred adoption of "universal norms." The ex-premier argued in an early 2007 article that China should unhesitatingly embrace *pushijiazhi*. "Democracy, a [fair] legal system, freedom, human rights, egalitarianism . . . are not unique to capitalism," Wen noted. "They are values that all humankind is jointly pursuing."[79] In a 2013 article, the Hunan Technological University economist Tang Zhijun echoed Wen when he contended that *pushijiazhi*—including democracy, freedom, and human rights—"are universal values sought by all mankind, and these ideals will not lose their values due to the different conditions in different countries."[80]

However, most establishment intellectuals and media commentators have insisted that China should go down its own road. In an August 2013 editorial, the conservative *Global Times* contended that "China cannot emerge from its preordained inferiority if it merely imitates the Western discourse." The Party mouthpiece cited the example of "democracy," which seemed to have a big following in China. The trouble, *Global Times* noted, was that the Western concept of "democracy" was inextricably linked to institutions such as rule of law, checks and balances, and multiparty competition. "These concrete institutions obviously cannot find parallels in China's conditions," it said.[81]

It is interesting to note, in view of this outlook, that in 2010 Xi sent his daughter, Xi Mingzhu, to Harvard University. An even more famous princeling, Bo Guagua, the son of Bo Xilai, has studied at Oxford, Harvard, and Columbia. The children of many other former PBSC members, including ex-president Jiang, ex-premiers Wen and Zhu Rongji, are also alumni of American universities.[82] The rationale, at least according to cynical netizens, seems to be that Chinese with a revolutionary bloodline would not easily succumb to the sugar-coated bullets of Western culture because they were born with built-in resistance to "bourgeois liberalization."

### Xi's Prescriptions for Running the Party—and the Country

#### *A Return to Ideological Struggles*

One of Deng Xiaoping's most important contributions to the Party and the country was that after taking over power in late 1978, he said good-bye to Mao's obsession with ideological purity and political struggles. Deng declared simply that "economic construction is the core task of the Party."[83] Xi, however, has reignited the ideological imperative, implying that the pursuit of the purest socialism was as important as building up the economy. Xi's concepts about *yishixingtai* (ideology and thought) were laid out in an address to a national meeting on ideology and propaganda held on August 19, 2013. In his talk, Xi gave equal billing to economic work, on the one hand, and upholding politically correct *yishixingtai*, on the other. "The core task of the Party is economic construction," Xi said. "Pursuits relating to *yishixingtai* are the Party's extremely important task." Added the ultraconservative *Beijing Daily*, "the fate of the CCP depends on whether it can defend the battlefield of ideology and thought."[84]

In his now-famous lecture, Xi admonished his comrades to work hard on "consolidating and boosting mainstream public opinion, propagating the leitmotifs [of socialism with Chinese characteristics], and spreading positive energy." *Yishixingtai* work was important, Xi said, because "the dissolution of a regime often begins in the field of ideas." Apparently referring to the Soviet Union, he added that "after the *yishixingtai* line of defense has been breached, other lines of defense will be difficult to hold." Xi went on to espouse the quintessentially Maoist stance of equating *dangxing* (the nature and characteristics of the Party) and *renminxing* (the nature and characteristics of the people). "*Dangxing* and *renminxing* have always been uniform and united," he said in his August speech. "We must uphold the correct political direction, stand firm on [proper] political views, and resolutely engage in propaganda for the Party's theories, lines, objectives, and policies," Xi added.

"We must resolutely remain in the highest degree of unison with the *zhongyang* [central authorities] and resolutely uphold central authority."[85]

The equation of *dangxing* and *renminxing*—the theory that Party members and citizens should not have ideas and aspirations different from those of the Party—was first celebrated by Mao. In his famous "Talks at the Yan'an Forum on Literature and Art" in 1942, Mao asked not only artists and writers but ordinary Party members to "cleave to the stand of the Party and *dangxing*." He urged all CCP affiliates to "further boost their [level of and] training in *dangxing,* so that they can subsume individual interests under the interests of the entire Party."[86]

Xi's apparent return to Maoist-style dogma has been affirmed by a number of Party mouthpieces. "*Dangxing* is the [result of the] refinement, sublimation, and synthesis of human nature," said an article carried by *Study Times*.[87] For the Beijing-based liberal scholar Mou Chuanheng, however, Xi was using high-sounding and politically correct language to circumvent tough questions on political reform, which had been mothballed for more than thirty years. "Xi Jinping is using the construction of *dangxing* to side-step the construction of constitutional governance," Mou wrote. "He has also advocated rectifying the Party's style to substitute the reform of institutions."[88] Alfred Wu, a specialist on Chinese politics at the Hong Kong Institute of Education, noted that Xi had embraced Maoist ideals and put political reform on indefinite hold. "Xi might also want to appeal to hardline elements in the Party so as to firm up his own power base," he said.[89]

Theoretical issues aside, what are the practical implications of Xi's apparent turning back of the clock? The president's ideological exercises serve to rally support of all Party members around the central authorities—in particular, around Xi himself. Not long after Xi's August 19 speech, the Beijing Party secretary Guo Jinlong published an article in *Seeking Truth* in which he called on his colleagues in Beijing to "always maintain a high degree of unison in terms of ideas and action with the Party central authorities with comrade Xi Jinping as general secretary." "We must self-consciously protect the authority of the central authorities," he added.[90]

Following a long-standing CCP ritual called *biaotai* (airing views by mid- to senior-ranking cadres to demonstrate their fealty to the top leadership), the heads of the Propaganda Departments of all of the country's administrative districts published statements endorsing President's Xi's strictures. Many of these declarations, however, amounted to an unreserved exaltation of Xi's putative wisdom and foresight. For instance, the director of the Tibet Autonomous Region Propaganda Department, Dong Yunhu, eulogized Xi for having "scientifically summed up" the Party's experience in ideological and propaganda work. President Xi had "enriched and developed Marxist theories on ideology as well as the Party's precepts on *yishixingtai* work," Deng asserted. The propaganda boss of Hainan Province, Xu Jun, went further. Xu proclaimed that in his August speech Xi had "awakened and enlightened the deaf and succeeded in profoundly illuminating people's minds."[91]

Although Xi's ability to elicit fairly obsequious expressions of support from regional officials testifies to his increasingly solid hold on power, ramping up ultraconservative norms could harm economic reform, which was the theme of the third plenum of the Eighteenth Central Committee held in November 2013. In his *biaotai* speech, the head of the Guangdong Propaganda Department, Tuo Zhen, repeated Xi's call on cadres in the media and related units to "foster and crystallize a social consensus [geared toward] demonstrating a bright future" for the province and the country.[92] Tuo's reputation as an orthodox commissar was burnished by his decision to kill an early 2013 cover story of the liberal paper *Southern Weekend* titled "Constitutional Governance Is Key to the Chinese Dream."[93] Yet intellectuals in Guangdong and Beijing were taken aback when Tuo asserted that "Guangdong is a double pacesetter: for reform and the open-door policy and for [political] struggle in the area of ideology and thoughts."[94] This ran counter to the commonly held belief that, particularly given its proximity to Hong Kong, Guangdong should serve as a window for all of China with respect to new ideas and thinking outside the box. It is significant that Xu Jun, the propaganda chief of Hainan—one of the five SEZs created by Deng in the early 1980s—also ruled out the island's function as a place where heterogeneous ways of thinking would at least be tolerated. "Hainan is an SEZ but not a 'special cultural zone,'" Xu noted in his *biaotai* speech.[95]

Tuo's views in particular have elicited vigorous criticism from the country's liberal intellectuals. Gao Yu, a respected political commentator who was detained by Beijing police in mid-2014, slammed Tuo for "trying to bring back Cultural Revolution-vintage political struggles." "Tuo and the Guangdong Propaganda Department have trampled upon the relatively liberal media in the province," Gao contended. "We are witnessing the rehabilitation of Mao-style ideology and thoughts."[96] The surprisingly conservative views of officials in Guangdong and Hainan—which used to be known as experimental zones for both economic and political reforms—may have dented these two provinces' reformist credentials in the eyes of foreign investors.

### A Twenty-First-Century Party Purge

President Xi has given the clearest indications to date of his political orientation and policy preferences by launching a Maoist-style rectification campaign geared toward "thoroughly cleaning up the work style" of the CCP's 85 million members. For a one-year period beginning in mid-2013, officials in civilian and military departments who failed to rid themselves of the undesirable traits of "formalism, bureaucratism, hedonism, and extravagance" would be penalized or kicked out of the Party.[97] The year-long *zhengfeng* (rectification) exercise, formally called the "Campaign on Mass-Line Education and Practice" was the largest-scale purge launched by Party authorities since the end of the Cultural Revolution.[98] In addition, a companion "thought education" movement aimed at "boosting grassroots-level cultural construction in the military forces" was launched within the PLA and the PAP. Regulations promulgated by the four PLA headquarters departments in June 2013 urged officers to "nurture the core values of the contemporary revolutionary soldier" through "doing a better job in educating, nurturing, and molding" the character of military personnel.[99]

In language that was reminiscent of the Chairman Mao's masterly blend of the metaphysical and the vernacular, Xi urged cadres and Party members to "purify themselves and to perfect themselves." "We must closely rely on the people and fully mobilize the enthusiasm, initiative and creativity of the broad masses," he said in the June 18 nationally televised speech that formally launched the *zhengfeng* crusade. "We must look in the mirror, tidy our attire, take a bath, and cure our sickness," added Xi.[100] In a commentary on the *zhengfeng* crusade, Xinhua pointed out that the Mao-style purge would serve the purpose of "bolstering the cohesiveness of the hearts of the Party and people—and consolidating the blood-and-flesh ties between the Party and the people." Shaanxi Party secretary Zhao Yongzheng compared Xi's ideological exercise to Mao Zedong's famous rectification movement in Yan'an in 1942, in which the Great Helmsman first tried to impose his uniquely authoritarian view of Marxism on the CCP's first batches of cadres. "The Yan'an Rectification movement was a smashing success," Zhao said while calling upon officials of today to learn from the campaign seventy-one years earlier. "It was the first great thought-liberation movement in CCP history," he asserted.[101]

One "innovation" introduced by Xi and advisers such as Politburo members Wang Huning and Li Zhanshu was the revival of the Maoist practice of "criticism and self-criticism" (*piping yu ziwopiping*), which was used extensively in the infamous "struggle sections" that were often presided over by Red Guards in the first half of the Cultural Revolution. "Criticism and self-criticism" were banned by Deng Xiaoping and used sparingly during ideological movements undertaken by Jiang Zemin and Hu Jintao.[102]

Xi, however, was so keen on reviving this Maoist institution that he performed a day-long "master class" in "struggle sessions" with members of the Hebei Provincial Party Committee in September 2013. He told the Hebei leadership team, headed by Party secretary Zhou Benshun and Governor Zhang Qingwei, that "criticism and self-criticism are a forceful weapon for resolving contradictions within the Party." This practice, Xi instructed, would "promote democratic centralism, bolster stringent rules for life within the Party, . . . and earnestly raise the ability of leadership teams to discover and solve problems."[103] In the course of these remarks, Zhou admitted to mistakes such as "a subjectivist style in decision-making," "having an inadequate knowledge of [the characters of] subordinates," and "lacking sufficient energy in carrying out [his job]." Zhou was criticized by one of his associates for "not paying enough attention to work for the poor." Governor Zhang, who is a much-decorated aeronautical engineer, admitted that he "sometimes succumbs to bureaucratic practices and raising himself over other cadres." A colleague of Zhang's then lambasted the governor for "being too satisfied with himself and not prone to taking the advice [of junior cadres]."[104]

It might be premature to assess whether these ritualistic sessions—described by liberal Beijing intellectuals as "political shows"—might live up to the billing of winnowing out bad sheep who were responsible for the alarming deterioration of cadres' morality and competence. It is significant, however, that in the footsteps of the Great Helmsman, Xi was resorting to Cultural Revolution-era ideological and propaganda campaigns to change the mind-set of cadres, rather than establishing institutions such as rule of law and universal-style checks and balances. As the legal expert Guo Wenjing argued in a commentary in the official *Legal Daily*, "critical to the success [of *zhengfeng*] is establishing solid institutions." Guo cited Deng's famous dictum about "the decisive role of institutions," namely, that "bad people cannot do evil within a good system, whereas it is possible for good people to do bad things within an evil system."[105] Similarly, the U.S.-based dissident scholar He Qinglian, who specializes in Party history and institutions, faulted Xi for "going after pleasing appearances rather than doing solid work." "The rectification exercise is itself a manifestation of formalism and bureaucracy," she contended. "What the CCP needs is the reform of political systems."[106]

In his speeches relating to the *zhengfeng* movement, Xi surprisingly shied away from concrete measures to eradicate rent-seeking and other corrupt activities particularly among top cadres and their kin. In his June 18 address, he made only one reference to tackling graft. "We must deeply implant in the thoughts and actions of all comrades of the Party the value of serving the people, sticking to reality, and being noncorrupt," he said. Xi's failure to properly address institutional malaise in the Party drew indirect flak even from academics within the CCP establishment. For example, Yao Heng, a politics professor at the Beijing Municipal Party School, pointed out in an interview with *People's Daily* that "without clean governance, adopting the mass line may become an empty phrase."[107]

Is the *zhengfeng* movement, then, a foil for old-style intra-Party power struggles that are aimed at boosting the authority of Xi, the putative "core" of the Fifth-Generation leadership? Zhang Lifan, a well-known Party historian, was convinced that "political campaigns waged in the name of the mass line are often symptomatic of factional strife within the Party." "It is possible that an internal power struggle is developing," he said.[108] Deng Yuwen, a respected media commentator who used to be a senior editor at the CPS, also thought that Xi might be using the rectification exercise to rid himself of political foes at both the central and local levels. "The *zhengfeng* crusade may become a loyalty drive that will enable Xi to establish his authority and flush out ideological opponents," he argued.[109]

A remarkable article in *Liberation Army Daily* in June 2013 seemed to lend credence to Zhang and Deng's views. In a piece titled "Self-Consciously Uphold the Authority of Chairman Xi Jinping," the commander and political commissar of the Second Artillery Corps (China's missile forces), Wei Fenghe and Zhang Haiyang, respectively, called upon officers and rank and file to "heed at any time and under any circumstances instructions from Party central authorities, the CMC and Chairman Xi." The two generals saluted the contributions made by Chairman Mao in "formulating and constructing the objectives for modernizing [China's] revolutionary army." They went on to note that in order to "ensure the army's superior nature, goals and essence," military personnel must "meet the challenges of reality and the requirements of inheriting 'red genes.'"[110]

It was the first time that senior staff in either civilian or military sectors had underscored the imperative of nurturing the Party's "red DNA." Given the commonly held beliefs among conservative sectors in the Party and army that "red genes" were found in the greatest abundance among cadres with a "revolutionary bloodline," the likes of Generals Wei and Zhang were in effect waging a loyalist campaign to enhance the status of princeling Xi as unquestioned leader of the Party, state, and military apparatuses. This is particularly glaring in light of the fact that a number of key Xi associates at the uppermost echelons of the Party and army, including PBSC members Yu Zhengsheng and Wang Qishan as well as General Zhang himself, are the relatives of illustrious Party elders.[111] The apparent veneration of "red genes" also manifested itself in the decision by a number of princelings in their twenties and forties to forgo relatively lucrative business careers for the world of politics. These newly minted regional cadres with a revolutionary bloodline include Deng Xiaoping's grandson, Deng Zhuodi (b. 1985), the son of ex-president Hu, Hu Haifeng (b. 1972), and the son of former NPC chairman Wu Bangguo, Wu Lei (b. 1978) (also see Chapter 1).[112]

Irrespective of the extent to which President Xi was committed to blowing the trumpet of cadres with "red genes," his adoption of Maoist values was criticized by the CCP's remnant liberal wing, which included Party elders as well as their children. Beijing's political circles were abuzz with the candid views of a number of retired cadres during a Chinese New Year intellectual salon in 2013 organized by the respected monthly *Yanhuang chunqiu*.[113] The second son of Hu Yaobang, Hu Dehua, blasted Xi's embrace of ultraconservative ideas, in particular his apparent refusal to push forward universal-style political reforms. Hu noted that instead of harboring nostalgia for the Cultural Revolution, Xi should emulate Taiwan's late president Chiang Ching-kuo, who instituted thoroughgoing political reforms on the island in 1986.[114] Zhong Peizhang, a retired senior cadre at the Party's Propaganda Department, urged Xi to take immediate steps to "reform the lawless Party and state systems laid down by Mao Zedong." While Xi has impressed observers inside and outside China with the speed with which he has consolidated his power base, the princeling has yet to convince his countrymen that he is committed to overhauling outdated institutions that underpin Party members' increasingly problematic "workstyle."[115]

### Centralized Power Key to Realizing Xi's "Chinese Dream"

The imperative of concentrating power at the top echelons of the Party-state apparatus is reflected in the fact that a number of key CCP and State Council agencies have been strengthened considerably. As Xi has reiterated since the Eighteenth Party Congress, a crucial challenge for the new leadership is to "ensure that [Beijing's] policies and directives are smoothly followed" by the entire country.[116]

Within the CCP's higher echelons, more power has been given to the Party's Central Committee Secretariat, which is the "work organ" of the supreme seven-member PBSC as well as the nerve center of the entire Party apparatus. The Secretariat under Xi consists of seven members—one more than that of the previous administration. For the first time in Party history, the State Council secretary-general has been inducted into the CCP Secretariat. This means that Yang Jing (b. 1953), who was appointed to this post at the NPC in March 2013, has to report to both Premier Li Keqiang and Liu Yunshan, who is the PBSC member in charge of the Secretariat. Since the office of the State Council secretary-general is deemed the nexus of the entire central government, both Liu and General Secretary Xi—who exercises overall control over Party affairs—can thus exert substantial influence over government operations.[117] Moreover, the ranking and authority of individual Secretariat members have been elevated. For example, Secretariat member Li Zhanshu concurrently serves as director of the Central Committee General Office. Li, who is Xi's premier troubleshooter, was inducted into the Politburo at the Eighteenth Party Congress. By contrast, Li's predecessors as director of the Central Committee General Office, who include luminaries including Wen Jiabao, Zeng Qinghong, Wang Gang, and Ling Jihua, were merely Central Committee members when they occupied that post. As discussed above, the fact that Li became secretary-general of the CNSC in early 2014 means that more clout than ever has been wielded by the Party Secretariat and its key members.[118]

Apart from Liu Yunshan, Li Zhanshu, and Yang Jing, other members of the Secretariat are in charge of hefty portfolios that embrace most Party and government functions. Liu Qibao (b. 1953), a Politburo member who doubles as director of the Party's Propaganda Department, handles issues ranging from ideology to policies toward the media. Politburo member Zhao Leji (b. 1957), who is also director of the Organization Department, supervises appointments and transfers of not only Party-state personnel but also senior managers in SOEs. Du Qinglin (b. 1946), who doubles as vice-chairman of the Chinese People's Political Consultative Conference (CPPCC), runs the Party and state's united front operations. Finally, Zhao Hongzhu (b. 1947), who is executive deputy-secretary of the Central Commission for Disciplinary Inspection (CCDI), is in charge of China's highest-level anti-corruption agency. The fact that Li Zhanshu, Zhao Leji, and Zhao Hongzhu are deemed Xi protégés testifies to the fact that Xi has been more successful at consolidating his power base than his predecessors Jiang Zemin and Hu Jintao.[119]

At his first international press conference at the NPC in 2013, Premier Li pointed out that his team would focus on "simplifying administrative [measures] and devolving powers to the regions," stressing that "we must change the nature of the government's function . . . Whatever can be done by society should be handled by society." At the same press conference a year later, he reiterated that "streamlining administration and delegating power [to localities and to enterprises] is a potent tool in energizing the market and stimulating social creativity." The head of government added that the market economy should be based on the rule of law. "We need to ensure that market forces can do anything that is not prohibited by the law, and government departments must not do anything unless it is mandated by the law," the premier noted.[120] However, both the structure and the modus operandi of the central government have yet to undergo major changes.

That the central government has sufficient clout to continue its long-standing interference in society and the marketplace is illustrated by the fact that two major departments of the State Council have assumed unprecedented authority. The first is the NDRC, which is often dubbed the "miniature State Council," because it is entrusted with the task of "macro-level adjustment and control" (*hongguan tiaokong*) for most aspects of the economy. The post-Eighteenth Party Congress lineup of the NDRC leadership comprises four full members of the Central Committee: NDRC minister Xu Shaoshi (b. 1951), Executive Vice Minister Jie Zhenhua (b. 1949), and two newly appointed vice ministers, Liu He (b. 1952) and Wu Xinxiong (b. 1949). By contrast, there is only one Central Committee member—usually the minister—in most ministerial-level agencies of the State Council. Under Premier Li, the NDRC has been given additional responsibilities, including overseeing the electricity-generation sector and engaging in long-term planning regarding population growth and urbanization.[121]

Given the top priority that the Xi administration has given to *weiwen* (preserving stability), it is perhaps not surprising that the power and staff establishment of the Ministry of Public Security (MPS), or police, have been augmented. The post-Eighteenth Party Congress MPS boasted three full members of the Central Committee. Apart from State Councilor and Minister Guo Shengkun (b. 1954), Executive Vice-Minister Yang Huanning (b. 1957) and Vice-Minister Li Dongsheng (b. 1955) were Central Committee members. Moreover, both Yang and Li, in addition to Vice-Minister Meng Hongwei, had the rank of full ministers. Like his predecessor Meng Jianzhu, Guo is not a career police officer. A former head of SOEs in the metallurgical sector, Guo was the Party secretary of Guangxi Province when he was named the country's top cop one month after the Eighteenth Party Congress. Executive Vice-Minister Yang, who holds a Ph.D. in criminal law from Peking University, is a veteran detective. After Li Dongsheng was arrested in December 2013 in connection with the Zhou Yongkang corruption case (see below), Vice-Minister Liu Jin'guo was given the rank of full minister.[122]

That the police apparatus has gained more responsibilities may have to do with the fact that President Xi is the PBSC member with direct oversight over the political-legal (*zhengfa*) hierarchy. Moreover, a number of cadres with experience in police and *zhengfa* work were promoted in the reshuffle after the NPC in 2013. For example, former secretary general of the Central Political-Legal Commission (CPLC) Zhou Benshun (b. 1953), a former police chief of Hunan Province, was appointed Party secretary of Hebei Province. Qiang Wei (b. 1953), a former head of the political-legal department of the Beijing Party committee, was named Party secretary of Jiangxi Province.[123] In the same vein, Du Jiahao (b. 1955), a former *zhengfa* secretary of Heilongjiang Province, became deputy Party secretary and governor of Hunan Province. Finally, Hao Peng (b. 1960), the former political-legal boss and deputy Party secretary of Tibet, became deputy Party secretary and governor-designate of Qinghai Province.[124]

The centripetal concern of the Xi administration has also manifested itself in the reshuffle of the administrative heads of China's thirty-one regions. Not counting the four directly administered cities and the five autonomous regions, half the governors of the twenty-two provinces who were appointed in the first half of 2013 were professional administrators who had served at the central level. Prior to their move to the provinces, they had been either ministers or deputy ministers on the State Council or the chairmen and CEOs of *yangqi* (SOE conglomerates; see Chapter 4).[125] From the beginning of the era of reform in 1978 until recently, most provincial governors or municipality mayors tended to be career Party apparatchiks or government functionaries who had worked their way up the hierarchy of regional administration.

Beijing's desire to arrest centrifugal tendencies was one reason behind the use of new criteria in gubernatorial appointments. Governors who had worked in central Party or government jobs are more aware of the thinking and requirements of the top leadership—as well as the imperative of dutifully implementing instructions from on high. Moreover, most of these "carpetbaggers" parachuted to local positions are professional administrators who at least in theory will be less liable to be entangled in the economic interests of local power blocs. Several of the newly appointed governors have valuable business and regulatory experience. For example, Shandong governor Guo Shuqing (b. 1956), is a former chairman of the China Securities Regulatory Commission and former chairman of the China Construction Bank. Fujian governor Su Shulin (b. 1962) is a former chairman of Sinopec, one of the three multinational oil-and-gas monopolies in the country.[126]

Yet another significant attribute of personnel changes since 2012 is the rise of the influence of the so-called Tibet Faction, a reference to cadres who first distinguished themselves while serving in mid- to senior-ranked posts in the restive region. Two veterans of the TAR, Guo Jinlong (b. 1947) and Hu Chunhua (b. 1963) were inducted into the Politburo at the Eighteenth Party Congress. A former Tibet Party secretary, Guo was appointed Beijing Party secretary in mid-2012. Hu, a former Tibet deputy Party secretary, was named Guangdong Party secretary. In March 2013, Zhang Qingli (b. 1951), who was Tibet Party boss from 2005 to 2011, was promoted to vice-chairman and secretary-general of the CPPCC. Yang Chuantang (b. 1954), another former Tibet Party secretary, became head of the expanded Ministry of Transport. Moreover, former TAR vice-chairman Qin Yizhi (b. 1965) was named first Party secretary of the CYL. A key factor behind the fast-track promotion of these cadres seems to be that their Tibet experience has testified to their ability to implement Beijing's directives under extremely tough conditions.[127]

Structural changes in the Party-state apparatus as well as personnel movements since the Eighteenth Party Congress have demonstrated the premium that the Xi leadership has put on a concentration of powers at the Party center as well as upholding sociopolitical stability. These developments also mark a departure from the dictums of Deng Xiaoping about devolution of powers to the regions as well as the separation of Party and government. President Xi, however, obviously favors a different approach to governance. As Zhang Ping, the recently retired NDRC minister, put it during the 2013 NPC session, "China's best advantage is that [the authorities] can concentrate the nation's resources and efforts to do big things." For Xi, it is apparent that the Leninist doctrine of "democratic centralism" is the best way to realize the Chinese Dream.[128]

This Leninist-style concentration of powers, however, has a serious downside. Given the fact that President Xi has ruled out universal norms ranging from multiparty politics to independence of the judiciary, an excessively top-heavy set-up might further militate against political liberalization. After all, decentralization of powers was a leitmotif of Deng's reforms. And past experience has pointed out that authoritarian leaders tend to make grievous mistakes in the absence of requisite checks and balances, including adequate feedback from the regions.[129]

### Cultivation of a Good Communist

Liu Shaoqi perished in the most ignoble circumstances in 1968, when he was hounded to death by Mao's Red Guards. Yet he still commands immense respect among Party members. One of his most famous books is a 1939 book called *On How to Be a Good Communist.* While Liu—and his close comrade Deng—became an implacable enemy of the CCP's conservative wing for advocating quasi-capitalist economic policies, he was a traditionalist with respect to most aspects of Party affairs.[130]

For example, Liu, together with the majority of Party leaders, believed that the key to good governance was "picking the right people to become cadres." This fit in with the "rule of personality" that was based in part on the Confucian belief that the apex of politics was persuading "saintly officials" to run the government.[131] Most Western political philosophies, however, put their emphasis on building institutions of checks and balances so as to limit the potential damages of despots. During the Mao era, the motto of the CCP Organization Department was grooming cadres to become "both red and expert." "Redness"—or revolutionary zeal—took precedence over expertise—or professional competence. In the era of reform, the slogan has changed to selecting officials who "possess both morality and ability—with priority given to morality." As Xi and former CCP Organization chief Li Yuanchao pointed out, morality meant "trustworthiness," political correctness, and, most importantly, the ability to toe the line laid down by the Politburo.[132]

Xi is famous for his many directives and articles about how to cultivate a cadre with unimpeachable moral qualities. Xi delivered a number of homilies about Confucian virtues when he was Party secretary of Zhejiang. In a memorable article in the Party mouthpiece *Seeking Truth,* he quoted both Confucius and Mao on the importance of *de* (morality) in governance—particularly as a yardstick for selecting worthy officials for high position. Xi cited the famous Confucian saying: "The official who practices *de* in politics is like the Northern Star; he is ensconced in his position even as other lesser stars surround him." And he cited Mao's crypto-Confucian dictum: "Running the country means disciplining officials. The qualities of propriety, righteousness, frugality, and sense of shame are the four faces of the nation."[133]

While he was waxing eloquent about the large number of Confucian qualities that cadres must cultivate, Xi often sounded like a quintessential *fumuguan* (lit. "an official who is like a father and mother"). On one occasion, Xi asked his underlings to "beware of 'making investments in friendships' and various types of 'public relations.'" "We must never be soft-hearted toward 'friends' who have ulterior motives," he said.[134] On another occasion, he admonished young cadres not to "spend too much time on entertainment and socializing" with their peers or well-established figures in society. Leading cadres should spend their time on their studies, including steeping themselves in history. Xi pointed out that "this will help them [officials] raise their cultural level as well as their aptitude in thoughts and policies." A knowledge of history would also enable cadres to "raise their working ability and leadership level," Xi instructed.[135]

Another major virtue preached by Xi was *tuanjiexue* (how to stay united) with fellow cadres. In modern language, *tuanjiexue* means camaraderie and teamwork; it also means playing it safe—and not voicing unpopular or unorthodox views that might threaten the Party's carefully cultivated façade of unanimity. In his interview with *China Profiles,* Xi pointed out that one thing he learned while working up the hierarchy in Fujian was "to be united with my colleagues." "Under any circumstances and predicaments, the art of being united is crucial," Xi said. "If you can manage human relationships well and get people to become united, your work will be smooth and easy," he said. "If colleagues are not united, everything will go awry." He explained that many heroes in history, including the founder of the Han dynasty (202 b.c.e.–220 c.e.) Liu Bang, the hero of *Sanguo yanyi (Romance of Three Kingdoms)* Liu Bei, and the leader of the legendary 108 heroes in the novel *Shuihu zhuan (Water Margin, Outlaws of the Marsh,* or *All Men Are Brothers),* Song Jiang, became great leaders primarily because of their ability to attract talented people and maintain a spirit of unity among their colleagues.[136] However, Xi seems oblivious to the fact that a senior cadre who pays too much attention to conforming with conventional wisdom is most unlikely to become a maverick leader—or one with visionary, out-of-the-box thinking.

Given Xi's views about propagating talent, it is not surprising that Xi wants to turn China's colleges into ideological bases where politically correct notions can be drummed into the heads of Party members, teachers, and students. While discussing "Party construction" at universities in late 2009, then-vice-president Xi urged cadres in higher education to "insist on arming Party members and imbuing students with the correct [knowledge about] the theoretical system of socialism with Chinese characteristics." Using language from an earlier era, Xi said: "We must uphold and perfect the responsibility system of the college president [working] under the leadership of the Party committee . . . and fully develop the core leadership functions of Party committees [at universities.]"[137] This runs counter to the spirit, endorsed at the Thirteenth Party Congress in 1987, of the separation between the Party and the government. It was former Party chief Zhao Ziyang who first advocated that the authority of Party committees be reduced. For example, at universities, full responsibility and powers should be held by administrative or professional heads—not Party functionaries.[138]

## Xi's Anti-Corruption Campaign and Factional Intrigue

Because corruption is widely admitted by ex-presidents Jiang Zemin and Hu Jintao as "a matter of life and death" for the CCP, Xi has from day one highlighted his resolve to fight the scourge. With the help of the capable and ambitious Wang Qishan, the PBSC member in charge of the CCDI—China's highest-level graft buster—Xi's score in nabbing corrupt officials has been better than that of his two predecessors. It can even be argued that the promotion of clean governance has to date been the single most notable achievement of the new administration.

Immediately after the Eighteenth Party Congress, Xi announced with great fanfare the "Eight-Point Regulations Against Extravagance." Cadres and PLA officers must avoid lavish banquets, liquor, or other kinds of conspicuous consumption. The stricture also said that "no welcome banners, no red carpets, no floral arrangements, or grand receptions" would be provided during the inspection visits to regional locations by senior cadres or generals. The latter were also expected to eat with rank-and-file staff and to stay in hostels, not five-star hotels. This has resulted in a precipitous drop in the sales of expensive gifts ranging from *maotai* liquor to European brand-name watches and fashion items. Business in luxury hotels and restaurants has plummeted.[139] Under PBSC member Wang, a former vice-premier in charge of finance, the CCDI has expanded its staff and operational parameters. The commission even set up its own Organization Department to recruit investigators and graft-busters. All five vice-secretaries of the CCDI, including Zhao Hongzhu, who doubles as a member of the Central Committee Secretariat, sit on the CLGCDR. This reflects the priority that Xi is giving to building up clean governance in the course of promoting "comprehensive reforms" in the economy and other sectors.[140]

Xi indicated in January 2013 that Party and state authorities were embarking on an anti-graft campaign that would last for most of his first five-year term. He pledged that "both flies and tigers" among miscreants in the Party, the government, and the army would be brought to justice. Xi also noted that clean governance was integral to the realization of the Chinese Dream. In 2013 alone, the CCDI and related departments such as the Ministry of Supervision and the Supreme People's Procuratorate arrested thirty-one *zhongguan* cadres (who report directly to Party headquarters), including twenty ministerial- and vice-ministerial-level officials. According to Cao

Jianmin, president of the Supreme People's Procuratorate, 51,306 officials were investigated for corruption and other "economic crimes" in 2013, up 8.4 percent over the number in 2012.[141]

The president's biggest triumph on the anti-graft front consists of investigations into the labyrinthine corruption ring centered on former PBSC member Zhou Yongkang (b. 1942), a tough bureaucratic infighter who was head of the CPLC from 2007 to 2012. Zhou was detained by anti-corruption and law-enforcement officers in December 2013. On July 29, 2014, the CCDI came out with a one-sentence statement confirming that Zhou was under investigation "on suspicion of grave violations of discipline" ("grave violations of discipline" is a widely used code for corruption and other economic crimes). The same day, the *People's Daily* ran a commentary saying that "Zhou Yongkang was a big tiger, and if even he can be brought down, any corrupt elements nursing delusions will understand: If they stretch out their hands, they will get caught." While in theory Zhou might only be subject to party discipline (such as being stripped of his party membership), it is almost certain that he will be put on trial—and that court procedures would start by early 2015 at the latest.[142]

Xi is a major beneficiary of Zhou's downfall because he was seen as determined and powerful enough to bend the unwritten Party regulation of *xingbushang changwei* (serving and retired PBSC members are exempt from prosecution—and that by extension, the immediate families of these Party elders would also enjoy some degree of immunity). This tacit rule is a "mutual protection clause" that is much-valued by former PBSC members. A major reason why it took several months before the CCDI confirmed that it was probing Zhou and his gang was opposition to Zhou's incrimination by a host of party elders and former PBSC members including Jiang Zemin, Hu Jintao, Wen Jiabao, former vice-president Zeng Qinghong, and former premier Li Peng. In the wake of Zhou's downfall, the big question on the anti-corruption front is: after having persuaded Jiang and others to acquiesce in the abrogation of the *xingbushang changwei* rule, would Xi move against other former PBSC members? The most-talked-about "next big tiger to be ensnared" is Zeng, who, like Zhou, began his remarkable career in the oil-and-gas sector. For reasons including preserving stability in the party, however, it seems unlikely that Xi will indict another PBSC member at least within the rest of his first five-year term of 2012–17. Deng Yuwen, a respected political analyst and former editor of *Study Times*, a CPS publication, noted that Xi having struck a deal with other party elders about circumscribing the scope of high-level corruption investigations after Zhou's downfall, "the possibility of [capturing another big tiger] … in the rest of Xi's first five-year term is close to zero." Moreover, there was evidence that Xi took measures to reassure the likes of ex-president Jiang that their offspring would not be affected. For example, in April the official media gave prominent coverage to President Xi while he was touring a Shanghai high-tech institute with Jiang's son, Jiang Mianheng. Most importantly, Xi invited fifteen former PBSC members—including ex-president Jiang, ex-vice-president Zeng, ex-premier Wen and ex-CCDI secretary He Guoqiang, all of whose sons are said to be under investigation for business irregularities—to a concert and banquet marking the October 1, 2014 National Day. This was seen as a carefully orchestrated show of unity and solidarity between Xi on one hand, and well-nigh all party elders who were fit to face the camera, on the other.[143] Yet even if Xi were to put a moratorium on nabbing top-level corrupt cadres, his accomplishment would still be phenomenal. The Zhou corruption scandal, which broke all records in terms of money involved and the number of senior officials arrested, has already become a milestone in terms of the CCP leadership's willingness to expose the nefarious crimes of a former PBSC stalwart.

From late 2012 until mid-2014, the CCDI detained for investigation close to 300 officials and business people who either worked under Zhou or were Zhou's relatives. At least RMB 90 billion in ill-gotten gains—including domestic and overseas bonds and stocks worth RMB 51 billion and 300 apartments and villas—were seized. The disgraced cadres include Zhou's colleagues and underlings throughout his long and successful career. Zhou, a native of Jiangsu Province, was a senior executive in the petroleum sector from 1988 to 1998. He was Party secretary of Sichuan Province from 1999 to 2002, after which he became minister at the MPS from 2002 to 2007 and PBSC member in charge of the CPLC (2007 to 2012).[144]

The Zhou-related investigations began just a month after the Eighteenth Party Congress, when Li Chuncheng, a former vice-Party secretary of Sichuan and crony of Zhou, was arrested. Two other Sichuan veterans with close connections to Zhou—former vice-governor Guo Yongxiang and former Party secretary Li Chongxi—were later detained. The CCDI then took action against several well-known stalwarts of the so-called Petroleum Faction, of which Zhou was a leader. These arrests climaxed in September with the detention of Jiang Jiemin, a former president of CNPC, who had been appointed chairman of the SASAC barely six months earlier. One of the best-known figures in China's oil industry, Jiang was charged with "serious disciplinary violations," a euphemism for corruption. Four other senior CNPC executives, including CNPC vice-president and Central Committee alternate member Wang Yongchun and deputy general manager Li Hualin, were also detained for investigation for graft-related offenses.[145]

By early 2014, the noose had tightened around the neck of Zhou's former colleagues in the security apparatus. Vice-Minister of Public Security Li Dongsheng and the head of the Beijing Municipal State Security Bureau, Liang Ke, were arrested in February. Other notable officials who fell victim to the purge included the vice-governor of Hainan Province, Ji Wenli, who was Zhou's secretary when the former PBSC member was in Sichuan and the MPS. In addition, Zhou's multimillionaire son, Zhou Bin, was brought in for questioning in late 2013. Zhou Bin, his wife, Huang Wan, and his mother-in-law, Zhan Minli, used to run fabulously profitable businesses relating to oil and gas as well as real estate. Other Zhou relatives, including his two brothers and their spouses, were also detained for questioning in early 2014.[146]

While Xi deserved credit for, as the Chinese like to say, touching the buttocks of a tiger, it is undeniable that he had not departed from the age-old CCP tradition of using corruption charges to bring down political foes, despite Xi's oft-repeated pledge that he would follow two broad criteria in eradicating corruption: following the rule of law with Chinese characteristics and "putting power back in the cage."[147] There was a close connection between Zhou and his ally Bo Xilai (b. 1948), the charismatic princeling who is a former Politburo member and Party secretary of Chongqing. Although the decision to detain Bo was made by the Hu Jintao-led Politburo in March 2012, Zhou and Bo were well-known political enemies of Xi. And even though rumors that the two tried to organize a coup d'état in early 2012 were unfounded, it was believed that the two did not agree with the succession plan enacted at the Eighteenth CCP Congress. In other words, Xi felt threatened by Zhou and Bo, who reportedly uttered disparaging remarks about Xi's fitness to become general secretary.[148]

There are eerie similarities between the Zhou and Bo cases, on the one hand, and the incrimination of two former Politburo members, Chen Xitong (1930–2013) and Chen Liangyu (b. 1946), on the other. Former Beijing Party secretary Chen Xitong and former Shanghai Party boss Chen Liangyu received jail terms of sixteen and eighteen years, respectively, for alleged corruption in 1998 and 2008. Yet the two Chens were first and foremost losers in CCP-style power struggles. Beijing's Chen ran afoul of the Shanghai Faction led by ex-president Jiang, and Shanghai's Chen was a political foe of both ex-president Hu and ex-premier Wen.[149] As the Beijing-based historian Zhang Lifan put it, "The anti-corruption effort is just a political weapon used to take down whoever they [the powers-that-be] want to take down." "Because when there is widespread institutional corruption, anti-graft efforts are not going to clean up the system," he explained. "They are above all a way to get rid of political opponents."[150]

The politicized nature of the Bo trial was partially illustrated by the inadequate handling of what some overseas Chinese commentators called the "trial of the century." After a rough five-day court procedure in Jinan, Shandong Province, in September 2013, Bo was sentenced to life imprisonment for bribe-taking and embezzlement involving RMB 26 million as well as abuse of power. The ill-gotten gains were provided mostly by two businessmen—Xu Ming and Tang Xiaolin—who became Bo's cronies and business partners when he was mayor of Dalian in the 1990s. The prosecution failed to explain why they did not go after Bo's allegedly corrupt activities when he was minister of commerce (2003–7) and Party secretary of Chongqing (2007–12), despite widespread reports that Bo and other senior municipal cadres confiscated huge sums from Chongqing businessmen who were detained on charges of being mafia bosses.[151]

Compared to predecessors Jiang and Hu, Xi has proven to be a much more aggressive graft-buster in the PLA. As of mid-2014, two military "tigers," the former Politburo member and ex-vice chairman of the CMC General Xu Caihou and his protégé, the former vice-commander of the General Logistics Department,

Lieutenant-General Gu Junshan, were taken into custody on corruption charges involving tens of billions of renminbi. At least a dozen other officers with the rank of major-general or above, including another former CMC vice-chairman, General Guo Boxiong, are believed to be under investigation.[152] It is, however, substantially more difficult for the Party leadership to wage an anti-corruption crusade within the defense establishment. Venal military officers are subject to less scrutiny than their civilian counterparts. For example, the CCDI and Ministry of Supervision do not have jurisdiction over the PLA, which has its own mechanism for disciplinary inspection. Lack of oversight is one reason corruption within the defense establishment is deemed at least as endemic as that in the Party-state apparatus.[153]

It is, of course, well-nigh impossible for Xi and the CCDI to perform what analysts call radical surgery on the corruption problem: There are simply too many corrupt officials, and mass arrests could lead to a political earthquake—and a gigantic backlash against Xi that could conceivably precipitate his downfall. According to Reuters, an unpublicized internal Party survey in 2013 showed that more than 30 percent of Party, government, and military officials were found to be involved in different categories of corruption and rent-seeking.[154] It seems most unlikely that Xi will probe the large number of princelings and other close kin of top cadres who are suspected of using their political ties to run lucrative businesses. No action has been taken against the relatives of current and former PBSC members whose business empires have been exposed by foreign media, including Bloomberg, the *New York Times,* Reuters, and the International Consortium of Investigative Journalists (ICIJ).[155] For example, Bloomberg reported in 2012 that Xi's relatives—mainly his sister, Qi Qiaoqiao, her husband, Deng Jiagui, and Qi's daughter, Zhang Yannan—were multimillionaire businesspeople (see Chapter 2).[156] Xi is also reluctant to go after high-ranking suspects who still enjoy the protection of influential Party veterans. Take, for example, the case of Ling Jihua, a key protégé of ex-president Hu, who is the director of the United Front Department. The wealth of his wife, the successful businesswoman Gu Lihua, and son, Ling Gu, was exposed in 2012, when Ling Gu died in a traffic accident while driving a Ferrari. The twenty-three-year-old Ling owned several of these expensive imported cars.[157]

Equally serious is the fact that China's anti-graft operation is not anchored upon sound institutions. As in past campaigns, the CCDI and its counterpart in the State Council—the Ministry of Supervision—deployed numerous "work groups" to investigate suspects in Party and government agencies at both the central and local level. An important innovation introduced by the Xi administration was that, for the first time, the authorities encouraged potential whistle blowers, including journalists, to report cases to the two major graft-busting units—or to simply put their stories on the Internet. For example, the NDRC's vice-minister Liu Tie'nan fell from power in 2013 due to detailed exposés about his "corrupt lifestyle" that were compiled by the deputy editor of *Caijing* (Finance and Economics), Luo Changping.[158]

Then there was the exposure of four senior judges of the Shanghai High People's Court, including the chief judge of the No. 1 Civil Tribunal, Chen Xueming, and deputy chief judge of the tribunal, Zhao Minghua. Businessman Ni Peiguo, who believes that he was a victim of a mistake by the Shanghai court, posted videos of the four cavorting with prostitutes in a local hotel. More reports on the Internet indicated that the four had also amassed assets through illegal means.[159] Less than a month after this episode, Cui Yadong, the newly appointed president of the Shanghai High People's Court, was accused of corruption when he was head of the Police Department of Guizhou Province from 2008 until early 2013. Seventy of his subordinates on the Guizhou police force wrote an Internet petition saying that Cui had, among other things, stolen more than 30 tons of expensive *maotai* during his tenure in the province.[160]

It has also become clear, however, that Xi's anti-corruption crusade suffers from severe institutional drawbacks. The authorities' sincerity in encouraging whistleblowers was cast in doubt due to the harassment of human-rights lawyers and NGOs that had done effective work in exposing corruption and other cases of the abuse of power. For example, in April 2013 police detained core members of an NGO called the New Citizens movement, which was active in exposing the rapacious and illegal activities of officials online. The ostensible reason was that members of the organization included pro-democracy lawyers and activists whom Beijing had accused of undermining political stability. Police also arrested three well-regarded Internet whistleblowers—Yuan Dong, Zhang Baocheng, and Ma Xinli—for their advocacy of a law obliging senior cadres to disclose their assets.[161]

Meanwhile, the Xi administration has indefinitely postponed the approval of a "sunshine" assets disclosure regulation. Since the late 2000s, liberal cadres and journalists have proposed an assets-declaration law that will oblige officials to publicize not only their assets but those of their immediate kin. One version of the proposal says senior cadres should also make known whether their spouses or children have overseas-residence rights. Of all Politburo members, only Yu Zhengsheng, chairman of the CPPCC, went on the record as supporting the "sunshine" legislation.[162]

Given Xi's reputation as consensus-driven politician who values unity and cohesion among the civilian as well as military cadres, it is unlikely that he will go after too many members of the red aristocracy. The "seven unmentionables" cited in Central Document No. 9 (see above ) included universal norms, press freedom, civil liberties and the independence of the judiciary, which are deemed integral components of successful market economies in Western as well as Asian countries. Corruption—one of the worst scourges of the Chinese economy and society—cannot be effectively eradicated without a free press and a non-Party-dominated legal and judicial system. It is perhaps for this reason that the Xi leadership has listed the "privileged capitalist class"—which comprises many senior cadres as well as princelings—as one of the "unmentionables."[163]

## Retrogression in Political Reform

### *"Good Social Governance" in Lieu of Democratization*

Immediately after becoming Party chief, Xi paid a visit to Guangdong—the province considered "ahead of the times"—in an apparent effort to highlight his reformist credentials. Xi wanted to show all Chinese—and the world—that he would carry the mantle of reform laid down by Deng Xiaoping. Xi held pep talks with cadres, including retired ones who had talked with Deng and executed some of Deng's ideas. "The decision made by Deng Xiaoping on the reform and open door policy is correct, and we will continue to walk down this correct road," he said. "This is the road toward a strong nation and rich citizenry. We will not only go down this road resolutely but also make new developments and reach higher levels."[164] At a Politburo study session in January 2013, Xi reiterated that "without the reform and open door policy, the China of today—and the China of tomorrow—would not exist."[165]

However, President Xi very seldom mentions political reform or democracy despite the fact that he has perfunctorily cited Deng's famous adage that "without democracy there would be no socialism or socialist modernization." Yet Xi never forgot to qualify this general statement by emphasizing that "we cannot develop socialism by copying things from foreign countries." At other times, he pointed out that "foreign ideas are, after all, nurtured in the soil of alien territory." "We cannot blindly copy [foreign ideas and institutions]," he said in another speech.[166] It seems evident that, by democracy, Xi means democracy under the Party's guidance—and not the "Western" ideal of multiparty politics and elections with universal suffrage.

Xi indicated early in his tenure that he was not interested in reforms that involved "universal values." In his now-famous internal talk given in Guangdong in December 2012, the Party chief accused Party members and intellectuals who favored "universal values" of having "misunderstood the nature of our reforms." "Some people have defined reform as [the adoption of] Western universal values," he said. "This is a misreading of concepts." Xi dropped strong hints that the moratorium on political reform since the Tiananmen Square incident in 1989 would continue indefinitely. Talking about the nature and directions of reform, he told Guangdong cadres: "The question is what to reform and what not to reform. There are some things that cannot and should not be changed even in the long term." Xi was making a clear reference to "Western-style" reforms that would dilute the CCP's monopoly on power.[167]

Indeed, Xi has always been careful about not stepping into the minefield of political reform. He has scant interest in political change—liberalization of ideology, modernization of cadres' mentality, or democratizing political institutions. This was made clear in an early 2013 speech that Xi made to the Politburo on the future directions of reform. "Reform being a case of systems engineering, we must uphold comprehensive reform," the Party chief indicated. "We must pay attention to the synergy of different types of reform as well as the benevolent interaction among them," he said. This was a bureaucratic way of saying that "controversial reforms" such as political liberalization should be stopped because they would upset the applecart of reforms favored by the conservative leadership. Xi also expressed the usual caveat about economic and political reform: "Stability is the prerequisite for reform, and we must insist upon the synthesis of reform, development, and stability." "Only when society is stable can reform be ceaselessly implemented," he said. "We must seek a unity between the force of reform, the speed of development, and the degree to which society can absorb [these changes]."[168] In other words, reforms that threaten stability—or the leadership and power of the CCP—must be put on the back burner.

It is significant that, instead of political reform, Xi has promoted the more mundane goal of *shehui zhili* (social governance). The Decision on Major Issues Concerning Comprehensively Deepening Reforms (hereafter, Decision) passed by the Central Committee in November 2012 has an entire section on "the innovation of the system of social governance." The watershed document pointed out that an innovative social governance system would include the goals of "safeguarding the basic interests of the broadest people, enhancing harmonious factors to the maximal extent, strengthening the vigor of social development, raising the level of social management . . . safeguarding national security, and ensuring that the people live and work in peace and contentment, and that society is stable and orderly." While the Decision encouraged the participation of the people and different social sectors in improving social governance, the emphasis was put on "boosting the leadership of Party committees and pushing forward the guidance of the government."[169]

In line with the CCP's nervousness about sociopolitical instability, much stress has been placed on the establishment of, first, "innovative systems to effectively prevent and defuse social contradictions" and, second, "comprehensive mechanisms to mediate and dissolve contradictions and disputes." The Central Committee document urged cadres to "persist in governance according to the law, strengthen rule-of-law guarantees, and to use rule-of-law methods to dissolve social contradictions." Moreover, the CCP leadership called for the establishment of "open and orderly mechanisms [for the people] to express their demands . . . to mediate contradictions and guarantee rights and interests, and to ensure that the problems of the masses can be reflected, contradictions dissolved, and [people's] rights and interests guaranteed."[170] Yet very little was said about participation of the citizenry by, for example, extending elections—which were first introduced at the village level by Deng Xiaoping in 1979—to higher levels such as townships and cities.

While talking to delegates at the NPC in March 2014, Xi pointed out that the goal of social governance—a "society that is stable and orderly"—can be achieved through "harmonious coexistence among the people." Then the Party chief gave a surprisingly simplistic recipe for *shehui zhili*. "The core of social governance resides in communities, in towns, and in villages," he said. "We must strengthen the routine management of cities and towns and aggressively go about curing the management woes of cities and towns."[171] While talking to another group of NPC delegates in 2014, Xi argued out that "social governance is a science." "We must consider a major task the nurturing of a corps of cadres who are experts in city management," he added. "We must construct and manage cities with a scientific attitude, advanced concepts, and professional knowledge."[172] There seems little doubt in Xi's mind that the most critical prerequisite for "good social governance" is strong leadership by the Party and the government—and not participation by the people. As for "contradictions among the people" that cannot be resolved, Beijing is relying upon its time-tested control apparatus to instill order. It is significant that the establishment of the CNSC was first mentioned in the section of the Decision dealing with "social governance" (see below).

Xi's lack of interest in political or ideological liberalization can be traced to his career in Fujian and Zhejiang. Having learned the lessons of the vicissitudes of his father—and fallen liberal leaders such as Hu Yaobang and Zhao Ziyang—Xi studiously steered clear of issues relating to political or democratic reform. The few references to political liberalization that Xi has ever made were couched in metaphorical language. A good example was his reference to the "Spirit of the Red Boat," a reference to the vessel in South Lake, Zhejiang, in which the First Party Congress was held in 1921. Immediately upon becoming Party secretary of Zhejiang in October 2002, Xi made a pilgrimage to South Lake. Xi indicated that "the spirit of the Red Boat" had served as "the source of inspiration and guidance of the Chinese Revolution." "It is the spirit of honestly making self-sacrifices for the people," he said. "The relationship between the Party and the people is like that between a boat and water," he added. "Water can support the boat, but it can also overturn it."[173] This ancient proverb was attributed to Confucius—and was used by various emperors to demonstrate their concern for the people.[174] Yet abiding by this Confucian precept does not mean a pledge to advance a democratic agenda. It simply means the Party leaders will avoid making grievous mistakes—such as the Cultural Revolution—that will turn the people against them.

Upon his induction to the PBSC at the Seventeenth Party Congress in 2007, Xi coined a new slogan regarding the relationship between the Party and the people: "Power [of the ruling Party] is entrusted by the people." This was an addition to a similar set of slogans first made famous by ex-president Hu not long after assuming power at the Sixteenth Party Congress: "Power should be exercised for the sake of the people, [cadres'] feelings should be tied to the people; profits should be sought on behalf of the people."[175] The idea that power came from the people was expressed in his talk to students at the CPS in September 2010. Xi urged cadres studying at the elite institution to "establish the correct view on power so that they can hold power and use power well for the sake of the people." "The power in the hands of Party members and leading cadres comes from the people," he said. "The philosophy behind our ruling Party is that the Party is established for the common good, and we administer for the sake of the people."[176] The premise for

Xi's populist pronouncements seemed to be that the CCP, as China's "perennial ruling Party," has the right to go on exercising power for the sake of the people; there is, therefore, no need to adopt mechanisms such as periodic general elections to ensure that the people still support the CCP.

In his April 2008 article in *Seeking Truth,* Xi made reference to the development of democracy, including "democracy within the Party." He argued that "we must fully develop democracy so as to be able to uphold [the goal of] thought liberation." The then-vice-president went on to say that "we must diligently cultivate within the Party, particularly among the cadre corps, the environment and atmosphere that are conducive to thought liberation, reform, and innovation. . . . We must promote the construction of democracy within the Party under the spirit of reform and innovation."[177] How exactly should "democracy within the Party" be implemented? Xi vowed that the Party leadership would "earnestly respect the individuality and self-sufficiency [*zhutidiwei*] status of Party members"—that is, that Party members are individuals who should be allowed to make up their own minds. "We will perfect the Party congress system and reform the system of elections within the Party," he wrote. "We must expand the parameters of direct elections within grassroots Party organizations so as to boost the creativity, cohesiveness, and combat worthiness of Party organizations." He also suggested using "democratic and open" methods of competition, examination, and selection to identify talents for the Party. At the same time, however, the then-vice-president vowed to "boost the construction of democratic centralism within Party committees."[178] "Democratic centralism" is a Leninist code word for the fact that while Party members have the right to air their views, the final decisions must be made by the top Party leadership.

It is notable that the call for "intra-Party democracy" was first made by ex-president Hu on the eve of the Seventeenth Party Congress. Hu's logic was that if democratic principles were fully developed within the Party of 85 million members—the elite of Chinese society—then the democratic spirit could gradually spread throughout the country.[179] In the early 2000s, experiments were conducted to allow Party members in towns and townships—which are just below the level of the county—to cast ballots to pick the town or township Party secretaries. However, no new experiments in elections have been contemplated since the mid-2000s. Moreover, Hu tried to invest substantial powers in different levels of the Party congress, which, according to the CCP constitution, is the highest-level decision-making body of the Party. The powers of Party congresses—especially the national Party congress—were largely removed by Mao Zedong, such that the only function of the national Party congress since the 1960s has consisted in electing the new Central Committee every five years. Hu raised the possibility that national Party congresses should be "institutionalized," meaning that they should meet at least once a year and that they should perform the function of supervising the work of the Central Committee and the Politburo. Experiments in the institutionalization of Party congresses were made in a few hundred counties, where local Party congresses meet every year to assess the performance of county Party committees.[180]

When he was Party secretary of Zhejiang, Xi made vague references to experiments regarding the revival and institutionalization of county-level Party congresses in his province. However, no efforts to broaden these experiments in institutional innovations have been made since Xi became Party chief in late 2012.[181]

## Constitutionalism and the Rule of Law

When he was Party secretary of Zhejiang Province from 2002 to 2007, Xi revealed his interest in rule of law with Chinese characteristics in the course of a dinner hosted by then U.S. ambassador to China Clark Randt. According to snippets of the conversation as revealed by Wikileaks, Xi told his host that his administration had proposed to central authorities a plan to make Zhejiang into "a province ruled by law" by 2006. "Laws are a basis for the socialist market economy," Xi reportedly said. "Provincial officials will promote public awareness of laws and do their best to enhance enforcement of laws." Xi added that the provincial people's congress would combine laws passed at the national level by the NPC with Zhejiang's local conditions. "The government and the Party will promote rule of law," Xi said.[182]

Since the Eighteenth Party Congress, on two occasions Xi has expressed views that could be construed as supportive of some form of rule of law. At a Politburo study session in early 2013, he underscored what Western analysts call rule by law with Chinese characteristics. "We must push forward scientific law-making in a comprehensive manner," he said. "We must seriously implement the law." "There must be a fair judicial system, and all citizens must abide by the law," Xi added. "We must insist on the simultaneous implementation of running the country according to law, [conducting] politics according to law, and [ensuring] public administration according to law." He noted that "all organizations and individuals must conduct themselves within the parameters of the law." It was made clear, however, that what Xi was referring to was "socialist rule by law." As he indicated, "we must uphold the unity, dignity, and authority of the socialist legal system." In the CCP tradition, a socialist legal system is different from a capitalist one because in the former, the Party controls the legislature and the courts.[183]

On the thirtieth anniversary of the promulgation of the 1982 Chinese constitution, Xi also made a solemn pledge regarding the imperative of upholding the constitution. "We must closely follow the principles of the constitution, propagate the spirit of the constitution and implement the mission of the constitution," he said. "No organization or individual has the special privilege of overriding the constitution and the law," he added. "All actions that run counter to the constitution and the law must be held to account." While this seemed a declaration of unreserved abidance by the rule of law, it is clear that the Fifth-Generation leader viewed the constitution as having crystallized the "will of the Party and the people." "Safeguarding the authority of the constitution means safeguarding the authority of the joint will of the Party and the people," he said. Xi added that the constitution had "endorsed the theoretical system of socialism with Chinese characteristics."[184] In other words, following the constitution—which, after all, lays down in its preamble that the people must observe "the leadership of the CCP and the guidance of Marxism-Leninism, Mao Zedong Thought, and Deng Xiaoping Theory"—means not straying from Party directives and the tenets of socialism with Chinese characteristics.[185]

Liberal intellectuals have urged the Xi administration to live up to its pledge of *xianzheng* (constitutional governance) by ensuring that all political organizations conduct themselves within the parameters of the constitution. Writing in response to Xi's statement, the retired liberal cadre Hu Deping argued that China should gradually adopt some form of tripartite division of power. "The authority of legislation, administration and the judiciary should be substantiated and legitimized under the constitution," he wrote. He added that *xianzheng* manifested itself in "administration according to the constitution, [undertaking] judicial procedures according to the constitution, and making laws according to the constitution."[186]

However, conservative commissars and ideologues responded with a rash of articles saying that the very idea of "constitutional governance" was a bourgeois-liberal concoction that applied only to capitalist countries. Writing in the official journal *Party Construction,* the theoretician Zheng Zhixue pointed out the ideal of constitutional governance was a plot to "sabotage the socialist regime in China." Zheng claimed that "constitutional governance," or "constitutionalism," was a distinctly capitalist concept that did not apply in China. "The goal of *xianzheng* is very clear," Zheng wrote. "It is to abolish the leadership of the Communist Party and to subvert the socialist regime."[187] In August 2013, *People's Daily* Overseas Edition ran articles on three days bashing the idea of "constitutional governance." The three pieces were titled "The Essence of *Xianzheng* Is a Weapon for Propaganda Warfare"; "The Name of American-Style *Xianzheng* Does Not Match Reality: It Is Not Compatible with Socialism"; and "Implementing So-Called *Xianzheng* in China Is Like Trying to Find Fish up a Tree." In one of the articles, Ma Zhongcheng, a CASS scholar, asserted that *xianzheng* was a propaganda tool that the United States sought to use to "globalize American liberal economics and legal system." "If socialist countries adopt American-style constitutional governance, this will open up the way for the capitalist class to take over political power," Ma wrote.[188] It seems clear that these conservative views were consistent with the mainstream opinion of the Party as well as the instructions of the Xi-led Politburo.

### Feeble Efforts in Judicial Reforms

To the surprise of many observers, the Decision of the third plenum of the Central Committee of late 2013 contained several weighty paragraphs on judicial and related reforms. The Central Committee document pledged that the authorities would "guarantee that judicial powers and prosecutorial powers are exercised according to the law, independently and fairly." The Party also committed itself "to reform judicial management systems, to promote the unified management of human resources in courts and procuratorates at the provincial and lower levels, to explore the establishment of judicial jurisdiction systems that are suitably separated from administrative areas, and to guarantee the uniform and correct implementation of state laws." The Decision made it clear, however, that the Party's goal is to put together a "high-efficiency and authoritative socialist judicial system," that is, one that upholds the values of socialism with Chinese characteristics.[189]

A number of specific reformist measures were introduced, and some of them were speedily implemented. For example, the much-maligned *laojiao* ("reform through labor" system, which allows the police to lock up suspects for up to four years) was officially abolished on January 1, 2014. However, in provinces like populous Henan, other penal institutions administered by the police such as "discipline and education centers" for petitioners still flourish.[190] Torture as a means of soliciting confessions was supposedly abolished. The number of crimes subject to the death penalty has also been reduced. By 2017 judges and prosecutors below the provincial level are supposed to be appointed by provincial courts and procuratorates—not by the local Party secretaries. Local courts and procuratorates are also due to be funded by provincial-level judicial and procuratorial authorities. Because the salaries of county and municipal judges and prosecutors are paid by Party and administrative agencies at the same level, the latter are often in a position to exert political control over the judicial system.[191]

The most crucial factor affecting whether judicial fairness can be assured, however, remains freedom of interference from powerful Party agencies such as the Party's CPLC—and the superagency CNSC set up at the third plenum of the Central Committee in November 2013 (see below). Since the early 1980s, the CPLC, which reports directly to the PBSC, has assumed ultimate control over the police, the prosecutor's offices, and the courts.[192] This is the case despite the fact that following the retirement and political demise of former CPLC secretary Zhou Yongkang—and the reduction in the membership of the PBSC from seven to five— the CPLC chief appointed at the Eighteenth Party Congress, Meng Jianzhu, is an ordinary Politburo member. A former minister of public security and Party secretary of Jiangxi Province, Meng is a member of the Shanghai Faction consequent to his long years of service in the East Chinese metropolis. It is significant that because of the overwhelmingly negative perception of the CPLC under Zhou, the Xi leadership has tried to revamp the mammoth *zhengfa* (political-legal) establishment.[193] One significant structural reform was that many provincial or municipal *zhengfa* secretaries no longer assume the additional role of head of police. In 2010, the *zhengfa* secretary doubled as the local police chief in fourteen provinces. As of late 2013, this overlapping of roles continued only in Hebei, Hunan, Gansu, and Ningxia.[194] This development could result in some form of checks and balances between regional-level heads of police, on the one hand, and *zhengfa* functionaries, on the other.

More significantly, Meng stated on different occasions since taking office in late 2012 that the CPLC would not tamper with judicial procedures. For example, Meng indicated at a nationwide meeting of law-enforcement officials in early 2013 that the CPLC would not interfere with individual cases and that procuratorial and judicial offices would be given full independence in enforcing the law. "China is a big country with 1.3 billion people," Meng pointed out. "The most fundamental guarantee of clean governance, social equality, and stability is the rule of law."[195] Reuters cited two senior law professors in Beijing on the fact that an internal regulation had been drafted by the CPLC to reduce "coordination"—meaning judges consulting with the CPLC and other Party agencies—in the process of adjudication. Peking University law professor Jiang Ming'an quoted Meng as saying in an internal meeting that "officials are not allowed to intervene in specific [court] cases."[196]

It is difficult to imagine the Party's not meddling in the judicial apparatus, which is an integral part of the *zhengfa* system. As Minister of State Security Geng Huichang put it in an early 2014 speech on upholding state security in the new era, "the *zhengfa* front must unequivocally safeguard Party leadership." Following Xi's—and Mao's—insistence that all aspects of administration must demonstrate *dangxing* (Party nature), Geng asked cadres in the political-legal field to "tightly grasp the clear-cut political nature and orientation of *zhengfa* work . . . and to maintain a high level of unison in thought, politics and actions with Party central authorities with comrade Xi Jinping as general secretary."[197]

Indeed, the tendency of the CCP to continue its interference particularly in politically sensitive judicial proceedings seems clear. Take, for example, the sensational case of Bo Xilai. Beijing touted the trial of the princeling as evidence of an increase in government transparency in general and rule of law in particular. "The Bo trial underscores China's resolve for rule of law," a Xinhua commentary stated, citing the microblog live feed provided to the public during the five-day court proceedings. *Guangming Daily* claimed that the Bo trial had showcased "a judicial system that is in the sunshine." "The new central leadership collective is self-consciously [implementing] rule of law and anti-corruption measures," the official newspaper said.[198]

As discussed above, the way in which the Bo trial was conducted seems consistent with a long-standing convention that senior politicians are subjected to punishment primarily because they are losers in high-level factional intrigue. And despite the availability of a microblog live feed, the five-day court proceedings as well as the announcement of the verdict were less transparent than official media made them out to be. For example, sensitive statements made by Bo—that he did not covet the position of prime minister and did not aspire to be "China's Putin"—were not released to the public. Moreover, Bo's protest when he heard the guilty verdict and the sentence of life imprisonment —"The trial is unjust and unfair; the verdict is not based on facts"—was also excised from the live blog.[199] By contrast, long video segments of the trial of the Gang of Four in 1980 and 1981 were broadcast on CCTV, including Jiang Qing's frontal challenge to the authority of the law as well as the legitimacy of the Deng Xiaoping administration.[200]

The Party's dominance over the due process of law is also evidenced by the large number of lawyers—especially rights-defense lawyers—who have been detained and prosecuted. In the year ending March 2014, at least 100 lawyers and NGO activists were harassed or arrested for reasons ranging from publicly supporting "constitutionalism" to defending dissidents. In July 2013 alone, some forty-four lawyers were beaten up or otherwise stopped by police and other security officials from routine operations such as meeting their clients. The incarcerated lawyers included Xi Zhiyong, an internationally recognized legal scholar and activist who had been at the forefront of expanding the watchdog function of China's inchoate civil society.[201]

However, cautious optimism about the improvement of particular areas of the judicial system was expressed when the former Party secretary of Hunan, Zhou Qiang, was appointed president of the SPC in March 2008. A master's of law gradu-ate from the respected Southwest University of Politics and Law, Zhou worked at the Ministry of Justice from 1989 to 1995 before joining the CYL. Considered a protégé of ex-president Hu Jintao, Zhou was at one point seen as a possible suc-cessor to Xi Jinping.[202] While Zhou's appointment as the equivalent of China's chief justice sidetracked him from promotion in the Party-state apparatus, it was welcomed by intellectuals who were highly critical of his immediate predecessor, Wang Shengjun. A former police officer with neither a law degree nor experience in the judicial system, Wang repeatedly urged the country's judges to follow Party edicts regarding the "scientific theory of development" and to place the highest priority on fostering a "harmonious society."[203]

After taking office, Zhou lost no time in trying to raise the low esteem with which the judiciary is held inside and outside China. "Transparency is our general principle—and nontransparency an exception," Zhou said at a conference of se-nior judges in July 2013. He added that the courts would uphold the law with the utmost vigor and that judicial fairness would be safeguarded. "We must ensure that every case is judged well, and particular attention will be paid to complex, controversial, and sensitive cases," he indicated. "Even if the courts make only one misjudgment out of 10,000 cases, this will result in 100 percent of injustice for the people involved," he added. Moreover, Zhou even made an oblique reference to "independence of the courts." "The people's courts will go about their adjudication independently and fairly in accordance with the law," he said.[204]

It is significant that Zhou often left out "guidance of the Party" in his pub-lic speeches. This was in sharp contrast to his predecessor, who often cited the "principle of the three priorities"—namely, that judges and judicial cadres should make their three priorities "the Party's enterprise, the interests of the people, and the constitution and the law." The precept of the three priorities, which subsumed the constitution and the law under the Party's interests, was first laid down by ex-president Hu in a nationwide conference of cadres in the political-legal apparatus in late 2007.[205]

Apart from the traditional issue of the Party dominating law enforcement, the judiciary has suffered from the dearth of qualified professional judges. The qualifications and aptitude of many regional-level judges appear questionable. Among the presidents of the people's high courts in China's major administrative districts, only eleven have degrees from law schools. Thirteen top regional judges boast diplomas from Party schools of different levels—but not degrees from fully fledged universities. Only one of them, Ma Xinfeng, the president of the Fujian People's High Court, has a designation as a lawyer. In terms of professional background, only ten have risen through the ranks of the judiciary. Two each used to work in the procuratorate and political-legal commissions, and three are former police officers. The other top local judges come from a variety of backgrounds. For example, four are former cadres in regional-level Party or government departments, four were specialists in "work with the masses," and two were senior railway staff.[206]

According to President Xi, "running the country according to law" and a fair judicial system are integral to the realization of the "Chinese Dream." As the *Procuratorial Daily* pointed out in an early 2014 commentary, "a just legal and judicial system provides a strong guarantee [for the attainment] of the Chinese Dream." "We must expand democracy within the judicial system," the official paper indicated. "We must advance judicial transparency and raise the [professional] ability of the judiciary."[207] The wide gulf between what the likes of Zhou Qiang, Meng Jianzhu, and President Xi have promised in terms of legal and judicial reform and the harsh reality seems to suggest that what the Xi leadership is interested in is not reform itself but tighter control of the legal-political apparatus now that Zhou Yongkang and his cronies have been elbowed aside. There is, after all, a long tradition of a CCP faction on the ascendancy—in this case Xi and his coterie of loyalists—getting rid of its opponents—in this instance, Bo and Zhou—in the name of high-sounding principles such as social justice and judicial fairness.

### The Xi Administration's Quasi-Police State Apparatus

#### The Role of the Central National Security Commission (CNSC)

The CNSC was set up at the third plenum of the Central Committee in November 2012 to uphold national security on both the domestic and foreign fronts. As President Xi noted at the plenum, "China is facing two pressures: internationally, the country needs to safeguard its sovereignty, security, and development interests; domestically, political security and social stability should be ensured." Xi noted that in view of the fact that "the variety of predictable and unpredictable risks has been increasing markedly; a powerful platform that can coordinate security-related work is needed." The main responsibilities of the national security commission include formulating and implementing national security strategies, assembling legal systems concerning state security, and conducting research as well as resolving major issues of national security.[208]

Although the CNSC shares its name in Chinese with the U.S. National Security Council, it is believed to be focused primarily on internal security, including ways to defuse challenges posed by "hostile anti-China forces from abroad." Within the Party's highest echelons, there are already two units—the Central Leading Group on Foreign Affairs and the less visible Central Leading Group on National Security—that perform coordinating roles like those of the U.S. NSC.[209] Given the CCP's long-standing belief that many destabilizing agents in China are abetted by "hostile foreign countries"—which seem bent on subverting the socialist system via mechanisms such as "color revolutions" or "peaceful evolution"—one of the CNSC's major objectives is to combat efforts by these "hostile countries" to infiltrate the country. This was best illustrated in the 2013 PLA video *Silent Contest,* whose main thrust was that the United States was trying to sabotage CCP rule under the guise of cultural exchange and other forms of engagement.[210]

More details of the CNSC's priorities were made public at its first meeting, held April 15, 2014. Commission chairman Xi indicated that his administration would devote the maximum resources toward maintaining state security in the following areas: politics, territory, military, economy, culture, society, science and technology, information, ecology, resources-related security, and nuclear power. "Upholding national security is of utmost importance in consolidating the Party's ruling status," said Xi. Although *weiwen* (preserving stability) has been a central concern to the CCP the past decade or so, Xi has argued that his new concept of *zongti guojiaanquan* (overall national security or mega-security) is a "road [map] for national security with Chinese characteristics" that will meet the growing challenges of the twenty-first century.[211]

What is new about "overall national security"? First, the CNSC takes a holistic and all-embracing approach to different aspects of security. As Xi put it, Beijing would "pay utmost attention to both external and internal security; territorial security as well as citizens' security; traditional and nontraditional security." Moreover, Xi added, the authorities would strike a balance between "the question of development and that of security." "The security of not only individual [citizens and units] but also the collective will be safeguarded," Xi added.[212]

As of mid-2014, the constituent units whose top representatives are sitting on the CNSC have not been announced. Semiofficial Chinese media, however, have cited the following agencies as having representation on the superagency: the PLA, the PAP, the Ministry of Foreign Affairs (MOFA), the MPS, the MSS, the Ministry of Trade, the CCP Department of Propaganda, and the CCP International Liaison Department (ILD). Cadres responsible for Tibet and Xinjiang will be represented. Given that the CNSC's interests include Taiwan and Hong Kong, the Taiwan Affairs Office and the Hong Kong and Macau Affairs Office—which are ministerial offices under the State Council—will have a presence in the commission.[213]

Foreign Ministry spokesman Qin Gang linked the CNSC to China's campaign against the "three evil forces," saying that the commission "will make terrorists, separatists, and religious extremists very nervous." The three evil forces are a crossover between foreign and domestic security concerns, usually described as sources of domestic instability caused by the "infiltration" of other countries or nonstate groups.[214] According to Li Wei, head of the Anti-Terrorism Research Center at the China Institute of Contemporary International Relations, the CNSC is "geared toward handling the increasing number of major incidents and mishaps that will impinge upon our country's security and interests." Li indicated that the CNSC's concerns included nontraditional security issues including economic and financial security, environmental safety, terrorism, and piracy.[215]

As the *Global Times* pointed out, "Social transformation has resulted in a profusion of contradictions within China." "Foreign forces are increasingly keen to challenge China by exploiting our internal problems—and their levers for doing so have become more numerous," the Party mouthpiece added. The paper cited as an example the growing number of incidents involving ethnic minorities, "which have turned ugly owing to China's radically changed external environment."[216] Given the leadership's growing awareness of what the *Global Times* calls "the megaconcept of security," the Party's long-standing organ for maintaining security—the Party's Central Political-Legal Commission, which is in charge of the police, the prosecutor's office, and the courts—seems to lack the requisite resources to cover all aspects of national security.

Quite a few liberal intellectuals are alarmed by the CNSC's apparent similarity to the all-powerful internal-security units in the Soviet Union. According to the economist Xia Yeliang, a former Peking University professor and noted public intellectual, "the authorities are very worried about stability despite the apparent achievements in economic development." "The CNSC will make better use of the military, the PAP, spies, and even anti-corruption agents to promote internal security," he told foreign media. "There are parallels between the CNSC and the KGB [in the Soviet Union]."[217] The internationally well-known dissident Hu Jia noted that the CNSC was a "much-strengthened version of the Central Political-Legal Commission." "The spirit of the KGB is alive and well in China," he asserted. The Beijing-based human-rights lawyer Liu Xiaoyuan asked this rhetorical question: "The CCP has set up the CNSC to preserve state security, but can we set up a people's security commission to safeguard the security of the people?"[218]

*A Labyrinthine Security Apparatus*

With respect to its domestic stability agenda, the CNSC is overseeing—and expanding—a labyrinthine *weiwen* apparatus that was put together by the Hu–Wen administration from 2002 to 2012. Since 2012, China's public security-related expenditure has exceeded the publicized budget of the PLA. The Finance Ministry budgeted RMB 850 billion for *weiwen* purposes in 2014, while the official PLA expenditure was only RMB 808.2 billion.[219]

When he was public security minister, Meng Jianzhu vowed that Beijing's goal was to construct a *fangkong* (prevention-and-control) grid that is "multidimensional, all-weather, and foolproof." Meng referred to several layers of anti-infiltration and anti-subversion networks: those based in streets and communities; internal security and anti-sabotage units in every government office, college, and commercial firm; CCTV and surveillance mechanisms, especially in big cities; coordination networks among security-related units in each province and region; and Internet-surveillance facilities.[220] For example, 2 million surveillance cameras were installed in the prosperous Pearl River Delta to target ordinary criminals, dissidents, foreign spies, and members of underground religious groups.[221]

Big and medium-size cities are setting up local-level State Security Leading Groups (SSLG), which will be headed by municipal Party secretaries. These leading groups set the agenda for police and security departments and ensure that enough vigilantes and voluntary informants can be recruited from the populace. SSLGs can also ask other government units to contribute funds and resources to help maintain overall stability. Smaller cities and county-level administrations are setting up big-brother units to ensure stability, called Offices to Maintain Social Stability and to Rectify Law and Order (OMSS).[222] In rich coastal cities, such organizations are being established in every district and on every major street. According to the official media, these groups are charged with ferreting out "anti-CCP elements" and "nipping all destabilizing forces in the bud." A key mandate of the OMSSs is to "get a firm grip on the activities of hostile forces within and outside China," particularly foreign NGOs and religious organizations that are seen as potential sources of subversion and sabotage. The OMSSs are also authorized to "prevent hostile elements from fomenting chaos by inflaming hot-button issues" in Chinese society. They have the power to coordinate the efforts of the police, state-security agents, and PAP officers to combat "anti-government forces"—and to recruit vigilantes and voluntary informants within their jurisdictions.[223]

The authorities have invoked Mao's people's warfare concept in an effort to defuse threats to state security and stability. The SSLGs and OMSSs are only the latest additions to a mazelike state-security apparatus that employs several million full-time police and spies and many more part-time informants. Since mid-2008, municipalities nationwide have been asked to emulate Beijing's security measures during the Olympics, when the city mobilized more than 1.5 million vigilantes and informants to safeguard security. Moreover, police and state-security agents in increasing numbers of cities are conducting regular training and operations in conjunction with private security staff employed by companies, factories, and universities.[224] Human rights organizations were shocked by the ubiquitous network of informants throughout China. In 2010, the police chief of Kailu County, Inner Mongolia, told the official media that he had recruited one of every thirty-three local residents as a part-time informant. Moreover, 12,093 of the county's 400,000 inhabitants are tasked with providing intelligence to the police if they become aware of suspicious characters—or destabilizing "plots"—that could jeopardize law and order.[225]

## Intensified Crackdown on the Internet

The Xi administration has upped the ante in enforcing control over the Internet, which conservatives regard as a potent threat to state security. In his now-famous August 19, 2013, speech on ideology and propaganda, Xi pointed out that "control over the Internet is a matter of life and death for the Party." Six months later, Xi established the Central Leading Group on Internet Security and Informatization (CLGISI) and became its head. The CLGISI takes charge of existing offices on Internet censorship and development of the IT industry such as the State Internet Information Office, the cyberpolice division of the Ministry of Public Security (MPS), and the Ministry of Industry and Information Technology.[226]

"No Internet safety means no national security," Xi pointed out in the inaugural meeting of the Leading Group, whose two deputy-heads are Premier Li Keqiang and PBSC member in charge of ideology and propaganda Liu Yunshan. "Cyberspace should be made clean," Xi stated, adding that "we should be fully aware of the importance and urgency of Internet security and informatization." China has to balance its need for developing information technologies (IT) and safeguarding Internet security, the president said, describing the two issues as "two wings of a bird and two wheels of an engine." By the end of 2013, China had 618 million Internet users, and the netizen population is projected to grow at 10 percent every year in the foreseeable future.[227]

Xinhua quoted Xi as calling for innovative methods to spread "discipline and mainstream values" and to stimulate positive energy while maintaining proper guidance of online opinions in terms of timing, intensity, and impact. Laws and regulations would be drawn up to "perfect Internet information content management," to help manage cyberspace, and to protect people's legal rights, he said. In 2013, the Xi administration introduced tougher measures to police the Internet. For example, the State Council passed a regulation that threatened legal action against netizens who spread rumors on microblogs such as Sina Weibo that are reposted more than 500 times or seen by more than 5,000 people.[228]

Even more draconian is the policy of targeting "Big Vs," Internet-based opinion leaders who boast at least 100,000 registered fans. They include controversial writers, businessmen, and professionals whose sharp views on social and political issues are often regarded by CCP censors as destabilizing or outright seditious. According to the 2014 *Blue Book on Social Development Trends* published by CASS, 300 Big Vs have dominated the microblog, and these opinion leaders could be more influential over the public than the official media.[229] In 2013, several Big Vs—the Chinese-American investor Charles Biqun Xue (aka Xue Manzi), the IT mogul Wang Gongquan, environmentalist Dong Xuejie, and Internet marketing whiz Yang Xiuyu and Qin Zhihui (Qin Huohuo)—were detained by the police for crimes including "disturbing the public order," "creating disturbances," illegal business activities, and spreading rumors. For example, Xue, whose blog has gained more than 10 million followers, was detained by the police in August 2013 for allegedly soliciting prostitutes. His supposed "confession" about "being addicted to prostitution" was aired on CCTV in an apparent attempt to smear his reputation. Xue was granted bail for medical reasons in April 2014 with the understanding that he might be detained again if he were to pose a threat to political stability. At the same time, however, Qin Zhihui was given a three-year jail term by a Beijing court for defamation and spreading rumors.[230]

Apart from enhanced scrutiny to rid the information superhighway of destabilizing elements, the CLGISI is expected to roll out new measures against hacking and "Internet-based terrorism." Claiming that China is a major victim of Internet sabotage, the authorities alleged that in 2013, hackers tampered with 16,388 Web pages in China—including 1,802 government Web sites—6.1 percent and 21.4 percent a year more than those of 2012, respectively.[231] Another major concern of the Internet police is fighting "Internet-based terrorism." In 2013 and 2014 alleged terrorist incidents by Uighurs flared up (see below), culminating in the Kunming Railway Station incident on March 1, 2014, in which twenty-nine civilians (as well as four perpetrators) were killed and more than 140 others were injured. The *Global Times* cited Li Wei, from the China Institute on Contemporary International Relations, as saying that "the importance of the Internet in terrorism activities has risen." "The Internet has become a convenient propaganda tool for extremist ideas," said Li. "It has raised the efficiency of spreading terrorist ideas in both speed and territorial coverage."[232]

In general, Xi's views on the Internet—and the control over news dissemination in general—does not depart from the classic CCP notion that information is a weapon that must be wielded by the state. After becoming general secretary, Xi has repeatedly called on Party and government offices handling the media to "deeply promote propaganda and education on socialism with Chinese characteristics, so that people of all nationalities can unite under the great flag of Chinese-style socialism." "We must strengthen [public education] on socialist core values," he noted in late 2013. "We must inculcate a superior atmosphere of positive values that places importance on devotion [to the Party] and fostering harmony."[233] *Seeking Truth* was even more straightforward. It said in a commentary at about the same time that "at this stage, China cannot sustain the consequence of the loss of control over public opinion."[234]

*No Evidence of Improvement in Law and Order*

Despite the fact that Xi Jinping—as well as the millions of cadres and law-enforcement officers working under the CNSC and the CPLC—has pulled out all the stops to foster "overall national security," there is no evidence that law and order has improved. Most estimates put the annual number of "mass incidents" (i.e., incidents ranging from riots and protests to mass killings) at between 150,000 and 180,000 in the early 2010s, up from 90,000 in 2006.[235] Moreover, instances of Chinese committing bloody rampages by using homemade bombs or, more frequently, cleavers and long knives, have been on the rise. These horrible acts are often perpetrated by disaffected elements of society that want to vent their frustrations on an authoritarian regime that has failed to carry out ex-president Hu's dictum about creating "harmonious society"—and Xi's instructions about "mediating and defusing social contradictions."[236]

The increasingly frequent and violent incidents attributed to members of the Uighur ethnic minority both inside and outside the Xinjiang Uighur Administration Region (XUAR) testify to the fact that Xi's strong-armed tactics to impose stability do not seem to be working. Killing sprees committed by Uighurs include the one at the Kunming Railway Station mentioned above and the bombing incident in downtown Urumqi two months later, which killed forty-three people and wounded ninety-four others, mostly local residents. That underground anti-Beijing groups were becoming more defiant was demonstrated by a blast at the Urumqi Railway Station on April 30, just a few hours after Xi and the largest civilian and military delegation in recent memory had finished a four-day inspection tour of the region that was meant to strike fear into the hearts of the exemplars of the three evil forces. That attack killed three people and wounded seventy-nine others.[237]

As in the past, Beijing has blamed all "violent and terrorist acts" perpetrated by Uighurs on separatists and jihadists who are being aided by the East Turkestan Islamic Movement and other "anti-China foreign forces."[238] Independent analysts of the Xinjiang situation in both China and the West, however, think that a large percentage of these incidents are not committed by separatists or religious extremists. They are a reaction against decades of suppression of cultural, linguistic, and, in particular, religious freedom in the XUAR, where Uighurs make up only 41.5 percent of the population of 21 million. According to Human Rights Watch Xinjiang expert Nicholas Bequelin, "the relationship between the Uighurs and the Han [Chinese] is best described as a relationship between the colonized and the colonizer. . . . Repression is always inbuilt into [Beijing's] Xinjiang policy."[239]

Since 2009, central and provincial authorities have boosted investments in the XUAR, ostensibly to boost employment and social welfare benefits. Yet many locals fear that these economic inducements are a front for "Sinicizing" Xinjiang. The rate of improvement of the living standards of ordinary Uighurs has fallen behind that of Han Chinese working in the region. Moreover, Beijing has imposed tight control over cultural and religious activities. Mosques in the XUAR are under heavy police surveillance; many Uighurs are not allowed to observe religious holidays such as Ramadan. According to Peking University law professor He Weifang, who worked in Xinjiang, Beijing's policy of "*weiwen* above all has led to a delay in solving problems such as contradictions between the Uighurs and the Han Chinese. . . . The result is that the tougher *weiwen* policies get, the more unstable the situation becomes."[240] Yet perhaps the worst part of the new "total national security" concept is that Beijing has cut off the voices of the moderate Uighur intellectuals who want to act as a bridge between the CCP authorities and ordinary Uighurs. A case in point was the incarceration in early 2014 of Ilham Tohti, a Beijing-based economics professor who had tried to promote Uighur-Han dialogue by, for example, hosting an Internet discussion platform. Tohti was sentenced to life imprisonment in September 2014 for alleged separatist activities. The harshness of the sentence drew criticisms from the American and EU authorities.[241]

A similar pattern of explosive unease can be found in the TAR and Tibetan counties in neighboring provinces such as Qinghai, Sichuan, and Gansu. The only difference is that Tibetans—particularly Buddhist monks and nuns who are victims of religious suppression—have largely chosen to vent their anger and frustration by burning themselves to death. CCP spokespeople, however, have labeled the more than 120 instances of self-immolation since 2009 as "acts of religious terrorism." The official media have accused the "Dalai Lama clique" of goading poor and young Tibetans to commit these acts of political protest. "It is brutal and terrorist behavior to incite young Tibetans" to self-immolate, said *China Daily*. Qin Feng, a commentator for the official China Tibet Net, contended that "instigating others to self-immolate" was a "violent and evil terrorist act."[242] In early 2013, eight Tibetans in the Sichuan district of Aba were given stiff punishments, even including the death sentence, for "instigating" a number of self-immolators.[243]

In Tibet, Xinjiang, and other places, then, President Xi seems to have abandoned the largely placatory policies that liberal Party elders including Hu Yanbang and his father, Xi Zhongxun, had used to improve Han Chinese relations with Uighurs and Tibetans.[244] It is probably not a stretch to argue that cadres running the CNSC, the CPLC, and other offices within China's gargantuan *weiwen* establishment are applying throughout the land essentially the same brand of oppressive, "stability-above-all-else" strictures that have spawned so much global opprobrium in Xinjiang and Tibet. After all, what Han Chinese and ethnic minorities alike are asking for are universal rights such as social justice, rule of law, equal opportunity, and freedom of religion and of expression.

## Conclusion: Holding Down the Fort vs. Ringing in the New

### *The Myth of Sisyphus with Chinese Characteristics*

In one of his many homilies about the art of governance, Xi had this to say about leadership. "A superb leader is steeped in the art of leadership," he wrote in a 2003 article in *Zhejiang Daily*. "He knows when to take which step. . . . He has a grasp of the laws and rhythms; he can lift a heavy object as though it were light." First-rate leaders, Xi went on, were capable of "creating things where none used to exist and solving problems before they get out of control." Xi also had this to say about second-rate but still passable cadres, namely, those who are diligent and self-sacrificing and "who make up in diligence what they lack in wisdom." The then-Party secretary of Zhejiang, however, was dismissive about third-rate cadres:

"They are slow to see things, and they react slowly. They are incapable of forestalling mishaps. And even if problems have arisen, they are either at their wits' end, or they just pretend that nothing has happened."[245]

Despite his lack of rigorous academic training and relatively limited exposure to modern political theories and practices, Xi has a very good understanding of Chinese reality. He grasps the problems that the CCP faces—and he certainly cannot be accused of "pretending that nothing has happened." However, the important thing is: Can he think outside the box and "create things where none used to exist"? "Can he lift a heavy object as though it were light?" So far, Xi's innovation in governance has consisted of getting into shape institutions such as the CLGCDR, the CNSC, and the CLGISI, all of which have tightened Xi's stranglehold on power at the expense of adding multiple layers of bureaucracy to the already-cumbersome Party-state apparatus.

There is, unfortunately, no indication that Xi is using his extra powers to promote novel ideas about reform. Using Xi's metaphor about how leaders deal with heavy burdens, it could perhaps be said that, somewhat like Sisyphus, senior CCP cadres are condemned to bear the baggage of more than sixty-five years of Party rule: There seems to be a severe deficit in ideas about how to ring in the new. On the one hand, there is a refusal to admit and recognize past mistakes: the June 4, 1989, crackdown seems to have been wiped out through Beijing-imposed collective amnesia; Party officials are still reluctant to face up to either the calamitous mistakes made by Chairman Mao or the lack of institutional checks and balances that made these blunders possible. Even more devastating is the Xi administration's refusal to consider solutions that smack of "international norms"—which Beijing has dismissed as "Western" or "American-led"—in order to solve the country's deep-seated problems.

Xi's paranoia about the sudden implosion of the Party or the obliteration of the mandate of heaven is well-known. Upon taking office, he lectured the Party faithful about avoiding the fate that befell the CPSU. As a well-read amateur historian, Xi on numerous occasions has also talked about the dynamics of dynastic cycles. In his speech on Mao's 120th birthday, Xi reiterated the Great Helmsman's warning: "We must never be another Li Zicheng." Li (1606–1645) was a peasant rebel leader who almost succeeded in overthrowing the Ming dynasty. After briefly capturing Beijing, however, Li's corrupt and dictatorial rule soon led to the demise of his short-lived empire.[246] So what should China do to reform? Again, Xi signaled his refusal to learn from global norms, saying that "if we were to merely follow others . . . we would definitely fail and become other people's subordinate vassal." Xi's solution is a kind of narcissistic self-perfectionism. "The Party must manage itself well and raise its administrative ability and leadership level," he said. "We must enhance the Party's [ability to] purify itself and to seek self-perfection, self-renewal, and self-resuscitation."[247]

In his two years in power, Xi has succeeded in seizing power to a much greater degree than either ex-president Jiang or ex-president Hu. As veteran Beijing-based scholar Chen Ziming pointed out: "Xi has tightened his grip on the reins of power. . . . .We still do not know enough about Xi to tell what he is about to do. . . . He can go down the road [of the reformist Taiwan president] Chiang Ching-kuo, or he could become another [Cambodian prime minister] Pol Pot."[248] The seminal problem with Xi and his conservative colleagues, however, is that "reform within a birdcage"—a reference to political and economic changes that will not jeopardize the CCP's near-total monopoly on power—will not get China very far. The result of "the modernization of social governance" with Chinese characteristics could be a vicious cycle of more repression fomenting more resistance. It is not a judicious way to bolster the Party's mandate of heaven.

### President Xi Compared to His Predecessors

Given that Xi's term as general secretary and commander-in-chief will last until late 2022 (and that of president until early 2013), it might be a bit premature to compare him with his predecessors. Yet several relatively radical ideas and policies of former presidents Jiang Zemin and Hu Jintao—as well as former premiers Zhu Rongji and Wen Jiabao—illustrate the kind of innovative if not unorthodox thinking that so far has eluded Xi.

Take, for instance, the decision by the Jiang administration (1989–2002) to radically revise Party dogma by allowing patriotic or otherwise exemplary members of classes other than workers and peasants to become members of the CCP, which, by definition, is the "vanguard of the proletariat." On July 1, 2001, the eightieth anniversary of the founding of the CCP, Jiang made the bold decision to allow private entrepreneurs—as well as members of the middle and professional classes—to be enrolled as CCP members. This measure, which clearly went against the cardinal tenets of Karl Marx, led to large protests within the CCP, particularly among its orthodox constituencies. Several thousand senior members of the CCP were reported to have threatened to resign from the Party.[249] In 1999, Jiang, together with ex-premier Zhu, made another unpopular decision: to speed up China's application for accession to the World Trade Organization (WTO) by making substantial trade concessions to the United States and other developed countries. Opposition to China's joining the WTO was intense within the ministries and in particular among provinces that were nervous about the influx of cheap—and superior—products from abroad. Most of the WTO-related negotiations between China and the United States were not released to the public. Then chief negotiator Long Yongtu—and premier Zhu—were subsequently labeled traitors by nationalistic Chinese.[250]

And then there were Wen Jiabao's many protestations of the imperative of political reform. Wen (b. 1942) was the only member of the Party elite to have repeatedly reminded the public that, as he said a year before leaving office, "economic reform can only go so far without commensurate political reform." "We cannot have thoroughgoing economic reform without achievements in political reform," Wen argued.[251] As we saw earlier, Wen, who had worked close to the two liberal icons of the Party—Hu Yaobang and Zhao Ziyang—was also the only Politburo-level cadre to have supported the introduction of *pushijiazhi* into China. It is true that for many reasons, including the fact that Wen's portfolio in the PBSC was economic policy and not ideology, "Grandpa Wen's" endorsement of relatively progressive ideas was strictly limited to rhetorical support. However, it took a lot of courage to go against the grain. And at least in internal meetings during the Hu Jintao era, Wen was a vocal opponent of efforts by careerists such as Bo Xilai to resuscitate Maoist norms.[252]

And how about ex-president Hu, who has been decried almost universally as the prime culprit for China's "ten lost years" (2002–12), when apparently no major initiatives were taken in various aspects of reform? Yet it cannot be denied that in the late 1990s, Hu did kick-start theoretical studies of possibly more liberal models toward which the CCP could evolve in the new century. Most of the brainstorming sessions were conducted behind closed doors at the CPS, of which Hu was president from 1998 to 2002. One of the topics hotly debated by CPS professors was whether the CCP could learn something from the social democratic parties in Western and Northern Europe. The CPS sent senior cadres and scholars to countries including Switzerland, Sweden, Norway, and Germany to study the creed and organizational principles of the social democratic parties in these countries.[253] Such studies encouraged several septuagenarian Party members—who used to work with Hu Yaobang and Zhao Ziyang—to think that it was not too early to give up hope for the liberal tendencies of the Hu-Wen administration. In the February 2007 issue of *Yanhuang chunqiu,* the theoretician Xie Tao published an article in which he argued that "only democratic socialism can save China," meaning that the CCP should adopt measures practiced by European countries such as Switzerland and those in Scandinavia.[254]

While there was no possibility that the CCP would evolve into a kind of a Chinese Social Democratic Party, Hu and his advisers thought that aspects of the social democratic model, ranging from values such as social justice to policies on social welfare, could help China's modernization under one-Party rule. Some of the ethos and practices underlying the social policies of Western European social democratic parties were incorporated in what Hu and ex-premier Wen called "the scientific outlook on development," especially the extension of medical and other social-welfare benefits from the cities to the countryside.[255]

Genealogy—and experience—however, is destiny. For cadres with a revolutionary bloodline, and particularly for princelings who maintain a proprietary mentality about power, it is very difficult to embark upon ventures that could change the color of the landscape. It is also important to note that Jiang and Zhu were able to make relatively bold departures due to their background. Both speak reasonably good English and know something about Western culture and mores. And both had spent long years handling foreign trade and talking to Western experts. By contrast, although Xi has some experience entertaining businessmen from Taiwan,

Hong Kong, and the West, he shares Mao's fondness for looking for solutions to modern-day problems by digging for analogies in the Chinese classics.

However, Xi the Maoist expert may have missed the intriguing conversation that the despot extraordinaire held with the liberal scholar Huang Yanpei, who was an authority on the rise and fall of dynasties. When he met Mao in Yan'an in 1945, Huang told him his views of Chinese history: "Some administrations that were vigorous and prosperous when they were on the upswing might collapse all of a sudden." "No regimes have been able to defy the dynastic cycle," Huang contended. To which Mao replied nonchalantly: "We have found a new road, which has enabled us to supersede the dynastic cycle." "This new road is democracy," Mao exclaimed. "The government dares not become lax if it is being supervised by the people. If everybody can play a responsible [role], the scenario of regime collapse can be avoided."[256] These and other grandiloquent promises made by Mao never came to pass. It is a pity that Xi's obsession with the superiority of the road, theories, and institutions of Chinese-style socialism, not to mention his fondness for unchecked power, have thus far prevented him from pursuing a new heaven and new earth.

**Notes**

1. For a discussion of Xi Jinping's use of words, see, for example, Cui Feng, "The eight characteristics of Xi Jinping's linguistic style," *People's Daily,* December 12, 2013, http://cpc.people.com.cn/pinglun/n/2013/1212/c241220-23825044.html. See also "Expert says Xi Jinping has a distinctive linguistic style that is suitable for profoundly explicating China's position," China News Service, March 26, 2013, www.chinanews.com/gn/2013/03-26/4676606.shtml.

2. Cited in "Brilliant quotations from Xi Jinping," CNTV News, June 5, 2013, http://news.cntv.cn/2013/06/05/ARTI1370433080862112.shtml. See also "Xi Jinping likes to use slang as well as quotations from Mao Zedong," *Ta Kung Pao* (Hong Kong), February 23, 2013, http://news.takungpao.com.hk/world/roll/2013-02/1454159.htm.

3. Cited in "Xi Jinping: We must ensure that our red heaven and earth will never change their color," CCTV News, July 13, 2013, http://news.sina.com.cn/c/2013-07-12/193327653764.shtml.

4. Cited in "Xi Jinping: Realizing the Chinese dream requires going down the China path," Xinhua News Agency, March 17, 2013, http://news.xinhuanet.com/2013lh/2013-03/17/c_115052693.htm.

5. For a discussion and interpretation of Xi's internal speech on the collapse of the Soviet party, see, for example, Chris Buckley, "Vows of change in China belie private warning," *New York Times,* February 15, 2013, www.nytimes.com/2013/02/15/world/asia/vowing-reform-chinas-leader-xi-jinping-airs-other-message-in-private.html?pagewanted=all&_r=0/; see also "Xi Jinping asks the CCP to beware of the lesson of the collapse of the Communist Party of the Soviet Union," BBC Chinese Service, February 16, 2013, www.bbc.co.uk/zhongwen/trad/china/2013/02/130216_china_xi_warning.shtml.

6. See "Xi Jinping: Ideological work is extremely important work for the party," Xinhua News Agency, August 20, 2013, http://news.sina.com.cn/c/2013-08-20/191028001307.shtml?from=hao123_news_index_paihang_news/.

7. For a discussion of how the two superagencies have helped Xi consolidate power, see, for example, Cary Huang, "How leading small groups help Xi Jinping and other party

leaders exert power," *South China Morning Post,* January 20, 2014, www.scmp.com/news/ china/article/1409118/how-leading-small-groups-help-xi-jinping-and-other-party-leaders- exert/; see also Jeremy Page, "China's President takes bigger security role," *Wall Street Journal,* January 24, 2014, http://online.wsj.com/news/articles/SB1000142405270230463 2204579340311352798346/.

8. For a discussion of how the formation of the three new central-level organs has added to Xi's powers, see, for example, Alice Miller, "How strong is Xi Jinping?" *China Leadership Monitor,* Hoover Institution, no. 43, 2014, http://media.hoover.org/sites/default/ files/documents/CLM43AM-2.pdf; see also Dexter Roberts, "China's president changes the rules, strengthens his hand," Bloomberg, February 27, 2014, www.businessweek.com/ articles/2014-02-27/chinas-president-xi-tightens-his-control-of-army-economy/; Paul Mozur, "China's Xi Jinping presides over Internet security committee," *Wall Street Journal,* February 28, 2014, www.theaustralian.com.au/business/wall-street-journal/chinas-xi-jinping-presides- over-internet-security-committee/story-fnay3ubk-1226840234654#/.

9. For a discussion of the composition of the Central Leading Group on Comprehensively Deepening Reforms, see, for example, "The name list of the Deepening Reforms Group has been revealed," *First Financial News* (Shanghai), March 10, 2014, http://news.163. com/api/14/0310/11/9MVLAPFO0001124J.html. See also "Composition of the Deepening Reforms Group revealed: Ma Kai, Wang Yang, and Zhou Xiaochuan are included," *Ta Kung Pao,* March 10, 2014, http://business.sohu.com/20140310/n396345762.shtml.

10. See "Li Zhanshu and Wang Huning are in charge of the general office of the National Security Commission and the Central Leading Group on Comprehensively Deepening Reforms," *Ta Kung Pao,* March 7, 2014, http://news.takungpao.com/2014lh/ article/2014-03/2330619.html.

11. For a discussion of Deng Xiaoping's concept of collective leadership, see, for example, Wang Chunxi, "Deng Xiaoping's contribution toward building a framework of central collective leadership system," *Party Archives,* no. 5 (2008), www.cnki.com.cn/Article/ CJFDTotal-DANG200805010.htm; see also Susan L. Shirk, *The Political Logic of Economic Reform in China* (Berkeley: University of California Press, 1993), pp. 70–91, 116–128.

12. See "Zhao Ziyang's political report to the Thirteenth Chinese Communist Party congress," *People's Daily,* October 25, 1987, http://cpc.people.com.cn/GB/64162/64168/645 66/65447/4526368.html. For a discussion of the evolution of the concept of the separation of party and government, see, for example, Shiping Zheng, *Party vs. State in Post-1949 China: The Institutional Dilemma* (Cambridge: Cambridge University Press, 1997), pp. 191–214.

13. For a discussion of Li Keqiang's shrinking power base see, for example, "Li Keqiang has become deputy head of the Central Leading Group on Comprehensively Deepening Reforms," *Ming Pao* (Hong Kong), January 23, 2014, http://premium.mingpao.com/cfm/ Content_News.cfm?Channel=ca&Path=168170027055/cab1.cfm. See also Jeremy Page, Bob Davis, and Lingling Wei, "Xi Weakens Role of Beijing's No. 2," *Wall Street Journal,* December 20, 2013, http://online.wsj.com/news/articles/SB1000142405270230447770 45 79252493857611618/.

14. For a discussion of Xi's relationship with two previous general secretaries, see, for example, Wu Jiaxiang, "Three characteristics in post-Eighteenth Congress politics that have not appeared in 20 years," News.ifeng.com, December 18, 2012, http://news.ifeng.com/exclusive/ lecture/special/wujiaxiang/shlu/detail_2012_12/18/20288211_0.shtml?_from_ralated/.

15. For a discussion of the sidelining of the CYL Faction, see, for example, Willy Lam, "Members of the Xi Jinping clique revealed," *China Brief,* Jamestown Foundation, vol. 14, no. 3, February 7, 2014, www.jamestown.org/programs/chinabrief/single/?tx_ttnews%5Btt_ news%5D=41933&tx_ttnews%5BbackPid%5D=25&cHash=c97424fda6de2f64e09ee0e2 456c6bb3/; see also Vaughan Winterbottom, "China's politics: Inside Xi Jinping's ruling clique," *Interpreter,* Lowy Institute for International Policy, February 12, 2014, www.

lowyinterpreter.org/post/2014/02/12/Chinas-politics-Inside-Xi-Jinpings-Ruling-Clique.aspx?COLLCC=3389665703&/.

16. For a discussion of Xi's inchoate personality cult, see, for example, Neil Conner, "Xi Jinping: Man of the people, or careful image builder?" AFP, March 15, 2014, www.google.com/hostednews/afp/article/ALeqM5iQFfz1i7MOzy3lCuOkfCjb39FFMw?docId=6286ba43-a821-40f0-946d-68009be6e75f/; Matt Schiavenza, "Why this seemingly innocuous photo of Xi Jinping is so important," Atlantic, July 23, 2013, www.theatlantic.com/china/archive/2013/07/why-this-seemingly-innocuous-photo-of-xi-jinping-is-so-important/278018/; Keith Richburg, "Fans of Xi Jinping fawn online over 'Pingping, China's new leader,'" Washington Post, December 13, 2012, www.washingtonpost.com/world/asia_pacific/xi-fans-fawn-over-pingping-chinas-new-leader/2012/12/12/f9aa5334-446f-11e2-8c8f-fbebf7ccab4e_story.html.

17. See "Scholar: Reformers need to solve eight major difficulties," Ta Kung Pao, February 24, 2014, http://news.takungpao.com/mainland/focus/2014-02/2295978.html.

18. Cited in "Xi Jinping has talked five times about the Chinese Dream," Wen Wei Po (Hong Kong), April 10, 2013, http://paper.wenweipo.com/2013/04/10/CH1304100038.htm. For a discussion of the meaning and significance of Xi Jinping's "Chinese dream," see, for example, Joseph Fewsmith, "Xi Jinping's fast start," China Leadership Monitor, Hoover Institution, Stanford University, no. 41, 2013, http://media.hoover.org/sites/default/files/documents/CLM41JF.pdf; Hoang Anh Tuan, "Understand Xi Jinping's renaissance, put it in historical context," Pacnet 22, Pacific Forum CSIS, April 1, 2013, http://papers.ssrn.com/sol3/papers.cfm?abstract_id=2305807/; Willy Lam, "Fierce debate erupts over the meaning of the 'China Dream,'" China Brief, Jamestown Foundation, April 25, 2013, www.jamestown.org/programs/chinabrief/single/?tx_ttnews%5Btt_news%5D=40782&tx_ttnews%5BbackPid%5D=25&cHash=b2e2c3b0b3b01acfe3684b43441a263c/.

19. For a discussion of Jiang Zemin's "Theory of the Three Represents," see, for example, Lam, Chinese Politics in the Hu Jintao Era, pp. 65–68.

20. For a discussion of the tradition of fuguo qiangbing in Chinese history, see, for example, Suisheng Zhao, "A tragedy of history: The Chinese search for democracy in the twentieth century," Journal of Contemporary China 2, no. 3 (1993): 18–37. See also Victoria Hui, "Building castles in the sand: A review of ancient Chinese thought, modern Chinese power," Chinese Journal of International Politics 5, no. 4 (Winter 2012): 425–449.

21. Cited in "Xi Jinping: Boldly march toward the goal of the great renaissance of the Chinese race," Xinhua News Agency, November 30, 2012, www.wenming.cn/xj_pd/yw/201211/t20121130_960796.shtml. See also Willy Lam, "Fierce debate erupts over the meaning of the 'China Dream,'" China Brief, Jamestown Foundation, April 25, 2013, www.jamestown.org/programs/chinabrief/single/?tx_ttnews%5Bpointer%5D=2&tx_ttnews%5Btt_news%5D=40782&tx_ttnews%5BbackPid%5D=25&cHash=11a68f3e86ade6ae7e51ddd6cb196786/.

22. Cited in "Xi Jinping's nine references to the 'Chinese Dream,'" Xinhua News Agency, March 17, 2013, http://news.xinhuanet.com/politics/2013-03/17/c_115054547.htm.

23. Cited in "Xi Jinping's 'Chinese Dream' reflects self-confidence in the 'Chinese road,'" People's Daily, December 6, 2012, http://hm.people.com.cn/n/2012/1206/c42272-19809939.html.

24. Cited in "General Secretary Xi Jinping explains the 'Chinese Dream,'" Xinhua News Agency, May 8, 2013, http://news.xinhuanet.com/ziliao/2013-05/08/c_124669102.htm.

25. Cited in "Wang Yiwei: Ten misunderstandings of 'the Chinese Dream,'" Xinhua News Agency, April 16, 2013, http://news.xinhuanet.com/2013-04/16/c_124587680.htm.

26. See "Beijing Daily commentator: Use 'the Chinese Dream' to create the strongest message of the times," Beijing Daily, December 18, 2012, http://cpc.people.com.cn/pinglun/n/2012/1218/c78779-19933965.html.

27. See "Bao Tong: Xi Jinping's Chinese Dream is 'the people's dream,'" DWNews. com, March 21, 2013, http://china.dwnews.com/big5/news/2013-03-21/59157761.html.

28. Cited in He Weifang: "What kind of dream should the Chinese Dream be?" He Weifang blog, March 29, 2013, http://blog.caijing.com.cn/expert_article-151302-49719.shtml.

29. See "Zhou Tianyong: The 21st-century Chinese Dream," China News Service, February 11, 2013, www.chinanews.com/cj/2011/02-11/2835459.shtml.

30. Cited in "Central Party School professor Xin Ming explains the 'Chinese Dream,'" People's Daily, March 27, 2013, www.legaldaily.com.cn/zt/content/2013-03/27/content_4315447_3.htm.

31. For a discussion of the rise of nationalism in contemporary China, see, for example, Suisheng Zhao, A Nation-State by Construction: Dynamics of Modern Chinese Nationalism (Stanford: Stanford University Press, 2004), pp. 1–34. See also Peter Hays Gries, China's New Nationalism: Pride, Politics, and Diplomacy (Berkeley: University of California Press, 2004), pp. 30–42, 116–134.

32. Cited in "Learn from the talk given by General Secretary Xi Jinping while viewing the Road to Renaissance exhibition," Xinhua News Agency, December 6, 2012, http://news.xinhuanet.com/politics/2012-12/06/c_113936084.htm; see also "Xi Jinping: Socialism with Chinese characteristics tallies with China's national conditions and it has a powerful life force," China News Service, July 24, 2012, www.chinanews.com/gn/2012/07-24/4056000.shtml.

33. Cited in "President Xi Jinping holds talks with Serbian president," August 27, 2013, http://news.xinhuanet.com/mrdx/2013-08/27/c_132664883.htm.

34. Cited in "Xi Jinping delivers speech at the Julius Nyerere International Convention Center in Tanzania, stressing that China and Africa will always remain reliable friends and faithful partners," Chinese Foreign Ministry Web site, March 25, 2013, www.fmprc.gov.cn/eng/zxxx/t1025803.shtml.

35. Cited in "President Xi Jinping gives joint interview to media from BRICS countries," Chinese Foreign Ministry Web site, March 19, 2013, www.fmprc.gov.cn/eng/zxxx/t1023070.shtml.

36. Cited in "What does Xi Jinping's Chinese Dream mean?" BBC News, June 5, 2013, www.bbc.co.uk/news/world-asia-china-22726375.

37. For a discussion of the military component of the "Chinese Dream," see, for example, Jeremy Page, "For Xi, a 'China Dream' of military power," Wall Street Journal, March 12, 2013, http://online.wsj.com/article/SB10001424127887324128504578348774040546346.html.

38. Cited in "The Chinese Dream is also a dream about a strong army," Liberation Army Daily, March 4, 2013, http://news.xinhuanet.com/mil/2013-03/04/c_124410762.htm.

39. For a discussion of the Chinese Dream as a "lowest common denominator," see, for example, Peter Martin and David Cohen, "Inside Xi Jinping's reform strategy," National Interest, March 20, 2014, http://nationalinterest.org/commentary/inside-xi-jinpings-reform-strategy-10087/.

40. Cited in "Xi Jinping: Dearth of ideals and faith will lead to 'calcium deficiency of the spirit' and result in 'soft bone disease,'" People's Daily, March 6, 2013, http://news.21cn.com/hot/cn/2013/03/06/14765193.shtml.

41. For a discussion of the "seven unmentionables," see, for example, Stanley Lubman, "Document No. 9: The party attacks Western democratic ideals," Wall Street Journal, August 27, 2913, http://blogs.wsj.com/chinarealtime/2013/08/27/document-no-9-the-party-attacks-western-democratic-ideals/.

42. See "Hu Jintao's address commemorating the thirtieth anniversary of the start of the reform and open-door policy," China Daily, December 18, 2008, www.chinadaily.com.cn/hqzg/2008-12/18/content_7318929_3.htm. See also Michael Bristow, "Chinese leader

rules out democracy," *BBC News,* March 10, 2011, www.bbc.co.uk/news/world-asia-pacific-12697997.

43. Cited in "Chongqing deputy Party secretary: Enemies within and outside China are colluding inside colleges," *Ming Pao,* February 4, 2014, http://news.mingpao.com/20140204/cac1.htm.

44. Cited in Willy Lam, "China's reform summed up: Politics, no; economics, yes (sort of . . .)," *China Brief,* Jamestown Foundation, vol. 13, no. 11, May 23, 2013, www.jamestown.org/programs/chinabrief/single/?tx_ttnews%5Btt_news%5D=40913&cHash=7853c7d8f9dfae95a6efcfc80a068698/.

45. Cited in "Xi Jinping: We must never jettison Marxism-Leninism and Mao Zedong Thought," Xinhua News Agency, November 19, 2013, http://news.cntv.cn/18da/20121119/100694.shtml.

46. Cited in Li Hainian, "Xi Jinping has summed up the lesson to be learned from the collapse of the Communist Party of the Soviet Union," *People's Daily,* March 1, 2013, www.people.com.cn/n/2013/0301/c33232-20645773.html.

47. Cited in Xi Jinping: "We cannot arbitrarily separate recent history into the pre-Cultural Revolution period and the post-Cultural Revolution period and then use one to negate the other," China News Service, January 5, 2013, www.chinanews.com/gn/2013/01-05/4460409.shtml.

48. See Qi Biao, "The important political significance behind the 'two cannot negates,'" *Guangming Daily* (Beijing), May 7, 2013. See also "*Qiushi:* Raise a clear-cut banner to negate historical nihilism," *Guangming Daily,* May 7, 2013, http://politics.gmw.cn/2013-05/07/content_7538912.htm.

49. For a discussion of Yang Jisheng and other researchers' works on the great famine, see, for example, Verna Yu, "Chinese author of book on famine braves risks to inform new generations," *New York Times,* November 18, 2008, www.nytimes.com/2008/12/18/world/asia/18iht-famine.1.18785257.html?pagewanted=all&_r=2&/.

50. See "Li Shenming: It is incorrect to say that the Mao Zedong period was totally worthless," *Red Flag Archives,* May 13, 2013, http://news.ifeng.com/mainland/detail_2013_05/13/25232777_0.shtml?qq-pf-from=qqconnect.share2qzone/.

51. Cited in "Tightly rally behind, uphold, and develop socialism with Chinese characteristics," Xinhua News Agency, November 18, 2012, www.gov.cn/ldhd/2012-11/19/content_2269332.htm.

52. For a discussion of the political motives behind Bo's "red culture campaign," see, for example, Jaime Florcruz, "'Red' culture campaign sweeps China," CNN, July 1, 2011, http://edition.cnn.com/2011/WORLD/asiapcf/06/30/china.red.campaign/index.html; see also Tania Branigan, "Red songs ring out in Chinese city's new cultural revolution," *Guardian,* April 22, 2011, www.theguardian.com/world/2011/apr/22/red-songs-chinese-cultural-revolution/.

53. Cited in Li Zhangjun, "Xi Jinping talks about attaching importance to classic works during ceremony to mark new semester at the Central Party School," *People's Daily,* May 14, 2011, http://politics.people.com.cn/GB/1024/14635203.html.

54. See "Xi Jinping: Why we should raise the name of Mao Zedong when thinking about party construction," *People's Daily,* September 10, 2008, http://news.xinhuanet.com/internet/2008-09/10/content_9892196.htm.

55. For an in-depth look at Xi Jinping's sentiments about the Daqing Oilfield and the model cadre Jiao Yulu, see "Xi Jinping's speech at the fiftieth anniversary of the discovery of oil in Daqing," *People's Daily,* September 22, 2009, http://energy.people.com.cn/GB/71899/152923/10110428.html; see also "Xi Jinping: We must propagate the spirit of Jiao Yulu while taking into considering new realities," *Seeking Truth,* May 18, 2009, http://theory.people.com.cn/GB/49169/49171/9316456.html.

56. See Zhang Quanjing, "We must unswervingly continue to uphold Mao Thought," *People's Daily,* March 30, 2011, http://theory.people.com.cn/GB/11253085.html.

57. See "Xi: Holding high the banner of Mao 'forever,'" Xinhua News Agency, December 26, 2013, http://news.xinhuanet.com/english/china/2013-12/26/c_132998764_2.htm.

58. Cited in "China marks Mao's 120th birthday with muted celebrations," VOAnews, December 26, 2013, www.voanews.com/content/china-marks-mao-120th-birthday-with-muted-celebrations/1817735.html.

59. For a discussion of the internecine bickering between the Gang of Princelings and Hu Jintao's Communist Youth League Faction, see, for example, Qiu Xiaotong, "Bo Xilai's campaign of hitting the triads and singing red songs has led to a schism within the CCP leadership," *Frontline* (Hong Kong), September 2011.

60. For a discussion of the rise of cadres with "revolutionary bloodlines," see, for example, Chen Pokong, "The CCP has elevated a large number of princelings," www.Chinesepen.org, December 9, 2007, www.chinesepen.org/Article/hyxz/200712/Article_20071209210450.shtml.

61. See "Xi Jinping emphasizes the need to develop the villages through reform and innovation, and to strengthen party construction by developing our superior tradition," CCTV, October 15, 2008, http://tv.people.com.cn/GB/61600/8179126.html.

62. See "Bo Xilai: We must remember forever the ideals and hot-bloodedness of our elders," *Chongqing Daily,* October 2, 2008, http://club.china.com/data/thread/1011/2344/86/22/3_1.html.

63. For a discussion of the activities of the Singing Troupe of 100 Offspring of Generals, see for example, "Offspring of the generals sing red songs; their enthusiasm spreads throughout the land," *Dazhong Daily* (Shandong), June 26, 2010, www.dzwww.com/shandong/sdnews/201006/t20100627_5679023.htm.

64. For a discussion of the "military princelings," see, for example, Lin Heli, "Factors behind Xi Jinping's consolidation of power," *Apple Daily,* August 24, 2011, www.boxun.com/news/gb/china/2011/08/201108241520.shtml.

65. For a discussion of Liu Yuan's assessment of Mao, see, for example, "How does General Liu Yuan assess Mao Zedong and his father, Liu Shaoqi?" *News Digest* (Beijing), January 10, 2013, http://history.chinaiiss.com/html/20131/10/a59f0f.html.

66. Cited in "Xi Jinping: Deeply study the theoretical system of socialism with Chinese characteristics; assiduously grasp the viewpoints and methodology of Marxism," *Seeking Truth,* April 1, 2010, http://theory.people.com.cn/GB/41038/11274357.html.

67. Cited in "Xi Jinping: On several points of understanding and observations while studying the theoretical system of socialism with Chinese characteristics," *Seeking Truth,* April 1, 2008, http://theory.people.com.cn/GB/49169/49171/7069468.html.

68. Ibid.

69. See "Xi Jinping: the party's ruling status cannot always be taken for granted," *Southern Metropolitan News* (Guangzhou), September 9, 2008, www.nfdaily.cn/china/shizheng/content/2008-09/09/content_4589087.htm.

70. Cited in "Tocqueville's advice on French revolution captures Chinese leaders' attention," *South China Morning Post,* January 22, 2013, www.scmp.com/news/china/article/1133212/tocquevilles-advice-french-revolution-captures-chinese-leaders-attention/.

71. Cited in "Xi Jinping: The road is the Party's life, and the revolution's ideals are higher than the heavens," Xinhua News Agency, January 5, 2013, www.hb.xinhuanet.com/2013-01/05/c_114258926_2.htm.

72. Ibid.

73. Cited in "Xi Jinping: Enthusiastically push forward the construction of a Marxist party geared toward learning," Xinhua News Agency, November 12, 2009, http://news.xinhuanet.com/politics/2009-11/12/content_12444075.htm.

74. For a discussion of the "Three Emphases" campaign, see, for example, "Jiang Zemin attends an education conference on the 'Three Emphases' and delivers major talk," Xinhua News Agency, February 21, 2000, http://news.sina.com.cn/china/2000-2-21/63516.html.

75. Cited in "Xi Jinping: The entire society should develop the spirit of innovation and raise its ability in innovation," Xinhua News Agency, September 20, 2009, http://news.xinhuanet.com/politics/2009-09/20/content_12081594.htm.

76. See "Xi Jinping: We must not go about construction by closing the door; we must absorb all the fruits of civilization," China News Service, November 18, 2009, www.chinanews.com/gn/news/2009/11-18/1970674.shtml.

77. Ibid.

78. For a discussion of Zhang Zhidong's views, see, for example, Xiaobai Shen and Robin Williams, "A critique of China's utilitarian view of science and technology," *Science, Technology and Society* 10, no. 2 (September 2005): 197–223.

79. See "Wen Jiabao: On several questions about the historical tasks of the preliminary stage of socialism and China's policy toward other countries," Xinhua News Agency, February 26, 2007, http://news.xinhuanet.com/politics/2007-02/26/content_5775212.htm. For a discussion of Wen Jiabao's views on universal values, see, for example, Tania Branigan, "Wen Jiabao talks of democracy and freedom in CNN interview," *Guardian,* October 4, 2010, www.theguardian.com/world/2010/oct/04/wen-jiabao-china-reform-cnn-interview/.

80. Cited in "Tang Zhijun: A bit less national conditions, a bit more international norms," *Global Times,* February 12, 2013, http://opinion.huanqiu.com/opinion_world/2013-02/3637529.html.

81. "Editorial: It will be difficult for China to change its preordained inferiority if it adopts Western discourse," *Global Times,* August 2, 2013, http://opinion.huanqiu.com/editorial/2013-08/4199969.html.

82. Cited in "Kids of Xi Jinping, Bo Xilai are different breed of Harvard student," *China Times* (Taipei), February 4, 2013, www.wantchinatimes.com/news-subclass-nt.aspx?id=20140203000037&cid=1101/.

83. Cited in "One central task, two fundamental points," *People's Daily,* September 24, 2008, www.ce.cn/xwzx/gnsz/szyw/200809/24/t20080924_16904185_1.shtml. For a discussion of Deng's focus on economic work, see, for example, Barry Naughton, "Deng Xiaoping: The economist," *China Quarterly,* no. 135 (September 1993): 491–514.

84. Cited in "Xi Jinping gives important address at National Conference on Ideological and Propaganda Work," China National Radio, August 21, 2013, http://china.cnr.cn/news/201308/t20130821_513374392.shtml; see also "The fate of the CCP depends on whether it can defend the battlefield of ideology and thought," *Beijing Daily,* September 3, 2013, http://news.xinhuanet.com/local/2013-09/03/c_125306949.htm.

85. Ibid. See also "Party journal: The dissolution of a regime begins in the area of ideology and thoughts," *Seeking Truth,* September 2, 2013, http://club.china.com/data/thread/1011/2763/76/58/2_1.html.

86. Cited in Mao Zedong, "Talks at the Yan'an Forum on Literature and Art," in *Selected Works of Mao Tse-tung,* www.marxists.org/reference/archive/mao/selected-works/volume-3/mswv3_08.html.

87. Cited in "*Dangxing* is the sublimation of human nature," *Study Times* (Beijing), August 19, 2013, http://news.china.com/domestic/945/20130819/18003473.html.

88. Cited in Mou Chuanheng, "China's history for the past 100 years consists of the struggle between constitutional governance and counterconstitutional governance," Minzhuzhongguo.org (Beijing), June 24, 2013, http://minzhuzhongguo.org/ArtShow.aspx?AID=34958.

89. Author interview with Alfred Wu, Hong Kong, September 17, 2013.

90. See "Guo Jinling: Ensure that the *zhongyang's* political orders are smoothly enforced; our political beliefs must remain unchanged under any circumstances," *Seeking Truth*, September 2, 2013, http://news.takungpao.com/mainland/focus/2013-09/1876667.html.

91. Cited in "31 regional party propaganda chiefs discuss their views on how to learn from the spirit of General Secretary Xi Jinping's important August 19 address," Xinhua News Agency, September 3, www.gd.xinhuanet.com/newscenter/2013-09/03/c_117202656.htm.

92. Ibid.

93. For a discussion of Tuo Zhen's battle with *Southern Weekend* journalists, see, for example, Teddy Ng, "Former *Southern Weekly* journalists want propaganda chief Tuo Zhen to go," *South China Morning Post*, January 8, 2013, www.scmp.com/news/china/article/1120199/former-southern-weekly-journalists-want-propaganda-chief-tuo-zhen-go/. See also Martin Patience, "China newspaper journalists stage rare strike," BBC News, January 7, 2013, www.bbc.co.uk/news/world-asia-china-20929826/.

94. Cited in "31 regional party propaganda chiefs."

95. Ibid.

96. Cited in Hai Yan, "Tuo Zhen's positioning of Guangdong as a pacesetter for ideological struggles has attracted attention," VOA Chinese Service, September 4, 2013, www.voafanti.com/gate/big5/m.voachinese.com/a/1742963.html.

97. See "Xi Jinping makes major speech during conference on the Campaign on Mass-Line Education and Practice," Xinhua News Agency, June 18, 2013, http://news.xinhuanet.com/politics/2013-06/18/c_116194026.htm.

98. For a discussion of the nature of political campaigns within the CCP, see, for example, Lowell Dittmer, "Patterns of elite strife and succession in Chinese politics," *China Quarterly*, no. 123 (September 1990): 405–430.

99. For a discussion of the Rectification Campaign within the People's Liberation Army, see, for example, "Commentator: Use the spirit of the Rectification Campaign to implement criticism and self-criticism," *Liberation Army Daily*, May 7, 2013, www.gov.cn/jrzg/2013-07/05/content_2440794.htm.

100. See "Render your behavior and attire proper: On the Campaign on Mass-Line Education and Practice," Xinhua News Agency, June 20, 2013, http://news.xinhuanet.com/politics/2013-06/20/c_116229156.htm.

101. Cited in "Zhao Zhengyong: Use the spirit of the Yan'an Rectification movement to implement the Campaign on Mass-Line Education and Practice," *People's Daily*, August 19, http://fujian.people.com.cn/n/2013/0819/c181466-19345079.html.

102. For a discussion of Deng Xiaoping's negative views about political campaigns, see, for example, "Why was Deng Xiaoping against political movements?" *Wen Wei Po* (Hong Kong), April 3, 2012, http://info.wenweipo.com/index.php/?action-viewnews-itemid-53745/.

103. Cited in "Xi Jinping: Use boldly the weapon of criticism and self-criticism," *People's Daily*, September 27, 2013, http://he.people.com.cn/n/2013/0927/c192235-19601657.html.

104. Ibid.

105. Cited in Guo Wenjing, "Using institutions to cure the 'four winds' is the essence of the mass line," *Legal Daily* (Beijing), June 20, 2013, http://opinion.people.com.cn/n/2013/0620/c1003-21909325.html.

106. Cited in Xiao Xun, "Analysis: Relationship between the CCP's Mass-Line Campaign and Party rectification," www.minzhuzhongguo.org, June 13, 2013, www.minzhuzhongguo.org/ArtShow.aspx?AID=34940/.

107. Cited in "Beijing Municipal Party School's Yao Heng on the practice of education on the mass line," *People's Daily*, June 28, http://theory.people.com.cn/BIG5/n/2013/0628/c40531-22008140.html.

108. Cited in "Is Xi Jinping rectifying the party or picking on individuals?" Mirrorbooks.com (New York), September 25, 2013, www.wenxuecity.com/news/2013/09/25/2684262.html.

109. Author interview with Deng Yuwen, Hong Kong, May 2013.

110. Cited in "Commander and political commissar of the Second Artillery Corps: Self-consciously uphold the authority of Chairman Xi," *Liberation Army Daily*, June 17, 2013, www.zgsyb.com/html/news/2013/06/639972038319_2.html.

111. For a discussion of Xi Jinping and the Gang of Princelings, see, for example, Yongnian Zheng, Gang Chen, and Liang Fook Lye, "China's politics: New leadership emerges from a tumultuous environment," *East Asian Policy* (Singapore) 5, no. 1 (January 2013): 5–13.

112. For a discussion of the rising political fortune of younger generations of "princelings," see, for example, "Deng Xiaoping's Duke Law alumnus grandson named county official," Bloomberg News, May 3, 2013, www.bloomberg.com/news/2013-05-03/deng-xiaoping-s-duke-law-alumnus-grandson-named-county-official.html; Lin Heli, "Princelings' grand scheme to take over heaven and earth," *Hong Kong Economic Journal*, June 13, 2013, http://forum.hkej.com/user/69312/201306/.

113. For a discussion of how liberal princelings view Xi Jinping's conservative ideology, see, for example, Su Renyan, "The children of Hu Yaobao break with Xi Jinping," Canyu.org, August 9, 2013, http://canyu.org/n78334c12.aspx; see also Ching Cheong, "Xi Jinping turns to the 'left,' resulting in a split among the Gang of Princelings," *Hong Kong Economic Journal*, June 27, 2013, http://forum.hkej.com/user/70348/201306/.

114. Cited in "Hu Dehua's speech at the gathering of *Yanhuang chunqiu*," China.com, June 17, 2013, http://club.china.com/data/thread/1011/2761/38/84/0_1.html.

115. For a discussion of Zhong Peizhang's views on reforms, see, for example, "Zhong Peizhang: Only democracy and constitutional governance can guarantee a long reign and perennial stability," 21ccom.net (Beijing), December 15, 2011, www.21ccom.net/articles/rwcq/article_2011121550426.html.

116. Cited in "Xi Jinping: We must stringently enforce discipline to ensure that policy directives are smoothly carried out," Xinhua News Agency, February 6, 2013, http://news.cntv.cn/2013/02/06/ARTI1360143222389583.shtml.

117. Cited in Wang Jun, "The powers of the Central Committee Secretariat have been boosted," *Ta Kung Pao*, March 17, 2013, http://news.takungpao.com.hk/mainland/zgzq/2013-03/1496196.html.

118. For a discussion of the career and traits of Li Zhanshu, see, for example, Benjamin Kang Lim, "China president to promote allies in sweeping reshuffle: sources," Reuters, www.reuters.com/article/2013/11/22/us-china-politics-reshuffle-idUSBRE9AL0DT20131122/; see also "Li Zhanshu: A troubleshooter with multiple facets of experience," *Ta Kung Pao*, September 3, 2012, www.takungpao.com/mainland/content/2012-09/03/content_1036483.htm.

119. For a discussion of personnel changes in the Secretariat, see, for example, Willy Lam, "All the general secretary's men: Xi Jinping's inner circle revealed," *China Brief*, Jamestown Foundation, February 15, 2013, www.jamestown.org/programs/chinabrief/single/?tx_ttnews%5Bpointer%5D=1&tx_ttnews%5Btt_news%5D=40461&tx_ttnews%5BbackPid%5D=25&cHash=28332dcad285c8fc89e8cc1ef02bca55/.

120. See "Li Keqiang talks about reforming the structure of departments: The core is to change the function of governance," China News Service, March 17, 2013, www.chinanews.com/gn/2013/03-17/4650143.shtml. See also "China to better handle relations between government, market: Premier Li," Xinhua News Agency, March 13, 2014, http://news.xinhuanet.com/english/special/2014-03/13/c_133183261.htm.

121. Cited in Liu Shan, "Keep expectations for NDRC reform limited," Caixin.com, March 12, 2014, http://english.caixin.com/2014-03-12/100650349.html.

122. Cited in "The Ministry of Public Security has three vice-ministers with rank of full ministers," *Ta Kung Pao,* February 12, 2014, http://news.takungpao.com/mainland/zgzq/2014-02/2272421.html.

123. For a discussion of the careers of Zhou Benshun and Jiang Wei, see, for example, "Media has exposed the backgrounds of the Party secretaries of Hebei and Jiangxi," China News Service, March 21.http://hebei.sina.com.cn/news/m/2013-03-21/140041043.html; see also "Former aide to Zhou Yongkang has parachuted into Hebei," *Ta Kung Pao,* March 20, 2013, http://news.takungpao.com/mainland/zgzq/2013-03/1502655.html.

124. For a discussion of the career of Hao Peng, see, for example, "The career of the head of the Political-Legal Committee of Tibet and where he is heading," Zhuisu.info (Beijing), February 14, 2013, www.zhuisu.info/renwu/ziliao/2013/0214/3029.html.

125. For a discussion of the series of appointments of governors after the Eighteenth Party Congress, see, for example, Ivan Zhou and Echo Hui, "Beijing steps up centralization of power to control provincial leaders," *South China Morning Post,* July 5, 2013, www.scmp.com/news/china/article/1275534/beijing-steps-centralisation-powercontrol-provincial-leaders/.

126. Cited in "General managers from state-owned corporations have been assigned to the provinces," China News Service, March 25, 2013, http://news.xinhuanet.com/politics/2013-03/25/c_115139066.htm.

127. For a study of senior cadres with a Tibet background, see, for example, "Many officials with a Tibet background have been promoted to state leaders," *Ta Kung Pao,* March 12, 2013, http://news.takungpao.com.hk/mainland/focus/2013-03/1486685.html.

128. Cited in "Zhang Ping: China's best advantage is [the authorities] can concentrate the nation's resources and efforts to do big things," *People's Daily,* March 6, 2013, http://business.sohu.com/20130306/n367946200.shtml.

129. For a discussion of the centrifugal tendencies of Deng's policies, see, for example, Hongbin Cai and Daniel Treisman, "Did government decentralization cause China's economic miracle?" *World Politics* 58, no. 4 (July 2006): 505–535.

130. For a discussion of the Confucian roots of Liu Shaoqi's ideas about cultivating a good Communist, see, for example, Wenxiang Gong, "The legacy of Confucian culture in Maoist China," *Social Science Journal* 26, no. 4 (1989): 363–374.

131. For a discussion of the mentality behind Liu Shaoqi's philosophy on educating good Communists, see, for example, Wenxiang Gong, "The legacy of Confucian culture in Maoist China," *Social Science Journal* 26, no. 4 (1989): 363–374. See also Frank N. Pieke, *The Good Communist: Elite Training and State Building in Today's China* (New York: Cambridge University Press, 2009), pp. 26–55.

132. Cited in "Xi Jinping: Officials must exercise morality when using power; they must follow [good] principles when making friends," Xinhua News Agency, October 4, 2004, http://news.sina.com.cn/o/2004-10-04/11303833187s.shtml.

133. See "Xi Jinping: Spend more time on thinking, studying, and working; don't spend time in entertainment and socializing," *People's Daily,* February 20, 2001, www.people.com.cn/GB/other4583/4597/4661/20010220/399338.html.

134. See "Xi Jinping: Leading cadres should establish a correct worldview as well as opinions on power and [building] careers," *People's Daily,* September 2, 2010, http://politics.people.com.cn/GB/1024/12610832.html.

135. See "Xi Jinping: Leading cadres should read about history," Xinhua News Agency, September 1, 2011, http://news.xinhuanet.com/politics/2011-09/01/c_121949418.htm.

136. Cited in Yang Xiaohuai, "Xi Jinping: How I got into politics," *China Profiles* (Beijing) July 2000, http://shuku.net/novels/zhuanji/sahqzwrpbj/zlsj55.html. See also Chan Fang, "The road of Xi Jinping: From party secretary of a work brigade to general secretary," Phoenix TV Net, November 15, 2012, www.sxdaily.com.cn/n/2012/1118/c219-5015788-1.html.

137. Cited in Guo Dongbo, "What are the implications of Xi Jinping's policy of 'strengthening and improving party construction at universities?" *People's Daily*, January 10, 2011, http://cpc.people.com.cn/GB/64093/64103/13689091.html.

138. For a discussion of the college president responsibility system and the power of the party secretary in colleges, see, for example, Ouyang Song, "The practice and reflection of the college president responsibility system under the leadership of the party committee," *Red Flag Archives*, March 7, 2011, www.qstheory.cn/hqwg/2011/201105/201103/t20110307_71236.htm. See also Qi Yeguo, "On the reform of the internal management system of universities," *China Education and Research Network* (Beijing), June 5, 2009, www.edu.cn/gj30years_8139/20090605/t20090605_382471.shtml.

139. For a discussion of Xi's austerity campaign, see, for example, "New CPC leadership rejects extravagance, bureaucracy," Xinhua News Agency, December 4, 2012, http://news.xinhuanet.com/english/china/2012-12/04/c_124047353.htm; Andrew Jacobs, "Elite in China face austerity under Xi's rule," *New York Times*, March 27, 2013, www.nytimes.com/2013/03/28/world/asia/xi-jinping-imposes-austerity-measures-on-chinas-elite.html?pagewanted=all&_r=0/; see also Don Lee, "Restraint is the new red in China," *Los Angeles Times*, May 19, 2013, http://articles.latimes.com/2013/may/19/world/la-fg-china-luxury-corruption-20130520/.

140. Cited in "Five deputy secretaries of the Central Commission on Discipline Inspection have appointments in the Central Leading Group on Comprehensively Deepening Reforms," China National Radio, January 24, 2014, http://news.jschina.com.cn/system/2014/01/24/020077231.shtml.

141. Cited in "Xi Jinping insists on hitting out at the 'tigers' and 'flies' at the same time," *People's Daily*, January 23, 2013, http://news.sina.com.cn/c/2013-01-23/040426098629.shtml. See also "The reports of the Supreme People's Court and Supreme People's Procuratorate reflect the campaign against graft," *Ming Pao*, March 11, 2014, http://news.mingpao.com/20140311/caa1h.htm. For a discussion of the ministerial and vice-ministerial level officials being nabbed for alleged corruption in 2013, see, for example, "Central authorities strike hard on corruption: eight tigers have been caught," *Ta Kung Pao*, August 22, 2013, http://news.takungpao.com/mainland/focus/2013-08/1845383_43.html.

142. Cited in Chris Buckley and Andrew Jacobs, "China says former security chief is being investigated for corruption," *New York Times*, July 29, 2014, www.nytimes.com/2014/07/30/world/asia/china-says-zhou-yongkang-former-security-chief-is-under-investigation.html?_r=0. For a discussion of Zhou's career and why he was involved in big-time corruption, see, for example, Emily Rauhala, "A purge in Beijing? China's former security czar may face trial," *Time*, December 22, 2013, http://world.time.com/2013/12/22/risky-business-jang-song-taek-zhou-yongkang-and-the-problem-with-political-purges/.

143. Cited in Deng Yuwen, "The future of tiger-hunting after the Zhou Yongkang case," *Ta Kung Pao*, July 29, 2014, http://news.takungpao.com/mainland/focus/2014-07/2638141.html. See also James T. Areddy, "China's leaders, new and old, turn out in show of Party unity for concert," *Wall Street Journal*, September 30, 2014, http://blogs.wsj.com/chinarealtime/2014/09/30/chinas-leaders-new-and-old-turn-out-in-show-of-party-solidarity-for-concert/; "Xi Jinping inspects Shanghai Lianying Medical Company: Jiang Mianheng provides explanations," *Ta Kung Pao*, May 26, 2014, http://news.takungpao.com/mainland/zgzq/2014-05/2496618.html. For a discussion of Jiang Zemin and Zeng Qinghong's opposition to prosecuting former PBSC members, see Lin Heli, "Struggle between forces who want to save Zhou and those who want to dump him," *Apple Daily*, February 17, 2014, http://hk.apple.nextmedia.com/news/art/20140217/18628291.

144. For a discussion of the number of suspects and amount of assets involved in the Zhou corruption ring, see, for example, Benjamin Kang Lim and Ben Blanchard "Exclusive: China seizes $14.5 billion assets from family, associates of ex-security chief: Sources," Reuters, March 30, 2014, www.reuters.com/article/2014/03/30/us-china-corruption-zhou-

idUSBREA2T02S20140330/. See also Michael Forsythe, Chris Buckley and Jonathan Ansfield, "Severing a family's ties, China's president signals a change," *New York Times,* April 19, 2014, www.nytimes.com/2014/04/20/world/asia/severing-a-familys-ties-chinas-president-signals-a-change.html?_r=0/.

145. For a discussion of Zhou Yongkang and his protégés and underlings, see, for example, Gillian Wong, "Chinese former vice-governor in anti-graft probe," Associated Press, June 24, 2013, www.businessweek.com/ap/2013-06-24/chinese-former-vice-governor-in-anti-graft-probe/. For a discussion of the Jiang Jiemin case, see, for example, Gabriel Domínguez, "China corruption probes reflect power struggle," Deutsche Welle, September 4, 2013, www.dw.de/china-corruption-probes-reflect-power-struggle/a-17065484/; see also Chen Aizhu and Charlie Zhu, "China investigates more top PetroChina executives over corruption," Reuters, August 27, 2013, www.reuters.com/article/2013/08/27/us-china-cnpc-idUSBRE97Q0DE20130827/.

146. For a discussion of Zhou relatives and *zhengfa* cadres implicated in the case of the former top cadre, see, for example, "Probe into Zhou family grows," *Global Times,* March 4, 2014, www.globaltimes.cn/content/846010.shtml. See also "China probes former aide to Zhou as investigations widen," Bloomberg, February 19, 2014, www.businessweek.com/news/2014-02-18/china-probes-former-zhou-yongkang-aide-as-investigation-widens/.

147. Cited in "Xi Jinping: Let power be locked up in the cage of institutions," Xinhua News Agency, January 22, 2013, http://news.xinhuanet.com/politics/2013-01/22/c_114459610.htm.

148. For a discussion of the power struggle behind the downfall of Zhou Yongkang and Bo Xilai, see, for example, Kerry Brown, "Xi Jinping vs. Zhou Yongkang: Xi Jinping's anti-corruption forces are closing in on Zhou Yongkang in a sensational example of Chinese politics," *Diplomat,* March 17, 2014, http://thediplomat.com/2014/03/xi-jinping-vs-zhou-yongkang/. See also Lin Heli, "Is Xi Jinping a paper tiger," *Hong Kong Economic Journal,* May 16, 2013, http://forum.hkej.com/user/69312/201305/.

149. For a discussion of the fall of Chen Liangyu, see, for example, Cheng Li, "Was the Shanghai Gang Shanghaied? The fall of Chen Liangyu and the survival of Jiang Zemin's faction," *China Leadership Monitor,* Hoover Institution, no. 20, 2007, http://media.hoover.org/sites/default/files/documents/clm20cl.pdf. For a discussion of the conflict between Chen Xitong and Jiang Zemin, see, for example, David Bachman, "Emerging patterns of political conflict in post-Deng China," in *China under Jiang Zemin,* ed. Hung-Mao Tien and Yun-han Chu (Boulder: Lynne Rienner, 2000), pp. 55–70.

150. Cited in Didi Tang and Gillian Wong, "Report: China to investigate former security czar," Associated Press, August 30, 2013, http://bigstory.ap.org/article/report-china-investigate-former-security-czar-0/.

151. For a discussion of the legal implications of the Bo trial, see, for example, Simon Denyer, "In China, Bo Xilai's political legacy may survive his downfall," *Washington Post,* September 22, 2013, http://articles.washingtonpost.com/2013-09-22/world/42299367_1_bo-xilai-mao-zedong-s-ousted-chinese/; see also Willy Lam, "Compromising the case against Bo Xilai," *Wall Street Journal,* August 20, 2013, http://online.wsj.com/article/SB100001424127887323608504579024320304674550.html.

152. For a discussion of the alleged corrupt activities of General Gu Junshan and his patron General Xu Caihou, see, for example, John Garnaut, "Rotting from within: Investigating the massive corruption of the Chinese military," *Foreign Policy,* April 16, 2012, www.foreignpolicy.com/articles/2012/04/16/rotting_from_within/.

153. For a discussion of disciplinary units within the PLA, see, for example, Zhao Lei, "PLA to improve disciplinary inspection," *China Daily,* November 20, 2013, www.chinadaily.com.cn/china/2013-11/20/content_17119137.htm. See also "Army disciplinary inspection eyes leading officials," Xinhua News Agency, November 19, 2013, www.globaltimes.cn/content/826032.shtml.

154. Cited in Benjamin Kang Lim and Megha Rajagopalan, "China's Xi purging corrupt officials to put own men in place: sources," Reuters, April 16, 2014, www.reuters.com/article/2014/04/16/us-china-corruption-xi-insight-idUSBREA3F1UT20140416/.

155. For a discussion of the wealth of top cadres such as Wen Jiabao and Xi Jinping, see, for example, David Barboza, "Billions in hidden riches for family of Chinese leader," New York Times, October 26, 2012, www.nytimes.com/2012/10/26/business/global/family-of-wen-jiabao-holds-a-hidden-fortune-in-china.html?pagewanted=all&_r=0/; see also James Bell, "China's princelings storing riches in Caribbean offshore haven," Guardian, January 21, 2014, www.theguardian.com/world/ng-interactive/2014/jan/21/china-british-virgin-islands-wealth-offshore-havens/.

156. See "Xi Jinping millionaire relations reveal fortunes of elite," Bloomberg, June 29, 2012, www.bloomberg.com/news/2012-06-29/xi-jinping-millionaire-relations-reveal-fortunes-of-elite.html.

157. For a discussion of allegations of corruption against the wife of Ling Jihua, see, for example, "Ling Jihua's wife probed for using charity as front: Report," China Times (Taipei), December 5, 2012, www.wantchinatimes.com/news-subclass-cnt.aspx?id=20121205000138&cid=1601/.

158. For a discussion of the Liu Tienan case, see, for example, Chris Buckley, "After a journalist's prodding, China investigates a top official," New York Times, May 13, 2013, www.nytimes.com/2013/05/13/world/asia/china-eyes-liu-tienan-an-official-challenged-by-a-journalist.html?_r=0/.

159. Cited in "Shanghai judges sacked over prostitution scandal," Xinhua News Agency, August 9, 2013, www.chinadaily.com.cn/china/2013-08/09/content_16882738.htm.

160. See Adrian Wan, "Seventy police make graft claims against top Shanghai judge," South China Morning Post, August 17, 2013, www.scmp.com/news/china/article/1297378/70-police-make-graft-claims-against-top-judge/.

161. For a discussion of the repression of the New Citizens' Movement and the trial of some of its members, see Tania Branigan, "Trials put nine Chinese activists in dock," Guardian, January 20, 2014, www.theguardian.com/world/2014/jan/20/nine-chinese-activists-trials/; see also "China: Verdicts and sentencing in trials of human rights defenders Mr. Yuan Dong and Ms. Hou Xin," Frontline Defenders, January 19, 2014, https://www.frontlinedefenders.org/node/24814/.

162. For a discussion of the relatively few senior cadres who support an assets-disclosure regulation, see, for example, "Official Chinese media suggest public disclosure of the assets of officials," BBC Chinese Service, November 13, 2012, www.bbc.co.uk/zhongwen/trad/chinese_news/2012/11/121113_china_anti_corruption.shtml.

163. For a discussion of the "privileged capitalist class," see, for example, Wu Jinglian, "China's privileged capitalism is become more serious," New Beijing Post (Beijing), November 12, 2010, http://news.163.com/10/1112/22/6LAT18G600012Q9L.html; see also "Xu Xiaonian: China is turning back the clock and marching toward 'privileged capitalism,'" Nanfeng Chuang (Guangzhou), August 30, 2010, http://business.sohu.com/20100830/n274583809.shtml.

164. Cited in "Xi Jinping vows no stop in reform, opening up," Xinhua News Agency, December 11, 2012, http://news.xinhuanet.com/english/china/2012-12/11/c_132034269.htm.

165. See "Xi Jinping: Use greater resolve to deepen important areas of reform," Xinhua News Agency, January 1, 2013, http://news.sina.com.cn/c/2013-01-01/175325940283.shtml.

166. Cited in "Xi Jinping: Retrospective and thoughts on party construction after thirty years of the reform and open-door policy," Xinhua News Agency, September 8, 2008, www.ce.cn/xwzx/gnsz/szyw/200809/08/t20080908_16739951.shtml. See also Zhang Feng, "The eight bright spots of General Secretary Xi's talk," Zhengzhou Daily (Zhengzhou), September 6, 2013, http://news.163.com/13/0906/20/9846PMU800014AED.html.

167. Cited in Buckley, "Vows of change in China belie private warning."

168. See "Xi Jinping: Use greater resolve to deepen important areas of reform."

169. See "Decision on major issues concerning comprehensively deepening reforms," Xinhua News Agency, November 16, 2013, http://news.xinhuanet.com/mrdx/2013-11/16/c_132892941.htm.

170. Ibid.

171. Cited in "Xi Jinping takes part in discussion among delegates to the NPC," China National Broadcasting Net, March 6, 2014, http://news.163.com/14/0306/07/9MKUP75800014JB5.html.

172. See "Xi Jinping: Nurture cadres who are experts in managing cities," *Chengdu Evening Post,* March 6, 2014, http://news.ifeng.com/gundong/detail_2014_03/06/34471032_0.shtml.

173. See "Xi Jinping: Develop the 'spirit of the Red Boat' and be at the forefront of the times," Xinhua News Agency, June 21, 2005, http://zjnews.zjol.com.cn/05zjnews/system/2005/06/22/006140772.shtml.

174. This saying was attributed to Confucius in the *Chronicle of the Late Han Dynasty,* written by Fan Hua (398–445), http://chengyu.soouu.com/list/chengyu_9106.htm.

175. For a discussion of Xi's view on the popular base of the party's power, see Deng Yuwen, "Xi Jinping's repeated emphasis on 'power being conferred by the people' has a very strong relevance," China News Service, April 4, 2011, www.chinanews.com/gn/2011/04-14/2972952.shtml.

176. Cited in "Xi Jinping: Leading cadres should firmly establish a correct worldview, view on power and view on [their] enterprise," Xinhua News Agency, September 2, 2010, http://opinion.people.com.cn/GB/157411/202005/202007/12611767.html.

177. Cited in "Xi Jinping: We must use the spirit of reform and innovation to construct intra-party democracy," China News Service, April 1, 2008, www.chinanews.com/gn/news/2008/04-01/1208300.shtml.

178. Ibid.

179. For a discussion of Hu Jintao's views on intra-party democracy, see, for example, Lam, *Chinese Politics in the Hu Jintao Era,* pp. 127–136.

180. For a discussion of Hu's reforms under the banner of "democracy within the party," see, for example, Lam, "Intra-party democracy with Chinese characteristics," in *Whither China's Democracy,* pp. 33–64.

181. For Xi's views on intra-party democracy and grassroots democracy, see Xi Jinping, *Work Hard on the Substance and Take the Lead* (Beijing: Central Party School Publishing House, 2006), pp. 369–385.

182. Cited in "U.S. embassy cables: China's next leader reveals taste for Hollywood movies," *Guardian,* December 4, 2010, www.theguardian.com/world/us-embassy-cables-documents/100934/.

183. Cited in "Xi Jinping stresses running the country according to law and administrating according to law," Xinhua News Agency, February 24, 2013, http://news.xinhuanet.com/politics/2013-02/24/c_114782088.htm.

184. Cited in "Xi Jinping's talk at the conference hosted by different circles in Beijing to commemorate the 30th anniversary of the promulgation of the 1982 constitution," Xinhua News Agency, December 4, 2012, http://news.xinhuanet.com/politics/2012-12/04/c_113907206.htm.

185. See "Constitution of the People's Republic of China (Full text after amendment on March 14, 2004)," www.npc.gov.cn/englishnpc/Constitution/2007-11/15/content_1372962.htm.

186. Cited in "Hu Deping: The constitution presupposes constitutional governance; without constitutional governance, the constitution itself will be sullied," *Economic Observer Post* (Beijing), August 10, 2013, http://nb.ifeng.com/gngj/detail_2013_08/10/1091519_0.shtml.

187. Cited in Zheng Zhixue, "The goal of constitutional governance is to abolish the leadership of the party," *Party Construction* (Beijing), May 30, 2013, http://news.takungpao. com/mainland/focus/2013-05/1651218.html.

188. Cited in Ma Zhongcheng, "The essence of 'constitutionalism' is a kind of weapon in propaganda warfare," *People's Daily,* August 5, 2013, http://money.163. com/13/0805/09/95GLMPT700254TI5.html.

189. See "Decision on major issues concerning comprehensively deepening reforms."

190. For a discussion of the *laojiao* system, see, for example, "China abolishes reeducation through labor," Xinhua News Agency, December 28, 2013, www.chinadaily.com.cn/ china/2013-12/28/content_17202294.htm; see also Fang Yang, "Reeducation returns in new form in Henan," *Global Times,* February 13, 2014, www.globaltimes.cn/content/842351.shtml.

191. For a discussion of legal-judicial reforms from late 2013 onward, see, for example, Stanley Lubman, "An encouraging sign for (limited) legal reform in China," *Wall Street Journal,* February 25, 2014, http://blogs.wsj.com/chinarealtime/2014/02/25/ an-encouraging-sign-for-limited-legal-reform-in-china/. See also Sui-Lee Wee and Li Hui, "With legal reforms, China wants less interfering in cases, fewer death penalty crimes," Reuters, March 9, 2014, www.reuters.com/article/2014/03/09/us-china-parliament-legal-idUSBREA2804S20140309/; "In China, brutality yields confessions of graft," Associated Press, March 7, 2014, www.usatoday.com/story/news/world/2014/03/07/china-brutality-yields-confession/6179431/.

192. For a study of the evolution and functions of the CPLC, see, for example, Zhou Yongkun, "The history and evolution of the Central Political-Legal Commission," *Yanhuang chunqiu,* September 2012, www.yhcqw.com/html/cqb/2012/96/23KG.html.

193. For a discussion of Meng Jianzhu's career, see, for example, Zhu Zhongyuan, "Meng Jianzhu runs the police with an iron fist," *Earth Biweekly,* no. 18, 2009, http://paper.people. com.cn/dd/html/2009-09/16/content_359860.htm.

194. Cited in "There are only four provinces where the *zhengfa* secretary doubles as the local police chiefs," *Ta Kung Pao,* August 20, 2013, http://news.takungpao.com/mainland/ focus/2013-08/1839517.html; see also "Putting vice heads of regional administrations in charge of police forces has become a trend," *Ta Kung Pao,* August 13, 2013, http://news. takungpao.com/mainland/focus/2013-08/1823715.html.

195. Cited in "The Central Political-Legal Commission will reform itself to ensure that it does not interfere with individual cases," *Southern Metropolitan News,* July 14, 2013, http://news.takungpao.com/mainland/focus/2013-07/1758629.html.

196. Cited in Sui-Lee Wee and Li Hui, "With legal reforms, China wants less interfering in cases, fewer death penalty crimes," Reuters, March 9, 2014, http://uk.reuters.com/ article/2014/03/09/uk-china-parliament-legal-idUKBREA2804V20140309/.

197. Cited in Geng Huaichang, "Keep up with the times in opening up new vistas for state-security work," *Seeking Truth,* March 16, 2014, http://theory.people.com.cn/n/2014/0316/ c83845-24646212.html.

198. Cited in "Bo's trial underscores China's resolve for rule of law," Xinhua News Agency, August 28, 2013, www.ecns.cn/voices/2013/08-28/78864.shtml; "The live broadcast of the Bo case shows the high confidence of central authorities," *Guangming Daily* (Beijing), August 23, 2013, http://news.xinhuanet.com/politics/2013-08/23/c_117059805.htm.

199. Cited in "Bo Xilai's last confession: I don't want to become China's Putin," *Apple Daily,* August 30, 2013, http://hk.apple.nextmedia.com/geocheck/cic/http__3A__2F__2Fhk. apple.nextmedia.com__2Frealtime__2Fnews__2F20130830__2F51685157/; see also "Bo Xilai shouted in court: The verdict is unjust," BBC (Chinese Service) September 23, 2013, www.bbc.co.uk/zhongwen/trad/china/2013/09/130923_boxilai_court.shtml.

200. For a comparison of the Bo trial to that of the Gang of Four, see, for example, Jaime FlorCruz, "From Gang of Four to Bo Xilai: Reporting from China's 'show trials,'" CNN,

August 28, 2013, http://edition.cnn.com/2013/08/28/world/asia/china-gang-of-four-trial-florcruz/index.html.

201. See Malcolm Moore, "China's lawyers targeted as Xi Jinping tightens control," *Daily Telegraph* (London), August 20, 2013, www.telegraph.co.uk/news/worldnews/asia/china/10254632/Chinese-lawyers-targeted-as-Xi-Jinping-tightens-control.html; see also Peter Ford, "With arrest, China signals limits to anti-corruption campaign," *Christian Science Monitor,* July 17, 2013, www.csmonitor.com/World/Asia-Pacific/2013/0717/With-arrest-China-signals-limits-to-anticorruption-campaign/.

202. For a discussion of Zhou Qiang's legal credentials and views, see, for example, Jiang Ping, "Zhou Qiang's respect for the law is recognized by the legal community," *China Business Journal* (Beijing), May 9, 2013, www.lawinnovation.com/html/zgfx50rlt/9125.shtml.

203. For a discussion of Wang Shengjun's views on the judiciary, see, for example, Willy Lam, "CCP tightens control over courts," *China Brief,* Jamestown Foundation, June 17, 2011, www.jamestown.org/programs/chinabrief/single/?tx_ttnews%5Bpointer%5D=7&tx_ttnews%5Btt_news%5D=38068&tx_ttnews%5BbackPid%5D=25&cHash=7749912f01b4f91bbb8eace0bca18a39/.

204. Cited in "Zhou Qiang: Transparency is our principle and nontransparency is the exception," Xinhua News Agency, July 5, 2013, http://news.xinhuanet.com/yzyd/local/20130705/c_116414014.htm?prolongation=1/; see also "Zhou Qiang: What people are most dissatisfied about the work of courts are unjust adjudication and corrupt judges," *People's Daily,* August 22, 2013, http://news.xinhuanet.com/politics/2013-08/22/c_117040139.htm.

205. For a discussion of the "three priorities," see, for example, "Wang Shengjun's address at the conference of the presidents of the higher courts," Xinhua News Agency, December 22, 2008, http://news.xinhuanet.com/legal/2008-12/22/content_10541536.htm. See also "Hu Jintao talks to senior judges and prosecutors in National Conference on Political-Legal Work," Xinhua News Agency, December 26, 2007, http://news.sina.com.cn/c/2007-12-26/032013143978s.shtml.

206. For a discussion of the qualifications of senior judges, see, for example, "Who says judges are not cognizant of the law?" *Ta Kung Pao,* August 14, 2013, http://news.takungpao.com/special/fyyz/.

207. Cited in "Justice in the judiciary is a strong guarantee for 'the Chinese dream,'" *Procuratorial Daily,* May 24, 2013, http://money.163.com/13/0524/10/8VKQRSG300254TI5.html.

208. Cited in "Decision on major issues concerning comprehensively deepening reforms." For a discussion of the role of the CNSC, see, for example, *Global Times,* "Keeping the nation secure from the top down," January 26, 2014, www.globaltimes.cn/DesktopModules/DnnForge%20-%20NewsArticles/Print.aspx?tabid=99&tabmoduleid=94&articleId=824883&moduleId=405&PortalID=0/; see also Radio Free Asia, "New Chinese agency to 'manage' social unrest," November 12, 2013, www.rfa.org/english/news/china/agency-11122013140403.html.

209. For a study of the roles of China's national security institutions, including the Central Leading Group on National Security and the Central Leading Group on Foreign Affairs, see, for example, Yun Sun, "Chinese national security decision-making: Processes and challenges," Brookings Institution Center for Northeast Asian Policy Studies, May 2013, www.brookings.edu/~/media/research/files/papers/2013/05/chinese%20national%20security%20decisionmaking%20sun/chinese%20national%20security%20decisionmaking%20sun%20paper.pdf.

210. For a discussion of the significance and implications of *Silent Contest,* see, for example, Miles Yu, "Inside China: A parade of paranoia about U.S. 'engagement' in China," *Washington Times,* November 7, 2013, www.washingtontimes.com/news/2013/nov/7/inside-china-a-parade-of-paranoia-about-us-engagem/?page=all/.

211. See "National security matter of prime importance: President Xi," Xinhua News Agency, April 15, 2014, http://news.xinhuanet.com/english/china/2014-04/15/c_133264574.htm.

212. Ibid.

213. For a discussion of the composition of the CNSC, see, for example, Willy Lam, "Terrorism fears push muscular approach to 'overall national security,'" *China Brief*, Jamestown Foundation, May 7, 2014, www.jamestown.org/programs/chinabrief/single/?tx_ttnews%5Btt_news%5D=42329&tx_ttnews%5BbackPid%5D=25&cHash=5c1918a6e2db6 5e194890b60f724a70a/.

214. Cited in "Ministry of Foreign Affairs spokesman on whether the National Security Commission is targeting Japan," Xinhua News Agency, November 13, 2013, http://news. xinhuanet.com/overseas/2013-11/13/c_125698870.htm?prolongation=1/.

215. Cited in Li Wei, "China needs a National Security Commission to formulate anti-terrorist strategies," China Daily Net, November 12, 2013, http://news.ifeng.com/mainland/special/sbjszqh/pinglun/detail_2013_11/12/31188911_0.shtml.

216. Cited in "Opening up China's mega-security framework through top-level design," *Global Times*, November 14, 2013, http://politics.people.com.cn/n/2013/1114/c70731-23539892.html.

217. Cited in Willy Lam, "Xi's power grab dwarfs market reforms," *Asia Times*, November 21, 2013, www.atimes.com/atimes/China/CHIN-01-211113.html.

218. Cited in "Hu Jia: The new National Security Commission will transform China into a police state," Now TV (Hong Kong), November 13, 2013, http://news.now.com/home/international/player?newsId=84873.

219. Cited in "*Weiwen* fee has reached RMB 815 billion," *Ming Pao*, March 8, 2013, http://news.mingpao.com/20140308/caa4.htm.

220. Cited in "Meng Jianzhu: Push forward the informatization of public security and construct a flawless network of prevention and control," China News Service, December 1, 2009, www.chinanews.com/gn/news/2009/12-01/1992812.shtml.

221. Cited in Fiona Tam, "2m spy cameras in Guangdong by 2015," *South China Morning Post*, June 15, 2012, www.scmp.com/article/1003992/2m-spy-cameras-guangdong-2015/.

222. For a discussion of grassroots *weiwen* units, see, for example, Karita Kan, "Whether *weiwen:* Stability maintenance in the Eighteenth Party Congress era," *China Perspectives* (Paris) January 2013 pp. 67–93, http://chinaperspectives.revues.org/6120. See also Jonathan Benney, "Stability maintenance at the grassroots: China's *weiwen* apparatus as a form of conflict resolution," Loewe Research Focus, Institute for U.S.-China Issues, University of Oklahoma, Working Paper no. 8, 2013, www.academia.edu/4949105/Stability_maintenance_at_the_grassroots_Chinas_weiwen_apparatus_as_a_form_of_conflict_resolution/.

223. Cited in Willy Lam, "China's new security state," *Wall Street Journal*, December 9, 2009, http://online.wsj.com/news/articles/SB10001424052748704240504574585120857399040/.

224. For a discussion of Beijing's revival of Mao's "people's warfare" concept so as to upgrade domestic security, see, for example, Willy Lam, "China has a blueprint for social order," *Asia Times*, March 31, 2011, www.atimes.com/atimes/China/MC31Ad02.html.

225. Cited in Tania Branigan, "Chinese police chief boasts of recruiting one in 33 residents as informants," *Guardian*, February 10, 2010, www.theguardian.com/world/2010/feb/10/china-police-informants-surveillance/.

226. Cited in "Xi Jinping: The Internet could lead to the collapse of the Party and the state," *Apple Daily*, November 6, 2013, http://hk.apple.nextmedia.com/news/first/20131106/18495692/. See also "Xi Jinping leads Internet security group," Xinhua News Agency, February 27, 2014, http://news.xinhuanet.com/english/china/2014-02/27/c_133148273.htm; "China's Xi to run Internet security body: State media," Reuters, February 27, 2014, www.reuters.com/article/2014/02/27/us-china-hacking-idUSBREA1Q1EX201402/.

227. Cited in "China has 3.5 million Web sites," Xinhua News Agency, March 22, 2014, http://news.xinhuanet.com/english/china/2014-03/22/c_133206625.htm; see also Charles Custer, "The demise of Sina Weibo: Censorship or evolution?" *Forbes*, February 4, 2014, www.forbes.com/sites/ccuster/2014/02/04/the-demise-of-sina-weibo-censorship-or-evolution/.

228. For a discussion of the new "gag order" on the Internet and *weibo*, see, for example, Megha Rajagopalan and Adam Rose, "China crackdown on online rumors seen as ploy to nail critics," Reuters, September 18, 2013, www.reuters.com/article/2013/09/18/net-us-china-internet-idUSBRE98H07X20130918/; see also "China must crack down on critical online speech—Party journal," Reuters, August 16, 2013, www.reuters.com/article/2013/09/16/net-us-china-internet-idUSBRE98A18Z20130916/.

229. Cited in "Chinese Academy of Social Sciences: 300 big Vs dominate 120 million users of weibo," *Ming Pao*, December 12, 2013, http://premium.mingpao.com/cfm/Content_News.cfm?Channel=ca&Path=201714894546/cac1.cfm.

230. For a discussion of the case of Charles Xue, see, "Four months after prostitution arrest, influential investor Charles Xue remains uncharged," *South China Morning Post*, January 11, 2014, www.scmp.com/news/china-insider/article/1403009/four-months-after-prostitution-arrest-influential-investor/. See also "China releases blogger on bail, jails another amid rumor crackdown," Reuters, April 16, 2014, www.reuters.com/article/2014/04/17/us-china-blogger-idUSBREA3G04A20140417/.

231. Cited in "China's cyber security under severe threat," Xinhua News Agency, March 19, 2013, www.chinadaily.com.cn/china/2013-03/19/content_16321007.htm.

232. Cited in Qiu Yu and Liu Chang, "Expert: The importance of the Internet in Xinjiang's terrorist activities has significantly increased," *Global Times*, January 26, 2014, www.mzb.com.cn/html/Home/report/140113333-1.htm.

233. See "Xi Jinping: We must do a better job in propaganda and ideological work," Gov. cn, August 20, 2013, www.gov.cn/ldhd/2013-08/20/content_2470599.htm.

234. Cited in "At this stage, China cannot sustain the consequence of the loss of control over public opinion," *Seeking Truth*, August 16, 2013, http://news.southcn.com/z/2013-08/16/content_76585189.htm.

235. Cited in "Control at the grassroots, China's new toolbox," European Council on Foreign Relations, June 2012, www.ecfr.eu/page/-/China_Analysis_Control_at_the_Grassroots_June2012.pdf. For a discussion of the scale of "mass incidents" in China in recent years, see, for example, Yanqi Tang and Shaohua Lai, *Social Protest in Contemporary China* (Abingdon, UK: Routledge, 2014), pp. 1–2; Alan Taylor, "Rising protests in China," *Atlantic*, February 17, 2012, www.theatlantic.com/infocus/2012/02/rising-protests-in-china/100247/.

236. For examples of vicious attacks and rampages, see, for example, "Man attacks children with a meat cleaver in Macheng, China," Huffington Post, May 21, 2014, www.huffingtonpost.co.uk/2014/05/21/man-attacks-children-with-meat-cleaver_n_5363683.html; "Villager slashes 22 kids with knife at elementary school gates in China," NBC News, December 14, 2012, http://worldnews.nbcnews.com/_news/2012/12/14/15901085-villager-slashes-22-kids-with-knife-at-elementary-school-gates-in-china?lite/.

237. For a discussion of mass killing incidents in Xinjing and other cities, see, for example, Jethro Mullen, "Terror attacks kill dozens in China's tense Xinjiang region," CNN, May 22, 2014, http://edition.cnn.com/2014/05/21/world/asia/china-xinjiang-explosions/; see also Andrew Jacobs and Chris Buckley, "China blames Xinjiang separatists for stabbing rampage at train station," *New York Times*, March 2, 2014, www.nytimes.com/2014/03/03/world/asia/china.html?_r=0/.

238. Cited in Jeremy Page, "China launches manhunt for alleged member of ETIM separatist group," *Wall Street Journal*, May 18, 2014, http://online.wsj.com/news/articles/SB10001424052702304422704579569772676469090/.

239. Cited in Michael Forsythe, "Q & A: Nicholas Bequelin on why tensions are rising in Xinjiang and beyond," *New York Times,* March 2, 2014, http://sinosphere.blogs.nytimes.com/2014/05/02/q-a-nicholas-bequelin-on-why-tensions-are-rising-in-xinjiang-and-beyond/#/.

240. Cited in "He Weifang on Xinjiang: Contradictions among ethnic groups should not be hidden," Phoenix TV Net, November 8, 2010, http://news.ifeng.com/mainland/special/xinjiang/baodao/detail_2010_11/08/3035552_0.shtml. For a discussion of Beijing's repressive measures in Xinjiang, see, for example, Peter Ford, "Uighurs: Who are they, and why are they unhappy?" *Christian Science Monitor,* November 9, 2013, www.csmonitor.com/World/Asia-Pacific/2013/1109/China-s-Uighurs-Who-are-they-and-why-are-they-unhappy/.

241. For a discussion of the career and work of Ilham Tohti, see, for example, Mihray Abdilim, "Three students of Uyghur scholar Ilham Tohti formally arrested," Radio Free Asia, February 26, 2014, www.rfa.org/english/news/uyghur/arrest-02262014185533.html; Eric Meyer, "Time is running out for ethnic peace and reconciliation in Xinjiang," *Forbes,* May 2, 2014, www.forbes.com/sites/ericrmeyer/2014/05/02/time-is-running-out-for-ethnic-peace-and-reconciliation-in-xinjiang/. See also Andrew Jacobs, "Uighur scholar's life sentence is seen as reining in debate on minorities in China," *New York Times,* September 24, 2014, www.nytimes.com/2014/09/25/world/asia/uighurs-sentence-seen-as-a-sign-of-narrowing-ethnic-debate.html?_r=0.

242. For a discussion of Chinese official views on self-immolations by Tibetans, see, for example, Holly Williams, "China: Immolations are terrorism in disguise," Sky News (London), March 6, 2012, http://news.sky.com/story/1268/china-immolations-are-terrorism-in-disguise/. See also Qin Feng, "Self-immolation: The ghosts of terrorism," China Tibet Net, February 18, 2013, www.tibet.cn/news/index/xzyw/201302/t20130218_1860767.htm.

243. See Olga Khazan, "China: Self-immolators and their abettors will be charged with murder," *Washington Post,* December 6, 2012, www.washingtonpost.com/blogs/worldviews/wp/2012/12/06/china-self-immolators-and-their-abettors-will-be-charged-with-murder/; Didi Tang, "Tibet Self-immolation convictions," Associated Press, January 31, 2013, www.huffingtonpost.com/2013/01/31/tibet-self-immolation-convictions-china_n_2590147.html.

244. For a study of Hu Yaobang's Tibet policy, see, for example, "Hu Yaobang issues a six-word dictum on Tibet policy," Phoenix TV, May 9, 2010, http://v.ifeng.com/his/201005/1b81be81-448d-4c06-b009-cc7e5f86e785.shtml; "Hu Yaobang inspects Tibet when he is 65; Deng Xiaoping says he is very bold," Phoenix TV, November 16, 2012, http://phtv.ifeng.com/program/zgjy/detail_2012_11/16/19243551_0.shtml. For a discussion of Xi Zhongxun's policies on ethnic minorities, see "The initiator of the party's policy toward ethnic minorities," *Shenzhen Special Zone Daily,* October 14, 2013, http://sztqb.sznews.com/html/2013-10/14/content_2648664.htm.

245. Cited in Xi, *Work Hard on the Substance and Take the Lead,* p. 553.

246. See "Xi Jinping: Talk in seminar in commemoration of the 120th birthday of comrade Mao Zedong," Xinhua News Agency, December 26, 2013, http://news.xinhuanet.com/politics/2013-12/26/c_118723453.htm.

247. See "Xi Jinping: Use the rectification spirit to develop the campaign of criticism and self-criticism," *China Youth Daily,* June 18, 2013, http://news.youth.cn/zt/qzxl/XiJinPingJH/201306/t20130620_3397630_2.htm.

248. Cited in "The National Security Commission has consolidated Xi's power," *Ming Pao,* November 13, 2013, http://news.creaders.net/headline/newsViewer.php?nid=591112&id=1314827/.

249. For a discussion of the significance of Jiang Zemin's allowing private businessmen to get into the CCP, see, for example, Gilles Guiheux, "The political 'participation' of

entrepreneurs: Challenge or opportunity for the Chinese Communist Party?" *Social Research: An International Quarterly* 73, no. 1 (Spring 2006): 219–244.

250. For a discussion of Long Yongtu as a "traitor," see Chen Jiang, "Long Yongtu: 'I'm neither a hero nor a traitor,'" *Southern Weekend,* December 31, 2010, www.infzm.com/content/54072/.

251. Cited in "Wen Jiabao: Without success in political reform, it is not possible to push through economic reform," Phoenix TV News, March 14, 2012, http://finance.ifeng.com/news/special/2012lianghui/20120314/5747030.shtml; See also "Wen Jiabao: Comprehensively push forward reform of the political and economic structures," CCTV News, March 5, http://news.cntv.cn/2013/03/05/ARTI1362451795837946.shtml.

252. For a discussion of Wen's views on Maoism, see, for example, Jamil Anderlini, "Wen lays ground for Tiananmen healing," *Financial Times,* March 20, 2014, www.ft.com/intl/cms/s/0/13c6fcb2-7285-11e1-9be9-00144feab49a.html#axzz2wqA0DKkQ/.

253. For a discussion of Hu Jintao's interest in socialist democratic parties of Europe, see, for example, Lam, *Chinese Politics in the Hu Jintao Era,* pp. 154–156.

254. Cited in Xie Tao, "The democratic socialist model and China's future," *Yanhuang chunqiu* 2 (2007), http://blog.renren.com/share/234535725/768916220/.

255. See Lam, *Chinese Politics in the Hu Jintao Era,* pp. 154–156. For a discussion of the influence of socialist democratic parties' theories on Hu's scientific outlook on development, see, for example, Yongnian Zheng, "Hu Jintao's road map to China's future," University of Nottingham China Policy Institute Briefing Series, no. 28, October 2007. https://southwellchurches.nottingham.ac.uk/cpi/documents/briefings/briefing-28-hu-jintao-road-map-party-congress-analysis.pdf.

256. Cited in "There can be no socialism in the absence of democracy," *People's Daily,* November 11, 2011, http://news.xinhuanet.com/comments/2012-11/11/c_113657446.htm.

# 4

# Economics vs. Politics

Beijing's Uphill Battle to Retool the Chinese Model

## Introduction: In Search of Sustainable—and More Equitable—Growth

The Xi Jinping administration should have been happy about the country's economic performance in its first year in office. China's GDP grew by 7.7 percent in 2013—the same rate as in 2012—but 0.2 percent higher than the goal laid down at the National People's Congress (NPC) of early 2013. Inflation was held down to a mere 2.6 percent, and 10 million new jobs were created. However, in 2013 the negative side-effects of the CCP leadership's obsession with a high growth rate became more apparent than ever. Environmental problems in cities with dazzling skyscrapers, such as Beijing and Shanghai, have become so serious that not only expats but Chinese professionals are thinking of relocating elsewhere. The gap between rich and poor is yawning wider. By mid-2014, the country's total debt (which includes government, corporate, and household borrowing as well as loans extended by "shadow banks") reached 250 percent of GDP.[1] Worst of all, the goal laid down by Li Keqiang—China's first "Ph.D. premier"—of "rebalancing" or improving the Chinese model by boosting the role of domestic consumption as a vehicle for growth is far from being achieved. Equally problematic is the fact that while Li is a keen advocate of market mechanisms, President Xi, who has apparently sidelined the premier as the ultimate arbiter of economic policy-making, is leaning toward boosting the Party-state apparatus's control over key sectors of the economy.

In 2013, "gross capital formation," or investment mainly by central and local governments, was responsible for 54.4 percent of the growth in GDP, compared with 47.1 percent in 2012. The contribution from consumption (both private and government) dropped from 55 percent in 2012 to 50 percent in 2013. Consumer spending made up a mere 35 percent of GDP.[2] Meanwhile, total bank loans in 2013 increased year-on-year by RMB 8.89 trillion, or RMB 0.69 trillion more than that of 2012. While M2, the broad measure of the money supply, rose in 2013 by 13.6

percent year-on-year—or 0.2 percent less than the comparable figure for 2012—it still remained at an unhealthily high level. Moreover, these figures did not take full consideration of shadow banking, which experts estimated to be in the region of RMB 36 trillion in late 2013.[3]

This chapter looks at efforts by the new administration to introduce market-oriented reforms to make economic growth more balanced and sustainable. There is in-depth discussion on the wide-ranging reform initiatives unveiled at the third plenum of the Eighteenth Central Committee, held in November 2013. Also analyzed are the future roles of SOEs as well as private-sector firms. The prospects for whether China can transform itself from a world factory to a global innovation hub are explored. Economic liberalization favored by Premier Li, however, is running up against the resistance of vested interests and power blocs. Aided by conservative elements in the top leadership, major clans within the "red aristocracy" and SOE conglomerates are trying the best they can to hold on to their quasi-monopolistic privileges. The conclusion assesses the future orientations of market-oriented reforms in the likely absence of thoroughgoing political and institutional changes.

## Market Reforms Introduced at the Third Plenum of the Eighteenth Central Committee

Most of the economic and social reforms introduced by the Xi administration in the rest of the 2010s were outlined in the Decision on Major Issues Concerning Comprehensively Deepening Reforms (hereafter, Decision), which was endorsed at the third plenum of the Eighteenth Central Committee, in November 2013. Although officials have compared the Decision to the radical liberalization measures kick-started by Deng Xiaoping at the third plenum of the Eleventh Central Committee, in December 1978, it is important to bear in mind the different historical contexts of the two landmark events. In 1978, China was still in the throes of the "command economy," in which the state had a stranglehold on industrial and agricultural production; private and foreign enterprises had yet to be revived or introduced. By late 2013, China had been a member of the WTO for twelve years, and most Chinese worked for non-state-sector firms rather than the government. Thus the third plenum of the Eleventh Central Committee virtually opened up a new heaven and earth—while the plenum thirty-five years later consisted of fine-tuning fairly extensive liberalization measures that had been rolled out in the previous three-plus decades.[4] Also significant is the fact that while the opposition that Deng faced was mostly ideological, the enemies of reform in the 2010s consist of holders of vested interests, including major clans within the "red aristocracy" who fear that a level playing field would eat into lucrative business empires that they have built up based on their sterling political connections.[5]

## The Market to "Play a Decisive Role in the Distribution of Resources"—and a New Deal for Private and Foreign Firms

The key clause in the Decision is that "the market will be a decisive force in the allocation of resources." "The [principle of the] market deciding the allocation of resources is a common law of market economics," the document said. "To complete the socialist market economy system, we must respect this law, and strive to resolve the problems of imperfect market systems, excessive government intervention and unsatisfactory supervision and management."[6]

A multipronged approach was adopted to boost the role of the market. As Li Keqiang indicated soon after becoming premier, the state should withdraw and "allow the market to do what it does best." Thus, several hundred government regulations would be slashed on top of the more than 300 fiats that had been abolished in the first half of 2013.[7] State control of the price of utilities—including electricity, water, and gasoline—would be incrementally curtailed. Interest rates charged by banks and other financial institutions would be gradually liberalized. The Decision pledged to open up in an orderly way the following areas to private and foreign companies: a number of manufacturing sectors in addition to services including finance, education, culture, health care, child care, elder care, architectural design, accounting and auditing, commerce and logistics, and electronic commerce.[8] Equally significantly, the Li cabinet pledged that central and local administrations would experiment with "management via negative lists." This means that the authorities will spell out sectors or activities that are out of bounds for private or foreign firms; anything outside the negative lists will be permissible. Moreover, Premier Li vowed that regional and local-level administrations, where more than 90 percent of civil servants are employed, would be told to drastically curtail their interference in the activities of enterprises. "Grassroots administrations represent what we call 'the last mile' [of reform]," said Li. The State Council chief also indicated that local governments would gradually stop investing in SOEs.[9]

However, whether market forces will have full play depends on the speed with which well-known limits and restrictions on economic liberalization are removed or minimized. While China has largely honored its commitments to the WTO regarding market-oriented reforms, the state—in terms of ministries and departments under the State Council—still controls "key sectors pertaining to state plans and people's livelihood." The 110 or so *yangqi* (centrally owned SOE conglomerates) enjoy monopolies in important sectors ranging from energy and finance to telecommunications and transport (see below).[10] In 2013 a number of big-name multinationals such as GlaxoSmithKline and Interdigital were penalized for alleged malpractices ranging from overcharging customers to using Chinese patents without adequate payments—despite the pledge made by Premier Li at a foreign investment forum in late 2013 that "China will continue to encourage foreign companies to invest and do business in China, and ensure that all companies have equal access . . . and equal treatment." So far, vested interests in the government as well as the state sector have been erecting obstacles that hinder foreign companies—particularly those in finance and other service sectors—from setting up shop in China.[11]

### Financial Reforms and the Full Convertibility of the Renminbi

Although Beijing has not announced a timetable for the full convertibility of the renminbi, it is expected that the Chinese currency will be freely traded on the world market by around 2020. The Decision pointed out that the band within which the renminbi's exchange rate with the U.S. dollar fluctuates will be further expanded. In early 2014 the renminbi was the eighth most frequently traded currency in the world. And it is no secret that Beijing wants the renminbi to gradually acquire the status of a currency that has wide global acceptance.[12] At the same time, controls over capital-account transactions will gradually be lifted. Chinese companies will be allowed to issue bonds and raise funds overseas, and Chinese citizens will find it easier to buy wealth-management products offered by non-Chinese financial firms. Equally significant was the pledge that Beijing would make it easier for companies, especially private firms, to launch an initial public offering (IPO) on the Shanghai and Shenzhen stock markets.[13]

In September 2013, Beijing set up its first free trade zone (FTZ) in Pudong, Shanghai, where financial reforms would be tried out on a larger scale. At least twelve additional FTZs were set to be established in coastal and hinterland cities in the coming year or so.[14] The Decision also called for more cooperation between the Hong Kong and Macau special administrative regions (SARs) and these zones. As of mid-2014, however, foreign firms operating in the Pudong FTZ remained limited. Even the domestic Chinese media reported that central-government ministries, on the one hand, and local governments, on the other, had different interpretations of the speed with which the zones would dovetail with global norms.[15]

A more ambitious step was taken in April 2014, when Beijing and Hong Kong authorities announced a trial that would allow cross-market stock trading by mainland Chinese and Hong Kong investors. This means that mainland investors would be able to buy and sell shares of selected companies listed on the Hong Kong Stock Exchange, and Hong Kong investors could trade designated stocks listed on the Shanghai Stock Exchange. The program permits Hong Kong investors to invest as much as RMB 13 billion a day in Shanghai-listed shares; the comparable quota for mainland investors is RMB 10.5 billion a day. The China Securities Regulatory Commission (CSRC) said the move represented a big step forward for internationalization of the renminbi as well as the incremental relaxation of capital-account transactions in and out of China.[16]

Beijing first experimented with interest rate liberalization in early 2013. Banks were allowed to vary interest rates on loans to different sectors and clienteles. A large majority of Chinese, however, are much more concerned about policies that would give banks more flexibility in setting interest rates on deposits, which totaled RMB 73.21 trillion in January 2014. Since the beginning of the reform era, bank customers have been getting fixed—and artificially low—interest payments on their deposits. For example, a one-year fixed deposit could only fetch a 3.3 percent yield. This not only allows the four *yangqi* banks to make huge profits but has also resulted in a kind of subsidy for SOEs, which are in a position to secure cheap loans.[17] Since mid-2013, however, e-commerce giants, including Alibaba and Tencent, have been offering investment fund-like products that will yield a return of at least 6 percent per annum. After the third plenum, state-run commercial banks, led by the Industrial and Commercial Bank of China (the world's largest bank by assets), have leaped into the fray by offering high-yield funds to customers. These developments would force all four *yangqi* banks to adopt a more flexible interest rate on deposits in the foreseeable future.[18]

### *A New Deal for Farmers and Faster Pace of Urbanization*

Although full details have yet to be spelled out, the third plenum in principle endorsed allowing farmers to monetize their private plots of land. Under the Chinese constitution, land in rural areas belongs to "the collective," meaning that individual households are not allowed to either sell their plots or borrow money from banks by using them as collateral. The Decision pointed out, however, that "under the precondition of conforming to regulations and managing the purpose of use, it is to be permitted that rural collective and construction land-use [rights] be sold, rented or leased."[19] "Construction land" is a technical term referring to land that is not used for production—for example, areas where farmers build their own houses. In actual practice, however, "construction land" and agricultural land may not be easy to distinguish. Moreover, farmers in a number of provinces and cities since the late 1990s have been allowed to sell the land-use rights of their agricultural plots on the open market. Tuliu.com, founded in 2009, is the country's largest private e-commerce platform that handles nationwide transactions of land-use rights. While it sold a mere 620,000 *mu* of land in 2009, in the first eleven months of 2013 it sold 17 million *mu*.[20]

The Decision further affirmed the importance of establishing "uniform urban and rural construction land markets." This was intended to allow peasants to get a better deal in selling their land-use rights. Some 60 percent of China's riots and disturbances have to do with "land grabs," in which unscrupulous local officials illegally sold off private plots owned by farmers to developers, during which process farmers received less than 10 percent of the money that their land could fetch on the open market.[21]

Apart from reducing the adverse impact of "land grabs," allowing farmers to sell their land-use rights is the best and least costly method for promoting urbanization, which is seen as a key engine of growth in the next decade. It is important to note, however, that the Xi administration lacked the political resolve to abolish the *hukou* (household residency permit) system. Established by Chairman Mao in 1955, the *hukou* prevents citizens born in the countryside from moving to the city. And even though more than 200 million peasants have become "migrant workers" in urban areas since the mid-1980s, they are not eligible for urban *hukou*—meaning that they and their offspring are barred from education, health, and retirement benefits that are only available to urban-born citizens.[22] Unfortunately, the Decision provided no indication as to when the discriminatory and unconstitutional regulation would be scrapped. Moreover, Chinese officials have warned that because megacities such as Shenzhen and Shanghai are already overcrowded, further urbanization will consist mostly of peasants moving to medium-size cities with a population of no more than a few million.[23]

### *Promoting Social Justice and Equality and Boosting Social Welfare*

Apart from economic and financial policies, the Decision also set forth a plethora of social measures in the interest of promoting "distributive justice," a reference to the fact that the economic pie should be sliced with equality in mind. The National Bureau of Statistics noted that China's Gini coefficient was 0.474 for 2012, having peaked at 0.491 in 2008. However, most independent social scientists have disputed this figure. For example, the Survey and Research Center for China Household Finance, a body set up by the Finance Research Institute of the People's Bank of China and the Southwestern University of Finance and Economics, pointed out in late 2012 that the figure in 2010 was close to 0.6, one of the highest in the world.[24] A key factor behind the yawning gap between rich and poor is artificially depressed salaries. According to the China expert Michael Pettis, while China's GDP increased by more than 10 percent annually through the 2000s, household income expanded by just 7 percent to 8 percent a year, while the state sector grew by nearly 15 percent per annum.[25]

The third plenum document mandated the formation of "rational and orderly income allocation structures," with priority given to the "protection of labor income," particularly the fact that wages should increase hand in hand with productivity growth. Another section of the Decision promised that Beijing would "establish fairer and more sustainable social security systems," especially a "basic old-age insurance system" to deal with the needs of an aging society. Other important social policies include partial relaxation of the one-child-family system: If either parent is a single child, the couple will be eligible to have more than one offspring.[26]

Details, however, are lacking regarding how the social security funds should be established—and the exact benefits for urban and rural residents. Better social-welfare benefits, especially regarding health insurance and pensions, are a key to boosting consumer spending. One reason for China's high savings rate is ordinary people's concern about inadequate social security payments. In 2013, social welfare spending comprised a mere 12 percent of government expenditures, compared with 37 percent in the United States. Even though Beijing plans to raise the level to 14 percent in five years, it could be a case of too little, too late with respect to promoting consumer spending.[27]

## Control vs. Let Go: Clashes Between Xi Jinping and Li Keqiang

Unlike the five-year plan, which has a specific time frame, the Decision did not spell out when a particular reform measure would come to fruition. Two social reforms—the abolition of the *laojiao* system and the liberalization of the one-child family planning policy—were launched on January 1, 2014. The timeline for most of the economic reforms, however, has remained murky. For example, the location of the twelve additional FTZs that would be set up—and the kind of dispensation to be accorded foreign enterprises operating in these zones—remains uncertain. The same is true for the number of private or foreign firms that will be allowed into the sectors that have been monopolized by SOE conglomerates. Moreover, the exact procedures by which farmers can monetize their farming plots and "construction land" have yet to be spelled out. No details have been released regarding the liberalization of procedures for private companies seeking a listing on the two Chinese stock markets.[28]

### *Xi's Insistence on Tight CCP Supervision of Reform— and the Establishment of the Central Leading Group on Comprehensively Deepening Reforms*

In line with Xi's broad governance philosophy, emphasis was placed on "top-level design" and the rolling out of reform measures under tight centralized supervision. "The comprehensive deepening of reforms necessarily requires strengthening and improving party leadership," the Decision said. "We must fully develop the core functions of the party taking charge of the whole situation and coordinating various [sectors]." The document also repeated Xi's ingrained belief in the "organic unification of the [principles of] leadership of the Party, the people mastering their own affairs and governing the country according to law."[29] In his interview with Russian television while attending the Sochi Olympics in January 2014, Xi characterized reform as "10 percent design and 90 percent implementation." The idea of "90 percent implementation" reflects his insistence that reform be calibrated and executed under the supervision of an elaborate Party-state apparatus.[30]

The Central Leading Group on Comprehensively Deepening Reforms (CLGCDR) was established at the third plenum to ensure the orderly and judicious promulgation of new policies. The Decision indicated that functions of the leading group—which is the largest and most powerful organ set up since the beginning of the era of reform—included "the overall design of reform, arranging and coordinating reform, pushing forward reform as a whole, and supervising the implementation of reform plans." Apart from the economy, the CLGCDR is also charged with planning and executing reforms regarding the political, cultural, social, and environmental structures as well as "Party construction."[31] Yet it is clear that, as Xi pointed out, economic reforms will provide the impetus for change on other fronts.

The focus of both Chinese and foreign media has been on the economics-related functions of the leading group.

A Politburo meeting in December 2013 appointed President Xi the chairman of the CLGCDR. The three vice-chairmen are PBSC members Li Keqiang, ideology and propaganda tsar Liu Yunshan, and Executive Vice-Premier Zhang Gaoli. The relationship between the CLGCDR and the Central Leading Group on Finance and Economics (CLGFE)—which is the country's long-standing top organ on economic policy-making—is unclear. The fact that Xi heads both leading groups, however, testifies to the president's overweening powers.[32]

Apart from the four PBSC members at the helm, members of the CLGCDR include ten Politburo members and thirteen other senior cadres from CCP head-quarters and the State Council. Party leaders sitting on the CLGCDR include the following Politburo members: director of the Central Committee General Office Li Zhanshu; director of the Organization Department Zhao Leji; director of the Propaganda Department Liu Qibao; secretary of the Central Political and Legal Commission (CPLC) Meng Jianzhu; and director of the Central Policy Research Office (CPRO) Wang Huning. The secretary-generals of the CLGFE as well as the Central Leading Group on Rural Affairs, respectively, Liu He and Chen Xi-wen, are also represented. Senior figures from the State Council include the three vice-premiers (who are also Politburo members) Liu Yandong, Ma Kai, and Wang Yang, as well as the governor of the People's Bank of China, Zhou Xiaochuan, the minister at the National Development and Reform Commission (NDRC), Xu Shaoshi, Minister of Finance Lou Jiwei, Commerce Minister Gao Hucheng and Minister of Public Security Guo Shengkun. Provincial and municipal CLGCDRs have also been established to speed up relevant reform measures in the regions.[33] Wang Huning, a political strategist who was credited with coining key political slogans for ex-presidents Jiang Zemin and Hu Jintao, will serve as secretary-general of the CLGCDR. And Wang's CPRO will double as the secretariat and clearinghouse for the leading group's many operations. The fact that day-to-day administration of this superagency will be handled by a secretive party organ—which is headed by somebody who is not a trained economist—does not seem to bode well for transparency, efficiency, and freedom from bureaucracy.[34]

The creation of the CLGCDR has confirmed that Xi has seized decision-making power over the economy from the premier and the State Council, despite the long-standing tradition that the premier is the PBSC member with particular responsibility for the economy.[35] As discussed in Chapter 1, Xi and Li come from different Party factions. And the fact that Li is the only member of the CYL Faction in the PBSC means that the protégé of ex-president Hu lacks the clout to claw back lost political territory. More importantly, Xi's revival of the Leninist doctrine of concentrating all powers at the apex of the Party amounts to a repudiation of Deng Xiaoping's many dictums about separation of the Party and the government as well as building transparent institutions to curb the formation of a cult of personality.[36]

Of more significance than the rivalry between Xi and Li is the effect that the president's top-down approach will have on the long-term prospects for reform. Chi Fulin, head of the China (Hainan) Reform and Development Research Institute, argued that concentrating powers in the CLGCDR and in President Xi would make it easier for the authorities to overcome obstacles to reform coming from "the vested interests of departments, [economic] sectors, and the regions."[37] However, the labyrinthine structure of the CLGCDR has raised the question of bureaucratic overkill: Can the free spirit of the market survive under the cumbersome and multifarious supervisory regimes? At the first meeting of the CLGCDR, in January 2014, Xi stressed that responsible departments and personnel must understand the "difficult, complex, and systematic nature" of reform—and that any new initiative would necessarily affect the ethos and structure of the Party-state apparatus. "While our pace must be fast, our steps must be stable," he counseled. The main reason for Xi's cautious approach, however, seems to be ideological. He went on to point out that CLGCDR-related cadres "must have a tight grip over the correct direction of reform." "We must take a resolute stance over fundamental questions such as the [nature of China's developmental] path, theories, and systems." In other words, the convoluted bureaucracy has been created to ensure that reform will not jeopardize the socialist path.[38]

Xi's preference for a cautious and steady pace of reform in order to preserve its socialist character was also evident in another talk that he gave at about the same time. "We must seek progress and accomplishments in the midst of stability," the president said. "If we do not give due regard to risks and difficulties and blindly go ahead [with new policy initiatives], not only will we fail to secure good results but our current achievements may go down the drain." What most concerned Xi is that "erroneous and overly hasty" measures might jeopardize the "socialist road." "Our direction must be correct, the navigation must be stable—and in particular we must avoid errors that would subvert [the socialist system]," he added.[39] Li Zhanshu, a close adviser to Xi, argued in a *People's Daily* article that "incremental reforms" suited China's conditions best. "We must avoid inadequate measures that would cause social upheaval," he wrote. "Our Party is in charge of the policy of reform and open door for a socialist developing country with 1.3 billion people," he added. "We must not allow subversive errors to appear in fundamental questions. After these errors have been made, it might be difficult to remedy [the situation]."[40]

Another factor that would predispose Xi toward a cautious approach to reform is his oft-repeated dictum about "striking a balance among reform, development, and stability." While meeting a group of foreign experts in late 2013, Xi noted that "we must handle well the relationship among reform, development, and stability." "We must summon greater political courage and wisdom in further liberating our thoughts . . . and boosting the innovative vigor of society," Xi added.[41] What usually happens, however, is that market-oriented reform policies will be decelerated if they are seen as infringing upon the sacrosanct goals of a reasonably high growth rate as well as sociopolitical stability.

### *The Short Shelf Life of Likonomics*

As the most liberal member of PBSC, Li is a well-known advocate of no-holds-barred market reforms. This is partly reflected by the premier's personal think tank, which consists mostly of liberal economists from Peking University, his alma mater. In the first half of 2013, the state media were replete with reports about "Likonomics," one of whose major thrusts was that Beijing should curtail bureaucratic intervention in the market—and that it should wean itself off the practice of relying on state injections of funds to sustain a relatively high GDP growth rate (see below).[42] "Likonomics," however, began to disappear from the official universe of discourse in the few months before the third plenum. Analysts were surprised that the high-level drafting group charged with putting together the Decision was headed by Xi, and that the two deputy heads were Liu Yunshan and Zhang Gaoli. This confirmed speculation that Li's authority in economic decision-making had to some extent been curtailed.[43]

According to the official Chinese media, Likonomics simply means using market-oriented measures to replace old-style administrative fiat, which tends to favor China's vested interest blocs. As *Southern Weekend,* the liberal Guangzhou-based paper, put it, Likonomics can be summarized in one sentence: "Let the economy again pick up its market track." Some of Li's reformist ideas were discussed publicly in a videoconference that he held in May 2013 with regional officials on how to wage a "national mobilization [campaign] for changing the institutions and functions of the State Council." The relatively young head of government made it clear that he was interested in "storming fortresses" so as to realize "big breakthroughs." "We must further stimulate the creative powers of the market and of society," Li noted, "The market is the creator of social wealth. Let go of the powers that should be let go." At an early 2014 talk to provincial leaders, the premier said: "We must believe in the market; we must believe in the boundless creativity of the masses."[44] In other words, the market and society—not the Party-state apparatus of which Xi is so enamored—should take center stage in twenty-first-century reform.

Unlike Xi and his conservative colleagues, Li wants the government to curtail direct interference in the economy. In his NPC Government Work Report of March 2014, Xi even talked about "self-revolution by the government," meaning that senior officials should selflessly go about curtailing the powers of their own offices. Pledging to "further simplify government [bureaucracy] and devolve powers" to the marketplace, Li noted that at least 200 "administrative approval procedures" would be slashed in 2014.[45] Talking to provincial officials a few months earlier, Li also indicated that "reform at the local level is a self-revolution," meaning that regional cadres should seize the initiative by giving market forces a bigger role in the allocation of resources.[46]

As in many of his previous speeches, Li argued that reform had entered a "critical stage and deep-water terrain." "We must closely rely on the people and summon the resolve of a warrior cutting off his own wrist . . . to smash mental shackles and break through the barriers set up by vested interests," Li noted. The key, he said, was to "break down barriers that constrain the vigor of the market" and to "allow the potential creativity of society to be fully released."[47] Pointing to the fact that some 60 percent of fixed-asset investment comes from the non-state sector, Li vowed to provide a level playing field for private firms by, for example, making more bank loans available and slashing government red tape. The State Council chief also promised to streamline government departments and cut state intervention in order to bolster the market's function in "nurturing superior enterprises and throwing out inefficient ones." "Enterprises must enthusiastically take part in market competition so that they will always be motivated to modernize technology and to create new products," he said.[48]

The premier, who leads the CYL Faction in Party politics, however, has made a big concession to his more conservative colleagues by paying tribute to the role of the government in his 2014 Government Work Report. "We must untangle the 'invisible hand' of the market and use well the 'visible hand' of the government," Li said. On the one hand, Li reiterated the "decisive role" of the market in the distribution of resources. But, on the other hand, the premier underscored the imperative of "developing well the functions of the government."[49] Another example of Li not having his way was the slow roll-out of reforms at the Pudong FTZ, which is considered the premier's brainchild. Due to the fact that a key mandate of the FTZ is to open the door wider to foreign companies in the financial services sector, the zone does not have the full support of China's cumbersome financial regulatory establishment and the four giant *yangqi* banks. On a trip to Shanghai in August 2013, Li asked Mayor Yang Xiong: "Does Shanghai want reform—or more [favorable] policies?" Li then told local cadres to "give top priority to reform as well as institutional innovation." While the FTZ opened according to schedule, Chinese and foreign observers were surprised that no Politburo-ranked official was on hand for the ceremony. As of mid-2014, only about a dozen foreign firms in the services sector had set up shop in the FTZ.[50]

## SOE Conglomerates Retain Clout

*Tackling the "National Champions"*

In the course of more than three decades of reform, central and regional authorities have closed down, sold off, or otherwise privatized hundreds of thousands of SOEs. The U.S.-based Peterson Institute of International Economics estimates that the business volume of state-controlled firms is equivalent to some 25 percent of China's GDP, though other analysts say they control an even larger chunk of the economy. By the end of 2011, China boasted 144,700 state-owned or state-controlled enterprises, which have total assets worth RMB 85.37 trillion. While these firms brought in revenues of RMB 39.25 trillion and profits of RMB 2.58 trillion that year, they are regarded as laggards in areas including efficient management and innovation. The program to whittle down the number of SOEs is expected to continue through the 2010s.[51]

What interests most foreign economists and businessmen, however, is the fate of the approximately 110 *yangqi*. They are rough equivalents of the *chaebol* (conglomerates) in South Korea, except that *yangqi* are "national champions" directly controlled by the central Party-and-state apparatus. And while many of them, including the three major oil corporations (CNPC, Sinopec, and China National Offshore Oil Corporation [CNOOC]) and the four commercial banks (Bank of China, Industrial and Commercial Bank of China, China Construction Bank, and Agriculture Bank), are listed on the Shanghai and Hong Kong stock markets, the government retains controlling interests in these so-called aircraft-carrier-type firms—and these state-held shares are not up for trading. As of 2010, the aggregate assets of *yangqi* were estimated at 62 percent of GDP. In that year, the combined profits of CNPC and the state-owned China Mobile were larger than those of China's 500 largest private firms combined.[52] Sixty-five of the seventy Chinese firms that broke into the 2012 Fortune Global 500 were *yangqi*. For example, the energy giant State Grid was the world's seventh-biggest company. The oil conglomerates Sinopec and CNPC, the parent of the publicly listed PetroChina, were ranked fifth and sixth, respectively.[53]

Despite its commitment to market reforms, the third plenum gave unambiguous support to the continued existence—even the further development—of the state-held sector, particularly the *yangqi*. The Decision stated that the authorities must "unwaveringly consolidate and develop the public economy, preserve the dominant position of public ownership, give full rein to the guiding function of the state-owned economy, [and] incessantly strengthen the vitality, control power and influence of the state-owned economy." It added in particular that *yangqi* in the following sectors would continue to enjoy monopolistic status: firms that "serve national strategic objectives," those that fall within "important sectors and key areas relating to national security or key branches of the national economy," and those that "provide public services, develop important and forward-looking strategic industries, protect the ecology and the environment . . . [and] support scientific and technological progress."[54] This meant in essence that the pace of privatizing the *yangqi* would be gradual and incremental at best.

One factor that could force Beijing's hand regarding *yangqi* reform is growing evidence that many of these behemoths are both corrupt and inefficient. The large-scale detention in 2013 of senior CNPC executives for corruption, embezzlement, and misuse of power has highlighted the sorry state of corporate governance of many of these conglomerates (see Chapter 3). In theory, all 110 *yangqi* report to the State Assets Supervision and Administration Commission (SASAC), which is a ministerial-level organ under the State Council. However, many *yangqi* chiefs have the rank of vice-ministers or above—and the conglomerates are so rich and powerful that they may not necessarily follow the instructions of the prime minister, let alone the SASAC chief.[55] The chummy relationship between the government and *yangqi* was illustrated by Jiang Jiemin, a former CNPC president who was appointed SASAC minister in March 2013. Six months later, however, Jiang and a handful of CNPC executives, including the deputy general managers Wang Yongchun and Li Hualin, were arrested for unspecified "economic crimes."

In all, some forty-five mid- to senior-ranked cadres associated with the oil giants were brought in for investigation. Moreover, *yangqi* chiefs have a poor record of clean governance. Top executives of the big-name state corporations Sinopec, China Mobile, and China National Nuclear Corporation—respectively Chen Tonghai, Zhang Chunjiang, and Kang Rixin—received heavy jail terms for graft-related offenses over the past few years.[56]

The Decision made it clear that the Party-state authorities wanted to overhaul the *yangqi* by introducing a modern management system. A few of the conglomerates may be restructured—and parts of them may be sold off to private or even foreign companies. As a sign of more stringent supervision, *yangqi* have to surrender 30 percent of their profits to the state by 2020; some of the funds will be used to underwrite social security payments.[57] The new SASAC minister, Zhang Yi, indicated that agencies under the commission should "forcefully implement structuring adjustments and transformation." Given that Zhang is a former senior cadre in the CCP Central Commission for Disciplinary Inspection (CCDI)—China's highest-level anti-graft watchdog—his role seems to be to clean up the mess in CNPC and other problematic SOE giants.[58]

Despite being the beneficiary of their monopolistic status, SOEs are notably less profitable than private enterprises. In 2012, the average return on assets for privately-owned enterprises (POEs) was 13 percent compared with just 5 percent for state-held firms. Moreover, recent research by a respected private Beijing think tank, Unirule, showed that SOEs had profited from numerous hidden subsidies. For example, they can get loans from state banks (which are themselves *yangqi*) at substantially lower rates than other firms. Moreover, the fact that these conglomerates get free land resources from the state amounted to a hefty hidden state subsidy worth some RMB 4 trillion. Unirule's veteran economist Mao Yushi pointed out after the third plenum that *yangqi* should surrender to the state a much higher percentage of their profits than the 30 percent goal stipulated in the Decision.[59]

### Support for Yangqi Runs Deep

Much of the impetus in reforming the *yangqi* has come from Premier Li, who is an ardent advocate of a level playing field for all enterprises in the country. Li indicated at a State Council conference in mid-2013 that private firms should gradually be allowed into several sectors dominated by *yangqi,* which include finance, oil and gas, electricity, railways, telecommunications, and the exploitation of mineral and other resources. At an earlier meeting, Li urged *yangqi* "to use reform-oriented methods and restructuring measures to solve existing problems." "They should raise management levels [and] make more efforts at boosting innovation," he added. "The government should build up 'sunshine *yangqi*' so that they can raise the value of state assets and acquit themselves well of their social responsibilities."[60] Moreover, Li noted in an internal talk in early 2013 that CNPC, Sinopec, CNOOC, China Telecom, and China Mobile were the five *yangqi* that required the most thorough reform. "If we do not restructure [these enterprises] and bring about major changes, there might be serious consequences for which no one will want to bear responsibility," Li said.[61]

Private entrepreneurs and advisers to Premier Li have also been pushing for a more rapid pace in reforming SOE groupings. At a Forum on Non-State Enterprises held in Beijing in March 2013, the Peking University economist Li Yining argued that "SOEs should become real enterprises" and not adjuncts of the state. Professor Li also urged SASAC to stop exercising direct control over *yangqi*. "Everything should be done according to laws and regulations," said Li, who supervised Li Keqiang's doctoral thesis. "Private enterprises should compete with SOEs in an environment of equality."[62] The Beijing-based real estate mogul Ren Zhiqiang, a vocal advocate of private enterprises' rights, also accused SASAC cadres of "failing to supervise [SOE] enterprises [due to] their lack of knowledge about running a business."[63]

Yet it is apparent that there is a divergence of views within the CCP's highest echelons as to the extent to which SOE conglomerates should be reformed or even privatized. This is evidenced by the plethora of articles in the official media that lobbied for the continuation of *yangqi*'s privileged status. The day after news broke of the detention of Jiang Jiemin, CCTV issued with a commentary defending the *yangqi* system. The editorial claimed that the CNPC scandal "has nothing to do with its monopoly status" and that there are many industries that could only be handled by state-controlled conglomerates. "It's not as though just anyone can get into the oil business," it said.[64] Equally significant was a series of five commentaries that appeared in the conservative *Economic Daily*. They warned advocates of privatization that weakening SOEs was tantamount to unsettling the foundation of the socialist state. "The purpose of SOE reform is not to abolish them but to make them better," it said. The paper praised President Vladimir Putin for renationalizing Russia's oil and gas operations "so that petroleum once again has become the pillar and foundation of the revival of Russia."[65]

Another major factor favoring the perpetuation of the *yangqi* system is the policy—which became evident at the turn of the century—of appointing *yangqi* executives to the CCP Central Committee as well as transferring them to administrative posts in the government or regional administrations.[66] At the Eighteenth Party Congress, a record number of serving or former CEOs of SOE conglomerates were picked as Central Committee members. In addition to then-president of CNPC Jiang, a former president of the Bank of China, Xiao Gang, joined the Party's ruling council. So did three former *yangqi* CEOs who were made provincial governors in 2013: Fujian governor Su Shulin, who is a former Sinopec president; Shandong governor Guo Shuqing, who used to run the China Construction Bank;

and Hebei governor Zhang Qingwei, who headed the Commercial Aircraft Corporation of China (COMAC). Also inducted into the Central Committee were the chief executives of four defense-industry and aerospace giants: Lin Zuoming of the China Aviation Industry Corporation; Xu Dazhe of the China Aerospace Science and Industry Corporation (CASIC); Ma Xingrui of the China Aerospace Science and Technology Corp (CASC); and Zhang Guoqing of Norinco. Zhang, whose company is China's largest importer and exporter of weapons and firearms, was later appointed deputy Party secretary of Chongqing, and Ma became a deputy Party secretary of Guangdong Province (also see Chapter 1).[67]

In his now-famous internal speech in December 2012, General Secretary Xi attributed the demise of the CPSU to the fact that the military "stood idly by" as "traitors" such as Mikhail Gorbachev and Boris Yeltsin plotted to overthrow the Party.[68] Conservative cadres such as Xi also seem convinced that in addition to the military, the CCP needs to maintain control over key sectors of the economy to ensure its status as China's "perennial ruling Party." Since early 2013, a number of official media have run commentaries on the imperative of having "the CCP run the economy" or "the Party impose tighter control on cadres" working in enterprises.

Yet liberal economists as well as entrepreneurs are adamant that China cannot afford to procrastinate on the restructuring of SOEs. At a forum on private enterprises held in August 2013, the tycoon Ren Zhiqiang criticized the concept of having the CCP control the economy. "If the Party is managing the economy, it will not be possible for Likonomics to exist," he said.[69] Zhang Weiying, a renowned economist at Peking University, was equally explicit about the choice that the Chinese economy has to make. "SOEs are a major factor behind the low innovative capacity of the Chinese economy," Zhang said. "Innovation requires resources, and our best resources have been taken up by SOEs." The liberal academic argued that China should not tolerate the prolonged existence of an economy marked by a mixed-ownership structure. "If the mixed-ownership economy becomes a stable, long-term arrangement, it will result in entrenched corruption," Professor Zhang noted.[70]

## The Uncertain Future of the Private Sector

### Xi Jinping and the "Red Capitalists"

As of the end of 2012, China had some 10.6 million POEs, with total registered capital of RMB 29.8 trillion. They contributed 60 percent of GDP, paid half of all commercial taxes, and provided 70 percent of the jobs nationwide.[71] As discussed earlier, however, non-state firms are still barred from many lucrative sectors, which remain the preserve of politically well-connected SOE conglomerates—despite the fact that President Xi had a lot of experience dealing with—and nurturing—POEs when he was the Party boss of Zhejiang, a major center of the non-state firms.

The private economy in Zhejiang, which is along the prosperous east coast, first developed in the mid-1980s. In those early days, quasi-capitalist enclaves such as Wenzhou and Yiwu had developed into important nodes of the world factory: Although largely spurned by Beijing's bureaucracy, entrepreneurs in these cities developed their "underground banks" as well as intimate connections with markets in Europe and the United States. By the time Xi arrived in 2002, the non-state sector already accounted for more than half the Zhejiang economy. Xi can claim some credit for further enhancing the role of POEs during his five-year stewardship of the prosperous province.[72]

Xi had high praise for the *minying* (run by the people) companies, which he thought could be more flexible and aggressive than state-held behemoths. "Don't think that the *minying* economy is backward," he said not long after taking up the Zhejiang post. "They are quick to adopt new technologies and are more sensitive [to market needs]. Our private firms are responsible for the use of new raw materials, new technologies, and the research and development of new products."[73] One of the beneficiaries of Xi's preferential policies toward POEs was Geely Motors, which made global news when it acquired the Swedish automaker Volvo in 2010. While visiting the headquarters of Geely in Linhai, Xi was impressed by the manufacturer's modern standards. "We must give preferential policies to domestic automobile manufacturers," he said. "We must create a favorable investment climate for *minying* enterprises." After touring Geely's facilities, Xi said, "If we do not support enterprises like Geely, who else should we support?"[74]

Xi was also a keen backer of the controversial Law on Private Property, which was finally enacted in 2007 after a gestation of some twenty years. While conservative cadres claimed that the law—which guarantees the inviolability of private property—was against the basic tenets of socialism, Xi gave it unqualified support. In 2007, he told then-U.S. ambassador to China Clark Randt that the law's passage was "needed to support the legal regime of China's socialist market economy. . . . The Property Law will equally protect state-owned and collectively owned assets as well as private properties. . . . The law should also prohibit the stripping of assets from state-owned enterprises and protect the general public's growing holdings of private property." Xi added that private assets played a leading role in Zhejiang's economic development, "so nearly everyone in Zhejiang agreed with passage of the Property Law."[75]

Despite Xi's apparent enthusiasm for POEs, he has not been able to reverse the trend of *guojin mintui* (SOEs advancing and POEs retreating), which started after the global financial crisis in 2008. For example, most of the RMB 4 trillion that the central government earmarked for resuscitating the economy in late 2008 was used to prop up state-controlled firms or to support infrastructure projects undertaken largely by SOEs.[76]

Despite the Decision's somewhat vague dispensations for POEs, systemic discrimination against the non-state sector could take years to reverse. The most-often-cited example is that private companies have difficulty securing credit from large commercial banks, which usually give priority to SOE clients. Particularly after the 2008 global financial crisis, many private firms have had to obtain loans from the gray, or shadow, banking sector. Hundreds of private companies in Zhejiang and other coastal provinces that failed to secure—or repay—loans went into default. The official media indicated that by early 2013, more than a hundred Wenzhou firms were on the brink of bankruptcy. The total value of loans incurred by business units in the city exceeded RMB 110 billion yuan.[77]

## The Politics of Private Bosses

By the mid-2000s, about a dozen private enterprises have become eye-catching multinationals. Not surprisingly, many of them are in the information technology area, where daring and nimble risk-takers find it easier to pull ahead of stodgy, unimaginative SOEs. Big names such as Alibaba, Tencent, Baidu, Huawei, and ZTE have become the first wave of PRC multinationals to burst onto the front pages of the *Financial Times* or the *Wall Street Journal*.[78] They complement a group of successful companies in more traditional areas, including Hai'er in Shandong Province, the maker of household appliances and other durable goods; the heavy machinery manufacturer Sany; and Geely, the "manufacturer of proletariat cars" in Zhejiang.[79]

It says much about the nature of the mixed-ownership economy with Chinese characteristics that the chairmen and CEOs of the vast majority of the multinational POEs have close links with the Party-state apparatus. And at least in their public appearances, these billionaires always come across as politically correct. Hai'er's chairman, Zhang Ruimin, has been an alternate member of the CCP Central Committee since 2002.[80] More than 30 of the approximately 2,200 delegates to the Eighteenth Party Congress in 2012 were private businessmen, compared with just 17 at the Seventeenth Party Congress in 2007. One of the best-known Eighteenth Party Congress delegates was the president of the Sany Group, Liang Wengen, who was thought to be China's richest man in 2011. Liang, whose company manufactures heavy machinery, narrowly missed induction into the Central Committee. Liang's case received much attention because until recently, private businessmen had been appointed only to "flower vase" (i.e., decorative) slots on the NPC or the CPPCC at both the national and regional levels. "Our firm takes as top priority the interest of the Party," said Liang, who admitted that Party membership was required of his senior staff. "My wealth and even my life belong to the Party, which represents the interests of the broad masses."[81]

It is not difficult to understand why, despite being multimillionaires, successful private entrepreneurs have to be seen as faithful followers of the Party. In October 2013, Wang Gongquan, the founder of the CDH Fund, was arrested on suspicion of providing financial support to the New Citizens movement, an NGO that had exposed the corrupt lifestyle of senior cadres. Appearing at a forum earlier that year, Wang had this to say about the relationship of *minying* bosses and the authorities: "Private entrepreneurs have a hard time dealing with the government. . . . The authorities have all the cards due to the inadequacy of rule of law." [82] Or as Wang Jianlin, the chairman of the Dalian Wanda Group, put it, the relationship between politicians and private businessmen was "very complicated." "It's very difficult for *minying* enterprises to grow big in China—many times more difficult compared to counterparts in the United States," he said. Liu Chuanzhi, the chairman of the information technology giant Lenovo, probably put it best when he said that "China's entrepreneurs are a vulnerable class. . . . Even when faced with the improper actions of government departments, entrepreneurs do not have either the courage or the ability to fight back. . . . All they can do is to minimize losses." [83]

Many private businessmen have tried to garner political respectability by becoming members of the CPPCC or Party-sanctioned organizations such as the Federation of Industry and Commerce. Particularly since non-state entrepreneurs were allowed to join the CCP in 2001, thousands of "red capitalists" have secured local-level positions such as heads of villages and townships. [84] Yet the most common way in which millionaire POE bosses hedge their bets is to move a portion of their assets—as well as their spouses and children—overseas. This accounts for not only capital flight but also severe brain drain among some of China's most creative and competitive entrepreneurs (see Chapter 6).

### Can China Innovate?

Both President Xi and Premier Li have given top priority to boosting Chinese innovativeness in industry and technology. "A country that only has a huge economy cannot be called strong," then-vice-president Xi said while talking to scientists at Tsinghua University in 2011. "Since we are a big power, we must not become dependent on other countries for know-how. We must be self-sufficient in critical fields of technology." [85] On a trip to the Tianjin Binhai New Area in December 2013, Premier Li encouraged young entrepreneurs and researchers to become China's Bill Gates and Steve Jobs. "Gates and Jobs started small," Li said. "Let ideas about setting up new ventures and concepts of innovation float freely." When asked whether the government would come to the aid of new start-ups, Li said his administration will provide "enhanced nutrients" to enterprises. [86]

Because of ballooning labor, land, and energy costs, even Chinese manufacturers are moving to countries such as Sri Lanka and Bangladesh and to Africa to build less expensive production bases. The only way for the Chinese world factory to continue to thrive is to move up the value chain. The Xi administration has committed itself to raising spending on research and development (R&D) to 2.5 percent of GDP by the end of the twelfth five-year plan (FYP) (2011–15). According to the Organization for Economic Cooperation and Development (OECD), in 2012 China earmarked 1.98 percent of GDP for R&D, which was slightly higher than the 1.96 percent figure for the twenty-eight members of the European Union (EU). Yet China still lagged behind the United States (2.8 percent) and Japan (3.3 percent). [87] In terms of the size of the talent pool, however, China is the undisputed world champion. The PRC boasts more than 500,000 high-level scientists and engineers who work in private firms, SOEs, as well as government institutions involved with high-tech pursuits. As of the late 2000s, Chinese universities were producing some 10,000 engineering Ph.D.s a year.[88]

Despite the huge investments, China's track record in innovation is checkered. China has surpassed the United States and Japan in terms of the number of patents filed for new products. According to the Geneva-based World Intellectual Property Organization (WIPO), companies and individuals in China filed 526,412 applications for patents in 2011, compared with 503,582 in the United States and 342,610 in Japan. However, quality matters much more than quantity. China suffers a huge deficit in patent trading: it bought significantly more patents from countries such as the United States than the other way around. Thus, in 2012, China suffered a record deficit in royalties and license fees of close to $17 billion—compared to an $82 billion surplus for the United States. This "intellectual property rights deficit" came about because China spent $18 billion on royalties and licenses but managed to sell only $1 billion worth of intellectual property rights (IPRs) to foreign countries.[89]

China does poorly in many respected measures of innovation assessment. In the Global Innovation Index for 2013 issued by Cornell University, the European business school INSEAD, and WIPO, China ranked thirty-fifth, just ahead of Slovakia, Croatia, and the United Arab Emirates. Not a single Chinese company made it to the 2013 Thomson Reuters Top 100 Global Innovators list, compared with twenty-eight firms from Japan, three from South Korea, and one from Taiwan. And although tens of Chinese multinationals—mostly *yangqi* like the three oil corporations and the four commercial banks—are on the Fortune 500 list, they can hardly be labeled innovators.[90]

This is not to say, of course, that the PRC—especially sectors either owned or affiliated with the Party-state apparatus—has not spawned spectacular technological breakthroughs. The country has produced the world's fastest computer and train; its missiles, jetfighters, and nuclear submarines are fast approaching the standard of the Russians; and it put a rover on the moon in late 2013.[91] In other words, China is doing well in what analysts call Soviet-style innovation, whose success is dependent upon huge state injections of funds and the ability of the administration to call up tens of thousands of scientists and engineers to work on priority projects. Indeed, the twelfth FYP incorporated long sections on goals and targets for science and technology. For example, it noted that "seven strategic sectors" would receive priority treatment: energy-saving and environmental-protection industries; next-generation IT; biotechnology; advanced equipment manufacturing; new energy; and new materials and clean-energy vehicles. According to the estimations of Zhou Zixue, an economic analyst at the Ministry of Industry and Information Technology, these seven industries will have sales of RMB 4.3 trillion by 2015 and RMB 11.4 trillion by 2020. It is expected that these emerging sectors will grow at an average year-on-year rate of 24.1 percent between 2011 and 2015 and 21.3 percent between 2016 and 2020.[92]

And the State Council periodically publishes game plans for advancements in specific cutting-edge sectors. President Xi is particularly keen to promote synergy between the R&D facilities of state-run military and aerospace industries, on the one hand, and civilian and private high-tech firms, on the other. For example, experts responsible for China's ambitious space exploration program are also involved in manufacturing commercial jets that are expected to compete with Boeing and Airbus in a decade or two.[93]

For a country that is the world's largest trading nation, relatively few technological champions come from the non-state sector. One of them is Huawei, the globally known IT company, which in 2013 displaced Ericsson as the world's largest telecommunications equipment maker. Its new generation of smartphones is expected to create a lot of competition for Samsung and Apple. Huawei, however, which was founded in 1988 by a former PLA engineer, Ren Zhengfei, is said to have close links with the government. This is one of the reasons it has faced problems in expanding into countries such as the United States, Australia, and India, which claim that use of Huawei products could pose a threat to national security.[94]

The large-scale involvement of the state in high-tech development has led to problems including favoritism for members of the privileged classes as well as large-scale corruption. It is not surprising that many princelings have played a big role in high-tech ventures largely due to their political connections. For example, Jiang Mianheng (b. 1951), the eldest son of ex-president Jiang Zemin, has been active in aerospace and IT-related industries. In the mid-2000s, he was a vice-commander of China's successful manned space program. Lately, Jiang, who is a vice-president of the Chinese Academy of Sciences (CAS) and chairman of the newly established Shanghai Technology University, has kept a low profile with respect to his business ventures.[95]

Looking into the future, the CCP leadership can derive confidence from the fact that a large proportion of the "returnees"—a reference to the 300,000 Western-educated Chinese who have returned to work in China—comprise well-trained engineers and entrepreneurs who are conversant with the values and business norms of global high-tech industries. Moreover, venture capital, which is essential to the development of private high-tech firms, has been rapidly growing. In 2011, non-state venture capital committed to technologically advanced Chinese companies reached $13 billion, which was almost half of the level invested in American firms.[96] It remains to be seen whether Chinese innovation can flourish in the absence of a free flow of information, which is considered a key factor underlying the success of Silicon Valley and other high-tech hubs around the world.[97]

### Retooling the Chinese Model

#### *Transforming the Locomotives of Growth— and Tackling a Debt Crisis*

Despite the stellar achievements of the Chinese economy since the third plenum of the Eleventh Central Committee, the problems created by the breakneck pace of development have become evident. The apparently irreversible degradation of the environment is only one of the many serious side-effects of what Deng Xiaoping called *cuguang* (rough and wild) style of growth, including an alarming deterioration of air and water quality, as shown by heavy smog in major cities such as Beijing and Shanghai. "Cancer villages" are cropping up all over the country. Crops and fisheries have been badly affected. The World Bank estimated in 2007 that environmental costs—including health bills incurred by workers laboring in unhygienic conditions—totaled at least 5.8 percent of GDP.[98] The situation has further deteriorated as the chase for GDP expansion intensifies.

However, Premier Li pointed out at a late 2013 State Council meeting that the country required a growth rate of at least 7.2 percent to provide enough employment and to prevent sociopolitical disorder. Li's figure was similar to the 7 percent that the then-premier Zhu Rongji stipulated in the 1990s as the minimum growth rate that the country could tolerate.[99] At his NPC press conference in March 2014, Li reiterated that although "we are not preoccupied with GDP growth," his adminis-tration "must create 10 million more urban jobs to ensure that the registered urban unemployment rate does not rise above 4.6 percent. . . . The growth that we want is one that brings real benefits to the people, helps raise the quality and efficiency of economic development, and contributes to energy conservation and environment protection."[100] The big question, however, remains that as China's economic base becomes bigger, the CCP leadership faces increasing difficulty in maintaining a rapid pace of growth while at the same time rationalizing the economic structure.

Since the mid-1980s, the government has relied mainly on trade and govern-ment investment to sustain high growth. Because prospects for exports to mature markets such as the United States and the European Union are limited, more weight than ever has been given to government input as well as consumer spending. Ac-cording to the National Bureau of Statistics, out of the 7.7 percent GDP growth in 2013, "capital formation" (mostly government investment) contributed 4.19 per-cent, while household consumption comprised 3.85 percent (with exports making up −0.34 percent). State capital outlays in 2013 made up close to 50 percent of GDP—while the finance costs for such investments were equivalent to 4 percent of GDP. By contrast, consumption's share of GDP was only 35 percent.[101] However, China's incremental capital output ratio—which is economists' measurement of the efficiency of investment in wealth creation—suffers from the law of diminish-ing marginal returns. According to the American ratings agency Fitch, RMB 1 of government investment yielded RMB 0.71 of GDP from 2005 to 2008; this level fell to just RMB 0.3 between 2009 and 2012. Nomura Securities Research reached a similar conclusion. From 1990 to 2011, an average of RMB 3.9 of investment produced RMB 1 of GDP; but from 2009 to 2011, this measure rose to RMB 5.[102]

Although since the global financial meltdown of 2008, much attention has fo-cused on the amount of "quantitative easing" in the United States and Japan, the CCP leadership has also pursued a relatively loose monetary policy. M2, the broad measurement of credit, jumped by 175 percent from 2007 to 2013. In 2013, debt incurred by the central government remained at a relatively low level of around

23 percent of GDP. Yet the country's total debt rose from 125 percent of GDP at the beginning of the world financial crisis to at least 225 percent of GDP in 2013, according to estimates by Western banks and ratings agencies. Fitch warned that the country's total credit-to-GDP ratio would reach 270 percent by the end of 2017. That would be comparable to the debt ratios of industrialized countries on the eve of the financial crisis. Meanwhile, interest owed by borrowers was equivalent to 12.5 percent of GDP in 2013, up from just 7 percent in 2008. Fitch estimated that this figure could climb to as much as 22 percent of GDP by the end of 2017.[103]

Particularly worrying was mushrooming debt piled up by local administrations and government-backed investment vehicles. The State Council announced in late 2013 that from the end of 2010 to June 2013, debt owed by grassroots administrations increased 67 percent to total RMB 17.9 trillion. Local debt was equivalent to 33 percent of GDP, up from about 10 percent in 2008 and almost nothing in 1997.[104] Moreover, direct liabilities sustained by these administrations reached RMB 10.6 trillion in 2013. Since budgeted revenues for local governments in 2014 were estimated at just RMB 6.7 trillion, the ratio of liabilities to income was 158 percent.[105] This proves that Beijing's stringent measures to control local-level government debt since the late 2000s have not been successful.

At least over the long term, Li wants to change the system in which the central authorities sustain growth using government injections and credit expansion. In June and December 2013, the Li administration allowed the seven-day interbank borrowing rate (repurchase or repo rate) to rise to 13.44 percent and 6.3 percent, respectively. (The rate is usually around 3 percent.) On June 20, 2013, the day that the repo rate hit its historic high, the State Council issued this statement: "While the economy faces many difficulties and challenges, we must promote financial reform in an orderly way to better serve economic restructuring."[106] Not long after each instance of raising the rate, however, the People's Bank of China (PBOC) injected liquidity into the market. It seems obvious that the Li cabinet had come under serious pressure to maintain growth at a reasonably high rate. As Zhang Yansheng, a top researcher attached to the NDRC put it, "The Chinese economy has to reduce its pace of expansion because the model of the past thirty years cannot sustain future development." However, Zhang admitted that stepping on the brakes had resulted in "pressure on the central government, local governments, enterprises, and the banks."[107]

That Premier Li has not departed from the long-standing strategy of using government input to bolster growth was demonstrated again in April 2014, when his cabinet announced another emergency package to ensure that the annual growth target of 7.5 percent would be met—in view of less-than-satisfactory first-quarter figures for exports, industrial expansion, and domestic spending. The Li cabinet announced that the central government would raise bonds worth RMB 150 billion to help build railways mainly in central and western China. Moreover, an extra "development fund" of RMB 200 billion to RMB 300 billion would be set up to underwrite rail finances for the rest of the year. Other measures to resuscitate the economy included a tax break for small and medium-size enterprises as well as a RMB 1 trillion war chest to rebuild slums in less prosperous cities. Given the fact that the railway system is already overleveraged, however, the wisdom of continuing the old-style strategy of utilizing public works to promote growth and create jobs has again been called into question.[108]

It has been a long-held goal of both the Hu Jintao and the Xi Jinping administrations to boost consumer spending—so that consumption, instead of government investment, will become the main engine of GDP expansion. As discussed earlier, however, the prospects for a leap forward in household spending are relatively dim for reasons including an inadequate social security net. For the foreseeable future, public and private injections of funds into areas such as infrastructure, industry, and real estate will remain the mainstay of economic growth. Apart from running up huge debts, this strategy has created more dislocation in the economy. For example, key sectors of the economy ranging from steel, aluminum, cement, and coal to solar panels and shipbuilding suffer from severe overcapacity. According to a 2013 survey of 3,545 enterprises by the State Council's Development Research Center, 71 percent of respondents called overcapacity "relatively serious" or "very serious."[109]

And the real-estate bubble, particularly in major cities along the coast, has remained unchecked despite the fact that apartment prices are so high that even members of the middle and professional classes find it hard to buy units within a reasonable distance of the central business districts. One reason for this phenomenon is that revenues from the sale of land and real-estate transactions account for at least half the income of many local administrations. This "build at any cost" psychology has been responsible for the appearance of "ghost cities," which are found not only in relatively remote Inner Mongolia but also near cities such as Zhengzhou and Wenzhou.[110]

Since late 2013, reports about defaults by companies ranging from green-technology firms to property developers have dented the aura of the "China economic miracle." In March 2014, the solar panel maker Shanghai Chaori Solar Energy announced that it could not make a RMB 89.9 million interest payment on a RMB 1 billion bond issued in 2012. This first case of a firm's defaulting in China's $4.2 trillion onshore bond market stoked speculation that other companies in industries with overcapacity might follow suit. Beijing's decision not to follow past practice by bailing out this failed firm showed that it was taking a tougher stance against inefficient, overleveraged companies.[111] At the NPC press conference in 2014, Li indicated that his government "has attached high attention to government debt and risks in this area are generally within control." Referring to the bankruptcies of a number of corporations, Li admitted that "avoiding a few individual cases would be difficult." But he vowed that more efforts would be made to prevent local governments and SOEs from exposure to the risk of high debt.[112] Unless the Chinese model is fundamentally retooled, however, the debt conundrum could worsen through the rest of the Xi Jinping era.

### *How to Jack Up Consumption*

In mature economies such as the United States, Germany, and Japan, household consumption typically makes up 60 percent or more of total economic output. China was not doing badly through the 1980s, when this figure hovered around 50 percent. In the early 2010s, however, consumer spending dropped to around 35 percent of GDP. This downward trend was also reflected in total retail sales figures. In 2008, total retail sales rose 21.6 percent over the level in 2007; the comparative figure for 2013 was a mere 13.1 percent.[113]

China's lack of distributive justice and equal opportunity have been cited as prime reasons behind ordinary citizens' reluctance to spend. The aggregate wages of workers as a proportion of GDP fell continually in the twenty-two years up to 2010, the latest year for which figures are available. According to Larry Hsien-Ping Lang, a finance professor at the Chinese University of Hong Kong and a popular lecturer in China, the total salaries of workers made up only 8 percent of GDP, significantly less than the 28 percent in Association of Southeast Asian Nations (ASEAN) member countries and 38 percent in Latin America.[114]

As discussed above, China's social security net—especially outside the big cities—has remained woefully inadequate despite more government spending on welfare during the twelfth FYP. According to the Texas A&M University economist Li Gan, who is a specialist on Chinese household consumption patterns, each dollar that the government spends on health insurance boosts consumption by $2.36 for rural citizens and $4.16 for urban employees. While in theory 90 percent of Chinese have health insurance coverage, entitlements for peasants are substantially lower than those for urban residents, which is at least partly responsible for the popularity of the "save for a rainy day" mentality. Chinese put away an average of 30.6 percent of their disposable income, up from 23 percent ten years ago.[115]

China's consumers also face institutional discrimination. Bank deposits by Chinese households are subject to an interest rate that is fixed by the government—and the yields are substantially lower than they could obtain if they were allowed to invest in fixed-deposit plans and other products offered by Hong Kong or foreign financial institutions. This non-market-oriented mechanism enables state banks to charge relatively low interest rates on loans made to SOEs. Consumer spending might rise if citizens could obtain more income from bank deposits. As Nicholas Lardy, a senior fellow at the Peterson Institute for International Economics, argued, "higher real deposit rates would increase household income, and, for any given saving rate, also increase household consumption as a share of GDP."[116] The Chinese media have reported that by 2016 the State Council might allow banks to offer their customers higher interest rates on deposits. This might also prevent those who are more well-off from buying dubious "wealth creation" products from both Chinese and overseas-based financial companies.[117]

High-end consumers—including private businessmen, professionals, and members of the middle class in general—are reluctant to spend too much in their own country for other, non-economic, reasons, such as worries about the lack of rule of law in general and inadequate legal protection of private property in particular. These concerns have led to a so-called elite emigration. According to the 2013 China Private Wealth Report, which was jointly compiled by China Merchants Bank and Bain Capital, China is home to over 840,000 people with more than RMB 10 million in investable assets. In this group, 56 percent of respondents said they had either completed procedures for emigrating to the West or were considering emigration. Another 11 percent said their children planned to emigrate.[118] In other words, well-heeled Chinese prefer to spend a sizable portion of their fortunes outside China—to buy permanent residency rights or to finance their children's education in the West. This mentality will, of course, make a dent in domestic consumption.

### Conclusion: State Capitalism with Chinese Characteristics

At an NPC press conference shortly after he became premier in March 2013, Li said somewhat professorially: "It's now more difficult to shake up vested interests than to touch the soul. . . . Yet we must cross the river no matter how deep the water is."[119] The heart of the matter, however, is that the premier—and reformist elements in the establishment—may not have enough clout to take on power blocs in the country. As discussed above, the establishment of the CLGCDR has demonstrated that conservative ideas associated with Xi are carrying the day. He seems to have opted for the perpetuation of "state capitalism with Chinese characteristics." First, this means essentially that while China will continue to integrate its economy with the global marketplace, the Party-state apparatus will retain ultimate control over major aspects of the economy. Second, while both Xi and Li have blamed "vested interests" for interfering with reform, there is no indication that the monopolistic privileges enjoyed by members of the "red aristocracy"—top cadres and their business cronies—are being curtailed.

### *Party-State Apparatus Retains Control over Key Sectors of the Economy*

The most obvious way that ideological and political requirements have infringed upon the workings of the market is manifested in the labyrinthine Party-and-state apparatus charged with "macro-level adjustments and control" regarding the economy. As the liberal economist Wu Jinglian has argued, the stumbling block to reform is "the question of systems and institutions. . . . The government is in control of too much power over the distribution of resources—and this has made economic restructuring impossible."[120]

Over the long term, it is unlikely that Premier Li will be able to claw back the reform initiative from Xi and his conservative advisers. Li's efforts to promote "small government, big market" or "small government, big society" began as soon as he was inducted to the PBSC in 2007. With the cooperation of then-premier Wen

Jiabao and ex-president Hu—who was his principal patron—Li tried to streamline the cumbersome State Council structure at the first session of the Eleventh NPC in March 2008, but without much success. Prior to his ascendancy to the premiership in March 2013, there was speculation that at least seven or eight ministries and departments would be slashed. However, only two of the twenty-seven ministerial units of the central government were eliminated at the first session of the Twelfth NPC at that time, even though Li had stressed that his team would focus on "simplifying administrative [measures] and devolving powers to the regions." The head of government also vowed that "we must change the nature of the government's function . . . Whatever can be done by society should be handled by society."[121]

Li also faces a daunting task of remolding the central government structure more in line with global practice. In the past decade or so, a few State Council offices were apparently modeled after U.S. government departments. For example, the Ministry of Foreign Trade and Economic Cooperation (MOFTEC) went through a reorganization in early 2003 and was renamed the Ministry of Commerce, whose organization and functions were partially modeled after the U.S. Department of Commerce. After the SARS (severe acute respiratory syndrome) outbreak in 2003, Beijing set up a Center for Disease Control and Prevention similar to the U.S. Centers for Disease Control and Prevention based in Atlanta.[122] Immediately after the Eighteenth Party Congress concluded, suggestions were raised by liberal economists that the PBOC incorporate characteristics of Western central banks and become less dependent on the Party-state apparatus.[123] However, the establishment of the CLGCDR—which rides roughshod over the State Council—could mean that no more administrative streamlining will be attempted during the tenure of President Xi.

### Obstruction from Powerful Clans in the Party

In a talk on the prospects of reform after the third plenum of the Central Committee in late 2013, Hu Deping, the son of Hu Yaobang, said, "If the reforms fail to be implemented, it must be due to obstruction by power blocs." Earlier that year, Hu, who has a liberal reputation, caused a stir when he said that "some interest groups are threatening the security of the Party and state." He urged CCP authorities to "sacrifice some of the Party's [own] interests and to be prepared for a protracted struggle with these interest groups."[124]

Who are these vested interests and power blocs? As a princeling, Hu is familiar with the way in which several dozen major clans at the apex of the CCP monopolize the economic and political resources of the country. Par contre, Chen Xiaolu, the son of revered Marshal Chen Yi, claims that the "red descendants" do not pack a big punch in Chinese politics or the economy. Using his definition of the *hong erdai* (second-generation red offspring)—the children of officials with the rank of head of a bureau or department before the beginning of the Cultural Revolution in 1966—Chen calculates that the loosely defined red aristocracy numbers no more than 40,000 people: "This is a negligible proportion of China's 1.4 billion people. . . . They [*hong erdai*] do not constitute a major political force."[125]

Yet this picture becomes different if we focus on the offspring of cadres who have held Politburo-level slots. A study conducted by Bloomberg in late 2012 showed that a majority of the 103 descendants of the "Eight Immortals"—Party elders including Deng Xiaoping, Chen Yun, Li Xiannian, Wang Zhen, Bo Yibo, and Song Renqiong—were multimillionaire entrepreneurs. Forty-three of these "red aristocrats" ran their own businesses or were senior executives at private firms. Twenty-six of the princelings held top positions at *yangqi*. According to public records accessed by Bloomberg, three princelings alone—Wang Zhen's son, Wang Jun; Deng's son-in-law, He Ping; and Chen Yun's son, Chen Yuan—"headed or still run SOEs with combined assets of about $1.6 trillion in 2011." This was equivalent to more than 20 percent of China's GDP for that year.[126] A January 2013 report by the International Consortium of Investigative Journalists (ICIJ) showed that more than a dozen close relatives of top Party and military leaders had stashed away huge levels of assets in bank accounts in the British Virgin Islands, a popular tax haven for the rich and powerful. These multimillionaires include the son of ex-premier Wen, Wen Yunsong, and the brother-in-law of President Xi, Deng Jiagui.[127]

Moreover, the offspring of later generations of leaders, such as ex-presidents Jiang Zemin and Hu Jintao and ex-premiers Zhu Rongji and Wen Jiabao, have also become savvy red capitalists. This was indirectly attested to by the fact that quite a few multinational banks and corporations have employed princelings mainly because of the high-level *guanxi* (personal connections) that the latter enjoy. In the second half of 2013, the Securities and Exchange Commission, the U.S. government's top securities regulator and financial watchdog, began investigations into the hiring practices of JPMorgan and at least four other multinational banks. JPMorgan reportedly ran a "Sons and Daughters" program to hire princelings who could parlay their political connections into lucrative business deals.[128]

### Limits on Free Communication in the Age of the Information Economy

That China's economic development could suffer from excessive political control is also evidenced by the formation in February 2014 of a Central Leading Group on Internet Security and Informatization (CLGISI), which is headed by President Xi. This Party superagency has two functions: to nurture the development of the IT industry and to purge the information superhighways of what Party ideologues call "spiritual pollution" or destabilizing elements. At the inaugural meeting of the group, Xi pointed out that "efforts should be made to build our country into a cyberpower." It is also clear, however, that China's IT industries and professionals must remain politically correct. "Building a cyberpower calls for domestically developed solid technology, rich and comprehensive information services, prosperous cybercultures, sound infrastructure, high-caliber talents working in Internet security and information, as well as international cooperation," said Xi, adding that he looked forward to propagating IT personnel who were "politically firm, professionally competent, and morally upright."[129]

It is true that some of China's most successful IT companies are highly energetic and profitable concerns. They include well-known firms such as Alibaba, Tencent, and Baidu. However, these private corporations, whose management teams are trusted by the Party, have mostly borrowed business models from foreign giants such as Amazon, Yahoo, and Google. Contrary to the spirit of China's pledges when it joined the WTO, the government has either barred foreign IT companies from setting up branches in China or kept these companies on a short leash. Beijing's interference in Google's China operations was the main reason that the American IT firm decided in 2010 to pull most of its operations out of the country.[130]

In a speech in Hong Kong in 2013, Google chairman Eric Schmidt argued that freedom of information and of expression was key to the development of a knowledge economy. "There should be freedom of speech to pursue one's goals for ideas," he said. Schmidt added that restrictions on mainland Internet access, which makes Google's search and email services unstable, would also hurt academic research in China. "My opinion is China wants to avoid the middle-income trap and in order to avoid that, they [sic] have to develop the openness, free speech . . . and the reason is in order to get there, you should have the debates about everything."[131]

In his perceptive book *Stumbling Giant: The Threat to China's Future*, the financier Timothy Beardson noted that "the platform is lacking for China to create an innovative economy." "This is for reasons of education, history, culture, ethics and politics," he wrote, adding that despite its impressive hardware, the country lacked "non-hierarchical scientific culture, fertile institutional framework and critical thinking" for top-notch innovation.[132] As long as the Party-state apparatus under President Xi is bent on thrusting its ever-more-visible hand into the business activities and daily lives of Chinese, the long-awaited restructuring and upgrading of China's economy will face very daunting challenges.

## Notes

1. Cited in Kevin Yao and Aileen Wang, "China's 2013 economic growth dodges 14-year low but further slowing seen," Reuters, January 20, 2014, www.reuters.com/article/2014/01/20/us-china-economy-gdp-idUSBREA0I0HH20140120/; "China's GDP up 7.7 pct in 2013," Xinhua News Agency, January 20, 2014, http://news.xinhuanet.com/english/china/2014-01/20/c_133058484.htm. See also Katie Holliday, "China's debt soars to 250 percent of GDP," CNBC.com, July 21, 2014, www.cnbc.com/id/101854344.

2. Cited in Bettina Wassener, "For China, a shift from exports to consumption," *New York Times,* January 20, 2014, www.nytimes.com/2014/01/21/business/international/for-china-a-shift-from-exports-to-consumption.html; Staff Reporter, "China reports 7.7% GDP in 4Q13," *Singapore Business Review,* January 21, 2014, http://sbr.com.sg/economy/asia/china-reports-77-gdp-in-4q13/; Dhara Ranasinghe, "Chinese consumers are still not spending enough," CNBC News, May 29, 2013, www.cnbc.com/id/100774903/.

3. See "Loans made in 2013 increased by 8.89 trillion yuan, a four-year high," Xinhua News Agency, January 5, 2014, http://news.xinhuanet.com/fortune/2014-01/15/c_118976751.

htm; see also Dexter Roberts, "China's shadow banking sector tops $5.8 trillion, Report says," *Businessweek,* May 8, 2013, www.businessweek.com/articles/2013-05-08/chinas-shadow-banking-sector-tops-5-dot-8-trillion-report-says/.

4. For comparison between the third plenum of the Eleventh Central Committee and the third plenum of the Eighteenth Central Committee, see, for example, Ching Cheong, "The third plenum of 1978 went further than the third plenum of 2013," *Hong Kong Economic Journal,* November 21, 2013, http://forum.hkej.com/user/70348/201311/.

5. For a discussion of the opposition of vested interests to reform, see, for example, Han Miao, Guo Xinfeng, and Cui Yuanlei, "China's new reforms must breach vested interests," Xinhua News Agency, November 4, 2013, http://news.xinhuanet.com/english/indepth/2013-11/04/c_132857921.htm. See also Megha Rajagopalan, "Vested interests won't block China's reforms: Party official," Reuters, November 22, 2013, www.reuters.com/article/2013/11/22/us-china-reforms-idUSBRE9AL0G120131122/.

6. Cited in "Decision on major issues concerning comprehensively deepening reforms—In brief," *China Daily,* November 16, 2013, www.china.org.cn/china/third_plenary_session/2013-11/16/content_30620736.htm; see also "Decision on major issues concerning comprehensively deepening reforms," Xinhua News Agency, November 16, 2013, http://news.xinhuanet.com/mrdx/2013-11/16/c_132892941.htm.

7. Cited in Lu Rucai, "Let the market play a decisive role," Chinatoday.com.cn, December 16, 2013, www.chinatoday.com.cn/english/report/2013-12/16/content_585007.htm.

8. See "Decision on major issues concerning comprehensively deepening reforms."

9. See "Li Keqiang: Local governments will in theory stop making investments in enterprises," Xinhua News Agency, November 8, 2013, http://news.nfdaily.cn/content/2013-11/08/content_84035918.htm.

10. For a discussion of SOE conglomerates, see, for example, Eve Cary, "Reforming China's state-owned enterprises," *Diplomat,* June 19, 2013, http://thediplomat.com/2013/06/reforming-chinas-state-owned-enterprises/; Gao Xu, "State-owned enterprises in China: How profitable are they?" Blogs.worldbank.org, March 2, 2010. https://blogs.worldbank.org/eastasiapacific/state-owned-enterprises-in-china-how-profitable-are-they/.

11. For a discussion of the deteriorating climate for foreign firms in China, see, for example, "From Starbucks to Audi, China clamps down on foreign companies," Bloomberg, December 27, 2013, http://articles.economictimes.indiatimes.com/2013-12-27/news/45626854_1_state-media-ndrc-foreign-companies/. See also Susan Decker, "InterDigital says China made threats over patent dispute," Bloomberg, December 16, 2013, www.bloomberg.com/news/2013-12-16/interdigital-ceo-says-chinese-threats-over-huawei-fight.html. For a discussion of Premier Li's attitude toward foreign firms, see Scott Neuman, "Chinese premier says foreign companies to get equal treatment," NPR.org, September 11, 2013, www.npr.org/blogs/thetwo-way/2013/09/11/221394449/chinese-premier-says-foreign-companies-to-get-equal-treatment/.

12. For a discussion of China's ambitions for the renminbi, see, for example, Jun Jie Woo and Suvi Dogra, "China's big currency strategy," *Diplomat,* September 23, 2013, http://thediplomat.com/2013/09/chinas-big-currency-strategy/; see also Robert N. McCauley, "Renminbi internationalization and China's financial development," *BIS Quarterly Review* (December 2011), www.bis.org/publ/qtrpdf/r_qt1312.htm.

13. For a discussion of China's IPO reforms, see, for example, Josh Noble, "China's reopened IPO highway proves a bumpy ride," *Financial Times,* January 20, 2014, www.ft.com/intl/cms/s/0/6a37e9ac-817a-11e3-b3d5-00144feab7de.html#axzz2qwsXnPMt/; see also Aileen Wang and Kevin Yao, "China central bank vows faster FX reform; IPO hopes tempered," Reuters, November 19, 2013, www.reuters.com/article/2013/11/19/us-china-reform-idUSBRE9AI0HU20131119/.

14. For a discussion of the potentials of China's FTZs, see, for example, John Sudworth, "Can Shanghai's free trade zone spur China's growth?" BBC News, January 19, 2014, www.bbc.co.uk/news/business-25774227/; see also "Shanghai free trade zone: The next Shenzhen?" *Economist,* October 5, 2013, www.economist.com/news/china/21587237-new-enterprise-zone-could-spark-wider-market-reformsbut-only-if-bureaucrats-ease-their-grip/.

15. For a critique of the Shanghai FTZ, see, for example, Li Yang, "Shanghai FTZ hasn't taken bold steps in financial reform," *China Daily,* April 11, 2014, http://usa.chinadaily.com.cn/epaper/2014-04/11/content_17427107.htm.

16. See Josh Noble, "Hong Kong and Shanghai unveil plan to link bourses," *Financial Times,* April 10, 2014, www.ft.com/intl/cms/s/0/ad708904-c077-11e3-8578-00144feabdc0.html#axzz2ygNav6pv/. See also Amy Li, Enda Curran, and Chao Deng, "China opens door wider to its stock markets, *Wall Street Journal,* April 10, 2014, http://online.wsj.com/news/articles/SB10001424052702303873604579492771531727000?mg=reno64-wsj&url=http%3A%2F%2Fonline.wsj.com%2Farticle%2FSB10001424052702303873604579492771531727000.html.

17. For a discussion of interest rate reforms, see, for example, Xiaoyi Shao and Kevin Yao, "China suggests full interest rate liberalization in two years," Reuters, March 11, 2014, www.reuters.com/article/2014/03/11/china-parliament-cenbank-idUSL3N0M72PK20140311/.

18. For a discussion of Chinese e-commerce giants offering high interest rates on deposits, see for example, Grace Zhu, "Chinese banks match tech firms in race for deposits," *Wall Street Journal,* February 24, 2014, http://online.wsj.com/news/articles/SB100014240527023048347045794025731286666330/.

19. Cited in "Decision on major issues concerning comprehensively deepening reforms."

20. Cited in Li Wei and Liu Ailin, "The growing pains of tuliu.com," *Twenty-first Century Economic Herald* (Beijing), November 13, 2013, http://finance.sina.com.cn/roll/20131113/022617302628.shtml.

21. For a discussion of land reform, see, for example, "China's top farm official reins in land reform expectations," Reuters, December 5, 2013, www.reuters.com/article/2013/12/05/china-agriculture-land-idUSL4N0J51GF20131205/; Dexter Roberts, "Is land reform finally coming to China?" *Businessweek,* November 20, 2013, www.businessweek.com/articles/2013-11-20/is-land-reform-finally-coming-to-china/.

22. For a discussion of *hukou* reforms, see, for example, Dexter Roberts, "China moves on reforming *hukou*?" *Businessweek,* June 28, 2013, www.businessweek.com/articles/2013-06-28/china-moves-on-reforming-hukou/; see also John Marshall, "China: Urbanization and *hukou* reform," *Diplomat,* October, 11, 2013, http://thediplomat.com/2013/10/china-urbanization-and-hukou-reform/.

23. For a discussion of China's urbanization plans, see, for example, "China to issue urbanization layout in 2013," Xinhua News Agency, March 6, 2013, www.chinadaily.com.cn/china/2013npc/2013-03/06/content_16283936.htm; see also "China sets out urbanization plans to support economic growth," Bloomberg, December 15, 2013, www.bloomberg.com/news/2013-12-15/china-sets-out-urbanization-plans-to-support-economic-growth.html.

24. Cited in "Gini out of the bottle," *Economist,* January 26 2013, www.economist.com/news/china/21570749-gini-out-bottle/; "China survey shows wealth gap soaring as Xi pledges help," Bloomberg, December 9, 2012, www.bloomberg.com/news/2012-12-09/china-s-wealth-gap-soars-as-xi-pledges-to-narrow-income-divide.html.

25. For a discussion of the growth of wages and household income, see Michael Pettis, *The Great Rebalancing: Trade, Conflict, and the Perilous Road Ahead for the World Economy* (Princeton: Princeton University Press, 2013), p. 74.

26. For a discussion of China's liberalization of its family-planning regime, see "China formally eases one-child policy," BBC News, December 28, 2013, www.bbc.co.uk/news/world-asia-china-25533339.

27. For a discussion of the relationship between social welfare and consumer spending, see, for example, Min Tang, "Social welfare system and consumption growth," China Development and Research Foundation, Beijing, January 2010, www.imf.org/external/country/chn/rr/2010/TANGE.pdf; see also Koh Gui Qing and Wayne Arnold, "China points to social welfare reforms needed for urbanization drive," November 13, 2013, Reuters, www.reuters.com/article/2013/11/13/us-china-reform-labour-idUSBRE9AB16020131113/.

28. For a discussion of liberalized IPO rules for private firms, see, for example, Charles Riley and Feng Ke, "China lifts IPO ban and relaxes rules," CNTV, February 8, 2014, http://english.cntv.cn/program/newsupdate/20140208/101983.shtml; see also "Xiao says China IPO rules to cut bureaucracy, boost markets," Bloomberg, November 19, 2013, www.bloomberg.com/news/2013-11-19/china-s-xiao-says-ipo-reform-to-cut-bureaucracy-boost-markets.html.

29. For example, Xi mentioned the integration of the three ideals at the end of the first post-Eighteenth Party Congress NPC session on March 17, 2013. See "Xi Jinping: We must uphold the organic unification of party leadership, the people mastering their own affairs, and governing the country according to law," Xinhua News Agency, March 17, 2013, www.chinadaily.com.cn/hqgj/jryw/2013-03-17/content_8518195.html. See also Commentator of *Study and Research,* "Foster the organic unification of party leadership, the people mastering their own affairs, and governing the country according to law," *Study and Research,* February 25, 2013, http://theory.people.com.cn/n/2013/0225/c49150-20593862.html.

30. See "Xi gives an interview to a Russian TV channel in Sochi," CNTV, February 8, 2014, http://english.cntv.cn/program/newsupdate/20140208/101983.shtml.

31. Cited in "The CCP Politburo met and decided to set up the Central Leading Group on Comprehensively Deepening Reform," Xinhua News Agency, December 30, 2013, www.gov.cn/ldhd/2013-12/30/content_2557318.htm.

32. See "The splendid line-up of the Central Leading Group on Comprehensively Deepening Reforms is unveiled," *Ta Kung Pao* (Hong Kong), January 23, 2014, http://news.takungpao.com.hk/mainland/focus/2014-01/2210204.html. For a discussion of the fact that Xi and not Li is the head of the Central Leading Group on Finance and Economics, see, for example, "Baidu.com has exposed the fact that Li Keqiang's power has been curtailed," *Ming Pao* (Hong Kong), March 8, 2014, www.mingpaotor.com/htm/News/20140308/tcad1.htm?m=0/.

33. For a discussion of the composition of the Central Leading Group on Comprehensively Deepening Reforms, see, for example, "Decoding the set-up of the Central Leading Group on Comprehensively Deepening Reform," *Ta Kung Pao,* January 23, 2014, http://news.takungpao.com/mainland/focus/2014-01/2236990.html.

34. For a discussion of the role of Wang Huning and his Central Policy Research Office, see Willy Lam, "New high-level groups threaten line between party and government," *China Brief,* Jamestown Foundation, April 9, 2014, www.jamestown.org/programs/chinabrief/single/?tx_ttnews%5Btt_news%5D=42208&tx_ttnews%5BbackPid%5D=25&cHash=9c04fb8086372aa9cd6deb00e61e01e7/. See also "Two new super organs come on stream," *Ta Kung Pao,* March 7, 2014, http://news.takungpao.com/2014lh/article/2014-03/2330619.html.

35. For a discussion of the tradition of the premier running the economy, see, for example, Zachary Keck, "Is Li Keqiang being marginalized?" *Diplomat,* January 7, 2014, http://thediplomat.com/2014/01/is-li-keqiang-being-marginalized/.

36. For a discussion of Deng's doctrine on the separation of party and government, see, for example, Zhu Hua, "An assessment of Deng Xiaoping's thoughts on 'separation of party and government,'" Club.china.com (Beijing), October 25, 2010, http://club.china.com/data/thread/5688138/2719/20/60/7_1.html. See also Qing Xiaohe, "Deng Xiaoping's

four historical contribution: Reform of the political structuring leading to the separation of party and government," *People's Daily*, September 8, 2013, http://forum.home.news.cn/detail/125961074/1.html.

37. See "Chi Fulin: The government has not let go enough of vital powers," *Jinghua Daily* (Nanjing), November 12, 2013, http://leaders.people.com.cn/n/2013/1112/c58278-23510468.html.

38. See "Xi Jinping: Reform must be pursued 'with a quick pace but steady steps,'" Xinhua News Agency, January 22, 2014, http://news.xinhuanet.com/politics/2014-01/22/c_119087717.htm.

39. Cited in "Xi Jinping: We must never allow subversive mistakes to take place over fundamental issues," Xinhua News Agency, February 24, 2014, www.gmw.cn/sixiang/2014-02/24/content_10485016.htm; see also "Comrade Xi Jinping's important statements on economic work since the Eighteenth Party Congress," Xinhua News Agency, February 22, 2014, http://china.huanqiu.com/roll/2014-02/4852207.html.

40. See "Director of the CCP Central Committee Li Zhanshu writes article on a major political topic," *Ta Kung Pao*, November 26, 2013, http://news.takungpao.com/mainland/focus/2013-11/2064461.html.

41. See "Xi Jinping: We must handle well the relationship between reform, development, and stability," CNTV, October 23, 2013, http://money.163.com/13/1023/20/9BT88V7B00253B0H.html.

42. For a discussion of "Likonomics," see, for example, "Likonomics is actually reform-oriented economics," *New Beijing Post*, July 27, 2013, http://news.163.com/13/0727/02/94OODMP200014AED.html. See also "'Likonomics has spearheaded the restructuring of the Chinese economy,'" *People's Daily*, July 9, 2013, http://finance.people.com.cn/n/2013/0709/c1004-22126643.html. "The three pillars of Le Keqiang economics," *Southern Metropolitan News* (Guangzhou), July 1, 2013, http://money.163.com/13/0701/08/92MFH86I00253B0H.html.

43. Cited in "Li Keqiang left out of the drafting committee on document on reform," BBC Chinese Service, November 15, 2013, www.bbc.co.uk/zhongwen/trad/china/2013/11/131115_china_xi_li_reform.shtml.

44. Cited in "Li Keqiang's talk at the video conference on changing the functions of State Council departments," *People's Daily*, May 15, 2013, http://cpc.people.com.cn/n/2013/0515/c64094-21483422.html. See also "Li Keqiang: Believe in the boundless creativity of the masses," Gov.cn (Beijing), March 28, 2014, www.gov.cn/guowuyuan/2014-03/28/content_2648798.htm.

45. See "Full text of Li Keqiang's government work report," Xinhua News Agency, March 5, 2014, http://news.china.com/2014lh/news/11151572/20140305/18375462.html.

46. Cited in "Li Keqiang: Local governments should in theory stop investing in enterprises," Xinhua News Agency, November 8, 2013, http://news.nfdaily.cn/content/2013-11/08/content_84035918.htm.

47. See "Full text of Li Keqiang's government work report." See also "Premier Li Keqiang's international press conference at the second session of the Twelfth NPC," Xinhua News Agency, March 13, 2014, http://news.xinhuanet.com/2014-03/13/c_119762407.htm.

48. See "Full text of Li Keqiang's government work report."

49. Ibid.

50. Cited in "Li Keqiang asks the Shanghai mayor: Do you want special policies or reform," *China Youth Daily*, August 12, 2013, http://news.youth.cn/gn/201308/t20130812_3680533_1.htm. For a discussion of Li and the Pudong FTZ, see, for example, George Chen, "Li Keqiang fought strong opposition for Shanghai free trade zone plan," *South China Morning Post*, July 15, 2013, www.scmp.com/news/china/article/1282793/li-fought-strong-opposition-shanghai-free-trade-zone-plan/; see also Dan Steinbock, "The rise

of Shanghai's free trade zone," Chinausfocus.com, September 18, 2013, www.chinausfocus. com/finance-economy/the-rise-of-shanghais-free-trade-zone/.

51. Cited in Cary, "Reforming China's state-owned enterprises." For a discussion of the future of SOE reform, see, for example, Simon Rabinovitch, "China's reform chip away at privileges of state-owned companies," *Financial Times,* November 19, 2013, www.ft.com/ intl/cms/s/0/42fc92d4-510a-11e3-b499-00144feabdc0.html#axzz2yqfxWqzV/; Bob Davis, "Beijing's state-owned sector gets a new boost," *Wall Street Journal,* February 23, 2014, http://online.wsj.com/news/articles/SB10001424052702303636404579369633232035544?mg=reno64-wsj&url=http%3A%2F%2Fonline.wsj.com%2Farticle%2F SB10001424052702303636404579396933232035544.html.

52. Cited in Stanley Lubman, "China's state capitalism: The real world implications," *Wall Street Journal,* March 1, 2012, http://blogs.wsj.com/chinarealtime/2012/03/01/chinas-state-capitalism-the-real-world-implications/; see also Derek Scissors, "Chinese state-owned enterprises and the U.S. policy on China," testimony before the U.S.-China Economic and Security Review Commission, Washington, DC, February 15, 2012, www.heritage.org/ research/testimony/2012/03/chinese-state-owned-enterprises-and-the-us-policy-on-china/.

53. Cited in Charlie Zhu and David Lague, "Special report: China's other power struggle," Reuters, October 16, 2012, www.reuters.com/article/2012/10/16/us-china-soe-idUSBRE89F1MP20121016/.

54. Cited in "Decision on major issues concerning comprehensively deepening reforms."

55. For a discussion of the reform of SOE conglomerates, see, for example, Willy Lam, "SOE links threaten China reform drive," *Asia Times,* October 31, 2013, www.atimes.com/ atimes/China/CHIN-03-311013.html.

56. For a discussion of graft-related cases at CNPC, see, for example, "148 disciplinary inspection officials at Petrol China present their reports," *Wen Wei Po* (Hong Kong), April 14, http://news.wenweipo.com/2014/04/14/IN1404140004.htm. For a discussion of high-profile SOE heads who have been arrested for corruption, see Chen Gang and Zhu Jining, "China's recent clampdown on high-stakes corruption," East Asian Institute Background Briefs no. 490, National Singapore University, November 2009, www.eai.nus.edu.sg/BB490.pdf.

57. For a discussion of *yangqi* surrendering a higher level of profits to central coffers, see, for example, "*Yangqi* to surrender 30 percent of bonus profits by 2020," *Beijing Morning Post,* November 16, 2013, http://news.163.com/13/1116/08/9DPNS87O00014AED.html; see also "A bigger proportion of profits surrendered by *yangqi* to be used to improve people's livelihood," *Wen Hui Bao* (Shanghai), November 20, 2013, http://finance.chinanews.com/ cj/2013/12-20/5644724.shtml.

58. Cited in "SASAC Party Secretary Zhang Yi: Resolutely carry out anti-corruption measures and hit out at both 'tigers' and 'flies,'" *People's Daily,* September 4, http://ccnews. people.com.cn/n/2013/0904/c141677-22803664.html.

59. Cited in "State-owned enterprises: The state advances," *Economist,* October 6, 2013, www.economist.com/node/21564274/; see also Davis, "Beijing's state-owned sector gets a new boost." For a discussion of Mao Yushi's views, see Zhang Fengjiao and Xiao Tong, "Mao Yushi: The question of SOEs is who is the boss?" Phoenix TV News Net, December 29, 2013, www.21ccom.net/articles/zgyj/gqmq/article_2013122997857.html.

60. See "Li Keqiang: On building 'sunshine *yangqi*,'" Xinhua News Agency, August 21, 2013, http://news.xinhuanet.com/politics/2013-08/21/c_117039025.htm.

61. Cited in Willy Lam, "SOE links threaten China reform drive," *Asia Times,* October 31, 2013, www.atimes.com/atimes/China/CHIN-03-311013.html.

62. Cited in Chen Yingying, "Li Yining: Private enterprises should compete with SOEs in an environment of equality," *China Securities News,* March 6, 2013, www.cs.com.cn/ sylm/jsbd/201303/t20130306_3887166.html.

63. Cited in Ren Yi, "Li Keqiang's adviser talks about reform of SOEs, and raises directions for reform," Phoenix TV News, October 11, 2013, http://blog.sina.com.cn/s/blog_4edc7a7b0102em69.html.

64. See "CCTV: The CNPC scandal has nothing to do with monopoly; the petroleum business is not something that any company can get into," CCTV News, September 2, 2013, http://news.china.com.cn/live/2013-09/02/content_22092648.htm.

65. See "Why state-held assets should not be distributed randomly," Economic Daily, August 13, 2013, www.chinasouth.com.cn/n29/n119/n133/c329221/content.html.

66. For a discussion of former SOE chiefs becoming cadres, see, for example, Russell Hsiao, "Red cadres and red-hat businessmen," Asia Times, June 26, 2010, http://atimes.com/atimes/China_Business/LF26Cb02.html. See also "From senior managers of yangqi to Central Committee members," China Economic Weekly (Beijing), November 6, 2012, www.ceweekly.cn/html/Article/201211067632949633107.html.

67. Cited in Willy Lam, "SOE background of rising leaders threatens reform," China Brief, Jamestown Foundation, October 24, 2013, www.jamestown.org/programs/chinabrief/single/?tx_ttnews%5Btt_news%5D=41525&tx_ttnews%5BbackPid%5D=25&cHash=c023e6f28f6017dbea14acf17a4c95e3/.

68. Cited in "Xi Jinping asks the CCP to beware of the lesson of the collapse of the Communist Party of the Soviet Union." See also Buckley, "Vows of change in China belie private warning."

69. Cited in "Ren Zhiqiang: If the party ran the economy, the government's economic [considerations] would come to no avail," Caijing Net (Beijing), August 14, 2013, http://fz.ifeng.com/money/cjtt/detail_2013_08/14/1106485_0.shtml.

70. See Zhang Weiying, "The mixed ownership system will in the long run bring about serious corruption," Caijing Net, April 8, 2014, http://finance.ifeng.com/a/20140408/12074457_0.shtml.

71. Cited in "China has 10m private enterprises," Xinhua News Agency, February 2, 2013, www.chinadaily.com.cn/business/2013-02/02/content_16195827.htm; Nini Zhang, "China to work on developing private sector," CNTV.cn, December 20, 2012, http://english.cntv.cn/program/bizasia/20121220/102630.shtml.

72. See in Xi Jinping, Work Hard on the Substance and Take the Lead (Beijing: Central Party School Publishing House, 2006), pp. 90–91.

73. See "Xi Jinping: The minying economy is where the vigor is," China Business Times, January 2, 2003, www.china.com.cn/chinese/OP-c/255672.htm.

74. Cited in Wang Zheng, "Xi Jinping: If we do not support enterprises like Geely, who else should we support?" People's Daily, January 8, 2003, www.people.com.cn/GB/jinji/32/178/20030108/904079.html.

75. See "Zhejiang Party secretary touts economic successes and work toward rule of law at ambassador's dinner, March 19, 2007," Wikileaks, https://www.wikileaks.org/plusd/cables/07BEIJING1840_a.html. See also "Special report: Cables show U.S. sizing up China's next leader," Reuters, February 17, 2011, www.reuters.com/article/2011/02/17/us-wiki-china-xi-idUSTRE71G5WH20110217/.

76. For a discussion of the guojinmintui phenomenon, see, for example, Simon Rabinovitch, "Private sector battles march of Chinese state," Financial Times, November 11, 2012, www.ft.com/intl/cms/s/0/eb5687c0-2bed-11e2-a91d-00144feabdc0.html#axzz2qkTG7NNc/; see also Patrick Chovanec, "China state enterprises advance, private sector retreats," Forbes, August 31, 2010, www.forbes.com/sites/china/2010/08/31/guo-jin-min-tui/.

77. Cited in Chen Zhouxi, "Wenzhou to face a wave of bankruptcies," First Financial Daily (Shanghai), March 24, 2013, www.cs.com.cn/cqzk/201303/t20130324_3917517.html.

78. For a discussion of the dominance of IT giants such as Alibaba and Tencent, see, for example, Kim Gittleson, "Tencent and Alibaba battle for internet dominance in China,"

BBC News, March 18, 2014, www.bbc.com/news/business-26540666/; see also Tom Risen, "China's tech giants eye Wall Street," USnews.com, March 21, 2014, www.usnews.com/news/articles/2014/03/21/chinas-tech-giants-eye-wall-street/.

79. For a discussion of the performance of Haier and Zany, see, for example, "Haier and higher," *Economist*, October 12, 2013, www.economist.com/news/business/21587792-radical-boss-haier-wants-transform-worlds-biggest-appliance-maker-nimble/; see also "Sany group growth pared as China slowdown cuts machinery demand," Bloomberg March 10, 2012, www.bloomberg.com/news/2012-03-10/sany-growth-pared-as-china-slowdown-cuts-machinery-demand.html.

80. For a discussion of Zhang Ruimin's career, see Christina Larson, "China's Jack Welch rethinks management strategies," *Businessweek*, October 11, 2013, www.businessweek.com/articles/2013-10-11/china-s-jack-welch-rethinks-management-strategies/; see also Hamish McDonald, "Communism-capitalism in crisis," *Sydney Morning Herald*, June 12, 2010.www.smh.com.au/federal-politics/society-and-culture/communismcapitalism-in-crisis-20100611/.

81. See "Liang Wengen: My properties and even my life belong to the Party," *Guangming Daily* (Beijing), November 12, 2012, http://news.ifeng.com/mainland/special/zhonggong18da/content-3/detail_2012_11/12/19047721_0.shtml.

82. Cited in Zhang Anran, "Entrepreneurs talk about the relations between politics and business," *Chinese Entrepreneur*, July 17, 2013, http://tech.ifeng.com/internet/detail_2013_07/17/27612851_0.shtml. See also Zhou Erjie, "Chinese entrepreneurs gain growing presence at Party congress," Xinhua News Agency, November 12, 2012, http://news.xinhuanet.com/english/special/18cpcnc/2012-11/12/c_131969008.htm.

83. Ibid. For a discussion of the influence of Wang Jianli, see, for example, Russell Flannery, "How China's richest man succeeds," *Forbes*, October 2, 2013, www.forbes.com/sites/russellflannery/2013/10/03/how-chinas-richest-man-succeeds/.

84. For a discussion of private businessmen becoming officials, see, for example, "On the phenomenon of entrepreneurs becoming officials," *First Financial News*, September 23, 2011, http://opinion.hexun.com/2011-09-23/133647909.html. See also Deng Yuwen, "How come private businessmen are interested in becoming officials," *Southern Metropolitan News*, August 2, 2004, http://news.sohu.com/20040802/n221324961.shtml.

85. See "Xi Jinping listens to work report of Tsinghua University and gives major speech," Tsinghua University Net, April 11, 2011, http://edu.qq.com/a/20110411/000211.htm.

86. See "Li Keqiang encourages entrepreneurs while inspecting Tianjin, saying the government will provide them with more nutrients," China National Radio, December 27, 2013, http://china.cnr.cn/gdgg/201312/t20131227_514511832.shtml.

87. Cited in Richard Van Noorden, "China tops Europe in R&D intensity," Nature.com, January 8, 2014, www.nature.com/news/china-tops-europe-in-rd-intensity-1.14476.

88. For a discussion of the number of technological personnel in China, see, for example, Geoff Colvin, "Desperately seeking math and science majors," *Fortune*, July 29, 2010, http://money.cnn.com/2010/07/29/news/international/china_engineering_grads.fortune/index.htm.

89. For a discussion of China's patents, see, for example, Lyric Hughes Hale, "China's innovation hurdle," Huffington Post, June 14, 2013, www.huffingtonpost.com/lyric-hughes-hale/chinas-innovation-hurdle_b_3435384.html; see also Valentina Romei, "Chart of the week: China's patent/royalty disconnect," *Financial Times*, May 6, 2013, http://blogs.ft.com/beyond-brics/2013/05/06/chart-of-the-week-chinas-patent-royalty-disconnect/#axzz2qFT62b1g/.

90. Cited in Li Jiabao, "China drops to 35 in Global Innovation Index," *China Daily*, July 5, 2013, www.chinadaily.com.cn/business/2013-07/05/content_16736750.htm; see also "Thomson Reuters names the world's Top 100 Most Innovative Organizations for

2013," Thomsonreuters, October 7, 2013, http://thomsonreuters.com/press-releases/102013/thomson-reuters-2013-top-100-global-innovators/.

91. For a discussion of China's achievements in certain areas of high technology, see, for example, James Wilsdon, Kirsten Bound and Tom Saunders, "What the world's fastest computer tells us about China's absorptive state," *Guardian,* October 7, 2013, www.theguardian.com/science/political-science/2013/oct/07/science-policy/. See also James T. Areddy and Norihiko Shirouzu, "China bullet trains trip on technology," *Wall Street Journal,* October 3, 2011, http://online.wsj.com/news/articles/SB1000142405311190435350457565 68983658561372/.

92. Cited in Xiaolei Gu, "China releases blueprint to promote seven emerging industries," China-briefing.com, June 1, 2012, www.china-briefing.com/news/2012/06/01/china-releases-blueprint-to-promote-seven-emerging-industries.html; "China eyes new strategic industries to spur economy," Reuters, July 23, 2012, www.reuters.com/article/2012/07/23/us-china-economy-strategic-idUSBRE86M03R20120723/.

93. For a discussion of synergy between civilian and military research and development in China, see, for example, David Yang, "Civil-military integration efforts in China," University of California at San Diego Institute on Global Conflict and Cooperation, Policy Brief no. 24, September 2011, http://igcc.ucsd.edu/assets/001/503248.pdf.

94. For a discussion for the problems faced by Huawei in expanding to certain foreign markets, see, for example, Simon Sharwood, "India joins list of nations vetting Huawei, ZTE," *Register* (U.K.), May 10, 2013, www.theregister.co.uk/2013/05/10/india_to_test_huawei_and_zte_kit/; see also "New Australian government upholds ban on China's Huawei," Reuters, October 29, 2013, www.reuters.com/article/2013/10/29/us-huawei-australia-idUSBRE99S01820131029/.

95. For a discussion of Jiang Mianheng's activities in the scientific and business arenas, see, for example, Mimi Leung and Yojana Sharma, "'Princeling' named head of new Shanghai university," Universityworldnews.com, March 9, 2014, www.universityworldnews.com/article.php?story=20140309162305896/.

96. Cited in Steve Blank, "Zhongguancun in Beijing—China's Silicon Valley," Berkeley.edu, April 15, 2013, http://blogs.berkeley.edu/2013/04/15/zhongguancun-in-beijing-chinas-silicon-valley/.

97. For a study of the Silicon Valley model and its applicability to countries including China, see, for example, AnnaLee Saxenian, *The New Argonauts: Regional Advantage in a Global Economy* (Cambridge: Harvard University Press, 2006), pp. 48–81.

98. Cited in World Bank, "Cost of pollution in China: Economic estimates of physical damages," February 2007, http://web.worldbank.org/WBSITE/EXTERNAL/COUNTRIES/EASTASIAPACIFICEXT/EXTEAPREGTOPENVIRONMENT/0,,contentMDK:21252897~pagePK:34004173~piPK:34003707~theSitePK:502886,00.html.

99. Cited in "China needs 7.2% growth to ensure employment," *Wall Street Journal,* November 15, 2013, http://online.wsj.com/news/articles/SB10001424052702303482504579179033609323974/.

100. Cited in "Chinese Premier Li Keqiang meets the press," Xinhua News Agency, March 13, 2014, http://news.xinhuanet.com/english/special/2014-03/13/c_133183041.htm.

101. Cited in Li Lei, "IMF says China's investment, at nearly 50 percent of GDP, is excessive," *New Beijing Post,* April 16, 2013, http://finance.qq.com/a/20130416/001093.htm; see also "Expert says state investment is close to 50 percent of GDP," *Economic and Nation Weekly* (Beijing), March 5, 2012, http://finance.sina.com.cn/china/hgjj/20120305/161811516957.shtml.

102. Cited in Tom Orlik, "China's credit bubble is swelling, not bursting," *Wall Street Journal,* April 4, 2013, http://online.wsj.com/news/articles/SB10001424127887323646604 5784017619429884/; see also Kate Mackenzie, "China's Pettis moment," *Financial Times,* April 16, 2013, http://ftalphaville.ft.com/2013/04/16/1461572/chinas-pettis-moment/.

103. Cited in "China leverage seen rising through 2016," Bloomberg, April 2, 2014. https://news.google.com/news/section?pz=1&cf=all&q=China&siidp=baf0d53eafcb738c1 2abf980a1c3bab8ce37&ict=ln/; Ambrose Evans-Pritchard, "Fitch says China credit bubble unprecedented in modern world history," *Telegraph*, January 16, 2013, www.telegraph. co.uk/finance/china-business/10123507/Fitch-says-China-credit-bubble-unprecedented-in-modern-world-history.html. See also "China's industrial-sized debt: Beijing continues to fuel economic growth with more credit," *Wall Street Journal*, September 25, 2013, http:// online.wsj.com/news/articles/SB10001424052702303759604579092720176345630/; Andy Xie, "When the giants unwind," Caixin.com, December 20, 2013, http://english.caixin. com/2013-12-30/100623528.html.

104. Cited in Charles Riley and Sophia Yan, "China local government debt hits $3 trillion," CNN, December 30, 2014, http://money.cnn.com/2013/12/30/news/economy/ china-local-debt/.

105. Cited in Wang Changyong, "Closer look: Rise in total government debt—to 30.3 trillion yuan—means change is needed," Caixin.com, December 31, 2013, http://english. caixin.com/2013-12-31/100624015.html; see also "Credit-driven China glut threatens surge into bank crisis," Bloomberg, November 19, 2013, www.bloomberg.com/news/2013-11-18/ credit-driven-china-glut-threatens-surge-into-bank-crisis.html.

106. Cited in Neil Gough and David Barboza, "Credit tightens in China as Central Bank takes a hard line," June 20, 2013, www.nytimes.com/2013/06/21/business/global/china-manufacturing-contracts-to-lowest-level-in-9-months.html?_r=0/; see also "Cautious monetary stance to remain," *China Daily*, June 20, 2013, http://europe.chinadaily.com.cn/ business/2013-06/20/content_16638714.htm.

107. Cited in Guo Fang, "Likonomics has received attention: Reformist zeal is comparable to the Zhu Rongji era," *China Economics Weekly*, July 9, 2013, http://news.163. com/13/0709/08/93B0UTMP00014JB6.html.

108. Cited in "China outlines measures to support growth as goal recedes," Bloomberg, April 2, 2014, www.bloomberg.com/news/2014-04-02/china-outlines-measures-to-support-growth.html.

109. Cited in Dexter Roberts, "Overcapacity threatens China growth," *Businessweek*, December 11, 2013, www.businessweek.com/articles/2013-12-11/overcapacity-threatens-china-growth; see also David Stanway, "China to ban new projects, strengthen market in new overcapacity plan," Reuters, October 15, 2013, www.reuters.com/article/2013/10/15/ us-china-overcapacity-idUSBRE99E05620131015/.

110. For a discussion of China's ghost cities, see, for example, Ivan Watson and Connie Yong, "Can China breathe life into 'ghost towns'?" CNN, May 28, 2013, http://edition.cnn. com/2013/05/27/world/asia/china-urbanization-house-prices/; see also Dinny McMahon, "China's gleaming ghost cities draw neither jobs nor people," *Wall Street Journal*, August 11, 2013, http://online.wsj.com/news/articles/SB10001424127887324412604578515382905495900/.

111. For a discussion of China's debt problem, see, for example, Rana Faroohar, "China's growing debt problem," *Time*, April 10, 2014, http://time.com/tag/debt/; see also "China gets first onshore bond default as Chaori doesn't pay," Bloomberg, March 7, 2014, www. bloomberg.com/news/2014-03-07/chaori-solar-fails-to-make-interest-payments-on-bond-wsj-says.html. For a discussion of the troubled real estate sector, see, for example, Sophia Yan, "China real estate firm at risk of bankruptcy," CNN, March 19, 2014, http://money. cnn.com/2014/03/19/news/economy/china-property-default/.

112. See "China's debt risk within control: Premier Li," Xinhua, March 13, 2014, http:// news.xinhuanet.com/english/special/2014-03/13/c_133182962.htm.

113. Cited in "Consumer spending increases only 13.1%; Beijing's targets not reached," *Ming Pao*, January 1, 2014, http://premium.mingpao.com/cfm/Content_News.cfm?Chann el=ea&Path=100902006213/eaa3.cfm.

114. Cited in "Wages' share of GDP continues to fall in 22 years," CCTV News, May 15, 2010, http://news.163.com/10/0515/00/66MEHTOM0001124J.html; see also Lang Xianping, "Why are Chinese citizens' income so low?" *Tencent Finance News,* February 4, 2010, http://finance.qq.com/a/20100204/003755.htm.

115. For a discussion of the relation between social welfare and consumer spending, see, for example, Li Gan, "Why China needs to spend more on welfare," CNN, March 5, 2013, http://edition.cnn.com/2013/03/05/opinion/china-economy-gan/; see also Dexter Roberts, "China's savers block the consumer economy," *Businessweek,* July 11, 2013, www.businessweek.com/articles/2013-07-11/chinas-savers-block-the-consumer-economy/.

116. Cited in "China seen to wait until 2016 to scrap cap on bank deposit rates," Bloomberg, September 27, 2013, www.bloomberg.com/news/2013-09-27/china-seen-to-wait-until-2016-to-scrap-cap-on-bank-deposit-rates.html/; see also Nicholas R. Lardy, *Sustaining China's Economic Growth After the Global Financial Crisis* (Washington, DC: Peterson Institute for International Economics, 2012), p. 82.

117. Cited in "Expert says it is difficult for marketization of interest rates on bank deposits to be accomplished in 2014," China News Service, December 16, 2013, www.chinanews.com/gn/2013/12-16/5624170.shtml; see also Jin Fenghui, "The wholesale implementation of China's financial system is ready to go in 2014," *Shanghai Securities News,* January 6, 2014, http://finance.sina.com.cn/money/bank/bank_hydt/20140106/023917850074.shtml.

118. Cited in Zheng Wang, "Why China's new rich want to emigrate," *Diplomat,* November 5, 2013, http://thediplomat.com/2013/11/why-chinas-new-rich-want-to-emigrate/comment-page-1/.

119. See "China's new premier presses reforms as 'biggest dividend,'" Xinhua News Agency, March 17, 2013, http://news.xinhuanet.com/english/china/2013-03/17/c_132240248.htm.

120. See "Wu Jinglian: The government's power in the allocation of resources is too big," *New Beijing Post* (Beijing), December 6, 2011, http://finance.ifeng.com/opinion/macro/20111206/5211947.shtml.

121. For a discussion of the streamlining of the State Council structure, see Wu Yao, "State Council units cut down to 25 departments," *Southern Metropolitan News,* March 11, 2013, www.chla.com.cn/htm/2013/0311/161369.html. See also "Li Keqiang: The market should as far as possible avoid becoming dependent on policy," Caijing.com, July 23, 2013, http://money.163.com/13/0723/07/94F1CBT100253B0H.html.

122. For a discussion of Western influence on bureaucratic streamlining in the State Council, see, for example, Martin Painter, Tom Christensen, Lisheng Dong, and Richard Walker, "Imitating the West? Evidence on administrative reform from the upper echelons of Chinese government," *Public Administration Review* 72, no. 6 (2012): 798–806.

123. For a discussion of the PBOC's relationship with the government, see, for example, Feng Jianmin, "People's Bank of China to back state progress," *Shanghai Daily,* April 12, 2014, www.shanghaidaily.com/business/finance/PBOC-to-back-state-progress/shdaily.shtml.

124. Cited in "Hu Deping: If the Decision can't be implemented, this is due to obstruction from interest groupings," *Ta Kung Pao,* December 8, 2013, http://news.takungpao.com/mainland/focus/2013-12/2092159.html; "Hu Deping: Some interests blocs are threatening the security of the party and state," *Ta Kung Pao,* April 3, 2013, http://news.takungpao.com/mainland/focus/2013-04/1526894.html.

125. Cited in "Chen Xiaolu: The number of the second red generation does not exceed 40,000," *Hong Kong Commercial Daily,* January 21, 2014, http://news.takungpao.com/mainland/zgzq/2014-01/2182083.html.

126. Cited in "Heirs of Mao's comrades rise as new capitalist nobility," Bloomberg, December 26, 2012, http://go.bloomberg.com/multimedia/mapping-chinas-red-nobility/.

127. Cited in James Ball, "China's princelings storing riches in Caribbean offshore haven," *Guardian,* January 21, 2014, www.theguardian.com/world/ng-interactive/2014/jan/21/china-british-virgin-islands-wealth-offshore-havens/.

128. Cited in Ben Protess and Jessica Silver-Greenberg, "On defensive, JPMorgan hired China's elite," *New York Times,* December 29, 2013, http://dealbook.nytimes.com/2013/12/29/on-defensive-jpmorgan-hired-chinas-elite/?_php=true&_type=blogs&_r=0/.

129. See "Xi Jinping leads Internet security group," Xinhua News Agency, February 27, 2014, http://news.xinhuanet.com/english/china/2014-02/27/c_133148273.htm.

130. For a discussion of the impact of Google's partial withdrawal from the China market, see, for example, Andrew Jacobs, "Google's threat echoed everywhere, except China," *New York Times,* January 13, 2010, www.nytimes.com/2010/01/14/world/asia/14beijing.html?_r=0/.

131. Cited in George Chen, "Free speech and Internet are key to China's reform, says Google's Eric Schmidt," *South China Morning Post,* November 4, 2013, www.scmp.com/news/hong-kong/article/1347382/free-speech-and-internet-are-key-chinas-reform-says-googles-eric?page=all/.

132. See Timothy Beardson, *Stumbling Giant: The Threat to China's Future* (New Haven: Yale University Press, 2013), pp. 79 and 114.

# 5

# China's Great Leap Outward

## Introduction: "Proactively Seek Achievements" vs. "Keep a Low Profile"

After China became a quasi-superpower in the second half of the Hu Jintao–Wen Jiabao administration (2007–12), it is evident that the country morphed from a status-quo power to one that is bent on aggressive global power projection so as to safeguard its growing national interests. This is despite the fact that as late as 2009, then-president Hu insisted that the Middle Kingdom was still sticking to Deng Xiaoping's famous dictum on foreign policy usually abbreviated as *taoguangyanghui* ("keeping a low profile" or "biding one's time"). Actually, Deng's entire instruction, given in the early 1990s, was: "We should make cool-headed observations [of the international scene], and remain sure-footed and exercise patience in countering [challenges]. We should take a low profile, be good at holding down the fort; we should never take the lead, and we should seek achievements [when circumstances allow]."[1]

While it can be argued that the reference to *yousuozuowei* (seeking achievements) does not render the Deng maxim necessarily passive or reactive, most references to this aphorism have focused on the quiescent, status quo-abiding *taoguangyanghui*. A small but significant revision of the instruction was made by ex-president Hu at a national meeting of diplomats held in July 2009. Hu rephrased Deng's dictum as "insist upon taking a low profile, and enthusiastically seek achievements." This line was repeated by then-state councilor Tang Jiaxuan later that year.[2] The emphasis had shifted from "biding one's time" to a more proactive agenda. The official *Guangming Daily* even warned in a 2011 commentary that "some comrades have begun to emphasize 'enthusiastically seeking achievements' while neglecting 'insisting upon taking a low profile.'"[3]

Wu Jianmin, an ambassador to France and a regular commentator on foreign affairs, argued in 2005 that Deng's instruction on *taoguangyanghui* "should be

maintained for at least a hundred years." Wu had this to say about those of his colleagues who wanted China to throw its weight around: "People all over the world
will think: since Chinese, whose per capita GDP is $3,000, have already become
so fierce, what would happen if their per capita GDP has jumped to $20,000?"
More recently, Wu lambasted intellectuals who asked: "Since China is no. 2 under
heaven, why should we still have to keep a low profile?" "This is the mentality of
an upstart," wrote Wu in 2012.[4] Renmin University international affairs expert Jin
Canrong pointed out the same year that "once the country has laid down major
goals such as peaceful development and taking a low profile, it should resolutely
hold on to them. . . . These goals should not be changed owing to controversies in
and out of China, or as a result of international conflict."[5]

By the time Xi Jinping became party general secretary and commander-in-chief at
the Eighteenth Party Congress in November 2012, however, the picture had largely
changed. Xi has never gone on the record repeating Deng's famous dictum. He has
talked instead about the foreign policy implications of his "Chinese Dream" mantra.
"The Chinese Dream is a dream about peace, development, cooperation, and win-
win [scenarios with other states]," Xi likes to say. "Irrespective of the winds of
change on the international stage, we want peace and not war, cooperation and not
confrontation."[6] Yet there is also an unmistakable dimension of nationalism—and
unabashed power projection—in the Chinese Dream. It is a blunt restatement of
Chairman Mao's "the Chinese people have stood up" mentality. Xi has reiterated
that his administration is seeking "the great renaissance of the Chinese people"
after a prolonged period of national humiliation since the Opium War of 1840. "The
Chinese Dream is a dream about a prosperous country," he noted while meeting
officers in the Guangzhou Military Region soon after taking office. "It is also a
dream about a strong military," he said. "We must uphold the synthesis between
a prosperous country and a strong army, and assiduously build up a solid national
defense and a powerful army."[7]

More specifically, Xi indicated at a key meeting on China's "peripheral
diplomacy"—meaning the country's relations with its neighbors—that "we must
be more proactive in seeking achievements in the conduct of our peripheral diplomacy." The expression that Xi used on this occasion—*fenfayouwei* (be proactive
in seeking achievements)—has become a new paradigm for China's much more
assertive foreign and national security policies—despite the fact that, to reassure
China's jittery neighbors, Xi has reiterated, as he did in May 2014 after a flare-up
in sovereignty disputes with Vietnam and the Philippines in the South China Sea,
that "the Chinese people do not have the gene . . . for invading others or dominating the world."[8]

This chapter investigates China's bold projection of hard and soft power as
it emerges as a quasi-superpower that is poised to challenge the U.S.-dominated
unipolar world order. China's major diplomatic principles, including the policy of
good-neighborliness and "economics-based diplomacy," are analyzed. Also discussed are the recent history and future development of China's relations with four

key countries and blocs: the United States, Japan, ASEAN, and Russia. Beijing's increasingly tense territorial disputes with a host of countries in the South China Sea and the East China Sea are examined. One section is devoted to the influence of the People's Liberation Army (PLA) on diplomacy and national security issues. The conclusion assesses the challenges that the Xi administration faces in trying to bring about a "de-Americanized world order."

## The Xi Administration's Assertive Foreign Policy

As we saw in Chapter 3, since the Eighteenth Party Congress in late 2012 Xi has pulled out all the stops to boost his power partly through the formation of super-agencies at the apex of the CCP, which ride roughshod over existing Party and government institutions. Having consolidated his authority within the Party-state apparatus, Commander-in-Chief Xi has come up with new concepts and strategies to facilitate the emergence of the quasi-superpower as a competitor to the United States in shaping the twenty-first-century world order.

Following Xi's enunciation of his *fenfayouwei* mantra, this new stance has been further elaborated on by officials and academics. Premier Li Keqiang said in his Government Work Report to the NPC in March 2014 that "we will fulfill the role of a responsible big country regarding major international and regional affairs and flashpoints." "Our influence abroad is being further raised," he added. Similarly, Foreign Minister Wang Yi indicated at the NPC that "China will give full play to the country's role as a major responsible country." In contradistinction to Deng's "keep a low profile" axiom, Wang indicated that China's foreign policy goal was "to seek achievements in a positive and proactive manner." Yan Xuetong, one of China's best-known theorists in international relations, said the evolution from "keeping a low profile" to "seeking achievements in a proactive manner" amounted to "a major change in China's foreign policy." "This can even be said to be a qualitative change," the Tsinghua University professor added. "We had to keep a low profile in the past because we were weak and you were strong. We told the international community that we would not interfere on all issues. Today's [slogan of] being proactive in seeking achievements is a way to tell our neighbors that 'we are strong and you are weak.'"[9]

### *Changing Definitions of Core National Interests—and a More Muscular Approach to Upholding Them*

#### *Ever-Expanding National Interests*

A major thrust of Xi Jinping's more assertive foreign policy is his reiteration that China's core national interests (*hexin guojialiyi*, abbreviated as *hexinliyi*) will never be sacrificed. As he said soon after becoming supreme leader: "China will stick to the path of peaceful development, but other countries should not assume that China will sacrifice its core national interests or that China will swallow the bitter pill of undermining its sovereignty, security, or development interests."[10] So what are China's core national interests? For example, Dai Bingguo, while state councilor in charge of diplomacy, pointed out in 2009 that "the core national interests of China are defending its fundamental systems and national security, preserving national sovereignty and unification, and maintaining the steady and sustainable development of its economy and society." This was confirmed in July 2010 by Foreign Ministry spokesman Qin Gang, when asked by foreign reporters to define the concept of core interests. "Areas relating to national sovereignty, security, territorial integrity, and developmental interests are all part of China's core interests," he said.[11]

On the surface, these definitions of *hexinliyi* do not differ much from earlier official statements on the same subject. However, it is clear that until the first half of the Hu administration (2002–7), Beijing's definition of core interests was basically static—and it involved mainly territorial integrity, namely, that China would not allow hostile foreign powers to "make trouble" in regions including Tibet, Xinjiang, Taiwan, and Hong Kong. However, by the second half of the 2000s, the concept of *hexinliyi* had taken a leap forward. In conversations with foreign officials or media statements, Chinese leaders began directly or indirectly to refer to contentious regions such as the South China Sea and the East China Sea—and even the Yellow Sea, wedged between China and the Koreas—as falling within China's core interests. For example, when the popular PLA commentator Major-General Luo Yuan explained Beijing's objections to war games being held there in 2010 by the United States and South Korea, he referred to the Yellow Sea as a virtual Chinese sphere of interest: "How can we let strangers fall sound asleep right outside our bedroom?"[12] The Foreign Ministry then lodged no fewer than nine protests with the U.S. government, which maintained that since the drills were in international waters, the United States was abiding by international law. On other occasions, senior cadres have dropped hints that the Diaoyu islets (known in Japan as the Senkaku islands) in the East China Sea fall within China's core interests.[13]

What is most worrying for China's neighbors is that as the country's clout—and vested interests—grows, so do its *hexinliyi*. The concept of the ever-expanding *hexinliyi* was propounded by military commentator Huang Kunlun. In a mid-2009 article in *Liberation Army Daily,* Huang introduced the notion of "the expanding boundaries of national interests." The nationalistic theorist argued that China's national interests had gone beyond its land, sea, and air territory to include areas such as the vast oceans traversed by Chinese oil freighters—as well as outer space. "Wherever our national interests have extended, so will the mission of our armed forces," Huang wrote. "Given our new historical mission, the military forces must safeguard not only the country's 'territorial boundaries' but also its 'boundaries of national interests'. . . . We need to safeguard not only national-security interests but also interests relating to [future] national development."[14]

Since the turn of the century, China's core interests have extended to outer space. Modern warfare demands command of the sky. China's space program is essentially run by the PLA, and military leaders are keen to apply whatever technology space scientists have developed for military use. Take, for example, China's moon program. According to the military expert Li Daguang, various techniques used in launching the Chang'e No. 3 expedition—which landed an exploratory rover on the moon in December 2013—could have military implications. "Techniques ranging from the propelling systems to remote-control mechanisms can be applied to missiles," he said. Other scientists even envisaged the eventual construction of a missile base on the moon.[15]

For strategic purposes, it is unlikely that Beijing will make known the full list of its core national interests. When Han Xudong, a national security expert at the National Defense University (NDU), stated that China should adopt a cautious attitude when staking out the country's "core interests," he seemed to argue against the "expansionist" definition of *hexinliyi*. Han pointed out that "our comprehensive national strength, especially military power, is not yet sufficient to safeguard all our core national interests." Yet he was only opposed to the premature proclamation of these core interests, recommending that Beijing release its list of *hexinliyi* in a phased, step-by-step fashion: "As China becomes stronger, we can publicize by installments those core interests that our country can effectively safeguard."[16] In other words, Han confirmed Beijing's adoption of a continuously expanding definition of core national interests.

*China as a "Maritime Power" and a New Formula for Settling Maritime Sovereignty Disputes*

A naval arms race is being conducted among powers in the Asia-Pacific region—and the CCP leadership seems confident that with its economic heft and single-minded devotion to military modernization, China will be in a position to dominate its surrounding seas in the not-too-distant future. China's ambition of becoming a "maritime power" was first declared in Hu's Political Report to the Eighteenth Party Congress in late 2012.[17] Commander-in-chief Xi has vowed to devote his undivided attention—and to earmark necessary resources—to building naval capacity that will not only surpass that of Japan and Russia but also close the gap with U.S. forces by the 2030s. Xi has also told China's naval officers to extend extra efforts to blunt the impact of President Barack Obama's "pivot to Asia," especially the U.S. decision to station as much as 60 percent of U.S. naval capacity in the Asia-Pacific region.[18]

Xi revealed more of China's maritime ambitions in a Politburo Study Session in early 2013 devoted to this topic. Experts including China National Overseas Oil Corporation (CNOOC) deputy chief engineer Zeng Hengyi and a professor at the China Institute for Marine Affairs, Gao Zhiguo, talked to the Politburo about how China could expand its influence in the seas and win sovereignty disputes with countries such as Japan, Vietnam, and the Philippines. Xi laid down the main strategy for the future: "We must promote better coordination between resources on land and at sea, and uphold the principle of building a rich country through exploiting maritime resources. . . . We must raise our ability to develop the ocean and expand areas of oceanic development. . . . We must let maritime economic development become a new locomotive of growth." Regarding the increasingly tense territorial and oceanic disputes with countries including Japan, Xi said, "We will not give up our rightful interests; we will never sacrifice core national interests."[19]

The China Defense White Paper of 2013, titled "The Diversified Employment of China's Armed Forces," contained a section called "safeguarding maritime rights and benefits." It called for no-holds-barred efforts to protect the approximately 1.16 million square miles (3 million square kilometers) of maritime territory claimed by China—including large swathes of the South China Sea and the East China Sea that are also claimed by Japan and various ASEAN member states.[20] According to Chinese statistics, some 463,000 square miles (1.2 million square kilometers) of China's ocean territory are subject to dispute with other countries, includings waters surrounding dozens of strategic islands that are occupied by the Philippines, Vietnam, and Malaysia.[21]

According to the vice-political commissar of the Navy, Wang Sentai, China has a long way to go before it can claim mastery over the oceans. Wang pointed out that due to improvement in equipment and in training in real-war conditions, "the combat power of the navy has been greatly raised." But he conceded that "while China is a big maritime power, it is not yet a strong maritime power. . . . We must build up oceanic power and construct a strong navy so as to realize the Chinese Dream. . . . History has told us that a weak navy portends a weak country, and a strong navy makes for a strong country."[22]

Apart from the PLA Navy, China has beefed up quasi-military forces under the State Oceanic Administration (SOA), which underwent a significant expansion in March 2013.[23] The SOA administers a new Chinese Coast Guard, which is the result of the amalgamation of the following units: the Marine Surveillance Unit under the SOA; the coast guard forces of the Public Security Ministry; the Fisheries Law Enforcement Command of the Agriculture Ministry; and the Maritime Anti-Smuggling Police of the General Administration of Customs. According to the SOA Web site, this new move was made to address the problem of low efficiency in maritime law enforcement, to improve protection and use of ocean resources, and to better safeguard the country's maritime rights and interests.[24]

On July 31, 2013, the eve of Army Day, the State Council published a plan for speeding up the structural change—and promoting the transformation and upgrading—of the shipping industry. A key section of the plan was "boosting technological innovation" and ensuring that the shipping industry was "innovation driven."[25] It is understood that state-owned shipping yards will receive more government subsidies in making naval vessels, including those to be used by the newly constituted Chinese Coast Guard.

*Resolving Conflicts Over Disputed Islands*

When explaining China's maritime ambitions, the Defense Ministry spokesman Geng Yansheng indicated in mid-2013 that China wanted to "raise its ability to exploit maritime resources, to develop the oceanic economy, and to safeguard the nation's oceanic rights and privileges. . . . We do not go for oceanic expansionism and we are not after oceanic hegemony." While words of reassurance of a similar nature have been repeated by senior cadres all the way up to President Xi, Beijing's assertive posture has exacerbated tensions with Vietnam, the Philippines, Japan, and other countries. For instance, Beijing's decision in April 2014 to move an oil rig into waters in the Paracel Islands in the South China Sea that are also claimed by Vietnam precipitated the largest anti-Chinese demonstrations in Vietnam since the Sino-Vietnam War in 1979 (see below).[26]

Indeed, for most of China's neighbors, Beijing's desire for oceanic hegemony is best illustrated by how the Xi administration is dealing with disputes in the South China Sea and the East China Sea. At the Politburo meeting on developing maritime resources, Xi laid down a dictum for the possible resolution of maritime sovereignty disputes: *zhuquanshuwo, gezhizhengyi, gongtongkaifa* (Upholding the principle that sovereignty belongs to China, setting aside disputes and pursuing joint development [with other countries]).[27] It is significant that Xi has expanded on and revised a comparable dictum expressed by Deng—"set aside [sovereignty] disputes and pursue joint development"—by adding the all-important premise that joint development was acceptable only under the precondition that other parties involved would at least acquiesce in Chinese sovereignty over the territories in question.[28]

Indeed, when Deng talked about the Diaoyu/Senkaku islands issue at a press conference in Tokyo in 1978, he made no reference to the imperative of upholding Chinese sovereignty. Deng merely said that such disputes should be shelved "until the next generation—which might have the wisdom to resolve [them]." Deng's emphasis was on the win-win scenario made possible by joint development, not hair splitting over sovereignty.[29] This approach, however, was revised by more hawkish strategists from both civilian and military units. According to Yang Yi at NDU, Deng's recommendation about joint development "must be based on the premise that sovereignty belongs to China." He warned unnamed countries that it was "dangerous" to assume that Beijing would not resort to force simply due to its concern over fostering peaceful development and polishing its international image. "Strong military force is a bulwark for upholding national interests," Yang pointed out. "The Chinese navy is a strong deterrent force that will prevent other countries from wantonly infringing upon China's maritime interests."[30]

According to Li Jinming, an expert on maritime rights at Xiamen University, the formula of "setting aside disputes and focusing on joint development" was responsible for China's "massive loss of oceanic sovereignty rights." "What has happened is that while China has suspended sovereignty disputes, other countries have proceeded to develop the disputed areas [without China's consent]," he said.[31] Major-General Luo Yuan noted that the *gezhizhengyi* mantra had become a "one-way street" that resulted in the marginalization of Chinese interests. "China must make known its sovereign rights so that neighboring countries will take note and beat a retreat," he said.[32] Luo did not explain why these neighbors would want to beat a retreat, but presumably they would do so because of the expansion of China's navy and its readiness to project power.

The Xi leadership hopes that now that China's naval capacity has taken a leap forward, it will be able to impose a solution, particularly on weak countries such as the Philippines. Thanks to close cooperation with Russia over the past decade, the PLA Navy's capacity to produce indigenously designed hardware, such as nuclear submarines, has improved significantly. It is believed that Chinese naval shipyards are building at least two aircraft carriers, which have selectively incorporated features of those in the Russian and American navies.[33] China's powerful generals have pointed to two recent developments—India's launch of the 37,500-ton INS *Vikrant* aircraft carrier and Japan's launching of the *Izumo*, which has been described by the Chinese media as a "semi-aircraft carrier"—to lobby for more state investment.[34]

### Avoidance of the "Thucydides Trap" and Policy of Good-Neighborliness

When Deng Xiaoping articulated his "keep a low profile" dictum, he was aware of the fact that the image of China as a fire-spitting dragon could be seen as threatening to its neighbors. Deng also coined the less famous "theory of opportunity," meaning that China has to take advantage of peace, especially in the Asia-Pacific region, to focus on internal economic development.[35] President Xi was referring to Deng's doctrine when he reiterated soon after taking power that "China needs a peaceful international environment to realize our goals. Without peace, China and the world cannot develop smoothly."[36]

Now that China has become a quasi-superpower, however, it has to expend more effort to defuse the "China threat" theory. As Foreign Minister Wang Yi put it in late 2013, "we are facing the major challenge of how to assuage the world's worries and doubts about China's future movements." Wang cited the Thucydides Trap, a reference to the fact that a rapidly growing power evokes so much anxiety among its neighbors that they may decide to join forces to contain the rising giant's ambitions. "We must break 'the law that a strong power will necessarily become imperialistic,'" Wang said. "We must reduce as much as possible obstacles to the renaissance of the Chinese race. We must try to realize our strategic goals while paying the smallest price."[37] The dynamics of the challenges of a rising power were stated succinctly by Cui Liru, a top researcher in the government-affiliated China Institutes of Contemporary International Relations (CICIR). "In the past ten years, China developed from a relatively weak posture to a relatively strong posture, and conflicts between China and the world were not particularly vehement," Cui said. "However, in the coming ten years, China will be progressing from a relatively strong posture to an even stronger posture. China's impact on the world will be bigger—and the world's worries about China will increase."[38]

Xi called a national conference on "diplomacy with peripheral countries" in October 2013, in which the top foreign policymaker laid down the principle of "a community of shared destinies." "We must insist upon the concept of bringing benefits to our neighbors [and] being partners with our neighbors," he said. "We must insist upon good-neighborliness, bringing peace and stability to our neighbors, and enriching our neighbors."[39] Xi listed four qualities that China would strive to demonstrate in its interactions with its neighbors: intimacy, sincerity, benefits, and tolerance. Building upon the theory and practice of his predecessors, Xi laid particular emphasis on two broad categories of efforts: economic cooperation and people-to-people diplomacy. He urged China's diplomats and related officials to "marshal resources in the area of economic [cooperation], trade, technology, and finance" so as to boost win-win strategic cooperation with neighboring countries. He cited the benefits of regional economic integration through setting up free trade areas (FTA) and regional banks. Xi also laid emphasis on "soft-power diplomacy," which included boosting publicity and pursuing public diplomacy and people-to-people diplomacy. "We must consolidate and expand the social and popular basis for the long-term development of relations with our neighbors," he said.[40]

China has common land borders with fourteen countries; it is also separated by narrow strips of water from neighbors such as Japan. In the past century, the country was involved in military conflicts of varying degrees with powers including Japan, India, Russia, and Vietnam. The Sino-Russian border agreement, which was negotiated largely by Jiang Zemin and then-Russian president Boris Yeltsin, succeeded in removing a potentially explosive bone of contention between the two erstwhile Communist allies.[41] In October 2013, Beijing and New Delhi signed a border defense cooperation agreement in an effort to lower tension along 2,485 miles (4,000 kilometers) of an ill-defined border in the eastern Himalayan region. The agreement consisted of enhancing confidence-building measures, such as mutual notification of patrols of border troops along the Line of Actual Control. The prospects for a border accord comparable to that signed between China and Russia, however, still remain uncertain.[42]

Beijing also made substantial efforts to cool tensions over their borders. During Premier Li Keqiang's visit to Hanoi in late 2013, both countries decided to set up three joint working teams for cooperation in the maritime, land, and financial sectors. "The establishment of the working team on the consultation of joint maritime development, in particular, is a positive signal sent by the two sides for cooperation in solving difficult problems," said a Ministry of Foreign Affairs (MOFA) spokesman. "This also shows that China and Vietnam have the capacity and wisdom to safeguard peace of the South China Sea, expand common interests and manage and narrow differences."[43] However, Hanoi, which had concluded deals with countries including India and Russia to jointly exploit oil and gas reserves in the South China Sea, was significantly less forthcoming about the potential of these working teams.

Beijing realizes full well that its peripheral diplomacy could meet with daunting challenges. "Most neighbors want to take shelter under the American protective umbrella and benefit from China's rapid economic development," said a commentary in *People's Daily*. "Vietnam, the Philippines, and Japan hope to thwart China's core interests by promoting cooperation with the United States in terms of security and defense, and to constrict China's maritime interests with the help of the United States," it said, adding that this "ambivalent mentality" would not change in the subsequent five to ten years.[44] According to Peking University professor Wang Dong, Beijing needs to avoid the mentality of an "upstart baron" in dealings with Southeast Asian countries. "China and ASEAN members are geographically close but psychologically distant," Wang argued in an early 2014 media forum. "China has never left Southeast Asia, but it has also never been part of Southeast Asia." He added that Southeast Asian countries' feelings toward China are less positive than those toward the United States and even Japan.[45]

Yet given the fact that the "China threat" theory could become a stumbling block to China's peripheral diplomacy, the aggressive power projection pursued by the Xi administration could prove counterproductive. Take, for example, Beijing's sudden establishment in November 2013 of an air defense identification zone (ADIZ) that covers the East China Sea region. The ADIZ, which partly overlaps with those of Japan and South Korea, drew negative reactions from countries including Japan, South Korea, the United States, and Australia.[46] While the ADIZ caused the highest level of alarm in Japan—due to the fact that it covers the Diaoyu/Senkaku islands—reactions from other countries were equally vehement. U.S. defense secretary Chuck Hagel called this a "destabilizing attempt to alter the status quo in the region." "This unilateral action increases the risk of misunderstanding and miscalculations," he said. Likewise, South Korean foreign minister Yun Byung-se argued that the Chinese ADIZ "made the already sticky situation [in Northeast Asia] more difficult to deal with."[47]

For Ren Xiao, director of the Center for the Study of Chinese Foreign Policy at Fudan University and a former Chinese diplomat in Japan, China's emergence is inevitable and there is nothing that its neighbors can do except to acknowledge its rise. "As China grows, China's maritime power also grows," Ren said, "China's neighboring countries should be prepared and become accustomed to this."[48] This apparently triumphalist mentality, however, is precisely what makes the Middle Kingdom's neighbors nervous in the first place.

### Economics-Based Diplomacy

Not too long ago, Beijing insisted on the principle of "the separation of politics and economics" in its relations with foreign countries. This precept was evidenced by tactics that Beijing used in applying for most-favored nation (MFN) status in the United States through the 1990s. China was repeatedly criticized by members of the U.S. Congress for its violations of human rights as well as its repressive

200 CHAPTER 5

policies in Tibet and Xinjiang. The Chinese government's response was that foreign governments should "separate politics and economics" when dealing with
China—that is, they should not let political considerations affect an issue that was
strictly economic in nature.[49]

Another example of Beijing's practicing the principle of "separating politics
from economics" was its handling of the anti-Japanese demonstrations in 2005 (see
below). Apart from the protests in the streets, ferocious anti-Japanese campaigns
were launched on the Internet. A Web-based petition asking all Chinese to boycott
Japanese products attracted more than 1 million signatures. The Chinese government, however, soon intervened. Bo Xilai, then minister of commerce, went on the
record saying that it was not advisable to mix politics and economics. Bo said that
in this world of globalization, an effort to boycott Japanese products could end up
hurting Chinese interests, including the millions of Chinese employed in Chinese
factories that were subcontractors of Japanese investors.[50]

Yet by the second half of the Hu–Wen administration, a clear-cut policy of
"economics-based diplomacy" had been hashed out. The top leadership's instruction
about this strategy was summed up by the official media as "using politics to boost
economics and using economics to boost politics so as to attain mutually beneficial
relations" with foreign countries.[51] "We should be skillful at a synthesis of political
friendliness and mutual trust, on the one hand, and economic cooperation, on the
other," then-premier Wen said in 2009. Wen also indicated that trade, investment,
and overseas foreign aid should be considered diplomatic weapons.[52]

China's much-enhanced economic status has rendered the CCP leadership much
more adept at making friends and neutralizing adversities on the global stage. The
crudest form of economics-based diplomacy is through overseas development aid
(ODA) and other kinds of grants and loans to foreign governments or corporations.
Much of China's ability to raise its profile in far-off continents such as Africa
and Latin America is through variations of "renminbi diplomacy." For example,
through the 2000s China forgave $3 billion worth of loans to African countries,
more than the entire Western world. At the Forum on Sino-African Cooperation
in Beijing in 2012, then-President Hu pledged $20 billion in new grants and loans
to a host of countries in Africa. Beijing even footed the $200 million bill for the
ultramodern new African Union Headquarters Building in Addis Ababa. When he
toured the continent in May 2014, Premier Li pledged an additional $12 billion in
development aid to Africa.[53]

One of the most efficacious items in the economics-based diplomacy playbook
is outbound foreign direct investment (OFDI). Since the early 2010s, top leaders
traveling abroad have invariably invoked the theme of China's contribution to the
growth of the world economy, including the fact that it will spend $500 billion in
OFDI in the 2013–18 period. China's OFDI rose 17.6 percent year-on-year in 2012
to reach a record US$87.8 billion, according to the Ministry of Commerce—despite
the fact that global OFDI declined by 17 percent in 2012 amid uncertainties facing

the world economy. China is now the world's third-largest investor in overseas projects, just behind the United States and Japan.[54]

Since the late 2000s, China has become the world's largest investor in the developing world. Because of its relatively short experience in "renminbi diplomacy," China has had its share of hits and misses. One reason is that, particularly in Africa and the Middle East, Beijing tends to form strategic political and economic alliances with authoritarian regimes that sometimes undergo a dramatic transformation. Take the case of Libya, where seventy-five Chinese companies—most of which were state-owned—had undertaken projects worth as much as $18.8 billion in 2011 on the eve of the demise of the Muammar Gaddafi regime. Beijing is now renegotiating relevant contracts with the post-Gaddafi administration, which no longer considers China a patron state. China's investments in Myanmar could also be threatened as the Thein Sein administration has apparently decided to reduce its dependence on Beijing and to seek investment from countries ranging from Japan to the United States.[55]

According to the U.S. think tank the Heritage Foundation, the bulk of China's OFDI from 2000 to 2011 went into the energy domain, which accounted for 47 percent of total outlay. The other big sectors included metals (20 percent), transportation (13 percent), and finance (9 percent).[56] One of the most effective formats of OFDI-related diplomacy is the so-called Tanzania Railway model: embarking on infrastructure projects, which often enable Beijing to kill several birds with one stone. During the Cultural Revolution, an impoverished China helped finance the $500 million Tazara Railway in Tanzania, which was the largest foreign aid project undertaken by Beijing. A key feature of infrastructure-related OFDI is that Chinese experts are involved in the construction—and very often the operation and maintenance—of the project. This will generate a lot of spillover benefits, including the promotion of "people-to-people diplomacy."[57]

Some of the most successful Chinese OFDI infrastructure projects have taken place in South and Southeast Asia. Take, for example, Beijing's multimillion-dollar investments in strategic infrastructure projects in Pakistan, Sri Lanka, Bangladesh, and Myanmar. These included the Gwadar Port on the western coast of Pakistan. A $1.18 billion project financed mainly by China, Gwadar will be managed by the China Overseas Port Holdings Corporation. While this facility is not envisaged as a naval base, it can service Chinese vessels of different categories. Equally strategic is the $1.5 billion Hambantoto Port in Sri Lanka, most of which is being bankrolled by Chinese SOEs. China's infrastructure forays in Bangladesh and Myanmar are represented by port projects in, respectively, Chittagong and Sittwe.[58] Given that Chinese engineers and other experts are usually involved in the construction and operation of infrastructure projects, they allow the Chinese to maintain a sizable and durable presence in these countries. Taken together, these four infrastructure schemes are critical elements of the "string of pearls" strategy geared toward "containing" India.[59] China's "infrastructure diplomacy" has even been extended to developed countries in the European Union. During a meeting with leaders from

Central and Eastern Europe in 2013, Premier Li inked an agreement to use Chinese technology to build a high-speed railway linking the capitals of Romania and Serbia. It was one of the most prestigious projects that China had secured in the EU.[60]

Moreover, the Chinese leadership has spearheaded the formation of regional economic-political blocs where China is destined to play a major role. While in theory China is still committed to being a nonaligned nation that will not enter into an alliance relationship with other countries, it has been active in nurturing business and geopolitical groupings with varying degrees of cohesiveness.[61] Apart from the goodwill that is being harnessed by symbiotic trade and investment activities, China sees itself as a mini-Middle Kingdom within these blocs: It has mapped out ambitious infrastructure schemes such as railways and highways (mainly in cases funded by China) that will bind the members together. The China-ASEAN FTA—the world's largest FTA by population—is a case in point (see below).

During a visit to four Central Asian states in September 2013, Xi raised the idea of a "New Silk Road Economic Belt" (NSREB) that would tie together China, on the one hand, and Kazakhstan, Tajikistan, Uzbekistan, Kyrgyzstan, and Turkmenistan, on the other. According to the latest statistics, China's trade with Central Asia (excluding Russia) was $46 billion in 2012, about a hundred times the level twenty-one years earlier. China is the largest trading partner of Kazakhstan and Turkmenistan and the second-largest trading partner of Uzbekistan and Kyrgyzstan. Xi noted that "since the total population of the Silk Road belt is 3 billion, the market potential is unique." A key motive behind forming the NSREB is that economic synergy could create political bonds between China and countries just across the border from its fractious northwest.[62] It is also significant that China is already linked with most of these countries within the framework of the Shanghai Cooperation Organization (SCO), which was formed in 2001. Encompassing China and Russia as well as Kazakhstan, Uzbekistan, Tajikistan and Kyrgyzstan, the SCO is, however, mainly a strategic and geopolitical organization that is sometimes known as the "Eastern NATO [North Atlantic Treaty Organization]." Moreover, internal competition between China and Russia has prompted Beijing to establish the NSREB, in which Chinese predominance is unrivaled (see below).[63]

China has also become an active member of economic and diplomatic groupings that include real or potential competitors. Take, for instance, the inchoate BRICS bloc, which comprises Brazil, Russia, India, China, and South Africa. Although the basic orientation of the BRICS bloc is geopolitical, it also has an economic dimension. The BRICS Development Bank (BDB) was established in 2013 to help finance infrastructure and other projects in the BRICS countries; it will also enable members to pool foreign currency reserves so as to prevent future financial crisis. China was due to contribute $41 billion to the BDB, whose initial capitalization would be $100 billion.[64] Yet another predominantly economic group masterminded by China also included India: the Bangladesh–China–India–Myanmar Economic Corridor. The framework covers 637,100 square miles (1.65 million square kilometers) of territory and encompasses an estimated 440 million people in Yunnan

Province in China, Bangladesh, Myanmar, and the Bihar District in northern India. The road, rail, water, and air linkages in the region are geared toward facilitating cross-border flows of people and goods, minimizing overland trade obstacles, and ensuring greater market access across the boundaries.[65]

However, there is a downside to China's aggressive projection of economic power. In early 2014, dock workers in Greece protested the Chinese transport giant China Ocean Shipping (Group) Company's (COSCO's) partial acquisition of the Piraeus port. Complaints that Chinese companies have exploited local workers have been raised by politicians and labor organizations in countries including Zimbabwe, Zambia, and Myanmar. Moreover, due to perceptions that IT multinationals including Huawei and ZTE have close connections to the Chinese government, their activities—including efforts to acquire control over high-tech firms in the United States and elsewhere—have generated controversies and ill feelings.[66]

## Projection of Soft Power

### China's Soft-Power Hard Sell

During the last five years of the Hu Jintao administration, China began to spend massively on "overseas propaganda" (*waixuan*)—mainly selling the "Chinese model" as well as other tidbits of Chinese civilization to the world. In 2009, the State Council earmarked RMB 45 billion for various *waixuan* facilities—including foreign-language television and print-media operations—to expand China's global footprint. As *Global Times* put it, "we must let the world see the thousand faces of China."[67] There is little question that the CCP leadership expects a leap forward in its spin-doctoring prowess. The image advertised by Beijing is a country that is embracing globalization and earnestly seeking a win-win solution to world issues. As the commentator Ding Gang has stated, "an important test in the course of China's globalization is how to use its power to shape the world's perception of China."[68]

Prominent state media including CCTV and Xinhua have vastly expanded programs and newsfeed in different languages for Western, Asian, and even Middle Eastern and African audiences. Particularly eye-catching have been news channels in English modeled after Al Jazeera that offer the Chinese take on issues ranging from politics and finance to culture and religion.[69] Beijing has also set up more than 400 Confucius Institutes around the world. Patterned after quasi-official language and cultural organizations, such as the Goethe Institute in Germany, Confucius Institutes spread Chinese culture in addition to acquainting foreigners with the latest Chinese policies. This "soft" approach is geared toward promoting people-to-people diplomacy in addition to enhancing the overall attractiveness of the Chinese model. Confucius Institutes, however, have been criticized by the American Association of University Professors for trying to exert political influence over the curriculum and pedagogy of universities that host them. In September 2014, the University of Chicago decided not to renew its contract with the Institute after more than 100 faculty members signed on to a letter that cast doubt on its political neutrality. At the same time, the number of foreign students studying in China is burgeoning. Chinese educational institutions hosted about 290,000 overseas students in 2011, an increase of 10 percent over the year before.[70]

A key thrust of Beijing's self-laudatory hard sell is exploiting the precipitous drop in the popularity of American-style, laissez-faire capitalism in the wake of the 2008 global financial crisis. The Xi leadership wants to convince the world that deficiencies of the American model have thrown into sharp relief the superiority of the Chinese way of doing things. According to a Xinhua commentary, the thirty years of Chinese reform have led to "the realization of innovation and creativity on a gargantuan scale . . . nothing less than an epic poem about fast-paced development. . . . Not only ordinary people but the media and academia in China and abroad have paid close attention to 'the Chinese miracle' or 'the Chinese model.'"[71]

Further, the Peking University political scientist Yu Keping claimed that the Chinese model had "enriched our knowledge about the laws and paths toward social development and promoted the multipronged development of human civilization in the age of globalization." Dong Manyuan, a researcher at the China Institute of International Studies, which is a Chinese Foreign Ministry think tank, argued that Chinese soft power was different from—and potentially more appealing than—the Western kind because it is based on a wholesome sense of "peace and harmony." "Characteristics of Chinese soft power include respect for the heterogeneity of world [cultures], openness and tolerance, friendliness and inclusiveness . . . respect for politeness and benevolence," he argued.[72] After Xi took over in late 2012, the spin doctors merged the "Chinese model" with the "Chinese Dream." As the Yunnan-based scholar Wang Xiaojun contended in early 2013, "the world needs the Chinese Dream—and the Chinese Dream is a prerequisite for the times. . . . Apart from 'Made in China,' the Chinese road of development and model of governance . . . have enriched and pluralized the world's development models."[73]

It seems obvious, however, that the attractiveness of Chinese culture and mores will have limits—as long as the CCP authorities refuse to tolerate universally accepted practices regarding human rights and freedom of expression. In an article on the difficulties facing the mass marketing of Chinese values, the well-known Tsinghua University media scholar Li Xiguang noted that "the soft power of a country is demonstrated by whether it has the power to define and interpret 'universal values' such as democracy, freedom, and human rights." Li pointed out that in order to enhance the attractiveness of "socialism with Chinese characteristics," "we must let the whole world hear the stories that Chinese citizens have to tell about their democracy, liberty, human rights, and rule of law. . . . The Chinese model has transcended the dichotomy between socialism and capitalism . . . It has broken down the universe of discourse on old-style market economy—and proven that there is no single narrative that is suitable for the whole world."[74]

The problem is that most intellectuals who are bold enough to air their views on democracy and political reform have been harassed if not jailed by the authorities. This is true of the dozens of well-known writers and professors who in early 2009 signed a manifesto called Charter '08, which asked the CCP leadership to do nothing more than let Chinese enjoy the civil rights enshrined in the Chinese constitution. And the incarceration of the Nobel prize-winning writer Liu Xiaobo has elicited protests from politicians and scholars around the world. Since Xi took over as general secretary, the police and other departments have stepped up their crackdown on not only dissidents but also "trouble-making" actors in China's inchoate civil society (see Chapter 3).[75]

*Beijing's Controversial "Red-Line Diplomacy"*

So-called Red-Line Diplomacy refers to Beijing's attempt to designate "taboo zones" around personalities—and, occasionally, issues—that the CCP administration does not want foreigners, particularly Western leaders and opinion leaders, to touch. This policy is based on the largely successful experience that the Party-state apparatus has accumulated in isolating Taiwan—including the two pro-independence bugbears, former presidents Lee Teng-hui and Chen Shui-bian—from the international community. Beijing successfully obliged even Western countries to openly profess their opposition to Taiwan independence and not to receive senior cabinet officials from the "breakaway province."[76] Given the remarkable thaw in relations between mainland China and Taiwan in the wake of the election of the Kuomintang's (or Guomindang's) Ma Ying-jeou as president in March 2008, Chinese diplomats have used the same tactic to circumscribe the international wiggle room of the Dalai Lama and Rebiya Kadeer, leaders of the Tibetan and Xinjiang exile movements, respectively.

Red-Line Diplomacy has been employed with a certain degree of success to isolate the Dalai Lama, the Nobel Peace Prize-winner who is the spiritual leader of Tibetans worldwide. In March 2009, the South African government barred the spiritual leader from participating in an international peace conference in Johannesburg. After Pretoria's surprise decision, several Nobel Prize-winners who were originally invited to the conference boycotted the session, which was then cancelled.[77] Beijing downgraded normal relations with the leaders of Germany, France, and the U.K. after their leaders' meetings with the Dalai Lama. The most recent case was British prime minister David Cameron's brief tête-à-tête with the Dalai Lama in early 2012. Beijing suspended normal relations with the U.K.—and the British leader was not allowed to visit China until December 2013.[78]

Since the international profile of the Uighur International Congress—and its leader, Rebiya Kadeer—was raised in the wake of the July 5, 2009, riots in Urumqi, Beijing has bent over backward to persuade different countries not to grant visas to the renowned dissident. Later that month, New Delhi obliged Beijing by refusing to allow her to visit India, and Chinese authorities were spared the embarrassment—

and colossal loss of face—that would have ensued from a get-together of the two prominent "splittists." However, Kadeer has since visited a number of countries, including Australia, Japan, and the United States.[79]

It is emblematic of China's global clout that the country has also sought to intervene in the activities of foreign NGOs and quasi-official organizations, despite the fact that it is contrary to the Five Principles of Peaceful Coexistence to interfere in the internal affairs of other countries.[80] In August 2009, the Chinese government raised eyebrows when it successfully pressured the organizers of the Frankfurt Book Fair to uninvite two Chinese dissident writers—Dai Qing and Bei Ling—who had been scheduled to speak at the famous forum.[81] Beijing reacted angrily when the Nobel Peace Prize Committee—an NGO over which the Norwegian government has no sway—awarded the Nobel Peace Prize to Liu Xiaobo in late 2010. Relations between China and Norway have remained tepid ever since.[82]

Beijing's draconian policy regarding the granting of visas to foreign academics and journalists could run counter to its soft-sell policy. Xi has continued the tradition set by ex-presidents Jiang and Hu of not allowing "anti-Chinese" academics—mostly Americans—from obtaining visas to attend conferences or conduct research in China.[83] For example, the thirteen authors of the acclaimed book *Xinjiang: China's Muslim Borderland,* published in 2004, are still denied entry to China. Other blacklisted China scholars include Perry Link at the University of California, Riverside, and Andrew Nathan at Columbia University.[84] After the Eighteenth Party Congress, the authorities penalized the *New York Times* and Bloomberg—which published stories about the wealth of the family members of ex-Premier Wen and President Xi—by making it difficult for their journalists to secure visas to the country.[85] As Joseph Nye, who coined the term "soft power" more than twenty years ago, pointed out, "China has had a limited return on its investment" despite having spent billions of dollars on advertising the Chinese model. "A recent BBC poll shows that opinions of China's influence are positive in much of Africa and Latin America, but predominantly negative in the United States and Europe, as well as in India, Japan and South Korea," wrote the Harvard professor. "What China seems not to appreciate is that using culture and narrative to create soft power is not easy when they are inconsistent with domestic realities."[86]

## China's Relations with the United States, Japan, ASEAN, and Russia

### U.S.–China Relations: "Fake Friends" or "Real Enemies"

The Xi leadership has articulated this list of foreign policy priorities for the country's diplomats: "Fostering relations with the big powers is the key; priority should be given to ties with peripheral countries; maintaining good relations with developing countries is the foundation; and the multilateral [arena] is an important stage."[87] Although the Xi administration seems to be paying more attention to its neighbors as well as international forums such as the Group of Twenty (G20), it is unmistakable that ties with the United States are still the preoccupation of Xi and his strategic advisers.

### "A New Model of Major-Country Relations"

The theory of a "new model of major-country relations" (*xinxing daguoguanxi*) with the United States was first put forward by Hu Jintao in the last year of his administration and then applied fully by President Xi. In his Political Report to the Eighteenth Party Congress in late 2012, Hu referred to "building a new model of major-country relations [with the United States] that will [ensure] a perennially stable and healthy development" in bilateral ties. During then-vice-president Xi's tour of the White House earlier that year, he said he envisaged building a "new model of major-country relations with the United States that was unprecedented and that would inspire later generations."[88]

This slogan, sometimes translated as "a new kind of great power relationship," basically argues that the emergence of China as a great power—and quasi-superpower—may not necessarily raise global tension in general and jeopardize ties with the status quo superpower in particular. This contrasts with the famous theories about power transition and "hegemonic stability" advocated by political scientists including A.F.K. Organski and John J. Mearsheimer—namely, that a would-be superpower will likely be sucked into a bitter power struggle with the status quo superpower. The typical examples cited were the rise of Germany and Japan and the devastating warfare that ensued.[89] There are, however, exceptions. When the United States replaced Britain as superpower, no inordinate degree of ill will was generated between the two countries. However, that might be due to the cultural and other commonalities between the two English-speaking democratic countries.[90] The ideological and cultural divide between China and the United States is, however, obvious.

A key message of Xi's visit to the United States both as vice-president in 2012 and as president in 2013 was that the rising quasi-superpower and long-reigning superpower could remain on friendly terms at least for the foreseeable future. According to a statement released by the Chinese government at the end of the Xi–Obama summit in California in June 2013: "China and the U.S. should go down a new road that is different from the old one of the confrontation between major countries in history."[91] Xinhua stated in a commentary on the summit: "The world has suffered too much pain in the seemingly doomed confrontations and wars between existing and emerging powers. It is high time that the vicious cycle be put to an end."[92]

The "new model of major-country relations" has been spelled out in more detail by State Councilor Yang Jiechi, a former foreign minister and ambassador to the United States, in an article written in English. Yang laid down three criteria for U.S.–China ties in the new era. The first was "nonconflict and nonconfrontation."

Yang wrote that both countries should "view each other's strategic intentions in an objective and sensible way . . . and properly handle their differences and disputes through dialogue and cooperation." The second criterion was "mutual respect." This meant that "the two sides respect each other's choice of social system and development path [and] respect each other's core interests and major concerns." The third was perhaps the most important: "win-win cooperation": "This requires the two sides to abandon a zero-sum mentality, accommodate the other's interests while seeking one's own . . . and continue to deepen the pattern of shared interests."[93]

Xi seemed fairly upbeat about the prospects of U.S.–Chinese relations on his watch. He mentioned at the end of his California summit with President Obama that "with an adequate degree of China-U.S. cooperation, this will become an anchor for world stability and a propeller for global peace."[94] Even though Beijing has vehemently resisted the concept of the Group of Two, Xi's characterization of a global order underpinned by U.S.–Chinese cooperation did contain elements of a "Chinamerica" or "AmeriChina" vision.[95]

What are the prospects for success of this "new model"? At first, the Obama administration seemed reluctant to embrace this particular formulation. In his remarks at the summit with Xi, President Obama made reference, in a rather casual manner, to working with Beijing to promote "the kind of new model of cooperation that we can establish for years to come." Not too long afterward, however, senior U.S. officials publicly used the Chinese-style characterization of bilateral relations. In her first address on Asian affairs after becoming U.S. national security adviser, Susan Rice said Washington was committed to "operationalizing a new model of major power relations" with China. "That means managing inevitable competition while forging deeper cooperation on issues where our interests converge—in Asia and beyond," she said. Vice-President Joe Biden also used the phrase when he visited Beijing at the end of 2013.[96]

In both theory and practice, both countries have found it easier to find common ground on economic, investment, and trade issues. As Xi pointed out after meeting President Obama in California: "economic relations are an important cornerstone of Sino–American relations." He characterized bilateral economic relations as "highly complementary" and marked by a "high degree of symbiotic interests." "We should deepen and expand our bilateral economic cooperation and assiduously discover new areas of confluence of interests and new areas of growth," Xi said.[97] It is true that a relatively large amount of give-and-take has been demonstrated in U.S.–Chinese economic relations. For example, Beijing has gone on buying U.S. government bonds despite the devaluation of the dollar. And although the annual U.S. trade deficit has remained around $300 billion, President Obama has resisted calls made by members of Congress and others that China be declared a "foreign-exchange manipulator."[98] Some senior U.S. officials even sympathized with Beijing's aspiration for a faster pace of globalization of the renminbi despite the fact that one long-standing financial goal of the CCP administration is to challenge—and eventually supplant—"dollar hegemony." For example, in 2010, during his tenure as president of the World Bank, Robert Zoellick, who served as deputy secretary of state under President George W. Bush, proposed a new global currency consisting of a basket of currencies including the dollar, the euro, the yen, pound sterling, the renminbi, and gold.[99]

As for "respecting each other's choice of social system and development path," the United States has also by and large lived up to Beijing's expectations. Although the State Department has continued to publish its annual report on the state of human rights in China, the U.S. government's criticism of China's treatment of dissidents as well as its policy on Tibet and Xinjiang has been muted. Human rights have largely ceased to be an item on the official agenda. During their visits to China, both President Obama and Vice-President Biden made only oblique references to the values of freedom and human rights when they met groups of Chinese citizens such as students.[100]

*"Fake Friends, Real Enemies"?*

It is much easier for China and the United States to observe the norms of "respecting each other's major concerns" and "accommodating the other's interests while seeking one's own" if the issues in question have no direct bearing on "core national interests." Thus, it is perhaps not too difficult for the United States to accept China's rapidly growing footprint in Africa. China displaced the United States as Africa's largest trading partner in 2009.[101] The United States has also largely acquiesced in China's growing presence in space. When in 2010 the PLA used a missile to knock out an aging weather satellite, Washington was taken aback by the potential this indicated that China could target American spy satellites and space-based missile defense systems. There was even speculation that some rogue generals had done this without the knowledge of then-general secretary Hu Jintao. As China's space program developed apace through the 2000s, however, the U.S. reaction to the seemingly never-ending reports about China's moon- and Mars-related ventures has died down. After all, outer space is big enough for the United States, Russia, Japan, China, and India.[102]

But in geopolitical issues—especially in the Asia-Pacific theater, which is a key area of interest for both powers—it is very difficult to engineer a meeting of minds. In her speech on Asia, National Security Adviser Rice indicated that both countries sought "the denuclearization of the Korean Peninsula, a peaceful resolution to the Iranian nuclear issue, a stable and secure Afghanistan, and an end to conflict in Sudan."[103] While Beijing has not been able to restart the long-stalled Six-Party Talks on denuclearizing the Korean Peninsula, it has consulted closely with the United States on ways to rein in the North Korean leader Kim Jong-un. In late 2013, representatives from China and the United States—together with diplomats from Russia, Britain, France, and Germany—persuaded Iran to freeze its nuclear program in return for the lifting of some sanctions. Washington and Beijing also talked about how to maintain peace in Afghanistan after the withdrawal of

U.S. and other Western forces. The two even cooperated in providing training for Afghan diplomats.[104]

The Asia-Pacific theater, however, remains a bone of contention despite Xi's often-repeated mantra that "the Pacific is big enough to accommodate [the interests of] both China and the United States." As Foreign Minister Wang Yi indicated in a speech at the Brookings Institution in September 2013, China did not want to challenge the superpower status of the United States. "We have never had the strategic intention to challenge, let alone replace, the U.S. position in the world," Wang said. Regarding the Asia-Pacific arena, Wang added: "We have never thought about pushing the U.S. out of the region. Rather, we hope the U.S. will play a positive and constructive role in safeguarding peace, stability, and development in the Asia-Pacific."[105] On other occasions, however, both Xi and Wang have harshly warned the United States not to "stir up trouble" in China's backyard. In his speech at the Boao Forum for Asia annual conference in April 2013, Xi warned: "No one should be allowed to throw a region and even the whole world into chaos for self-ish gain." In a similar vein, Wang pointed out, largely with reference to Asia, that "the Chinese side will definitely not allow [other countries] to foment incidents and chaos; we definitely will not accept any interference in and interruptions to China's course of development."[106]

The reality, however, is that the Xi administration is paranoid about the apparent tightening of the Obama administration's policy aimed at "containing" China. Barack Obama, the "first Pacific U.S. president," as part of his "pivot to Asia" strategy has strengthened defense ties with long-standing allies in Asia such as Japan, South Korea, the Philippines, and Australia—and with new friends such as India and Vietnam. Beijing was taken aback by President Obama's tour of Japan, South Korea, Malaysia, and the Philippines in April 2014. In Tokyo, Obama stated in no uncertain terms that the disputed Senkaku islands (which China calls the Diaoyu islands) fall within the parameters of the U.S.–Japan defense pact. It was the first time that a U.S. commander-in-chief had given such unambiguous support to Japan in the dispute with China over sovereignty of the islands.[107] President Obama also signed a ten-year Enhanced Defense Cooperation Agreement with the Philippines, which would provide for the stationing of more U.S. troops in the strategic archipelago. Although President Obama reiterated on this trip that Washington had no intention of containing China, there was little doubt that, as then-secretary of state Hillary Clinton stated, Washington sees the South China Sea as very much part of U.S. "national interests."[108] Chinese leaders and strategists are convinced that "the United States is forming a 'C-shaped encirclement ring' round China." As an expert on the United States, Jin Canrong, put it, the United States is pursuing a two-pronged strategy that includes both "containment" and "engagement." "Washington's ultimate goal is to mold China into a partner that can fit American rules," he argued in late 2013. Meanwhile, the official media have continued to highlight alleged attempts by the U.S. government as well as NGOs to topple the communist government using "peaceful evolution" or "color revolution" mechanisms. The CCP leadership has even accused the United States of fomenting a "color revolution" in Hong Kong through funneling subtle support to pro-democracy, anti-Beijing political groups there.[109]

Intensified competition between China and the United States in the Asia-Pacific region has thrown into sharp relief then-secretary of state Condoleezza Rice's characterization of United States and China as "strategic competitors," which are predisposed to cross swords through the twenty-first century.[110] Regarding U.S.–Chinese relations in the Asia-Pacific region, it is hard not to agree with the assessment of two leading China specialists, the American professor David Shambaugh and the Chinese scholar Yan Xuetong. Shambaugh, a professor of political science and international affairs at George Washington University, noted in a late 2012 article that, despite the frequent meetings of top leaders from both sides, "the competitive elements in the relationship are growing and now becoming primary, while the cooperative ones are secondary and declining." Professor Yan characterized bilateral ties as ones in which "enmity outweighs friendship." While noting that the two countries shared common interests mainly regarding the economy and trade, Yan contended that such commonalities were overshadowed by rapidly growing rivalry in a number of geopolitical hotspots. "China and the United States are active competitors and passive cooperative partners," he argued. Yan indicated that "both sides do not want to openly admit that their conflict outweighs common interests." While he noted that the two countries "want to maintain [the facade of] fake friendship," he implied that this won't last very long.[111]

The crux of the matter seems to be that, contrary to senior cadres' protestations about nurturing win-win scenarios, the not-so-subtle intention of Beijing is someday to supplant the United States as the arbiter in the Asia-Pacific. Patriotic intellectuals seem franker about China's motive, which is to change the America-centric status quo. According to Liu Jianhua at the Zhongnan University of Economics and Law, "China should seize upon the opportunity provided by the shrinkage in America's strategic [resources]" by expanding its international exposure. He pointed out that, in the coming decade or so, "America's needs for China will grow and its ability to contain China will decline." And Beijing should not miss this golden opportunity to pursue more proactive foreign policies so as to stake out a larger global presence.[112] As Shambaugh writes: "As China's global footprint has emerged on to every continent, it is increasingly bumping up against longstanding American interests—thus adding a global dimension [of bilateral competition that] the relationship has never had."[113]

In the foreseeable future, direct clashes between the world's No. 1 and No. 2 do not seem likely. It will take about two decades for China to close the gap with the United States in either industrial technology or the military. In the short term, friction can be attenuated to some extent by a comprehensive architecture of frequent personnel exchanges. For example, there are more than ninety intergovernmental mechanisms, including the U.S.-China Strategic and Economic Dialogue (S&ED) and high-level consultation on cultural and educational exchanges, which provide the institutional underpinning for exchanges of views and crisis prevention. At the people-to-people level, there are 220 pairs of sister provinces, states and cities between China and the United States, and there are growing numbers of Chinese students in the United States and American students in China. Moreover, many members of China's "red aristocracy"—including "princelings" such as the son of Deng Xiaoping, Deng Zhifang, and the daughter of the late Politburo Standing Committee member Huang Ju, Huang Fan—have become U.S. citizens. Former president Jiang Zemin's son, Jiang Mianheng, is a business partner of relatives of former president George W. Bush.[114]

In 2012, Henry Kissinger had this to say about U.S.–Chinese competition: "Just as Chinese influence in surrounding countries may spur fears of dominance, so efforts to pursue traditional American national interests can be perceived as a form of military encirclement. . . . Both sides should be open to conceiving of each other's activities as a normal part of international life and not in themselves as a cause for alarm. . . . The inevitable tendency to impinge on each other should not be equated with a conscious drive to contain or dominate, so long as both can maintain the distinction and calibrate their actions accordingly."[115] The momentum, however, seems to favor the exacerbation of adversarial contest under an elaborate and ritualistic guise of "feigned friendship."

### Sino-Japanese Relations: Badly in Need of New Thinking

Ceremonies in 2014 marking the 120th anniversary of the first Sino-Japanese war threw into sharp relief fast-deteriorating Sino-Japanese ties. Questions were raised about whether skirmishes if not full-fledged warfare would again break out between the two neighbors. To understand the severity of the downward spiral in which bilateral ties seem to be trapped, it is instructive to look at how Beijing and Tokyo not too long ago were able to set aside differences and strike a "win-win" deal over sovereignty disputes in the East China Sea. Although the agreement reached in 2008 between then-president Hu Jintao and then-prime minister Yasuo Fukuda is now practically a dead letter, the Hu–Fukuda pact serves as a reminder of the fragile and vulnerable nature of the relationship between Asia's two most powerful countries.

During his visit to Tokyo in May 2008, then-president Hu reached an understanding with then-prime minister Fukuda with regard to the joint exploration of gas fields under the East China Sea. Disagreements about the boundaries of the two countries' exclusive economic zones (EEZs) have arisen primarily because Tokyo uses the "median-line" concept to divide the ocean into two exact halves. China, however, prefers the continental shelf theory, which makes its EEZ substantially larger. The Hu–Fukuda accord was a breakthrough to the extent that no mention was made of sovereignty disputes. Both sides referred to their determination to make the East China Sea "a sea of peace, cooperation, and friendship." They agreed to "conduct cooperation [in exploiting gas resources] in the transitional period prior to delimitation [of boundaries] without prejudicing their respective legal positions." "The two sides will, through joint exploration, select by mutual agreement areas for joint development . . . under the principle of mutual benefit," the agreement said. What was even more extraordinary was that the agreement allowed Japanese companies to invest in the Chunxiao Oilfield "under Chinese law." (The Chunxiao Oilfield lies west of the median line, so even using Japanese criteria, it is located on the Chinese side of the ocean.)[116]

Unfortunately, the goodwill generated by the Hu–Fukuda agreement lasted only a short while. Chinese opinions expressed on the Internet were overwhelmingly negative, which prompted Beijing to delay turning the agreement into a treaty. Fukuda, deemed a China-friendly politician, was soon replaced as prime minister by Taro Aso, who belonged to the same right-wing faction that includes the current prime minister, Shinzo Abe, and former prime minister Junichiro Koizumi.[117] And although bilateral ties blossomed briefly after the ascendency in late 2009 of the Democratic Party of Japan (DPJ)—which had a "China-friendly" reputation—the rapprochement proved short-lived.

*Dispute Over the Diaoyu/Senkakus Becomes a Test of Wills Between Two Old Enemies*

Sino-Japanese relations went into a tailspin—and an apparently irrevocable vicious cycle—after then-prime minister Yoshihiko Noda of the DPJ decided in September 2012 to use government funds to buy three major islets in the Senkaku archipelago from a rich Japanese family. From 1971 to September 2012, Beijing largely acquiesced in Tokyo's *de facto* administration of the Diaoyu/Senkakus while not recognizing Japanese sovereignty.[118] Indeed, during talks leading to the re-establishment of bilateral ties in 1972, then-prime minister Kakuei Tanaka raised the issue of the Senkakus with then-premier Zhou Enlai, and Zhou's reply was that resolution of the issue should be postponed. Deng Xiaoping repeated Zhou's stance—that this question should be "left to a later generation"—when he visited Tokyo in 1978, when the two countries signed a Treaty of Peace and Friendship.[119]

The reactions from the Chinese government were stern. "Japan's 'purchase of the islands' is illegal and invalid," then-president Hu said. "The Japanese side must fully consider the seriousness of the matter and not make a mistaken decision."[120] In a matter of weeks, Beijing took swift action to assert its claims over the East China Sea. The Chinese government publicized for the first time the geographical coordinates for the Diaoyu/Senkakus—and other parts of the East China Sea according to the continental shelf criterion. More important, Beijing began to contest Tokyo's *de facto* administration of the Diaoyu/Senkakus: Vessels from offices such as the Fisheries Administration, Marine Surveillance, and the Anti-Smuggling Unit of the Ministry of Public Administration made frequent forays to within 12 nautical miles of the islets. Tense confrontations with the Japanese coast guard vessels took place regularly. Chinese "patrols" of the Diaoyu/Senkakus became even more frequent after Beijing decided in March 2013 to merge different maritime defense units into the *haijing* (marine police; or the Coast Guard). Even the Chinese air force got into the act. In September 2013, a Chinese drone flew to the vicinity of the Diaoyu/Senkakus. Tensions rose further in November 2013 after Beijing unveiled an ADIZ, which covered the Diaoyu/Senkakus—and partially overlapped with that of Japan and South Korea. Potentially dangerous cat-and-mouse games between jetfighters from both sides frequently took place in narrow air corridors over the East China Sea.[121]

The Hu—and particularly Xi—administration turned this sovereignty dispute into a test of wills between the two erstwhile political foes for several reasons. First, Japan provides the best "foil" for the success of Xi's "Chinese Dream"— particularly with respect to economic and military prowess. Since the two countries began to interact in the Tang dynasty, it had always been clear which one was the "big brother" or even the teacher—and hence also the leader in all Asia. From the seventh century until the 1880s, Japan played the role of a student. But from 1895, when China suffered defeat in the Sino-Japanese naval battle, until the end of the twentieth century, Japan was unquestionably the more advanced and powerful country. In the eyes of many Chinese, the pendulum began to swing in 2010 when China overtook Japan as the world's second-largest economy: China is on course to become the predominant actor in the Asia-Pacific region.[122]

It has also been suggested that the Xi administration can buttress its legitimacy by stoking the flames of anti-Japanese sentiment. Films about Japanese atrocities during World War II are a staple on Chinese television. While the Chinese government has frequently targeted Japanese textbooks for whitewashing the activities of the Japan Imperial Army, students in Chinese high schools and colleges are often given an exaggerated picture of "the revival of Japanese militarism."[123] Moreover, it seems "safer" for the Xi administration to pump up Chinese nationalism against Japan. Given the relatively large number of offspring of top cadres who have either studied in the United States or have done business with American firms, a nationalist movement that was anti-American could easily morph into a campaign against "unpatriotic" cadres.[124]

According to Feng Zhaokui, a leading Japan expert at the Chinese Academy of Social Sciences (CASS), "the comparative strength of China and Japan is a basic factor determining changes in bilateral relations." Feng indicated that at least in the first two decades of the twenty-first century, a rough parity would still obtain regarding the overall capacity of the two powers. He cited a report by the Chinese Academy of Sciences (CAS) showing that in the late 2000s, Japan ranked second only to the United States in the CAS's comprehensive modernization criteria, while China ranked seventy-eighth. Feng postulated that only when China's GDP became ten times that of Japan would the two neighbors be at peace. The CASS scholar foresaw two scenarios: a win-win scenario involving "rational, judicious policies" and "irrational, heavy-handed, and even emotion-laden policies," which would lead to a lose-lose situation and even military confrontation.[125]

*The China–Japan–U.S. Triangle*

Particularly in light of President Obama's "pivot toward Asia" policy, animosity between China and Japan has flared up in large measure due to Beijing's perception that Japan is playing a big role in Washington's supposed "containment policy" toward China. A prime reason for the massive anti-Japanese riots in 2005 was that earlier that year, the U.S.-Japan Defense Guidelines for the first time mentioned the Taiwan Strait: "instability in the Taiwan Strait area" would be sufficient cause for the two countries to join forces and thwart China's ambitions.[126] During the five years that Koizumi was prime minister of Japan (2001–2006), that country, together with Australia, was seen as a zealous backer of then-president George W. Bush's aggressive foreign policy.

Despite the deterioration of Sino-Japanese ties throughout the Koizumi years— during which ministerial-level visits were suspended—a handful of Chinese intellectuals advocated a "new thinking on Japan." Shi Yinhong, an international relations expert at Renmin University in this group, argued that China should persuade Japan to shed its overdependence on the United States and instead build up a solid relationship with China. Shi pointed out in articles in *People's Daily* and *Strategy and Management* that, thanks to a beefed-up relationship with Japan, "China can improve its security environment and its diplomatic position." Shi suggested that Beijing improve bilateral ties with Japan by not belaboring the issues over history textbooks and by supporting Japan's bid for a permanent seat on the UN Security Council.[127]

During the anti-Japan demonstrations in 2005, Shi and two like-minded intellectuals—*People's Daily* commentator Ma Licheng and CASS's Feng Zhaokui— were labeled "three big traitors." However, some politicians and intellectuals in Japan came to espouse views similar to Shi's. In September 2009, a seismic shift took place in Japanese politics when the DPJ came to power. The first DPJ prime minister, Yukio Hatoyama, was an "Asianist" who proposed a "policy of equidistance": that is, while the U.S.–Japan alliance should be maintained, Tokyo should also prioritize improving relations with China. This was how Hatoyama phrased Tokyo's balancing act: "How should Japan maintain its political and economic independence and protect its national interest when caught between the United States, which is fighting to retain its position as the world's dominant power, and China, which is seeking ways to become dominant?"[128] That Beijing appreciated Hatoyama's views was evident when then-DPJ secretary-general Ichiro Ozawa led an unprecedentedly large delegation of Japanese politicians and businessmen—including 146 members of the Japanese legislature, the Diet—to China in December of that year. Ex-president Hu shook hands with each and every Japanese guest at their reception at the Great Hall of the People.[129]

The CCP-DPJ "honeymoon" was short-lived. Hatoyama had to resign in June 2010 because of his failure to persuade Washington to withdraw U.S. troops from the Futenma Airbase in Okinawa—which was a key campaign promise of the DPJ a year earlier. A few months later, Sino-Japanese relations began to deteriorate when a Chinese fishing vessel was captured near the Diaoyu/Senkaku islands and its captain, Zhan Qixiong, was detained by Japan for more than two weeks. Since that point, Tokyo has put more emphasis on relying on the United States to fend off perceived Chinese encroachment.[130]

The Chinese government seems confident that while the United States has appeared to stand solidly by its ally, the day will come when the benefits from Sino-American give-and-take are so great that Washington will be willing to "sacrifice" its junior Asian partner. In an unusually provocative editorial published on the occasion of Japan's "nationalization" of the Diaoyu/Senkaku islets, *Global Times* stated: "If Japan is willing to become a plaything of the United States, it will end up being played by both China and the United States." This meant that someday, when the United States and China decide to lay their cards on the table, the result of this "showing of hands" will be "smashing up the plaything." In other words, if Beijing has something really substantive to offer the United States, Washington might be willing to sacrifice the interests of Japan.[131]

But there is no indication that the United States is prepared to abandon its key ally in the Asia-Pacific region. It is true that the U.S. government has expressed displeasure over Abe's visit to the Yasukuni Shrine in December 2013 as well as controversial statements made by Japanese officials about the issue of "comfort women" during World War II. However, during his visit to Japan in April 2014 President Obama stated in no uncertain terms that the Diaoyu/Senkakus fall within the parameters of the U.S.-Japan security treaty. This was the first time that a U.S. president has made an explicit commitment to help Japan defend the disputed islets. Obama and other U.S. officials have also expressed support for a more active international role to be played by Japan's self-defense forces. Moreover, Washington has given tacit support for increasing Japan's defense budget and boosting exports of Japanese-made military hardware.[132]

*Cold Politics, Hot Economics: The Prospects for*
*People-to-People Diplomacy*

The two countries' close economic links are a major factor in favor of a possible Sino-Japanese rapprochement. China is Japan's largest trading partner, while Japan is China's fourth-most-important trading partner, after the EU, the United States and ASEAN. Due in part to the Diaoyu/Senkaku crisis, in 2012 total trade between the two countries fell 3.9 percent, to $329 billion, the first drop in three years. Japan's exports to China declined year-on-year by 8.6 percent.[133]

Since the time of Mao Zedong, Beijing has to a significant extent relied on the strategy of *yimin cuguan, yishang cuzheng* (using [Japanese] people to put pressure on the government; using [Japanese] businessmen to weigh in on diplomatic developments) to manage its relations with Japan.[134] Before the establishment of ties between the two countries in 1972, trade and other activities were conducted through people-to-people contacts. During periods when official relations were frosty, the Chinese government has relied on "China friendly" elder statesmen as well as business and community leaders in Japan to keep bilateral relations on an even keel.[135]

"New thinkers on Japan" such as Feng Zhaokui have suggested that the two countries emulate France and Germany by using close economic cooperation to bury the hatchet from the past.[136] Despite the fact that China relies substantially on American and European firms to obtain high technology, the Fifth-Generation leadership is interested in Japanese know-how. While Xi served in Fujian, he toyed with the idea of using Japan's bullet-train technology to build long-distance railways in the province. During his visit to Japan in 2009, the then-vice-president toured firms such as Yaskawa Electric Corporation, a well-known manufacturer of robots and machine tools. Xi was particularly interested in Japan's experience with striking a good balance between industrialization and preservation of the environment.[137]

People-to-people diplomacy in general, however, has become less effective as a vehicle of last resort. Since the turn of the century, most China hands in Japan—and Japan hands in China—have retired or passed away. Due in part to the fact that since the mid-1980s the Chinese elite have been pursuing higher education and business opportunities largely in English-speaking countries, the number of younger Chinese cadres, businessmen, and intellectuals with personal knowledge of Japan is dramatically smaller than in generations past. Zeng Qinghong, China's vice-president from 2003 to 2008, was the last high-level official to have a large network of Japanese friends. During the Koizumi era, Zeng was able to smooth relations through private talks with influential Japanese such as former chief cabinet secretary Hiromu Nonaka, who was known as the "shadow shogun" within the Liberal Democratic Party (LDP). Since Zeng's retirement from the Politburo in 2007, there have been no high-level interlocutors on either side.[138] Beijing has to rely on "China-friendly" former senior officials—including former prime ministers Yasuo Fukuda and Yukio Hatoyama, as well as the daughter of Tanaka, former foreign minister Makiko Tanaka—to pass their message to the powers-that-be in Tokyo. Yet these figures can do rather little, given their lack of political connections with the Abe administration. Hatoyama was labeled a "traitor" by members of the Abe cabinet after he indicated during a Beijing trip in early 2013 that there was indeed a historical dispute between the two countries over the Diaoyu/Senkakus.[139]

What is most alarming about the future of Sino-Japanese relations is the rapid growth of mutual animosity between the two peoples. According to a 2013 poll conducted by *China Daily* and Genron NPO, a Japanese think tank, in a survey of 2,542 Chinese, 92 percent of respondents harbored negative feelings toward Japan, twenty-eight points higher than in a similar poll a year earlier. And a survey of 1,805 Japanese found that 90.1 percent of respondents held a negative attitude toward China, an increase from 84.3 percent in 2012.[140] In the early days of China's open-door policy, Japanese engineers and other experts in business and other projects in China built bridges despite the checkered history of relations between the two countries. For example, the Baogang Steel Mill—now the world's fourth largest— benefited from not only Japanese investment but also technical support from Nippon Steel. In the first few years after its establishment, as many as 700 Japanese engineers were on hand in Shanghai, and more than 2,400 Chinese workers received on-the-job training at Nippon Steel facilities in Chiba and plants in other locations in Japan.[141] In the past decade, such close collaboration has become rare.

### China–ASEAN Relations: Business Opportunities vs. Security Concerns

Much of the challenge that China faces in improving relations with the ten members of ASEAN is encapsulated in the advice given by Singapore's former prime minister, Lee Kuan Yew, to Barack Obama in 2009. "The size of China makes it impossible for the rest of Asia, including Japan and India, to match it in weight and capacity in about 20 or 30 years," Lee told the then-newly elected U.S. president. "So we need America to strike a balance," said Lee. "I think if the U.S. does not recognize that the Asia-Pacific is where the economic center of action would be and it loses that economic superiority or lead that it has in the Pacific, then it would lose it worldwide."[142]

Compared to his predecessors Jiang and Hu, Xi seemed more eager to devote resources to building up a systematic and structured relationship with the ASEAN bloc.[143] He vowed to foster a "community of common destiny" with the Southeast Asian states, in most of which the ethnic-Chinese populations figure prominently particularly in the business field. During his visit to Indonesia in October 2013, Xi indicated that China and ASEAN "are bound by the same destiny" and that Southeast Asia would be the first region to share economic benefits accruing from China's rapid development. Beijing has upgraded relations with several ASEAN member states, including Indonesia, Thailand, Malaysia, Laos, and Cambodia, to "comprehensive strategic partnerships." This theoretically puts China's relations with these countries on par with the PRC's ties with Russia.[144] Xi then laid out a five-point program for future developments focused on trust, good-neighborliness, "win-win cooperation," and people-to-people relations. Xi did not shy away from the one potential obstacle, namely, territorial disputes with the four ASEAN members Vietnam, the Philippines, Malaysia, and Brunei. With regard to the disputes over sovereignty, Xi noted that "peaceful solutions should be sought, and differences and disputes should be properly handled through dialogue on an equal footing and friendly consultation in the overall interests of bilateral ties and regional stability."[145]

Beijing is pursuing a multipronged approach toward winning hearts and minds among ASEAN members. First, it hopes to bond China and ASEAN via economic and infrastructure ties, based on the China–ASEAN Free Trade Area (CAFTA). The Xi leadership's expectation is that ASEAN members that have become dependent on economic cooperation with China will not be drawn into Washington's "containment policy" toward China. Regarding territorial disputes, Beijing is willing to negotiate settlements with the disputant countries on a one-on-one basis. The CCP leadership has also warned "outside parties" such as the United States and Japan against getting involved in China's disputes.[146]

*Boosting Economic Ties*

China became the first Asian giant to form a free trade agreement with ASEAN—CAFTA, which became operational in 2010. It is the largest FTA in the world in terms of population. The Xi leadership has vowed to work toward an "enhanced version of CAFTA" in the coming decade. At the sixteenth ASEAN summit with China, which took place in Brunei in 2003, Premier Li Keqiang unveiled plans for a "diamond decade" of economic cooperation between the two. China is ASEAN's largest trading partner, and ASEAN is China's third-largest trading partner. Li called on both sides to redouble efforts to ensure that trade reaches $1 trillion by 2020, or two-and-a-half times the level in 2012. Bilateral investment is expected to increase by $50 billion over the next eight years.[147]

In Brunei, Li also proposed the so-called 2+7 framework to enhance China–ASEAN ties. Relations would be based on two principles: "deepening political mutual trust and enhancing good-neighborly friendship" and "focusing on economic growth and expanding mutual benefit." In addition, Li made a seven-point proposal with respect to China-ASEAN economic and political cooperation. First, a "treaty on good-neighborliness, friendship, and cooperation" would be signed. This would in theory provide legal and institutional safeguards for China–ASEAN strategic cooperation. The second dealt with confidence-building measures in the security field. "We need to strengthen exchange and cooperation in security," said Li. "We need to improve the mechanism of ASEAN–China defense ministers' meetings and deepen cooperation in disaster prevention and relief, cybersecurity, combating transnational crimes, joint law enforcement, and other nontraditional security fields." The other four points related to boosting cooperation in trade, finance, and infrastructure. For example, a China–ASEAN Banking Consortium would be set up to facilitate currency swaps in trading as well as providing loans to SMEs in the region.[148]

Also in 2013, Beijing unveiled proposals for a "Maritime Silk Road" between China and ASEAN members. "We should work together to build the Maritime Silk Road of the twenty-first century and intensify cooperation on marine economy, maritime connectivity, marine environmental protection and scientific research, maritime search and rescue, and fishery," said Li at the Brunei meeting. Beijing and ASEAN agreed to establish a China–ASEAN Maritime Cooperation Fund, to which Beijing would make the biggest investment. The fund would help ASEAN members, particularly in maritime infrastructure and other projects. The corollary of this initiative is that if maritime cooperation is successful, China and the rival claimants to islets in the South China Sea might find it easier to settle for win-win scenarios such as joint development of oil and gas resources.[149]

Geography is destiny. Beijing's most effective strategy is perhaps to further leverage its proximity to ASEAN by constructing a series of rail, highway, air, and river links with most of its Southeast Asian neighbors. The highest priority has been put on railway links—and Chinese officials are pulling out all the stops to persuade ASEAN countries such as Thailand, Indonesia, Vietnam, and Malaysia to use Chinese high-speed railway technology despite the fact that countries including Japan and France have also been promising special deals to these countries in the same transport sector. Work on a railway linking cities in Myanmar with Kunming, Yunnan Province, has already started. Beijing is convinced that if China is linked with ASEAN members through a comprehensive infrastructure network such as a high-speed rail link from Kunming to Singapore, Southeast Asia countries will see their future destiny as friendship with China rather than cooperation with the United States or Japan.[150]

The Xi administration is also trying to make it difficult for Washington to put together the Trans-Pacific Partnership (TPP) Free Trade Area, which excludes China. Even though Washington has not officially opposed China's membership in the TPP, U.S. officials have hinted that the socialist country would be hard pressed to meet its entry requirements, ranging from intellectual property rights protection to labor rights. It is understood that the Chinese leaders have lobbied their ASEAN friends to give higher priority to the proposed Regional Comprehensive Economic Partnership (RCEP), which will group ASEAN together with China, Japan, South Korea, India, Australia, and New Zealand. Negotiations on the RCEP FTA are set to conclude by the end of 2015.[151]

*Exacerbated Tension Over Territorial Disputes in 2014*

The efficacy of much of the policy of good-neighborliness as well as "economics-based diplomacy" implemented by the Xi administration, however, was called into question by the sudden upsurge of tension in May 2014 between China, on the one hand, and Vietnam and the Philippines, on the other. In late April, Chinese authorities moved a deep-sea oil rig into waters near the Paracel Islands, which are also claimed by Vietnam. The $1 billion drilling platform owned by the oil giant CNOOC was 120 nautical miles east of Vietnam's Ly Son Island—in other words, well within Vietnam's EEZ.[152] Beijing also speeded up the construction of a runway on Johnson Reef, one of the Spratly islets close to the Philippines. The mini-islet is called Mabini Reef by the Philippines and Chigua Reef by China. This compounded the already tense standoff between navies of the two countries in the vicinity of Mischief Reef (called Huangyan in Chinese), which started in early 2013. Mischief Reef is within the 200-nautical mile EEZ of the Philippines.[153]

Beijing's assertive tactics—which are perceived by critics of China as efforts to change the status quo in the South China Sea—have provoked a series of anti-Chinese incidents, whose vehemence has not been seen in the past decade. Anti-Chinese protests in Vietnam in mid-May morphed into mob attacks on more than 400 Chinese and Taiwanese factories in different Vietnamese cities. At least 2 Chinese workers were killed and 140 others were injured. This was the largest-scale series of anti-Chinese riots since the Sino-Vietnamese war in 1979. On May 19, Chinese vessels dispatched by Beijing repatriated some 4,000 Chinese workers.[154]

Of greater significance to China-ASEAN ties, however, is that two heavyweight countries in the bloc—Malaysia and Indonesia—are seen as moving closer to the stance that ASEAN should adopt a more unified and clear-cut posture toward negotiating with China over territorial disputes. Compared to disputes that China has with Vietnam and the Philippines, Malaysia's territorial disputes with China are of a smaller scale—and until recently Kuala Lumpur kept a low profile regarding sovereignty disputes with Beijing.[155] As for Indonesia, it was only in early 2014 that Jakarta announced that China's so-called nine-dash-line demarcation of the South China Sea infringed upon the EEZ zone of the Indonesian island chain of Natuna. This development practically meant that Jakarta could no longer play the role of disinterested third party between China and its South China Sea adversaries. Significantly more aggressive measures like those that Beijing has employed toward Vietnam and the Philippines could even predispose individual Malaysian and Indonesian politicians to join the chorus of criticism of Beijing's hard-power projection.[156]

Within ASEAN's membership, only Laos, Cambodia, and, to a lesser extent, Myanmar are seen as unreserved supporters of China's South China Sea gambit. It was due to the intervention of Laos and Cambodia that the ASEAN meeting of foreign ministers in Myanmar in May 2014 did not criticize China by name. But a joint statement referred to the group's "serious concerns over the ongoing developments in the South China Sea."[157] China's enhanced posture in the South China Sea dominated a meeting of ASEAN defense ministers on May 20. The ten defense ministers reaffirmed ASEAN's commitment to consolidating defense cooperation that "contributes to the realization" of the ASEAN Community 2015. It is understood that the generals also discussed a proposal that the defense ministers of any two ASEAN members could, after consultation, decide on a course of action to resolve an emergency in the South China Sea without having to seek the approval of the entire ASEAN membership.[158]

At the same time, the United States has made clear its opposition to China's moving the oil rig into seas close to Vietnam. Secretary of State John Kerry told Chinese foreign minister Wang Yi in a telephone exchange that the Chinese move was "provocative" and "aggressive." It is likely that the United States will enhance its defense cooperation not only with Vietnam and the Philippines but also ASEAN members such as Malaysia, Indonesia, and Singapore. One of the achievements of Obama's April trip to four Asian countries was the conclusion of a ten-year defense pact with the Philippines that would provide for the stationing of more U.S. trips in bases in the strategic Philippine archipelago.[159]

The Xi administration is expected to stick to time-honored ploys to try to impose a solution on the South China Sea. First, Beijing will persevere with its divide-and-rule tactics by emphasizing that it will settle sovereignty disputes with individual ASEAN members on an individual basis—and that the South China Sea is not an issue between China and ASEAN as a whole. As Premier Li pointed out in 2013, "the South China Sea disputes are not an issue between China and the ASEAN, and they should not and will not affect the overall China-ASEAN cooperation."[160] Second, the Xi administration will continue to rely on economic inducements to defuse tension with hostile ASEAN members such as Vietnam and the Philippines. After the anti-Chinese riots in Vietnam, Xinhua published a commentary calling on Hanoi to "think of the bigger picture" of Sino-Vietnamese cooperation. "By immediately stopping the violence and any further provocations, Vietnam can work with China to tap the full potential of their economic cooperation in such areas as financial services and industry transfer," said the commentary.[161]

In the meantime, parties to sovereignty rows with China can only hope that there will be more examples in the South China Sea of applying Deng Xiaoping's formula of "pursuing joint development while [temporarily] putting aside sovereignty disputes." In mid-2013, CNOOC, one of the three Chinese oil monopolies, signed preliminary agreements with a Brunei state oil company to jointly exploit petroleum in the vicinity of islets claimed by both countries. In late 2004, when Sino-Filipino relations were better during the Hu Jintao and Gloria Arroyo administrations, oil companies of the two countries were close to hammering out joint-exploitation deals in seas close to the Philippines.[162]

Yet Beijing should also realize that suspicions about Chinese intentions run deep among its Southeast Asian neighbors. The official China News Service contended that because of the attractiveness of China-related economic advantages, "the Abe administration has become ostracized [in Asia]."[163] That Japan—backed by the United States—is still able to play the "China threat game" to good effect was evidenced by the Japan–ASEAN summit held in Tokyo in December 2013. Freedom of navigation in the South China Sea was discussed at the meeting even though the ostensible focus of discussions was economic issues. In a joint statement, the eleven countries underscored their concern over "maritime security and safety, freedom of navigation, unimpeded commerce . . . and resolution of disputes by peaceful means in accordance with universally recognized principles of international law" in the Asia-Pacific region. Clearly, the majority of ASEAN members wanted to boost their room for maneuver on the South China Sea issue by seeking at least ad hoc assistance from regional powers, including Japan and India.[164]

The major problem with China's approach to resolving sovereignty disputes is that the Beijing leadership has never provided a legal rationale for its much-criticized nine-dash-line demarcation of the South China Sea, according to which China claims ownership of some 90 percent of the maritime territory. In January 2013, the Philippines took the case to the United Nations' Permanent Court of Arbitration. Manila's position, backed by 40 maps and 4,000 pages of evidence, is that the Chinese claims violated the United Nations Convention of the Law of the Sea. Beijing, however, has refused to take part in the arbitration. In June 2013 Foreign Minister Wang Yi argued during a trip to Bangkok that disputes could be resolved only "through negotiations on the basis of respecting historical facts and international law."[165] As the Southeast Asia expert Ian Storey noted, "governments across the region have been unnerved by China's emphasis on history over international law, and have quietly applauded the Philippines' U.N. submission, which they hope will provide clarity on the issue."[166]

Another factor contributing to the unease of the ASEAN bloc is apparent attempts by the Xi administration to drag its feet over consultations on a long-stalled Code of Conduct (CoC) in the disputed waters. While agreeing in principle to a China–ASEAN CoC, which will lay down confidence-building measures so that military, fishing, and commercial vessels from countries in the vicinity can go about their business in an unimpeded fashion, Beijing has reiterated that the protocol requires painstaking negotiations.[167] "China believes that there should be no rush," said Wang Yi in August 2013. "Certain countries are hoping that CoC can be agreed on overnight. These countries have unrealistic expectations and unserious attitudes." Wang also claimed that some ASEAN members—apparently Vietnam and the Philippines—had been creating "disturbances." "Instead of making disturbances, parties should make efforts that are conducive to the process so as to create necessary conditions and atmosphere," said Wang.[168]

### Sino-Russian Relations: Hot Politics vs. Cold Economics

Sino-Russian relations for the past decade have been marked by two traits: "enthusiasm at the top and coolness at the grassroots" and "hot politics and cold economics."[169] Because the two countries had a period of estrangement from the early 1960s to the late 1980s—and the fact that relatively few Chinese speak Russian—people-to-people communication has lagged behind increasingly cozy ties between the two leaderships. And although ex-president Hu Jintao, who had a "pro-Russian reputation," consolidated a "comprehensive strategic partnership" with Moscow, economic relations lag behind. Bilateral trade in 2013 totaled $89.21 billion, an increase of only 1.1 percent over that of 2012. In light of the fact that comparable year-on-year trade growth figures for 2010, 2011, and 2012 were 43.1 percent, 42.7 percent, and 11.2, respectively, the prospects for long-term economic ties do not look good. Moreover, although China is Russia's largest trading partner, Russia ranks only eleventh for China among its trading partners.[170]

### President Xi Risks Big by Putting So Many Eggs in the Russian Basket

Since its founding, the PRC has prided itself on not forming alliances with other countries. However, the Xi administration has obviously tilted toward Russia. He has called his country's relationship with Russia one "characterized by the most solid foundation, the highest level of mutual trust, and [having] the greatest regional and global influence."[171] In February 2014, Xi became the first Chinese head of state to participate in the inauguration of a foreign sporting event: the Sochi Olympic Games. Xi's purpose was to underscore China's "all-weather, all-rounded strategic partnership" with Russia by giving Putin face, particularly in light of the fact that the Sochi Games had been severely criticized by most American and European media. *People's Daily* even called Xi's "sports diplomacy" "a responsible action in sustaining international morality."[172]

Xi has clearly staked his reputation on the continuous amelioration of ties between the two authoritarian states. Russia was the first country that Xi visited upon becoming head of state in March 2013. On that occasion, he signed a contract worth $3.5 billion for the purchase of twenty-four Sukhoi Su-35 fighters and four Amur-class conventional submarines. It was the largest purchase of Russian arms by China in the past decade.[173] Ties between Xi and Putin were so intimate that the usually dour-looking Chinese head of state took along a big cake for Putin's birthday, which was observed while they were attending the Asia-Pacific Economic Cooperation (APEC) forum in Indonesia in October 2013. Xi's visit to Sochi and subsequent private meeting with Putin was their sixth meeting since Xi became China's leader in late 2012.[174]

Xi's pro-Russian strategy appeared to pay off to some extent in May 2014, when Putin visited China to take part in the Conference on Interaction and Confidence-Building Measures in China (CICA) and to inaugurate with Xi a seven-day Sino-Russian naval exercise.[175] Putin told Chinese reporters that the bilateral relationship had "reached the highest level in its centuries-long history" and that China was "Russia's unconditional foreign policy priority." Xi and Putin signed a joint statement on "a new stage of comprehensive strategic partnership" between the two giants. They signed agreements on cooperative ventures ranging from designing commercial aircraft to manufacturing military hardware. Major projects envisaged included a $400 million cross-border bridge over the Amur River, as well as oil refinery and liquefied natural gas facilities.[176]

Perhaps more significant was the breakthrough on a $400 billion gas deal that had been negotiated for ten years in which Gazprom, the Russian gas monopoly, would supply state-owned CNPC with 38 billion cubic meters of gas annually. That would represent about a quarter of China's current annual gas consumption of nearly 150 billion cubic meters. Although full details regarding costs and other arrangements had yet to emerge, this had the makings of a win-win deal. Gazprom, which had to reduce its dependence on the EU market in view of deteriorating relations with Western Europe caused by the Ukraine crisis, was willing to give China price concessions.[177]

Examples of economic synergy notwithstanding, it is clear that what draws China and Russia together is their common perception of growing threats from the United States. The United States—and the EU—imposed tough sanctions on Moscow after Russia's annexation of Crimea in March 2014. And the naval war games could be construed as the two quasi-allies' joint thumbing of their noses at the Obama administration. However, subtle but important incongruities between China and Russia were never far from the surface even at this celebratory event. The two leaders' joint statement condemned "unilateral sanctions" relating to Ukraine, a reference to those imposed on Russia by the West. They called for de-escalation of tensions in the former Soviet republic and for "peaceful, political ways to resolve existing problems" in the country.[178] However, consistent with China's abstention from the UN Security Council vote in March regarding the secession referendum in Crimea, Beijing has stopped short of endorsing Moscow's expansionist ambitions toward its western neighbor.[179] In Beijing, there was no shortage of Russian experts who had grave reservations about Putin's adventurist stance on Ukraine. Some have even drawn parallels between the Crimea referendum and that held in Mongolia (known then in China as Outer Mongolia) in 1945, which led the former Chinese "protectorate" to become a satellite state of the Soviet Union. As Xiao An argued in a commentary in the *Global Times,* the Crimea referendum was "[an instance of] one country refusing to recognize the sovereignty of another country, a new example of a big power adopting double standards on the question of countering secessionism."[180]

In his interview with the Chinese press, Putin indicated that he and Xi "share an idea that it is unacceptable to revise the results of [World War II], as the consequences will be extremely grave." While this looked like indirect support for Beijing's contention that the Abe administration in Japan had tried to subvert international agreements ending World War II, Putin has consistently refused to support Beijing's claims to the Diaoyu/Senkaku islands (see below).[181]

Despite the bear hugs, both leaders have failed to find a platform for deepening their partnership beyond a joint desire to push back against the United States. Although since the end of the cold war Moscow has fought the eastward expansion of NATO, the Xi administration is equally nervous about Washington's perceived "pivot toward Asia," which it regards as a conspiracy against China. As Peking University foreign affairs expert Niu Jun pointed out, "the reason the official media are eulogizing Putin and Russian expansionism is substantially due to [China's] hostility against the West." Examples of China and Russia joining hands to counter American diplomatic initiatives included their joint stance on Syria and Iran. For example, Beijing and Moscow have consistently opposed the use of force by the U.S.-led Western Alliance to tame the two rogue regimes.[182]

Yet it is well known in diplomatic circles in Moscow and Beijing that powerful sectors of the Russian polity—including military officers as well as administrators of regions that border China—harbor suspicions about China's intentions. Russia has always been nervous about the influx of Chinese businessmen and workers to its thinly populated Far East. In July 2013, the Russians conducted a large-scale war game in Siberia and the Far East—which involved 160,000 troops, 1,000 tanks, and 130 aircraft—that was interpreted as a show of force against potential Chinese encroachment. Alexander Khramchikhin, a Moscow-based military analyst, argued that the exercises "were intended to discourage China from harboring expansionist plots."[183]

In Central Asia, China and Russia are competitors as much as they are collaborators.[184] Both Beijing and Moscow want to be the elder brother in the SCO bloc, which consists of the two Asia-Pacific giants in addition to four Central Asian countries. A major trade initiative by the Xi administration—the formation of the NSREB with several Central Asian states—does not include Russia (see above). Because of Beijing's massive investments in energy and mining projects in Central Asia, China has displaced Russia as the most important economic partner of Kazakhstan, Kyrgyzstan, Tajikistan, Turkmenistan, and Uzbekistan. These developments can only appear disturbing in the eyes of Russian oligarchs and state corporations that are expecting to reap big profits through helping Central Asian countries—which used to be Soviet republics—develop oil and gas reserves.[185]

*Sino-Russian Differences Over Japan, India, and Vietnam*

Whether Xi's high-profile embrace of Russia is paying off may hinge on Moscow's relations with the three Asian countries that are at loggerheads to varying degrees with China. Consider the intriguing triangular relationship among China, Russia, and Japan. One goal that Beijing is anxious to achieve is forging a kind of united front with Russia against Japan. Chinese officials have hinted that in return for Moscow's support of Chinese claims over the Diaoyu/Senkaku islands, China would support Moscow's claims over the Four Northern Islands (known in Russia as the Southern Kurils). Xi also wants Putin to echo Beijing's allegations that Japan is the "biggest troublemaker" in the Asia-Pacific region.[186]

Putin, however, has failed to deliver on these fronts. The Russian dictator has never given unequivocal support for China's claims over the disputed islets. Moreover, Putin seems to be following the long-standing Soviet and Russian tradition of playing China off against Japan—and playing Japan off against China—depending on the circumstances.[187] This was illustrated by the warm reception that Putin gave Prime Minister Abe when he took part in the inauguration of the Sochi Games. The two leaders held an informal meeting at Putin's summerhouse in Sochi. Although Putin and Abe did not mention China when they met the press, it seemed clear that the Russian leader was not following Beijing's script about belittling Japan. Moreover, despite animosity over their overlapping sovereignty claims over the islands north of Hokkaido, the Putin and Abe administrations seek to boost trading and investment links. In early 2014 several Chinese Web sites posted stories comparing the U.S.–Japan alliance to the partnership between China and Russia. The conclusion was that "if war were to break out between China and Japan, the United States would definitely come to Japan's aid, while Russia would very likely stay neutral."[188]

Beijing is also unhappy with Russia's entrenched defense ties with India, which is engaged in some kind of arms race with China. Intimate Russo-Indian relations, which began at the start of the cold war, have not been affected by the dramatic improvement in ties between New Delhi and Washington since the late 1990s. India is the largest buyer of Russian arms, with contracts worth $30 billion between 2000 and 2010. It is believed that the Russian defense establishment has little hesitation about selling state-of-the-art weapons to India, something that cannot be said for China.[189] The Chinese response to this development is to try to engineer a three-way *entente cordiale* under the auspices of two mechanisms: the inchoate BRICS bloc, which includes China, Russia, and India, and the annual meeting of the foreign ministers of the three countries, which began in 1996.[190]

Perhaps even more than Russo-Indian ties, Beijing harbors grave misgivings about the rapid improvement of relations between Moscow and Hanoi. Vietnam has placed multibillion-dollar orders from Russia for Su-30MK2 jetfighters as well as naval vessels. In 2012 Moscow announced its interest in renting naval facilities at Vietnam's strategically located Cam Ranh Bay.[191] Even more provocative in China's view is the deal signed by Gazprom to explore two parcels of Vietnam's continental shelf near the Paracel Islands. Beijing's response to the Gazprom venture was relatively muted compared to Indo-Vietnamese cooperation in oil and gas exploration in the South China Sea. Without naming Russia or Gazprom, the Chinese MOFA called upon "countries and enterprises outside the region to avoid being implicated in any way in South China Sea-related disputes."[192]

Over the long term, Sino-Russian relations could be hurt by the lack of a firm popular base. Most Chinese intellectuals look to the United States and the EU—not Russia—as pacesetters in areas ranging from the development of democracy to high technology. Moreover, it cannot be disputed that the Xi administration's pro-Russian tilt relies on Beijing's concealment of many seamy aspects in the recent history of the two former Communist allies, such as the role played by Josef Stalin in persuading Mao Zedong to enter the Korean War, which liberal Chinese historians regard as the first major blunder of the then-new communist government. Chinese intellectuals are also indignant over the lack of transparency in the negotiation of the 2008 Sino-Russian border treaty. Veteran Hong Kong-based China watcher Ching Cheong noted that the agreement in effect legitimized Russian seizure of huge tracts of land—roughly forty times the area of Taiwan—since the days of the tsars.[193]

## Large-Scale PLA Involvement in China's Foreign Policy

Under Xi Jinping, the PLA will be playing a significantly larger role in foreign and national security policies despite the fact that senior generals have gone out of their way to emphasize the "Party's absolute leadership over the army." Moreover, the 2011 White Paper on National Defense underscored the "defensive nature" of China's military forces: "China will not engage in arms race with any other country, and it does not pose a military threat to any other country."[194]

The overweening diplomatic posture of the generals was already evident during President Hu Jintao's last few years in office. Take, for example, the hawkish statements made by senior military personnel during Hu's much-anticipated state visit to Washington, DC, in January 2011. A key goal of Hu's tour was to restore military-to-military ties between the two countries. The China-U.S. Joint Statement issued by Hu and Barack Obama had this to say about defense relations: "Both sides agreed on the need for enhanced and substantive dialogue and communication at all levels [and] to reduce misunderstanding, misperception, and miscalculation."[195] While Hu was apparently making nice with his American hosts, a number of PLA hawks were engaged in spirited America bashing.

NDU expert Yang Yi told the official Chinese media on the eve of the Hu visit that "while China and the United States are mutually dependent economically, it's still a zero-sum game in the military sphere. . . . I don't think we should let go of our strategic goals and let America's misgivings affect our [military] progress. . . . What needs to be done should be done." According to popular military commentator Peng Guangqian, "the U.S. has not changed its hegemonic logic. . . . Recent reports coming out of the United States have shown that Washington has positioned China as a major strategic opponent that will challenge American [national] interest in the future. . . . the U.S., fearing the loss of its hegemonic status, is speeding up its activities in Asia to impede China's development."[196]

At the very least, PLA generals seem to be maximizing the threat posed by the United States and other countries so as to win bigger budgets every year. Yang, a former military attaché at China's embassy in Washington, DC, argued that the Chinese military needs more spending on advanced weaponry to blunt U.S. forces' "hegemonic expansion" into Asia. He argued that "China must construct aircraft carriers to safeguard regional peace."[197] On a deeper level, the generals are having a big say in the definition of concepts such as national security and "core interests," which testifies to their pivotal role in foreign policy-making. There seems little question that, within China's foreign policy establishment, the clout of the top brass is expanding at the expense of traditional stakeholders, such as career diplomats.[198]

The use of both coast guard vessels and jetfighters to assert China's *de facto* administrative rights over the Diaoyu/Senkaku islands is only one example of how Beijing is using the threat of military action to assert its foreign policy goals. Hawkish media mouthpieces, especially the *Global Times*—a subsidiary of *People's Daily*—have given the views of military hawks such as Luo Yuan, Dai Xu, and Long Tao a great deal of exposure. Major-General Luo Yuan said the South China Sea issue was tantamount to a "knife in the chest of the Chinese." Responding to the relatively frequent war games that Hanoi has staged to assert its sovereignty claims on the Paracels, Luo said that the Chinese might lose their patience and "take out that knife." Luo, the son of the intelligence whiz Luo Changqing, also indicated that the PLA was adamant about becoming a blue-water fleet capable of rapid worldwide deployment. He said that efforts by unnamed countries to "render China the dragon into China the worm" would be futile.[199]

## Factors Behind the Rise of the Generals' Say in Diplomatic Affairs

Unlike most countries, China's foreign and security policy is not made by MOFA but by a shadowy Party organ, the CCP Central Leading Group on Foreign Affairs (CLGFA), which is headed by the Party general secretary—that is, Xi Jinping and, before him, Hu Jintao and Jiang Zemin. The CLGFA comprises representatives from agencies and departments such as the PLA, MOFA, the CCP International Liaison Department (which handles the Party's relations with foreign political parties), the Ministry of State Security (MSS), Ministry of Commerce, and agencies with responsibility for energy, overseas propaganda, and other aspects of China's international activities. The CLGFA's secretariat—which functions like the U.S. National Security Council—is headed by State Councilor Yang Jiechi. (In China, a state councilor is halfway between a vice-premier and a minister.) Although Yang is often described as China's top diplomat, his role is to coordinate the policy preferences of all members of the CLGFA.[200] The Central National Security Commission (CNSC), which was set up at the third plenum of the Central Committee in November 2012, is believed to be focused primarily on domestic security, even though the PLA, the PAP, the MOFA, the MSS, and others are represented in this top-level decision-making and coordinating agency (see Chapter 3).[201]

Decisions by the CLGFA are carried out by MOFA, which has a very limited policy-making role. Given that China publishes no public records relating to CLGFA deliberations, it is not easy for observers to determine the dynamics—including competition and infighting—among various stakeholders represented in the secretive agency. One example, however, clearly illustrates the diplomats' relative lack of clout. A series of Wikileaks documents published in 2011 indicated that a number of ambassadorial-level career diplomats had a very low opinion of the Kim Jong-il regime in North Korea—and that they were not in favor of the kind of unconditional support that Beijing had given Pyongyang over the past few years. For historical and other reasons, however, the generals seemed to favor strong backing for the Kim dynasty irrespective of the worsening of Pyongyang's roguish behavior particularly after 2010.[202] The generals have also enjoyed a larger-than-usual say on relations with countries including Pakistan and Iran, whose militaries have cooperated with the PLA for decades. Since the late 2000s, however, the PLA's input on diplomacy regarding a number of key countries and regions—including the United States, Japan, and ASEAN—clearly has increased.[203]

One possible reason for MOFA's apparent lack of authority is that because Minister Wang Yi is not a member of the ruling Politburo, his overall voice in the establishment is deemed weak. By contrast, according to tradition the PLA has two seats on the Politburo. Its influence on diplomatic and security matters has expanded in direct proportion to the leaps-and-bounds growth of China's military might—and the government's desire to seek a level of hard power projection commensurate with the country's quasi-superpower status. The bigger say that generals have gained in security-related policies is evidenced by the fact that a relatively large number of senior PLA officers, in addition to military commentators, have dominated the electronic and print media with their pugilistic views on diplomacy. When asked about the preeminence of military voices in foreign policy, Major-General Xu Guangyu indicated in 2010 that "it's natural for the PLA to speak out first on these issues." Xu, a researcher at the China Arms Control and Disarmament Association, added, "It's the PLA's sacred duty to defend China's territory and interests."[204] Because the PLA—which is the bastion of the Gang of Princelings—is Xi's primary power base (see Chapter 1), it is probable that he is giving the generals more authority over security matters in return for their backing.

According to Air Force Senior Colonel Dai Xu, China's military capacity is simply not equal to the task of maintaining national security or protecting the country's vast global interests. Dai, a popular online commentator on military affairs, compared the U.S. defense force to an eagle—"which stands tall and has unimpaired vision"—and that of Russia to an ostrich, "which can't fly too high but can run very fast." The PLA, by contrast, "can neither fly nor run fast." Yet Dai was confident that the Chinese military machine would catch up soon in light of the priority that the Party leaders had placed on narrowing the military gap with the United States.[205]

### Xi Is More Ready to Use Military Means to Attain Diplomatic Goals

In an apparent revision of Deng Xiaoping's well-known "keep a low profile" diplomatic dictum—or of the "peaceful rise" mantra posited by ex-president Jiang Zemin and his advisers—China's military officers and analysts are saying that to attain a global status commensurate with China's comprehensive strength, the PLA should not only seek sophisticated weapons but also be constantly primed for warfare to defend China's core interests.

According to General Zhang Zhaoyin, the deputy commander of a Group Army in the Chengdu Military Region, the PLA must abandon the outdated doctrine of "building a peace-oriented army at a time of peace." Writing in *Liberation Army Daily*, General Zhang argued that "preparing for battle, fighting wars, and winning wars have always been the fundamental tasks of the army. . . . The PLA must never deviate from the doctrine of 'being assiduous in preparing for warfare, and seeking to win wars.'"[206] Strategist Jin Yi'nan has posited the theory that "China cannot emerge in the midst of nightingale songs and swallow dances," a reference to the placid pleasures of peacetime. General Jin, who teaches at NDU, indicated that China had to "hack out a path through thorns and thistles" in its search for greatness. "When a country and a people have reached a critical moment, the armed forces often play the role of pivot and mainstay," in ensuring that national goals are met, Jin noted. That these theorists were articulating mainstream opinion within the leadership was made clear when Jin was invited in July 2009 to give a lecture to the Politburo on military strategy.[207]

As a general principle, Xi subscribes to Deng's theory that China should take advantage of peace to focus on economic development. But compared to ex-presidents Jiang and Hu, he is much more willing to use hard-power projection—or flexing military muscles—to attain diplomatic goals. Xi's preoccupation with raising the PLA's combat-readiness was reflected in the 2013 Defense White Paper, called Diversified Employment of China's Armed Forces. "China's armed forces firmly base their military preparedness on winning local wars under the conditions of informatization, make overall and coordinated plans to promote military preparedness in all strategic directions . . . and enhance war-fighting capabilities based on information systems," the paper said.[208]

Upon becoming CMC chairman at the Eighteenth Party Congress, Xi lost no time in touring all the military divisions. Xi has laid down essentially two tenets for PLA personnel. The first one is their loyalty to Party leadership. "Troops must be absolutely loyal, absolutely pure, and absolutely reliable," he said. "They must abide by the instructions of the Party central leadership and the CMC in whatever they do." The second one relates to combat-readiness. "Officers and rank and file should strengthen the ideology that they become soldiers for the sake of fighting wars and that [officers] provide guidance to and train soldiers for the sake of fighting wars," added Xi. PLA personnel should "go about military construction and preparations in accordance with the requirements of fighting wars."[209]

On another occasion, Xi gave this bellicose instruction to officers: "We must devote the utmost effort to expanding and deepening preparations for military struggle," he said. "We must ensure that the troops are ready when called upon and that they can fight effectively and win wars."[210] He also laid down this twenty-first-century axiom: "Combat ability is the only and fundamental criterion" for evaluating the strength of the armed forces." "Troops should focus all their thoughts on warfare," Xi said on the eve of Army Day in 2013. "All types of endeavors should be geared toward warfare. . . . the idea of raising combat ability should take a deep root in the brains of officers and soldiers."[211] Indeed, Xi has proven a relentless taskmaster in raising the combat-readiness of soldiers. While meeting with division commanders of the Jinan Military Region in late 2013, Xi pointed out that frequent drills were critical for beefing up the PLA's war capability and that "training must focus on what is needed to fight a war and what is lacking most. . . . Training should include educating troops about their duty to the nation and should be conducted under simulated war conditions."[212]

Xi raised the bar of military preparedness even higher during his talk with PLA delegates to the NPC in March 2014. Xi called upon officers to "tightly rally around the goal of building up a strong army and insist upon focusing different kinds of work on fighting wars. . . . We must uphold the correct political orientation, and fulfill the goal of [the PLA] being combat-ready and capable of winning wars." Xi expressed confidence that more thorough "thought liberation" would "further liberate and develop the fighting ability [of the troops]." Moreover, *Liberation Army Daily* has published numerous articles on the imperative of "getting rid of the inertia and habits of peacetime." A November 2013 article criticized unnamed army officials for lacking an "awareness of always being ready to fight. . . . Soldiers under their command have not been trained hard enough and the quality of military training is not good enough. . . . Leading soldiers in battles should be the primary task and ultimate duty of military leaders at all levels. . . . Everything the army does should be about fighting, and it all counts for nothing if the army cannot win battles."[213]

At the same time, the PLA has become more transparent in telling the world about state-of-the-art weapons that it is developing. Through calculated leaks to the unofficial media, the defense establishment has shown the world prototypes of new weapons, ranging from Jian-10 jetfighters and nuclear submarines to the DF-21 missile, which is said to be aimed at battling aircraft carriers.[214] Major-General Xu Guangyu was not shy about China's ambitious plans regarding aircraft carriers. Reacting to foreign reports about China's plans for constructing several of them, Xu said the PLA navy was aiming to develop capacities "equivalent to those of other permanent members of the UN Security Council." And while denying that China was building a naval port at Gwadar in western Pakistan, Xu noted, "It is only a matter of time before China owns foreign bases."[215]

### Why the PLA Hawks' Voices Are Expected to Grow

The generals (from the PLA and, to a lesser extent, the PAP) have always packed a disproportionately big political punch in the polity. Since the end of the Cultural Revolution, 20 percent of the seats on the ruling Central Committee have been reserved for senior military officers. And the two vice-chairmen of the CMC are always concurrently Politburo members. Of the six *yangqi* heads inducted to the Central Committee at the Eighteenth Party Congress, four were from the defense industry and aerospace giants (see Chapters 1 and 5).[216]

Xi is also an enthusiastic supporter of the Maoist doctrine of "a synthesis of peace and war," meaning that even in peacetime, there should be synergy between, for example, economic construction and defense modernization. The same idea was discussed by ex-president Hu at a Politburo meeting in 2009.[217] Thus infrastructure projects such as airports and container terminals should be designed with military uses in mind. There should also be ample cross-pollination between the R&D departments of the PLA, on the one hand, and those of state-owned enterprises, on the other. Even putatively private IT firms, such as Huawei and ZTE, are said to have contributed their research capacity for military use. After all, when Xi proposed the notion of the "Chinese Dream" in late 2012, he waxed eloquent about the unity of the goals of "a rich country and a strong army." "The Chinese Dream is a dream about a strong country," he said. "For the military, this is also a dream about a strong army."[218]

This is not to say, of course, that liberal and conciliatory messages about China's foreign policy—and overall role in the world—were nowhere to be found. For example, in late 2011 *Global Times* published a distinctly "pacifist" article written by Sun Peisong, director of the Linyungang Research Institute, a think tank of the Jiangsu government. Sun noted that the Chinese government should exercise the utmost caution to avoid war. "As a major country in the region, and as a big power with nuclear weapons, China must not raise lightly the possibility of war regarding small countries or those that do not have nuclear weapons. . . . If China can withstand the temptation [to use force] and if it is not tricked into warfare, then this will constitute China's victory. . . . China's biggest soft power consists in being conciliatory and benevolent."[219]

Some analysts have suggested that the government is playing the usual "good cop–bad cop" game. This means that the generals' pugilistic statements are meant to intimidate China's opponents as part of psychological warfare. The more conciliatory lines spelled out by civilian cadres and opinion-makers are meant to reassure the Western alliance as well as China's neighbors that the Chinese government is committed to being a responsible stakeholder in the global order. This line of thinking, however, presupposes that the "good cop" is in a position to counterbalance the "bad cop." Since the late 2000s, however, the voices of the military have been in the ascendant.[220]

Looking beyond the South China Sea, an expanded PLA role in China's foreign policy-making could exacerbate tensions over flashpoints in the overall Asia-Pacific region—and beyond. For example, the army may have a vested interest in speeding up the political reunification of Taiwan with the mainland. After all, preserving national unity has always been one of the raisons d'être of the PLA, as well as an effective pretext for lobbying for a bigger budget. The Chinese defense establishment has a long-standing partnership with regimes in nondemocratic and rogue states including North Korea, Myanmar, Iran, and Pakistan; China's security and military ties with these countries could be widened in the short to medium term. Looking further afield, the arms—and space—race between China, on the one hand, and countries including India, Japan, Vietnam, and the United States, on the other, is expected to intensify for the rest of the decade.[221]

**Conclusion: Can China Usher in a "De-Americanized World"?**

*China Roots for a "New World Order"*

An October 2013 commentary published by Xinhua sent ripples across the world. Addressing the temporary U.S. government shutdown—which was triggered by the failure of the president and Congress to agree on ways to resolve America's budget deficit—the commentary suggested that it was time for the world to consider ushering in "a de-Americanized world." "Under what is known as Pax Americana, we fail to see a world in which the United States is helping defuse violence and conflicts, reduce poverty and displaced populations, and bring about a real and lasting peace," it said. Instead, it argued, "a self-serving Washington has abused its superpower status and introduced even more chaos into the world by shifting financial risks overseas [and] instigating regional tensions amid territorial disputes." The commentary called for a "new world order" in which "the key interests [of] all nations, large and small . . . are respected and protected on an equal footing." It made three specific proposals: that all military actions require a UN mandate, that developing and emerging market economies be given more say in major international financial institutions such as the World Bank and the International Monetary Fund, and that a new international reserve currency be created to replace the U.S. dollar.[222] And in a late 2013 speech on a de-Americanized world order, the Tsinghua University professor Yan Xuetong appealed for the introduction of "new international rules." "We should develop new international norms to maintain world order and bring collective power to bear on countries that break these rules," he said. It would be a world order, in other words, in which the United States cannot impose its rules on others.[223]

In more ways than one, by 2014 Beijing had come a long way toward promoting a multipolar world order. Given that much of China's achievement is in the economic field, it is not surprising that the Chinese leadership has thrown its weight around on ways to mend the post-2008 international financial architecture. After all, the global financial tsunami has been blamed on America's apparent failure to rein in the rapacious deals—and dubious products such as junk bonds and overleveraged securities—of its banks and insurance companies. China, which accounts for some 23 percent of world economic growth, seems to have good reason to claim that the "Beijing consensus" or "Chinese model" is superior to the "Washington consensus."[224] At the G20 meeting in April 2009, the governor of the PBOC Zhou Xiaochuan fired the first salvo by demanding that the world consider using a new global currency to replace the dollar. And although Zhou's proposal—the use of special drawing rights of the International Monetary Fund (IMF)—failed to gain traction, the renminbi has made respectable headway as an international currency. Although the Chinese currency is traded mostly via swap agreements in bilateral trade, by early 2014 it had become the eighth-most-frequently-used currency in the world. Four countries to date, including Australia and the U.K., have decided to hold part of their foreign exchange reserves in renminbi.[225]

With the help of other members of the BRICS bloc, Beijing has successfully lobbied for more senior positions at the World Bank and the IMF for officials from developing countries. China's voting rights at both institutions have doubled. During recent G20 meetings, Beijing has turned the table on the United States and the EU regarding the valuation of currencies. Considering the level of quantitative easing undertaken by the U.S. Federal Reserve, Washington apparently thought better of lecturing China on the alleged undervaluation of the renminbi.[226] However, if China is determined to participate proactively in shaping the global financial architecture, it has to do more in terms of fulfilling obligations to norms regarding fair trade and opening its door wider, particularly to foreign firms in the services sector. It was not until the third plenum of the Eighteenth Central Committee held in November 2013 that pledges were made to set up a phalanx of FTZ, where market forces would play a dominant role. Yet in light of the fact that liberalized policies in the first such FTZ, established in Pudong, are being rolled out slowly, the Xi leadership's commitment to integration with the international marketplace has been questioned (see Chapter 4).[227]

### China as a Responsible Stakeholder in the Global Community

Apart from taking a larger role in maintaining the global financial order, Beijing needs to do more to show that it is a responsible stakeholder if not also a peacemaker on the world scene. This involves a radical revision of the Chinese leadership's long-standing position of "noninterference in the internal affairs of other countries." Although this principle has provided Beijing with a good excuse for maintaining relations with rogue regimes, including North Korea and Zimbabwe, it is also clear that the nonintervention mantra has prevented China from establishing itself as a proactive player on the international stage. As the French sinologist François Godement argued, "non-interference may have hampered Chinese diplomacy by preventing nimble responses and protecting stodgy thinking. . . . But moving to a more committed policy that is not afraid to take sides and favor particular domestic outcomes opens up a gulf of doubts and different answers. . . . Little by little, China's strategists are discovering the dilemmas of an imperial power."[228]

In fact, since the mid-2000s the Chinese government has made significant changes in its noninterference doctrine. From 2003 to 2007, Beijing hosted the Six-Party Talks on denuclearization of the Korean Peninsula. Although Beijing's track record in reining in the excesses of the Kim dynasty has been spotty, China is generally considered to have exerted a moderating influence on the Pyongyang regime. China is the biggest contributor of volunteers to UN-mandated peace-keeping forces. In late 2013, Beijing participated in talks that led to a partial relaxation of sanctions imposed on Iran.[229] However, given its economic and military size, there is little question that Beijing can do more, particularly in the developing world.

A case in point is the crisis that erupted in South Sudan in late 2013 due to disputes between forces loyal to President Salva Kiir and those supportive of Vice-President Rick Machar. China is South Sudan's largest investor, with interests in oil, construction, and telecommunications. China also imports 66 percent of the oil produced in Sudan and South Sudan. However, although the United States, Norway, and Britain have joined the UN in trying to restore peace, China was nowhere to be seen. "By not being proactive and taking a public position for peace [in Sudan], China will be vulnerable to criticism that it prizes profit over lives," wrote Steven Kuo, while a visiting scholar at Shanghai International Studies University. Earlier, the Chinese government was heavily criticized for its failure to condemn the

Sudanese government for engaging in ethnic cleansing against millions of members of non-Arab minorities in the country.[230]

China's bid for greater international influence has been impeded by its low capacity for supplying global public goods. This is due not only to Beijing's "noninterventionist tradition" but also to the fact that the government has refused to recognize international norms, including values enshrined in UN documents such as the International Covenant on Civil and Political Rights. As the veteran China expert Howard French put it, "China needs to develop a public goods side of its appeal, and a set of values to propose to the rest of the world commensurate to the dimensions of hard goods it already offers. . . . That's China's fundamental problem." Indeed, one factor that has impaired the country's ability to endear itself to its Southeast Asian neighbors is the paucity of public goods-related services. As Xiong Jie, a researcher at the CPS argued, the United States and Japan had done much better in this crucial arena. "China's contributions of public goods in Southeast Asia are not commensurate with its status," Xiong noted.[231]

### *A Realistic Calibration of the Gap Between China and the United States*

Beijing still lacks the ability to launch a frontal challenge to U.S. supremacy. Despite the decline in the U.S. economy—and the fact that China has become America's greatest creditor—there is still a big gap between the economic and military strengths of the two countries. Moreover, global standards in areas ranging from banking and accounting to advertising and medicine are still set by the U.S.-led Western alliance. However, judging by the rhetoric of a number of Chinese opinion leaders, the Chinese government seems convinced that China is within striking distance of rivaling and even overtaking the United States. Even though Party and state leaders still insist that China is a developing country, the core meaning of "a new model of major-country relations" with the United States rests on the assumption that China is virtually on par with the superpower. Although official discourse about "the great renaissance of the Chinese people" legitimizes Communist Party rule—and panders to feel-good, nationalistic feelings, particularly of the *fenqing* (angry young men and women)—serious consequences could follow from a miscalculation of the relative strengths of the two countries.[232]

Firstly, an exaggeration of China's hard power would predispose leaders—especially top cadres like Xi, who are close to the military—to take a hard stand against not only the United States but also its allies in Asia. As far back as 2010, popular military commentator Dai Xu advocated an "eye for an eye" strategy to counter what he perceived as Washington's containment policy against China. Calling the United States a warlike country that was obsessed with real or imaginary foes, Dai indicated that "China must use the full force of the state to warn the United States and to rebuff [its provocative policies]." "Only by so doing can we earn the respect of the United States," he told Xinhua.[233] Long Tao, a media commentator with military ties, even warned the Obama administration that the entire United States was within range of Chinese missiles. "China's arsenal includes not only ICBMs [intercontinental ballistic missiles], but our missile-equipped submarines go everywhere," he said. "For China's enemies, there is no refuge anywhere in the world."[234]

Moreover, Beijing's increasingly harsh tactics against two long-standing American allies in Asia—Japan and the Philippines—could give force to the "China threat theory" throughout the Asia-Pacific region. This, in turn, would prompt relatively neutral countries to seek the help of Washington to guard against the fire-spitting dragon that China seems to have become. Take, for example, the belligerent rhetoric of *Global Times* editorialists. The paper has warned that sovereignty claimants to South China Sea such as Vietnam and the Philippines should "mentally prepare for the sound of cannons. . . . China should not give pride of place to force and use the military option as its national policy. . . . Yet China must also not rely solely on negotiations. In times of exigencies, it should 'kill one to scare off the hundred.'"[235]

However, some more balanced analysts are aware that China stands to gain the largest room for maneuver if it is not seen as challenging the superpower status of the United States head on. The veteran Chinese diplomat Sha Zukuang pointed out in late 2013 that "China cannot become a center [of the world]—nor is there a necessity for China to become such a center. . . . The question of a power transition does not exist between the United States and China." The subtext of Sha's argument was that China should focus on economic and social reforms instead of seeking to undermine the U.S.-led world order.[236] Wang Yiwei, who heads the International Relations Department at Tongji University, shares a similar view: "It is not necessarily good to go too fast. If China is perceived as being too proud of its achievements and going its own way, it will not only get away from the mainstream [of global public opinion] but also face greater obstacles from different quarters of the globe." Wang counseled that in the course of China's rise, "direction is more important than speed; and morality and rationality are more important than strategy."[237]

### Chinks in the Armor of the Chinese Model

Whether China can become a superpower may hinge more on the viability of twenty-first-century Chinese culture than the number of aircraft carrier battle groups under the command of the PLA. In an article in *Foreign Affairs,* the Peking University expert on international relations Wang Jisi noted that if China was said to have a "grand strategy," it was not undermining American world leadership but fixing domestic problems. "If an organizing principle must be established to guide China's grand strategy, it should be the improvement of the Chinese people's living standards, welfare, and happiness through social justice. . . . A China with good governance will be a likeable China," he wrote.[238] Kenneth Lieberthal, a sinologist who was a senior official in the Clinton administration, agrees. "To a remarkable extent, domestic concerns structure the strategic objectives of China's formal impact and objectives."[239]

The foreign policy scholar Xiao Yang touches on the same subject, albeit from a different vantage point, in his new book *Boundless Power: Analysis of the Driving Force of China's Rise.* "China might be the loneliest of all the rising powers in history," he wrote. Xiao pointed to the supreme importance of soft power. He noted that before the "Chinese model" could win more converts around the world, "China should develop its own strategic culture and make this the basis for influencing the thoughts and culture of society . . . [so as] to achieve a national rejuvenation."[240] That something is missing in the Chinese order or Chinese model is indirectly attested to by the fact that when elaborating on his Chinese Dream, President Xi noted that the vision of China's becoming "a modern socialist country that is prosperous, strong, democratic, culturally advanced and harmonious" could be realized only by the mid-twenty-first century.[241]

One serious problem is that the Chinese system so ferociously promoted by the CCP leadership may militate against the emergence of a "democratic, culturally advanced, and harmonious" China. In light of the country's authoritarian political institutions, particularly the ruthless suppression of freedom and rights recognized by the UN Charter, can Beijing persuasively argue that the "Beijing consensus" is superior to the "Western model"? Moreover, top leaders from ex-president Hu and to President Xi have reiterated that China will "never go down the deviant path" of adopting Western institutions such as universal suffrage and multiparty politics. All that the CCP has promised the country in the way of political reform is that it will assiduously go about "perfecting the socialist system."[242]

Apart from the Beijing leadership's systematic violation of the civil liberties of Chinese citizens, there are salient areas in which China's domestic politics undercut its international appeal. Consider the country's neglect of the environment. Given the accelerated pace of globalization, no country can claim that its environmental policy is solely part of its "internal affairs." Since the turn of the century, China has been subject to increasing criticism for spreading acid rain and dust to areas including Japan, South Korea, and even the western United States. These and other countries have also complained that mercury and other metallic and chemical substances that originated in China have polluted neighboring fishing grounds. And because a number of international waters, including the Brahmaputra and the Mekong, originate in mountains in western China, the PRC has been blasted by countries including Vietnam, Laos, and India for selfishly overexploiting water and hydraulic resources in the upper reaches of these waterways.[243]

Then there is the problematic nature of the PLA, which is sometimes called a "state within a state" in the Chinese polity. In the past decade, the PLA's clout has grown because of its role not only in bolstering China's global reach but also in suppressing an estimated 150,000 incidents of protesting, rioting, and other disturbances that erupt annually. Unlike military forces in most countries, the PLA is a "Party army," not a state army.[244] This means that it is answerable only to a handful of top CCP cadres such as Xi, who requires the top brass's backing to maintain the preeminence of his own faction. The absence of any meaningful checks and balances to which the Chinese armed forces might be subject has raised fears among China's neighbors that the generals could, for their own benefit, push the country to adopt an expansionist foreign policy. The government's refusal to give up Maoist norms such as the "Party's absolute leadership over the armed forces" and "the synthesis of [the requirements of] peace and war" has diminished the global appeal of the Chinese model—and reduced the credibility of Beijing's quasi-superpower diplomacy.

### The Disturbing Rise of Nationalism

As we saw in Chapter 3, integral to President Xi's Chinese Dream is an appeal to nationalism, which is one of the few cohesive forces in Chinese society. The realization of the Chinese Dream means essentially that China as an economically prosperous and militarily powerful country can claim its place at the head table of the community of nations. While Xi has reiterated Beijing's commitment to the "peaceful rise of China," the high-decibel celebration of "the great renaissance of the Chinese people" could, at least in the eyes of China's nervous neighbors, smack of a vengeful triumphalism.

Major manifestations of nationalism over the past decade have included anti-Japanese demonstrations in 2005 and 2012 as well as the anti-French protests in 2008. A number of reports in the Western press have accused Beijing of providing support to the demonstrators from behind the scenes. And although the Chinese government has repeatedly criticized Japan for embellishing the country's World War II war crimes, references to Japan in Chinese textbooks and movies can hardly be called neutral.[245] Given the increasing irrelevance of socialism and communism, the CCP may find it necessary to bolster its legitimacy—and consolidate its "perennial ruling-class status"—by pandering to citizens' patriotic and even jingoistic feelings about the greatness of the Chinese nation. Chatrooms online are filled with xenophobic attacks on countries and politicians that are seen as belittling China's achievements or finding shortcomings in the Chinese model. At the same time, the leadership has cited popular support for military modernization to justify its decision to spend billions of renminbi on expensive weapons such as nuclear submarines or aircraft carriers.[246]

Xi's apparent wielding of the "nationalist card" against the Japanese could invite criticism that his administration is trying to bolster its support by invoking ordinary citizens' kneejerk reactions against what some netizens are now calling "Japanese devils." Nowhere is this more evident than in attempts by Xi and his colleagues to remind their citizens of the atrocities committed by the Japanese Imperial Army during World War II. The ostensible reason for opening up these old war wounds was to expose what Beijing calls the right-wing, militaristic tendencies of the administration of Prime Minister Abe. Beijing also wants to establish a linkage between Tokyo's claims over the Diaoyu/Senkaku islands and the Japanese government's alleged refusal to accept the outcome of the war.[247] It is true that Abe's visit to the controversial Yasukuni Shrine in December 2013 and his administration's apparent bid to revise the Japanese "Peace Constitution" have elicited criticism from not only China but also South Korea. For example, South Korean president Park Geun-hye has refused to have a one-on-one meeting with Abe. However, the Xi leadership's Machiavellian use of the "victimization narrative" risks conjuring up emotions especially among young Chinese that could degenerate into hate-filled rhetoric.[248]

A case in point is Xi's efforts to use his March 2014 visit to Berlin to underscore the sharp difference between Germany's thorough atonement for Nazi war crimes and Japan's alleged refusal to apologize for its wartime atrocities. German chancellor Angela Merkel made no secret of the fact that she did not want Germany to be sucked into a propaganda war between China and Japan. Berlin turned down Chinese requests that German officials accompany Xi to visit two Holocaust memorials in the capital.[249] Xi nonetheless mentioned Japanese aggression twice at a speech at the Korber Foundation in Berlin. "The war of aggression committed by Japan militarism alone inflicted over 35 million Chinese military and civilian casualties," Xi told an audience of politicians and business leaders. "These atrocities are still fresh in our memory . . . China needs peace as much as human beings need air and plants need sunshine."[250]

As a fervent student of Mao Zedong, Xi should perhaps be reminded that the late chairman had repeatedly told Japanese politicians and intellectuals that it was no longer necessary for them to make amends about those wartime atrocities. While meeting a delegation of Japanese parliamentarians in 1955, Mao said there was no more need for Japan to tender an apology to China. "You have already said you were sorry; there is no need to give an apology every day," he indicated. And while meeting another group of Japanese politicians in 1964, Mao went so far as to say that "it can be said that the Japanese invasion was a good thing because this helped us [the Party] a great deal. Look, the Chinese people have seized power." The Great Helmsman added: "Had it not been for the occupation of the majority of China by the Imperial Army, the Chinese people would not have become united in combating Jiang Jieshi [Chiang Kai-shek], and the Chinese Communist Party would not have come to power."[251]

While talking about the global dimensions of the Chinese Dream, Xi has highlighted the commonality between China's aspirations and those of other countries. The Chinese leader has underscored the fact that the Chinese Dream is compatible with the American Dream, the French Dream, or the African Dream. For example, while meeting President Obama in mid-2013, Xi pointed out that the "Chinese Dream" is "a dream about peace, development, cooperation, and win-win [scenarios]" and that "the Chinese dream is interlinked with the beautiful dreams of peoples around the world, including the American Dream." And when he was in Paris in early 2014, Xi told President François Hollande that both their countries should endeavor to realize the "Sino-French dream."[252] Yet until the Xi leadership makes a solid commitment to uphold universal values—and to stop revving up nationalism particularly among young Chinese—China will not get very far with its great leap outward.

## Notes

1. Cited in Liu Daqiao, "Keep a low profile while seeking achievements: China's thinking on foreign policy in the past thirty years," *People's Daily*, October 6, 2009, http://news.qq.com/a/20091215/002532.htm. For a discussion of China's newfound status as a quasi-superpower or the up-and-coming superpower, see, for example, Peter Ford, "China wants to be the world's next superpower: True or false," *Christian Science Monitor*, December 12, 2013, www.csmonitor.com/World/Security-Watch/Reality-Check/2013/1212/China-wants-to-be-the-world-s-next-superpower.-True-or-false/; Charles Riley, "China seen surpassing U.S. in superpower shift," CNN, July 18, 2013, http://money.cnn.com/2013/07/18/news/economy/china-us-superpower/. See also David Shambaugh, *China Goes Global: The Partial Power* (New York: Oxford University Press, 2013), pp. 45–120; Zhiqun Zhu, *China's New Diplomacy: Rationale, Strategies, Significance* (Burlington, VT: Ashgate, 2010), pp. 1–20, 215–232.

2. Cited in "Insist upon taking a low profile; proactively seek achievements," Xinhua News Agency, November 6, 2010, http://news.xinhuanet.com/politics/2010-11/06/c_12745081.htm.

3. Cited in "'Keeping a low profile' is a broad and deep philosophy," *Guangming Daily* Net (Beijing), November 7, 2011, www.gmw.cn/sixiang/2011-11/07/content_2918276.htm.

4. Cited in "Wu Jianmin: China must uphold the goals of insisting on taking a low profile and seeking achievements," China News Service (Beijing), September 27, 2005, www.chinanews.com/news/2005/2005-09-27/8/631955.shtml; Wu Jianmin, "The world's prejudice against the Chinese Communist Party remains deep," *People's Daily*, December 11, 2012, http://star.news.sohu.com/20121211/n360065368.shtml.

5. Cited in "Jin Canrong: Foreign policy goals such as 'keep a low profile' should be resolutely upheld," *People's Daily*, September 17, 2012, http://politics.people.com.cn/n/2012/0917/c30178-19025710.html.

6. For a discussion of the various facets of the "Chinese dream" as interpreted by Xi Jinping, see *Xi Jinping's Talks on Realizing the Chinese Dream of the Great Renaissance of the Chinese People* (Beijing: CCP Archives Research Office, 2013), pp. 65 and 69.

7. Ibid., p. 4.

8. See "Xi Jinping makes major speech at work conference on peripheral diplomacy," Xinhua News Agency, October 25, 2013, http://news.163.com/13/1025/22/9C2JM8UB00014JB5.html. For a discussion of Xi's new philosophy on diplomacy, see, for example, Li Ying, "Chinese foreign policy: From taking a low profile to seeking achievements in a proactive manner," *International Herald Leader* (Beijing), January 4, 2014, http://ihl.cankaoxiaoxi.com/2014/0114/331003.shtml. See also "'No gene for invasion in Chinese people's blood,' says Xi, amid Sino-Vietnam tensions," *Businessweek*, May 16, 2014, www.businessweek.com/printer/articles/201416-no-gene-for-invasion-in-chinese-peoples-blood-says-xi-amid-sino-vietnam-tensions/.

9. Cited in "Li Keqiang's government work report for 2014," *Economic Observer* (Beijing), March 5, 2013, http://finance.ifeng.com/a/20140305/11810549_0.shtml; see also "China to act as major responsible country 'more actively': FM," Xinhua News Agency, March 8, 2014, http://english.peopledaily.com.cn/90883/8559174.html; Yan Xuetong, "From 'take a low profile' to 'be proactive in seeking achievements': China's rise cannot

be stopped," *China Economics Weekly* (Beijing), November 11, 2013, http://finance.ifeng.com/a/20131111/11054882_0.shtml.

10. See "Xi Jinping: We will never sacrifice our country's core interests," *People's Daily,* January 30, 2014, http://news.cntv.cn/2013/01/30/ARTI1359504038874467.shtml.

11. Cited in "Dai Bingguo: China's core interests consist of upholding its basic system and national security," China News Service, July 29, 2009, www.chinanews.com.cn/gn/news/2009/07-29/1794984.shtml. See also "Spokesman of the Ministry of Foreign Affairs elucidates the parameters of China's core interests," July 13, 2010, http://china.huanqiu.com/roll/2010-07/924984.html.

12. For a discussion of military reactions to U.S. maneuvers in the Yellow Sea, see, for example, "Chinese major-general blasts the U.S., 'If people offend us, we'll certainly punish them,'" *Ming Pao* (Hong Kong), August 13, 2010; Chris Buckley, "Chinese admiral says U.S. drill courts confrontation," Reuters, August 13, 2010, www.reuters.com/article/idUS TRE67B11W20100813?type=politicsNews/.

13. For a discussion on whether Beijing has formally labeled the Diaoyus a "core interest," see for example, Zachary Keck, "Did Xi call Diaoyu/Senkakus a 'core interest'?" *Diplomat,* June 14, 2013, http://thediplomat.com/2013/06/did-xi-call-diaoyusenkakus-a-core-interest/.

14. Cited in Huang Kunlun, "Our army must transcend concepts of [the protection of] territorial integrity so as to safeguard national security," *Liberation Army Daily,* April 1, 2009, www.hlkmil.com/news/milcn/200901/20090104093409_5.html.

15. For a discussion of the military significance of China's space program, see, for example, "Expert: The rocket technology of the Chang'e III program is very advanced and can be applied to the manufacture of missiles," *Jinghua Times* (Beijing), December 3, 2013, http://news.sina.com.cn/c/2013-12-03/033428870991.shtml

16. Cited in Han Xudong, "We should be careful with the concept 'national core interests,'" *Outlook Weekly* (Beijing), July 25, 2010, http://news.xinhuanet.com/world/2010-07/25/c_12369991.htm.

17. See "Full text of Hu Jintao's report to the Eighteenth Party Congress," Xinhua News Agency, November 17, 2013, http://news.xinhuanet.com/english/special/18cpcnc/2012-11/17/c_131981259.htm.

18. Cited in Jane Perlez, "Panetta outlines new weaponry for Pacific," *New York Times,* June 2, 2012, www.nytimes.com/2012/06/02/world/asia/leon-panetta-outlines-new-weaponry-for-pacific.html?_r=0/.

19. See "Xi Jinping on upholding maritime rights: Sovereignty belongs to China while disputes can be set aside to facilitate joint development," CCTV News, August 1, 2013, www.qingdaonews.com/node_92031/2013-08/01/content_9895716.htm.

20. See "Full text: The diversified employment of China's armed forces," Xinhua News Agency, April 16, 2013, http://news.xinhuanet.com/english/china/2013-04/16/c_132312681.htm.

21. Cited in "China has 1.2 million sq km of oceanic territory that is in dispute with other countries," *Global Times,* March 14, 2009, http://news.hunantv.com/x/j/20090313/168883_2.html.

22. Cited in "Deputy political commissar of the Navy: China is a big maritime power, but not yet a strong maritime power," China News Service, May 13, 2013, http://military.people.com.cn/n/2013/0513/c172467-21458117.html.

23. See "China's new oceanic administration in operation," Xinhua News Agency, July 22, 2013,, www.china.org.cn/china/2013-07/22/content_29491818.htm. See also Marianne Brown, "Vietnam Accuses China of ramming vessels in S. China Sea," VOA News, May 7, 2014, www.voanews.com/content/chinese-ships-ram-vietnamese-vessels-in-south-china-sea/1909349.html.

24. For a discussion of the reinforced Chinese coast guard, see, for example, *Andrew Erickson and Gabe Collins,* "New fleet on the block: China's Coast Guard comes together," *Wall Street Journal,* March 11, 2013, http://blogs.wsj.com/chinarealtime/2013/03/11/new-fleet-on-the-block-chinas-coast-guard-comes-together/. See also Bonnie Glaser and Brittany Billingsley, "The promise and peril of China's new Coast Guard," *Diplomat,* August 7, 2013.http://thediplomat.com/2013/08/the-promise-and-peril-of-chinas-new-coast-guard/.

25. Cited in "Plan for the implementation of speeding up the structural change and promoting the transformation and upgrading of the shipping industry (2013–2015)," www.gov.cn, August 4, 2013, www.gov.cn/zwgk/2013-08/04/content_2460962.htm.

26. See Zheng Ming, "Expert: The premise of 'setting aside disputes and joint development' is 'sovereignty belongs to China,'" *China Maritime Times,* September 3, 2013, www.chinanews.com/mil/2013/09-03/5239574.shtml; see also "'Sovereignty belongs to China': China confirms the twelve-character dictum to protect its maritime power," Xinhua News Agency, August 1, 2013, http://big5.xinhuanet.com/gate/big5/forum.home.news.cn/thread/124506542/1.html#/.

27. Cited in "Ministry of Defense: China is not seeking maritime hegemony when it aims to become a maritime power," Ministry of Defense Web site, November 29, 2012, www.mod.gov.cn/affair/2012-11/29/content_4415431.htm.

28. For a discussion of the principle of "setting aside disputes while taking part in joint exploration," see "Official of Ministry of Foreign Affairs: 'setting aside disputes and joint exploration' tallies with international law," China News Service, February 20, 2013, http://news.21cn.com/caiji/roll/a/2013/0220/19/14697728.shtml.

29. Cited in "Set aside disputes and pursue joint development," Chinese Foreign Ministry, November 17, 2000, www.fmprc.gov.cn/eng/ziliao/3602/3604/t18023.htm.

30. Cited in "New ideas required for China's oceanic strategy," *International Herald Leader* (Beijing), March 3, 2009, http://news.xinhuanet.com/world/2009-03/03/content_10932738.html.

31. See "Half of oceanic territory where we have sovereignty has been taken," *International Herald Leader,* March 3, 2010, www.360doc.com/content/09/0303/20/62146_2701298.shtml; see also Li Wei, "The internationalization of the South China Sea," *Hong Kong Economic Daily,* August 23, 2010.

32. See "PLA major-general: The United States has formed a 'crescent moon' circle to contain China," *Guangzhou Daily,* July 18, 2010, http://club.bandao.cn/showthreadm.asp?boardid=101&id=1604283/.

33. For a discussion of China's aircraft carrier program, see, for example, Zachary Keck, "China says it's building more aircraft carriers and ballistic missiles," *Diplomat,* September 7, 2013, http://thediplomat.com/2013/09/china-says-its-building-more-aircraft-carriers-and-ballistic-missiles/; see also "China to build two more aircraft carriers: Taiwan," AFP, May 21, 2012, www.defensenews.com/article/20120521/DEFREG03/305210003/.

34. For a discussion of Chinese reactions to the launch of the Izumo, see, for example, "The Izumo: Japan's nostalgia about the imperial era," *Global Times,* August 7, 2013, http://opinion.huanqiu.com/editorial/2013-08/4215770.html.

35. For a discussion of the "theory of opportunity," see, for example, "Learn from Deng Xiaoping's 'theory of opportunity' and seek leap-forward development," *Hunan Daily,* August 23, 2004, http://news.sina.com.cn/s/2004-08-23/09563468516s.shtml. See also Guoguang Wu and Helen Lansdowne, *China Turns to Multilateralism: Foreign Policy and Regional Security* (London: Routledge, 2008), p. 224.

36. Cited in "Xi Jinping makes major speech at work conference on peripheral diplomacy," Xinhua News Agency, October 25, 2013, http://news.163.com/13/1025/22/9C2JM8UB00014JB5.html.

37. See Wang Yi, "Resolutely go down the road of peaceful development, and nurture a benevolent international environment for the renaissance of the Chinese people," Ministry of

Foreign Affairs, November 22, 2013, www.fmprc.gov.cn/mfa_chn/zyxw_602251/t1101579. shtml. See also Clifford Kiracofe, "US, China must avoid Thucydides trap," *Global Times*, July 11, 2013, www.globaltimes.cn/content/795537.shtml#.UpDPRbCwpBg/.

38. Cited in Cui Liru, "The possibility of China developing conflicts with the world is greater than in the past," *Global Times*, July 22, 2009, http://opinion.huanqiu.com/roll/2009-07/523024.html.

39. See "Xi Jinping makes major speech at work conference on peripheral diplomacy." For a discussion of Xi's new-look foreign policy, see Chen Jimin, "The motivations for China's new periphery strategy," November 18, 2013, www.chinausfocus.com/foreign-policy/the-motivations-for-chinas-new-periphery-strategy/.

40. Ibid.

41. Citied in "Yeltsin, Jiang become borderline friends," *Moscow Times*, November 11, 1997, www.themoscowtimes.com/news/article/yeltsin-jiang-become-borderline-friends/297834.html; see also "Jiang Zemin and Yeltsin issue joint press communiqué," *People's Daily*, December 11,1999, http://english.people.com.cn/english/199912/11/eng19991211A103.html.

42. Cited in "China, India sign deal aimed at soothing Himalayan tension," Reuters, October 23, 2013, www.reuters.com/article/2013/10/23/us-china-india-idUSBRE99M04J20131023/.

43. Cited in Foreign Ministry spokesperson Hua Chunying's regular press conference on October 15, 2013, http://milano.china-consulate.org/eng/fyrth/t1089830.htm; see also "China, Vietnam agree to take strategic partnership to next level," Vietnamese News Agency, October 15, 2013, http://vietnamnews.vn/politics-laws/246235/china-viet-nam-agree-to-take-strategic-partnership-to-next-level.html.

44. Cited in "What are the difficulties in China's peripheral diplomacy?" *People's Daily*, November 26, 2012, http://english.peopledaily.com.cn/90883/8033393.html.

45. Cited in Li, "Chinese foreign policy."

46. For a discussion of the reasons behind Beijing's decision to set up the ADIZ, see, for example, Bryce White, "Washington's 'Asian pivot' and China's Air Defense Identification Zone (ADIZ): US-China Power Play in the South China Sea," Globalresearch.ca, December 13, 2013, www.globalresearch.ca/washingtons-asian-pivot-and-chinas-air-defense-identification-zone-us-china-power-play-in-the-south-china-sea/5362329/.

47. Cited in Bonnie S. Glaser, "China's ADIZ undermines regional stability," *Asia Times*, January 26, 2013, www.atimes.com/atimes/China/CHIN-01-261113.html. See also "Air defense zone issue worsens Northeast Asian situation: S. Korea," Xinhua News Agency, November 27, 2013, www.china.org.cn/world/Off_the_Wire/2013-11/27/content_30722682.htm.

48. Cited in David Lague, "Special report: China's navy breaks out to the high seas," Reuters, November 27, 2012, http://uk.reuters.com/article/2013/11/27/us-china-navy-specialreport-idUKBRE9AQ04220131127/.

49. For a discussion of Beijing's strategies while negotiating the MFN with the United States, see, for example, Maggie Farley, "U.S.-China pact was won the hard way," *Los Angeles Times*, March 6, 1995, http://articles.latimes.com/1995-03-06/business/fi-39372_1_intellectual-property-rights/.

50. See "Commerce Minister Bo Xilai cools off campaign to boycott Japanese products," *China Business Times*, April 26, 2005, www.qzwb.com/gb/content/2005-04/26/content_1625015.htm.

51. For a discussion of China's economics-based diplomacy, see, for example, Zhang Shuguang, "A study of China's economics-based foreign-policy strategies," *Wen Hui Bao* (Shanghai), August 20, 2012, http://finance.ifeng.com/opinion/macro/20120820/6925545. shtml. See also "China to deepen, broaden economic diplomacy," Xinhua News Agency,

December 26, 2013, www.chinadaily.com.cn/business/2013-12/26/content_17199106. htm.

52. Cited in Ren Yuanxi, "Economic diplomacy: The most basic and important aspects," China.com.cn, September 10, 2009, www.china.com.cn/international/txt/2009-09/10/ content_18501056.htm.

53. See "China to extend over $12 bln in aid to Africa," Reuters, May 9, 2014, www. reuters.com/article/2014/05/09/us-china-africa-idUSBREA4802320140509/. For a discussion of China's largesse for African states, see, for example, Ousman Murzik Kobo, "A new world order? Africa and China," *Origins, Current Events in Historical Perspectives* 6, no. 8 (May 2013), http://origins.osu.edu/article/new-world-order-africa-and-china/.

54. Cited in "China now world's third largest investor behind U.S. and Japan," *Press Trust of India,* September 10, 2013, http://timesofindia.indiatimes.com/business/ international-business/China-now-worlds-third-largest-investor-behind-US-and-Japan/ articleshow/22455956.cms/.

55. For a discussion of Chinese investments in Libya and Myanmar, see, for example, "China seeks compensation in Libya," *Global Times,* March 7, 2012, http://china-wire. org/?p=19295/; Peter Birgbauer, "China lessons for Myanmar investors," *Diplomat,* October 27, 2013, http://thediplomat.com/2013/10/china-lessons-for-myanmar-investors/.

56. Cited in Derek Scissors, "China's steady global investment: American choices," Heritage Foundation Issue Brief 3990, July 16, 2013, www.heritage.org/research/ reports/2013/07/china-s-steady-global-investment-american-choices/.

57. For a discussion of China's investment in the Tanzanian railway, see Daniel Semberya, "Tanzania: China injects US$40 million in Tazara Railway," *East African Business Week* (Kampala), September 5, 2011, http://allafrica.com/stories/201109052414.html.

58. For a discussion of the significance of China's investments in Gwadar and Hambantoto, see, for example, Qaswar Abbas, "Pakistan's Gwadar port may get special 'China' status," *Daily Mail* (London), August 31, 2013, www.dailymail.co.uk/indiahome/indianews/ article-2408121/Pakistans-Gwadar-port-special-China-status.html#ixzz2nLo8sB25/. See also Vikas Bajaj, "India worries as China builds ports in South Asia," *New York Times,* February 15, 2010, www.nytimes.com/2010/02/16/business/global/16port.html?_r=0/.

59. For a discussion of Beijing's "string of pearls" strategy, see, for example, Iskander Rehman, "China's string of pearls and India's enduring tactical advantage," Institute for Defence Studies and Analysis (New Delhi), June 8, 2010, www.idsa.in/node/5468/493/.

60. Cited in "China signs railway deals with Romania, Hungary, Serbia," China.org.cn, November 26, 2013, www.china.org.cn/world/2013-11/26/content_30703634.htm.

61. For a discussion of whether China should fine-tune its policy of non-alignment, see, for example, Wang Yusheng, "Should China abandon non-alignment?" *People's Daily,* November 4 2012, http://english.peopledaily.com.cn/90883/8003975.html.

62. For a discussion of the New Silk Road Economic Belt, see, for example, Raffaello Pantucci and Li Lifan, "Shanghai Cooperation Organization: Not quite the new Silk Road," *Diplomat,* September 12, 2013, http://thediplomat.com/2013/09/shanghai-cooperation- organization-not-quite-the-new-silk-road-2/.

63. For a discussion of Sino-Russian discord within the SCO, see, for example, Michael Lelyveld, "Russia-China rivalry in energy-rich Central Asia denied," Radio Free Asia, September 20, 2013, www.rfa.org/english/commentaries/energy_watch/ rivalry-09302013104945.html.

64. Cited in "BRICS agree to capitalize development bank at $100bn," RT.com, September 5, 2013, http://rt.com/business/russia-brics-bank-g20-468/.

65. For a discussion of the Bangladesh-China-India-Myanmar corridor, see, for example, Tridivesh Singh Maini, "India and China: Different approaches to the border," *Diplomat,* September 17, 2013, http://thediplomat.com/2013/09/india-and-china-different-approaches- to-the-border/; see also Harun ur Rashid, "BCIM economic corridor: A giant step towards

integration," Institute of Peace and Conflict Studies, November 12, 2013, www.ipcs.org/article/india/bcim-economic-corridor-a-giant-step-towards-integration-4172.html.

66. See "Greek dock workers protest against privatising Piraeus port," AFP, February 26, 2014, https://au.finance.yahoo.com/news/greek-dock-workers-protest-against-103105711.html. For a discussion of allegations of Chinese companies "exploiting" workers in Africa, see "Chinese companies free to exploit workers in Zimbabwe," Equaltimes.org, September 24, 2012, www.equaltimes.org/in-depth/chinese-companies-free-to-exploit-workers-in-zimbabwe-2/; see also "You'll be fired if you refuse: Labor abuses in Zambia's Chinese state-owned copper mines," Human Rights Watch, November 4, 2011, http://m.hrw.org/reports/2011/11/04/you-ll-be-fired-if-you-refuse/. For a discussion of Huawei's failed acquisition bids in the United States, see David Benoit, "Huawei already can't get deals done," *Wall Street Journal*, October 8, 2012, http://blogs.wsj.com/deals/2012/10/08/huawei-already-cant-get-deals-done/.

67. Cited in "China plans global media expansion: officials," AFP, January 14, 2009, www.google.com/hostednews/afp/article/ALeqM5juSqW75T9CV55CR1AN52DTTfMdeg/.

68. Cited in Willy Lam, "Chinese state media goes global: A great leap outward for Chinese soft power?" *China Brief*, Jamestown Foundation, January 22, 2009, www.jamestown.org/programs/chinabrief/single/?tx_ttnews%5Btt_news%5D=34387&cHash=64c53060b0/.

69. For a discussion of the quality of English-language media set up by CCP authorities, see, for example, Zachary Keck, "Destined to fail: China's soft power push," *Diplomat*, July 1, 2013, http://thediplomat.com/2013/01/destined-to-fail-chinas-soft-power-offensive/1/.

70. For a discussion of the impact of Confucius Institutes, see, for example, Su-Yan Pan, "Confucius Institute project: China's cultural diplomacy and soft power projection," *Asian Education and Development Studies* (Hong Kong) 2, no. 1(2013): 22–33. See also Stuart Leavenworth, "UChicago ends China-funded program over remarks by Chinese official," McClatchy News, September 27, 2014, www.sacbee.com/2014/09/27/6738599/amid-concerns-about-academic-freedom.html#.

71. Cited in Lam, "Chinese state media goes global."

72. Cited in Yu Keping, "The 'Chinese model' and thought liberation," *Beijing Daily*, November 18, 2008, http://news.xinhuanet.com/theory/2008-11/18/content_10373496.htm; Dong Manyuan, "How to extend soft power with Chinese characteristics," *Outlook Weekly* (Beijing), December 8, 2008, http://news.xinhuanet.com/politics/2008-12/08/content_10473539.htm.

73. Cited in Wang Xiaojun, "Discussing the Chinese model and searching for the Chinese dream," Culture.yunnan.cn, March 8, 2013, http://culture.yunnan.cn/html/2013-03/08/content_2645172.htm.

74. Cited in "Li Xiguang: How to solve the discrepancy between the right of discourse of the rich and poor," Xinhua News Agency, May 4, 2012, www.china.com.cn/news/txt/2012-05/04/content_25303064.htm; see also Li Xiguang, "Major difficulties facing the construction of Chinese soft power," *People's Daily*, January 5, 2009, http://unn.people.com.cn/GB/22220/142506/8625983.html.

75. For a discussion of Xi's treatment of dissidents and human rights lawyers, see, for example, Stephanie Nebehay and Sui-Lee Wee, "China crackdown under scrutiny at U.N. rights review," Reuters, October 22, 2013, www.reuters.com/article/2013/10/22/china-rights-idUSL3N0IC2AB20131022/; Malcolm Moore, "Chinese lawyers targeted as Xi Jinping tightens control," *Telegraph* (London), August 20, 2013, www.telegraph.co.uk/news/worldnews/asia/china/10254632/Chinese-lawyers-targeted-as-Xi-Jinping-tightens-control.html.

76. For a discussion of Taiwan's limited diplomatic wiggle room, see, for example, Vincent Wang, "Bush snubs democracy in Taiwan," *Taipei Times*, December 17, 2003, http://taiwantt.org.tw/taipeitimes/DOC/2003/12/20031217.doc; "Taipei's costly search for

friends," Associated Press, April 27, 2006, www.asiafinest.com/forum/index.php?showtop
ic=72985&pid=1792334&mode=threaded&start=/.

77. Cited in "Dalai Lama's South Africa conference ban causes uproar," *Guardian*
(London), March 23, 2009, www.guardian.co.uk/world/2009/mar/23/dalai-lama-south-
africa-world-cup-ban/.

78. Cited in Andrew Osborn, "Cameron to make first China visit since Dalai Lama row,"
Reuters, November 12, 2013, http://uk.reuters.com/article/2013/11/12/uk-britain-china-
cameron-idukbre9aa0wn20131112/.

79. For a discussion of Kadeer's botched trip to India, see, for example, Kanishk
Tharoor, "India, don't kowtow to China," *Guardian,* July 28, 2009, www.theguardian.com/
commentisfree/2009/jul/28/india-china-rebiya-kadeer-human-rights/. For a discussion of
her overseas activities, see, for example, Julie Harbin, "Rebiya Kadeer: American grand
strategy should care about the Uyghurs," IslamiCommentary.org, March 12, 2013, http://
islamicommentary.org/2013/03/rebiya-kadeer-american-grand-strategy-should-care-about-
the-uyghurs/.

80. Cited in "The five principles of peaceful co-existence," *People's Daily,* June 28, 2004,
http://english.peopledaily.com.cn/200406/28/eng20040628_147763.html.

81. Cited in "Furor over Chinese dissidents at Frankfurt Book Fair symposium," Deutsche
Welle News, September 12, 2009, www.dw-world.de/dw/article/0,,4675700,00.html.

82. For a discussion of Beijing's pressure on Norwegian authorities regarding Liu Xiaobo,
see, for example, "Nobel arms-twisting," *Wall Street Journal,* October 1, 2010, http://online.
wsj.com/article/SB10001424052748703882404575520912261103800.html; see also Pavol
Stracansky "Chinese dissident wins more backing for Nobel," IPS News, February 10, 2010,
http://ipsnews.net/news.asp?idnews=50278/.

83. For a discussion of scholars banned by China, see, for example, Jay Nordlinger,
"Scholars with spine: Notes from the field of China studies," Initiativesforchina.org, August 27,
2012, www.initiativesforchina.org/?p=1206/; see also Yan Sun, "Wary of Western intentions,"
*New York Times,* September 2, 2011, www.nytimes.com/roomfordebate/2011/09/01/can-us-
colleges-defend-academic-freedom/china-is-wary-of-western-intentions/.

84. Cited in Daniel Golden and Oliver Staley, "China banning U.S. professors elicits
silence from colleges employing them," Bloomberg, August 11, 2011, www.bloomberg.com/
news/2011-08-11/china-banning-u-s-professors-elicits-silence-from-colleges.html.

85. Cited in Jaime FlorCruz, "Western journalists' China visa dramas: Don't shoot
the messenger," CNN, December 22, 2013, http://edition.cnn.com/2013/12/21/world/
asia/china-journalists-jaime-florcruz/; see also Damian Grammaticas, "Will China expel
foreign journalists?" BBC News, December 11, 2013, www.bbc.co.uk/news/blogs-china-
blog-25314241/.

86. See Joseph Nye, "Why China is weak on soft power," *New York Times,* January
18, 2012, www.nytimes.com/2012/01/18/opinion/why-china-is-weak-on-soft-power.
html?_r=0/.

87. Cited in Ji Shuoming, "China's foreign policy goes along a new path," *Ta
Kung Pao* (Hong Kong), March 28, 2014, http://news.takungpao.com/opinion/
highlights/2014-03/2384937.html. For a discussion of U.S.-China relations, see, for example,
Michael Swaine, *America's Challenge: Engaging a Rising China in the Twenty-First
Century* (Washington, DC: Carnegie Endowment for International Peace, 2011); Thomas
Fingar, "China's rise: Contingency, constraints, and concerns," *Survival* 54, no. 1 (2012):
195–204; Henry Kissinger, "The future of U.S.-Chinese relations: Conflict is a choice, not
a necessity," *Foreign Affairs* 9, no. 2 (March/April 2012), 44–55, www.foreignaffairs.com/
articles/137245/henry-a-kissinger/the-future-of-us-chinese-relations/.

88. Cited in "Full text of Hu Jintao's report to the Eighteenth Party Congress." See also
"China, U.S. should increase strategic trust, respect mutual core interests: Chinese VP,"
Xinhua News Agency, February 16, 2012, http://news.xinhuanet.com/english/china/2012-

02/16/c_122707589.htm. For a discussion of the implications of the "new model of major-country relationship," see, for example, Bonnie Glaser and Alison Szalwinski, "Major country diplomacy with Chinese characteristics," *China Brief* 13, no. 16 August 9, 2013, www.jamestown.org/programs/chinabrief/single/?tx_ttnews%5Btt_news%5D=41253&tx_tt news%5BbackPid%5D=25&cHash=a5216a9cfe8baa1f122fe1689df686ad/; see also David Lampton, "A new type of major-power relationship: Seeking a durable foundation for U.S.-China ties," Chinausfocus.com, September 21, 2013, www.chinausfocus.com/foreign-policy/a-new-type-of-major-power-relationship-seeking-a-durable-foundation-for-u-s-china-ties/. For a Chinese point of view, see Pang Zhongying, "A 'new type of great power relationship' between China and U.S.," Chinausfocus.com, July 2, 2013, www.chinausfocus.com/foreign-policy/a-new-type-of-great-power-relationship-between-china-and-us/.

89. For a discussion of the power transition theory (or the hegemony stability theory), see, for example, Steve Chan, *China, the U.S. and the Power-Transition Theory: A Critique* (London: Routledge, 2007), pp. 1–26; Mark Beeson, "Hegemonic transition in East Asia? The dynamics of Chinese and American power," *Review of International Studies* 35, no. 1 (January 2009): 95–112; and Ronald L. Tammen et al., *Power Transition: Strategies for the 21st Century* (New York: Seven Bridges Press, 2000), pp. 153–182. See also Aaron L. Friedberg, *A Contest for Supremacy: China, America, and the Struggle for Mastery in Asia* (New York: W.W. Norton, 2011); Peter Shearman, ed., *Power Transition and International Order in Asia: Issues and Challenges* (London: Routledge, 2013).

90. For a discussion of the transition of power from the UK to the United States, see, for example, Feng Yongping, "The peaceful transition of power from the UK to the U.S.," *Chinese Journal of International Politics* 1, no. 1 (2006): 83–108, http://cjip.oxfordjournals.org/content/1/1/83.full.pdf+html.

91. Cited in "Xi, Obama meet for first summit," Xinhua News Agency, June 8, 2013, http://news.xinhuanet.com/english/china/2013-06/08/c_132440860.htm.

92. Cited in "Commentary: Xi-Obama summit opens new chapter in China-U.S. relations," Xinhua News Agency, June 10, 2013, http://news.xinhuanet.com/english/china/2013-06/10/c_132444854.htm.

93. Cited in Yang Jiechi, "Implementing the Chinese dream," *National Interest*, September 10, 2013, http://nationalinterest.org/commentary/implementing-the-chinese-dream-9026?page=1/.

94. Cited in "Remarks by President Obama and President Xi Jinping of the People's Republic of China before bilateral meeting," White House, June 7, 2013, www.whitehouse.gov/the-press-office/2013/06/07/remarks-president-obama-and-president-xi-jinping-peoples-republic-china-/.

95. For a discussion of the "AmeriChina" concept, see, for example, Victor Gao, "'AmeriChina' looking for trust at the top," CNN, June 7, 2013, http://edition.cnn.com/2013/06/07/opinion/china-america-summit-gao/.

96. Cited in "Remarks by President Obama and President Xi Jinping of the People's Republic of China before bilateral meeting"; See also "U.S. seeks to 'operationalize' new model of major-country ties with China: Official," *Global Times*, November 21, 2013, www.globaltimes.cn/NEWS/tabid/99/ID/826597/US-seeks-to-operationalize-new-model-of-major-country-ties-with-China-official.aspx.

97. See "Xi-Obama summit opens new chapter in China-U.S. relations."

98. Cited in "U.S. declines to label China a currency manipulator," Associated Press, November 27, 2012, www.foxnews.com/politics/2012/11/27/us-declines-to-label-china-currency-manipulator/.

99. Cited in "World Bank chief surprises with gold standard idea," Reuters, November 8, 2010, www.reuters.com/article/2010/11/08/us-gold-zoellick-idUSTRE6A70D720101108/.

100. For example, during his first trip to China, Obama only mentioned human rights during a "town-hall meeting" with students in Shanghai. See, for example, François Bougon,

"Obama's China visit leaves dissidents disappointed," *Telegraph* (London), November 19, 2009, www.telegraph.co.uk/expat/expatnews/6604567/Obamas-China-visit-leaves-dissidents-disappointed.html.

101. For a discussion of China's fast-growing trade and other relations with Africa, see, for example, "More than minerals," *Economist*, March 23, 2013, www.economist.com/news/middle-east-and-africa/21574012-chinese-trade-africa-keeps-growing-fears-neocolonialism-are-overdone-more/; see also Marcin Grabowski, "China and the U.S. in Africa: Conflict or Collaboration?" *Journal of American Studies*, no. 12 (2011): 64–85.

102. For a discussion of a possible space race between the United States and China, see, for example, Daryl Morini, "The coming U.S.-China space race," *Diplomat*, August 15, 2013, http://thediplomat.com/2012/08/a-u-s-china-space-race-in-the-offing/.

103. See "Remarks as prepared for delivery by National Security Advisor Susan E. Rice," White House, November 20, 2013, www.whitehouse.gov/the-press-office/2013/11/21/remarks-prepared-delivery-national-security-advisor-susan-e-rice/.

104. Cited in Nike Ching, "U.S., China partner to train Afghan diplomats," VOA, September 23, 2013, www.voanews.com/content/us-china-partner-train-afghan-diplomats/1755357.html; see also "U.S., China launch 2nd joint training program for Afghan diplomats," Xinhua News Agency, September 10, 2013, www.globaltimes.cn/content/809978.shtml.

105. Cited in "Remarks by President Obama and President Xi Jinping of the People's Republic of China before bilateral meeting."

106. Cited in "Full text of Xi Jinping's speech at the opening ceremony of the Bo'ao Forum for Asia," Xinhua News Agency, April 4, 2013, http://english.boaoforum.org/mtzxxwzxen/7379.jhtml; see also "Wang Yi, Resolutely go down the road of peaceful development."

107. Cited in Justin McCurry, "Obama says U.S. will defend Japan in island dispute with China," *Guardian*, April 24, 2014, www.theguardian.com/world/2014/apr/24/obama-in-japan-backs-status-quo-in-island-dispute-with-china/.

108. Cited in Emily Rauhala, "Obama in the Philippines: 'Our goal is not to contain China,'" *Time*, http://time.com/78779/obama-philippines-china/. For a discussion of Washington's policies toward the South China Sea, see, for example, Edward Wong, "China hedges over whether South China Sea is a 'core interest' worth war," *New York Times*, March 30, 2011, www.nytimes.com/2011/03/31/world/asia/31beijing.html?_r=0/; Elsa Kania, "The South China Sea: Flashpoints and the U.S. pivot," *Harvard Political Review*, January 11, 2013, http://harvardpolitics.com/world/the-south-china-sea-flashpoints-and-the-u-s-pivot/. See also "Stirring up the South China Sea," International Crisis Group, Asia Paper 223, April 23, 2012, www.crisisgroup.org/~/media/Files/asia/north-east-asia/223-stirring-up-the-south-china-sea-i.pdf.

109. Cited in "The world power distribution is changing, China should have a big vision," *Global Times*, December 12, 2013, http://opinion.huanqiu.com/opinion_world/2013-12/4654086.html. For a discussion of Chinese perception of Washington's "containment policy," see, for example, "The U.S. is forming a 'C-shaped encirclement ring' around China," *Guangzhou Daily* (Guangzhou), August 14, 2010, www.chinanews.com.cn/gj/2010/08-14/2467638.shtml; "Editorial: Beware of the emergence of a psychological 'Asian NATO,'" *Global Times*, August 11, 2010, http://opinion.huanqiu.com/roll/2010-08/1003401.html. For a discussion of the "color revolution conspiracy" in Hong Kong, see, for example, Thomas Chan, "Hong Kong and color revolution," *China Daily* (Hong Kong ), October 11, 2013, www.chinadaily.com.cn/hkedition/2013-10/11/content_17022301.htm.

110. Cited in Condoleezza Rice, "Promoting the national interest," *Foreign Affairs* 79, no. 1 (January/February 2000), www.mtholyoke.edu/~jwestern/ir319/condoleezza_rice.htm.

111. Cited in David Shambaugh, "The rocky road ahead in U.S.-China relations," Chinausfocus.com, October 23, 2012, www.chinausfocus.com/print/?id=20902/; "Yan Xuetong: The China-U.S. relationship is one in which 'enmity outweighs friendship,'" Xinhua News Agency, March 22, 2010, http://world.people.com.cn/GB/11193945.html. See

also Yan Xuetong, "Let's not be friends: Obama and Xi will work better together if they both acknowledge they don't trust each other," *Foreign Policy,* July 6, 2013, www.foreignpolicy. com/articles/2013/06/05/lets_not_be_friends_us_china_trust#sthash.HX2l5bvT.dpbs/.

112. Cited in "China should seize the opportunities provided by America's strategic retreat," *Global Times,* September 10, 2010, http://news.xinhuanet.com/world/2010-09/09/c_12535628_2.htm.

113. See Shambaugh, "The rocky road ahead in U.S.-China relations."

114. For a discussion of official dialogue mechanisms and people-to-people relationship between the two countries, see, for example, Chen Xiangyang, "Three grave challenges facing China-U.S. relations," Chinausfocus.com, June 21, 2012, www.chinausfocus.com/print/?id=29485/. For a discussion of the "princelings'" global business activities, see for example, Patrick Tyler, "China's first family comes under growing scrutiny," *New York Times,* June 2, 1995, www.nytimes.com/1995/06/02/world/china-s-first-family-comes-under-growing-scrutiny.html; see also "A Bush in hand is worth . . . a lot," *Businessweek,* December 14, 2003, www.businessweek.com/stories/2003-12-14/a-bush-in-hand-is-worth-dot-dot-dot-a-lot/.

115. Cited in Kissinger, "The future of U.S.-Chinese relations."

116. Cited in "China, Japan reach principled consensus on East China Sea issue," Xinhua News Agency, June 18, 2008, http://news.xinhuanet.com/english/2008-06/18/content_8394206.htm. For a discussion of the Hu-Fukuda agreement on the East China Sea, see, for example, James Manicom, "Hu-Fukuda summit: The East China Sea dispute," *China Brief,* Jamestown Foundation, June 6, 2008, www.jamestown.org/programs/chinabrief/single/?tx_ttnews%5Btt_news%5D=4968&tx_ttnews%5BbackPid%5D=168&no_cache=1/.

117. For a discussion of relations between Fukuda and hawkish members of the LDP establishment, see, for example, Masami Ito, "Hawks expected to push Fukuda hard," *Japan Times,* September 24, 2007, www.japantimes.co.jp/news/2007/09/24/national/hawks-expected-to-push-fukuda-hard/.

118. For a discussion of the significance of the Diaoyu-Senkaku crisis, see, for example, Reinhard Drifte, "The Senkaku-Diaoyu dispute between Japan and China: Between the materialization of the 'China threat' and Japan 'reversing the outcome of World War II,'" UNISCI Paper 52, May 2013, http://international.uiowa.edu/files/international.uiowa.edu/files/file_uploads/drifte_senkaku_article_1.pdf. See also Akio Takahara, "Japan should join Sino-U.S. dialogue," *Asahi shimbun,* July 12, 2013, https://ajw.asahi.com/article/views/opinion/AJ201207120066/; Yakushiji Katsuyuki, "Structural shift in Japan-China relations," Tokyo Foundation, December 2, 2013, www.tokyofoundation.org/en/articles/2013/shift-in-japan-china-relations/.

119. For a discussion of Zhou Enlai and Deng Xiaoping's views on the Diaoyu/Senkaku islets, see, for example, Wu Li, "Prime Minister Zhou uses six words to move Kakuei Tanaka during negotiations for establishment of diplomatic ties between China and Japan," *Southern Weekend* (Guangzhou), October 24, 2010, http://history.people.com.cn/GB/198305/198865/13032878.html; see also "Japan denies consensus with Deng Xiaoping over setting aside of sovereignty," China News Service, October 18, 2012, http://news.qq.com/a/20121018/000568.htm. For a discussion of Deng's dictum on the Diaoyus and related developments in the tussle with Tokyo, see, for example, Zhongqi Pan, "Sino-Japanese dispute over the Diaoyu/Senkaku Islands: The pending controversy from the Chinese perspective," *Journal of Chinese Political Science* 12, no. 1 (March 2007): 71–92, www.springerlink.com/content/b2306611125nw526/.

120. Cited in "Hu Jintao makes known China's stance on China-Japan relations and the Diaoyu Islands," *People's Daily,* September 9, 2012, http://politics.people.com.cn/n/2012/0909/c1024-18959058.html.

121. Cited in Michael Cole, "China flies bombers and drone near Japanese skies," *Diplomat,* September 10, 2013, http://thediplomat.com/2013/09/china-flies-bombers-and-drone-near-japanese-skies/.

122. For a discussion of the impact of China's GDP exceeding that of Japan in 2010, see, for example, "Kato Chihiro: China's GDP overtaking that of Japan is a watershed in China-Japan relations," *Global Times,* March 14, 2011, http://opinion.huanqiu.com/dialogue/2011-03/1561197.html.

123. For a discussion of the quality of Chinese history textbooks, see, for example, Mark Magnier, "Like Japan's, Chinese textbooks are adept at rewriting history," *Los Angeles Times,* May 8, 2005, http://articles.latimes.com/2005/may/08/world/fg-history8/.

124. For a discussion of Chinese nationalism, see Peter Hays Gries, *China's New Nationalism: Pride, Politics, and Diplomacy* (Berkeley: University of California Press, 2004), pp. 86–134.

125. Cited in Feng Zhaokui, "China and Japan will not be at peace until China's economy is ten times that of Japan," *Global Times,* February 11, 2013, http://finance.sina.com.cn/review/sbzt/20130211/210214548297.shtml.

126. For a discussion of the 2005 revision of the U.S.-Japan Defense Guidelines, see, for example, James Auer and Tetsuo Kotani, "Reaffirming the 'Taiwan clause': Japan's national interest in the Taiwan Strait and the U.S.-Japan alliance," National Bureau of Asian Research, Washington, DC, October 2005, www.nbr.org/publications/nbranalysis/pdf/vol16no1.pdf.

127. Cited in Peter Hays Gries, "China's 'new thinking' on Japan," *China Quarterly,* no. 184 (December 2005): 831–850; Shi Yinhong, "China-Japan rapprochement and 'revolution in foreign policy,'" *People's Daily,* August 13, 2003, www.people.com.cn/GB/guandian/1033/2015190.html.

128. Cited in Yukio Hatoyama, "A new path for Japan," *New York Times,* August 26, 2009, www.nytimes.com/2009/08/27/opinion/27iht-edhatoyama.html?pagewanted=all&_r=0/.

129. Cited in "Hu meets secretary-general of Japanese DPJ," Xinhua News Agency, December 11, 2009, www.china.org.cn/world/2009-12/11/content_19046400.htm.

130. For a discussion of the Zhan Qixiong incident, see, for example, Akio Takahara, "The Senkaku fishing trawler collision incident, September 2010," in *The Okinawa Question: Futenma, the U.S.-Japan Alliance and Regional Security,* ed. Akikazu Hashimoto, Mike Mochizuki and Kurayoshi Takara (Okinawa: Nansei Shoto Industrial Advancement Center, 2013), pp. 91–102. See also Andy Yee, "The Diaoyu/Senkaku dispute: Japan's quiet power," *East Asia Forum* (Canberra), September 21, 2010, www.eastasiaforum.org/2010/09/21/diaoyu-senkaku-dispute-japans-quiet-power/.

131. Cited in "If Japan is willing to become a plaything of the U.S., it will end up being played by both China and the U.S.," *Global Times,* September 14, 2012, http://opinion.huanqiu.com/1152/2012-09/3117037.html.

132. See Luis Ramirez, "Obama reaffirms U.S.-Japan defense commitment," VOA News, April 24, 2014, www.voanews.com/content/obama-senkaku-islands-fall-under-usjapan-defense-treaty/1899996.html. For a discussion of American commitment to defend the Diaoyu/Senkakus, see, for example, James Rosen, "Hagel: U.S.-Japan mutual defense treaty covers islands China also claims," McClatchy News Service, November 27, 2013, www.mcclatchydc.com/2013/11/27/209998/hagel-us-japan-mutual-defense.html.

133. See Zhang Yunbi, "China-Japan trade will pick up: Report," *China Daily,* May 22, 2013, http://usa.chinadaily.com.cn/business/2013-05/22/content_16517836.htm.

134. For a discussion of the policy of *yimincuguan, yishangcuzheng,* see, for example, Feng Zhaokui, "China-Japan relations depend on interactions between the people and officials," *World Affairs* (Beijing), October 23, 2006, http://news.sina.com.cn/c/pl/2006-10-23/144611310978.shtml; See also "Tang Jiaxuan: The future of China-Japan relations depends on the people of both countries," *People's Daily,* October 26, 2013, http://money.163.com/13/1026/15/9C4E3KKJ00254TI5.html.

135. For a discussion of trade between China and Japan before their normalization of relations in 1972, see, for example, Chalmers Johnson, "The patterns of Japanese relations with China, 1952–1982," *Pacific Affairs* 59, no. 3 (Autumn 1986): 402–428.

136. Cited in Feng Zhaokui, "How can China and Japan learn from Europe," *People's Daily,* August 18, 2012, www.people.com.cn/GB/paper68/7007/679895.html.

137. Cited in "Vice President Xi Jinping visited Yaskawa Electric Corporation to admire the energy of science during the period of his visiting Japan," Web.ysr-motoman.cn (Beijing), December 22, 2009, http://web.ysr-motoman.cn:8383/en/contents/40/189.html.

138. For a discussion of the "informal diplomacy" conducted between Zeng Qinghong and Hiromu Nonaka, see, for example, Ming Wan, *Sino-Japanese Relations: Interaction, Logic and Transformation* (Stanford: Stanford University Press, 2006), pp. 142–144.

139. Cited in Elizabeth Yuan, "Former Japanese prime minister slammed as 'traitor' at home," CNN, January 18, 2013, http://edition.cnn.com/2013/01/18/world/asia/japan-hatoyama-china/.

140. Cited in "The ninth Japan-China public opinion poll," Genron-NPO Net (Tokyo), August 13, 2013, www.genron-npo.net/english/index.php?option=com_content&view=article&id=59:the-9th-japan-china-public-opinion-poll&catid=2:research&Itemid=4/; "Bad feelings between Chinese, Japanese worst in a decade: poll," UPI, August 8, 2013, www.upi.com/Top_News/World-News/2013/08/08/Bad-feelings-between-Chinese-Japanese-worst-in-a-decade-poll/UPI-35351375978657/; "Poll: Two-thirds of Chinese boycotted Japanese goods over Senkaku dispute," Kyodo News, January 6, 2013.www.japantimes.co.jp/news/2013/01/06/national/poll-two-thirds-of-chinese-boycotted-japanese-goods-over-senkaku-dispute/#.Up2RT7Cwrq0/.

141. Cited in Toru Sugawara, "Retirement of Chinese Japan hands narrows Sino-Japan pipeline," *Nikkei shimbun,* October 25, 2013, http://asia.nikkei.com/Viewpoints/Milestone/Retirement-of-Chinese-Japan-hands-narrows-Sino-Japan-pipeline/.

142. Cited in P. Parameswaran, "U.S. must engage Asia to maintain global power: Lee," AFP, October 27, 2009, http://yoursdp.org/news/us_must_engage_asia_to_maintain_global_power_lee/2009-10-29-1398.

143. For a discussion of relations between China and Southeast Asia, see, for example, Ian Storey, *Southeast Asia and the Rise of China: The Search for Security* (London: Routledge, 2011), pp. 38–98; Zhu, *China's New Diplomacy*, pp. 165–194.

144. Cited in "Xi's Indonesia visit lifts bilateral ties, charts future cooperation," Xinhua News Agency, October 4, 2013, http://english.people.com.cn/90883/8416789.html; for a discussion on China's new strategies regarding relations with Thailand, Indonesia and Malaysia, see Kavi Chongkittavorn, "China's rebalancing strategies to ASEAN," *Nation* (Bangkok), October 21, 2013, www.nationmultimedia.com/opinion/Chinas-rebalancing-strategies-to-Asean-30217545.html.

145. Cited in "China vows to build community of common destiny with ASEAN," Xinhua News Agency, October 3, 2013, http://news.xinhuanet.com/english/china/2013-10/03/c_132770494.htm.

146. For a discussion of the bilateral versus multilateral approach to the solution of sovereignty disputes in the South China Sea, see, for example, Julian Barnes, "China rejects multilateral intervention in South China Sea disputes," *Wall Street Journal,* August 29, 2013, http://online.wsj.com/news/articles/SB10001424127887323324904579042742806878158/; see also Chen Jipeng, "News analysis: Confusion of bilateral, multilateral efforts on South China Sea," Xinhua News Agency, July 1, 2013, http://news.xinhuanet.com/english/indepth/2013-07/01/c_132501866.htm.

147. Cited in Li Xiaokun, "Li proposes ASEAN plan," *China Daily,* October 10, 2013, www.chinadaily.com.cn/china/2013livisiteastasia/2013-10/10/content_17019003.htm. For a discussion of the impact of the CAFTA on ASEAN countries, see, for example, Jose L.

Tongzon, "ASEAN-China free trade area: A bane or boon for ASEAN countries?" *World Economy* 28, no. 2 (2005): 191–210.

148. Cited in "Foreign Ministry spokesperson Hua Chunying's regular press conference on October 10, 2013," Chinese Ministry of Foreign Affairs, October 10, 2013, www.fmprc.gov.cn/eng/xwfw/s2510/t1086912.shtml.

149 For a discussion of the Maritime Silk Road, see, for example, "China to pave way for Maritime Silk Road," Xinhua News Agency, October 11, 2013, http://news.xinhuanet.com/english/china/2013-10/11/c_132790018.htm.

150. For a discussion of railway networks linking China and ASEAN, see, for example, "Railway connecting Nanning and Guangzhou has been finished; Beijing is hoping to link up with ASEAN," *Ming Pao*, December 11, 2013, http://premium.mingpao.com/cfm/Content_News.cfm?Channel=ca&Path=134476489484/cca1.cfm.

151. For a discussion of China's attitude toward the TPP, see, for example, Evelyn Shyamala Devadason, "The Trans-Pacific Partnership (TPP): The Chinese perspective," Social Science Research Network, July 6, 2012, http://papers.ssrn.com/sol3/papers.cfm?abstract_id=2101839/; Ellen Frost, "Strategic implications of TPP: Answering the critics," *Asia Pacific Bulletin,* East-West Center, Hawaii, July 9, 2013, http://scholarspace.manoa.hawaii.edu/bitstream/handle/10125/29568/APB%20no.%20220.pdf?sequence=1/. For a discussion of the prospects for the RCEP, see, for example, Yoshifumi Fukunaga and Ikumo Isono, "Taking ASEAN+1 FTAs towards the RCEP: A mapping study," Economic Research Institute for ASEAN and East Asia, Tokyo, Discussion Paper 2, 2013, www.eria.org/ERIA-DP-2013-02.pdf.

152. For a discussion of the impact of the oil rig incident, see, for example, Hilary Whiteman, "How an oil rig sparked anti-China riots in Vietnam," CNN, May 19, 2014, http://edition.cnn.com/2014/05/19/world/asia/china-vietnam-islands-oil-rig-explainer/.

153. See Jim Gomes, "Manila says China reclaiming land in disputed sea," Associated Press, May 13, 2014, www.stripes.com/news/pacific/manila-says-china-reclaiming-land-in-disputed-sea-1.282941/; see also Wendell Minnick, "Is China laying down stakes at disputed Scarborough shoal?" Defensenews.com, September 6, 2013, www.defensenews.com/article/20130906/DEFREG03/309060013/.

154. See Hau Dinh and Chris Brummitt, "Chinese ships evacuate workers from Vietnam after deadly riots," Associated Press, May 19, 2014, www.680news.com/2014/05/19/chinese-ships-evacuate-workers-from-vietnam-after-deadly-riots/. For a discussion of the status quo changing nature of the oil rig incident, see, "Editorial: A Beijing power play in the South China Sea is met with U.S. inaction," *Washington Post,* May 12, 2014, www.washingtonpost.com/opinions/a-beijing-power-play-in-the-south-china-sea-is-met-with-us-inaction/2014/05/12/f0602134-d9ef-11e3-b745-87d39690c5c0_story.html.

155. For a discussion that more ASEAN members may side with Vietnam and the Philippines, see, for example, Cai Penghong, "ASEAN should not touch the base line of neutrality in the South China Sea," *Global Times,* May 14, 2014, http://opinion.huanqiu.com/opinion_world/2014-05/4994410.html. See also Edgar Yuen, "China-Vietnam confrontation may affect ASEAN neutrality," *Ming Pao,* May 18, 2014, http://news.mingpao.com/20140518/caf1.htm; "The South China Sea question leads to 'dissension' within ASEAN: Malaysia shifts to support Vietnam," *Ta Kung Pao,* May 14, 2014, http://news.takungpao.com/world/exclusive/2014-05/2476340.html9/.

156. Cited in *Jakarta Globe,* "Indonesia's military flexes muscle as South China Sea dispute looms," March 13, 2014, www.thejakartaglobe.com/news/indonesia-military-flexes-muscles-china-sea-dispute-looms/. For a discussion of the implications of Chinese-Indonesian territorial disputes, see Anne Marie Murphy, "The end of strategic ambiguity: Indonesia formally announces its dispute with China in the South China Sea," CSIS.org, April 1, 2014, https://csis.org/files/publication/Pac1426.pdf.

157. For a discussion of lack of ASEAN unity on the South China Sea issue, see, for example, Mike Ives and Thomas Fuller, "Vietnam fails to rally partners in China dispute," *New York Times,* May 11, 2014, www.nytimes.com/2014/05/12/world/asia/vietnam. html?_r=0/.

158. Cited in "ASEAN defense ministers adopt three-year work program," Xinhua News Agency, May 20, 2014, http://news.xinhuanet.com/english/world/2014-05/20/c_133348203. htm.

159. See "Kerry: China's oil rig in South China Sea 'provocative,'" VOA News, May 13, 2014, www.voanews.com/content/kerry-chinas-oil-rig-in-south-china-sea-provocative/1913329.html. For a discussion of the ten-year defense agreement between the United States and the Philippines, see, for example, "Obama in Asia: Military deal tops Philippine agenda," BBC News, April 28, 2014, www.bbc.com/news/world-asia-27183976.

160. See "Li Keqiang vows China-ASEAN 'diamond decade,'" Xinhua News Agency, September 4, 2013, http://news.xinhuanet.com/english/indepth/2013-09/04/c_132688776. htm.

161. See Shang Jun, "Commentary: Vietnam to take economic hit for violent protests," Xinhua News Agency, http://news.xinhuanet.com/english/china/2014-05/18/c_133342717. htm. See also "Editorial: The South China Sea is a big vista, interests are more important than emotional satisfaction," *Global Times,* May 14, 2014, http://opinion.huanqiu.com/editorial/2014-05/4994409.html.

162. See Chua Guan Cheong, "Brunei, China to step up maritime, energy ties," *Brunei Times,* October 12, 2013, www.bt.com.bn/news-national/2013/10/12/brunei-china-step-maritime-energy-ties/. For a study of China-Philippine discussions on joint oil exploration in 2004, see, for example, Willy Lam, "China's petroleum diplomacy," in *China Turns to Multilateralism,* pp. 231–232. For a discussion of China's negotiation tactics regarding sovereignty rows, see, for example, Huy Duong, "Negotiating the South China Sea: China and Southeast Asian nations have very different negotiating strategies in the South China Sea disputes," *Diplomat,* July 20, 2011, http://thediplomat.com/2011/07/negotiating-the-south-china-sea/.

163. "The economic card of China has defeated Japan's political card—it will be difficult for ASEAN to join the ranks of anti-China forces," China News Service, October 11, 2013, http://finance.huanqiu.com/data/2013-10/4436502.html.

164. Cited in Elaine Lies and Kiyoshi Takenaka, "Japan-ASEAN call for freedom of air and seas, with tensions high over China," Reuters, December 14, 2013. http://www.reuters.com/article/2013/12/14/us-japan-asean-idUSBRE9BD01F20131214/.

165. Cited in "Philippines files case to UN in South China Sea dispute," BBC News, March 1, 2014, www.bbc.com/news/world-asia-26781682; see also "Chinese FM: South China Sea disputes could be solved with three ways together," Xinhua News Agency, August 3, 2013, http://news.xinhuanet.com/english/china/2013-08/03/c_125110225.htm.

166. See Ian Storey, "China runs rings around ASEAN," *Wall Street Journal,* October 2, 2013, http://online.wsj.com/news/articles/SB10001424052702304906704579110781140446244/.

167. For a discussion of the significance of a code of conduct in the South China Sea, see, for example, Deep Pal, "A code of conduct for the South China Sea?" *Diplomat,* September 25, 2013, http://thediplomat.com/2013/09/a-code-of-conduct-for-the-south-china-sea/.

168. See "China warns against rush to set code of conduct in the South China Sea," Xinhua News Agency, August 5, 2013, http://news.xinhuanet.com/english/china/2013-08/05/c_132603785.htm.

169. For a discussion of the "hot politics, cold economics" phenomenon in Sino-Russian ties, see, for example, "2013: Sino-Russian relations are characterized by 'hot politics and

not-cold economics," *Wen Hui Bao* (Shanghai), January 4, 2013, http://news.xinhuanet.com/world/2013-01/04/c_124182902_2.htm.

170. Cited in Ge Wanqing and Wang Zuokuei, "Pluses and minuses in China-Russian trade in 2013," Xinhua News Agency, December 30, 2013, http://business.sohu.com/20131230/n392660722.shtml.

171. Cited in "Xi hails development of Sino-Russian ties," Xinhua News Agency, February 9, 2014, www.globaltimes.cn/DesktopModules/DnnForge%20-%20NewsArticles/Print.asp x?tabid=99&tabmoduleid=94&articleId=841226&moduleId=405&PortalID=0/.

172. See "The international community has a positive estimation of China's sports diplomacy," *People's Daily,* February 5, 2014, http://world.huanqiu.com/regions/2014-02/4807689.html.

173. See David Lague, "China eyes $3.5 billion Russian arms deal despite ire over Sukhoi copy," Reuters, March 27, 2013, www.reuters.com/article/2013/03/27/us-china-russia-arms-idUSBRE92Q0PE20130327/.

174. For a discussion of the six meetings between Xi and Putin, see, for example, "An assessment of the six 'Xi-Putin meetings,'" *Ta Kung Pao,* February 7, 2014, http://news.takungpao.com/world/bright/2014-02/1370846.html.

175. For a discussion of the bilateral naval exercises, see, for example, "China, Russia show off naval forces amid disputes," AFP, May 20, 2014, www.channelnewsasia.com/news/asiapacific/china-russia-show-off/1113906.html.

176. Cited in "Interview: Russia sees expansion of ties with China undoubted diplomatic priority: Putin," Xinhua News Agency, May 19, 2014, http://news.xinhuanet.com/world/2014-05/20/c_1110779099.htm; see also Liu Hua, Hu Hao and Wu Yu, "Xi Jinping holds talks with President Putin: Stress put on expanding and deepening pragmatic cooperation," Xinhua News Agency, May 20, 2014, http://news.xinhuanet.com/world/2014-05/20/c_1110779099.htm.

177. Cited in Louise Watt and Vladimir Isachenkov, "Gazprom: China, Russia sign 30-year gas deal," Associated Press, May 21, 2014, http://abcnews.go.com/International/wireStory/gazprom-china-russia-sign-30-year-gas-deal-23807568?singlePage=true/.

178. Cited in "Russia & China: 'No to sanctions rhetoric, regime change in other countries,'" Rt.com (Moscow), May 20, 2014, http://rt.com/news/160128-russia-china-sanctions-rhetoric/.

179. For a discussion of China's attitude toward the Crimea and Ukraine crisis, see, for example, Jaime FlorCruz and Paul Armstrong, "Russia may find ally in China—albeit a passive one for now," CNN, March 6, 2014, http://edition.cnn.com/2014/03/05/world/asia/china-russia-ukraine-analysis/. See also Somini Sengupta, "Vote by U.N. General Assembly isolates Russia," *New York Times,* March 27, 2014, www.nytimes.com/2014/03/28/world/europe/General-Assembly-Vote-on-Crimea.html?_r=0/.

180. For an example of a Chinese expert condemning Moscow's actions in Ukraine, see Xiao An, "Crimea referendum should not get our applause," *Global Times,* March 17, 2014, http://opinion.huanqiu.com/opinion_world/2014-03/4910014.html.

181. See Simon Denyer, "Russia and China unite around the memory of World War II," Washington Post, May 20, 2014, www.washingtonpost.com/blogs/worldviews/wp/2014/05/20/russia-and-china-unite-around-the-memory-of-world-war-ii/.

182. See Niu Jun, "'The ghost of the West' in China's overseas propaganda," *Ming pao,* March 26, 2014, http://news2.mingpao.com/pns/%E7%89%9B%E8%BB%8D%EF%B9%95%E4%B8%AD%E5%9C%8B%E5%A4%96%E5%AE%A3%E4%B8%AD%E7%9A%84%E3%80%8C%E8%A5%BF%E6%96%B9%E5%B9%BD%E9%9D%88%E3%80%8D/web_tc/article/20140326/s00013/1395771529943/.

183. Cited in "Russia holds biggest war games in decades," Associated Press, July 16, 2013, http://cnsnews.com/news/article/russia-holds-biggest-war-games-decades/. See also Vladimir Radyuhin, "Love in the water, fear on land," *Hindu,* July 30, 2013, www.thehindu.com/opinion/op-ed/love-in-the-water-fear-on-land/article4967343.ece/.

184. For a discussion of Sino-Russian rivalry in Central Asia, see, for example, Baktybek Beshimov, "The struggle for Central Asia: Russia vs. China," Aljazeera, March 12, 2014, www.aljazeera.com/indepth/opinion/2014/02/struggle-central-asia-russia-vs-201422585652677510.html. See also Marlene Laruelle, "Moscow's China dilemma: Evolving perceptions of Russian security in Eurasia and Asia," in *Eurasia's Ascent in Energy and Geopolitics: Rivalry or Partnership for China, Russia, and Central Asia?* ed. Robert Bedeski and Niklas Swanstrom (London: Routledge, 2012), pp. 76–91.

185. For a discussion of China's trade and investment links with Central Asian countries, see, for example, Simon Denyer, "China envisions new 'Silk Roads' to West by land and by sea," *Washington Post,* November 1, 2013, www.japantimes.co.jp/news/2013/11/01/asia-pacific/china-envisions-new-silk-roads-to-west-by-land-and-by-sea/.

186. For a discussion of China's perception of Russo-Japanese ties, see, for example, "Expert: Joint Sino-Russian effort to counter the United States and Japan is just a posture," *Ming pao,* February 7, 2014, http://news.mingpao.com/20140217/tba2.htm; see also Richard Weitz, "China's relations in the Asia-Pacific: Russia," *Diplomat,* February 10, 2011, http://thediplomat.com/2011/02/russia/.

187. For a discussion of Moscow's "two-faced policies" toward China and Japan, see, for example, "Opportunistic Russia is sitting on the fence: China and Japan will suffer losses if they put their trust in Russia," *Ming pao,* February 12, 2014, http://premium.mingpao.com/cfm/Content_News.cfm?Channel=ta&Path=134536616164/tbb1_er.cfm.

188. Cited in "People fear that if a Sino-Japanese war takes place, the Russian military will not help China," Armystar.com (Beijing), January 28, 2014, www.armystar.com/jspl/2014-01-28_14581.html.

189. Cited in "Russia, India sign weapons deals worth billions," Associated Press, December 24, 2012, www.dawn.com/news/773687/russia-india-sign-weapons-deals-worth-billions/.

190. For a discussion of strategic cooperation among China, Russia, and India, see, for example, Shenali Waduge, "China-India-Russia strategic geopolitical alliance," *Tribune International* (Australia), April 13, 2013, http://tribune-intl.com/?p=2086/.

191. For a discussion of latest developments in Russo-Vietnamese relations, see, for example, Stephen Blank, "Russia's growing ties with Vietnam," *Diplomat,* September 19, 2013, http://thediplomat.com/2013/09/russias-growing-ties-with-vietnam/.

192. For a discussion of Chinese reactions to Russian participation in oil exploration in disputed territories close to Vietnam, see Jen Alic, "Gazprom-Vietnam: All hands on deck in South China Sea," Oilprice.com, April 20, 2012, http://oilprice.com/Energy/Energy-General/Gazprom-Vietnam-All-Hands-on-Deck-in-South-China-Sea.html. See also "Ministry of Foreign Affairs' reaction to plans by Russia and Vietnam to jointly develop oilfields in the South China Sea," Ministry of Foreign Affairs, April 10, 2012, http://news.china.com/focus/nhctsj/11101498/20120410/17138556.html.

193. For a discussion of Mao Zedong's decision to get into the Korean War, see, for example, Xu Zerong, "Six motives behind Mao Zedong's 'Fight the Americans and Support the Koreans,'" Chinainperspective.com, August 30, 2009, www.chinainperspective.com/ArtShow.aspx?AID=2598/. See also Shen Zhihua, "The Korean War was Mao's biggest mistake," *Cultural Forum* (Beijing), March 21, 2008, http://culture.china.com/zh_cn/history/kaogu/11022843/20080321/14740401.html. For a discussion of the China-Russian border treaty, see Jin Zhong, "How China lost 150 million square kilometers of territory," *Open* (Hong Kong), July 27, 2008, www.open.com.hk/old_version/0808p20.html.

194. See "China defense policy 'defensive in nature': White paper," Xinhua News Agency, September 6, 2011, http://news.xinhuanet.com/english2010/china/2011-09/06/c_131102682.htm.

195. Cited in "U.S.-China Joint Statement," White House, January 19, 2011, www.whitehouse.gov/the-press-office/2011/01/19/us-china-joint-statement/.

196. Cited in Willy Lam, "The military maneuvers of Xi Jinping," *Wall Street Journal*, January 14, 2011, http://online.wsj.com/news/articles/SB10001424052748704698004576103513580674214/; see also Peng Guangqian: "The nature of China-U.S. relations has changed; military conflict is not impossible," Xinhua News Agency, December 24, 2011, www.sinonet.org/news/military/2011-12-24/178343_2.html.

197. Cited in Yang Yi, "The Chinese aircraft carrier has taken the first step in a Long March," *International Herald Leader*, January 19, 2012, http://news.xinhuanet.com/herald/2012-01/09/c_131344347.htm.

198. For a discussion of the PLA's role in foreign policy-making, see, for example, Michael Swaine, "China's assertive behavior: The role of the military in foreign policy," *China Leadership Monitor*, Hoover Institution, no. 36, 2012, http://media.hoover.org/sites/default/files/documents/CLM36MS.pdf; Trefer Moss, "PLA influence over Chinese politics: Fact or fiction?" *Diplomat*, August 10, 2012, http://thediplomat.com/2012/08/pla-influence-over-chinese-politics-fact-of-fiction/. See also D.S. Rajan, "PLA's influence in foreign policy making in China and implications for India," Chennai Centre for China Studies (India) Paper 874, September 28, 2011, www.c3sindia.org/india/2582/.

199. Cited in "Major-General Luo Yuan: Vietnam must not force China to unsheathe the sword and brandish it," Xinhua News Agency, June 16, 2011, http://news.ifeng.com/mil/2/detail_2011_06/16/7045490_0.shtml.

200. For a discussion of the role of the CLGFA, see, for example, Linda Jakobson and Dean Knox, "New foreign policy actors in China," SIPRI Policy Paper 26, September 2010, http://books.sipri.org/files/PP/SIPRIPP26.pdf; Chin-Hao Huang, "Assessing the role of foreign policy elites in China: Impact on Chinese foreign policy formulation," University of Southern California, U.S.-China Institute, September 12, 2011, http://china.usc.edu/ShowArticle.aspx?articleID=2569/.

201. For a discussion of the possible functions of the CNSC, see, for example, Willy Lam, "Xi's power grab dwarfs market reforms," *Asia Times*, November 21, 2013, www.atimes.com/atimes/China/CHIN-01-211113.html.

202. For a discussion of how some Chinese diplomats view North Korea, see, for example, "Wikileaks cables reveal China 'ready to abandon North Korea,'" *Guardian*, November 29, 2010, www.theguardian.com/world/2010/nov/29/wikileaks-cables-china-reunified-korea/.

203. For a discussion of the generals' influence in foreign policy, see, for example, Jeremy Page, "China's army extends sway," *Wall Street Journal*, October 4, 2010, http://online.wsj.com/news/articles/SB10001424052748703466104575529810234851000/; see also Willy Lam, "China's hawks in command," *Wall Street Journal*, July 1, 2012, http://online.wsj.com/news/articles/SB10001424052702304211804577500521756902802/.

204. Cited in Willy Lam, "Hawks vs. doves: Beijing debates 'core interests' and Sino-U.S. relations," *China Brief*, August 19, 2010, http://freerepublic.com/focus/f-news/2579043/posts/.

205. Cited in Dai Xu, "China's army must have a game plan for breaking out of encirclement," *Global Times*, July 24, 2009, http://mil.sohu.com/20090728/n265548282.shtml.

206. Cited in "Deputy army head in Chengdu Military Region publishes article on the concept of 'winning wars,'" *Singtao Daily* (Hong Kong), December 17, 2008, www.stnn.cc/glb_military/200812/t20081217_942388.html.

207. Cited in Jin Yinan, "China's rise cannot be accomplished in the midst of nightingale songs and swallow dances," *Liberation Army Daily*, December 31, 2008, http://news.xinhuanet.com/mil/2008-12/31/content_10585102_1.htm.

208. See in "Full Text: The Diversified Employment of China's Armed Forces."

209. Cited in Wang Shibin and An Puzhong, "Xin Jinping puts emphasis on ceaselessly raising the scientific standard of Party construction within the army," *Liberation Army Daily*, July 11, 2013, http://chn.chinamil.com.cn/jwjj/2013-11/07/content_5634818.htm. See also

"Xi Jinping asks the troops to be absolutely loyal and to undergo preparations in accordance with the requirements of combat," China News Service, March 11, 2013, http://news.china.com/focus/2013lh/news/11136226/20130311/17723102.html.

210. Cited in "Xi calls for stronger strategic reserve forces," Xinhua News Agency, November 30, 2013, www.ecns.cn/military/2013/11-30/90691.shtml.

211. See "Xi Jinping inspects the Beijing Military Region on the eve of August 1st Army Day," Xinhua News Agency, July 29, 2013, http://news.xinhuanet.com/politics/2013-07/29/c_116729110.htm.

212. Cited in "To win battles: PLA newspaper," Xinhua News Agency, November 19, 2013, http://news.xinhuanet.com/english/china/2013-11/19/c_125722577.htm.

213. See "Xi Jinping: We must never give up upholding the country's forthright interests; we will never sacrifice the nation's core interests," Xinhua News Agency, March 11, 2014, http://news.xinhuanet.com/politics/2014-03/11/c_119721043.htm.

214. For a look at China's nuclear submarine program, see "China reveals long-secret nuclear sub fleet," Global Times, October 28, 2013, www.globaltimes.cn/content/820840.shtml#.Uq75V7Cwrq/; see also "China tests 'aircraft carrier killer' and simulates the destruction of an American aircraft carrier," Eastday.com (Shanghai), January 15, 2013, http://military.people.com.cn/n/2013/0125/c1011-20321528.html.

215. Cited in "Gwadar: The first overseas base of the PLA?" International Herald Leader (Beijing), June 8, 2011, http://news.xinhuanet.com/herald/2011-06/08/c_13915407.htm.

216. Cited in "Four CEOs of military enterprises have been inducted to the Central Committee," Ta Kung Pao, December 3, 2012, http://news.takungpao.com/mainland/zgzq/2012-12/1301743.html.

217. "Hu Jintao stresses the importance of the fusion of military and civilian development at a Politburo collective study session," Xinhua News Agency, July 24, 2009, www.chinesetoday.com/news/show/id/266967/.

218. Cited in Xi, Selected Talks on Realizing the Chinese Dream, p. 4.

219. Cited in Sun Peisong, "China must be ready to grin and bear it," Global Times, September 27, 2011, http://world.huanqiu.com/roll/2011-09/2038480.html.

220. For a discussion of the "good cop, bad cop strategy," see, for example, Andrew Chubb, "Good cop, bad cop with China's generals," Asia Times, July 27, 2013, www.atimes.com/atimes/China/CHIN-01-290713.html.

221. For a discussion of the space race between China and other countries, see, for example, Chris Zappone, "Asian powers open new chapter in space race," Sidney Morning Herald, January 3, 2014, www.smh.com.au/technology/sci-tech/asian-powers-open-new-chapter-in-space-race-20140104-30at2.html.

222. See "Commentary: U.S. fiscal failure warrants a de-Americanized world," Xinhua News Agency, October 13, 2013, http://news.xinhuanet.com/english/indepth/2013-10/13/c_132794246.htm.

223. Cited in Ken Moriyasu, "China envisions smaller U.S. role in world affairs," Nikkei shimbun (Tokyo), November 11, 2013, http://asia.nikkei.com/magazine/20131023-Casino/Blogs-Columns/China-envisions-smaller-U.S.-role-in-world-affairs/.

224. For a discussion of the rise of the China model in the wake of the global financial crisis of 2008, see, for example, Dirk Schmidt, "The financial crisis and its impact on China," China Analysis, www.chinapolitik.de, no. 27, January 2009, www.chinapolitik.de/studien/china_analysis/no_67.pdf. See also Wayne Morrison, "China's economic rise: History, trends, challenges and implications for the United States," Congressional Research Service, March 2, 2014, https://www.fas.org/sgp/crsrow/RL33534.pdf.

225. Cited in "China's yuan falls behind Swiss franc as 8th most-used currency-SWIFT," Reuters, March 26, 2014, www.reuters.com/article/2014/03/26/china-offshore-yuan-idUSL4N0MN13T20140326/. See also Angelo Young, "Australia says it will hold 5% of its reserves in yuan," International Business Times, April 24, 2013, www.ibtimes.com/australia-

becomes-third-country-establish-direct-currency-trading-china-says-it-will-hold-5-its/; "UK to become first Western government to issue renminbi bond," Reuters, http://uk.reuters.com/article/2014/09/12/uk-britain-debt-renminbi-idUKKBN0H71TA20140912.

226. For a discussion of China's views on quantitative easing in the United States see, for example, Gao Changxin, "'Tapering' of QE by U.S. would benefit world: Economists," *China Daily,* November 21, 2013, http://usa.chinadaily.com.cn/business/2013-11/21/content_17122360.htm; see also "China says Fed may floor world with 'hot money'" Bloomberg, November 8, 2010, www.bloomberg.com/news/2010-11-08/fed-easing-may-flood-world-economy-with-hot-money-chinese-official-says.html.

227. For a discussion of the potentials of the free trade zones, see, for example, John Sudworth, "Can Shanghai's free trade zone spur China's growth?" BBC News, January 19, 2014, www.bbc.com/news/business-25774227. See also "Shanghai free trade zone: The next Shenzhen?" *Economist,* October 5, 2013, www.economist.com/news/china/21587237-new-enterprise-zone-could-spark-wider-market-reformsbut-only-if-bureaucrats-ease-their-grip/.

228. Cited in François Godement, "China analysis: The end of non-interference?" ECFR Publications, October 24, 2013, http://ecfr.eu/page/-/China_Analysis_The_End_of_Non_interference_October2013.pdf. For a discussion of China's possible revision of its non-interventionist tradition, see, for example, Pichamon Yeophantong, "Governing the world: China's evolving conceptions of responsibility," *Chinese Journal of International Politics* 6, no. 4 (Winter 2013): 329–364, http://cjip.oxfordjournals.org/content/6/4/329.full/.

229. For a discussion of Beijing's role in the Six-Party Talks on de-nuclearization of the Korean Peninsula, see, for example, Scott Snyder, "Persistent support for the six-party talks," *Atlantic,* September 19, 2013, www.theatlantic.com/china/archive/2013/09/chinas-persistent-support-for-the-six-party-talks/279827/. See also "Iran nuclear deal complete after days of talks, ministers confirm," *Guardian,* November 24, 2013, www.theguardian.com/world/2013/nov/24/iran-nuclear-deal-completed-foreign-ministers/.

230. See Steven Kuo, "China's soft power suffers a blow in South Sudan," Caixin (Beijing), March 1, 2014, http://english.caixin.com/2014-01-03/100625127.html.

231. Cited in Kelly Chung Dawson, "China needs to export 'public goods': Expert," *China Daily,* October 17, 2013, http://usa.chinadaily.com.cn/epaper/2013-10/07/content_17012134.htm; see also Li, "Chinese foreign policy."

232. For discussion of the discrepancy between the "comprehensive strength" of China and that of the United States, see, for example, "Huang Ping: A nation's GDP is not equivalent to its comprehensive strength," Xinhua News Agency, November 6, 2012, http://news.xinhuanet.com/english/indepth/2012-11/06/c_132313195.htm.

233. Cited in Dai Xu, "We can only earn America's respect if we use the entire country's forces to warn [the United States] and to retaliate," Xinhua News Agency, August 4, 2010, http://news.xinhuanet.com/mil/2010-08/04/content_13965369.htm.

234. See Long Tao, "If the U.S. wants to pin down China, it can't escape China's deterrence," *Global Times,* November 25, 2011, http://news.xinhuanet.com/mil/2011-11/25/c_122336903_2.htm.

235. See "Don't take peaceful approach for granted," *Global Times,* October 25, 2011, www.globaltimes.cn/NEWS/tabid/99/ID/680694/Dont-take-peaceful-approach-for-granted.aspx.

236. Cited in "Chinese scholars debate global power transition: The fate of the world lies in our hands," *Global Times,* December 12, 2013, http://news.ifeng.com/mil/4/detail_2013_12/12/32064905_0.shtml.

237. See Wang Yiwei, "China should transcend both left and right; China's rise should not be too hasty," *Global Times,* June 2, 2011, www.21ccom.net/articles/qqsw/zlwj/article_2011060236745.html.

238. Cited in Wang Jisi, "China's search for a grand strategy: A rising great power finds its way," *Foreign Affairs* 90, no. 2 (March/April 2011), 68–79, www.foreignaffairs.com/articles/67470/wang-jisi/chinas-search-for-a-grand-strategy/.

239. See Kenneth Lieberthal, "How domestic forces shape the PRC's grand strategy and international impact," in *Domestic Political Changes and Grand Strategy,* ed. Ashley Tellis and Michael Wills (Washington, DC: National Bureau of Asian Research, 2007), p. 29.

240. Cited in "International outlook required to maintain momentum of China's rise," *Global Times,* December 12, 2013, www.globaltimes.cn/content/831797.shtml.

241. Cited in "What is the Chinese dream; how to interpret the Chinese dream," *People's Daily,* April 26, 2013, http://sznews.zjol.com.cn/sznews/system/2013/04/26/016367871.shtml.

242. For a discussion of the "self-perfection" of the socialist system, see, for example, "Focus on Xi Jinping's reform ideas: Re-establish institutional modernity and absorb world experience," China National Radio, July 24, 2013, www.cnr.cn/gundong/201307/t20130724_513140967.shtml.

243. For a discussion of China's water-related conflicts with the Mekong's lower riparian countries, see, for example, Parameswaran Ponnudurai, "Water wars feared over Mekong," Radio Free Asia, September 30, 2012, www.rfa.org/english/commentaries/east-asia-beat/mekong-09302012160353.html. See also "India expert claims China wants to use water resources to control India," *Global Times,* August 11, 2009, http://world.people.com.cn/GB/9834712.html.

244. For a discussion of the implications of the PLA being a "party army," see, for example, Willy Lam, "China to roll out the big guns," *Asia Times*, August 14, 2009, www.atimes.com/atimes/China/KH14Ad01.html. See also Party Military History Research Center of National Defense University, "Why we must resolutely counter [efforts to] delink the army from the party," *Liberation Army Daily*, May 4, 2009, www.chinamil.com.cn/site1/xwpdxw/2009-05/04/content_1749539.htm.

245. Cited in Mu Duosheng, "Less anti-Japanese dramas should be staged," *Global Times,* September 8, 2011, www.360doc.com/content/11/0909/17/1147381_147089878.shtml; for a discussion of Beijing's use of nationalism to pursue diplomatic goals, see, for example, "Strained China-Japan ties: Beijing's drive to instill nationalism fires up the young," *Straits Times,* February 23, 2014, www.stasiareport.com/the-big-story/asia-report/china/story/strained--china-japan-ties-beijings-drive-instill-nationalism-f/. See also Jane McCartney, "French supermarket Carrefour faces wrath of Chinese protesters," *Times*, April 21, 2008, www.timesonline.co.uk/tol/news/world/asia/china/article3784932.ece/; Paul Mooney, "Internet fans flames of Chinese nationalism," *YaleGlobal,* April 4, 2005, http://yaleglobal.yale.edu/display.article?id=5516/.

246. For a discussion of the impact of the rise of nationalism, see, for example, "China's rulers look to space to maintain Olympic pride," AFP, September 10, 2008, http://afp.google.com/article/ALeqM5it_tnj1X28nnzGHNwh4WgORD1v-w/; "China's risky support of Internet activism," Stratfor.com, April 15, 2008, www.stratfor.com/memberships/114779/analysis/chinas_risky_support_internet_activism/.

247. Beijing's point of view is that the Diaoyu/Senkaku islets should have been returned to China as part of the territories that Japan illegally acquired from the late nineteenth century to the end of World War II—and that the Cairo and Potsdam declarations testified to Chinese sovereignty rights over these islets. For a discussion, see "China: Declaration supports China's Diaoyu Islands sovereignty," Xinhua News Agency, December 1, 2013, http://news.xinhuanet.com/english/video/2013-12/01/c_132932696.htm; "Potsdam declaration: Diaoyu islands belong to China," CNTV News, September 19, 2012, http://english.cntv.cn/program/asiatoday/20120918/104071.shtml.

248. For a discussion of the "victimization complex" in Chinese nationalism, see, for example, Suizheng Zhao, "Chinese pragmatic nationalism and its foreign policy implications,"

paper delivered at the General Meeting of the American Political Science Association, August 28–31, 2008, www.lsu.edu/artsci/groups/voegelin/society/2008%20Papers/Suisheng%20 Zhao.pdf. See also Robert Sutter, "China's self-absorbed nationalism," *Diplomat,* August 31, 2012, http://thediplomat.com/2012/08/chinas-self-absorbed-nationalism/; Gries, *China's New Nationalism.*

249. See "Xi Jinping's Germany trip: Berlin nixes Holocaust memorial request," *Der Spiegel,* March 1, 2014, www.spiegel.de/international/germany/no-holocaust-memorials-for-china-president-xi-on-trip-to-berlin-a-956574.html.

250. See "Wartime memories still fresh in memory, President Xi Jinping says in Berlin," *South China Morning Post,* March 30, 2014, www.scmp.com/news/china/article/1460649/ wartime-atrocities-still-fresh-memory-president-xi-jinping-says-berlin?page=all/.

251. Cited in "Mao Zedong's talks with Japanese politicians," 21ccom.net (Beijing), October 1, 2010, www.21ccom.net/articles/lsjd/jwxd/article_2010100120704.html.

252. See Xi, *Selected Talks on Realizing the Chinese Dream of the Great Renaissance of the Chinese People,* p. 71. See also "Xi Jinping's speech at the meeting to commemorate the fiftieth anniversary of the establishment of relations between China and France," Xinhua News Agency, March 27, 2014, www.dzwww.com/2013/zgm/xwbd/201403/ t20140328_9915239.htm.

# 6

# Conclusion

## Xi Jinping and the Closing of the Chinese Mind

### Introduction: Trajectory of the Development of a Problematic Quasi-Superpower

China observers familiar with the robotic mannerisms of ex-president Hu Jintao are struck by the robust activism and zealousness of his successor, Xi Jinping. Two years after coming to power, Xi and his senior colleagues have achieved at least one major aspect of the Chinese Dream: a *fuqiang* (economically prosperous and militarily strong) China that is increasingly influential in international affairs. In 2014, the centenary of the outbreak of World War I, politicians and scholars alike have compared China to Germany in the run-up to the apocalyptic showdown in the Western world.

At a speech before the World Economic Forum in Davos in early 2014, Japanese prime minister Shinzo Abe compared relations between Japan and China to those between Britain and Germany before World War I. "Germany and the U.K. went to war despite their strong economic ties," said Abe, adding that there were similarities between the two relationships.[1] At about the same time, President of the Philippines Benigno Aquino III likened China to Germany during World War II. Aquino asked the global powers "not to repeat the old error" by adopting a policy of appeasement toward the expansionist PRC.[2]

Even more significant are the views of power transition theorists that an epic struggle for supremacy is shaping up between the United States, as the status quo superpower, and China, which is challenging it on almost every front. The University of Chicago political scientist John Mearsheimer is convinced that "China will try to dominate the Asia-Pacific region much as the United States dominates the Western Hemisphere." Moreover, he argued that, in light of the increasingly pugnacious statements made by Chinese diplomats and generals alike, "China cannot rise peacefully."[3] However, there are reasons for believing that in the coming decade, the Xi administration will think twice about going beyond high-decibel sovereignty claims over islets in the East China Sea and the South China Sea. As the Harvard professor Joseph Nye indicated in an early 2014 article, "the U.S. remains decades ahead of China in overall military, economic, and soft-power resources. . . . Too adventuresome a policy would jeopardize China's gains at home and abroad."[4]

Equally significant is the fact that any inordinately aggressive moves by China—for example, the outright takeover of islets that are also claimed by Vietnam and the Philippines—will further fuel the "anti-China containment conspiracy" purportedly led by the United States and supported by China's nervous Asia-Pacific neighbors. As Mearsheimer noted, "most of China's neighbors, to include India, Japan, Singapore, South Korea, Russia, Vietnam—and Australia—will join with the United States to contain China's power."[5] It is also significant that in early 2014, Xi expressed worries that perceptions of "the China threat" could lead countries in the region to gang up on his country. In an interview with the Huffington Post, Xi reiterated his administration's commitment to "peaceful rise," saying "the argument that strong countries are bound to seek hegemony does not apply to China. . . . This is not in the DNA of the country given our long historical and cultural background." He offered a historical reference to Sparta and Athens: "We all need to work together to avoid the Thucydides trap—destructive tensions between an emerging power and established powers, or between established powers themselves."[6]

Even assuming that Xi's protestations are credible, however, China's preponderance will appear disturbing simply because of the country's refusal to jettison its outdated "state capitalism" and, in particular, its political ethos and structure marked by Leninist authoritarianism. If one were to compare China with world-class powers in the past two to three centuries—Britain, France, Germany, Russia, the United States, and even Japan—a single trait stands out. For much of the past century, Chinese politicians and establishment intellectuals have chosen a system of ideology and governance that is at odds with global norms. Before Germany and Japan succumbed to totalitarian and militaristic temptations, both countries for at least a generation or so had embraced Western democratic values. In fact, what made possible Japan's emergence as Asia's kingpin was the decision by the Meiji-era aristocracy in the 1860s to adopt a strategy of "all-out Westernization."[7] Until the eve of the Bolshevik Revolution in 1917, Russia was at least partially a Europeanized country. This "European DNA" in the Russian body politic perhaps explains that the-erstwhile general secretary Mikhail Gorbachev could introduce *glasnost* and *perestroika*.[8] The Chinese government—particularly one led by an ardently conservative honcho such as Xi—however, seems to have decided to move further away from global values by ensuring that the ill-fated Westernization campaigns attempted by reformist then-general secretaries Hu Yaobang and Zhao Ziyang in the 1980s can never make a comeback.[9]

China is different from previous world powers as well because of its surprisingly meager cultural accomplishments in the past century, especially since 1949. Only two Chinese citizens have won the Nobel Prize. Liu Xiaobo, who was awarded the Nobel Peace Prize in 2010 for his advocacy of nonviolent political change, languishes in jail after having been convicted on trumped-up charges.[10] The 2012 winner of the Nobel Prize for Literature Mo Yan is an apparatchik in the official cultural establishment, one of whose missions is to ensure the political loyalty of the country's literati (see below). How can China—in particular Xi's "Chinese Dream"—win world approval when the CCP is embarking on policies that seem to run counter to a number of UN covenants? Moreover, given the Chinese government's long-standing policy of controlling the thinking of intellectuals and constricting the growth of civil society, the possibility that "new thinking" will triumph over crypto-Maoist standards remains low.

Even more than factors such as shifts in China's foreign and defense policies, therefore, the most important determinant of the trajectory of China's development in the twenty-first century will be domestic questions. Foremost is whether and when China will pick a development path that favors the construction of a real market economy and a just, compassionate society that embraces values such as the rule of law and equal opportunity.

As the Peking University professor Wang Jisi argued, most of China's problems have grown out of institutional and conceptual defects of one kind or another. Wang urged the CCP leadership to unhesitatingly "seek common values in the global arena, such as good governance and transparency. . . . The country's continued resurgence depends on greater transparency and accountability, as well as on a firmer commitment to the rule of law, democracy, and human rights, all values that are widely shared throughout the world today."[11] Similarly, Ma Yong, a historian at the Chinese Academy of Social Sciences (CASS), noted that curing the many ills afflicting the country depended on "politics," meaning the development of internationally recognized institutions and norms. "If China can pull it off on the political front, other matters can be tackled," Ma said in a 2012 interview with a Chinese newspaper. "Political solutions include constitutional governance, democratization, and going down the path on which all humankind has trodden."[12]

The connection between domestic developments, on the one hand, and China's room for maneuver on the world stage, on the other, is obvious. A key factor underpinning the "China threat" is that the PLA is a "Party army" that answers only to the seven-member Politburo Standing Committee (PBSC). As we saw in Chapter 5, the generals now have an unprecedentedly big say in foreign affairs. Then there is the familiar scenario of a dictatorial regime—which lacks so-called ballot box legitimacy—trying to extend its "mandate of heaven" by appealing to nationalism. Undemocratic governments have a long tradition of diverting the attention of their discontented and maltreated populace by engaging in expansionist activities abroad. All things being equal, an authoritarian administration—particularly one like China, where an estimated 150,000-odd incidents of riots and disturbances occur every year—is more prone to adopt an aggressive foreign policy.[13] Then there is the state of the civil society and intelligentsia: Are China's academics, public intellectuals, opinion-leaders as well as NGO activists in a position to prod the Party-state apparatus toward adopting values and standards that are compatible with those that are practiced not only in the West but in an increasing number of Asia-Pacific countries?

This concluding chapter looks into the weighty issues of Chinese governance and civilization. What measures has the CCP leadership taken to close the Chinese mind so as to ensure the Party's "long reign and perennial stability"? In light of the rhetorical pledges made by the third plenum of the Eighteenth Central Committee on different aspects of reform, will the Xi administration move closer to a market economy and a rule-based society? Given the increasingly close global linkages forged by Party, government, military, business, and academic sectors, how high is the possibility that Beijing will adopt a more tolerant attitude toward universal values? Will the country's universities and research institutes be equipped to nurture a younger generation that might be more open minded than Xi and his colleagues? Are China's increasingly vocal intellectuals and NGO activists able to fight back— and shatter Chairman Mao's notorious "one-voice chamber"? Or have disillusioned members of China's growing middle and professional classes chosen to vote with their feet by emigrating to Western countries that offer greater freedom for the individual? For the foreseeable future, China's economic and military might will continue to expand. Yet the corollary of the PRC's daunting soft-power deficit is that the country will be feared, not loved.

## The Deceleration of Reform and Institutional Innovation

### Why the Privileged as Well as Disadvantaged Classes Have Lost Interest in Reform

During an interview with Russian television while attending the Sochi Olympic Games in early 2014, Xi had this to say about the prospect of reform: "Pushing through further economic reforms will prove tough, and there may be dangerous times ahead. The easier reforms that could make everybody happy have already been completed. The tasty meat has been eaten up. The rest are tough bones to crack. We should dare to gnaw even rough bones and dare to ford dangerous rapids." On another occasion, addressing the imperative of "seeking breakthroughs in reform," Xi said: "We need to harness all our energy and vigor. Hesitation and doubt not only will hinder our progress but may result in total failure."[14]

Xi seems confident about the prospects for reform because he has vowed to pull out all the stops to create an innovative state and society. Since he became Party boss in late 2012, hardly a week has passed by that either Xi or some other senior cadre does not make an impassioned pep talk about the virtues of an innovative approach to governance. When he was president of the Central Party School (CPS) from 2007 to 2012, Xi waxed eloquent about "developing an innovative spirit and raising the innovative ability [of the government and society]. . . . We must uphold an independent and creative road with Chinese characteristics, and lay solid foundation for the masses to build an innovative country." And while inspecting central

Hunan Province in late 2013, Xi pointed out that "the way out for the deep-seated contradictions and problems [in China] is innovation. . . . The future and fate of the Chinese race depends on a strategy of innovation-driven development."[15]

It seems unlikely, however, that the Xi administration will "breach the fortresses" through innovative approaches. Since early 2013 he reiterated that while reformers should be bold, "the steps we take must be steady." A key message that Xi delivered at the APEC meeting in Indonesia in October 2013 is that "while China must make bold explorations [in reform] and be brave in opening up new vistas, we must also be prudent and cautious, and take actions only after due consideration." Xi has repeatedly cited the danger of "subversive errors." "China is a huge country," he told a gathering of business leaders in Bali. "We cannot afford to make subversive mistakes over fundamental questions. If such errors were to happen, they can never be remedied."[16]

What Xi meant by "subversive mistakes" are economic, social, or political policies that would compromise the monopoly on power that is enjoyed by the CCP—or more specifically the Party's ruling elite, also known as the "red aristocracy." From the point of view of China's upper crust, the best example of an "irremediable error" are the economic and political reforms undertaken in the last days of the Soviet Union by Mikhail Gorbachev and Boris Yeltsin. As the conservative ideologue Wang Xiaoshi pointed out in a Xinhua article, "if China is struck with instability, the end result will be worse than [what happened to] the Soviet Union." However, what CCP cadres fear most is the loss of their special privileges. As the Beijing Technology University professor Zhao Xiao argued, "the resistance to reform comes from interest blocs and newly minted privileged classes. . . . These people have used their power to obtain immense benefits from reform—and they want to preserve the status quo."[17]

Equally significant is Xi's self-serving interpretation of why economic reform has become an uphill struggle. He attributed this to the fact that because "low-hanging fruit" and "tasty meat" have been snapped up, not many Chinese are willing to make an extra effort to tackle the "tough bones" that remain. The reality, however, is that the first ten or so years of reform took place when China was still a relatively equal society, therefore not only people with power and education but also members of the "lower classes" managed to get a relatively satisfactory share of the expanding economic pie. By the mid-1990s, however, the privileged classes—including big clans within the Party and their business partners—had become entrenched, and almost all kinds of reform have become impossible. Members of this so-called red aristocracy are more interested in preserving the status quo—which automatically guarantees them the lion's share of the pie—rather than new policies and arrangements that could make a dent in their vested interests. And how about the lower classes? Having been losers for more than three decades of reform, disadvantaged social sectors have lost trust in the Party leadership's ability to improve their lot through more reforms. They believe that the next wave of changes will only benefit the "unholy alliance" of senior cadres and commercial interests. As the CASS historian Ma Yong put it in 2013, "Everyone is talking about reform, but in fact everyone fears reform."[18] The only way to revive people's enthusiasm for reform, according to Hu Deping, the liberal son of Hu Yaobang, is to seek a "synthesis between top-level design and the applause of the masses. . . . If we were to give the bonus of reform to ordinary people—for example, investing the bonus of reform in areas including pensions, education, and health services—there will be sufficient backing and motivation for the next stage of reform."[19] Unfortunately, not many senior cadres—and certainly not the princelings—share Hu's liberal vision.

According to the Tsinghua University sociologist Sun Liping, in an interview with the *Economic Observer,* the emergence of the market economy in the 1980s and early 1990s brought tangible benefits to "people occupying disadvantaged and marginalized positions in society." Yet, Sun said, after the mid-1990s the very nature of reform had been "twisted and distorted by vested interests." The result was that, instead of constructing a newer, fairer socioeconomic order, "reform [policies] have brought about an irrational distribution of economic benefits" that favored the powerful and the privileged. "Each reform that involves the well-being of the great majority of Chinese has degenerated into a war involving the pillage of interests and wealth," Sun added. As an example, he cited housing reform in the 1990s and 2000s, which spawned unprecedented levels of wealth for the politically well-connected property developers—as well as untold millions of victims of land grabs.[20]

A 2012 study by a group of reform specialists at Tsinghua University also pointed out that China risked falling into a "trap of transformation." Referring to Deng Xiaoping's well-known dictum about reform being a process of "crossing the river while feeling for stones," the report said that even though China was, at best, halfway across the river, people in responsible positions "have lost the desire for making it to the other side." The report disputed perceptions that "reform has become more difficult because it has entered a deep-water zone." The crux of the matter, it said, was that "vested-interest groupings have emerged in the course of reform and transformation. . . . These groupings want to block further reforms. . . . They want the system in transition to coagulate and solidify—so that their interests can be preserved and maximized."[21]

## *The Party-State Apparatus Refuses to Cede the Initiative for Reform to the Market—or the People*

A large part of the difficulty of Xi-style reform is that he insists on a Leninist top-down approach, what he calls *dingceng shezhi* (top-level design). The reason the Xi-led Politburo established the Central Leading Group on Comprehensively Deepening Reform (CLGCDR) was to create a highly centralized command structure. Xi pointed out that reform involved "playing the piano with all ten fingers," meaning that detailed, thoroughgoing guidance and supervision from the Party-state apparatus was essential. This belies Xi's pledge in early 2013 that the success of reform hinged on "the massive liberation of society's creative energy." The president vowed at that time to "arouse the enthusiasm of various [social] sectors, boost to the utmost society's developmental vigor, and give full play to the masses' creativity."[22]

As discussed in Chapter 4, however, the establishment of the CLGCDR has added multiple layers of bureaucracy to the task of running the economy in general and implementing reform measures in particular. Yet neither Xi nor his public-relations experts have explained why the State Council alone—one of whose main tasks is designing and implementing economic reforms—should not be able to do the job. According to Wang Changjiang, a specialist on "Party construction" at the CCP CPS, the makeup of the CLGCDR is marred by conflicts of interest because cadres responsible for designing reforms are also those in charge of executing them. Professor Wang said it was better for relatively independent and neutral experts such as academics, think-tank members, and non-Party members to participate in the design of new measures. "At this stage, the CLGCDR comprises the heads of various departments and commissions," Wang said. "If problems arise, the same departments and commissions will be involved in [their solutions] . . . in such a way that the old road of the [self-serving] trading of vested interests will be repeated."[23]

The State Information Center expert Jiang Zhiyong contended that instead of following a top-heavy approach, the CCP leadership should let society play a bigger role in reform. The liberal official noted that a key to the success of reform was "handling well the relationship between the government and society." He added that, apart from curtailing interference in the market, central authorities "should interfere less in society and fully develop the functions of society [in implementing reform]."[24] Zhang Wenhui, a researcher at the Development Research Center of the State Council, agrees. "Practice in the past 30 years has shown that the wisdom and impulse of reform come from the grassroots," he said. "Delegating the power of reform to lower-level units is very important."[25]

Indeed, the experience of China's development since 1978 shows that it would be foolhardy to let the fate of reform rest on the mushrooming Party-state apparatus. Questions of inefficiency, procrastination, and, of course, corruption could derail particularly those reforms that will dramatically alter the way in which wealth is distributed. As the Fudan University economist Wei Sen argued, the chief task of reform is to address the absence of checks and balances regarding state author-ity. "If the problem of checks and balances of government power is not resolved, China may even go through a depression," he said.[26] Within the current leadership, Premier Li has stood out as the only cadre who has advocated some form of "small government, big market" and "small government, big society." As we discussed in Chapter 4, however, the pro-market inclinations of Premier Li have been curbed by the whiplash of a crypto-Maoist restoration masterminded by Xi.

The era of reform is replete with examples of how, owing mostly to the perpetu-ation of vested interests, the Party-state bureaucracy has repeatedly delayed reforms that are seen as urgent, ranging from the abolition of the *hukou* system to allowing private companies to enter sectors monopolized by SOE conglomerates.[27] Beijing has also been dragging its feet over other crucial socioeconomic—not to mention political—problems. Apart from the off-again, on-again crusade against real-estate profiteering, examples include the failure to replace the decades-long "petitions system" with legal aid so that disadvantaged citizens can settle their grievances through legal processes.[28]

Yet the one phenomenon whose resolution has persistently been put on the back burner is the "land grab," in which residents in urban and rural areas are evicted from their homes by real-estate companies in the absence of adequate compensation. In almost all cases, the developers are acting in cahoots with corrupt local officials. Land grabs, which account for some 60 percent of the riots and disturbances that break out every year, started in the late 1990s. However, the Party-and-state apparatus waited until 2011 to issue an administrative regulation against the illegal expropriation of land. As late as 2014, incidents in which peasants committed suicide or were killed in the course of a land grab were still frequently reported in the media.[29]

## The CCP's Feet of Clay: A Superpower with an Alarming "Civilization Deficit"

The CCP has a long tradition of valuing and promoting culture. Chairman Mao called his orgy of power struggle and wholesale degradation of morality the "Cultural Revolution," during which untold numbers of historical and contemporary works of art and literature were burned or otherwise destroyed. Ex-president Jiang Zemin's "Theory of the Three Represents" ordained that in order to survive in the twenty-first century, the CCP and its members must "represent the most advanced culture."[30] It is therefore not surprising the President Xi—who, like Mao, has a passion for classical Chinese learning—has an interest in boosting the cultural level of Chinese. A key thrust of the Decision on Major Issues Concerning Comprehensively Deepening Reforms (hereafter, Decision), which was released after the third plenum of the Eighteenth Central Committee in November 2013, was "pushing forward the innovation of the cultural system and mechanism."[31]

According to the Decision, the authorities committed themselves to "constructing a country with a strong socialist culture and strengthening cultural soft power." The Central Committee added that the Party must "uphold the progressive direction of socialist advanced culture, uphold a cultural developmental path [that is imbued with] socialism with Chinese characteristics, foster a socialist core value system, and consolidate the leading position of Marxism in the ideological arena." There is also a subsection on "perfecting cultural management structures," meaning that Party-and-state organs should be more efficient in promoting socialist culture and combating unwholesome, nonsocialist values.[32]

Judging by China's rich history and long civilization alone, the country will always be considered a cultural heavyweight. This perhaps underlies the fact that, in a project called "China Modernization Report 2009—A Study on Cultural Modernization," experts at the Chinese Academy of Sciences (CAS) put the PRC's cultural influence as No. 7 in the world, behind the United States, Germany, the UK, France, Italy, and Spain.[33] However, efforts in "cultural engineering" by the administrations of ex-president Hu and President Xi may not have been effective. As Wang Jisi put it, China has to understand that "soft power cannot be artificially created: Such influence originates more from a society than from a state."[34]

### Rejection of Global Values

President Xi has exacerbated the trend, which began during the Hu Jintao era, of saying "no" to universal values, particularly those that pertain to political and democratic principles. Hu warned against the danger of "going down the path of evil" if China were to adopt "Western" norms of governance.[35] Xi has gone even further in celebrating a kind of "Chinese exceptionalism": His version of the Chinese dream is that the great Chinese civilization can sail from triumph to triumph while spurning globally recognized principles and values, including those enshrined in various UN covenants (see Chapter 3).

President Xi has pointed out on numerous occasions that his administration will not adopt the "foreign method of all-out Westernization." "We must adopt a developmental path that is suitable to our characteristics," he pointed out, adding that this was due to "China's unique cultural heritage, unique history and fate, and unique national conditions." While vowing to follow the Maoist principle of converting foreign knowledge and tradition to meet China's specific needs, Xi noted that "our road [of development], theories, and systems have their clear-cut traits and obvious superiority. . . . Copying the West will only lead to indigestion and will definitely fail."[36]

The CCP administration's logic for dismissing universal values seems as fallacious as it is misleading. Because each country must follow a path that dovetails with its unique circumstances, it seems logical for Beijing to insist that it will not unthinkingly copy the experience of other countries. However, it cannot be denied that there are universal values and practices, such as freedom of expression, freedom of religion, rule of law, independence of the judiciary, and universal-suffrage elections that are respected—and transparent—not only in the West but in countries and regions not too far from China. Taiwan, Japan, and South Korea—which are all influenced by Confucianism and myriad kinds of "Oriental despotic" values—are only three examples of Asian countries and societies that have embraced "American" or Western values.[37]

Perhaps more important is the fact that a large number of liberal cadres and scholars are convinced that many political precepts and methods of governance can be applied universally. As mentioned in Chapter 3, Wen Jiabao made an impassioned plea for respecting and adopting values that all humankind is pursuing. Wen's argument was reminiscent of Deng Xiaoping's insistence that market mechanisms—as a universal principle—could be applied in both socialist and capitalist countries. "The market economy does not equal capitalism because you can also find the market economy in socialism," Deng said during his famous "southern tour" in 1992.[38] A form of this idea can even be found in the third plenum Decision of 2013, which said that the principle of "the market deciding resource allocation is a common law of market economics . . . [and] we must respect this law." In a mid-2013 talk with technological personnel, Xi pointed out that "science has no national boundaries."[39] It seems Xi is perfectly willing to recognize the universality of certain principles and phenomena—as long as they are not values such as democracy that would erode the CCP's stranglehold on power.

### The PRC's Exclusionism Is a First in Chinese History

Deng Xiaoping famously said that even as China's economy becomes integrated with that of the West, Beijing must keep out "the flies and mosquitoes," otherwise known as the "sugarcoated bullets of capitalism."[40] After the Cultural Revolution, the Tiananmen Square massacre could be considered a milestone in a protracted pogrom against "bourgeois-liberal values" that has culminated in the draconian and exclusionary measures adopted by Xi and his colleagues. Apart from censoring the Internet, Beijing has taken more heavy-handed measures to control the flow of information into China, including harassing the few hundred foreign correspondents based in Beijing, Shanghai, and other cities.[41]

The narrow-mindedness of CCP rule in general and the Xi administration in particular perhaps can be best gauged if we compare the current regime's lack of tolerance for Western ideas with dynastic China. Despite the fact that from the Han dynasty (206 B.C.E.–220 C.E.) onward, Chinese emperors and the cultural elite revered Confucianism as a failsafe guide to morality and the art of governance, both the aristocracy and men of letters of the Tang and Song dynasties were remarkably open-minded about exotic ideas, learning, and customs from the Western, Central Asian, and Middle Eastern traditions.[42]

China first earned the distinction as the "Middle Kingdom" during the Tang dynasty (618–907), when a hundred flowers bloomed. Underpinning the multisplendored development of Chinese civilization was the nobility and literati's passion for cross-pollination with different alien cultures. Buddhism, Islam, and other religions took root, often under the auspices of emperors. Gifted foreigners from Japan, Korea, Persia, and other realms not only lived happily in the capital, Chang'an, and other big cities but even became officials and generals. Some seventy-two foreign countries sent envoys to Chang'an. The Tang authorities even designed civil-service exams solely for the benefit of "new immigrants." Emperor Xuanzong (685–762) had this to say about interactions with the outside world: "Coexistence is the fairest path, and collaboration is the essence of peace."[43]

Also consider the case of the Song dynasty (960–1279), which seemed to pale beside the Tang in terms of strength and global influence. Song emperors frequently promoted communication with foreign countries by sending emissaries overseas to seek dialogue as well as business opportunities. According to *Song shi* (History of the Song), Emperor Taizong (939–997) dispatched eight envoys to the islands of the South Seas in an attempt not only to purchase foreign goods but also to promote cultural and diplomatic ties.[44] The contemporary historian Xiao Jianshan argued that the Song represented "the apex of ancient Chinese civilization." Historical evidence showed, Xiao said, "a free and open country marked by an active and healthy multifaceted society."[45] Quanzhou, a coastal city in modern-day Fujian Province, was in the 1110s designated a center for commerce with some thirty-five countries. By the 1270s, as many as 300,000 foreigners lived in the city. Language schools were set up to allow foreigners to learn Chinese and the Chinese to study the foreign tongues. It was also during the Song dynasty that a large number of Jews living in China became Sinicized.[46]

Perhaps due in part to the fact that the rulers of the Qing dynasty were Manchus and not Han Chinese, they continued the tradition of earlier dynasties of being relatively unbiased toward Western learning. Missionaries, scientists, and other learned foreigners were recruited into imperial service. The German Jesuit and noted astronomer Johann Adam Schall von Bell became director of the Imperial Observatory and the Tribunal of Mathematics under Emperor Shenzhi (1638–1661). Ferdinand Verbiest (1623–1688), a Belgian Jesuit scholar, was made a personal adviser to Emperor Kangxi (1654–1722) in astronomy and other sciences. The British consular official Robert Hart (1835–1911), who helped the throne design a modern customs service, was among the foreigner-mandarins of the late Qing period.[47] After China's humiliating defeat at the hands of the British in the Opium War of 1840, reformist nobles and ministers thought seriously of following the example of Japan's Meiji reforms in 1868. These Westernization efforts culminated in Emperor Guangxu's Hundred Days' Reform of 1898, which was unfortunately crushed by Empress Dowager Cixi. Avant-garde intellectuals of the era, including Kang Youwei and Liang Qichao, laid the foundation for the 1919 May Fourth movement, whose slogan was "Let's introduce Mr. Sai [science] and Mr. De [democracy] to China."[48]

China was cut off from the West for much of Mao's reign. During the era of reform started by Deng Xiaoping in 1978, several top cadres were keen students of Western economics and governance. Zhao Ziyang was an unabashed supporter of market-oriented economics.[49] After his fall from grace in the wake of the Tiananmen Square crackdown, Zhao was criticized by the conservatives for his meeting in 1988 with Milton Friedman, during which Zhao lavished praise on the work of the Nobel laureate. A year earlier, Zhao gave approval for George Soros to set up a branch of the Open Society Foundation in Beijing.[50]

After the June 4, 1989, crackdown, Beijing became even more paranoid about the spread of "bourgeois-liberal ideas" in China. The official verdict of the 1989 student movement was that it was a conspiracy of "hostile forces outside China" to overturn the CCP with the help of intellectuals, who had succumbed to blandishments from the West. Jiang Zemin, however, was knowledgeable if not appreciative of global norms. Because he attended college before 1949, his English was reasonably good. During his visit to Washington, DC, in October 1997, the then-President Bill Clinton showed him a copy of Abraham Lincoln's Gettysburg Address. Jiang immediately recited the first sentence in English.[51] Zhu Rongji was educated in part by American professors at Tsinghua University before 1949. He played a key role in expediting China's accession to the WTO. In 2001, Zhu broke with tradition by hiring a Chinese-American lawyer, Laura Cha, for the post of vice-chairperson of the China Securities Regulatory Commission (CSRC).[52] Xi's overall hostility toward Western values appears all the more jarring when compared to the commitment of his predecessors Jiang and Zhu to learning from the West.

### The CCP's Self-Serving Revival of Ancient Culture and Beliefs

Since the end of the Cultural Revolution, the Chinese government has tried to revive ancient Chinese wisdom—mainly Confucianism, Buddhism, and Daoism—so as to fill the spiritual vacuum of citizens who have lost faith in communism. The socialist regime's resuscitation of Confucianism parallels efforts by Singapore's Lee Kuan Yew in the 1980s to revive Confucian teachings such as filial piety and respect for authority.[53]

Ex-president Jiang pronounced in the mid-1990s that the three centuries-old beliefs were representative of *guocui* (the essence of national wisdom) that should be taught in schools and propagated in society. The establishment of several hundred Confucius Institutes overseas testifies to the newfound respect that supposedly "anti-feudalist" Communist leaders have accorded the pillar of traditional Chinese learning.[54] Many policies of Jiang as well as Hu Jintao have clear-cut Confucian roots. This is particularly true of measures aimed at boosting the qualifications of cadres as well as the Party's relationship with the people. Jiang in 2001 put forward the doctrine of "running the country according to moral values."[55] That the ruler should try to win over the populace through moral acts and policies is a well-known Confucian doctrine. And in the mid-2000s, Hu unveiled his ambitious goal of nurturing a "harmonious society," which is a distinctively Confucian ideal.[56] According to the U.S.-based historian Ying-shih Yu, the CCP establishment is "sloughing off Mao Zedong Thought and making a move toward [adopting] Confucianism, even though it will not admit this openly." Yu saw the revival of Confucianism as a "cultural strategy as well as a means of boosting control" over intellectuals and citizens.[57]

Most nonofficial intellectuals do not see an insurmountable contradiction between Confucianism and liberalism even though a popular slogan during the May Fourth movement was "Smash the Confucius Shop." A number of Confucian scholars inside and outside China have chosen to focus on the liberal, even pro-democracy, teachings of Confucius, such as this famous dictum: "Water supports a ship—but it can also overturn the vessel." For example, the Fudan University philosopher Bai Tongdong does not think that Confucianism and liberalism have irreconcilable differences. "Confucians have, apart from the functions of the political elite, consistently stressed the importance of the will of the people," he argued. "Ideally, Confucian politics is one that encourages the participation of both elite and popular opinion."[58]

President Xi, however, seems bent on following his predecessors in exploiting anything in Confucianism that could bolster regime legitimacy. In a nationally televised visit to the temple in Confucius's home at Qufu, Shandong Province, in late 2013, Xi noted that "the Chinese race has a long-running traditional culture, and our people can definitely create new heights for Chinese civilization." He urged scholars at the site to adopt a utilitarian approach to fostering Confucian studies. "We should use the old to serve the modern and keep the elixir while discarding the dross . . . so that Confucianism can provide positive contributions" to twenty-first-century China, Xi indicated. Speaking at the 2,565th birthday of Confucius in September 2014, Xi vowed that Chinese Communists—being "faithful inheritors of China's superior traditional culture"—will definitely embrace love of peace and other time-tested values of Confucianism.[59]

Because of his father's friendship with Buddhist monks, including the Dalai Lama (b. 1935) and the Panchen Lama (1938–1989), Xi had early exposure to Buddhism. One of his most famous sayings on the art of being a good cadre is: "Do not get too cozy with businessmen; you can only get to a high level [of learning] when you meditate before the wall and become a Buddha."[60] Yet following the Party's long-standing tradition of using religion as a "united front" tool for promoting national cohesiveness under CCP leadership, most of Xi's instructions regarding Buddhism relate to preventing Tibetan Buddhism from fueling separatist sentiments in Tibet. While speaking at a Buddhist function in Tibet in 2011, the then-vice-president pointed out that "we hope religious personalities will propagate the superior patriotic tradition of Tibetan Buddhism." He added that, apart from pursuing religious studies, Buddhists should "enthusiastically take up their social responsibility and self-consciously uphold national unification and the unity of the nationalities."[61] Increasing state interference in the monasteries has resulted in at least 200 self-immolations by monks and nuns who saw no future in the freedom of religion in the Tibetan Autonomous Region and Tibetan counties in neighboring provinces.[62]

While seeming to be anxious about reviving traditional Chinese culture, the CCP authorities have failed to preserve the rich heritage that is fast slipping away in the countryside despite the fact that according to the twelfth FYP, 700 museums every year should be built mostly in urban areas particularly for the purpose of showcasing the fruits of ancient Chinese civilization. However, the majority of the recently constructed museums have remained empty.[63] According to a recent cataloguing project undertaken by the government, China boasts 9,700 examples of "intangible cultural heritage," which includes traditions and art forms such as songs, dances, rituals, martial arts, cuisines, and theater. About 80 percent of these heirlooms are located in rural areas. Under the whiplash of urbanization and relentless property development, however, villages have disappeared in the past decade at the rate of about 300 a day. Equally damaging to local culture is the exodus of young men and women to the cities. "Chinese culture has traditionally been rural-based," says Feng Jicai, a well-known author and scholar. "Once the villages are gone, the culture is gone."[64]

## Reasons Why China Is a World Power Without a World-Class Culture

### *The "Nobel Prize Complex" and the State Sponsorship of Talent*

In late 2012, CCP leaders finally got what they had spent enormous resources to attain: a Nobel Prize awarded to a member of the establishment. Mo Yan, a novelist renowned for his colorful and idiosyncratic use of language, received the Nobel Prize for literature. The Swedish Academy citation said that "through a mixture of fantasy and reality, Mo Yan has created a world reminiscent in its complexity of those in the writings of William Faulkner and Gabriel Garcia Marquez."[65] What has emerged as the Mo Yan phenomenon, however, is emblematic of the failure of the Chinese system to nurture world-class talents who dare to challenge orthodox values.

After much prodding from the Western and Hong Kong media, not long after receiving the prize Mo indicated that he hoped Liu Xiaobo would be freed. But he refused to sign a petition calling for his release, which prompted Salman Rushdie to call Mo "a patsy of the regime." During the awards ceremony in Stockholm, Mo even defended censorship, saying it was necessary to curb rumors and defamation.[66] In his Nobel lecture as well as interviews with the media, Mo focused on the traditional art of story-telling in rural China. He made no comments on Chinese politics except to say in a circumspect way that literature should not be involved with politics. Ai Weiwei, the well-known artist and dissident had this to say about Mo's behavior: "Mo Yan's talk about story telling is about covering things up and hiding. . . . it was powerless, disgraceful, a betrayal and a sellout."[67]

That Mo did not want to be seen as challenging the CCP is easy to understand. He is a long-standing CCP member as well as a vice-chairman of the China's Writers' Association (CWA), whose goal is to ensure that China's writers make "positive contributions" to socialism with Chinese characteristics. On the occasion of the seventieth anniversary of Mao Zedong's infamous "Talks at the Yan'an Forum on Literature and Art" (see below), the Party-controlled CWA asked a hundred well-known authors and intellectuals to hand-copy the Mao text, which was later published in a special anniversary edition. Writers who took part in this task included Mo, former minister of culture Wang Meng, and Tie Ying, chairwoman of the CWA and a member of the CCP Central Committee.[68]

A look at Beijing's "strategic plan" to nurture world-class academics and professionals—in particular, potential Nobel prizewinners—has exposed the CCP's problematic attitude toward raising the quality of human resources. According to a late 2013 report in the *Global Times,* the CCP Central Coordinating Group on Talent-Related Work (CCGTW), Party and government agencies as well as research and academic institutions were tasked with identifying and nurturing 10,000 "talents," particularly in the fields of science and technology. Special subsidies in terms of salaries and research funding would be given to these high-caliber personnel. Most interestingly, the CCGTW has set about identifying 100 top researchers and professors "with the capacity to breach the Nobel threshold." Although the official media has not disclosed either the names of these "potential Nobel prizewinners" or the funds that the government is making available to them, it is clear that Beijing is following the time-honored top-down approach in what might be called human-resources engineering.[69]

Ample independent studies, however, have demonstrated that this quintessentially Soviet approach to propagating scientists and researchers might succumb to bureaucratic malaise—and corruption (see Chapter 4). Government-sponsored talent programs have a much lower chance of success in fields that demand original thinking: These range from the humanities and social sciences to the performing arts and IT. Much has been written about the Chinese quasi-miracle in engineering huge numbers of Olympic medalists within a relatively short time. Western experts have pointed out that the Chinese sports establishment has successfully incorporated the "East German model" in producing sports champions.[70] Although compared to aspiring writers, economists, or scientists, sports aces might derive substantial benefit from state-enforced regimentation, a number of notable cases have demonstrated that the Chinese approach can also militate against the emergence of world-class athletes.

A ferocious battle between the tennis champion Li Na and Beijing's sports establishment has struck a chord among not only athletes but also other professionals who have raged against the tight leash of state sponsorship. Unable to withstand what she considered the hypocrisy and demeaning political demands of the Party-run All-China Sports Association (ACSA) and its affiliates, Li left the official Chinese team in 2004 and struck out on her own. She won the French Open in 2010 and the Australian Open in 2014. The famously willful Li had this to say about her breaking away from the state sports bureaucracy. "Having spent so much time in [official] sports circles, I have seen too much ugliness and shame," she wrote in 2012. Citing what a sports apparatchik had told her—"without our national sports system, you will go hungry"—Li said: "I am not yet 30, but I have experienced [the vicissitudes] of a 60-year-old."[71]

### *The Dubious Quality of Chinese Institutes of Learning*

#### *Universities Handicapped by "Academic Corruption"*

Chinese scientists and technology personnel have attained stunning breakthroughs in areas including supercomputers, missiles, and space exploration. Yet China excels mainly in what experts call Soviet-style innovation, which is based on strong government funding and guidance, as well as the cross-pollination of civilian and military research and development (see Chapter 4).

The standards of Chinese institutes of learning, however, are not commensurate with a country that is both a quasi-superpower and a follower of Confucian educational ethos. First, the government's tight control of the universities has stifled original thinking among both educators and students. According to the vice-president of the China Metallurgical University, Jiang Yaodong, "China has only one university—the Education Ministry University—and we are all its branches," he said. "Unless universities rid themselves of bureaucracy, there is no way that college education can work."[72]

Apart from excessive control, education standards have been degraded by malpractice, such as plagiarism and influence peddling. Experts at Wuhan University estimated that the "industry" of plagiarism, fabricated research, and fake journals was worth $150 million in 2009, as much as five times more than just two years earlier. It is not uncommon for professors even at the top-ranked universities to practically offer master's and doctorates to senior cadres, whose theses are often written by their personal secretary and other hired hands.[73] Other favored modus operandi are for thesis advisers to pay their junior colleagues or research students to compile the dissertation for these VIP graduate students. Perhaps the most discussed incident of this nature is President Xi's dissertation, "A Tentative Study on China's Rural Marketization," which earned him a Doctor of Laws degree from Tsinghua University in 2002. The *Sunday Times* of London quoted Chinese experts as saying that the 161-page thesis "appeared to combine extracts from government reports with translations from foreign works in a leaden Marxist style, suggesting it was drafted by a group and finalized by the author."[74]

To a significant extent, the quality—and authenticity—of papers published by Chinese academics has been called into question. China ranks second behind the United States in the number of papers published every year in domestic and foreign academic journals. Yet the large number of papers based on dishonest or fraudulent research has raised eyebrows. In 2010, the respected British medical journal *Lancet* took the unusual step of publicly calling on authorities in Beijing to intervene. "China's government must assume stronger leadership in scientific integrity," *Lancet* said, citing dozens of suspect papers that Chinese academics had submitted to the journal.[75]

The Harvard mathematician Shing-tung Yau, who has been active in helping to set up math centers at Chinese universities, is highly critical of what he called "academic corruption." "This is serious enough to keep the development of China's advanced science from success," he said in 2010. Yau contended that "academic corruption," which was unique to China, was more serious than mere plagiarism or fraud, as it includes using unethical means to secure awards, degrees, research grants, and promotions, as well as covering up for academic counterfeiters. "The problem is that those who are found to plagiarize and cheat don't get punished," he added in an interview with *China Daily.* "How can others be persuaded not to [do the same]?"[76] Lin Songqing, a researcher at the CAS, agreed. "Academic corruption is gradually eroding the marvelous and well-established culture that our ancestors left for us 5,000 years ago," wrote Lin in *Learned Publishing,* a British-based journal.[77]

Many academics seem to be bending over backward to prove their patriotic credentials, especially senior professors and top administrators. Take, for example, the president of Peking University (Beida), Zhou Qifeng. The acclaimed chemist and member of the prestigious CAS caused a stir during a talk a few years ago to high school students from his native Hunan Province. When asked to compare Chinese universities to those in the United States, Zhou asserted that "American education is in a mess. . . . U.S. presidents just do not know how to respect other people. . . . Every American president is bent on imposing his views on other people."[78] Zhou's views came across as relatively moderate when compared to those of Professor Kong Qingdong, a "neo-leftist" in the Chinese Language Department at Beida. While making comments on a TV program about the frequency with which Hong Kong citizens criticize the "uncivilized" and occasionally illegal activities of tourists from the mainland, Kong blurted out: "Hong Kong people are dogs." Pointing to the fact that mainland tourists are essential to propping up the Hong Kong economy, the professor added that residents of Hong Kong are "disgraceful and ungrateful."[79]

Peking University, of course, also boasts liberal professors who are critical of the regime. But they know that the price for carrying out a professor's social responsibility is often outright dismissal. Consider the case of economics professor Xia Yeliang, who often talks to the foreign and overseas Chinese press about the failings of the Chinese government. In mid-2013, he was fired by the university on account of his "consistently low scores" in internal assessments of his teaching. Xia, however, indicated that the real reason was that he did not buckle under to pressure from the Party committee at Beida to stop bad-mouthing the government. He told the Western media that the Party secretary at the School of Economics had scolded him immediately before his dismissal. "You could make suggestions and recommendations, and we can send them to the leaders," Xia recalled being told. "But you don't have to say it this way in public. This is ruining the image of the Party and the government."[80] The phenomenon of freethinking professors being lectured to by commissars based at their universities—and even fired—is a common occurrence.

*Overall Educational Standards Are Still a Big Problem*

In 2012 at the Program for International Student Assessment (PISA) organized by the OECD, junior high school students in Shanghai ranked first in the world in reading, mathematics, and science. By contrast, the UK and the United States ranked, respectively, 26th and 36th among students from sixty-five countries. Shanghai schools were exceptional not only for the high quality of teachers and equipment but also the "strong drive and self-belief of students," according to PISA expert Andreas Schleicher.[81]

However, Shanghai is not China. Data from the Rural Education Action Program (REAP) at Stanford University provides a stark picture of how Shanghai's education success is not being replicated in China's less wealthy interior. Although 84 percent of high school graduates in Shanghai go to college, less than 5 percent of the rural poor do the same. In the 1970s, 50 percent of first-year students at Tsinghua University, President Xi's alma mater, were from relatively impoverished regions, according to Yang Dongping at the Beijing Institute of Technology. In 2010, that figure was down to 17 percent. High school attendance is just 40 percent in much of China's agrarian hinterland.[82]

Jiang Xueqin, currently the deputy principal of Tsinghua University High School, pointed out that "kids in the rural regions are at a huge disadvantage. . . . Teachers and schools are under-resourced." This is compounded by the fact that it is common for parents in rural areas to move to work in the cities, leaving their children behind in the villages to be taken care of by poorly educated grandparents. This has resulted in a severe shortage of parental support and guidance. "Students in rural schools are subject to a lot of cultural stigma," Jiang said. "No one in China believes they will succeed."[83] According to figures provided by the All-China Women's Foundation, 61 million "left-behind" children—one in five nationally—grow up without one or both of their parents. A disproportionately high percentage of these underprivileged children do not go to school—and are easily recruited by criminal gangs that are active in the countryside.[84]

In theory, China has accomplished the goal, first laid down in 1993, of spending 4 percent of GDP on education. However, the quality of education for rural children is vastly inferior to that in the big cities. In Beijing, for example, in 2011, annual expenditure per primary school pupil was about RMB 20,000 compared with a mere RMB 3,000 in Henan, an agricultural province in Central China.[85] One of the reasons for this yawning gap is that the responsibility of funding rural schools falls on local administrations, at least one-quarter of which are either bankrupt or close to it. The result is that regional officials often levy illegal "education charges" on farming households. This is why free education for nine years—which is enshrined in the Chinese constitution—is not observed in agrarian provinces such as Guizhou, Guangxi, Ningxia, Qinghai, and Gansu.[86]

### The Alarming Decline of Morality

Compared to education, the state of morality in China is perhaps even more significant for the future of the country—particularly given the fact that the country is affecting the world in more ways than one. President Xi has cited morality as a basic "core value of socialism with Chinese characteristics. . . . We must provide guidance to the people on paying attention to morality, respecting morality, abiding by morality, and pursuing the ideal of lofty morality."[87] The

CCP authorities, however, are at least partly responsible for the alarming morality deficit in Chinese society.

The series of calamities caused by Mao—which climaxed in the Cultural Revolution—created the PRC's first "lost generation." Schooling was disrupted by the Great Leap Forward and, of course, the Great Famine. Universities and high schools nationwide were largely closed during the years of the Cultural Revolution—and did not reopen until 1979. Since the 1980s Chinese students have been subjected to intensive "patriotic education," which, according to liberal intellectuals, is responsible for the closing of the Chinese mind.[88] According to the historian Yuan Weishi, the cumulative aberrations of the Party and the fact that there was no opposition among the intelligentsia to Mao's erroneous policies have produced generations of Chinese who "grew up drinking wolf's milk." "So-called wolf's milk refers to the extreme nationalism and [efforts to] render class struggle absolute and one-sided" in the polity, the Zhongshan University professor explained. Yuan argued that, in addition to providing the basis for authoritarianism, this phenomenon will "prevent China from absorbing the advanced culture of the world."[89]

A good example of "wolf's milk civilization" is the celebration of "war culture" by General Liu Yuan, Xi's princeling crony who is political commissar of the PLA General Logistics Department. Liu argued in a controversial 2010 article that war culture "has crystallized the most time-honored and most critical intelligence of mankind. . . . We should harbor a devout heart and a worshipper's fealty toward war and the actors in warfare. . . . They are just too splendid, too great!"[90] Within the military establishment, Liu's views were a worthy precursor of Xi's theory that "combat power is the only and fundamental criterion" for the army. In the broader universe of discourse of Chinese society, however, Liu's apparent glorification of naked power and Machiavellianism could exacerbate the already serious tendencies toward amorality in Chinese society.

By the turn of the century a severe decline of morality among ordinary Chinese had become evident. In the wake of the death of communism with the turn to more market-oriented economics, more Chinese have taken up the worship of money. Even the state media have deplored the "integrity deficit" that has plagued not only the business world but ordinary social interactions. A 2002 report by the official media indicated that a lack of *chengxin* (integrity or honesty) was responsible for economic losses of RMB 585 billion a year, including not only unsettled "triangular debts" incurred by unscrupulous business and irresponsible government agencies but also the prevalence of counterfeit products and migrant workers not being paid by employers. Although no such surveys have been conducted since the early 2000s, *chengxin*-related crimes committed in cyberspace have presumably soared given the exponential growth of e-commerce.[91]

The *chengxin* calamity has also affected the quality of life of even the middle and professional classes. Much has been written about the profusion of counterfeit wine, medicine, infant formula, and other food and beverages in China, to the point that well-off consumers drink only imported water and buy infant formula in Hong

Kong or overseas.[92] Much more alarming is the fact that farmers, growers of pigs and chickens as well as breeders of pond fish, shrimp, and crabs, routinely use huge amounts of chemicals, including growth hormones and antibiotics to cut costs and speed up production. In an article widely circulated online in early 2014, the internationally acclaimed agriculture specialist Yuan Longping wrote: "Is it really true that what we eat is okay? Rational considerations tell us that big problems have already arisen, and that it has become difficult to redress [the trend]."[93]

Consider the horrific state of the medical profession throughout China. Despite the fact that hospital and clinic fees are in many cities as expensive as those in Hong Kong or Taiwan, patients routinely pay bribes to medical professionals to ensure that they can get the "best treatment." Many doctors and administrators, however, have to hire bodyguards due to the increase in the number of disgruntled patients beating up—and, in some cases, maiming or killing—medical professionals out of a belief that they have been cheated. In early 2014, the Chinese Medical Doctors' Association, the Chinese Medical Association, the Chinese Hospital Association, and the China Health Law Society issued a joint appeal to patients to stop resorting to violence and, instead, use legal and civilized methods to air their grievances against the medical system.[94]

Yet another manifestation of the rising tide of amorality in Chinese society is the lack of human feelings that people display toward one another. Chinese seem to have lost what Mencius called *cerenzhixin* (an inborn compassion for one's neighbors who are in dire straits). Cases of onlookers doing nothing upon seeing people drowning in rivers and lakes—or victims of car accidents receiving no help from passersby—have become so routine they rarely make the front pages. Only extreme instances of callousness can make commentators wring their hands at the alarming compassion deficit in Chinese society. Take, for example, what happened to two-year-old Yueyue, a resident of Foshan, Guangdong Province, on October 13, 2011, when she was knocked down by a truck. Footage from a nearby security camera revealed that for the next seven minutes, eighteen passersby pretended not to see the critically injured infant lying in the street. By the time a shabby ragpicker finally came to her rescue, Yueyue had been run over a second time by another vehicle. Yueyue died in a nearby hospital eight days later, by which time the Chinese Google site had registered more than 8 million hits regarding the incident. Xu Qingqing, a commentator for the state-run China News Service, called for a "moral enlightenment movement" to ameliorate the "shabby aspects of the Chinese psyche."[95]

There is, of course, no shortage of philanthropists in the world's second-largest economy. Consider billionaire Chen Guangbiao, a PR-savvy CEO of recycling factories who became known internationally in 2014 after he expressed an interest in buying a $1 billion stake in the *New York Times*. (The *Times'* proprietors said "no thanks.") Over the past decade, the Chinese, Taiwan, and Hong Kong press have given Chen abundant coverage every time he put on a charity show. In 2010, Chen built a "wall of money" out of huge stacks of 100-renminbi bills before donating the funds to poor peasants from Guizhou, Sichuan, and Yunnan Provinces. A year later, Chen stopped traffic in Taipei when he handed out red envelopes—reportedly totaling $250,000—to the needy who had queued up for hours to receive his largesse. The flamboyant do-gooder was so successful with PR that even his business card attracted global coverage because he identified himself on it as the "Most influential person of China"; "Most charismatic philanthropist of China"; "China moral leader"; "Most well-known and beloved China role model"; "China earthquake rescue hero," and so forth.[96]

### Key Factors Behind the Retrogression of Chinese Culture

#### Dangxing vs. Individualism: Citizens as Cogs in the Socialist Machine

Perhaps the most undemocratic aspect of Maoism is that it not only consigns every Chinese to the role of a slave of the Party machinery but also insists that all knowledge be politically correct and in service to the regime. Following Marx and Lenin, Mao indicated that every person has a "class nature." The goal of the Party-state apparatus is to ensure that citizens—particularly those who belong to "black categories" such as capitalists and bourgeois-liberal intellectuals—undergo self-transformation until they have acquired a bona fide "proletarian class nature." Mao also demanded that not only CCP members but all Chinese should acquire the requisite *dangxing* (Party nature), meaning that their thoughts, goals, and aspirations should all be for the sake of the Party.[97]

In his infamous "Talks at the Yan'an Forum on Literature and Art" in May 1942, the Great Helmsman argued that the triumph of *dangxing* would "curtail 'individualism,' 'heroism,' or anarchy" among less committed Party members.[98] The corollary of this insistence on "pure upon pure *dangxing*" is that every Party cadre and member should be transformed—through brainwashing and other means—into a figure like Lei Feng, an altruistic proletariat lionized by Mao in the 1950s.

Mao also underscored the fact that the *dangxing* theory applied to all kinds of knowledge. He admonished proletarian writers and artists to "take the stand of the Party, take the stand of *dangxing* and the Party's policies." According to Mao, art—and other forms of knowledge and expertise—has no innate self-sufficiency: It must serve the higher cause of the revolution. "There is in fact no such thing as art for art's sake, art that stands above classes, or art that is detached from or independent of politics. . . . Proletarian literature and art are part of the whole proletarian revolutionary cause; they are, as Lenin said, cogs and wheels in the whole revolutionary machine."[99] This ethos applied to intellectuals of different backgrounds and sectors as well as their specialized knowledge. Since knowledge—and what goes through people's minds—must dovetail with *dangxing*, it is not surprising that Mao devised all sorts of thought control techniques to help CCP members and even ordinary citizens get rid of politically suspect ideas. As Mao put it in another speech during the Yan'an era, there are many fully registered CCP members "who in their thoughts have not fully joined the Party—or who have not joined the Party at all." He pointed out that the brains of these unqualified members were full of *zang dongxi* (dirty things), such as those of the exploitative classes.[100]

Mao's fans included President Xi, who has endorsed many of the tyrant's most insidious proclivities. Xi gave strong reaffirmation to the *dangxing* theory in his August 19, 2013, talk to cadres in charge of ideology and propaganda, pointing out unequivocally that "*dangxing* and *renminxing* [the nature of the people] have always been uniform and unified. . . . Upholding *dangxing* means upholding the nature of the people. . . . There is no *dangxing* that is alienated from the nature of the people, and similarly there is no nature of the people that has forsaken *dangxing*."[101] In other words, ideas and aspirations of the people that do not align with the Party's interests must be banished (see Chapter 3). The Marxist theorist Yang Faxiang even claimed that *dangxing* is superior to *renminxing* or *renxing* (human nature). "*Dangxing* serves as guidance to social development and is acquired and followed by advanced members of society," Yang claimed. "People with high-quality *renxing* may not qualify to be a superior Party member, yet those with high-quality *dangxing* must necessarily evince *renxing*."[102]

Xi also wants Party authorities to ensure that all branches of learning—and their impact on individuals' thinking—must serve the cause of the revolution. First, knowledge as discussed in schools and the media must be politically above reproach. Even more importantly, schools, newspapers, the Internet and people's thoughts are *zhendi* (battlegrounds) that the ideological police must oversee and correct. "If we do not occupy the *zhendi*, other people will do so," Xi said. He divides knowledge and thinking into three categories: red, black, and gray. Ideas and inclinations that are red, or politically correct, should be safeguarded by censors and commissars. "Black" areas refer to information and knowledge that have been corrupted by Western standards. "We must be bold enough to lay siege to black terrain and gradually implement a change of colors," Xi said. As for gray areas, Xi's recommendation is to turn them red—and prevent them from degenerating into black. In a genuflection to Mao's totalitarian views on "ideology and thought work," Xi told propaganda cadres in early 2014 that the Party's mass-education campaigns must be so thorough and all-enveloping that "core socialist values"—shorthand for patriotism, loyalty to the Party leadership, and undying support for Chinese-style socialism—"should be as ubiquitous as the air."[103] As we shall see, Xi also aims to be as effective as Mao in exterminating "dirty things" in the minds of the unfaithful.

Despite Xi's claim to be a disciple of Deng Xiaoping, there is a fundamental difference between the two leaders in terms of epistemology and worldview. It is true that Deng was adamant about Party members heeding the "Four Cardinal Principles" of socialism and CCP leadership. Yet at least before the Tiananmen Square crackdown, Deng adopted an open-minded—and near-heretical—approach to theories and doctrines, including how to run the economy and society. Unlike Xi, who stresses that everything must be conceived and executed using *dangxing* as a measure, Deng advocated the famous "doctrine of the noninsistence of surnames." This variation of the "two cats theory" meant that when the Party evaluates goals and policies, it should not be bogged down by arguments as to whether they are "surnamed socialist or surnamed capitalist." All that matters is whether the goals and policies in question are capable of producing beneficial results.[104] Using Deng's figure of speech, Xi would have second thoughts about economic and social policies that were "surnamed capitalist."

### *The CCP's Historical Opportunism*

While talking to the media in New York in early 2014, Cui Jian, China's best-known rock singer, said about his country: "As long as the Mao Zedong portrait still hangs over the Tiananmen Square rostrum, times have not changed. . . . The Cultural Revolution still rages on," Cui indicated.[105]

Leaders ranging from Deng Xiaoping to Xi Jinping have milked the Mao legacy to prop up the CCP's legitimacy (see Chapter 3). There is, however, a big price to pay. The maintenance of the Party's mandate of heaven hinges on what critics have called historical amorality or nihilism, which has led to the hiding, molding, and whitewashing of the many mistakes by the CCP, from China's entry to the Korean War to the Tiananmen Square massacre. After all, the Machiavellian use of information and propaganda—including self-serving interpretations of history—is one of the three key factors that have underpinned the CCP's success. (The other two are naked force—"power grows out of the barrel of the gun"—and united front tactics.) Following Mao, President Xi thinks that history has a "class nature and *dangxing*." This means that, first, only historical knowledge that accords with the Party's goals should be taught in schools and talked about in the media. Second, the Party is more than justified in deleting, whitewashing or repackaging past events.[106]

In a 2010 lecture on compiling and doing research on the history of the Party, the then-vice-president Xi pointed out that historians must "uphold the synthesis of *dangxing* and the scientific nature of historiography."[107] This essentially meant that the study, teaching, and overall dissemination of historical ideas and knowledge must be in sync with the Party's interests. By "scientific," Xi meant "the scientific nature of the laws of China's social movements"—not "scientific methodology," as is understood in the Western social sciences tradition. While marking Mao's 120th birthday in December 2013, Leng Rong contended that scholars must "uphold an all-around and correct view of history and provide a scientific assessment of Mao Zedong as well as Party history." Leng, who is the director of the CCP Archives Research Office, said the Party's conclusions on Mao's contributions and other major historical events had demonstrated the CCP's "resolute political stand and clear-cut political attitude."[108]

According to the veteran political commissar Shi Zhongquan, although academics and Party cadres should adopt a "seek truth from facts" approach to historiography, it is clear that the CCP favors a kind of historical opportunism: Suppress whatever is not conducive to building up the Party's glorious image.[109] Zhu Xueqin, a liberal historian at Shanghai University, argued that "history books used in schools and universities have distorted history. . . . Students who grow up studying these books are equivalent to those who have consumed wolf's milk all their lives."[110] Beijing has never followed the global norm about the declassification of official documents twenty-five to thirty years after a particular event has elapsed. Even archives going back to the early 1950s—for example, those relating to Chairman Mao's decision to participate in the Korean War—are still classified as confidential or "state secrets." A collective amnesia has been imposed with regard to the Tiananmen Square massacre. Although individual textbooks or articles in the official press might make brief references to the "turmoil" of 1989, the emphasis was on "bad elements" in society challenging the Party with the help of "hostile foreign forces."[111]

The meager official accounts of the Three Years of Famine (1958–61) offer perhaps the best examples of the CCP's strategic distortion of history. Most official accounts of the famine attributed the disaster to the weather—and not to the erroneous policies of Mao and his ultraleftist colleagues. Indeed, the official term for the famine remains the "Three Years of Natural Disasters."[112] And even though well-respected scholars in China and the West, such as Yang Jisheng and Frank Dikötter, have pointed out in their books that at least 36 million people perished in the manmade catastrophe, CCP officials have yet to reveal the official casualty figures. So far, only cadres with great stature, such as Yuan Longping, have openly talked about the millions of farmers who perished in what some describe as "the Chinese holocaust."[113]

Officially sanctioned distortions of past events are also evidenced by CCP accounts of the controversial Anti-Rightist movement (1957–59). Official reports that some 550,000 intellectuals were labeled rightist (or anti-Party elements) were not too far off the mark. The well-known blogger Han Han, however, disputed the CCP's theory that the Anti-Rightist movement was justified because there were indeed "people who are going against the Party and socialism." The Party, therefore, would say only that while it may have erred in labeling so many intellectuals as rightists, central authorities were absolutely right in launching the political campaign to get rid of them. Han's comment was that this peculiar "Chinese logic"—"[the interests of] political parties and ideologies overriding people's lives and rights"—was inhumane in the extreme.[114]

It is a testimony to the skills of censors and spin doctors that such a well-documented event as the Cultural Revolution could have been swept under the carpet despite the fact that, since the late 2000s, several high-profile former Red Guards who are princelings—including Chen Xiaolu and Song Binbin, respectively the son and daughter of Party elder Chen Yi and Song Renqiong—have issued public apologies for their activities during that period.[115] Yet CCP authorities have shied away from thorough acts of atonement, such as building a museum to record the barbaric acts that were committed. As Yu Hua put it, "In the immediate aftermath of the Cultural Revolution, many sought to repudiate it, but when our leaders realized that this kind of critique detracted from their own authority, they immediately suppressed such criticisms." The post-1980s generation has little means to find out what really happened. "In June 2012, members of the graduating class of Central China Normal University in Wuhan took a graduation photo, all dressed in Red Guard uniforms," wrote Yu. "To these young people, the Cultural Revolution seems to have been nothing more than one huge party."[116]

The Xi administration's nihilistic attitude toward history is best illustrated by the unprecedented steps taken by the security apparatus to prevent intellectuals from doing anything—including totally private gatherings in homes or restaurants—to mark the twenty-fifth anniversary of the June 4, 1989, massacre (see below). According to the veteran journalist Louisa Lim, who published her book, *The People's Republic of Amnesia: Tiananmen Revisited*, in the United States on June 4, 2014, Xi and his colleagues wanted to scrub away the tiniest reminder of the massacre not only because it damaged the Party's legitimacy but even more because the current leaders were the beneficiaries of a plot to liquidate the Party's liberal wing. "China's leaders are personally vulnerable because they trace their lineage to the winners of the power struggle that cleaved their party in 1989," Lim wrote. "Party leader Xi Jinping's refusal to repudiate Chairman Mao Zedong effectively rules out any acts of historical reevaluation. . . . The party's ultimate goal is ensuring its own survival, and it has clearly decided that it needs to keep a lid on discussion about Tiananmen in public, in private and in cyberspace."[117]

### The Party's Pogrom Against Liberal Intellectuals

Intellectuals such as Xu Jilin, Bao Tong, and Liu Xiaobo are fully aware of the myriad strategies that the Party is using to tame and neuter citizens who refuse to toe the line. They also know very well that their battle against the propaganda establishment as well as the police-state apparatus is an asymmetrical war, in which the authorities wield most of the weapons. Much has been written about the fact that illustrious artists and writers who established solid reputations in the 1920s and 1930s invariably disappeared from public view after 1949. Master novelists such as Mao Dun (1896–1981), Ba Jin (1904–2005), and Lao She (1899–1966) basically abandoned creative writing after the establishment of the People's Republic. Lao She committed suicide at the start of the Cultural Revolution. The talented author Shen Congwen (1902–1988), who was nominated for a Nobel Prize but did not win, turned to archeology and art history. The polyglot man of letters Qian Zhongshu (1910–1998) managed to produce several important works of literary criticism after 1949, but he was also obliged to spend time translating Chairman Mao's works into English.[118] As the Zhonghan University historian Yuan Weishi argued, "a great number of established authors have failed to produce remarkable works after 1949. . . . The reason is simple: their spirits have been weighed down by oppression."[119]

The respected painter and critic Chen Danqing summed up the pernicious impact of authoritarianism on artists and intellectuals at a 2013 conference on the great painter Xu Beihong (1895–1953) when he said that it would be all but impossible for world-class talents to emerge after 1949. Chen noted that Xu was able to win over warlords as well as Kuomintang (Guomindang) officials during the Republican period. Referring to the stifling political and artistic atmosphere after 1949, Chen said: "It is well-nigh impossible for a great master to be nurtured in our era. . . . I am glad for Mr. Xu that he passed away soon after our [Communist] era began." The critic noted that Xu's key motto was "I stick to my way in defense of my beliefs." "Who among our fellow artists dare to go it alone?" asked Chen. "Moreover, we don't even have beliefs that we can call ours."[120] It should also be pointed out that, thanks to the Party's sixty-five-year control over the study, research, and public discussion of politics, economics, history, and related topics, relatively few Chinese academics in the humanities and social sciences who trained in China and are based there have gained a worldwide reputation.

Beijing intensified its draconian treatment of dissidents—as well as NGO activists and human rights defense lawyers—during the second half of the Hu Jintao era (2007–12). The reasons included heightened security concerns in the run-up to the Olympic Games in 2008, celebrations of the sixtieth anniversary of the founding of the PRC in 2009, and the Shanghai Expo in 2010. Ethnic unrest in Tibet and Xinjiang flared up in, respectively, March 2008 and July 2009. Then came the series of Arab Spring revolutions in countries such as Tunisia, Libya, and Egypt. This revived the CCP's paranoia—first precipitated by the Solidarity movement in Poland in the early 1980s—that China could become the target of a "color revolution conspiracy."[121] Another factor that prompted the police to crack down harder on "destabilizing forces" was Liu Xiaobo's winning the Nobel Peace Prize in 2010. As discussed earlier, this was interpreted by the CCP leadership as an instance of "collusion" between dissidents and their "Western patrons." Yu Jie, a talented author who was writing Liu's biography, was severely beaten by police. He fled to the United States in 2012. In an op-ed article in the *Washington Post,* Yu quoted his secret police tormentor as saying that the authorities had a list of "200 anti-Communist Party intellectuals" nationwide—and that, if need be, the state apparatus could easily round them up and bury them alive within a day or two.[122]

Is Xi considerably harsher than Hu in violating the human rights particularly of dissidents, liberal academics, lawyers, and NGO activists? The police and *weiwen* apparatus under Xi has in some areas followed established practice. Take, for example, the "red line" associated with the formation of an underground organization. On occasion, the authorities display a modicum of tolerance toward outspoken public intellectuals if they are considered to be acting on their own. Yet once these individuals form a citywide or cross-provincial political organization, the standing order for the police is to break up the "underground gangs" immediately. This was true of the police's harsh treatment of the New Citizens movement, a group of civic-minded citizens who championed the enactment of an "assets-disclosure law" that would oblige senior officials to publicize their wealth and that of their immediate family members. Prominent rights lawyers cited an internal document of the Supreme People's Procuratorate, which said that the police should search for any "illegal assembly" or "crowd-gathering."[123]

In several areas, however, the Xi administration has gone beyond the Jiang Zemin or Hu Jintao era in trying to eliminate "destabilizing elements" in society—for example, the punishment of the close relatives of noted dissidents. The wife of Liu Xiaobo, Liu Xia, has been kept under house arrest, and her brother, Liu Hui, was given a three-year jail term on what human rights organizations called trumped-up charges. The nephew of the blind legal activist Chen Guangcheng—who was granted asylum in the United States in 2012—was imprisoned for three years in late 2012 for allegedly assaulting police officers.[124]

Xi has also begun targeting multimillionaire private businessmen who have gone beyond making liberal comments on political issues to providing dissident groupings with financial support. A case in point is billionaire real-estate and IT businessman Wang Gongquan, who was detained by police in September 2013 for allegedly "organizing a mob to disturb public order." Wang's real "crime," however, was that he is a keen supporter of civil society and human rights activists, such as well-known legal scholar Xu Zhiyong. Wang has also used online petitions to press the CCP leadership to restart political liberalization.[125] President Xi and his colleagues are very nervous about private businessmen getting involved in activities that can be construed as politically destabilizing. Several entrepreneurs were behind the large-scale antinuclear demonstrations held in mid-2013 by more than 1,000 residents of Jiangmen, Guangdong. Provincial authorities were forced at least temporarily to shelve a plan to build a nuclear power plant on the outskirts of the city.[126]

There is evidence that the Xi administration intensified its harsh treatment of "trouble-making" intellectuals after the establishment of the Central National Security Commission (see Chapter 3). In the run-up to the twenty-fifth anniversary of the Tiananmen Square crackdown in mid-2014, a few hundred academics, lawyers, NGO activists, online opinion-makers, and retired liberal cadres were hauled in for questioning by the police. More than a dozen critics of the regime, including the prominent lawyer Pu Zhiqiang, who was Ai Weiwei's counsel, were subjected to "criminal detention," meaning that they were likely to be formally charged after a month or so. The official pretext for harassing these intellectuals, whose "crime" was holding meetings in restaurants or hotels to reminisce about the twenty-fifth anniversary of the massacre, was that they were engaged in *xunxin zishi* (picking quarrels and provoking troubles), which could earn them up to five years in jail if convicted (which was a virtual certainty). A week or so after Pu and four friends were picked up for participating in a private Tiananmen-related salon on May 6, his own lawyer, Qu Zhenheng, as well two journalist friends, Wu Wei and Xin Jian, were detained by police in Beijing.[127] During the same period, the authorities also arrested the respected former journalist Gao Yu for allegedly revealing to a Hong Kong publication the contents of Central Document No. 9 of 2013, which forbids college teachers to discuss seven politically sensitive topics. Also detained was the freelance writer Xiang Nanfu, who was accused of supplying anti-government articles to the U.S.-based Boxun.com. Yet what scandalized China's legal scholars and professionals the most was that in contradiction to Xi's apparent advocacy of judicial fairness and due process, the CCTV broadcast detailed "confessions of guilt" by Gao and Xiang when they were interrogated by the Beijing police.[128]

### Zizhuxing vs. Dangxing: Intellectuals Fight Back the Best They Can

Men of letters and public intellectuals who have ambitions and aspirations beyond being a "cog in the revolution" have fought back with gusto. Even well-educated and politically alert Chinese, however, have found it difficult to challenge CCP orthodoxy—and the virtual police-state regime behind it. Zhu Yongjia, a noted scholar and one-time adviser to the Gang of Four radicals, used a familiar proverb to express the intimate connection between intellectuals and the powers-that-be: hair growing on the skin. "There is this old saying that if the skin is no more, from where can hair draw its sustenance?" said Zhu. "In traditional Chinese society, intellectuals have little choice other than working for the administration. There were few other means of making a living."[129] According to the writer and historian Wu Xiaobo, "Chinese in their heart of hearts are calling out for dictators. . . . There is an old saying that goes 'it's better to be a dog in times of peace than a human being in times of upheaval.'. . . Chinese politics is the art of control: central authorities control localities even as [various levels of] government exercises control over the masses."[130]

Overwhelming odds not withstanding, free-thinking Chinese have made a Herculean effort to wean the individual off political control and to confer independence and self-sufficiency on the intellectual. In an essay titled "The Quintessence of Global Values Is to Treat the Individual as an Individual," Bao Tong, the former secretary to Zhao Ziyang, pointed out that one of the greatest failings of the CCP was precisely its refusal to treat the people as individuals who can pursue agendas separate from those of the state. "The Four Cardinal Principles [of Marxism and Party leadership] have led to the degradation of the individual," he wrote.[131]

Xu Jilin, a noted liberal philosopher at Shanghai's Huadong Normal University, for the past ten years or so has waged a valiant battle against efforts by the Party's leaders to shackle and subjugate the Chinese intellectual. Xu pointed out that independent, self-respecting intellectuals must not only preserve their distinctive personality (*zizhuxing;* innate self-sufficiency); they must also ensure the *zizhuxing* of knowledge itself. "The *zizhuxing* of knowledge and learning is fundamental to intellectuals' ability to reach [the goal of improving] public life and to implement the critique of the politics [of the day]," he added. The knowledge and values propagated by intellectuals must be "independent of religion, politics, economics, and other spheres of influence," he wrote.[132]

On the one hand, few intellectuals are naive enough to think that their actions can make a big dent in the current system of one-Party authoritarian rule. On the other hand, new horizons are opening up. The public sphere has expanded. For instance, the number of NGOs exceeds 500,000. Despite the fact that these organizations are tightly monitored by the state, the profusion of NGOs could make possible the popularization of ideas that challenge the CCP's "echo chamber."[133] Ousted Peking University Professor Xia Yeliang is convinced that a bigger role for public intellectuals and NGO participants is possible despite Beijing's strict prohibition on forming political parties. "It's well-nigh impossible for an 'opposition party' to be established in China," he wrote in 2013. "It is also not possible for a foreign-based opposition party to affect developments in China. We can only rely on [the growth of] the civil society." He argued that through means such as the Internet, "a kind of 'unorganized state of organization' has been formed." This meant that although China's public sphere lacks organizations with specific names and addresses, "once the opportunity comes, [concerned citizens] can quickly come together to influence events," he added.[134]

Is Professor Xia too optimistic? Maybe. Xi Jinping has continued ex-president Hu's attempt to squeeze civil society to the point that dissenting voices have all but been flushed out of the system. As of mid-2014, there is no evidence of any civil society organization potent enough to force the hand of the CCP on significant issues. In terms of informal groupings, followers of Hu Yaobang and Zhao Ziyang—many of whom are associated with the liberal journal *Yanhuang chunqiu*—have urged the Xi administration to pick up on the threads of political reform. Hu Deping personally lobbied Xi to boost the degree of "intra-Party democracy" within the CCP apparatus.[135] The activities of these septuagenarian and octogenarian remnants of the CCP's liberal wing are tolerated partly because most of them are veteran Party members who do not challenge the CCP's status as China's "perennial ruling party." Yet it seems they can do little since Xi has made clear his preference for an ultraconservative path.[136]

The second group of intellectuals who occasionally rock the boat of Party-imposed stability consists of members of China's minuscule number of unofficial think tanks. According to the Think Tanks and Civil Societies Program at the University of Pennsylvania, the PRC has 426 think tanks, second only to the 1,828 in the United States.[137] Yet the vast majority of these organizations are adjuncts of Party and government departments, including civilian and military intelligence agencies. Only a small proportion of think tanks, for example, the Unirule Institute of Economics and the World and China Institute (WCI), are bona fide private organizations. The fact that Mao Yushi (b. 1929), a founder and principal researcher at

Unirule, is subject to surveillance by state security agents illustrates the difficulty of running unofficial think tanks.[138]

As discussed in Chapter 3, the Xi administration has set up the CLGISI partly to prevent the Web from becoming a destabilizing force. Tight surveillance on the *weibo* and other microblogging sites is seen as a reason that subscribers to social-networking media declined for the first time in 2013.[139] While there is little question that the Internet has opened the eyes of Chinese—and robbed the authorities of their monolithic control of information—the CCP has demonstrated that it can to a considerable extent use it as a method of stabilizing the regime. As the Chinese Internet specialist Scott Greene pointed out, "the Internet can serve as a tool for the state" by providing Beijing with a good gauge of public opinion. At least for the less sophisticated, the Internet can give state propaganda extra mileage. "The Internet can actually produce a more dynamic propaganda state," added Greene.[140] Moreover, given that cyberpolice are closely monitoring the communications of dissidents, rights lawyers, NGO activists, and "separatists" in Tibet and Xinjiang, the Internet can provide clues for the police to track down "troublemakers." Said Gady Epstein, an expert on the Chinese information superhighway: "The internet was expected to help democratize China. Instead, it has enabled the authoritarian state to get a firmer grip [on society]." Moreover, the Internet can serve as a safety valve for the regime. Popular grievances that are so widely expressed on *weibo* and other channels have alerted the government about what they must do to defuse imminent political crises.[141]

**Disturbing Reasons for "Elite Emigration"**

"What makes possible [good] governance over heaven and earth is talent," said President Xi in a 2013 speech marking the hundredth anniversary of the Western Returned Scholars Association (WRSA). Xi was citing a famous aphorism of the Song dynasty educator Hu Yuan (993–1059). "Talents are a major criterion for assessing a country's comprehensive national strength," he indicated. While appealing for more students who have studied in countries including the United States, Europe, Australia, and Japan to return to work in the motherland, Xi made a pledge about his administration's respect for well-educated personnel. "It has been a long-standing objective of the Party and government to respect labor, respect intellectuals, respect talents, and respect creativity," he said.[142] Xi's plea followed similar speeches by earlier leaders about Beijing's willingness to invest more in nurturing and retaining talent. For example, in 2010 Wen Jiabao said that the government would give greater support to "high-caliber, creative experts who are urgently needed in China."[143]

For reasons outlined in earlier sections, particularly the demands made by the Party that all talents serve the powers-that-be like a cog in a machine, China has experienced a worrisome exodus of the best and the brightest, particularly among the educated, professional, and entrepreneurial classes. China's migration deficit—the number of people leaving China compared with foreigners settling in the country—hit a peak of 8.49 million in 2013.[144] The mass departure of highly educated Chinese signals that, at the very least, President Xi's "Chinese Dream" is not very attractive. Moreover, elite emigration will deplete the number of Chinese who are willing and able to expand China's civil society and pave the way for a more pluralistic and tolerant society.

China became the biggest worldwide contributor of emigrants in 2007, and official statistics showed that 81,784 Chinese secured immigration or permanent-residency status in the United States in 2012, as well as 33,018 in Canada and 25,509 in Australia. Chinese were outnumbered only by Mexicans as the largest ethnic group that acquired green cards in the United States that year.[145] Particularly in the area of investment-related emigration to major Western countries, Chinese are expected to become the largest cohort by the mid-2010s. The Canadian government's sudden decision in early 2014 to stop all investment-category immigration applications seemed to reflect Ottawa's concern about a disproportionately large number of Chinese using Canada as a "safe haven" for their assets as well as their children. Then there are middle-class and affluent Chinese who take advantage of liberalized travel regulations to give birth to children in the United States and other Western countries. The magnitude of the *huaqiao* (Chinese diaspora), estimated by the Overseas Affairs Office of the State Council at more than 45 million, is expected to grow significantly in the 2010s.[146]

Despite the downturn in Western economies in the wake of the global financial crisis, more Chinese students are expected to stay on in the West after getting degrees and professional qualifications. According to statistics reported by the Xinhua News Agency, out of the 2.64 million students who went abroad for further education from 1978 to 2012, 41.29 percent, or 1.09 million, have returned. At least on paper, the "return rate" seems to have gradually improved. An earlier statistic given in the 2010 White Paper on China's Human Resources pointed out that of the 1.62 million Chinese who went abroad for higher education from 1978 to 2009, some 497,000, or 30.68 percent, returned to China.[147] However, it is difficult to estimate whether the "returnees"—many of whom have already acquired overseas residency status, if not foreign citizenship—are returning for good. Moreover, other reports in the official media give the strong impression that the return rate among top-quality personnel in fields such as technology and finance is much lower than the overall figures would suggest. For example, in 2012 only 5.9 percent of foreign-trained specialists with doctorates and solid research experience indicated a desire to return to China.[148]

Xinhua pointed out in 2013 that China "suffers from 'brain drain' more than any other country." Citing materials from the CCGTW, it disclosed that "a staggering 87 percent of China's scientists and engineers are choosing to stay abroad rather than work in China." An expert at CCGTW was quoted as saying that "35 percent of chief technology officers and laboratory directors in Silicon Valley are from China."[149]

What are the reasons for the exodus of professors, engineers, and managers as well as private businessmen? The official Chinese media admit that members of the middle and professional classes are leaving the country due to dissatisfaction with the harrowing contradictions in Chinese politics and society. In other words, because China is a country that does not recognize global norms such as civil and democratic rights, many of its best-trained, most qualified citizens seem to be voting with their feet by settling in the West. A 2010 Xinhua commentary admitted that many members of China's elite had chosen Western countries "in search of a sense of safety"—a way out of "the pain and aberrations brought about by social transformation" in the previous decade.[150] Nie Xiaoyang, deputy chief editor of *Globe* magazine, noted that emigrants destined for the United States were not aiming only for a higher standard of living. "A very important point is the tolerance and energy of American society," Nie argued. "Its multifaceted cultural environment can give people more confidence."[151] An article on the China Broadcasting Corporation Web site noted that the authorities must "boost their respect for talents and furnish them with more humanistic concern" so as to persuade top-flight personnel to remain in China. The commentary also cited the importance of "a transparent system of regulations and a sense of security" as well as "a fairer environment in which people can develop their talent."[152]

In a 2010 article published by Xinhua, Ran Wei saluted American soft power, particularly the country's ability to attract gifted personnel from different countries. Apart from the allure of top-notch universities and cutting-edge high-tech firms, Ran pointed to institutions and systems that "encourage gifted people to achieve breakthroughs. . . . America puts a lot of stress on the rational use of human resources and on retaining outstanding personnel. . . . Much emphasis is put on the free flow of talents and the abolition of restrictions and discrimination."[153]

China's brain drain and "talents deficit" are a blow to the prestige and credibility of the Chinese government. This phenomenon belies the claims made after the global financial crisis, for example, by the PBSC member in charge of ideology and propaganda, Liu Yunshan, that "the Chinese system is incomparably superior. . . . The China model has demonstrated strong vigor and energy."[154] The apparent exodus of business people, professionals, and other members of the elite begs the question of how superior the Chinese model is.

In mid-2010, in part to counter the worsening brain drain, the State Council unveiled a "Mid- to Long-Term National Plan for the Development of Talents," which covers 2010 to 2020. For example, universities, research institutes, and laboratories have been given more government funds so as to persuade well-educated Chinese to conduct academic and industrial research in their homeland. In January 2009, Beijing launched the "Thousand Talents Program" to lure back accomplished Chinese who had settled overseas.[155] Then-director of the Department of Organization Li Yuanchao claimed that "China is going through the third wave of talents returning to the motherland." Li said that the first wave, which included "Father of the Republic" Sun Yat-sen and Zhou Enlai, returned from abroad to overthrow feudalism. The second wave was a reference to scientists such as the physicists Qian Xuesen and Qian Sanqiang, who left high-paying jobs in the United States and Europe in the 1950s. "The third wave is taking place now," Li said, adding that more foreign-based Chinese than ever were eager to contribute to modernization of the country.[156]

Statistics, however, do not seem to indicate that initiatives to encourage overseas-based Chinese talents to return home are working very well. As of the end of 2013, a mere 4,180 "top-tier talents" had agreed to return to China and develop their careers in the motherland under the "Thousand Talents Program."[157] In view of the expected worsening of "social contradictions" in the Xi Jinping era, this exodus could become more serious by the end of this decade.

## Conclusion: Why the Chinese Dream Remains Illusory

### Authoritarian Nonresilience Under Xi Jinping

A useful prism through which students of China have looked at the rapidly developing quasi-superpower in the past decade is the idea of authoritarian resilience or how the CCP leadership has maintained power and upheld political stability through institutional changes that stop short of democratization. In a much-noted 2003 article in the *Journal of Democracy,* the veteran sinologist Andrew Nathan cited "institutionalization of orderly succession processes, meritocratic promotions, bureaucratic differentiation and channels of mass participation and appeal" as *modus operandi* that the Party-and-state apparatus could employ to prolong its mandate of heaven without introducing real democracy.[158]

Moreover, as Minxin Pei, a respected professor of government, has argued, after the collapse of the Soviet Union Beijing adopted stability-oriented policies, including "reviving the country's stagnant economy; . . . ending international isolation; placating the intelligentsia; and boosting the confidence of the business community." "But the measures that helped to keep the regime in power during the tumults of the late twentieth century are not necessarily working as well" from the mid-2000s onward, wrote Pei, who believed that CCP rule was "fragile rather than resilient."[159] As discussed in this and earlier chapters, it is evident that the Party leadership has hardly passed muster in implementing even the limited reforms suggested by Nathan and Pei. That China remains potentially highly unstable is attested to by the fact that the number of "mass incidents" remains high—and that the *weiwen* budget has kept mounting. As Nathan argued in the same journal in 2013, "there is a sense of impermanence that we do not find in mature political systems . . . whose members operate on the assumption, wise or not, that their system is lasting."[160] Yet at least for the foreseeable future—say, up to the end of the Xi era, which is the Twentieth Party Congress, in late 2022—it is likely that the Party-state apparatus can maintain the CCP's "perennial ruling party status" through rigid, nonresilient means such as the familiar tactics of suppression of dissent mixed with appeals to the nationalist sentiments of ordinary Chinese.

Nathan pointed to the possibility that "a Chinese Vladimir Putin might emerge to reconsolidate authoritarian or semi-authoritarian institutions."[161] Xi, who appears to be a great admirer of Putin's, has actually gone beyond merely consolidating authoritarian mechanisms that the Party has used since the beginning of the era of reform. He has reinstated several Maoist precepts and practices. And he has been "innovative" enough to create new authoritarian institutions such as the CNSC and the CLGISI in order to bolster the country's already formidable quasi-police state apparatus. As we saw above in this chapter, China's educated class, considered a key group for spearheading possible political changes, has been largely cowed into submission. Moreover, vast members of the middle, professional, and entre-preneurial classes have signaled their terminal distrust of the system by emigrating to Western and even other Asian countries.

### Institutional and Cultural Deficiencies Militate Against the Renaissance of the Chinese People

At a speech at the College of Europe, Belgium, in March 2014, Xi stuck to his favorite theme: that only socialism with Chinese characteristics works for China. "Constitutional monarchy, imperial restoration, parliamentarianism, a multiparty system, and a presidential system, we considered them and tried them, but none worked," Xi said. He added that because of China's unique historical and social conditions, the PRC could not copy a political system or development model from other countries "because it would not suit us, and it might even lead to catastrophic consequences."[162]

Xi was being economical with the truth. Marxism-Leninism—a creed imported from Europe that many consider alien to the Chinese tradition and mentality—was planted in Chinese soil with disastrous consequences. Consider, for example, the intra-Party purge and power struggle undertaken by Mao that was partly lifted from the playbook of Lenin and Stalin. Chinese industry and agriculture also suffered because of misguided efforts to copy the Soviet model. As discussed in Chapter 3, Xi's obsession with the concentration of power in his own hands smacks of Lenin's "democratic centralism" and other dictatorial precepts. Xi's claim that China has fully experimented with parliamentarianism, a multiparty system, and a presidential system is simply not true. Only in brief periods during the Republican era (1911–49) was some semblance of so-called Western-style democracy tried out in various Chinese regions.[163] It is true that in the 1940s Mao told Chinese intel-lectuals and Western journalists alike that he would introduce real democracy after the CCP came to power. For example, in September 1945 Mao told Reuters that after the Communist victory, "all levels of government up to the central govern-ment will be produced through universal, equal, and anonymous elections." Yet he never kept his word.[164]

For the rest of the decade, the political landscape is likely to be marked by a bundle of contradictions. China's GDP will soon overtake that of the United States, and the gap between Chinese and American high technology and military prowess may progressively narrow. However, the Chinese Dream, especially aspects having to do with social equality, the rule of law, and political participation, will remain a distant prospect. Even more illusory is the renaissance of Chinese civilization.

More and more Chinese intellectuals have come to the realization that soft power is the Achilles' heel of China's modernization. Renmin University's international relations expert Pang Zhongying was forthcoming enough to note that "the situation of Chinese soft power is not too optimistic." He argued that China needed to do more regarding "political systems and political models, including political reform."[165] Yu Keping, a one-time informal adviser to ex-president Hu on political reform, is convinced that President Xi's ideal of seeking the renaissance of the Chinese people will be possible only after China has developed a "political civilization in addition to material, spiritual, and environmental civilizations. . . . Without a highly developed democracy and rule of law, it will be impossible for the Chinese people to achieve a great renaissance."[166] For the Shanghai-based historian Xu Jilin, the major problem with CCP rule in the past few decades is that "China has lost its culture and civilization." The renowned thinker noted that China will be able to play a responsible role on the world stage only if officials and intellectuals refamiliarize themselves with the concepts and vocabulary of world civilization. Xu's stark message for the leadership is that the country must first remedy the fact that "China has lost the heaven and earth of civilization."[167]

For General Liu Yazhou, the renowned military strategist who supports political reform, the most urgent task for China is not to win wars or boost national strength but to improve the quality and cultural standards of every Chinese. He cited the Qing dynasty reformer Liang Qichao on the fact that "competition between countries takes place not between nations but between [the qualities of] peoples." Speaking on the occasion of the 120th anniversary of the outbreak of the first Sino-Japanese War, Liu pointed out that Japan won not because of its navy but because of the superior education of its people. "From the Meiji Restoration [1868] until today, the priority [of Japanese authorities] has been the education of its people," he said. Liu noted that the most critical factor behind national strength and global competition was the "human spirit. . . . The power of thought is overwhelming." [168] Similarly, the military historian Major-General Pi Mingyong argued that China lost the war with Japan in 1894–95 not so much because of inferiority of weaponry as because of "the deficiency of cultural power." Pi noted that cultural power meant "the force of thoughts, concepts, and spirit."[169] Yet if, as this chapter argues, what Xi has accomplished is the closing of the Chinese mind, one can hardly be sanguine about the prospects of a cultural reawakening and enlightenment in his country.

## Notes

1. For a discussion of Prime Minister Abe's comparison of China with Germany during World War I, see, for example, Isabel Reynolds and Takashi Hirokawa, "Abe comparing China ties to pre-war Europe fuels tensions," Bloomberg, January 24, 2014, www.bloomberg.com/news/2014-01-23/abe-comparing-china-to-pre-world-war-one-germany-fuels-tensions.html. See also "Editorial: Will World War 1 repeat itself in East Asia: Who wants to frighten who?" *Global Times,* January 15, 2014, http://opinion.huanqiu.com/editorial/2014-01/4755047.html.

2. Cited in Keith Bradsher, "Philippine leader sounds alarm on China," *New York Times,* February 4, 2014, www.nytimes.com/2014/02/05/world/asia/philippine-leader-urges-international-help-in-resisting-chinas-sea-claims.html?_r=0/; see also Sanat Vallikappen and Rosalind Mathieson, "Abe, Aquino views on China unhelpful, says U.S. General Carlisle," Bloomberg, February 9, 2014, www.bloomberg.com/news/2014-02-09/abe-aquino-views-on-china-unhelpful-says-u-s-general-carlisle.html.

3. John J. Mearsheimer, "The gathering storm: China's challenge to U.S. power in Asia," *Chinese Journal of International Politics* 3, no. 4 (2010): 381–396, http://cjip.oxfordjournals.org/content/3/4/381.full.pdf+html/.

4. Cited in Joseph Nye, "1914 revisited?" *Project Syndicate,* January 13, 2014, www.project-syndicate.org/commentary/joseph-s-nye-asks-whether-war-between-china-and-the-us-is-as-inevitable-as-many-believe-world-war-i-to-have-been/.

5. Ibid.

6. Cited in Nicolas Berggruen and Nathan Gardels, "How the world's most powerful leader thinks," Huffington Post, January 21, 2014, www.huffingtonpost.com/2014/01/21/xi-jinping-davos_n_4639929.html.

7. For a discussion of the reforms under the Meiji emperor, see, for example, W.G. Beasley, *The Meiji Restoration* (Stanford: Stanford University Press, 1972), pp. 71–116.

8. For a discussion of Gorbachev's role in shaking up the CPSU, see, for example, "The Great Dissident," BBC News, August 12, 2011, www.bbc.co.uk/news/world-europe-14507036/.

9. For a discussion of the fate of Zhao Ziyang's political reforms, see Guoguang Wu and Helen Landsdown, *Zhao Ziyang and China's Political Future* (London: Routledge, 2013), pp. 32–57.

10. For a discussion of the cultural aspects of China's rise, see Gungwu Wang, "The fourth rise of China: Cultural implications," *China: An International Journal* 2, no. 2 (September 2004): 311–322; see also Bates Gill and Yanzhong Huang, "Sources and limits of Chinese 'soft power,'" *Survival: Global Politics and Strategy* 48, no. 2 (2006): 17–36. For a discussion of Beijing's views of the values of a Nobel Prize for literature, see Julia Lovell, *The Politics of Cultural Capital: China's Quest for a Nobel Prize in Literature* (Honolulu: University of Hawaii Press, 2006), pp. 3–40.

11. See Wang, "China's search for a grand strategy."

12. See "Ma Yong: Constitutional governance and democratization is a path that all mankind must take," News.21cn.com (Beijing), September 1, 2013, http://news.21cn.com/zhuanti/domestic/nzpd/my/a/2013/0109/18/14326327.shtml.

13. For a discussion of how regimes can divert the attention of the public from internal issues to external ones, see, for example, Taylor Fravel, "The limits of diversion: Rethinking internal and external conflicts," *Security Studies* 19 (2010): 307–341.

14. Cited in "Xi Jinping interviewed by Russian television," *People's Daily,* February 9, 2014, http://cpc.people.com.cn/n/2014/0209/c64094-24303725.html; see also Keith Chai, "Further economic reforms a tough task, warns Xi Jinping," *South China Morning Post,* February 10, 2014, www.scmp.com/news/china/article/1424863/further-economic-reforms-tough-task-warns-xi-jinping/.

15. Cited in "Xi Jinping puts emphasis on building an innovative country," *Liberation Daily* (Shanghai), September 20, 2009, http://epaper.jfdaily.com/jfdaily/html/2009-09/20/content_253959.htm; see also "Xi Jinping stresses while inspecting Hunan Province that the goal is to realize economic and social development through deepening reform and pushing forward innovation," *Legal Daily,* November 16, 2013, www.legaldaily.com.cn/locality/content/2013-11/06/content_4996779.htm?node=31464/.

16. See "Xi Jinping attends APEC leaders' meeting and makes important address," China News Service, October 7, 2013, www.chinanews.com/gn/2013/10-07/5347314.shtml.

17. See Wang Xiaoshi, "If China is struck with instability, the result will be worse than the Soviet Union," Xinhua News Agency, August 1, 2013, http://opinion.huanqiu.com/opinion_china/2013-08/4196579.html; Zhao Xiao, "History must not repeat itself; reform is as urgent as ever," *People's Daily,* December 7, 2012, http://theory.people.com.cn/n/2012/1207/c40531-19818585.html.

18. See "Ma Yong: Constitutional governance and democratization is a path that all mankind must take." See also Buckley, "Vows of change in China belie private warning."

19. See Hu Deping, "Some interest blocs are severely threatening the safety of the party and the state," *Ta Kung Pao* (Hong Kong), April 3, 2013, http://news.takungpao.com/mainland/focus/2013-04/1526894.html.

20. See "Sun Liping: Consensus for reform has basically been fractured," *Economic Observer,* December 8, 2010, www.21ccom.net/articles/zgyj/ggzhc/article_2010120825947.html.

21. Cited in "Tsinghua University report: China must beware of 'losing the desire to cross the river in the course of reform,'" *China Youth Daily,* January 9, 2012, http://china.huanqiu.com/roll/2012-01/2336366.html.

22. Cited in "Xi Jinping interviewed by Russian television." See also "China's way of thinking about comprehensive reform has basically coalesced," China News Service, February 20, 2013, http://oversea.huanqiu.com/economy/2014-02/4847163.html; "Xi Jinping: Reform has entered the deep-water zone," China News Service, July 25, 2013, http://business.sohu.com/20130725/n382529715.shtml.

23. See "CCP think tank member: Xi Jinping will become a Deng Xiaoping-like strongman," Phoenix TV net, March 11, 2014, http://finance.ifeng.com/a/20140311/11852944_0.shtml.

24. See "Jiang Zhiyong: Social reform should be the breakthrough for China's reforms," *Ta Kung Pao,* March 25, 2014, www.rmlt.com.cn/2014/0325/249442.shtml.

25. See "Zhang Wenhui: 'Reform leading groups' should break through the vested interests of departments," Caixin.com (Beijing), November 15, 2013, http://opinion.caixin.com/2013-11-15/100605445.html.

26. Cited in "Wei Sen: If the question of the checks and balance of governmental power is not solved in the course of reform, a depression could occur," Phoenix TV News, September 14, 2013, http://finance.ifeng.com/a/20130914/10685782_0.shtml.

27. For a discussion of the reform of the *hukou* system, see for example, Dexter Roberts, "China moves on reforming *hukou?*" See also "China to accelerate *hukou* system reform: Document," Xinhua News Agency, November 15, 2013, http://news.xinhuanet.com/english/china/2013-11/15/c_132892030.htm.

28. For a discussion of China's petition system, see, for example, Lucy Hornby, "China's modern take on an ancient petition system," *Financial Times,* November 28, 2013, www.ft.com/intl/cms/s/0/ebab4304-580c-11e3-a2ed-00144feabdc0.html#axzz2ygNav6pv/; see also "Official pledges reforms to China's petition system," Xinhua News Agency, November 28, 2013, http://english.cntv.cn/20131128/105434.shtml.

29. See "The case of land expropriation in Pingdu, Shandong: Villagers say the village administration committee has played a seamy role," *Southern Metropolitan News* (Guangzhou), March 22, 2014, http://news.163.com/14/0322/05/9NTUC9K30001124J.html.

For a discussion of the land grab situation, including the 2011 regulation to curb irregularities in land requisition, see, for example, Chris Hogg, "China law to limit home demolitions and evictions," BBC News, July 1, 2011, www.bbc.co.uk/news/world-asia-pacific-13986456/; see also "China issues new regulations on house expropriation," Xinhua News Agency, January 22, 2011, www.chinadaily.com.cn/china/2011-01/22/content_11900647.htm.

30. Cited in "The important theory of the Three Represents," Xinhua News Agency, January 21, 2003, http://news.xinhuanet.com/ziliao/2003-01/21/content_699933.htm.

31. See "Decision on major issues concerning comprehensively deepening reforms," Xinhua News Agency, November 16, 2013, http://news.xinhuanet.com/mrdx/2013-11/16/c_132892941.htm.

32. Ibid.

33. See "China's cultural influence ranks 7th in the world," *People's Daily*, March 31, 2009, www.chinadaily.com.cn/life/2009-03/31/content_11569271.htm.For a discussion of China's cultural influence, see, for example, Nicholas Dynon, "History and culture not enough to drive China's soft power," *Global Times*, October 15, 2013, http://mobile.globaltimes.cn/content/817948.html.

34. See Wang Jisi, "China's search for a grand strategy."

35. Cited in "Hu Jintao's speech at meeting commemorating the thirtieth anniversary of the Reform and Open Door policy," Xinhua News Agency, November 18, 2008, www.chinadaily.com.cn/hqzg/2008-12/18/content_7318929_3.htm.

36. Cited in "Xi Jinping: Introduce well the China narrative; propagate well China's voice," Xinhua News Agency, August 21, 2013, http://news.xinhuanet.com/zgjx/2013-08/21/c_132648439.htm.

37. For a discussion of the possibilities of democratic development in countries with authoritarian cultures, see, for example, Becky Shelley, *Democratic Development in East Asia* (London: RoutledgeCurzon, 2005), pp. 8–43. See also Lucian W. Pye, *Asian Power and Politics: The Cultural Dimensions of Authority* (Cambridge, MA: Belknap Press, 1988), pp. 182–247.

38. Cited in "Deng Xiaoping redefines market economy during his southern tour," Sina. Finance (Beijing), November 15, 2007, http://finance.sina.com.cn/hy/20071115/10034176845.shtml.

39. Cited in *Xi Jinping: Selection of Talks on Realizing the Chinese Dream of the Great Renaissance of the Chinese Race* (Beijing: CCP Central Committee Archives Research Office, 2013), p. 39.

40. Cited in Ezra F. Vogel, *Deng Xiaoping and the Transformation of China* (Cambridge: Harvard University Press, 2011), p. 96.

41. For a discussion of Beijing's treatment of foreign reporters, see, for example, Michael Calderone, "China foreign press crackdown prompts calls for visa retaliation," Huffington Post, December 10, 2013, www.huffingtonpost.com/2013/12/10/china-press-crackdown-visa-reciprocity_n_4420253.html; see also Madeline Earp, "Disdain for foreign press undercuts China's global ambition," Committee to Protect Journalists (New York), February 2013, http://cpj.org/2013/02/attacks-on-the-press-china-tightens-control.php.

42. For a discussion on the spread of foreign culture and religions into China in the Tang and Song periods, see, for example, Yi-Jie Tang, *Confucianism, Buddhism, Daoism, Christianity and Chinese Culture* (Washington, DC: Council for Research in Values and Philosophy, 1991), pp. 89–160. See also Song Qianggang, "The reasons behind the cultural diversity of the Tang dynasty and the traits of interaction between Chinese and foreign culture in the Tang period," *Journal of Sichuan College of Education* 2 (1994): 50; Zhou Shangbing, "The characteristics and historical significance of the Tang dynasty's opening to the world," *Journal of Liaoning Normal University (Social Sciences Edition)* 4 (2001): 95–96.

43. Cited in Ouyang Xiu, Song Qi, and Yang Jialuo, ed., *Xintangshu* (Beijing: Zhonghua, 1975), vol. 135, p. 4577; Liu Xu and Yang Jialuo, ed., *Jiutangshu* (Beijing: Zhonghua,

1975), vol. 8, p. 184. See also Fang Yaguang, "Discussion on the Tang dynasty's openness to foreign affairs," *Journal of Jiangsu Social Sciences* 6 (1997): 107.

44. See Toqto'a, *Song shi* (Beijing: Zhonghua, 1977), vol. 186, p. 4559. For a discussion of the Song dynasty's commerce with foreign countries, see Wang Jia, "The social fundamental of the development of marine trade in both the southern and northern Song," *Dongjiang Journal* 4 (2000): 40.

45. Cited in Xiao Jianshan, *Chinese History Revisited* (Hong Kong: New Century Press of Hong Kong, 2009), p. 188.

46. Cited in Shi Xuanyuan, "The status and influence of Quanzhou in Chinese history," *Guangming Daily* (Beijing), April 11, 2012, http://fj.qq.com/a/20120411/000333.htm.

47. For a discussion of the introduction of Western culture and science into China during the Qing dynasty, see, for example, Catherine Jami, "'European science in China' or 'Western learning'? Representations of cross-cultural transmission, 1600–1800," *Science in Context* 12, no. 3 (Autumn 1999): 413–434. See also "Some foreigners who served the Chinese emperors in the Qing dynasty," Chinagaze.com, August 13, 2013, www.chinagaze.com/2013/08/13/qing-dynasty-part-1/.

48. For a study of the contributions of Kang Youwei and Liang Qichao to democracy, see, for example, Young-Tsu Wong, "Revisionism reconsidered: Kang Youwei and the reform movement of 1898," *Journal of Asian Studies* 51, no. 3 (August 1992): 513–544. See also Orville Schell, "China's hidden democratic legacy," *Foreign Affairs* 83, no 4 (July/August 2004): 116, www.foreignaffairs.com/articles/59927/orville-schell/chinas-hidden-democratic-legacy/.

49. For a discussion of political reform contemplated by Zhao Ziyang and his followers, see, for example, Wu Guoguang, *Political Reform Under Zhao Ziyang* (Taipei: Vista Press, 1997), pp. 168–207.

50. For a discussion of Zhao's meeting with Soros, see, Zhang Weiying, "Soros insists on pushing forward the liberalization and democratization of mankind," Sina.com (Beijing), February 25, 2012, http://finance.sina.com.cn/hy/20120225/152411453854.shtml.

51. Cited in Karla Crosswhite and Kevin Bohn, "Clinton welcomes Jiang to White House," CNN, October 29, 1997, http://edition.cnn.com/ALLPOLITICS/1997/10/29/clinton.jiang/.

52. For a discussion of Laura Cha's career in China, see, for example, "China's iron lady," *Institutional Investor,* May 1, 2002, www.institutionalinvestor.com/Popups/PrintArticle.aspx?ArticleID=1027445/; see also Willy Lam, "China's dice-roll on casino culture," CNN, February 21, 2001, http://edition.cnn.com/2001/WORLD/asiapcf/east/02/20/stockmkt.reform/index.html.

53. For a discussion of Singapore's Confucian education campaign, see, for example, Colin Campbell, "Singapore plans to revive study of Confucianism," *New York Times,* May 20, 1982, www.nytimes.com/1982/05/20/world/singapore-plans-to-revive-study-of-confucianism.html.

54. Cited in Yao Jianping and Gong Lianying, "Taking lessons from history: The spirit and wisdom of CCP administration," *People's Forum* (Beijing), April 11, 2011, http://paper.people.com.cn/rmlt/html/2011-04/11/content_804571.htm?div=-1/.

55. Cited in "President Jiang Zemin emphasizes running the country according to moral values," China News Service, January 10, 2011, www.chinanews.com/2001-01-10/26/65768.html.

56. For a discussion of the Confucian roots of Hu Jintao's "harmonious society," see, for example, Yongnian Zheng and Sow Keat Tok, "'Harmonious society' and 'harmonious world': China's policy discourse under Hu Jintao," China Policy Institute, Nottingham University, October 2007, http://nottingham.ac.uk/cpi/documents/briefings/briefing-26-harmonious-society-and-harmonious-world.pdf.

57. Cited in "Taiwan scholar Yu Yingshi: Mainland China is reviving traditions in search of national identity," Sina.com.cn, April 26, 2007, http://news.sina.com.cn/c/2007-04-26/102111720034s.shtml.

58. Cited in "How can Confucianism and liberalism find common ground amid differences?" Huaxiajingwei Net (Shanghai), October 19, 2011, http://big5.huaxia.com/zhwh/gxjd/2624710.html.

59. Cited in "Xi Jinping inspects the Confucius Temple at Qufu: We must create new glories for Chinese civilization," Xinhua News Agency, November 27, 2013, www.sd.xinhuanet.com/whsdw/2013-11/27/c_118310888.htm. See also "Xi Jinping's talk on the 2,565th birthday of Confucius," China Youth Daily, September 25, 2014, http://edu.people.com.cn/n/2014/0925/c1053-25731131.html.

60. For a discussion about Xi Zhongxun's friendship with the Panchen Lama, see, for example, Shui Xinying, "Xi Zhongxun's friendship with the tenth Panchen Lama," People's Daily, January 15, 2014, http://dangshi.people.com.cn/n/2014/0115/c85037-24125805.html. See also "Xi Jinping: We can only raise our level [of wisdom] by meditating before a wall and becoming Buddha," Yangzi Evening Post (Nanjing), March 9, 2013, http://news.e23.cn/content/2013-03-09/2013030900288.html.

61. Cited in "Xi Jinping: Buddhism provides immense wisdom for our behavior and work," Phoenix TV News, December 24, 2013, http://fo.ifeng.com/special/lingdao/foyuan/detail_2013_12/24/32430677_0.shtml?_from_ralated/.

62. For a discussion of how the Xi leadership handles the self-immolations in Tibet, see, for example, Saransh Sehgal, "Xi unmoved by Tibetan self-immolation," Asia Times, www.atimes.com/atimes/China/CHIN-02-190313.html.

63. Cited in "Mad about museums," Economist, December 21, 2013, www.economist.com/news/special-report/21591710-china-building-thousands-new-museums-how-will-it-fill-them-mad-about-museums/.

64. Cited in Ian Johnson, "In China, 'Once the villages are gone, the culture is gone,'" New York Times, February 1, 2014, www.nytimes.com/2014/02/02/world/asia/once-the-villages-are-gone-the-culture-is-gone.html?_r=0/.

65. Cited in Alison Flood, "Mo Yan accepts Nobel prize, defends 'necessary' censorship," Guardian, December 11, 2012, www.theguardian.com/books/2012/dec/11/mo-yan-nobel-prize-censorship/.

66. For a discussion of Mo Yan's political attitudes, see, for example, Perry Link, "Does this writer deserve the prize?" New York Review of Books, December 6, 2012, www.nybooks.com/articles/archives/2012/dec/06/mo-yan-nobel-prize/?pagination=false/.

67. For a discussion of Ai Weiwei's views on Mo Yan, see, for example, Nick Clark and Clifford Coonan, "Ai Weiwei brands Nobel Prize for literature decision an 'insult to humanity' as China's Mo Yan named winner," Independent, October 11, 2012, www.independent.co.uk/arts-entertainment/books/news/ai-weiwei-brands-nobel-prize-for-literature-decision-an-insult-to-humanity-as-chinas-mo-yan-named-winner-8207109.html.

68. Cited in Zhang Hong, "Tie Ying, Wang Meng, and other writers do hand copies of Mao Zedong's 'Talks at the Yan'an Forum on Literature and Art,'" China News Service, May 28, 2012, http://news.ifeng.com/mainland/detail_2012_05/28/14869452_0.shtml.

69. Cited in "Party authorities will select 100 talents who have the potential to get the Nobel Prize," People's Daily, October 30, 2013, http://china.huanqiu.com/politics/2013-10/4509068.html.

70. For a study of China's formidable state sports complex, see, for example, Uri Berliner, "China's sports machine mints Olympic gold," NPR, August 18, 2008, www.npr.org/templates/story/story.php?storyId=93707032/; Klaus Nielsen and Rasmus Storm, "Olympic predictions: China can become the undisputed Olympic champion," Playthegame.org, July 27, 2012, www.playthegame.org/news/detailed/olympic-predictions-china-can-become-the-undisputed-olympic-champion-5425.html.

71. Cited in Li Na, "Even dirty words can't express your meanness," Canyu.org (Beijing), February 3, 2014, www.canyu.org/n84415c10.aspx. For a discussion of Li Na's unorthodox career, see, for example, Hannah Beech, "The meaning of Li Na," *Time*, May 15, 2014, http://time.com/100575/the-meaning-of-li-na/; see also Brook Larmer, "Li Na: China's tennis rebel," *New York Times*, August 22, 2013, www.nytimes.com/2013/08/25/magazine/li-na-chinas-tennis-rebel.html.

72. Cited in "CPPCC member says China only has one university—the Education Ministry University," *Yangzi Evening Post*, March 4, 2013, http://edu.takungpao.com/q/2014/0304/2319790.html.

73. Cited in "A flawed system for judging research is leading to academic fraud," *Economist*, September 28, 2013, www.economist.com/news/china/21586845-flawed-system-judging-research-leading-academic-fraud-looks-good-paper/.

74. For a discussion of Xi Jinping's PhD dissertation at Tsinghua University, see Michael Sheridan, "Xi Jinping's law degree questioned as claims he was 'helped,'" *Times of London*, August 11, 2013, www.theaustralian.com.au/higher-education/xi-jinpings-law-degree-questioned-as-claims-he-was-helped/story-e6frgcjx-1226695022265#/.

75. Cited in Doreen Walton, "*Lancet* urges China to tackle scientific fraud," BBC News, January 8, 2010, http://news.bbc.co.uk/2/hi/8448731.stm.

76. Cited in Guo Jiaxue, "Academic corruption undermining higher education: Yau Shing-tung," *China Daily*, June 2, 2010, www.chinadaily.com.cn/hkedition/2010-06/02/content_9919871.htm.

77. Cited in Lin Songqing, "Why serious academic fraud occurs in China," *Learned Publishing* 26, no. 1 (January 2013): 24–27(4).

78. Cited in "Peking University president: American education is in a mess; American presidents do not respect other people," Xinhua News Agency, December 25, 2011, www.wenxuecity.com/news/2011/12/25/1579057.html.

79. Cited in "Peking University professor: Hong Kong people are dogs," *Oriental Daily News* (Hong Kong), January 21, 2012, http://orientaldaily.on.cc/cnt/news/20120121/00174_001.html.

80. For a discussion of the career of Xia Yeliang, see, for example, David Feith, "Xia Yeliang: The China Americans don't see," *Wall Street Journal*, October 25, 2013, http://online.wsj.com/news/articles/SB10001424127887323308504579085611270637836/.

81. For a discussion of Shanghai students' terrific test scores, see, for example, "Evaluating Shanghai's high test scores," *Economist*, January 21, 2014, www.economist.com/blogs/analects/2014/01/chinese-schools/.

82. Cited in "Not educating the masses," *Economist*, January 4, 2014, www.economist.com/news/china/21592664-proportion-rural-students-university-has-declined-dramatically-not-educating-masses?zid=306&ah=1b164dbd43b0cb27ba0d4c3b12a5e227/.

83. Cited in Jiang Xueqin, "The cost of Shanghai's education success story," CNN, December 16, 2013, http://edition.cnn.com/2013/12/04/opinion/china-education-jiang-xueqin/.

84. Cited in April Ma, "China raises a generation of 'left-behind' children," CNN, February 5, 2014, http://edition.cnn.com/2014/02/04/world/asia/china-chil/.

85. Cited in "Not educating the masses."

86. For a discussion of the provision of nine-year free education, see, for example, Liu Yandong, "Providing better compulsory education for rural children," *Qiushi* 5, no. 4 (October 1, 2013), http://english.qstheory.cn/leaders/201311/t20131113_290374.htm.

87. Cited in "Xi Jinping: enthusiastically provide guidance to the people to pay attention to morality and to pursue the ideal of lofty morality," Xinhua News Agency, February 25, 2014, http://news.qq.com/a/20140226/000094.htm.

88. For a discussion of "patriotic education" in Chinese educational institutes, see, for example, Suisheng Zhao, "A state-led nationalism: The patriotic education campaign in

post-Tiananmen China," *Communist and Post-Communist Studies* 31, no. 3 (September 1998): 287–302.

89. Cited in "Yuan Weishi on history textbooks: We grew up drinking wolf's milk," *China Youth Daily*, April 21, 2010, http://news.ifeng.com/history/zhuanjialunshi/yuanweishi/detail_2010_04/21/538099_0.shtml. See also Guo Yuhua, "On the sociological concept of 'wolf's milk,'" Aisixiang.com (Beijing), February 1, 2010, www.aisixiang.com/data/31621.html.

90. Cited in "Liu Yuan: Why we need to retool our views on culture and history," *People's Daily Forum*, August 3, 2010, http://theory.people.com.cn/GB/41038/12328791.html.

91. Cited in "Everybody has to pay for the absence of integrity and honesty in society," *China Youth Daily*, June 16, 2006, http://edu.sina.com.cn/l/2006-06-16/1130134240.html. For a discussion of Internet-based crime, see, for example, Kathrin Hille, "Chinese cyber crime: More crooks than patriots," *Financial Times*, May 19, 2013, www.ft.com/intl/cms/s/0/20442304-bedb-11e2-a9d4-00144feab7de.html#axzz2ygNav6pv/.

92. For a discussion of Chinese parents' preference for foreign infant formula, see, for example, Alanna Petroff, "China draining world infant milk supply," CNN, April 10, 2013, http://money.cnn.com/2013/04/09/news/world/china-baby-milk-rationing/. See also Edward Wong, "Chinese search for infant formula goes global," *New York Times*, July 25, 2013, www.nytimes.com/2013/07/26/world/asia/chinas-search-for-infant-formula-goes-global.html?pagewanted=all&_r=0/.

93. Cited in Yuan Longping "Is China's biggest catastrophe unavoidable?" China.com, January 2, 2014, http://club.china.com/data/thread/1011/2767/03/89/0_1.html.

94. Cited in "With violence on rise, doctors and nurses sign joint petition to save themselves," *Ming Pao*, March 15, 2014, http://premium.mingpao.com/cfm/Content_News.cfm?Channel=ca&Path=235440282357/cha1_er.cfm. For a discussion of medical violence in China, see "Violence against doctors: Why China? Why now? What next?" *Lancet* 383, no. 9922 (March 22, 2014), www.thelancet.com/journals/lancet/article/PIIS0140-6736(14)60501-8/fulltext?rss=yes/.

95. See "A moral enlightenment? The 'Little Yueyue affair' has elicited a big rethink in public opinion," China News Service, October 21, 2011, www.chinanews.com/gn/2011/10-21/3406136.shtml.

96. Cited in Adam Taylor, "The incredible business card of the Chinese millionaire who wants to buy *The New York Times*," *Business Insider*, January 8, 2014, www.businessinsider.com/chen-guangbiaos-incredible-business-card-2014-1#ixzz2uiq1MmzQ/.

97. For a discussion of Mao's views on *dangxing*, see "Mao Zedong talks about party construction: On individual characteristics and party characteristics," *Research on Party Construction* (Beijing), November 20, 2004, www.wutnews.net/news/news.aspx?id=4804/.

98. See Mao Zedong, "Talks at the Yan'an Forum on Literature and Art," in *Selected Works of Mao Tse-tung* Online, www.marxists.org/reference/archive/mao/selected-works/volume-3/mswv3_08.htm.

99. Ibid.

100. Cited in Wang Youtai, "Mao Zedong calls for 'raising the level of *dangxing*' and becoming a resolute Communist fighter," *People's Daily*, July 11, 2008, http://cpc.people.com.cn/GB/85037/85038/8619079.html.

101. Cited in "Xi Jinping: Ideological and propaganda work is an extremely important work of the party," Xinhua News Agency, August 20, 2013, http://news.xinhuanet.com/politics/2013-08/20/c_117021464.htm.

102. Cited in Yang Faxiang, "Party nature is the amelioration, sublimation and crystallization of human nature," *Study Times* (Beijing), August 19, 2013, http://opinion.hexun.com/2013-08-19/157199427.html.

103. Cited in "Xi Jinping: Ideological and propaganda work is an extremely important work of the party." See also "Xi Jinping: Ensure that the effect of core socialist values will be as ubiquitous as the air," Xinhua News Agency, February 26, 2014, http://news.takungpao.com/mainland/focus/2014-02/2303281.html.

104. For a discussion of the "controversy over the surnames," see "Deng Xiaoping's talk in southern China has cut the dead knot about 'surnamed socialist' vs. 'surnamed capitalist,'" Xinhua News Agency, November 18, 2011, http://news.xinhuanet.com/theory/2008-11/18/content_10373415.htm.

105. Cited in "Cui Jian: As long as the Mao portrait hangs over Tiananmen Square, the times have not changed," *Ming Pao*, February 9, 2014, http://news.mingpao.com/20140209/cab1.htm.

106. Cited in Shi Zhongquan: "Research of party history is the synthesis of the nature of the party and the nature of science," *People's Daily*, July 30, 2010, http://theory.people.com.cn/GB/12303209.html.

107. Ibid.

108. Cited in Leng Rong, "National conference begins on stressing *dangxing*, putting emphasis on moral behavior and putting up demonstrations," *People's Daily*, August 30, 2013, http://cpc.people.com.cn/n/2012/0830/c64094-18870360.html.

109. Shi, "Research of party history is the synthesis of the nature of the party and the nature of science."

110. Cited in "Scholar Zhu Xueqin thinks new history textbooks have shown some improvement," Xinhua News Agency, October16, 2006, http://news.xinhuanet.com/edu/2006-10/16/content_5206428.htm.

111. For a discussion on the controversy over the origin of the Korean War, see, for example, Shen Zhihua, "The China-Soviet alliance and the origin of the Korean War," Culture.21ccom.net, February 21, 2014, http://news.takungpao.com/history/dongjian/2014-02/2292026.html. For a discussion of how the CCP has imposed a collective amnesia on the Tiananmen incident, see, for example, Louisa Lim, *The People's Republic of Amnesia: The Legacy of Tiananmen Square* (New York: Oxford University Press, 2014).

112. For a discussion of the Three Years of Famine and Beijing's spin-doctoring on this dark period of history, see, for example, Ian Johnson, "Finding the facts about Mao's victims," *New York Review of Books*, December 20, 2010, www.nybooks.com/blogs/nyrblog/2010/dec/20/finding-facts-about-maos-victims/; see also Susanne Weigelin-Schwiedrzik, "Trauma and memory: The case of the great famine in the People's Republic of China (1959–1961)," *Historiography East and West* 1, no. 1 (2003), https://uscholar.univie.ac.at/get/o:291770.pdf.

113. For a discussion of Yang Jisheng's research on the three years of famine, see, for example, Verna Yu, "Chinese author of book on famine braves risks to inform new generations," *New York Times*, November 18, 2008, www.nytimes.com/2008/12/18/world/asia/18iht-famine.1.18785257.html?pagewanted=all&_r=0/. See also Zeng Xiangrong and Guan Jiayun "Yuan Longping: It is difficult to uphold the red line of 1.8 billion *mu* of arable land," *Guangzhou Daily*, April 8, 2009, http://gzdaily.dayoo.com/html/2009-04/08/content_528349.htm.

114. Cited in Du Junli, "Logic and Han Han's logic," Aisixiang.com (Beijing), February 27, 2013, www.aisixiang.com/data/50608.html. For a discussion of the anti-rightist movement, see, for example, Judith Shapiro, *Mao's War Against Nature: Politics and the Environment in Revolutionary China* (New York: Cambridge University Press, 2001), pp. 21–66.

115. See Jane Perlez, "A leader in Mao's Cultural Revolution faces his past," *New York Times*, December 7, 2013, www.nytimes.com/2013/12/07/world/asia/a-student-leader-in-maos-cultural-revolution.html?_r=0/; Tyler Roney, "Famous princeling apologies for Cultural Revolution," *Diplomat*, January 16, 2014, http://thediplomat.com/2014/01/famous-chinese-princeling-apologies-for-cultural-revolution/.

116. See Yu Hua, "China waits for an apology," *New York Times*, April 10, 2014, www.nytimes.com/2014/04/10/opinion/yu-hua-cultural-revolution-nostalgia.html?emc=edit_tnt_20140409&nlid=16428923&tntemail0=y&_r=1/.

117. Cited in Louisa Lim, "Dangerous memories of Tiananmen Square," *Washington Post*, May 16, 2014, www.washingtonpost.com/opinions/dangerous-memories-of-tiananmen-square/2014/05/16/16dfe888-d9de-11e3-bda1-9b46b2066796_story.html. See also Lim, *The People's Republic of Amnesia*.

118. For a discussion of how famous writers suffered from Mao's strictures and persecution, see, for example, Ranbir Vohra, *Lao She and the Chinese Revolution* (Cambridge: Harvard University Press, 1974), pp. 148–167. See also Hong Zicheng, *A History of Contemporary Chinese Literature* (Leiden: Brill, 2009), pp. 21–63. For a discussion of Shen Congwen's struggles with CCP authority, see, for example, Jeffrey Kinkley, *The Odyssey of Shen Congwen* (Stanford: Stanford University Press, 1987), pp. 228–275. See also Li Jingrui, "Master in the margins: How the world rediscovered one of China's most accomplished writers," *News China Magazine* (Beijing) (March 2013), www.newschinamag.com/magazine/master-in-the-margins/.

119. See Yuan Weishi, "Thoughts on the controversy over China's history textbooks," Xinhua News Agency, March 6, 2006, http://news.21cn.com/today/PK/2006/03/06/2491358.shtml.

120. See "Chen Danqing: My views about Xi Beihong," Netease.com (Beijing), December 30, 2013, http://fashion.163.com/13/1230/00/9HA6721S00264MK3.html.

121. For a discussion of Beijing's fear of color revolutions, see, for example, "Head of Xinhua says Western media pushing revolution in China," Reuters, September 4, 2013, www.reuters.com/article/2013/09/04/us-china-media-idUSBRE9830DW20130904/. See also Eric Li, "China's 'color revolution' is red," *New Perspectives Quarterly* 28, no. 2 (Spring 2011): 7–9.

122. Cited in Edward Wong, "From Virginia suburb, a dissident Chinese writer continues his mission," *New York Times*, February 25, 2012, www.nytimes.com/2012/02/26/world/asia/yu-jie-dissident-chinese-writer-continues-his-work-in-us.html?pagewanted=all/.

123. Cited in Malcolm Moore, "Chinese lawyers targeted as Xi Jinping tightens control," *Telegraph*, August 20, 2013, www.telegraph.co.uk/news/worldnews/asia/china/10254632/Chinese-lawyers-targeted-as-Xi-Jinping-tightens-control.html.

124. For a discussion of the mistreatment of Liu Xiaobo's wife and relatives, see, for example, "Jailed Nobel dissident's wife weeks treatment in Beijing hospital," Radio Free Asia, February 20, 2014, www.rfa.org/english/news/china/liu-xia-02202014172456.html. See also "Liu Xiaobo's brother-in-law Liu Hui to serve 11 years after losing appeal," *Guardian*, August 16, 2013, www.theguardian.com/world/2013/aug/16/liu-hui-loses-appeal-11-years-liu-xiaobo/. For a discussion of the treatment of Chen's relatives, see, for example, Andrew Jacobs, "Chen Guangcheng's nephew given 3 years in prison for assault," *New York Times*, November 30, 2013, www.nytimes.com/2012/12/01/world/asia/nephew-of-chinese-dissident-chen-guangcheng-given-3-years-in-prison-for-assault.html?_r=0/.

125. For a discussion of the career of entrepreneur-activist Wang, see, for example, Simon Denyer, "In China, citizens rights activist Wang Gongquan is formally arrested," *Washington Post*, October 21, 2013, www.washingtonpost.com/world/chinese-citizens-rights-activist-wang-gongquan-is-formally-arrested/2013/10/21/888909ca-3a73-11e3-b0e7-716179a2c2c7_story.html.

126. Cited in "Report says that entrepreneurs from nearby cities are leaders in the anti-nuclear protests in Jiangmen," Guancha.cn, July 22, 2013, www.guancha.cn/Industry/2013_07_22_160148.

127. For a discussion of Beijing's tough tactics towards intellectuals in the run-up to the 25th anniversary of the June 4, 1989 crisis, see, for example, Verna Yu, "Human rights lawyer among four detained over Tiananmen commemoration event," *South China Morning Post*,

May 6, 2014, www.scmp.com/news/china/article/1505724/activists-held-questioned-police-after-commemorating-tiananmen-crackdown/. See also Dexter Roberts, "'Picking quarrels and provoking troubles'—the crime sweeping China," *Businessweek,* May 12, 2014, www.businessweek.com/articles/2014-05-12/picking-quarrels-and-provoking-troubles-the-crime-sweeping-china/; "Pu Zhiqiang's lawyer is detained," VOA News, May 16, 2014, www.voacantonese.com/content/pu-zhiqiang-lawyer-detained/1915825.html.

128. For a discussion of the incarceration of Gao Yu and Xiang Nanfu, see, for example, Dexter Roberts, "Detained Chinese journalists forced to make televised confessions," *Businessweek,* May 14, 2014, www.businessweek.com/articles/2014-05-14/detained-chinese-journalists-forced-to-make-televised-confessions/; see also Scoot Murdoch, "TV 'confession' from senior Chinese journalist and activist Gao Yu," *Australian,* May 9, 2014, www.theaustralian.com.au/news/world/tv-confession-from-senior-chinese-journalist-and-activist-gao-yu/story-e6frg6so-1226910890599#/.

129. Cited in Zhang Jianfeng, "Memorable things about the Shanghai writing team during the Cultural Revolution," *Southern Reviews* (Guangzhou), April 14, 2010, http://news.163.com/10/0414/17/648ECOQT00011SM9.html.

130. See "Scholar Wu Xiaobo: Chinese in their heart of hearts are calling out for dictators," *National Humanity History* (Beijing), December 3, 2013, http://news.takungpao.com/mainland/focus/2013-12/2081847.html.

131. Cited in Bao Tong, *A Collection of Essays by Bao Tong* (Hong Kong: New Century Media, 2012), p. 479.

132. Cited in Xu Jilin, "From the specialized to the common: The possibility of the emergence of public intellectuals in the age of specialization," *Theoretical Studies of Intellectuals,* vol. 1 (Nanjing: Jiangsu People's Press, 2002), www.aisixiang.com/data/37021.html?page=1/.

133. For a discussion of China's NGOs, see, "Chinese civil society: Beneath the glacier," *Economist,* April 12, 2014, www.economist.com/news/china/21600747-spite-political-clampdown-flourishing-civil-society-taking-hold-beneath-glacier. See also Catherine Morton, "The emergence of NGOs in China and their transnational linkages: Implications for domestic reform," *Australian Journal of International Affairs* 59, no. 4 (2005): 519–532.

134. Cited in "Xia Yeliang: The future of China depends on a coalescing civil society," Radio Free Asia, January 18, 2013, www.rfa.org/mandarin/yataibaodao/ck1-01182013103115.html.

135. For a discussion of how liberal princelings are lobbying Xi for political reform, see, for example, Edward Wong and Jonathan Ansfield, "Many urge next leader of China to liberalize," *New York Times,* October 22, 2012, www.nytimes.com/2012/10/22/world/asia/many-urge-chinas-next-leader-to-enact-reform.html?_r=0/.

136. For a discussion of the views of party elders associated with *Yanhuang chunqiu,* see, for example, Edward Wong and Jonathan Ansfield, "Reformers aim to get China to live up to own constitution," *New York Times,* February 4, 2013, www.nytimes.com/2013/02/04/world/asia/reformers-aim-to-get-china-to-live-up-to-own-constitution.html.

137. Cited in "Think tanks sinking," *Global Times,* February 23, 2014, www.globaltimes.cn/content/844235.shtml.

138. For a discussion of Mao's views on Chinese politics and economy, see, for example, Simon Montlake, "China's 'privilege powers': An interview with Mao Yushi," *Forbes,* April 25, 2013, www.forbes.com/sites/simonmontlake/2012/04/25/chinas-privilege-powers-an-interview-with-mao-yushi/. See also Didi Tatlow, "Standing at the center of China's war of words," *New York Times,* May 15, 2013, www.nytimes.com/2013/05/16/world/asia/16iht-letter16.html?_r=0/.

139. See Didi Tang, "China loses 27.8 million microblog users in 2013," Associated Press, January 17, 2014, http://bigstory.ap.org/article/china-loses-278-million-microblog-users-last-year-0/.

140. See Scott Greene, "Double-edged sword: Internet proliferation, information control, and the domestic legitimacy of the Chinese Communist Party," B.A. thesis, Middlebury College, 2009, http://middarchive.middlebury.edu/cdm/ref/collection/scholarship/id/248/. For a discussion of Internet censorship in China, see, for example, "Freedom on the Net 2013," Freedom House, http://freedomhouse.org/report/freedom-net/2013/china/.

141. See Sophie Roell, "Gady Epstein on China and the Internet," Fivebooks.com, June 16, 2013, http://fivebooks.com/interviews/gady-epstein-on-china-and-internet?print/.

142. See "Xi Jinping: Give ample scope for returnees to develop their abilities," Xinhua News Agency, October 21, 2013, http://news.xinhuanet.com/politics/2013-10/21/c_117808372.htm.

143. See "Hu Jintao and Wen Jiabao give important talks at the National Conference on Work related to human resources," Xinhua News Agency, May 26, 2010, http://news.xinhuanet.com/politics/2010-05/26/c_12145780_2.htm.

144. Cited in *Blue Book of Global Talent: Annual Report on Chinese International Migration* (Beijing: Centre for China and Globalization and Social Sciences Academic Press, 2014), p. 9.

145. Ibid. For a discussion of the current emigration wave, see, for example, Li Ying, "Millions of members of the elite are staying overseas; China has become the country with the most serious brain drain," *Guangzhou Daily,* July 21, 2010, http://china.huanqiu.com/roll/2009-07/520573.html; Li Jing, "Members of the Chinese elite are rushing to immigrate to rich countries; this wave of emigration has led to China losing both talents and funds," China Economics Net, July 21, 2010, http://business.sohu.com/20100721/n273656807.shtml.

146. Cited in Sophia Yan, "Canada kills investor visa popular with Chinese," CNN, March 25, 2014, http://money.cnn.com/2014/02/12/news/canada-chinese-immigration/. See also Huang Chong, "The third wave of emigration has exposed the urgency of the idea of 'making China more livable,'" *China Youth Daily,* July 15, 2010; Wang Xin, "American media say Chinese are using a thousand and one ways to let their children be born in the United States," *Global Times,* November 23, 2010, http://world.huanqiu.com/roll/2010-11/1281438.html.

147. Cited in "Xinhua insight: China struggles to retain talents," Xinhua News Agency, July 29, 2013, http://news.xinhuanet.com/english/indepth/2013-07/29/c_125084713.htm; "More than 1.6 million students have gone abroad for studies since the start of the era of reform," China News Service, September 10, 2010, www.chinanews.com/edu/2010/09-10/2525611.shtml.

148. See "The Ministry of Education: The rate of well-trained graduates returning to China is low," *China Youth Daily,* August 6, 2013, www.1000plan.org/qrjh/article/38725/.

149. See "China struggles to return talents."

150. Cited in Zhang Haowen, "The wave of emigration by China's elite has led to soul-searching: Experts say the emigrants are looking for a sense of security," Xinhua News Agency, July 12, 2010, http://news.qq.com/a/20100712/001090.htm.

151. Cited in "Experts talk about China's new wave of emigrants; more research and discussion need to be done on allegations about brain drain," China National Radio Net, June 29, 2010, www.cnr.cn/china/newszh/yaowen/201006/t20100629_506652198.html.

152. Ibid.; see also "Third wave of emigration has appeared in China: Members of pillar sectors are leaving en masse," Xinhua News Agency, June 4, 2010, http://news.qq.com/a/20100604/001861.htm.

153. See Ran Wei, "The United States is luring elites from around the world," Xinhua News Agency, July 23, 2010, http://news.xinhuanet.com/world/2010-07/16/c_12340554_2.htm.

154. Cited in Willy Lam, "Beijing's glorification of the 'China model' could blunt its enthusiasm for reforms," *China Brief,* Jamestown Foundation, November 18, 2008, www.jamestown.org/single/?no_cache=1&tx_ttnews%5Btt_news%5D=34139/.

155. Cited in Jane Qiu, "China targets top talent from overseas: Package aims to entice high-flyers back home," www.Nature.com, January 28, 2009, www.nature.com/news/2009/090128/full/457522a.html.

156. See "Li Yuanchao: The wave of overseas talents returning to China is increasing ceaselessly," China News Service, May 30, 2010, www.chinanews.com/gn/news/2010/05-30/2312390.shtml.

157. See "China's 1,000 Talents Campaign has brought back 4,180 foreign-trained talents," Xinhua News Agency, February 19, 2014, http://news.xinhuanet.com/2014-02/19/c_119413038.htm.

158. Cited in Andrew J. Nathan, "Authoritarian resilience," in *Will China Democratize?* ed. Andrew J. Nathan, Larry Diamond, and Marc F. Plattner (Baltimore: Johns Hopkins University Press, 2013), p. 74.

159. See Minxin Pei, "Is CCP rule fragile or resilient?" in *Will China Democratize?* p. 110.

160. See Andrew J. Nathan, "Foreseeing the unforeseeable," in *Will China Democratize?* p. 133.

161. Ibid.

162. See "Xi elaborates on Chinese civilization at College of Europe," Xinhua News Agency, April 1, 2014, http://news.xinhuanet.com/english/china/2014-04/01/c_133230738.htm.

163. For a discussion of democratic experiments in the Republican period, see, for example, Suzanne Ogden, *Inklings of Democracy in China* (Cambridge: Harvard University Press, 2002), pp. 60–90.

164. Cited in Yan Changgui, "Mao's interview with Reuters correspondent in 1945," *Yanhuang chunqiu* (Beijing), October, 2008, http://club.history.sina.com.cn/thread-2769189-1-1.html.

165. See "Speech made by Renmin University international relations Professor Pang Zhongying at the *Global Times* annual conference," *Global Times,* December 13, 2013, http://china.huanqiu.com/hot/2012-12/3377530.html.

166. See Yu Keping, "Reform cannot be energized without self-confidence," Phoenix TV Net, December 19, 2012, http://news.ifeng.com/exclusive/lecture/special/yukeping/.

167. Cited in "Xi Zilin: China has lost the 'heaven and earth' of civilization," Phoenix TV Net, January 12, 2014, http://book.ifeng.com/shuhua/detail_2014_01/12/32941510_0.shtml.

168. See "Defeat of a great power: General Liu Yazhou on the Sino-Japanese War of 1894," www.21ccom.net (Beijing), April 15, 2014, www.21ccom.net/articles/qqsw/zlwj/article_20140415104386.html.

169. See Pi Mingyong, "China's loss in the Jia Wu war was a defeat of 'cultural power,'" Xinhua News Agency, March 12, 2014, www.chinanews.com/gj/2014/03-12/5941411.shtml.

# About the Author

**Willy Lam** is an adjunct professor in the History Department and the Center for China Studies, Chinese University of Hong Kong. He is also an adjunct professor in the Master of Global Political Economy Program of the same university. In addition, Lam is a senior fellow of Jamestown Foundation, a think tank in Washington D.C.

Dr. Lam has more than thirty years of experience researching and writing about China. His areas of expertise include elite Chinese politics, economic and political reforms, foreign policy and the People's Liberation Army. Lam's views on China are frequently sought by global news agencies and major newspapers and TV stations. He is the author of *Chinese Politics in the Hu Jintao Era* (2006) and *The Era of Jiang Zemin* (1999).

# Index

rectification and purge of by Xi 96–9;
self-serving revival of ancient culture
and beliefs 273–5
CCTV 59, 118, 123, 203
Central Asia: China's trade with 202
Central Commission for Disciplinary
Inspection *see* CCDI
Central Committee 112, 116; and
Eighteenth Party Congress 8–10
Central Committee Secretariat 25, 55, 82,
100
Central Coordinating Group on Talent-
Related Work (CCGTW) 276
Central Leading Group on
Comprehensively Deepening Reforms
*see* CLGCDR
Central Leading Group on Finance and
Economics *see* CLGFE
Central Leading Group on Foreign Affairs
*see* CLGFA
Central Leading Group on Internet
Security and Informatization *see*
CLGISI
Central Military Commission *see* CMC
Central National Security Commission *see*
CNSC
Central Party School see CPS
Central Political-Legal Commission *see*
CPLC
*cerenzhixin* 281
Cha, Laura 273
Changle International Airport 47–8
Charter'08 205
Chen Danqing 287
Chen Deming 9
Chen Guangbiao 281–2
Chen Guangcheng 288
Chen Liangyu 55, 56, 108
Chen Min'er 62
Chen Xi 62–3
Chen Xiaolu 176–7, 285–6
Chen Xitong 108
Chen Yun 23, 44
Chen Zhu 21
Chen Ziming 129
*chengxin* 280
Chi Fulin 159
Chiang Ching-kuo 99
China Institute of International Studies 204
China Mobile 162
'China Modernization Report (2009)' 270
China Ocean Shipping (Group) Company
203

*China Profiles*: Xi's interview with 43, 104
China Securities Regulatory Commission
(CSRC) 154
'China threat' theory 197, 199, 222, 237,
263, 264
China-ASEAN Free Trade Area *see*
CAFTA
China-ASEAN Maritime Cooperation
Fund 219–20
China's Writers Association (CWA) 275
Chinese Academy of Sciences *see* CAS
Chinese Academy of Social Sciences
(CASS) 63
Chinese Coast Guard 195
Chinese Communist Party *see* CCP
Chinese Dream 76, 81–5, 105, 120, 191,
204, 232, 239, 240, 262, 270, 296
Chinese model: shortcomings 237–9
Ching Cheong 227
civil society 264, 290
CLGCDR (Central Leading Group on
Comprehensively Deepening Reforms)
xiii, 19, 78, 79, 80, 128, 157–9, 175,
176, 267–8
CLGFA (Central Leading Group on
Foreign Affairs) 77, 121, 229
CLGFE (Central Leading Group on
Finance and Economics) 62, 158
CLGISI (Central Leading Group on
Internet Security and Informatization)
78, 124–5, 128, 177, 291, 295
Clinton, Hillary 210
CMC (Central Military Commission) xi,
4, 5, 8, 13, 25, 36, 42–3, 57–60, 62, 75,
77–79, 98, 108–9, 231
CNOOC (China National Offshore Oil
Corporation) 164, 220, 222
CNPC (China National Petroleum
Corporation) 10, 22, 107, 162, 163, 164,
224
CNSC (Central National Security
Commission) xiii, 70, 76–7, 78, 79, 117,
120–2, 128, 229, 288, 295
communism: collapse of 23
Communist Party of the Soviet Union *see*
CPSU
Communist Youth League *see* CYL
Faction
company defaults 173
Confucius Institutes 203
Confucius/Confucianism 11, 103–4, 113,
271, 273–4
constitution (1982) 115